LIVING
DANGEROUSLY
IN KOREA

LIVING DANGEROUSLY IN KOREA

The Western Experience 1900–1950

Donald N. Clark

EastBridge

Norwalk

EastBridge

The Missionary Enterprise in Asia

Copyright © 2003 by EastBridge

EastBridge is a nonprofit publishing corporation, chartered in the State of Connecticut and tax exempt under section 501(c)(3) of the United States tax code.

Second Printing

Both the author and the publisher gratefully acknowledge the support of the Korea Foundation for this volume. The opinions, findings, conclusions or recommendations are those of the author and do not necessarily reflect those of the Korea Foundation.

Library of Congress Cataloging-in-Publication Data

Clark, Donald N.
    Living Dangerously in Korea : The Western Experience, 1900–1950 / Donald N. Clark.
    p. cm. — (The Missionary Enterprise in Asia)
Includes bibliographical references and index.
    ISBN 1-891936-11-5 (pbk. : alk. paper) — ISBN 1-891936-21-2 (hardcover : alk. paper)
    1. Korea—History—Japanese Occupation, 1910–1945. 2. Korea—History—Allied Occupation, 1945–1948. 3. Aliens—Korea—History—20th century. I. Title. II Series.

DS916.55.C553 2003
951.9'03—dc21   2003000169

Printed in the United States of America

Earlier versions of passages in this manuscript have appeared in the following articles:

Donald N. Clark, "Surely God Will Work Out Their Salvation: Protestant Missionaries in the March First Movement," *Korean Studies* (University of Hawaii), XIII (1989), pp. 42-75.

Donald N. Clark, "Vanished Exiles: The Prewar Russian Community in Korea," *Korean Studies: New Pacific Currents*, ed. Dae-Sook Suh (Honolulu: Center for Korean Studies, University of Hawaii, 1994), pp. 41-58.

Dedication

Remembering my grandparents

Charles Allen Clark and Mabel Craft Clark,
residents of Seoul and P'yŏngyang, 1902-1941, and
Stacy Lippincott Roberts and Evelyn Millen Roberts,
residents of Sŏnch'ŏn and P'yŏngyang, 1907-1938;

and my parents,

Allen DeGray Clark (1908-1990), born in Seoul, and
Eugenia Roberts Clark (1908-1996), born in Sŏnch'ŏn,
residents of P'yŏngyang, Hsinpin, Ch'ŏngju, and Seoul, 1933-1973.

Contents

Preface

This book is the story of the Western presence in Korea; about the lives of ordinary people who went halfway around the world to live extraordinary lives during the turbulent first half of the twentieth century. It is also an account of Korea under Japanese rule and after, during the revolutionary early years of Liberation. The observers were missionaries, traders, diplomats, and a miscellaneous lot of travelers, adventurers, and refugees from other wounded lands. They were the Western component of the wave of modernization that swept Korea after the fall of the Chosŏn kingdom in 1910 and their legacy endures in the Korea of the twenty-first century.

Today, the Korea of their time is difficult to imagine. Conditions were primitive. Authority was arbitrary and the nation's institutions were in crisis. Illiteracy and ill health were rampant and class conflict was endemic. What could have prompted so many outsiders to devote their lives to changing such an inhospitable place? Who were they, why did they come, how did they live and die, and what difference did they make?

This book began with questions that formed in my mind during my upbringing as the son of Presbyterian missionaries in Seoul during the 1950s. The Korean War had just ended, and the wretchedness of Korea at that time beggars description: the hills were brown and stripped for firewood; sick and injured people were everywhere; entire city blocks lay in rubble. Everywhere one looked there was meagerness and suffering. I had been taught that there was a just and loving God and that Korea was a land that loved God; but if that was so, how could such terrible tribulation have been allowed to come upon the Korean people? At the time I was told that the Korean War had been a necessary defense of South Korea from Communist attack; and yet to my childish mind it seemed that the remedy had been too severe. At the time I knew better than to question the firm beliefs of the grownups around me and in time I was to learn to comprehend things more deeply. I started to fathom the injustices and deep hatreds that had caused the Korean War. I learned that complicated questions can have seemingly contradictory answers, and that Korea was a land that was full of contradictions. Among these was the role of the West in the shaping of Korean history, and within that role, the part played by my parents and grandparents as Christian missionaries.

My questions led to fascination with the history that I saw being made all around me. Much of this had to do with American power, which was everywhere in my environment, from the small U.S. Army transportation base temporarily using the school compound across the street, to the great Eighth Army headquarters base at Yongsan. I admired the stalwart GIs who drove the deuce-and-a-halfs that dominated the city's relatively few paved streets. In this context it was easy to regard America as Korea's strong friend, the rescuer that had saved the South from communist domination.

The history that I witnessed also had to do with politics and diplomacy. My earliest heroes were American ambassadors: Walter Dowling, who took a grandfatherly interest in my Boy Scout troop and organized hot dog roasts for us in the garden of his historic home in Chŏng-dong; and Walter McConaughy, a clarinetist who gathered Korean musicians on Saturday afternoons and played chamber music in the house's front parlor, inviting in visiting American teenagers to listen. It was the clarinetist, Walter McConaughy, whom I saw one day in April 1960 passing in his Cadillac Fleetwood en route to Kyŏngmudae to tell President Syngman Rhee that it was time for him to resign. How amazing, I thought, that the American Ambassador could command events in such a way!

Interspersed with these experiences were frequent lessons about the good that my own people, the missionaries, had done and were still doing in Korea. For my parents, who were themselves children of missionaries and had grown up in the North where the Communists now ruled and persecuted Christians, there was an unceasing sadness, as if we too were exiles, barred from our native place by the national division. My father often spoke of the way Korean Christians had resisted Japanese oppression during his youth, and he used our daily family prayers at breakfast to remember the Christians who had been left behind in North Korea under Communist rule.

Eventually I was exposed to a different side of Korea. Korean friends invited me to homes and introduced me to a style of family life that was anything but sorrowful. In these encounters I met their parents and learned something new about upper-class refinements.[1] I also had an extraordinary history teacher at Seoul Foreign School, Hope Diffenderfer, who taught a

1. For a lyrical expression of this style, see Hi-soo Shin Hepinstall, *Growing Up in a Korean Kitchen* (Berkeley: Ten Speed Press, 2001).

four-semester sequence of courses on Far Eastern History that featured extended field trips throughout Korea. Fording rivers and sleeping in *yogwans* my classmates and I acquired our own understanding of what was important to Koreans and how their national life had evolved. Everywhere we learned that, though the recent war had been terrible, the ordeal of Japanese colonialism between 1910-1945 had in some ways been worse. In their colony the Japanese had tried to steal the Koreans' souls, robbing them of their livelihoods and autonomy, imposing their national and religious ideologies, and finally even canceling their identities by forcing them to assume Japanese names. These indignities had generated an abiding hatred that trumped just about everything in Korea's national life. It at least was consistent with what my parents taught me about the period of their own childhood, when good things had been Korean things and bad things had been Japanese.

Since learning these early lessons, I have studied much more about how modern Korea came to be the way it is, and the part played by foreigners—Japanese and Americans in particular—in its development. While doing all the typical academic things I have wanted to pursue a more personal study—to learn what my family and the people whom we knew contributed to the story of Korea today. I have wanted to find out how they got there, what they accomplished, what it cost them, and, at some level, whether it was worth it. This book is the result of that pursuit, and I invite the reader to help me assess the meaning of what they did and the importance of what they left behind.

Caelum non animum mutant qui trans mare currunt, wrote the poet Horace in the first century B.C. "They change their skies but not their souls who cross the ocean." In Horace's time, people rarely went abroad unless they were in trouble or on some imperial errand, and, if he is to be believed, they remained unchanged by the experience. Twenty centuries later, it was common to find enclaves of foreigners spending their lives in countries half a world away from home. In these communities of the colonial world, from Africa to India to China and Korea, Western people preserved their homelands' values and transplanted themselves in foreign parts.

But Horace was wrong about their not changing their souls. The Westerners in this book, many of whom spent thirty or more years in Korea, were profoundly changed by the experience. Though most ultimately retired to their countries of origin, their retirements were filled with longing for Korea and the friends who had shared their lives there. Though they did not go as immigrants and never sought to "be Korean," during their careers they created a way of life, an imaginary town of foreigners like themselves, who were also engaged in the business of changing Korea. Their imaginary town was doomed from the beginning—though some will say that it vanished only recently—yet the work of its inhabitants is significant in the history of modern Korea. The purpose of this book is to reconstruct the story of the town's inhabitants and to reflect upon their humanity, experience, and resilience.

Korea today is a country still struggling with its modern destiny, divided by external forces into rival republics battling to advance themselves under separate political and economic systems. Both North and South Korea are fiercely nationalistic and somewhat embarrassed that the West ever looked upon their country as a place that needed missionaries, aid workers, advisors of all kinds, Peace Corps Volunteers, and other necessary (but not necessarily welcome) do-gooders. Korean social scientists look back at the story of the West in Korea as a chapter in the history of imperialism that was hardly better than Japan's colonial rule. They see the Allied occupation after 1945 as an especially violent disruption of their national life by foreigners and blame Americans for decades of military dictatorship in the South. Ideology exaggerates the colors, making the evildoers more evil, the innocents more innocent, and the people from the colonial and postcolonial powers more selfish and cynical than they actually were. Stereotypes are useful; the problem is that they are only partly true.

Colonies were the norm during the era covered by this book. Great Britain had India, Burma, Malaya, Singapore, Hong Kong, and spheres of influence in China. Germany had a sphere of influence in Shantung until World War I. Until after World War II, the Dutch ruled the Indies, France had Indochina, and America had the Philippines. And Japan had Korea. Japan shaped every aspect of modern life in Korea: its political and administrative pattern, its way of doing business, its educational system, its police and legal system, and its modern language, literature, reading habits, popular music, clothing, and food. During this period, Korea's Westerners lived as sojourners, not only among the Koreans but also under the Japanese. They worked with Japanese permission and succeeded only insofar as the Japanese allowed it. As their years passed in Korea they were always conscious that the Japanese could take it all away at any time.

This was a strange situation for Caucasians who were used to making their own imperial arrangements with the help of their own gunboats. But in Japanese-occupied Korea, the Western missionaries and businessmen had to balance the need to win government tolerance against their distaste for Japanese oppression of the Koreans. Koreans sometimes criticize the West for doing so little to stop Japanese aggression on the mainland. There is a controversy over whether Westerners in Korea did enough to promote human rights during the period, whether the missionaries' religious teachings were not actually an opiate to help Koreans endure oppression while they waited for salvation in the next life. In the years leading up to World War II, Korea's foreign residents confronted this problem, weighing whether to risk being deported against the cost of acquiescing in Japan's colonial oppression. All attempts to compromise and solve the contradiction failed when the foreign community evacuated from Korea in 1940-41, leaving the Koreans to their wartime fate. This part of the story is a variation on a classic theme of colonialism.

The last chapters of the book are about South Korea under the U.S. Army and the emergence of the Republic of Korea as an American client state in the cold war. In this era it was the Americans who were on an "imperial errand," taking a heavily Japanized Korea and trying to reorganize it as a democracy with a capitalist economy. The occupiers' ends may have been honorable but their means were lacking. They were poorly prepared and underinformed, and they had to resort to repression. In contrast, the returning missionaries were eager to be "home" again and tried to resume the rhythm of life before the war. However, they found things radically changed. In the confusion of the period following liberation they found Korea's Christians on the conservative side. With the defense of Korean Christianity as the foremost goal, they made common cause with American military authorities in a crusade against Soviet-backed Korean Communism tolerating every kind of human rights abuse as the state tried to crush the South Korean left wing. The same Westerners who criticized the Japanese regime for brutality against Koreans this time took sides with the right against the left, in effect becoming participants in Korea's incipient civil war. Under the circumstances, and given the choices as they appeared to be, compromise once more seemed pointless. The story is a lesson in the contradiction between idealism and reality that has been so visible in the relations between the West and the wider world in the modern age.

I have been fortunate to find and interview many people who have personal knowledge of events described in this book and I have listed their names in a section of the bibliography. I want to thank them for taking the time and trusting me with their histories and stories of their loved ones.

While writing I have depended on the advice and encouragement of many friends and mentors, foremost among them Horace G. Underwood, Horace H. Underwood, Lew Young-Ick, and the late George Paik, all of Yonsei University; Yi Manyŏl of Sookmyung Women's University; and Lee Kwangnin of Sŏgang University. In addition to these, Victoria Yankovsky, Colonel James H. Hausman, Professor Allan R. Millett of Ohio State University, and my aunt and uncle Katherine and Timothy Hong opened doors for me at crucial moments and contributed key pieces of information. The book would lack much of its detail and personal flavor if it had not been for their generous help.

I am grateful for the financial support of Trinity University, the Korean-American Educational [Fulbright] Commission in Seoul, and the National Endowment for the Humanities. I want to thank the archivists and librarians who opened materials for my use: Fred Heuser and Amy Roberts at the Presbyterian Historical Society in Philadelphia and Bill Bynum at the Presbyterian Church (USA) Department of History in Montreat, North

Carolina; Martha Smalley and Joan Duffy of the Day Missions Library at Yale University; Johanne Pelletier and Ian Mason of the United Church of Canada Archives at Victoria University in Toronto; Sister Grace Krieger and her staff at the Maryknoll Mission Archives in New York; Ruth Kirk of the Whitley County (Indiana) County Museum; Sally Marks and Kathy Niicastro of the Diplomatic Branch of the National Archives in Washington, D.C.; Oliver Hoare of the Public Record Office in Kew, Surrey, and his father, Dr. James E. Hoare of the Foreign and Commonwealth Office in London (and lately of the British Legation in P'yŏngyang); Dagmar Getz of the YMCA Archives at the University of Minnesota; Yi Myŏnghŭi and the late Sunny Murphy of the U.S. Army's Command Reference Library at Yongsan, Seoul; the late Sung-ha Kim and his successor Choong Nam Yoon at the Harvard-Yenching Library of Harvard University, and Yu Yŏngyŏl of Soongsil University's Museum of Christianity.

Thanks, too, to those who read the manuscript and offered critical suggestions: Horace G. Underwood, Laurel Kendall and Homer Williams, Elizabeth Underwood, Sheila Miyoshi Jager and Jiyul Kim, Sam and Eileen Moffett, Virginia Bell Somerville, Tom Fenton, and Eunice Herrington. Their thoughtful comments have added immeasurably to the book as it has taken shape. Some of the people who helped me will not agree with all of the book's interpretations. The interpretations are mine, of course, along with the responsibility for any errors that may have escaped me.

During the preparation of this book my wife Linda and our daughters Jennifer and Joanna experienced two family relocations to Korea. As they lived in Seoul, they too became part of the story of the West in Korea, successors to some of the characters in this book. Relating to the story in their own way, they contributed much in the way of feedback and insight. Their loving patience, interest, and support over the years have invested the research and writing with enormous personal meaning. I am sincerely thankful to (and for) all three of them. Finally, I dedicate the book to the memory of my parents, Allen and Eugenia Roberts Clark, and their parents, Charles and Mabel Clark and Stacy and Evelyn Roberts. Their decisions to go to Korea a hundred years ago when they were young marked the real beginning of this project.

Donald N. Clark
October 2002

LIVING
DANGEROUSLY
IN KOREA

PART I

IN JAPANESE-OCCUPIED KOREA

--1--

Half a World Away from Home

Charlie Clark stepped out of his cabin on the *Shinano Maru* and gazed over the railing at the dock below. The rain had stopped, and his nose twitched at the pungent mix of Yokohama port smells: fish, wet wood, coal smoke, and soy sauce. Japanese stevedores in G-strings were swarming over the ship's main deck heaving cargo, and the vessel vibrated with the noise of winches and cables lifting crates and barrels from the hold. Jelly-fish bobbed between the ship and the dock while the wooden pilings groaned from the pressure of the hull in the current.

Charlie looked past the pier to the street beyond. On this September day in 1902, it seemed a great accomplishment to have crossed the vast Pacific as far as Japan. Now only a few days remained before he and his bride Mabel would be stepping ashore in their intended destination in Korea.

Although Charlie and Mabel had come more than six thousand miles to commit their lives as missionaries in Korea, they still had never met a Korean. Indeed, the mission board could have sent them anywhere—to the Congo, India, China, or any of the denomination's overseas fields—and they would have accepted the assignment. But Korea had been Charlie's first choice and he felt fortunate to be going there even though he knew next to nothing about it. He only knew that he was destined to work in a newly opened sphere of operations that was sure to be full of opportunities and rewards, and at the age of twenty-six, he was eager to get to "the field" and start preaching the gospel.

From the Heart of Minnesota

Charles Allen Clark had begun life as the son of a farmer in Spring Valley, Minnesota. When his father moved to Minneapolis to become a contractor,

Charlie Clark learned about building houses. He worked hard and was a good apprentice, but he liked school too. He went to college and in time decided on a career in the ministry. This choice grew out of a deep spiritual yearning that was caused by a string of childhood tragedies, notably his mother's death from tuberculosis when he was only ten, and his brother Burton's accidental drowning when he was seventeen.

Charlie Clark found religion at a time when American churches were putting great emphasis on foreign missions. In the 1890s, missions were being "celebrated as manifestations of America's national beneficence as a Christian and democratic society."[1] They seemed to represent the country at its best–a blending of the highest form of politics, democracy, with the highest form of religion, Christianity. Americans enjoyed thinking of themselves as the best of the Anglo-Saxon race, charged with a unique obligation to civilize and Christianize a world in darkness. After a century of continental expansion, they were now being challenged to look across the oceans for new visions of their Manifest Destiny.[2]

For Charlie Clark, answering the call to the ministry included the possibility that he might end up going to the foreign mission field. This disturbed and frightened him. He had never been away from home and he had no appetite for the sacrifices associated with missionary life. However, he felt guilty when he realized that he could not be a sincere Christian if he did not surrender himself completely to the will of God. He believed that he should be willing to do whatever he was called to do, even if it meant a life of loneliness in some foreign land. He felt that it was profane in church to sing the missionary hymn entitled "I'll go where you want me to go, dear Lord, o'er mountain or plain or sea," when in his heart he was saying, "I'll go where you want me to go, dear Lord, as long as it's within the United States."

But Charlie could not escape the powerful messages that were aimed at Christian youth by speakers from the Student Volunteer Movement, the interdenominational missionary recruiting movement that held rallies across America on campuses and in civic auditoriums. In the 1890s, the SVM challenged standing-room-only audiences of young people to fulfill the Biblical promise of the Second Coming. It had a slogan—"The evangelization of the world in *this* generation!"—which referred to the pre-millenarian expectation that the messiah would return and usher in the millennium as soon as the gospel had been presented in every land and language and the world's people had been offered a chance to accept salvation. One of the speakers, the great evangelist Josiah Strong, put it this way: "I believe it is fully in the hands of the Christians of the United States, during the next ten

1. Patricia R. Hill, "The Missionary Enterprise," in *Encyclopedia of the American Religious Experience*, ed. Charles H. Lippy and Peter W. Williams, III (New York: Charles Scribner's Sons, 1988), p. 1696.
2. For the flavor of the era see Josiah Strong, *Our Country: Its Possible Future and Its Present Crisis*, rev. ed. (New York: Baker and Taylor, 1891), pp. 222-223.

(Left) Samuel A. Moffett (1864-1939). Pioneer missionary in Korea, 1890-1934. Clark Collection.
(Right) Horace G. Underwood (1859- 1916). Pioneer missionary in Korea, 1885-1916. Clark Collection.

or fifteen years, to hasten or retard the coming of Christ's kingdom in the world by hundreds, and perhaps thousands, of years. We of this generation and nation occupy the Gibraltar of the ages, which commands the world's future."[3]

As Charlie Clark veered from his career path in the Minneapolis construction business toward the church, he enrolled first at the University of Minnesota, where he studied philosophy and imagined becoming a professor. The steady call to Christian service then diverted him directly into pre-ministerial studies and he transferred to the Presbyterian Church-related Macalester College in St. Paul. He graduated with a B.A. in 1899 and went on to spend the next three years at McCormick Theological Seminary in Chicago.

Each one of these steps involved much inner pain. In his conscience, Charlie Clark continued to feel that his selfish refusal to go abroad was keeping him from growing into a fully consecrated Christian. He became obsessed with the idea that he was predestined for the foreign field. In prayer he tried to bargain with God, promising to live a life of unselfish dedication as a homeland pastor if he could just be spared the call to foreign service.

But McCormick Seminary was not the place to avoid talk of missions. The institution hosted a procession of missionary speakers whose messages simply aggravated Charlie's anguish. In Charlie Clark's senior seminary year, McCormick hosted two particularly effective missionary visitors named Horace G. Underwood and Samuel A. Moffett. Underwood and Moffett told of their pioneering work in the ancient Asiatic kingdom of Korea, a nation with a highly developed culture, a conservative ruling class, and a vast class of commoners who were obliged to labor all their lives without education or hope of advancement. Underwood and Moffett explained that Korea's native religions—notably Buddhism, Confucianism, and the country's mélange of folk beliefs—had become degraded, and that since the advent of Protestant missions in 1884 the people of Korea had been responding gladly to the Christian Gospel. Charlie was especially im-

3. Strong, *Our Country*, p. 227.

pressed with Underwood's declaration that millions of
Koreans would become Christians if there were only
enough missionaries to present the gospel to them.

Soon after hearing the call from Korea, Charlie
stopped resisting. In his last semester at McCormick
Seminary, he offered himself to the Presbyterian Board
of Foreign Missions as a missionary candidate. "I'll go
where you want me to go," he prayed, now adding that
he hoped it could be Korea. Indeed, Underwood and
Moffett had done their work well. Out of McCormick's
1902 graduating class of 44, eighteen seniors volunteered to be sent to Korea. Of these, the Board accepted two: Charlie Clark and his best friend Carl
Kearns.

Charles Allen Clark in
1912. Clark Collection.

Earlier at seminary, Charlie Clark had signed up for an internship in
western Chicago at the Faith Mission, an urban charity of the Austin Presbyterian Church in Oak Park. Charlie was put in charge, preaching twice on
Sundays and leading the midweek prayer service. As he developed the Mission he also developed a relationship with a volunteer pianist named
Mabel Craft. He learned that Mabel too had felt called to the mission field
and was thinking about volunteering. Her parents, however, were dead set
against her going far away, partly because of the danger and partly because
they thought she was not strong enough to face the hardships of mission life.
A long family argument had ended in a compromise: Mabel's parents would
allow her to volunteer for missionary work in México but nowhere farther.

As he prepared for his Korea missionary assignment, Charlie Clark knew
that he was taking on a lifetime commitment. The Board wanted people
who were prepared to spend long terms—as long as seven years at a
time—on the field. Married men were regarded as more stable, more effective, and more likely to remain on the field long enough to justify the investment in their training, and Charlie knew he needed to find a wife. In
March 1902 he proposed to Mabel Craft and she accepted, agreeing to join
him in Korea. Mabel's parents, however, put up a spirited resistance. Why
shouldn't Charlie change *his* plans and go to México? Why should he take
their only daughter half a world away from home to run unimaginable risks
and live in unimaginable misery, to satisfy his newfound interest in the Orient? Charlie and Mabel's engagement announcement was not a very happy
occasion for the Crafts. While Charlie argued with his future in-laws about
the wisdom of going to Korea the family engaged in a flurry of conspiracies
and correspondence. Mabel's father got the family pastor to write the
Board describing his daughter as frail, lacking in initiative, and possessing
few missionary abilities. Meanwhile Mabel wrote the Board asking that her
pending México application be redirected to Korea. Charlie wrote for information about Korea that might help convince Mabel's parents. His class-

mate Carl Kearns and Kearns's new bride Daisy were enlisted to show that Charlie and Mabel would have familiar friends in Korea. Charlie even came close to giving up Korea and agreeing to go to México himself when the Board's decision arrived in the mail. The couple were to go to Korea for assignment as the mission there saw fit.

So it was that on June 19, 1902, while on a trip to New York for career orientation and with little support from either of their families, Charlie Clark and Mabel Craft were married in the Crafts' ancestral church in Brooklyn. In August they said their final goodbyes in Chicago and Minneapolis and reported to the port of Seattle for embarkation on the steamship *Shinano Maru*.[4]

Yokohama Morning

On the Yokohama dock, from around the corner of the warehouse there came a white-robed man in a tall black hat, followed by a youth who appeared to be his servant.

"Mr. Clark," came a voice beside him. One of the ship's European officers had appeared on deck.

"Take a good look. There's a Korean for you. There's a lot more like that where he came from. This one's a nobleman. You can tell by the hat."

Charlie focused on the man approaching the ship. The man walked with a strut, affecting great dignity and looking neither right nor left, as if his surroundings would take care of themselves. As he made his way up the gangplank, Charlie saw that the hat was actually made of wiry horsehair, and that underneath it was an inner cap containing a thick topknot.

"Funny," he thought to himself. "I heard they'd all cut their topknots." It struck him that the man was probably one of the more conservative types from the aristocratic class known as the *yangban*. In his left hand the Korean carried a long bamboo pipe with brass fittings for the bowl and mouthpiece. The boy behind him carried a bundle of his possessions.

"I wonder if he sees the rope," Charlie thought to himself as the man headed across the deck between a winch and one of the cranes. The winch operator was getting ready to haul back on his lever, tightening the rope. He appeared not to notice the Korean. Passengers were not supposed to be on deck during loading. Such rules, however, were for ordinary people, and Charlie remembered being told that Korean *yangban* lived by their own rules. In a moment that seemed suspended in time, the Korean straddled the rope and the operator hauled back on his lever. Charlie wrote, "For a second, he didn't understand but as he rose from the ground, his

4. Information on Charles and Mabel Clark is from letters, diaries, and other materials in the possession of the author and from personnel records and correspondence in Record Groups 140 and 401 in the archives of the Presbyterian Historical Society in Philadelphia.

dignity went to the winds, he wildly grabbed at the rope, turned upside down, let go and came down with a thump right on that precious hat of his. He picked himself up and sneaked off to his quarters. It was wicked to laugh but impossible not to. We observed the Korean from all angles."

The officer guffawed and slapped Charlie on the back.

"You see?" he exclaimed. "You're in for a life of entertainment!"

Landfall at Chemulp'o

When things on deck had returned to normal, Charlie reflected on their trans-Pacific crossing. It had been interminable. Two days before, after sighting the Japanese coastline, Charlie had thought he understood how Columbus must have felt upon sighting land in 1492. The Orient had become real, but only after a miserable sea voyage. Already Charlie was dreading the return to America, due in 1909 at the end of their first seven-year term in Korea.

The trip had started with a cruise through placid Puget Sound, but on the open sea the *Shinano* had begun to pitch and roll. By the second afternoon Mabel had reported feeling queasy and had gone to her bunk, become violently ill, and had not risen again for fifteen days. Unbeknownst even to herself she was already pregnant, but under the circumstances she was believed to be suffering from raging seasickness. She could not eat solid food and it was a struggle merely to keep her hydrated. She grew weak and depressed as nothing seemed to help. Charlie watched over her and read to her and kept her drinking fluids, but Mabel was completely, pathetically, miserable.

Charlie had taken his own meals in the ship's dining room in the company of the fellow-missionaries on board: "...the Wrights of China, the Kearns of Korea, the McKays of Laos, the Johnsons of Japan, the Whites of Laos, and the Hicks of Peking. Besides, there were single missionaries, Misses Hall, Franz, Corbett, and Wynne, and Messrs. Fisher,...Guy,...Dr. Todd, Armstrong; and returning folks, Mr. and Mrs. Forman and Mr. and Mrs. Campbell with two children to Laos, Mrs. Whiting and Mrs. Mattox, with her little girl to China, Mr. and Mrs. Sprague of the Congregational Mission, also to China, and Mr. And Mrs. Moore and little girls, Lutherans, to Yokohama."

The *Shinano* was an early version of a "combi," a freighter of the Japan Mail Line that accommodated a limited number of passengers in first-class comfort. Missionaries were prominent on the manifests of trans-Pacific ships in those days, and thirty-eight of the forty passengers on the *Shinano* that September were heading to, or back to, missionary assignments in the Far East. "The captain was a heathen and forbade either singing or speaking a grace," Charlie wrote, but he was unable to keep them from using the smoking room for regular prayer services. Apart from prayers and meals, however, there had been little to do but read and watch the sea. Seagulls had trailed the ship for many days diving for garbage in the *Shinano's* wake. On occasion there had been porpoises and once a group of spouting whales. Charlie spent hours at the railing watching the sea. On September 3 they had crossed the International Dateline and skipped a Wednesday. They had grazed a typhoon and spent a day watching waves breaking over the deck. Then finally, during breakfast on September 11, someone had called down from the bridge that land was in sight.

Yokohama was dry land at least, and during their layover in port Charlie and Mabel ventured onto terra firma. Mabel had rallied during her last days at sea and in Japan she gamely mounted a rickshaw and allowed herself to be pulled through the alleys in search of local sights. Her seasickness was gone but the nausea returned at times, as when the rickshaw passed through clouds of steam rising from streetside seafood stands. Halfway through that day in Yokohama the thought struck her that perhaps it had not been seasickness at all, but morning sickness. She comforted herself by thinking, "How wonderful it would be to start a new life in Korea with a new life in the family!"

The final crossing from Kobe to Korea was a step down from the *Shinano Maru*. The ferry was much smaller and the cabin assigned to Charlie and Mabel was just a four-by-six-foot cell. The Inland Sea was smooth and Mabel was well enough to sit on deck and enjoy the passing scenery. Charlie used his camera to take snapshots of the shore, bringing on his first brush with Japanese law. A ship's police officer caught him taking pictures of a lighthouse and accosted him. "Security prohibition," he said. "No pictures allowed!"

The ferry stopped at Moji and again at Nagasaki before heading across the open sea to Korea. The water was rough and according to Charlie half the passengers became seasick right away. "The boat had eight distinct motions all at once," he wrote. "I would have been all right only I rose at daylight to get the first sight of Korea. I went out on the stern, where the motion was terrific [and] had to get back to my berth to save myself. We got into [Pusan] harbor just then."

In Pusan and then with their final arrival at Chemulp'o on September 22, Charlie filled his diary with powerful first impressions. "Our first impression of the Koreans, on landing, was taken up with Billy-goat whiskers and black hats. They did look queer. The jickies [the *chigye*, or A-frame, is used for carrying heavy loads], too, were queer. Kearns alarmed Mrs. Galloway very much by telling her that those were Korean jinrickshas and she must ride on one."

At Chemulp'o the ferry had to anchor in the outer harbor because of the great tides, and sampans carried the passengers and baggage the final four

miles to the dock. Unloading the ship took several trips, each with a powered launch pulling a string of sampans connected with hawsers. Charlie
sent Mabel ashore first and waited to watch all the baggage get safely transferred. "I watched them out of sight. Just as they entered the inner harbor,
a big wave hit them. Their rope broke loose. The Koreans got excited. They
shipped a big wave. Everybody yelled. It looked for a minute like a tip-over
but gradually things righted and they pulled in...." When Charlie reached
the dock, "200 yelling jickiemen pounced" on his personal effects fighting
to carry them to the railroad station. "I saw a feat of strength that I had
never seen before. A slender little boy, not over 16 years old, picked up my
biggest trunk as easily as could be on his jickie [A-frame] and walked off
with it. It must have weighed 350 pounds."

> As the train passed out of Chemulp'o, off to the left we saw the great salt
> marshes where the Koreans dry the sea water for the salt. In one place, the
> hills on each side of the marsh run away back on each side until they seemed
> to meet near the ocean, making a sort of pocket. Just as we passed, the most
> beautiful rainbow I ever saw dropped one end down in that pocket. It was
> simply marvelous. Down below was the mud of the marsh. Off to one side,
> the mud huts of the Koreans. And out of it all a glory rising up to God's beau-
> tiful heaven, such a dispensation of grace granted to us, a promise for our life
> in Korea.

Pioneering in Korea

From their train to Seoul, Charlie and Mabel Clark looked out on a country
that had been open to Western contact for barely two decades. When the
"Hermit Kingdom," as Korea was often called, first opened its doors in the
1880s, nobody had expected to see people like the Clarks arriving to make
a life for themselves in Seoul. Korea was a Chinese tributary state. The King
of Korea was accustomed to paying tribute to the Chinese emperor to sym-
bolize his country's submission to the greater Imperial power in exchange
for recognition and protection. Tributary status meant promising the Chinese court that Korea would make no alliances and have no dealings with
other nations. Until the 1880s Korea had kept itself isolated from the world
except for the occasional mission to Japan. The king of Korea had referred
approaches and inquiries from all foreigners to the court in Peking.

However, after being forced to sign a treaty of "friendship and commerce" with Japan in 1876, Korea shifted to a more modern stance and
opened diplomatic relations on its own with other nations. Chinese advisors told the Korean court that times had changed and it would be better to
spread their favors around. In 1882 Korea signed its first Western treaty,
with the United States, and opened its closed capital to residence by Western diplomats.

In 1884, the newly arrived U.S. Minister Lucius Foote became the first Westerner to acquire property in Seoul. He paid $2,000 to members of the royal family for a house that once had housed ladies of the king's harem.[5] The house was in the historic Chŏng-dong neighborhood between the auxiliary Kyŏng'un (now Tŏksu) Palace and the city wall on the west side of Seoul, a district distinguished by homes of government officials, royal relatives, and the T'aep'yŏng-gwan, the hall for hosting envoys from Peking. Following Foote's lead, other Western governments bought compounds of their own in Chŏng-dong, as did the missionaries who soon followed. Lucius Foote's house became the American Legation. Next door, the British built two imposing China-coast-style buildings for their establishment. The French built an elaborate Renaissance-style mansion for theirs; and the Russians made the most of their property atop Chŏng-dong hill by building a tower that commanded a view of the entire city. By the end of the 1880s the foreign community was calling Chŏng-dong the "Legation Quarter," Peking-style, and the main alleyway "Legation Street."

Protestant missionaries outnumbered all other early arrivals. Nearly all of them were young, in their twenties, fresh from the atmosphere of church camp meetings and missionary recruiting sermons, launched on their adventures by proud families and friends. In most cases their travels had involved a certain amount of romance and the glamour of crossing the ocean on a luxury liner with the rich and powerful. But then they arrived at their squalid Korean ports to be conveyed by primitive means of transportation to places of work that were, after all, as promised: lonely, often dangerous to health and safety, and invariably frustrating.

In 1885, such had been the journey of Horace G. Underwood, age 26, the first ordained Presbyterian missionary to Korea, as he traveled around the world to Chemulp'o.[6] By the time Charlie Clark arrived in Korea in 1902, Horace Underwood and his fellow-pioneer Samuel Moffett already were legends in missionary circles, a fact that had been noted when they visited McCormick Seminary on the recruiting trip that persuaded so many

5. Foote, who faced the urgent problem of a proper place to live, paid this out of his own pocket. Three years later, when Congress got around to appropriating funds for a U.S. Legation in Seoul, he sold it to the State Department for $4,400. Gregory Henderson, "A History of the Chong Dong Area and the American Embassy Residence Compound," *Transactions of the Korea Branch of the Royal Asiatic Society,* hereafter referred to as *TKBRAS,* XXXV (1959), pp. 23-25.

6. For Horace G. Underwood see Lillias Horton Underwood, *Underwood of Korea* (New York: Fleming H. Revell, 1918). His Korean-language biography is Yi Kwangnin, *Ch'odae Ŏndo'udu sŏn'gyosa-ŭi saengae* (Seoul: Yonsei University Press, 1991). A slightly more critical treatment of Underwood in his early days in Korea, through the eyes of one of his colleagues, is found in Fred Harvey Harrington, *God, Mammon, and the Japanese: Dr. Horace N. Allen and Korean-American Relations, 1884-1905* (Madison, Wisc.: University of Wisconsin Press, 1966), pp. 77-79 and passim.

seminary seniors to volunteer for the foreign field. The British-born Underwood had grown up in New York where his older brother John had started an ink-making business that eventually grew into the Underwood Typewriter Company. The Underwoods were religious people, and with the family business prospering under brother John, brother Horace had been free to pursue a religious calling. After his education at New York University and at the Dutch Reformed Seminary in nearby New Brunswick, Horace Underwood had volunteered for foreign service under the Presbyterian Board. His first choice had been India, part of a vision that had been in his head since the age of four when he had heard a missionary from India speak. The Board, however, needed someone to open a new field in the little-known kingdom of Korea and after being persuaded that Korea could turn out to be an even better opportunity than India, Underwood set out to meet the challenge. In a spirit of devotion and youthful hubris he had put his fate in the hands of God and set out to meet his destiny in the "Hermit Kingdom."[7]

Horace Underwood arrived at Chemulp'o together with Methodist pioneers Henry and Ella Appenzeller on Easter Sunday, 1885, only months after the Korean government's lifting of the official ban on Christianity. Until 1885, missionary strategists had been forced to resort to subterfuge to get their people into Korea. The first missionary doctor, Horace N. Allen, had been transferred to Korea from the Presbyterian Mission in Shantung but took diplomatic cover as physician to the American Legation during his first months in the country. Over the winter, Allen ingratiated himself with the Korean royal family by tending the wounds suffered by Prince Min Yŏng'ik during an attempted palace coup. The king had rewarded the doctor by granting his wish to start a clinic, to which he contributed a number of *kisaeng*-class palace women as "nurses." He also agreed to tolerate missionary co-workers—on the understanding that they would come primarily as teachers. Soon thereafter came the Reverends Underwood and Appenzeller, both beginning their work by founding schools.[8]

The Korean government officially lifted the ban on Christianity in 1887, under urging from the French government, which obtained an official tol-

7. Underwood, *Underwood of Korea*, pp. 24-36. A favorite joke in the Underwood family is the remark by an associate of the London Missionary Society who, when told that Horace was being assigned to Korea, said, "Korea, Korea; let me see, I believe we sent a man out there some twenty years ago and he was never heard from again." Ibid., p. 36.

8. For the beginnings of Protestant mission work in Korea, see Martha Huntley, *To Start a Work: The Foundations of Protestant Mission in Korea (1884-1919)* (Seoul: Presbyterian Church of Korea, 1987), and Everett N. Hunt Jr., *Protestant Pioneers in Korea* (Maryknoll, N.Y.: Orbis Books, 1980). Also see Harrington, *God, Mammon, and the Japanese;* Underwood, *Underwood of Korea*, and Daniel M. Davies, *The Life and Thought of Henry Gerhard Appenzeller, 1858-1902* (Lewiston, Me.: The Edwin Mellen Press, 1988).

eration clause in one of their treaties. The Catholics then resumed the work that had been interrupted by the bloody purge of Christians in 1866, returning in 1890 with a bishop and a contingent of French fathers from the Société des Missions Étrangères-de Paris (SME). Meanwhile, the Korean government itself hired a cadre of foreigners, advisors who, together with an adventuresome few investors and traders, formed the third element of the Western community in Korea, the nonofficial, nonmissionary contingent traditionally referred to as "the business people."

The early missionaries, though no longer officially persecuted after 1885, found that they were still unwelcome in much of the country. Korea's 1886 treaty with France had legalized the practice of Christianity in Korea, and the citizens of other countries gained the same privilege through their most-favored-nation clauses. Officials and other upper-class Koreans, however, continued to see Westerners in general and missionaries in particular as troublemakers. District magistrates sometimes issued orders—which the court in Seoul quickly overruled—decreeing death for all foreign and Korean Christians. Travel in the interior was especially problematic, since treaty provisions technically applied only to Westerners in the treaty "ports," namely Seoul, Chemulp'o, and Pusan, leaving the rest of the country closed to missionary exploration. This did not keep certain intrepid missionaries from obtaining "passports" for travel in the interior, usually without incident. However, there were occasional antiforeign outbreaks such as the 1888 riot over rumors that mission orphanages were kidnapping Korean children and using their organs for food, medicine, photography, and other works of science.[9] And when the French Catholics started their cathedral in Chong-hyŏn (now Myŏng-dong) in the 1890s, there was an outcry from the official class against their building a steeple high enough to spy on the royal palace.

The missionaries accepted adversity as part of the bargain when they answered to call to work in Korea. Anyone volunteering for a career there needed courage and perseverance in order to endure the crowds, the food, having to sleep on hot *ŏndol* floors in the heat of summer, the vermin, and the constant bouts of illness.[10] However, a fine line separated courage and perseverance from stubbornness and excessive zeal. Schisms

9. This was a serious matter for any Westerner who remembered how similar rumors in Tientsin, China, had led to a massacre of missionaries in 1870. For the Korean "baby riots" of 1888, see *Hulbert's History of Korea*, ed. Clarence Norwood Weems II (New York: Hilary House, 1962), p. 245, and Horace N. Allen, *Things Korean* (New York: Fleming H. Revell, 1908), pp. 226-227.

10. For a catalogue of conditions see James Scarth Gale, *Korea in Transition* (New York: Young People's Missionary Movement of the United States and Canada, n.d.), pp. 164-170.

developed among the missionaries as they argued over petty points.[11] They irritated their nonmissionary peers with pieties about their "calling," inviting taunts about Korean "rice Christians" who joined the church only because they thought the missionaries could find them jobs or other material benefits. American Legation Secretary William Franklin Sands was one who thought that the missionaries were silly to claim that conversion to Christianity made much difference in the lives of ordinary Koreans. He used the ancient village ritual of stone fighting to illustrate his point:

> Nothing ever equaled the joy with which the native Christians sailed into each other with clubs and stone slings. One had a complete miniature of the religious wars of Europe, with the village scalawags thumping each other heartily in the cause of rival clergymen, for the sake of the particular side on which the butter was spread for them.[12]

But Korea's tiny band of Westerners could ill afford much feuding. They were surrounded by locals who were hard-pressed to figure them out. What kind of people would abandon their own parents to live in a foreign land? Perhaps they were exiles or fugitives from justice, or somehow rejects from their own societies. Yet oddly, they seemed rich. They claimed to be teachers and carried themselves like members of an upper class, yet they were ignorant of the Confucian *ye* (rituals), mixed men and women, married and unmarried, and altogether seemed like anything but people to respect in the traditional way.

Koreans who associated with the Westerners were also suspect. In the 1880s and '90s, the few Koreans who had been abroad returned with stories that seemed fantastic to ordinary listeners. Some of the returnees started reform movements but then were frustrated by the entrenched conservatism of the government and the ruling *yangban* class. A group of young Koreans inspired by the Meiji thinker Fukuzawa Yukichi tried to reorient Korea toward reform in 1884 and were routed by conservative forces. Another Japanese-inspired group held power briefly in the mid 1890s but lost it during the backlash against the murder of Queen Min by Japanese agents. Western-educated reformers had not gotten much farther. Reform had been the object of the Independence Club (*Tongnip Hyŏphoe*) led by American-educated Sŏ Chaep'il [Philip Jaisohn] and Yun

11. James Scarth Gale wrote about the intensity and contentiousness of the relationships among the early foreigners in Korea in a novel entitled *The Vanguard: A Tale of Korea* (New York: Fleming H. Revell, 1904). See also Paik, pp. 118-120.

12. William Franklin Sands, *Undiplomatic Memories* (London: John Hamilton, n.d.), p. 93. After reading Sands's mocking account, Charlie Clark wrote a chapter into one of his books in which a village of Christians, after being challenged to a stone fight by a neighboring village, responded by refusing to fight and expressing friendship and a desire for forgiveness for whatever offense had brought on the challenge. Charles Allen Clark, *First Fruits in Korea* (New York: Fleming H. Revell, 1921), pp. 193-209.

Ch'iho, but these stalwarts had offended many important *yangban* with their calls for social change and political realignment. Sŏ and Yun had used their bilingual Korean-English newspaper, *The Independent* (*Tongnip Sinmun*), to address both the Western resident community and the top tiers of the Korean intelligentsia. They had tried to boost Korean nationalism by erecting a symbolic "Independence Gate" (*Tongnimmun*) on the road once used by Korean tribute envoys heading for Peking, to signify the end of Korea's vassalage to the Chinese throne. These mild gestures had been controversial enough, but when the Independence Club leaders started staging street rallies to demonstrate their bond with the populace, the conservative government came after them with hired peddlers from Seoul's marketplaces who broke up the rallies and scattered the participants. Shortly thereafter the Independence Club had collapsed, and with it Korea's first Western-oriented reform effort.

Communicating with the Koreans

Charlie and Mabel Clark and their Chicago friends Carl and Daisy Kearns arrived in Seoul to be gathered into the bosom of the missionary circle. On arrival, Charlie was apprenticed to help the Reverend Samuel Forman Moore in Seoul's Central Presbyterian Church. This church was already famous as a case of social engineering by the missionaries. Its founding in 1895 had coincided with a sweeping set of government-ordered reforms that included the abolition of social classes. Moore had proposed using the Central Church to demonstrate the benefits of this and to model democratic values in the church context. Hoping to make the point that all are equal in the sight of God, he sent out invitations to members of the *paekch'ŏng*, the lowest Korean caste commonly called "butchers" because of their work with meat and leather, to join the congregation. He went so far as to encourage them to put their hair up in the dignified topknot and come wearing hats, the badges of dignity normally identified with *yangban* aristocrats.

The commoners and few *yangban* who already belonged to Moore's church were torn between following their foreign pastor and their traditional prejudice against the *paekch'ŏng*. They took special offense at Moore's attempt to get them to call each other "Brother." No Korean would have attempted to integrate the classes in that manner, and the presence of the *paekch'ŏng* brought church growth to a screeching halt. Moore's efforts continued until he was felled by illness in 1906, but Charlie Clark could see from the start that the project was doomed, and when he took over the church in 1906 he put a stop to it. Meanwhile the butchers were isolated in the Central Church congregation and asked not to visit other churches "on the plea that they had blocked the way into the Kingdom of many high class people," according to Charlie. "Only after this step had been taken did the work in that part of [Seoul] show signs of healthy growth." In fact, "few [of the butchers] really repented of their sins, which were of the grossest sort."[13]

The Presbyterian Mission obtained a house for Charlie and Mabel in Kongdan-kol, across the palace square from the Legation Quarter, and with some hand-me-down furniture and the help of a Korean maidservant, Mabel began fashioning a home.[14] Charlie meanwhile was given a Korean tutor and set to work on the language. The tutor came to the Clarks' *sarangbang* receiving room each morning and spent hours drilling Charlie on memorized vocabulary lists and short set speeches. The intent was to send him out on the street to hand out tracts and deliver memorized homilies in Korean as soon as possible, and to work up to delivering meditations and sermons in church as his aptitude allowed. The absence of textbooks of any kind complicated the job. The earliest Protestant missionaries had learned everyday speech quickly enough, but "street Korean" had its limits. The Korean language was a tricky business even for the most senior missionaries, one of whom was famous for having preached an entire sermon on the sin of *ttam* (sweating) when he meant to preach on the sin of *t'am* (envy).[15]

The need for better tools for learning Korean was so urgent that a team of pioneer missionaries led by Horace Underwood early on set about creating a dictionary. This had been controversial among the missionaries because it diverted the energies of the most capable missionaries away from "true" missionary work for a period of many months in 1888-89. Some thought it silly to expect young men with so little experience in the country to organize the language into any kind of useful dictionary. But Underwood had set reasonable goals for the project, creating a small handbook-type reference that was based on the Korean-French dictionary that had been compiled by Catholic missionaries earlier in the century. The Canadian missionary James Scarth Gale helped him over the summer of 1889 as they worked in a pavilion loaned by King Kojong himself on the banks of the Han River at Yanghwajin.

The dictionary had been published in Japan with Underwood supervising the production of fonts for printing the Korean *Han'gŭl* alphabet at

13. Harriet E. Pollard, "The History of the Missionary Enterprise of the Presbyterian Church, U.S.A., in Korea, with Special Emphasis on the Personnel" (unpublished M.A. thesis, Department of Education, Northwestern University, 1927), p. 32. For Samuel F. Moore's experiment, see also Allen D. Clark, *Avison of Korea* (Seoul: Yonsei University Press, 1979), pp. 97-103, and *The Korean Repository*, II (1895), pp. 279-280. The church in question was the Sŭng-dong Presbyterian Church, later pastored by Charles Allen Clark and still located near Pagoda Park. For an assessment of the experiment see Charles Allen Clark, *The Korean Church and the Nevius Method* (New York: Fleming H. Revell, 1930), pp. 99.

14. The house was on a plot of land that is now underneath the Lotte Hotel, off City Hall Plaza.

15. Allen, *Things Korean*, pp. 76-77.

Kelly & Walsh in Yokohama. It was an instant success and became the foundation for training the hundreds of Westerners who followed.[16] Underwood, Gale, and their Methodist colleague Homer Hulbert had gone on to
found the Korean Tract Society, which later became the Christian Literature
Society, an important conduit for Christian and Western ideas throughout
the twentieth century.

With the advent of publication facilities, the missionaries made text production a part of their own language learning—with the help of their Korean tutors as co-authors. The Methodist educator Mary Scranton produced a catechism in *Han'gŭl*, a book published in traditional Korean format, right-to-left, on rice paper with oilpaper covers and stitched binding
on the right. Others produced handbooks for the study of various books of
the Bible and aids for worship. Many missionaries wrote Sunday School
materials. They also conjured up their own college studies and devised
textbooks in secular subjects like botany, zoology, and geography for Korea's mission schools. Ella Appenzeller's geography text was an eye-opener
for children who could hardly imagine a world beyond their shores. She
used the question-and-answer ("*mundap*") format of the catechism for
memorization:

> "What do we call the areas that contain much water?" (*Muri manhi mŏ'in
> gosi muŏsinya?*)

> "They are called oceans." (*Taeyang'ira handa.*)[17]

16. The dictionary project is a good example of the pioneer missionaries' practical adaptation of existing work. Underwood started with the Société des Missions
Étrangères de Paris, *Dictionnaire Coréen-Français* (Yokohama: Kelly and Walsh,
1880). His own first edition was the 239-page *Concise Dictionary of the Korean
Language* (Han-yŏng chajŏn), Vol. 1, by H.G. Underwood, assisted by Homer B.
Hulbert and James S. Gale (Yokohama: Kelly and Walsh, 1891). This was followed
by James Scarth Gale's own *Korean-English Dictionary* (Han-yŏng chajŏn) (Yokohama: Kelly and Walsh, 1897), an expanded version of the Underwood team's first
edition published together with a separate Chinese-English section giving the basic
list of characters used in Korea with their Korean readings and English definitions
adapted from Herbert A. Giles's classic *Chinese-English Dictionary*. Later editions
of Gale's dictionary were published between 1911 and 1931 in Yokohama and
Seoul, in varying formats with assorted appendices. L.H. Underwood, *Underwood
of Korea*, pp. 94-95; Richard Rutt, *James Scarth Gale and His History of the Korean
People* (Seoul: Royal Asiatic Society, Korea Branch), pp. 15, 18, 373-374.

17. Many of these early texts are preserved in Soongsil University's Museum of
Christianity, including two separate translations of the Gospel of John by Horace
and Lillias Underwood, H.G. Underwood's 1894 hymnbook, James Gale's 1895
translation of *Pilgrim's Progress* (Ch'ŏllyŏ yŏkjŏng), destined for hard use as a
Sunday School text for many years thereafter. By the 1910s there were substantial
texts for secondary and higher students on the Gospels of John (M.B. Stokes,
1913), Matthew (J.S. Gale, 1916), and Joshua, Judges, and Ruth (by W.D. Reynolds). Seminary-level texts for pastoral training had also been written: e.g.,

Underwood and Gale's dictionary research hideaway at Yanghwajin was one of several spots where Korea's early Westerners tried to escape the heat and pestilence of Seoul during the summer months. Although filth and disease were problems all over the late nineteenth century world, the summer environment in Korea was especially perilous.[18] Despite precautions, members of the foreign community regularly died of diseases such as typhoid, cholera, malaria, sprue, or tuberculosis. Nor were the foreign doctors themselves safe: in fact the first Protestant missionary to die in Korea was a medical doctor named John Heron, in July 1890. Heron's death provided the occasion for King Kojong to donate a plot of his land at Yanghwajin to the foreign community for use as a cemetery. In the years to come, Yanghwajin was destined to become the final resting place for more than four hundred Western residents of Seoul, some of whom died literally within days of their arrival in a country where they had meant to spend decades of their lives in service to God and humankind.[19]

The Cost of the Calling

By September 1903, a year after arriving at Chemulp'o, Charlie and Mabel Clark felt like they had already spent a lifetime in Korea. Their first year was a roller coaster, beginning with an open quarrel among the senior missionaries about where to assign them. Then they were forced to board with others until their Korean house in Kongdan-kol could be readied for occupancy in December. Soon they were playing host themselves, taking in a single woman missionary in February and then in March the recently widowed Walter Johnson. Johnson's wife had fallen ill on the sea voyage and had died in Japan. Walter Johnson himself arrived in Seoul with an incipient case of smallpox that burst into a fever on his second day in the Clarks' house. As Charlie wrote in his diary,

Charles Allen Clark's *Sŏlgyohak* (Homiletics: The Art of Preaching).

18. Witness Isabella Bird Bishop's famous description of Seoul (which she compared favorably with Peking): "For a great city and a capital its meanness is indescribable....[A]n estimated quarter of a million people are living on "the ground," chiefly in labyrinthine alleys, . . .further narrowed by a series of vile holes or green, slimy ditches, which receive the solid and liquid refuse of the houses, their foul and fetid margins being the favorite resort of half-naked children, begrimed with dirt, and of big, mangy, blear-eyed dogs, which wallow in the slime or blink in the sun." *Korea and Her Neighbours* (New York: Fleming H. Revell, 1898), p. 40.

19. On the subject of health conditions and health problems, see *The Korea Mission Field*, XVIII:8 (August, 1922). On the subject of the cemetery at Yanghwajin and its association with foreigners, missionaries, and as an execution ground for mid-nineteenth century Catholics, both Koreans and foreigners, see Donald N. Clark, comp., *The Seoul Foreigners' Cemetery at Yanghwajin: An Informal History* (Seoul: Seoul Union Church, 1998).

We gave him our bed, which was the only one we had. By the doctor's orders, later we moved him to the old church building on the compound. I nursed him three days and nights alone as no one would help. Then Miss [Katherine] Wambold came and took the days and I took the nights, twelve hours each. On the 14th day, just as he passed the crisis, he died. We laid him to rest in the foreign cemetery, five miles outside the gate, on the banks of the Han. Two weeks later, on April 3rd, our Burton was born, the jolliest little laddie God ever sent to brighten homesick folks' hearts.

Three weeks after Burton was born, Charlie took his first trip into the hinterland. Mabel and the baby stayed behind, being cared for by a houseguest. Charlie's trip, from Seoul to P'yŏngyang, involved a boat ride down the Han River to the estuary, then up the Imjin River to Paech'ŏn. "It was Buddha's birthday the day we left, and we passed several large boats full of picnickers with their dancing girls making merry. The weird music of the pipes had an uncanny sound as evening came on. The gentle zephyrs blew down our necks and the water bugs danced in the bedclothes, but the lullaby of the waves put us to sleep."

For this trip Charlie was paired with Arthur Welbon, a veteran of three years in Korea. After going ashore at Paech'ŏn they continued on foot 60 *li* (fifteen miles) to a church where they were obliged to disentangle a marriage complication: a backslidden Christian who had reverted to his concubine and had to be suspended from membership. The next day they walked another 60 *li* farther to Kimch'ŏn where they spent several days. A boat full of liquor had just crossed from China, creating a scene of debauchery that appalled them. "Every man we passed had a jug or basket of jugs. Men drunk lying even in the mud of the rice fields and squarely across the path along the dikes."

Next they turned up the main road to P'yŏngyang along which traveling missionaries were becoming a common curiosity. "Know how animals in a cage feel. They packed the court so the boy couldn't get dinner. On the outside, women punched 20 holes in the paper windows in five minutes and the men did the same on the court side." People had heard about medical missionaries. "Several sick people were brought to us to heal, one with some mysterious neck disease, most loathsome. Syphilis is very common in Korea. The next village was full of typhus. Two people had died in the church, so we merely stopped a couple of hours and went on."

After crossing into South P'yŏng'an Province they came to a village with another marriage complication. Here their human instincts got the better of them, though they were overruled on appeal.

There was a man with two wives, one 55 years old and barren, one 35 years old, ten years married and having three children. All had believed [become Christians]. The man was caring for both but living only with No. 2. They all wanted to be baptized and were willing to do whatever we said. The man was 45. [The church's] rule says that the man must put away No. 2 in a separate house and maintain her; must live with No. 1 only. Welbon couldn't find it in his heart to order such a thing, now that No. 1's relatives and she herself were satisfied with things as they are. Referred it up to the Seoul Committee of the Council. Later Council's policy was reaffirmed.

In the summer, Charlie, Mabel, and Baby Burton together journeyed by rail to P'yŏngyang to house-sit for a missionary family on furlough. It was a happy vacation break visiting with friends and learning lore about the ancient Korean city:

> Saw Kija's tomb, the new palace being built for the king by his loving subjects, the boat-like city with the two mooring pillars out in the meadow behind, the island in the river which floated down from above, one day long ago. The peak where the Chinese made their last stand in '94, the battlefield of the Chinese and Japanese, the apricot orchards, the old wall built in Solomon's time, the city gate with the anchor chains of the old American boat *General Sherman* hanging up, etc. There was a great amount of rain during the summer. Nearly the whole P'yang community went up the river on flat houseboats for a month. We did not go because of the baby. The river rose perpendicularly 15 feet in one night after a terrible rain, flooded the lower end of the city and destroyed about 200 houses.

At the end of the summer of 1903, Carl and Daisy Kearns and their newborn baby Joey were assigned to the newly opened mission station at Sŏnch'ŏn, in North P'yŏng'an Province near the Manchurian border. Charlie volunteered to accompany the Kearneses north to their new location. The summer rains had washed out the road and bridges in many places, requiring ingenious, usually dangerous, ways of crossing. In an early mishap, the pack pony carrying most of their food fell in deep water and was swept away in the current, reducing the traveling party to buying food along the way. The only safe items to be had were chickens, eggs, and rice, and it was this trip, with chickens, eggs, and rice several times a day, that put Charlie off eggs for the rest of his life. Daisy Kearns, meanwhile, became dehydrated and failed to produce enough milk for Joey, forcing them to improvise a formula based on boiled water, rice, and eggs. The nights were even worse than the days.

> Got to an inn. Got two rooms, each 6 by 6. Mine was right next to the kitchen, so all the heat from cooking twenty suppers went into my stone floor. Only by sleeping on my whole outfit, not spread out, could I bear the heat. The bedbugs were by the hundreds on the floor, dropping down from the ceiling. There was also a bug which looked like a bedbug but was as large as one's thumb-nail, which my teacher cheerfully told me wouldn't kill me if it bit but would just make a bad sore. There were scores of them, too.

After several days of soggy crossings and buggy inn rooms, they approached Sŏnch'ŏn:

We offered the coolies untold wealth if they would make the remaining 57 miles by the following night, but it was a physical impossibility. We made 20 *li* more, that night, but could do no better. We felt then that we had drained the dregs, but, next day, was worse yet. The road was entirely flooded with from a few inches to four feet of water, all bridges were gone and, in the bottom of the water was from two to four inches of mud. Horrors! Every foot stuck where it was put. The baby cried nearly all the time. Money could not have done to those coolies what the baby's crying did. In spite of that awful road, when they dropped their loads at 7 p.m., they had made 34 awful miles. They simply dropped, when they laid the chair down. And we *still* ate chickens, eggs, and rice.

Mabel had thought the Sŏnch'ŏn trip too risky for her own health, but back in the relative safety of P'yŏngyang she came down with a case of malaria. Charlie was shocked when he got back and saw her. "Nursing the baby took so much of her strength, so he had been weaned and he was sick, with a white face and black rings under his eyes. Mabel looked like a ghost. Mrs. Moffett had taken her to her house and had been very good to her as, in fact, was everyone else." But Charlie was about to demonstrate a character trait that became typical of his career in Korea. Though Mabel's abilities were limited, in this case by illness and the need to care for the baby, Charlie felt himself under an obligation to carry on with "the Work" regardless of the cost. Accordingly, he wrote, "The next day I took my written language exam and Tuesday my oral. The terrific strain of the previous 15 days was hard on the result but I passed. Mabel could not try either, of course."

Mabel's malaria calmed down, the summer ended, and the time came for the Clarks to return to Seoul. They took a steamer from a landing just below Man'gyŏngdae, on the outskirts of P'yŏngyang, and when it hit the open sea it began to buck and roll, sending even Charlie to his bunk to hold on for dear life. "Existed till morning. Mabel pretty bad, also, but not too bad as she didn't try to rise. Couldn't lift my head in the morning. Only one of the 15 foreigners on board that was not sick was [William] Bull of Kunsan. He took care of Burt. Later in the day, McCutcheon, a new man, assisted. We were all sick till we reached Chemulp'o at 10 p.m. Saturday night. Went home. Set to work."

While in Sŏnch'ŏn with the Kearnses, and after only eleven months in the country, Charlie Clark had preached his first Korean language sermon. When he passed his language exam the Presbyterian Mission elders assigned him to preach in a country territory, "itinerating" along the south fork of the Han River eastward toward Wŏnju. Here he spent weeks at a time walking between established churches in the villages of Hoengsong, Toegyewŏn, Munaemi, and Sangsimni, accompanied by his Korean teacher, an assistant, and several pack ponies to carry his gear, which included a stock of Bibles and other religious books for sale.

At churches along his circuit Charlie stopped and examined applicants for membership. These "catechumens" had to memorize the series of *mundap* questions and answers that covered the basic points of Presbyterian doctrine. They also had to show that they had renounced a number of practices that were forbidden to church members, including concubinage, ancestor worship, idols of all kinds, opium, alcohol, and tobacco. On one ten-day trek Charlie preached twenty-four times in sixteen villages, suspended two male church members for deserting their wives and taking concubines, and "helped Pak the powder maker burn his household idols, one for each room in the house and some for the yard."

Meanwhile, when in Seoul, he staged "street chapels" and preached to raffish crowds of peddlers and urchins along the city's avenues. After speaking he would give away printed leaflets ("tracts") coaxing people to accept them when they seemed afraid that they contained "devils." He helped with services at his own Sŭng-dong Church as well as at the Tong-hyŏn and Yŏn-dong churches. He taught calisthenics at the Presbyterian Boys' Academy and Sunday School at the foreigners' church. And he started using his Minneapolis construction experience by designing and building a house for single women missionaries on mission property in Chŏng-dong, the first of a long list of building projects that he supervised during his Korean career.

While Charlie busied himself with these projects, Mabel nourished Burton and struggled to maintain her own health. The Clarks hired an "amah" to watch the baby so Mabel could hold up her end of the couple's missionary call, an obligation that Charlie regularly emphasized to her. Mabel invented her own kind of "women's work," inviting the ladies of the neighborhood into her home and allowing them to poke through her possessions while she tried to turn their visits into social occasions. Seated on the floor with tea in cups she would summon every word in her Korean vocabulary and try to tell them Bible stories. On days when this was too much she simply would simply teach them English words for things: "table," "chair," "clock," "blanket," "flower," and "spoon." Baby Burton was an asset: the women were full of the secrets of motherhood and they were quick to impart advice, however unintelligible, to the young American woman.

In the spring of 1904 the Clarks took in a boarder, an American who had come to teach the city's Western children. Mabel's friend Daisy Kearns also joined the household, having left Sŏnch'ŏn with Baby Joey to escape the Russo-Japanese War. For a few happy weeks there was laughter and friendship in the house. But Daisy and Joey went home in June, traveling on a tiny steamer that tossed and heaved in the fog along the coast skirting rocks and courting disaster the whole way to Chinnamp'o. By the time they made port, mother and child were near death from vomiting and dehydration. The last leg of the trip from P'yŏngyang to Sŏnch'ŏn by road was a replay of the "chicken, eggs, and rice" experience that left Joey so weak that he could not recover. In October he died from meningitis.

Unaware of what Daisy Kearns and Joey were suffering, Charlie, Mabel, Burton and four of the mission's single women missionaries went up into the Pukhan Mountains north of Seoul to spend the hottest summer weeks in cooler air. They went with James Scarth Gale, the scholarly Canadian missionary who by 1904 had become deeply interested in Korean culture and was writing a history of the Korean people. The group stayed in a Buddhist monastery within the walled fortress that had been built as a refuge for the king in case of invasion. Gale amused himself by reading to the group in the evenings and spending afternoons teaching Charlie about Korea. Their conversations with the monks that summer planted in Charlie the interest in Korean religions that he later turned into a master's thesis at the University of Chicago and finally his book, *Religions of Old Korea,* published in 1932.

However, these were Charlie's singular delights. In July Mabel became sick to her stomach once again and after two weeks of suffering was carried down the mountain to see the doctor. The doctor put an end to the vacation and sent Mabel to bed, where her condition worsened despite numerous medical experiments. The pain turned to real agony and after eight weeks, as Charlie described it in his diary, she "got out of her head." The mission doctor ordered round the clock feedings and gradually she began keeping food down. She regained her strength slowly, and it was December before she was physically—if not mentally—back to normal.

Mabel's health kept Charlie close to home but in fact he too was badly worn down. He had his own bouts of malaria, interspersed with days when he went out to distribute gospel tracts and work in the mission bookstore selling gospel prints, textbooks, and other little volumes, sales of which kept doubling month by month. The houseguests who came and went were a mixed blessing, adding to the chores but also helping Mabel and the amah with baby Burton, who by now could walk and was developing an 18-month-old's vocabulary in Korean and English.

However, on December 21 one of the guests awoke with a rash and temperature, sure symptoms of scarlet fever. In the afternoon of the same day baby Burton, who for several days had been fussy and thought to be teething, developed his own rash followed by a skyrocketing temperature. The suddenness of the illness and the virulence of the fever were beyond anything Charlie and Mabel had ever seen, and they spent a shocked evening cradling their baby as he died. "It was the hardest blow we ever received," wrote Charlie, "and we understand Matthew 19:29 now as never before: 'And everyone that hath left houses, or brethren, or sisters, or father, or mother, or children, or lands for my name's sake, shall receive a hundred fold and shall inherit eternal life.'"

Charlie and Mabel got little respite from demands that would not leave them alone in their grief. Mabel's summertime illness had masked a pregnancy that became obvious in the fall, and after Burton's death she focused on getting ready for the new baby that was due in April. Meanwhile, the guest with scarlet fever needed seventeen days in isolation but recovered, following which another boarder developed a "nervous disorder" that turned out to be sprue. While caring for this patient Charlie himself developed "nervous prostration" and had to be forced to rest in bed for many weeks, some of them in the hospital. Much of the time Mabel was the ablest person in the house, though she had debilitating bouts with depression. Her pregnancy went more smoothly toward the end, and on April 6, 1905 she bore her second son, Gordon. "We were tremendously busy just then," wrote Charlie. "We had begun to move across the compound the day before Gordie came. Had to finish and move Gordie and his ma on a cot three days after birth. Just got settled and were ordered to move again by June 15, as the Japanese wanted the house."

Springtime had brought them much relief. On May 12, according to Charlie's diary, "Mabel's mind came back." On the same day, Gordie gave his first smile in response to his parents' cooing. In June they made a temporary move to Dr. Underwood's riverside cottage at Yanghwajin, near Burton's grave, where they benefited from the breeze and regained much of their strength. Charlie, however, could not be happy just resting in the vacation cottage. He returned to town to supervise the new Central Church building in Sŭng-dong. He drafted plans and ordered materials for the building of a two-story, Western-style brick house for the family in "Yonmotkol," the site that was to become the main Presbyterian Mission compound at Yŏn-dong near East Gate. On days when he stayed by the river he delighted in Baby Gordie, happy and relieved that the baby had not been sick a day since birth.

But then in September at the annual mission conference, Gordie began having trouble with his digestion. His condition worsened and no one could figure out the cause, though there were theories that it was a water-borne microbe of some kind from the terrible flooding that happened that month in Seoul. "We tried every possible baby food, but he could not assimilate any of it. He suffered terribly; his pitiful little cry was agony itself. Drs. Avison and Hirst did everything possible for him. We had a Korean wet nurse, but it was all to no avail. On October 29, his pain was all over and he went to his brother. Poor little laddie. He did so much for us, when we needed him so much. Lots of grownups do less in a lifetime than he did in his six months and 23 days. He was put to sleep beside his brother in the foreign cemetery five miles out from Seoul."

-- 2 --

Vigil for a Dying Kingdom

In 1907, after five hard years, Carl and Daisy Kearns decided to leave Korea and rebuild their lives back home in Chicago. Mabel Clark would have been glad to go with them. The deaths of her two children had taken away her zest for mission work and she had retreated to the interior world where she was destined to spend the rest of her life. Charlie, on the other hand, had found his stride. He was fascinated by the happenings all around him and relished his place in the unfolding drama of Korea, despite the primitive conditions and recurring illness. He was not entirely heedless of Mabel's comfort, however: by 1907 he had built her a proper American-style house on the Presbyterian compound. The two-story brick structure within sight of Seoul's ancient East Gate would have fit well in Chicago with its porches, balustrades, wood floors, radiators, American bathrooms, and spacious living and sleeping rooms. It looked out over the city from the highest point on the compound and everything about it was light and airy, exactly the opposite of the oppressive Kongdan-kol cottage with its tiny rooms and hot floors in the heart of the malodorous city. Mabel of course was delighted, and she immediately installed herself in the main bedroom where she whiled away the hours in her rocking chair reading the Bible and gazing out the window at Namsan, the city's South Mountain.

The Great Game of Empire in Korea

When the Clarks first arrived in Korea, the country had been trapped as a pawn in the "Great Game of Empire" between Russia and Japan. At the time, Japan had just strengthened its hand by signing the Anglo-Japanese Alliance. This placed a barrier in the way of Russia's expansion in East Asia and boosted Japan's own plans for hegemony. It was especially bad news

Sŏnch'ŏn Presbyterian missionaries. Clark Collection.

for Korea, which had lost Chinese protection in 1895 and was desperate for help to maintain its independence. Korea needed friends but had none. France was preoccupied in Indochina; Germany was establishing its foothold across the Yellow Sea in Shantung; and the United States was busy crushing the independence movement in the Philippines. A handful of Westerners in Korea had individual investments in the peninsula and all the Western governments maintained diplomatic missions in Seoul, but altogether these amounted to little more than a symbolic presence. Only Czarist Russia stood in the way of Japan's plans for domination in Korea.

For a while it had seemed that Russia might rescue Korea. The Japanese had seriously overreached in the aftermath of their victory over China. They had sent agents and operatives to Seoul to take virtual control of the Korean royal government and its policies, and Japanese sōshi, or "men of determination," had actually broken into the palace and assassinated Queen Min, one of their main opponents. The murder of the queen had backfired badly, sending King Kojong into the arms of the Russian Minister, Karl Waeber. Living in the Russian Legation, the terrified king had been a willing listener to the Russian Minister's schemes to promote Russian influence on the peninsula.

Russia's period of ascendancy in Korea had been brief but busy. In the background was the Trans-Siberian Railroad connecting European Russia with the Pacific, nearing completion and requiring warm water ports to project Russian power into the Pacific. On the other hand was the rise of Meiji Japan with national security concerns that required it to possess Korea, both for its inherent value and to deny it to any rival power. For a while it appeared that Russia would gain a Korean port as a naval base; then came the Nishi-Rosen Agreement of 1898 limiting Russia's interest in Korea and redirecting it to Port Arthur and the building of the South Manchurian Railway. Russian influence in Korea ended for good, however, when the Japanese won the Russo-Japanese War of 1904-05. With the Treaty of Portsmouth, Russia pulled out of the "Great Game of Empire" in Korea and left the peninsula, in effect, to the Japanese. The United States made a separate deal of its own with Japan, promising not to interfere with Japanese power in Korea if the Japanese would stay out of the Philippines. Not long thereafter, Japan established a protectorate over Korea and then annexed it outright, maintaining it as a colony until the end of World War II.

The events of the Russo-Japanese War created much excitement in Korea's foreign community. The arrival of the Japanese fleet at Chemulp'o on February 8, 1904, and the sinking of the Russian warships *Variag* and *Koryetz,* were major spectacles, the explosions being heard in Seoul, twenty-two miles inland. The trains that carried Japanese soldiers northward to face the Russians also brought journalists from the West, including Jack London, writing for the *San Francisco Examiner.*[1]

During lulls in reporting from the front, London and his fellow reporters told about the isolated Westerners living near the battle lines. This meant human-interest stories on American Minister Horace Allen, Russian civilians fleeing Seoul and other points, and the movement of Western refugees within Korea. The spotlight shone briefly on Korea, and the foreign community basked in the world's attention.[2]

The world was fascinated with the Russo-Japanese War because the Asiatic Japanese had taken on a major white power and were defeating it with modern, Western-style weapons. Great Britain kept a watchful eye, sending the cruiser HMS *Phoenix* to the tiny northeast Korean port of Sŏngjin to

---

1. Jack London's visit to Korea was the occasion for much excitement in the Seoul foreign community, which hosted a reception and a reading for him at the Seoul Union Club. Some of London's souvenirs and letters from Korea are preserved in the museum at his former home in the Valley of the Moon, Sonoma County, California. For a critique of London's view of Koreans, which were frankly racist, see James S. Lee, "Jack London: War Correspondent in Korea," *Korean Culture,* XV:1 (spring 1994), pp. 26-33.

2. See *The Russo-Japanese War: A Photographic and Descriptive Review of the Great Conflict in the Far East* (New York: P. F. Collier and Son, 1905).

evacuate two Canadian missionary couples.[3] At Sŏnch'ŏn, on the opposite
coast, the American Presbyterians sighted Russian scouts on February 16,
and a 5,300-man cavalry contingent that followed on February 20. U.S.
Minister Horace Allen in Seoul and mission chairman Samuel A. Moffett in
P'yŏngyang urged the missionaries—including Carl and Daisy Kearns—to
evacuate Sŏnch'ŏn. But the Russians had already passed through the town
heading south and it seemed pointless to follow them toward the battle.
Instead the Sŏnch'ŏn missionaries considered going into the hills where
there was an American mining camp. They thought of asking for a ship to
evacuate them to China. But some decided to stay, since a general evacuation would have left the station open to vandalism—and the station's
prized milk cow might be stolen.[4]

Sŏnch'ŏn had a mission hospital tended by Alfred Sharrocks, and during
the course of the war Dr. Sharrocks took in wounded men from both armies as they fought along the rail line. The Sŏnch'ŏn missionaries had
front row seats for one battle at the end of March, when the Japanese were
preparing to force the Russians northward beyond the Yalu River. Sharrocks described it in a letter to Horace Allen:

Tuesday morning before daybreak the wounded began to come in on their
stretchers and I was sorry to find among them an English speaking lieutenant
who had been up to the house for dinner a couple of times and with whom
we had become very good friends. From him…I learned that the Russian loss
was about 10 killed and from 20 to 30 wounded. He said that the Japanese
charged up the hill most bravely and that they [the Russians] had learned that
their enemy were good soldiers. He said that they were about 600 strong
while the Japanese were over a thousand. He also said that the Japanese
losses were much heavier than their own. From the Koreans, however, we
learned that this was not so and from the diary of a Japanese which was lost
here in [Sŏnch'ŏn] we learned that the Japanese loss was 5 killed and 18
wounded.…

The [Russian] troops stopped here [at the Presbyterian compound] that day
and at 1:00 there was a call to arms and suddenly the greatest running
around. Russians were running to their camp. Sentinels were coming from
the hills and Koreans were running everywhere. A few scouts had met a few
Japanese 15 li out and came back saying the enemy were coming. The troops
lined the top of the ridge where the rifle pits had formerly been dug and the
horses were tied at the base down in back. We sat on our front porch, which
commands a view of the town, and with field glasses in hand awaited developments. For three hours we expected any moment to be the first foreigners

3. A. Hamish Ion, *The Cross and the Rising Sun: The Canadian Protestant Missionary Movement in the Japanese Empire, 1872-1931* (Waterloo, Ontario: Wilfrid
Laurier University Press, 1990), p. 167. The Canadian missionaries were taken to
the port of Wonsan.
4. This account follows Marian A. Sharrocks Intemann et al., *In Syen Chun, Korea, during the Russo-Japanese War of 1904* (Santa Rosa: n.p., 1984), pp. 2 ff.

to be treated to a view of a battle. At about 4:00 the tension lessened and at 5:00 the troops began to move off. This was the last we saw of them in any numbers and in a couple of days this part of the country was entirely given over to the Japanese.[5]

The picture of the Americans on their porches in Sŏnch'ŏn waiting with binoculars for the battle in the town below is indicative of the position of Americans in Korea at the time: fascinated and vulnerable, yet oddly detached from the actual events. What they saw at least taught them to take the Japanese seriously. Many other people in the world—non-Westerners, particularly—likewise invested Japan's campaign against Russia with great significance, since it seemed to disprove the language of white supremacy that had been so much a part of world politics in the late nineteenth century.

In America itself, the war was not much more than journalistic entertainment. In Washington, D.C., the Theodore Roosevelt administration took a cold-eyed, realistic view of events in Korea, siding with Japan as England's ally, lauding Japan's success and progress from feudal state to world power, and accepting Japan as the logical hegemon in East Asia. Certainly Roosevelt saw no reason for the United States to intervene or take a stand to help Korea ward off Japanese domination. He was the one who brokered the Russo-Japanese treaty that recognized Japan's "special interest" in Korea. Later in the year 1905 his secretary of state, William Howard Taft, signed a separate agreement with Japanese Foreign Minister Katsura Tarō conceding Japanese control over Korea in return for Japan's acceptance of American control in the Philippines. Roosevelt believed that it was a matter of nature taking its course. "We cannot possibly interfere for the Koreans against Japan," he said. "They could not strike one blow in their own defence."[6] Consequently the United States was disinclined to object in November 1905, when the Japanese forced Korea to accept a protectorate, an arrangement whereby Korea turned its defense and foreign affairs over to a Japanese super-ambassador to be known as the "Resident-General of Chōsen."

5. Intemann, pp. 68-70.
6. Howard K. Beale, *Theodore Roosevelt and the Rise of America to World Power* (Baltimore: The Johns Hopkins University Press, 1956), p. 280. In retrospect, many Koreans are offended by the way Roosevelt belittled their armed struggle against the Japanese and he is often denounced as one who helped the Japanese take over Korea. The deeper truth, however, is that the United States was completely without means to deter the Japanese. With its fleet in the Atlantic and its army tied down in the Philippines, it is hardly conceivable that Congress would have committed forces to defend Korea, a little-known country where there were virtually no American interests at stake.

Korea's own top officials signed the protectorate treaty with Japan in Seoul's Tŏksu Palace, literally at swordpoint. Charlie Clark recorded the
events of late November in his diary:

> Six thousand Japanese soldiers surrounded the Korean palace and com-
> pelled the king to sign a request to them for aid in governing his kingdom.
> On our Thanksgiving Day, November 30, there was a big riot in Seoul, by the
> Big Bell, caused by the suicide of Min Yonghwan, one of the former minis-
> ters. Leaders of the mob were from among the Pyengyang Christian academy
> boys. The Japanese dispersed the mob with pistols and swords, wounding
> several. The next day, the Japanese had a mock battle on the drill ground
> near the East Gate, using all their artillery to scare the Koreans stiff. Also on
> November 30, at the American Legation, there was a farewell reception to all
> Americans and the final closing of the Legation in Korea, all foreign affairs in
> the future to be carried on from Tokyo.[7]

Champions of a Lost Cause

Of the Westerners in Korea at the time of the protectorate treaty, three
—Horace Allen, Homer Hulbert, and Ernest Bethell—are remembered for
having spoken out against Japan. Horace Allen, who had been appointed
U.S. minister to Korea in 1897, argued for years that the United States
should take a more active stance against Japanese imperialism in Korea.
Furthermore, as an American official charged with the promotion of American commerce abroad, he was convinced by 1905 that Japan's takeover of
Korea would be a step toward closing the Open Door to American trade all
over East Asia. For this reason, as well as out of loyalty to the cause of Korean independence, Allen wanted the Roosevelt administration to work
with Russia to check Japan. He expressed this to the president during a
1903 visit to the White House, and the ensuing argument marked him as
disloyal and led to his replacement as minister at the beginning of Roosevelt's second term in the spring of 1905. Allen therefore was off the stage by
the time of the Portsmouth negotiations and without influence as Roosevelt stood aside and let Japan take Korea.[8]

7. American Consul Willard Straight described the midnight signing ceremony
itself: "At half past one I went out for a stroll around the compound. There was a
rattling of rickshaws and on looking over the wall I saw the Japanese going
away…the palace compound full of Japanese policemen and gendarmes….Kore-
ans in court dress were fluttering to and fro but little was said. It seemed impossible, as I stood there in the moonlight behind the hedge, that the fate of a nation had
been sealed within fifty yards of where I stood, that an independent Empire of
12,000,000 people had subjected themselves to bullying and exploitation without
a struggle. Yet the Ministers had signed." Quoted in Herbert Croly, *Willard Straight*
(New York: Macmillan, 1925), p. 182.
8. Harrington, *God, Mammon, and the Japanese,* pp. 302-318. Allen opposed
Japanese hegemony in Korea not because he advocated Korean independence but
because Japan's rule would be bad for American influence in the peninsula. He felt

The second Western defender was Homer Hulbert, who had come to Korea in 1886 to teach in the Korean government's English language school and subsequently joined the Methodist Mission. Hulbert made a hobby of collecting historical lore about Korea and left a considerable literature to future generations in the *Korean Repository,* the *Korea Review,* and two books on Korean history. This identification with Korea led to his involvement in resistance against Japanese encroachment. In particular, he is remembered for having arranged a secret Korean appeal to the 1907 world peace conference at The Hague. The appeal came from the Korean monarch and was meant for presentation at The Hague by a delegation headed by Yi Chun (1858-1907), a trusted ex-official. Homer Hulbert went along as special advisor. He hoped the appeal might embarrass Japan into restoring some of the Korean court's authority, at least, and perhaps even lead to political recognition by some of the other nations represented at the conference.

Japanese intelligence got wind of the Yi Chun mission before it left Seoul, however, and Hulbert was under surveillance the entire time.[9] In May 1907, as the delegation was leaving Korea for the rail trip across Russia, the Japanese started trying to discredit Hulbert by publishing reports on his finances, pointing out that he had arrived in Korea penniless but was leaving with a fortune made from real estate speculation while ostensibly a missionary. At the same time, Japanese diplomats at The Hague were put on alert. When the Koreans arrived and tried to present their credentials on June 27, the Conference rejected them on grounds that the Korean ruler was under Japan's protection and no longer had any diplomatic standing of his own. Yi Chun thereupon collapsed and died, and Homer Hulbert continued on his way home to the United States, never to see Korea again until 1949, after the Japanese had finally left. In America, Hulbert wrote about Korea in many newspapers and gave numerous speeches before civic gatherings, all in the hope of getting the American public interested in

that Korea's subjugation by some foreign power or other was inevitable, but given a choice he would have preferred the Russians.

9. Hulbert was the actual courier of the documents from the Korean emperor on his trip to Europe via the Trans-Siberian Railway. From Vladivostok to Moscow he shared a wagonlit compartment with the W.F. Bulls, a Southern Presbyterian missionary family from Kunsan, Korea. According to Mrs. Bull, Hulbert confided that he was carrying papers from Emperor Kojong to be delivered (as she understood it) to President Theodore Roosevelt and Secretary of State Elihu Root. In her trip journal she wrote, "Dr. Hulbert knew the Japanese were watching him closely and was uneasy for fear that his baggage would be searched and the papers found and matters made even worse for Korea. He told us his trouble. I spoke up and told him to bring the papers and that I would put them in cases where the children's clothes were. He accepted the offer. I was able to give them [back] to him in Moscow." Journal of Libby Alby Bull, May 1907. My thanks to Virginia Bell Somerville for giving me access to the journal.

the cause of Korean independence; but he was usually followed by Japanese agents who refuted his assertions in letters and speeches of their own. Hulbert had little impact either on the public or the U.S. government, which came to regard him as a familiar type of agitator: the longtime expatriate so sentimentally attached to his adopted country that he lost all perspective on world affairs.[10]

The third Westerner whom Koreans associate with the resistance was Ernest Bethell, a Britisher who originally came to Korea as a *London Daily News* correspondent during the Russo-Japanese War and stayed on to edit a short-lived English paper called the *Korea Times.* In 1908, he tried again with the *Taehan Mae'il Sinbo,* which had an English edition called the *Korea Daily News.* In these papers Bethell openly criticized Japanese policy in Korea and he quickly wore out his welcome. British officials, mindful of the Anglo-Japanese Alliance, tried without success to soften his position, and in 1908 he was arrested along with his Korean co-editor Yang Kit'ak. The British navy obligingly removed the pair to Shanghai, where they were briefly imprisoned, but within months Bethell was back in Seoul, no less full of political fire. "My fight for Korea is heaven-ordained," he announced. "I will work, regardless of my personal safety." His ringing declaration is famous among Koreans; but like Horace Allen and Homer Hulbert, Bethell was undone by his own flaws. In Bethell's case it was alcohol, which is believed to have been the reason for his death in 1909 at the age of 36. Ironically, the Japanese bought his paper and turned it into the official organ of the colonial regime.[11]

Some of the news about what the Japanese were doing to Korea percolated through to the West. Homer Hulbert wrote a book about it entitled *The Passing of Korea.*[12] Frederick A. McKenzie, a reporter for the *London Daily Mail,* published an impassioned account of Japanese abuses in Korea from the Kanghwa Treaty of 1876 through the murder of Queen Min in 1895 to the period of the Japanese Protectorate between 1905 and 1910. McKenzie first discovered Korea during the Russo-Japanese War and then

10. The Acting Secretary of State was quoted as saying of Hulbert, "We are familiar with the method of those agitators. We shall know exactly how to deal with them." See Hilary Conroy, *The Japanese Seizure of Korea: 1868-1910. A Study of Realism and Idealism in International Relations* (Philadelphia: University of Pennsylvania Press, 1960), pp. 347-349. Hulbert's own account of the Japanese takeover of Korea is *The Passing of Korea* (Garden City, N.Y.: Doubleday, 1906, reprint Seoul: Yonsei University Press, 1969), especially pp. 169-224; biographical data about him is collected in Clarence Norwood Weems's introduction to *Hulbert's History of Korea,* I, pp. ED23-ED62.

11. *Taehan Mae'il Sinbo,* 1 (August 1904-March 1905), reprint, with introduction (Seoul: Inmunhwasa, 1976), pp. 4-5. Chong Chin-sok, "E. T. Bethell and the Taehan Maeil Sinbo," *Korea Journal,* XXIV:4 (April 1984), pp. 39-44.

12. Homer Hulbert, *The Passing of Korea* (Garden City, New York: Doubleday, 1905).

returned to witness the events of the Protectorate era. His exposé, *The Tragedy of Korea*,[13] was aimed at British and American readers who liked to devour accounts of exotic lands and adventures on the fringes of Western civilization, a market wider than for missionary books, including Hulbert's histories with their impenetrable detail. Of particular interest was McKenzie's account of trips into the Korean countryside to watch the rebellious soldiers of the disbanded Korean army fight guerrilla actions against the occupying Japanese. These were the "righteous troops," the *ŭibyŏng*, disarmed by the puppet emperor Sunjong in 1907 and re-armed with whatever rusting weapons they could scrounge: bird guns, horse pistols, wartime souvenirs, and antique Chinese muzzle-loaders. With donations from villagers and dispirited local *yangban*, these *ŭibyŏng* harried patrols of disciplined Japanese regular army troops in the years of the protectorate. They inflicted damage, but in the end they were no match for the invaders. Their doomed resistance was inspiring to McKenzie, and he portrayed them as true heroes:

> A pitiful group they seemed—men already doomed to certain death, fighting in an absolutely hopeless cause. But as I looked the sparkling eyes and smiles of the [Korean] sergeant to the right seemed to rebuke me. Pity! Maybe my pity was misplaced. At least they were showing their countrymen an example of patriotism, however mistaken their method of displaying it might be.[14]

But not everyone saw the *ŭibyŏng* in such a favorable light. The fighting between the Japanese and the righteous troops devastated the countryside, and often the Korean fighters were as hard on the people as the Japanese. Charlie Clark, who spent much of the year 1907 riding a circuit of country churches east of Seoul in the valleys of Kyŏnggi and Kangwŏn provinces, observed the results in his assigned mission territory.

> I saw the ruins of hundreds of houses burned either by the Japanese or the "euipyungs," for both are in the business. At Yanggeun, 300 houses, at Tuksoo, 80, Yongmoon, 80, and so on. These were the largest towns but every day we passed isolated houses and small villages burned in whole or in part. Hundreds are living in caves. Hundreds more are crowded into houses that were hastily patched together after it got cold and, as the mud is not dry, it is impossible to heat them. The Japanese have been very cruel, in some places, but on the whole, no worse than the other side. The "euipyungs" are the real oppressors of the poor. Some months ago, there was a faint spark of patriotism in this movement and it no doubt lingers in some individuals, but my conclusion, from what I saw, is that 90% of them are in it for Number One and not for the sake of the country. They have never, so far as I could find, sought the Japanese to fight them. From the beginning, they have gone around in bands of 30 to 1500 men, going from village to village, summoning the leaders of the town and demanding great sums of money. Wherever they

13. F.A. McKenzie, *The Tragedy of Korea*, 2d. ed. (London, 1908).
14. Ibid., p. 201.

were refused, they murdered or tortured without limit. In Hong Sung Eup alone, they have squeezed a total in money and goods of 46,000 nyang, or over 5,000 yen, as the exchange now is. They have actually taken the clothes off the backs of the poor, where no money was available. When the Japanese appear, they scatter and run. The Japanese have put about 2500 or so soldiers in every county. These are often in bands of 5 or 10, who go out fearlessly against hundreds of "euipyungs" and the latter run. Occasionally the "euipyungs" get cornered and have to fight and these are the battles that we hear about in Seoul.

The Japanese, in two places, have shown themselves hostile to our churches. In Yong-moon, they came in on Sunday while the people were worshipping, tore the flag off the flagpole and set fire to the church. In Tangmi, they scraped the crosses off the front doors of the Christian houses. In Noramteul, however, though they set fire to the whole town, they spared the church. Two Christians only have been harmed. The "yoo-sa" of Noramteul was shot while gambling with a "euipyung" at midnight, and the leader of the Tangmoroo group was killed because he lied to the Japanese in answer to a question.

The "euipyungs" have taken food and clothes and money from the Christians and they burned one Christian village near Whang-sang-kol, but they have not as yet harmed any of our people physically. The most disturbed of all the places I saw was Hong Sung County (in western Kangwŏn Province) and I have just received a letter saying that the conditions there are even worse, now. Not a day passes there without battles. The Japanese work in relays and the "euipyungs" are having a lively time of it. Our groups in Hong Sung are badly broken up. Everyone who could come to Seoul left months ago.[15]

Later in the year he wrote again,

The whole area has been passing through a reign of terror. All the opponents of the Japanese from the 13 provinces have assembled here because the mountains make it hard for the Japanese to catch them. The guerrilla fighters have roamed around in bands living off the land. The Japanese have followed them wherever they could get any knowledge of them. Night and day, for months, continuous skirmishing has gone on. No mercy was shown on either side. Anyone suspected of helping either side was at once shot by the other, if caught. Every house or village that entertained either side was at once burned by the other. Almost any day, one could hear shooting. Members of the pro-Japanese Korean society, the Ilchinhoe, spent their time paying off old grudges, getting the Japanese to jail off their private enemies by pretending that these enemies were "euipyungs." It has put the church through a test by fire.[16]

15. Charles Allen Clark, Personal Report to the Korea Mission for 1906-07, in the C.A. Clark papers.
16. Charles Allen Clark, Personal Report to the Korea Mission for 1907-08, in the C.A. Clark papers.

The Japanese did not hide their intentions once they had pacified the angry Koreans. They expected to take the land. "How do the Japanese treat the Koreans?" asked Charlie Clark. "On the hills near us are fields, and along the borders of nearly every field little stakes marked with Japanese names of those who will be along to buy, whether the owner wants to sell or not. Some fields have been in the family for generations, but the Koreans cannot roll back the tide."[17]

The Protectorate as an Opportunity

As Korea's Westerners watched Japan steal Korea's independence, they wondered if the protectorate arrangement might not actually be to their advantage. There was a consensus that the country was in wretched shape after generations of rule by *yangban* whose vaunted Confucian ethics were nothing but a corrupt façade.[18] "Behold Korea," wrote the missionary editor of the *Korean Repository* in 1895, "with her oppressed masses, her dirt and filth, her degraded women, her blighted families–behold all this and judge for yourselves what Confucianism has done for Korea."[19] The need for reform was obvious, and it seemed unlikely that ordinary Koreans would do worse under Japanese rule. In fact many thought they might actually do better.

The Koreans' own appetite for change was shown in the reform movements at all levels of society during the nineteenth century—reform ideologies that elicited powerful responses.[20] Some of the ideas came at least indirectly from the West. Thousands of Koreans had become Catholics in the nineteenth century despite the direst persecutions and thousands remained faithful despite all obstacles. In the 1890s Koreans responded to Protestant Christianity the same way, giving the missionaries a sense of his-

17. Charles Allen Clark to Arthur Judson Brown, letter, March 18, 1905, in the C.A. Clark papers.
18. For a scathing assessment of *yangban* in general, though not perhaps as artful as some traditional Korean satires on the same theme, see Homer Hulbert's "The Rise of the Yangban," in the *Korean Repository* (December 1895), pp. 471-474.
19. *Korean Repository* (November 1895), p. 403. Foreigners were not the only ones with these opinions. For example, see *Yun Ch'iho Ilgi*, hereafter referred to as *YCH* (Seoul: Kuksa p'yŏnch'an wiwŏnhoe, 1973-1988), IV, p. 82 and passim. Also see Spencer John Palmer, *Korea and Christianity* (Seoul: Royal Asiatic Society, 1967), p. 717, for a sampling of contemporary lamentations from the turn of the century, ending with the suicide letter of Prince Min Yŏnghwan.
20. These included the Silhak "Practical Learning" school, which had helped infiltrate Catholicism illegally into the country; local peasant revolts such as that of Hong Kyŏngnae in 1811; larger peasant uprisings such as the Tonghak Movement of the 1860s and the subsequent rebellion in the 1890s; the ill-fated reform efforts of the pro-Japanese faction in 1894-95; and the progressive agitation of the Independence Club in 1895-98.

toric opportunity.[21] Their schools and training institutes attracted commoners who were hungry for education. Their church organizations created new communities. New converts learned to read the Bible through the missionaries' literacy campaigns, empowering women as well as men, the poor as well as the rich. Many missionaries undoubtedly appreciated the democratic implications of mass literacy as well. But to commoner Koreans above all, it meant access to the power of the written word—a privilege previously reserved by the *yangban* class. The rate of conversions therefore began to accelerate in the 1890s, and by 1910 the Protestant community claimed nearly 200,000 members out of a total population of 13 million.[22]

Missionary work, however, was not universally successful. Christianity sank deeper roots in the northwest than in the south, and there were more converts in the countryside than in the cities. One reason for the receptivity in northwestern Korea was the traditional resentment felt by northerners against the royal government in Seoul, which was packed with southern *yangban*. Resentment against discrimination by southerners simmered steadily throughout the nineteenth century. Another factor may have been the fact that the Korean northwest was an area frequently traveled by foreigners and therefore less xenophobic than the more isolated south. For a generation, Japanese merchants had been flooding the northwest with imported products, adding to the market pressure already being exerted by Chinese merchants from across the Yalu. The Japanese railroad being built between Pusan and Sinŭiju on the border brought many more outsiders to the region. All these things fueled social and political unrest in northwestern Korea and created a climate hospitable to change. Into this regional culture Western missionaries introduced ideas and ways of life that seemed like alternatives to what was being offered by the Japanese and Chinese, and certainly by the waning Korean system.

As Koreans expressed their grief and anger over the collapse of the traditional order, many flocked to Christian churches to be caught up in the "Great Revival" of 1907.[23] One missionary explained it in terms of historical opportunity: "Many are realizing the failure of the ancient civilization of their fathers in the stress of the twentieth century. They see that the nations styled Christian are the ones that today possess the highest civilization and

21. "Continued Progress," in the *Korean Repository*, II (1895), p. 268.
22. *The Korea Mission Field*, VI:10 (October 1, 1910), p. 249, put the number of Protestants at 173,000. L. George Paik, writing later, put the figure for the same year at 200,000 in *The History of Protestant Missions in Korea, 1832-1910*, rev. ed. (Seoul: Yonsei University Press, 1971), p. 423.
23. An eyewitness account of the Great Revival in P'yŏngyang can be found in Blair, *Gold in Korea*, pp. 66-68. Martha Huntley provides a composite of reminiscences about it in *Caring, Growing, Changing: A History of the Protestant Mission in Korea* (New York: Friendship Press, 1984), chapter VI.

culture...."[24] But this was a temporal explanation. The missionaries who witnessed the waves of emotionalism that broke over their congregations in 1907 saw it as nothing less than a mighty sweeping of the Holy Spirit over Korea. It began in the Methodist churches of Wŏnsan and spread to the Presbyterian churches of P'yŏngyang, where it became a national phenomenon. As the movement took on a life of its own, hundreds of church people, mostly men, were gripped by guilt and went into frenzies of prayer, confessing sins and begging forgiveness both from God and from those they had wronged. Missionaries began the services but they soon erupted spontaneously, with Korean pastors and laymen leading them.

Kil Sŏnju, one of the first Presbyterian pastors, was especially effective in the P'yŏngyang meetings, and Charlie Clark decided to invite him to bring the revival to the Central Church in Seoul. Kil quickly ignited the congregation into a white heat of grief and passion. "The people seemed on fire with a loathing for sin and wild to tell it and get rid of the burden," wrote Clark.

> Every day we saw them with tears confessing one to the other and begging forgiveness....Men would confess part of their sin and the very vision of the vileness of it all would seem to get hold of them and they would fall on their faces before God fairly writhing in agony....As in Pyeng Yang,...prayer aloud went on all the time all over the church, 300 to 500 people praying aloud all at once....Two or three would be on their feet at once shaking from head to foot in agony as only a repentant sinner can before an angry God....Back and forth over the church would go the sound of weeping and praying dying down and then rising as some poor soul confessed to his God....

The effects of the revival awed Charlie Clark even though his straitlaced Presbyterian soul recoiled at the wild emotions that he saw in the meetings. In his country travels he had watched Korean villagers reduced to babbling simpletons by illness or insanity and he had seen their conditions aggravated by folk healers and shamans. He noticed certain coincidences between Korean folk religion and what he saw in the 1907 revival and it made him uncomfortable.

In his seminary days in Chicago, Charlie had belittled the idea of demon possession, chalking the symptoms up to "insanity or nervousness or an injudicious lack of discipline in childhood." But an experience one day during the revival at the Central Church changed his mind. A man in the back of one of the meetings had started banging on his Bible and raving, trying to disrupt the service and lashing out at anyone who tried to control him. Charlie Clark and Kil Sŏnju left the platform and went to the back to deal with the disturbance. They were obliged to haul the man to an outer room.

24. C.E. Sharp, "Motives for Seeking Christ," *The Korea Mission Field*, II:9 (July 1906), p. 182. See also Allen, *Things Korean*, p. 120, and Roy E. Shearer, *Wildfire: Church Growth in Korea* (Grand Rapids, Mich.: William B. Eerdmans, 1966), p. 50.

When he got there he began to rage like a wild beast. He smashed his own hat
and ripped off his coat, tore open his leggings, and then started to demolish
the room. He fell on his face on the floor....Just then he saw a box in the
room shaped somewhat like the ancestral worship boxes for tablets and he
prostrated himself before it....The veins of his neck swelled till it seemed
they must burst. Finally I became convinced that it was a devil's manifestation...so I went to him, took firm hold of his shaking hands, and ordered him
in Jesus' name to be still....Then I prayed and almost at once he became
quiet. I prayed again and he subsided. After lying quietly for about 10 minutes while we prayed beside him he seemed suddenly to wake up and I will
testify that he was as sane as any Korean I know. He gave us his name. Said he
had been believing seven weeks. He did not have a very clear idea of what he
had done but when he saw his head smashed and his clothes all torn he felt
terribly. After prayer again we let him out a back way and he went home....

The previous summer Charlie had read an account of a missionary's
"casting out devils" in China and he had regarded it as nonsense. There
had to be a medical or scientific explanation. But it seemed clear to him
that the spirit he had seen in the Korean man at the Central Church was an
agent of Satan. "The Holy Spirit was doing so great a work that I firmly believe the devil entered into that man to make him break up the meeting,"
he wrote. "As sure as I believe there is a Holy Spirit who can 'convince men
of sin and righteousness and judgment' I am convinced that the devil can
work now in opposition to Him exactly as he did 1900 years ago."[25]

It was in the Great Revival of 1907 that Korean Protestantism acquired
much of its emotional tradition of public confession, prayer, and renewal.
The missionaries themselves were amazed by what took place. And to this
day, Korean Protestants look back on the events of that year as a crisis that
created the momentum in their movement and gave it the morale that enabled it to survive the decades of trial that were to follow.[26]

In this way the success of Protestant Christianity paralleled the Japanese
conquest of Korea. The political situation undoubtedly contributed to the
movement's growth. But if Koreans were reacting against the coming of
the Japanese, quite a few missionaries saw the Japanese as reformers who
would improve conditions and perhaps even make missionary work eas-

25. Charles Allen Clark, "Dear Friends" letter, Seoul, March 1, 1907, in the C.A.
Clark papers.
26. This growth spawned an ambitious "million movement" to build the church
membership even more rapidly through 1910. However, non-missionary sources
note that in the aftermath of the annexation a significant number of Koreans, perhaps 50,000, stopped coming to church, causing some retrenchment. U.S. Consul-General Leo Bergholz to the Secretary of State (hereafter "SecState"), March 16,
1919, in U.S. Department of State, "Correspondence Relating to the Internal Affairs
of Korea, 1910-1929," a part of Record Group 59, Archives of the Department of
State in the National Archives and Records Service, Washington, D.C., file number
895.00/589. Department of State documents are hereafter cited by document title
and date, followed by the file number in parentheses.

ier.[27] They assumed that events in Korea were divinely ordained and must be accepted by Christians as instructed by the Apostle Paul in his epistle to the Romans, chapter XIII, verses 1-3:

> Let every person be subject to the governing authorities. For there is no authority except from God, and those that exist have been instituted by God. Therefore, he who resists the authorities resists what God has appointed, and those who resist will incur judgment. For rulers are not a terror to good conduct but to bad....

The Japanese reciprocated. In 1910, the newly appointed governor-general, Terauchi Masatake, assured the missionaries that he too believed in the separation of church and state and that the new regime would smile on their work:

> Freedom of religion will always be respected and I am ready to extend due protection and facilities to the propagation of all religious doctrines, provided they do not interfere with politics. I am one of those who fully appreciate the good work of foreign missionaries, and as we have the same object in view as they, the improving of the general conditions of the people, their work will by no means be subjected to any inconvenience. I need scarcely say that all the vested rights of foreign residents will be fully respected.[28]

27. Arthur Judson Brown, *The Mastery of the Far East* (London: G. Bell and Sons, 1919), pp. 354-362. Pioneer missionary James Scarth Gale was among those who hoped that the Japanese would improve things for everyone, the Koreans and missionaries, as well as themselves. Consul-General Thomas Sammons (Shanghai) to SecState, July 22, 1919 (895.00/653). Gale later was greatly disillusioned, especially by the suppression of the March 1 Independence Movement in 1919.

28. Quoted in George H. Scidmore (U.S. consul-general, Seoul), to assistant secretary of state, September 1, 1910 (895.00/501).

-- 3 --

The Great Independence Uprising

When Japan annexed Korea in August 1910, Resident-General Terauchi Masatake became the head of a new colonial regime to be known as the Government-General of Chōsen. The name "Chōsen" was the Japanese pronunciation of "Chosŏn," the ancient Sino-Korean name of the Korean kingdom. The administrative structure that had developed under Terauchi and his predecessor Itō Hirobumi was expanded, and Japan sent a full complement of bureaucrats to staff it. The man at the top of this structure was uniquely powerful. Once appointed by the imperial government in Tokyo, the governor-general of Chōsen was Korea's chief executive, its only legislator, and its supreme judge. In theory, the citizens of Chōsen were Japanese imperial subjects who enjoyed the rights and duties set forth in the Meiji Constitution. In reality, they were subjects of the governor-general.

Relations with foreign residents in Chōsen became the responsibility of the Foreign Affairs Bureau of the Government-General. This bureau was headed by a succession of urbane, English-speaking officials whose abilities impressed Korea's Western residents. They made an especially favorable impression when compared to Korea's former government officials. An example of their commonsensical approach was the way they handled licensing for Western missionary doctors and nurses. The former Korean government had not bothered to issue licenses. The Japanese required them but found that the rules required that exams be taken in Japanese. This was beyond the ability of Korea's missionary medical personnel, so Foreign Affairs Bureau Chief Komatsu Midori and U.S. Consul-General Ransford Miller worked out an exception to enable them to continue their work by taking their qualifying exams in English. Many potential conflicts between the Japanese and other foreigners in Korea were avoided through consultations and good will. Both sides wanted to find ways to show that they could coexist under the new regime.[1]

In the provinces it was a different story. Lower-ranking provincial officials were not as well educated and had less authority than the ones in Seoul, and they erred on the side of caution, enforcing regulations in ways designed to please their superiors rather than to serve the public. The convenience of foreigners was low on their priority list, and dealing with them became an endless story of frustration and conflict. Law enforcement and investigations of infractions were the business of Japan's colonial gendarmerie, or *kempeitai*.[2] In a typical case of *kempeitai* diligence, a gendarme might notice a mission clinic flying a Red Cross flag and order that it be taken down.[3] A missionary teacher's Korean student assistant might be detained for interrogation about cameras and "spy equipment" in the foreigner's home. An investigator might demand a list of publications being received on the foreign compound. The police might order the foreigners not to slaughter any of the compound hogs for food without first obtaining a meat inspector's license.[4] A detective might listen in on a missionary's classes and report his Bible stories as anti-Japanese allusions, thereby bringing on a police investigation.[5] The police pounced on any failure to register overnight guests. At the post office they intercepted letters and packages and subjected the recipients to interrogation. When permits such as drivers' licenses came up for renewal in the provinces, it could take

1. Komatsu Midori to Ransford Miller, July 9, 1914, enclosed with Miller to SecState (895.1281/3). Also Ransford Miller to Ambassador George Guthrie (Tokyo), January 18, 1915, in the same file.

2. In Korea, the Japanese had a regular police force comprised of Japanese and Korean officers, the outgrowth of a merger between civil and military police forces in 1910. The *kempeitai* were gendarmes, part of a separate military police-type force commanded by the colony's chief of police but employing military methods to keep order. As Ching-chih Chen has written, "The unwillingness on the part of the Japanese [Government-General] to switch from the gendarme-dominated policing system to a [civilian] police system. . .accounted for the Japanese failure to prevent what was originally a localized demonstration from developing into a nation-wide, anti-Japanese movement in March 1919." "Police and Community Control Systems in the Empire," in *The Japanese Colonial Empire, 1895-1945*, ed. Ramon Myers and Mark Peattie (Princeton: Princeton University Press, 1984), p. 222.

3. Consul-General George Scidmore (Seoul) to SecState, January 30, 1912 (895.142). In fact it was illegal under U.S. law, and presumably under Japanese law, for persons not associated directly with the Red Cross to fly the Red Cross flag. Scidmore to Rev. William C. Kerr (in Chaeryŏng), January 30, 1912 (895.142).

4. C.N. Weems, Songdo (Kaesŏng), to George Scidmore (Seoul), June 17, 1911 (file number illegible).

5. Among many such examples is an investigation of George S. McCune of Sŏnch'ŏn, reported by Consul-General Ransford Miller (Seoul) to Ambassador George Guthrie (Tokyo), January 16, 1916 (895.00/557).

months for an approval that could be gotten in Seoul within half an hour. Anything that required a "chop"—the personal stamp that served as an official signature—was likely to involve questioning, rudeness, and delays. Nuisances like these reminded the foreigners that they were in Korea only at the pleasure of the Japanese.

While the missionaries were learning to live under Japanese colonial rule there were two serious confrontations with the Government-General. One was the so-called Conspiracy Case of 1911-15, in which the government accused a group of Koreans, mainly Christians, of plotting to assassinate Governor-General Terauchi Masatake. The investigation focused on the Sinsŏng School (the Hugh O'Neill Academy) in Sŏnch'ŏn, where Presbyterian missionary George Shannon McCune was principal, and the indictment named him as an instigator. Though McCune and his students were eventually exonerated, six Korean adults spent several years behind bars, including the Methodist Yun Ch'iho and the journalist Yang Kit'ak, Ernest Bethell's former co-editor on the *Korea Daily News*. Their trial embarrassed the Japanese when the story went around that the accused had been tortured into confessing and had recanted their confessions in open court. In 1915 even the six were granted amnesty; but in the meantime the Japanese put the Christian community on notice that it was being watched, and that many Japanese regarded the Korean church as a hotbed of sedition.[6]

Another case of pressure on foreign and Korean Christians was a list of school regulations that came out in 1915. By that time the missionaries had built a network of schools across Korea, a network supplemented by dozens of informally organized schools attached to churches throughout the country. Their purpose was to teach Korean Christians to read the Bible in their easy *Han'gŭl* alphabet, then known as *ŏnmun*. The teachers were church members whose sole qualification often was that they could read better than their pupils, and few had anything like higher education. Some schools were better than others, but there were no standards for teacher training and no consistent plan for teaching. The curriculum in many church schools was simply literacy and religion.[7]

The new educational ordinances decreed standards for teacher training and denied accreditation to schools that did not meet the standards, including many Christian schools. They also forbade the teaching of religion in accredited schools, which constituted an attack on the raison d'être of

6. Sources on the Conspiracy Case include *The Korean Conspiracy Trial: Full Report of the Proceedings in Appeal, by the Special Correspondent of the "Japan Chronicle"* (Kobe: The Japan Chronicle, 1913), Yun Kyŏngno, *Paek-o-in sakŏn gwa Sinminhoe yŏn'gu* (Studies on the "105 Incident" and the New People's Association) (Seoul: Ilchisa, 1990), and F.A. McKenzie, *Korea's Fight for Freedom*, reprint edition (Seoul: Yonsei University Press, 1969), pp. 218-238.

7. Horace H. Underwood, *Modern Education in Korea* (New York: International Press, 1926), pp. 94-99.

Christian schools. Some missionaries tried to get around the rule by taking religion classes out of the daily schedule and offering them on an extracurricular basis. This upset the missionary faction that considered mission education a diversion from the main business of evangelism. They argued that without religion in the curriculum the schools should be closed altogether.

Negotiations ensued between the missionaries and the Government-General. As a conciliatory gesture the Japanese offered a ten-year grace period during which the missionaries might either redesign their curriculum or phase their schools out. Some missions—the Methodists at Paejae Boys' Academy, for example—dutifully went about conforming to the new standards and dropped religion classes from the daily routine. The Northern Presbyterians, however, decided to keep religion in the daily schedule as long as possible and then to close their schools by the 1925 deadline.[8]

Agitators Unawares

By 1919, most of the missionaries in Korea had become convinced that their goals were at odds with those of the Japanese. The Conspiracy Case proved that the freedoms guaranteed by the Meiji Constitution were not to be extended to the Koreans, and perhaps least of all to Korean Christians under the influence of foreigners. The educational regulations served to warn the missionaries that they could not expect any special treatment or privileged protection for their work.

These points came home with special force on March 1, 1919, with the outbreak of the Korean independence movement. This was a carefully planned wave of anti-Japanese demonstrations timed to coincide with the funeral of the former king, Kojong, who had died in January. The movement was the product of many things: a rumor that the Japanese had poisoned the old king; political agitation by Korean students in Japan who were impatient with their country's subjugation; the inspiration of the Russian revolution and Lenin's calls for an end to imperialism; the Versailles conference and President Woodrow Wilson's call for self-determination and democracy around the world; the coordinated planning of student and youth groups in Korea; and the willingness of religious leaders to step out in front and lead the call for liberation from Japan. The king's funeral, scheduled for March 2, 1919, had brought thousands of Korean mourners

8. There is extensive correspondence on the subject of the school regulations negotiation in the files of the Presbyterian Historical Society in Philadelphia and in the State Department files from the Consulate-General in Seoul at the National Archives in Washington, D.C. In New York, Arthur Judson Brown, the secretary of the Board of Foreign Missions of the Presbyterian Church, U.S.A., took a personal interest in the issue and wrote his analysis in a chapter entitled "Japanese Nationalism and Mission Schools," in *The Mastery of the Far East*, pp. 586-610.

to Seoul to witness the stately procession that was to convey Kojong's body to the specially prepared tomb in Kŭmgok, east of Seoul. On March 1, the day before the funeral, a committee of thirty-three religious leaders representing the Korean Ch'ŏndokyo sect, the country's Christian denominations, and the Buddhist clergy, met at a restaurant to sign a Declaration of Independence that was then proclaimed during the afternoon at a rally in a park on the main street of the scheduled funeral procession. When the colonial police and *kempeitai* arrived to break up the rally, sympathy demonstrations started up around the city and within a few days copies of the Declaration of Independence had been dispersed throughout the country and illegal demonstrations had taken place in towns along the entire length of the peninsula. The Japanese met the demonstrations with force and struggled to retain control, arresting thousands and resorting to torture to extract information about perpetrators. Korean sources claim that there were 47,000 arrests, 7,509 deaths, and 15,951 injuries during the course of the uprising. Japanese sources admit to many fewer. The outbreaks did not cease until late 1920.

The independence uprising surprised the Western community in Korea as much as it surprised the Japanese. Most foreigners sympathized with the idea of Korean independence and admired the organizers' willingness to risk everything as they coordinated efforts to rally support for freedom. The demonstrators' signature chant was "Taehan tongnip mansei!" (Korean independence forever!), and because of the word *mansei* (lit. "ten-thousand years," meaning "forever," the word more famous as *banzai* in Japanese) the Westerners called the rallies "*mansei* demonstrations."

A few foreigners had picked up clues that an anti-Japanese demonstration was in the works, but no one had been expecting a general uprising.[9] Most saw the Koreans after a decade of Japanese rule as being too intimidated to strike back in any organized fashion. Thus, when the Koreans did

---

9. Chōsen Christian College professors Bliss Billings, Herbert Owens, and Arthur Becker had all heard rumors of an impending Korean independence campaign, and all three had taken pains to warn their students not to participate because there was likely to be violence. Owens called the idea "madness." Becker apparently knew that the site of the movement was to be Pagoda Park and warned against it since the demonstrators would be vulnerable to Japanese police if they kept to an enclosed area. Becker and Billings told YMCA secretary Pak Hŭido to stay out of the demonstrations because the YMCA couldn't do without him, and stressed that if there was to be a movement it must be nonviolent. Pak was one of the Christian signers of the Declaration of Independence and ended up spending two years in prison. Ku Dae-yeol, *Korea Under Colonialism: The March First Movement and Anglo-Japanese Relations* (Seoul: Royal Asiatic Society, Korea Branch, 1985), pp. 170-171 and C.I. Eugene Kim, "Nationalist Movements and Students," in *Korea's Response to Japan: The Colonial Period, 1910-1945*, ed. C.I. Eugene Kim and Doretha Mortimore (Kalamazoo: Center for Korean Studies, Western Michigan University, 1977), p. 271.

rise up, they shared the amazement expressed by American Consul-General Leo Bergholz, both at the Koreans' courage and at the ineptitude of the Japanese authorities in failing to preempt the movement.

> Considering the docility, the ready obedience to the law, and the childlike simplicity shown by the Koreans, it is surprising to an occidental that the Government General under Marshal Count Hasegawa so signally failed to comprehend the psychology of the Koreans, a people they had governed for nearly ten years, and who are of a kindred race to the Japanese, and between whom there are no religious differences as western powers must contend with in their African and Near Eastern possessions. The pacific demonstrations in March of this year did not take the Government General by surprise as Mr. Yamagata [Isaburō], the then Administrative Superintendent, and a very capable and humane man, stated that a movement for independence had been continuous since the annexation. If so why could the Japanese not have met the question at its inception by granting certain of the fundamental demands of the Koreans and promising to take others into careful consideration, thus preventing the uprising from reaching national proportions?[10]

Bergholz wanted Americans in Korea to avoid showing sympathy with the uprising, but because so many Korean Christians, especially students at mission schools, were part of the movement, the missionaries could not help becoming associated with it. Some openly praised the demonstrators. A few sheltered their students from the police. Mission hospitals treated the wounded and reports from missionaries all over the country painted a picture of repression for the foreign press that contributed to a public relations disaster for Japan. Students used mission school facilities to hold meetings and print handbills, usually without permission, making unwitting accomplices of their foreign teachers.[11]

There were some who discovered that Korean activists were using them without their knowledge to support the uprising. In Taegu, for example, independence handbills circulated that the police felt sure were being produced on the Presbyterian Mission compound. Many students from the mission's Kyesŏng Boys' School were known to be active in the demonstrations, and one night the police decided to raid the school for incriminating evidence. Rousting principal Harold Henderson out of bed and using his skeleton key, they conducted a thorough search, opening every door and

10. Bergholz to SecState, October 27, 1919, p. 8 (895.00/667).

11. For discussions of missionary involvement in the March First Movement see Donald N. Clark, "'Surely God Will Work Out Their Salvation:' Protestant Missionaries in the March First Movement," *Korean Studies* (University of Hawaii), XIII (1989), pp. 42-75; Frank Baldwin, "Missionaries and the March First Movement: Can Moral Men be Neutral?" in *Korea Under Japanese Colonial Rule*, ed. Andrew C. Nahm (Kalamazoo: Center for Korean Studies, Western Michigan University, 1973), pp. 193-219; Samuel H. Moffett, "The Independence Movement and the Missionaries," in *TKBRAS*, LIV (1979), pp. 13-32; Ku, *Korea under Colonialism*, pp. 169-198; and Huntley, *To Start a Work*, pp. 537-552.

examining every nook of the school building, and yet found nothing. Later that night, as Henderson lay awake replaying the raid in his mind, it occurred to him that one door had been passed over—the door to the closet in the senior class lounge. Immediately he got up, collected a flashlight and a neighbor and went to see what the Japanese had missed behind that one door. In his memoir he wrote,

> [The door] opened into a closet long and narrow, which had nothing in it but litter on the floor. The litter was made up of dozens of used mimeograph stencils and a small hand mimeograph....
>
> It made my blood run cold. Here would have been complete evidence that the school was deeply involved in it all.... We carefully picked up the sheets and took them down to the furnace room and burned them, little by little so as not to make too much smoke....The mimeograph we threw back under a part of the building that had not been excavated.... I never told this story to anyone until after the Koreans secured their independence in 1945.[12]

Harold Henderson did not want to be drawn into the conflict between the Koreans and the Japanese, but he was caught between sympathy for his students and the need to protect his school from Japanese reprisals. This was the missionaries' essential dilemma throughout the independence movement, from the Methodist missionaries at Ewha Girls' School who barred the gates in an unsuccessful attempt to keep their students from joining the demonstrations, to the Presbyterian missionaries who were caught unawares in the midst of a political rally in chapel at their boys' school. That incident took place in P'yŏngyang on March First during what was meant to be a memorial service for the former King Kojong. It began as a religious service, with a scripture lesson from 1 Peter III:13-17 that begins, "Now who is there to harm you if you are zealous for what is right? But even if you do suffer for righteousness' sake, you will be blessed." Missionary Charles Bernheisel's diary describes what happened as the lector read the passage,

> it was evident from his intonation as he read that something serious was on the docket. Then Chong Il-sun, a graduate of the college...took the platform and said he had an important communication to read. He said it was the happiest and proudest day of his life...a great cheer went up from the audience. He then proceeded to read what was virtually a declaration of independence of the Korean people.[13]

12. Clara Hedberg Bruen, comp., *Forty Years in Korea* (n.p., Family Memoir [1987]), pp. 253-255.

13. Charles F. Bernheisel, "Forty-one Years in Korea," newsletters 1900-1941, quoted in Huntley, p. 539.

The Americans found it dangerously easy to look like part of the independence agitation. Here is Bernheisel's diary of events later in the day on March First, when he and several colleagues took a stroll in the direction of downtown:

> After walking for some distance…I happened to look behind us and found that we were leading a long procession. As soon as we had quit the school grounds the crowd…unknown to us, had fallen in behind us and we were thus in the position of leading the procession down the main street of the city. I told the brethren that we must not continue in this position, and they agreed, so we scooted off into an alley and allowed the crowd to follow other leaders.[14]

Even then, Bernheisel should have realized that the missionaries could not avoid association with the movement. Nearly half the signers of the Declaration of Independence on March First had been Christians, eleven of them ordained ministers and former students in the Presbyterian and Methodist theological seminaries. Several had close personal ties with missionaries. Signer Kil Sŏnju, the foremost Korean minister in P'yŏngyang, for example, was the closest protégé of Samuel A. Moffett, the Presbyterian pioneer whom P'yŏngyang Christians were said to obey "as they would Jesus himself."[15] Small wonder, then, that the Japanese considered the missionaries a malign influence on the local people. In the newspaper they continued their diatribe against the foreigners:

> Outside the West Gate of Pyeng Yang there are some houses—some of brick, some in the Korean style—some high and some low. These are the houses of the foreigners. There are about 100 of them. Outwardly they manifest love and mercy but if their minds were investigated, they would be found to be filled with intrigue and greed. They pretend to be here for preaching but they are secretly stirring up political disturbances and foolishly keep passing on the vain tales of the Koreans and thereby foster trouble. These are really the homes of devils…. This is the center of the present Korean uprising. We feel certain it is in the church schools—a certain college and a certain girls' school in a certain compound of these foreigners—really this community is very vile.[16]

Officially, the colonial government refrained from accusing the foreigners of instigating the rebellion. Unofficially, however, the Japanese establishment in Korea thought otherwise. On March 10, the Japanese-language

14. Huntley, p. 540.

15. *Chōsen Shimbun*, quoted in "A Plea for Korea by an Eyewitness," (no date), file microfilm collection on the March 1 Independence Movement compiled by the Presbyterian Historical Society, Philadelphia.

16. *Chōsen Shimbun*, March 10, 1919, quoted in "A Plea for Korea by an Eyewitness."

Chōsen Shimbun attacked the missionaries' character and blamed them for the uprising:

> If one enquires into their learning, their personality, their character, they are failures from home, given a paltry three hundred gold dollars, sent out all the way to the thirteen provinces of Korea.... As was expected, it is they who have planned the present disorder. Then inciting the ignorant mob which constitutes the Chon-do-kyo followers, disturbances have been planned which have now unexpectedly taken a wrong turn.[17]

Japanese and Koreans alike saw missionaries as extensions of their governments' foreign policies, so it was hard to convince them that there was nothing political in their actions. After all, President Woodrow Wilson was known to be a Christian—in fact the son of a Presbyterian minister—and his brand of foreign policy was often labeled "missionary diplomacy." Wilson's statements about independence for colonial peoples in his famous Fourteen Points speech were cited in the Korean Declaration of Independence on March 1. On reflection it seemed plausible that the American community in Korea had been laying the groundwork for the rebellion all along by planting seditious ideas in the minds of Christian youth. For proof one had only to recall the circumstances of the Conspiracy Case: the way George McCune had preached to his students about David and Goliath and the way his fellow missionaries hid their students from the police. Missionaries talked about the separation of church and state but their actions demonstrated clear sympathy with the Koreans against the Japanese.

Wilsonian idealism, of course, was only one of the external influences on the March First Movement. Korean students in Japan itself were more important in getting it organized, and they drew their inspiration from Japanese nationalism itself. Other Korean youth were influenced by the iconoclasm of Chinese young people in what was soon to be known as the May Fourth Movement. The Russian revolution inspired the movement's left wing. But Wilson's ideas had a special place in the uprising.[18] Many Koreans thought that Wilson was personally interested in their cause, and some even hoped for direct American intervention. A group of Seoul schoolgirls wrote Wilson a petition that closed, "Mr. Wilson, President of Great Amer-

17. *Chōsen Shimbun*, cited in Ku, *Korea under Colonialism,* 177-178. For a discussion of the idea that Westerners went abroad to compensate for failures at home, see Arthur Schlesinger Jr., "The Missionary Enterprise and Theories of Imperialism," in *The Missionary Enterprise in China and America,* ed. John King Fairbank (Cambridge, Mass.: Harvard University Press, 1974), pp. 340-342.

18. One reason was Wilson's leadership at the ongoing Versailles peace conference where Koreans hoped to get a hearing before the world community. The Japanese, however, were in a position to ensure that they got no such hearing. Japan had been offended at the West's refusal to insert a racial equality clause in the final treaty, and the powers were determined not to offend Japan further by making declarations about Korean independence.

ica, we look on you as a father. 'Hear our declaration of independence and tell it to the world,' is our prayer."[19] Rumors circulated that Wilson was about to arrive in an airship to lead the Koreans' fight for independence,[20] or, alternatively, that he was about to land at Inch'ŏn with an army to liberate the peninsula.[21] For a while, Wilson was so popular in Korea that the Japanese actually resorted to snipping footage of him out of movie newsreels "as they evoke much enthusiasm among the Koreans in the audience."[22]

The Americans in Korea watched in horror as the colonial police and *kempeitai* cracked down on the demonstrators. Their greatest shock came in April 1919 with the discovery of the smoking ruins at Che'am-ni, a village of about fifty houses near Osan south of Seoul, by a group of foreign residents that included Horace H. Underwood of Chōsen Christian College, U.S. Consul Raymond Curtice, and businessman A.W. Taylor acting as a stringer for the Associated Press. The three were responding to rumors of church burnings in the area when they happened on Che'am-ni and found that the previous day, Japanese army troops had gathered up the Christian and Ch'ŏndokyo men of the village,[23] herded them into the local Methodist church, and there had beaten, stabbed, and shot them, finishing by burning down the building and part of the village. Thirty-five men had died in the church, and with them two protesting wives who were shot dead in the street outside. As they questioned the villagers, the Amer-

19. "A Letter to President Wilson and the Members of the Peace Conference from Korean School Girls," March 10, 1919, Presbyterian Historical Society, Philadelphia.

20. Leo Bergholz, "The Present Movement for Korean Independence," date uncertain (895.00/612).

21. Rumor cited in letter from Frank Herron Smith, Methodist Mission, Seoul, to Sidney Gulick, Secretary of the Commission on Relations with the Orient of the Federal Council of Churches of Christ in America, October 16, 1919, Presbyterian Historical Society, Philadelphia. This curious rumor foreshadows a similar one that circulated in the city of Kwangju, during the civil uprising in 1980, when many citizens apparently believed that the United States was about to deploy forces to rescue them from a martial law assault by the forces of General Chun Doo-hwan. See Linda Lewis, "The 'Kwangju Incident' Observed: An Anthropological Perspective on Civil Uprisings," in *The Kwangju Uprising: Shadows over the Regime in South Korea*, ed. Donald N. Clark (Boulder, Colorado: Westview Press, 1988), pp. 23-24.

22. Bergholz to SecState, April 4, 1919 (895.00/612).

23. Most missionary accounts since 1919 have left the impression that the Che'am-ni massacre victims were Christians, but contemporary accounts indicate that two-thirds of them were Ch'ŏndokyo. (Missionaries also knew this at the time. See, for example, O.R. Avison to A.E. Armstrong, April 30, 1919, Methodist Mission archives, Drew University.) Horace Underwood wrote a transcript of conversations he had with villagers, in which Che'am-ni was identified as a "Christian village." This may be the origin of the idea that the victims were exclusively Christian. See discussion in Ku, *Korea under Colonialism*, pp. 11-114. The full transcript of this and other conversations between Underwood and various villagers is filed at the Presbyterian Historical Society, Philadelphia.

icans learned that the Japanese had similarly attacked a dozen or more other nearby villages.[24]

Consul Curtice's presence on the Che'am-ni expedition forced Consul-General Leo Bergholz to make an official issue of Japanese brutality. He reported Curtice's findings immediately to Foreign Affairs Director Hisamizu Saburō. Hisamizu pled ignorance but promised to investigate, and when he checked with the police and army he got a different version of the story. The police said that they had invited the men of the village to the church to "listen to advice." The villagers had gotten angry and attacked the officers and had overturned a lamp in the melee, setting fire to the church, whereupon amid the chaos it had been necessary for the officers to shoot in self-defense.[25]

The Japanese account, however, did not hold up. Other foreigners visited the area and found that the *kempeitai* and regular soldiers had burned no fewer than eighteen villages. The attacks were said to have been reprisals for the killing of a gendarme in the district some days earlier.[26] However, no orders could be traced to authorize the killings and village burnings, and the likeliest interpretation of the burnings continued to be that the local *kempeitai* had gone on a rampage.

Though U.S. Consul-General Leo Bergholz lacked authority to take his protest any higher, the nonofficial community was able to do more. A group of senior missionaries got an audience with Governor-General Hasegawa Yoshimichi and delivered their objections in person. Hasegawa expressed sorrow for what had happened and assured the missionaries that the responsible police and military officers were being disciplined. He even reached into his pocket for ¥1500 ($750.00) to rebuild the Che'am-ni church.[27]

24. Bergholz to SecState, April 23, 1919 (895.00/625). Consular reports say that the victims were both Christians and adherents of Ch'ŏndokyo.
25. Bergholz to SecState, May 12, 1919 (895.00/642).
26. Police reports of conditions in the Osan area just prior to the massacre were that area villagers had killed a Korean gendarme and a Japanese policeman, and there had been demonstrations and destruction of Japanese town offices, postal facilities, and homes, and many Japanese residents had been forced to flee. Although the Korean demonstrators were unarmed, fire was effective as an anti-Japanese weapon and some of the destroyed buildings had been torched. People brandished torches during demonstrations and lit beacons, a traditional Korean war signal, atop hills. Ku, *Korea under Colonialism,* p. 81.
27. Bergholz to SecState, May 12, 1919 (895.00/642). The donation was from Hasegawa's discretionary fund. When the *Japan Advertiser* learned of it, apparently from Methodist missionary W.A. Noble and/or Consul-General Bergholz, the governor-general was "instantly" recalled to Tokyo, according to Frank Herron Smith, an American missionary with contacts in the Japanese community. The gift looked embarrassingly like an indemnity or admission of guilt. F.H. Smith to Sidney Gulick (New York), January 10, 1920, letter, Presbyterian Historical Society, Philadelphia.

The Che'am-ni massacre endures as the arch-symbol of Japanese cruelty toward Koreans during the colonial period. Accounts of it, along with reports about the wounds being inflicted by Japanese guns, swords, and firefighters' hooks, all pointed to a Japanese policy of terror designed to make examples of innocent people. Senior missionary James Scarth Gale, who had started out in 1910 thinking that the Japanese would do Korea some good, was completely disillusioned. Commenting on what he saw as a trend toward cultural genocide, he wrote,

> Old Korean literature is full of the voices of great men. It marshals a host of great masters whom the world may rejoice to see. There is interest unbounded in its pages. Today all this is gone. The government would seem to say, "If the Korean's mind cannot be Japanized let it be foully poisoned and so rendered innocuous to the state."[28]

Witnessing the Independence Movement

The name of Canadian missionary Frank Schofield is significant in the lore of the Korean independence movement. Schofield was a doctor at Severance Hospital in Seoul whose photographs of the demonstrations on March First itself and reports of Japanese brutality in Korea circulated widely abroad. Remembering these efforts, Koreans still refer to him as the "Thirty-fourth patriot," following the thirty-three Korean signers of the March First Declaration of Independence. When he died they buried him with honors in the South Korean National Cemetery in Tongjak-dong, Seoul.[29]

Frank Schofield associated himself with the Korean independence movement by playing the part of protector. He wrote about how the Japanese were "syphilizing," rather than "civilizing," the Koreans. He took his camera out on the street and photographed the way the Japanese were suppressing the Korean demonstrators.[30] He tricked some Japanese policemen into admitting that the Government-General had imported agents (euphemistically called *shishi*, "men of action," colloquially known as *sōshi*, connoting thugs) to manhandle Koreans. Schofield reveled in the notoriety. The Japanese "hate me like sin," he wrote to a friend, "because I

28. "Dr. Gale's Statement on Press Laws and Regulations," undated, enclosed with Frank Brockman to John R. Mott, June 22, 1919, YMCA Archives, University of Minnesota.
29. See Doretha E. Mortimore, "Dr. Frank W. Schofield and the Korean National Consciousness, in *Korea's Response to Japan*, pp. 245-261. For Schofield's own account see "What Happened on Sam Il Day, March 1, 1919," in *The Feel of Korea*, ed. Inha Jung (Seoul: Hollym Corp., 1967), pp. 271-280.
30. Independence Declaration signer Yi Kapsŏng approached Schofield the day before the uprising and asked him to be downtown on March 1 with his camera to document the events. Interview with Yi Kapsŏng, *The Korea Times*, March 2, 1969, p. 2.

have recently been exposing their torture and stunts."[31] It was said that the governor-general himself regarded Schofield as "a most dangerous man."[32] All this caused his employers in Toronto to fret that he was jeopardizing the entire Canadian Mission in Korea. However, the accumulated strains of doctoring at Severance Hospital and keeping up his personal political crusade cost Schofield dearly. Schofield and wife Allie both developed health problems and their marriage foundered. In 1920, Allie Schofield took their infant son home with her to Canada. Frank followed later that winter and found that Allie had become so mentally unbalanced that she had to be committed to an institution. Under the circumstances, he decided to resign and stay in Canada.[33]

Frank Schofield was a member of the Korea Mission of the Presbyterian Church of Canada (later part of the United Church of Canada), a mission founded in 1897 and deployed primarily along the northeast coast of Korea and inland to serve the Korean emigrant population in the southeast Manchurian region called Chientao (Korean: Kando).[34] Though Schofield's assignment was to be part of the missionary consortium operating Severance Union Medical College in Seoul, most of the Canadians occupied stations in the northeastern provinces of North and South Hamgyŏng, namely Wŏnsan, Hamhŭng, and Sŏngjin on the coast, and Hoeryŏng and Lungchingtsun (Korean: Yongjŏng) on opposite sides of the Manchurian border. In this Nova Scotia-sized territory, they witnessed incidents less famous than the Che'am-ni massacre but no less cruel. Their letters home to Canada describe burnings, shootings, the especially horrifying impaling of demonstrators on firefighters' pikes, and rapes of schoolgirls. Their descriptions frequently compared what they were seeing to the infamous atrocities of the World War. One missionary called the Government-Gen-

31. Frank Schofield to "Bob," December 16, 1919, Archives of the United Church of Canada Mission in Korea, hereafter referred to as "UCCA," at Victoria University of the University of Toronto, Toronto, File Number 79.204C, Box 3, File 53.

32. *Japan Advertiser*, December 10, 1919.

33. For a while, Schofield entertained thoughts of returning to Korea, partly to carry on his fight for the Koreans, and partly as a protest against what he saw as degeneration in the Canadian church. His state of mind is suggested by these lines written to the Board from Halifax in 1921, while he was thinking about what to do next: "As to my getting into politics in Korea when I return, there is little danger. I have received such a shock from observing the worldliness of the church and the paganism of the State in our so-called Christian land that my enthusiasm for political reform as a means of bringing in the Kingdom of God has received a—well almost—a death blow. However should the Japanese do something very bad—worse than the Black and Tans in Ireland—then I might also do something bad, but there need be little fear on this account." Frank Schofield to A.E. Armstrong, March 7, 1921. UCCA, 79.204C, Box 6, File 84.

34. See William Scott, "Canadians in Korea: A Brief Historical Sketch" (1975), unpublished manuscript in the United Church of Canada Archives manuscript collection, UCCA, Toronto.

eral in Korea a "German Machine" and noted its "Prussian" characteristics. Back in Canada, church officials lodged protests with Canadian government and with Japanese diplomats in Ottawa.

The Canadians in the Korean northeast kept up a show of political neutrality, which put them in a now-familiar dilemma. "So far as possible we have kept anything of a political nature out of our schools and churches," wrote A.H. Barker in Hoeryŏng. "The Japanese want us to tell them if we hear of [demonstrations brewing], but we did not come to be political spies, and had to tell them so. Because we take that stand they suspect us of having something to do with this...."[35]

It was easy to be discouraged by the futility of it all. As Sŏngjin missionary Robert Grierson wrote,

> Of course, their demonstration will have been in vain. There is no nation on earth ready to fight to give Korea her independence, even if there were assurances that independence would be good for her and not an opening of the door to squabbles like China is still experiencing.... So the Koreans' demonstration will surely prove to be a useless expenditure of life and effort, as we could have told them from the first, had they asked our opinion or advice on the matter.[36]

Based as they were in the far northeast, the Canadian missionaries saw what happened when the Independence Movement spread to Chientao, the area around the mission station at Lungching. As Dr. Stanley Martin of St. Andrew's Hospital reported, "In the month of March [1919], our in-patient department was without warning taxed to its utmost in taking care of about forty serious cases. Many of these were fatal from the outset, having been fired on at point-blank range and shot through the brain and other vital organs."[37]

But the worst was yet to come. In the autumn of 1920, Koreans attacked the Japanese at Hunchun near the Russian border. In the "Chientao Incident" of 1920,[38] the Korean attackers were partisans of Yi Tonghwi, the Shanghai-based Korean leftist who was calling for armed struggle in Korea.

35. A.H. Barker to Board Secretary R.P. Mackay, March 20, 1919 (UCCA, 79.204C, Box 4, File 61).

36. Robert Grierson to A.E. Armstrong, May 30, 1919, UCCA, 79.204C, Box 4, File 62.

37. Undated Report entitled "Medical Work, Yongjung–Dr. S.H. Martin," UCCA, 79.204C, Box 6, File 85. The paragraph concludes, "We are glad to report that except those who died within a few days of admission the patients all returned home good earnest Christians."

38. For the Chientao Incident of 1920 see Ku, *Korea under Colonialism,* pp. 266-291, and A. Hamish Ion, "Defenders of the Faithful: Canadian Presbyterian Missionaries and the Korean Independence Movement in Chientao 1919-1931," in *Canadian Missionaries and Korea: Two Case Studies in Public Opinion,* Geoffrey Johnston and A. Hamish Ion (Toronto: University of Toronto-York University Joint Centre for Asia Pacific Studies, 1988), pp. 34-69.

Yi's call-to-arms was easier to follow in Chientao than in Korea itself where Japanese control was more firmly established. Many Manchurian Koreans were happy to join the attacks. The Korean organization at Hunchun easily recruited enough members to become a threat, and by the middle of 1920 it had deployed numerous guerrillas in the field. The Japanese answered by sending troops to Chientao: six battalions and some 450 *kempeitai* gendarmes. This show of force reflected Japan's most basic fear, that an enemy power—either Chinese nationalism or Russian Bolshevism—would enter the power vacuum in Manchuria and threaten her security from across the Japan Sea. The Japanese were determined to permit no slackening of control exactly at the point where these forces might converge with the Korean spirit of rebellion.[39]

The Japanese used the term "bandits" to refer to anyone who opposed their rule in Chientao. The generic word for "bandits" was *hung hu-tzu*, meaning "Red Beards," a label originally applied to lawless Russians who had plundered Manchurian villages in the 1800s. By 1920 the Red Beards were long gone but the term "*hung hu-tzu*" continued in the regional vocabulary.[40] On September 12, 1920, more than a year after the outbreak of the Korean independence movement, Korean *hung hu-tzu* tried to raid Hunchun and were driven off by a combined force of Japanese and Chinese troops. On October 2, however, a second *hung hu-tzu* band attacked the town and burned the Japanese consulate. This brought the Japanese 19th Division over the border from Korea in what amounted to a Japanese invasion of Chientao.

The Japanese story was that "Korean revolters, Chinese bandits, and Russian bolsheviki" had gone on a rampage burning and looting the "foreign trade quarter" of Hunchun and killing Japanese police officers, men, women, and children. Revolutionaries were recruiting young Koreans in Chientao and had established barracks and training schools for them, "taking advantage of the notorious laxity of the Chinese police administration in that region and getting weapons and ammunition from Russian anarchists." If a village had to be wiped out by the Japanese it was because it harbored these "revolters" and if churches were burned it was because

---

39. These factors included Japanese frustration over a lack of success in the Siberian Expedition and the strategic aim of blocking the extension of Red rule to the Far East; the Manchurian warlord Chang Tso-lin's success in getting control of the Chinese Eastern Railway through Harbin and his general lack of cooperation with Japanese strategic plans in Manchuria and north China, and a Japanese determination to establish unshakable control over southeastern Manchuria along the Korean and Russian borders. These points are summarized by A. Hamish Ion, in "Defenders of the Faithful," pp. 40-48.

40. Chong-Sik Lee, *Revolutionary Struggle in Manchuria* (Berkeley and Los Angeles: University of California Press, 1983), pp. 82-83.

they were rendezvous points for outlaws.[41] The retribution was widespread and indiscriminate. In Lungchingtsun, fifty miles to the west, the Canadian missionaries at St. Andrew's Hospital reported a "reign of terror." Dr. Stanley Martin described it, again comparing Chientao with wartime France:[42]

> There are now over 8,000 troops in this district with 4,000 at Ninguta on their way here from Siberia. Koreans are daily being shot and whole villages being burnt.

> [Myŏngdong] Academy [was] the Korean Souvain [Louvain]. [It was a school of] 300 boys. Has only its brick walls standing like the Cloth Hall at Ypres. The Elders House [is] now useless and all the young men in the whole district fled. Chung Dong Academy [was] burnt. 12 People shot (Christians) for giving food to compatriots. Sorangtong, 30 *li* from Kainei [Hoeryong]: 17 shot (10 Christians); a village 5 *li* from there, 14 shot. Kooseidong [*sic*] where the people built their church before building their own houses: partly burnt fire put out by women after soldiers left...school and houses burnt. Only one house burnt that is not Christian. Yangmoo chun cha [*sic*]. School burnt. Besides this all families connected with independence soldiers houses burnt out with their crops.

It was said that Japanese retribution had been especially terrible at the nearby village of "Norapawie" (aka Kanchang'am). Early in November when things were calmer, the Canadians went to see what had happened. Dr. Martin wrote,[43]

> I saw an old man who had been quietly walking down a valley road when he was shot at by some Japanese troops encamped on the hillside. He was shot in two places but an operation later at our hospital saved his life. Two days later on Nov. 5th seventeen Jap soldiers and 3 policemen (one Korean) arrived at the village and began pulling down the walls of the burned houses and covering up as much as possible of the hideousness of the place. Men (all the men of this village being dead) were ordered in from a neighbouring village and forced to gather in bodies of thirty-one of the victims from their temporary graves....

---

41. Consul-General S. Shimazu (Toronto), Letter to the Editor, the *Toronto Globe and Mail*, December 8, 1920, p. 4.

42. Stanley Haviland Martin to A.E. Armstrong, October 26, 1920. UCCA, 79. 204C, Box 5, File 79. St. Andrew's Hospital's statistics for 1920 suggest its scale of operations: Dr. Martin, his Canadian nursing chief, and a small Korean medical staff dealt with 22,000 outpatients, 380 inpatients, performed 418 operations under chloroform, and 100 more under local anesthetic, and made 1,496 house calls. Nearly half of the patients treated were Chinese. Only 474 of the total were professing Christians and the staff distributed 6,000 tracts. "Medical Work among Koreans in Manchuria," leaflet, UCCA 79.204C, Box 6, File 87.

43. Stanley Haviland Martin to A.E. Armstrong, December 6, 1920. UCCA, 79. 204C, Box 5, File 81.

The villagers were then forced to gather the remaining wood in the village…from the ruins of the houses and pile the bodies on it, after which the women and children looking on, the bodies were once more committed to the flames. (There's nothing so repulsive to Koreans than having their dead treated with disrespect.) The widows were then called into a room and vigorously questioned re their dead, after which they received a portion of ashes of the bodies and were made to sign a paper stating that they would never again disturb the ashes of the dead, etc. [and] that they would confess their sins to the Japanese….

So about a week ago a special commission from Tokyo visited this spot and at this time an old man stating that he was the Principal Leader of the independence movement in the district presented the colonel in charge with three banners and an ox. On the banners was inscribed the words, "Thanking the Japanese soldiers for the peace they have brought to our village in protecting them against independence soldiers."

Dr. Martin treated anyone who came in wounded, whether Korean, Chinese, or Japanese. His feelings, however, ran strongly against the Japanese. During the ensuing army investigation, the Japanese commander, Colonel Mizumachi Takeso, criticized Dr. Martin and the Canadians for their anti-Japanese attitude. He warned that Japan might find a way to retaliate in kind—perhaps by helping beleaguered fellow-Buddhists in British colonies who were having to suffer persecutions such as the Amritsar massacre.[44]

Many missionaries shared Dr. Martin's feelings about the political struggle, but not all were so single-mindedly sympathetic. Frank Herron Smith, a Methodist missionary assigned to work among Japanese in Korea and who had a reputation for being what the Koreans call "pro-Japanese," protested that there was another side to the story. "In Dr. Martin's report of these later atrocities," he wrote, "I find no mention of the scores of raids made from this section of Manchuria into Korea. These raids were made, and people were constantly being robbed, killed and their houses burned. If he undertook to write anything he ought to write all….Why did not Dr. Martin…give the reason for these reprisals?"[45]

Back in Canada, Board Secretary A.E. Armstrong forwarded reports from the missionaries in Korea to the government and to S. Shimizu, the Japanese consul-general in Ottawa. Canada, being part of the British empire and therefore an ally of Japan, was in no position to do anything official, but Armstrong managed to get an interview with Shimizu to discuss the Korean issue. The consul-general assured the board secretary that many Japanese were unhappy with the behavior of the authorities in Chōsen. He conceded privately that there had been a lot of violence, the

44. *Gendaishi Shiryō*, cited in Ion, "Defenders of the Faithful," p. 48.
45. Frank Herron Smith to A.E. Armstrong, June 25, 1921 and related correspondence, UCCA 79.204C, Box 6, File 87.

army had overstepped, and that reforms were called for; but he also cautioned Armstrong against thinking that Japan would ever grant Korea its independence.[46]

Perhaps aware of the political damage in the West, the Japanese in Chientao undertook to win the Canadians over. There were dinner invitations from the Japanese consul and from General Higashi, the area's top military commander. A Japanese delegation called at St. Andrew's Hospital to offer thanks for the ministrations of the medical staff. An officer from Chōsen Army headquarters in Seoul brought the Martin family a tin of English biscuits and some Cadbury's chocolates. The provincial government also sent presents. Even the investigator Colonel Mizumachi waxed generous with a 100 yen donation for the hospital, which Dr. Martin applied to the treatment of patients wounded in what he called the "Imperial Japanese slaughter."[47]

Learning from the Independence Movement

By the time the Japanese had finished crushing the Independence Movement in late 1920, Korea's foreign residents had learned some lessons. Most of them resolutely feigned neutrality in public however much they loathed the Japanese in private. However, they remained underinformed about the dynamics of what had happened, mainly because they were undereducated about Japan, its political system, and Korea's place in the Japanese political economy. The Korean Independence Movement arose during the liberal administration of Japanese Prime Minister Hara Kei, a time generally thought to have been the high point of democracy in prewar Japan. Although the governor-general in Korea normally was a law unto himself, the March First uprising in Korea represented a policy failure that was serious enough to be an issue in Japan's domestic politics. At the time there was considerable tension within Japan between the authoritarian tradition and the more "modern" liberal ideals of constitutional democracy and human rights. The foreign community in Korea, having taken on a Korea-centric viewpoint that failed to consider the degree to which the Korean independence movement could be exploited as a *domestic* issue in Japan, put its efforts into mobilizing public opinion in the disinterested West rather than in Japan where there was considerable public concern about colonial policies in Korea.[48] Although some of the reports reaching

---

46. See correspondence, UCCA, 79.204C, Box 5, Files 84-87.
47. Martin to Armstrong, February 4, 1921. UCCA, 79.204C, Box 6, file 83.
48. Clark, "Surely God Will Work Out Their Salvation," pp. 58-61. A few missionaries did make abortive attempts to exploit Japanese public opinion. In April 1919, the Presbyterian Mission sent two representatives to Tokyo for meetings with Christians and missionary counterparts in hopes of reaching powerful people in the government. Upon arrival in Tokyo the pair called upon U.S. Ambassador

the West led to a certain embarrassment for Japan, the moderation of colonial rule in Korea after 1919 came about because the Japanese themselves concluded that change was necessary, not because sympathetic foreigners in Korea had been effective in pressuring Tokyo to reform the administration. The appointment of a new, relatively liberal governor-general in the summer of 1919, for example, was a pragmatic decision designed to enhance the effectiveness of Japanese control over the Korean people. That was the primary, and really the only significant, motive.

The missionaries' ignorance of Japanese affairs was one result of their home churches' decisions to continue separate missions in Korea when they could have combined them with their Japan missions at the time of the 1910 annexation.[49] The biggest group, the Korea Mission of the Presbyterian Church, U.S.A. (or "Northern Presbyterians"), had no institutional relationship with its counterpart in Japan but answered directly to the Presbyterian Board in New York. No one ever seriously suggested that the Japan Mission colonize the Korea Mission. Confined to the Korean peninsula, it was natural for the Northern Presbyterians to identify with the interests of Koreans, a tendency that developed easily into a bias against Japan. This helped associate Christianity with Korean nationalism in the minds of Koreans but it disturbed many people who had a broader view. Frank Herron Smith, the Methodist who worked with the Japanese in Korea, compared the attitudes of missionaries in Japan and Korea as follows:

1. Japan missionaries love Japan generally. Korea missionaries may love a few [Japanese] individuals.
2. Japan missionaries know there is a fight in Japan [between rightists and liberal/moderate factions], but they trust in her and think she will do right in the

Roland Morris to discuss their purpose. Morris, who was interested chiefly in keeping Americans neutral in Korea, "practically forbade" them from talking politics with anyone in Japan, whereupon their only accomplishment appears to have been a seven-page letter to the Board of Foreign Missions in New York. The Canadians did a little better: Oliver R. Avison of Severance Union Medical College had a visiting Canadian board secretary stop by Tokyo enroute home to talk with liberal Diet members, and they reportedly relayed Avison's views to Prime Minister Hara Kei, but with no discernible result. The Presbyterian emissaries were Gordon Holdcroft and Walter Erdman. See their report to Arthur Judson Brown, April 7, 1919, Presbyterian Historical Society, Philadelphia. For A.E. Armstrong's report see his "Notes on the Korean Uprising for Independence," copy in Methodist Mission archives, Drew University. I wish to thank Professor Yi Manyŏl for sharing his microfilm copy of this source with me.

49. There were exceptions. In the early years, the Methodist Episcopal Mission in Korea was under an American bishop in Tokyo, but the missions themselves were separate. To be sure, there was plenty of logic to keeping separate missions in Korea. Missions were not political entities and did not have to reflect political changes; separate regional missions within countries were common in large fields such as China and India. Other reasons included the separate Korean language and in some cases a separate Korean church structure.

end. Korea missionaries think Japan is a second Germany.

3. Japan missionaries have respect [for] Japan's honor in what they write and say. Korea missionaries—some of them—think that to defame Japan is to do God's service.[50]

American officials also disagreed about the benefits of Japanese rule in Korea. U.S. Consul-General Ransford Miller, who was reassigned to Seoul to succeed Leo Bergholz in November 1919 after an absence of several years, returned believing that Bergholz had overstated reports of Japanese brutality during the Independence Movement.[51] Miller remembered the good relationship he had enjoyed with Foreign Affairs Director Komatsu Midori a few years earlier and he worried that the foreigners' reports about the Independence Movement in 1919 would poison Japanese-American relations. There was enough friction already, and he wanted to foster harmony.[52] But once back in Seoul he was soon persuaded that Japanese rule had turned into something evil. It had become so harsh that the Koreans had been justified in their uprising.[53] He even empathized with the missionaries as they tried to carry on their work after the uprising. "They have succeeded to a remarkable degree," he wrote, "in maintaining a discreet and neutral attitude in a most difficult situation, the factors of which have tended to draw their hearts and their heads in opposite directions."[54]

Admiral Saitō and the Velvet Glove

Before the end of 1919 Korea got a new governor-general and a less repressive regime. In place of *budan seiji* ("martial rule") under army generals Terauchi and Hasegawa, the colony entered a new period of *bunka seiji* ("cultural rule") under relatively humane navy admirals. The first was Admiral Saitō Makoto, who arrived in Seoul in September 1919 and served two terms, 1919-1927 and 1929-1931.

Saitō's first moments in Seoul were nearly fatal. A would-be assassin rolled a bomb under his carriage at the railroad station and nearly killed him on the spot. The incident helped Saitō focus on the problem of public order in Chōsen, which he approached by giving ground to the Koreans. Although in fact he merely sheathed the iron fist in a velvet glove, he did

50. Frank Herron Smith to Sidney Gulick, October 16, 1919, Presbyterian Historical Society, Philadelphia. By 1919, Smith, who had been in Korea since 1905, had a reputation as an apologist for the colonial regime.

51. Bergholz left Korea with much goodwill from American citizens there. When he was transferred, a group of missionaries got together a petition to Washington to let him stay. Ku, p. 191n.

52. Cablegram, Morris to SecState, March 15, 1919, (895.00/572).

53. Miller to Morris (Tokyo), December 26, 1919 (895.00/673).

54. Miller to Morris, personal letter, December 26, 1919 (enclosed with 895.00/673).

succeed in lulling many Koreans into acquiescence and even collaboration during his two terms in office. The 1920s, therefore, were a decade of concessions—of toleration for Korean ideas, publications, education, and even political movements. Important Korean institutions were begun and even flourished during the Saitō years: the newspapers *Tong'a Ilbo* (East Asia Daily) and *Chosŏn Ilbo* (Korea Daily); magazines such as *Kaebyŏk* (Creation); Posŏng College, which is now Korea University; intellectual associations such as the Hŭngsadan (Society for Fostering Activists); and even an avowedly political group, the Sin'gan-hoe (New Korea Society), which welcomed members from all points on the political spectrum including the far left. Limited permission was granted for many kinds of expression, and many Koreans were willing to settle for this much from the Government-General. Others, however, continued to be angry about losing their land to Japanese developers, or injustices of various kinds during the 'teens, or, most of all, the brutality of the Independence Movement suppression. Many of these joined displaced farmers migrating northward to Manchuria in search of land and jobs. There, in the Chientao area, Koreans concentrated just over the border from Japanese-controlled Chōsen and the hated *kempeitai* and Korean radical politics began their gestation period.

Historians see the 1920s as the beginning of the schism between Korean leftists and rightists that has been behind the confrontation between North and South Korea ever since the country was divided in 1945. The left wanted revolution—violent resistance against Japanese imperialism and an end to the privileges of landowners and former *yangban*. Leftists in Manchuria, next door to Soviet Russia, tried to put this into action by organizing an armed struggle against Japanese border outposts. But others in the Korean right and center rejected violence in favor of the "cultural nationalist" approach to independence, resisting Japanese domination by maintaining Korean heritage, while keeping Korea's traditional social and economic arrangements more or less intact. During the twenties the approaches of left and right proved to be incompatible. During meetings of the Sin'gan-hoe, for example, leftists accused the "cultural nationalists" of collaboration and forsook the debating platform in favor of the battlefield, leaving the organization in shreds. Shortly thereafter came the Manchurian Incident of 1931, Japan's turn to the right and its slide into militarism, and a new colonial regime in Korea that embarked on a program of total assimilation that amounted to cultural genocide. Consequently, despite the contributions of "cultural nationalism" to the safekeeping of Korean traditions, the leftists turned out to be correct in their assertion that only violence—ultimately in the form of the Allied victory—would succeed in eliminating the Japanese threat to Korean national identity.[55]

55. See Michael E. Robinson, *Cultural Nationalism in Colonial Korea, 1920-1925* (Seattle: University of Washington Press, 1988), esp. pp. 48-77; Bruce Cumings,

Although Koreans met him with a bomb, the foreign community greeted Admiral Saitō with relief and hope. His appointment was thought to be due in part to their efforts to publicize the Independence Movement in the world press. It was said that Saitō was a moderate, a member of the Navy faction of the Japanese government; and unlike his predecessors, Generals Terauchi and Hasegawa, he had a genuine appreciation of Westerners and Western culture. He was a gracious host who conversed easily in English and could make his foreign guests feel both comfortable and important when he asked for their advice. He used his deputy, Civil Administrator Mizuno Rentarō, to gather suggestions from the missionaries on improving relations with the Koreans. These attentions represented a renewed effort to co-opt the foreigners and to tempt them to think that Japanese rule was being made palatable to the Koreans. And the effort was at least partially successful. Methodist Bishop Herbert Welch was especially sanguine:

> The people of the country itself, while by no means at rest, apparently appreciate the wisdom of settling down to the slower processes of education, moralization, and training in the art of government, with an eye to the future and its larger responsibilities, whatever the form of government. I cannot help thinking that if the Irish question is brought to a settlement that leaves Ireland an integral part of the British Empire, this will have a quieting effect upon Korea.[56]

Saitō's policies included rescinding the order prohibiting the teaching of religion in mission schools after 1925. This gave the Northern Presbyterian Mission, which had already voted to close its schools before the 1925 deadline, a reprieve, and the missionaries took it as a conciliatory gesture. Local officials continued to annoy foreigners in the hinterland with petty aggravations, but the impetus to make life difficult for them no longer seemed to be coming from the top. This was a great relief to the consular corps, which was voluble in its praise for Saitō. U.S. Consul-General Ransford Miller put it this way:

> [Since his arrival], Viscount Saito (he seldom uses the title "Admiral" here) has shown himself so approachable, straightforward, broad-minded, kindly, patient, conscientious and fair that he has won the confidence and respect of all classes, whether Japanese, Koreans, or foreigners. There doubtless are individual exceptions to this general statement but they are comparatively few and I personally know of none.[57]

The Origins of the Korean War, Vol. I: *Liberation and the Emergence of Separate Regimes* (Princeton: Princeton University Press, 1980), pp. 3-38; and Chong-Sik Lee, *The Politics of Korean Nationalism* (Berkeley and Los Angeles: University of California Press, 1963), pp. 257-260.

56. Herbert Welch (Seoul) to William McDowell (Washington), enclosed with McDowell to SecState, August 18, 1921 (895.00/695).

57. Quoted in C.H. Stephan (Seoul) to SecState, December 9, 1927 (895.001/9).

Saitō started a program to educate the missionaries about Japan. In 1926 he asked the selected mission schools to nominate faculty members to go on an expense-paid tour of schools in Japan. The trip took place during cherry blossom season, April 19 to May 13, touching at Miyajima, Kyōto, Nara, Tokyo, Nikkō, and Kamakura, among other prime spots. The missionaries knew it was a public relations ploy but appreciated it nonetheless. "The chief impression of our trip so far," wrote one traveler from Ōsaka, "is the unfailing courtesy and heartiness of the Japanese people." They met mayors and officials, saw sights, and accumulated presents from their hosts along with the gift purchases (*omiyage*) for the folks back in Korea. And they drew the right conclusions: "[T]hese first class schools are the ones which must become the standard for us and that we will have to approximate to their standard if we are going to be able to justify our existence and commend the Christian faith to the country at large."[58]

Public relations thus made Saitō's early years a time of harmony between the Western community and the colonial regime. The governor-general spoke at missionary schools and ribbon-cuttings and ordered his staff to cooperate in solving business problems. Meanwhile he pushed a progressive-looking public works program highlighted by the completion of the new Government-General headquarters, Seoul's new Japanese-Baroque railway station, the provincial office building that is now City Hall, and the colony's main Shintō shrine on South Mountain.

58. William Scott to A. E. Armstrong, April 24, 1926 (UCCA, 83.006C, Box 1, File 9).

-- 4 --

Living in Admiral Saitō's Korea

Seoul's Chŏng-dong neighborhood was still the hub of Western life in the 1920s. The old "Legation Quarter" continued green and wooded with foreign-looking structures appearing among the trees: the white tower of the Russian consulate; the Romanesque square tower of the Anglican Cathedral of St. Mary and St. Nicholas; the flagpole with the Stars and Stripes flying over Lucius Foote's old house at the American consulate, and, until 1935 when it was demolished to make way for an elementary school, the original French consulate building in French Renaissance style, by common consent the most beautiful European building in the city.[1]

Elsewhere within the old walled city were the missionary compounds, enclaves that included—in addition to schools, churches, and other venues of mission work—clusters of Western-style homes for the foreigners themselves. These were on hill land, bought cheap because of the difficulty of raising water. The foreigners solved this problem with drills, pumps, and pipes and built their out-of-scale foreign buildings in a way that made them conspicuous in an urban landscape where even the finest *hanok* homes of the Korean upper class were one-story structures. Foreign homes—even the ones built in a pseudo-Korean style—were large because of the space required to live Western-style and because they doubled as hostels for visitors and boarders at a time when decent hotel lodgings were nonexistent. Most foreign homes were never without guests, either overseas visitors or colleagues from within Korea who were traveling on business.

Except for the hours when students were milling in and out, a bucolic quiet covered the Presbyterian compound with its lawns, paths, vegetable

1. Yun Ilju, *Han'guk Yangsik kŏnch'uk p'alsimnyŏn-sa: haebang-jŏn p'yŏn* (History of eighty years of Western-style architecture in Korea: Before liberation) (Seoul: Yajŏng munhwasa, 1965), passim.

gardens, and row of servants' houses just inside the perimeter wall. Other foreign preserves were similarly tranquil: the staff compound at Severance Hospital, the foreign faculty houses at Chōsen Christian College, the Methodist compounds in Chŏng-dong, Sajik-dong, and Naengch'ŏn-dong, the Seventh Day Adventist compound in Hoegi-dong, and the Oriental Missionary Society compound at what is now Ch'ungjŏng-no 3-ga.

Korean visitors came and went throughout the day, spending time with the missionaries in their *sarang* parlors, an architectural feature adapted from upper-class Korean homes where the men of the house had outer rooms enabling them to entertain friends while shielding their family quarters from public view. The rest of the house was a haven from the rigors of Korea, a place for family life in old home style.

From time to time a new arrival would express a wish to renounce compound living and "live among the people." Old timers would respond with admonitions about filth and disease and stories about the Westerners who had ended up being buried in the local foreign cemetery, some of them within weeks and even days of arrival. Soon enough the newcomer would be attacked by one of Korea's tough little microbes and then would reconsider. Certainly if children were involved, their needs soon swung the balance in favor of compound living.

Living in protected enclaves, though necessary for health and sanity, emphasized the social distance between Westerners and Koreans. Life apart made it easy to get by without using much Korean, one reason why so many missionaries, especially those with families, never learned the language well enough to exchange ideas with educated local people. Instead they learned specialized vocabularies such as "work Korean" or "kitchen Korean," while their children learned "childhood Korean."

For missionary children (generically known as MK's [missionary kids] and in Korea as "Korea Kids"), life went on in a special kind of bubble. Their families struggled to prepare them for higher studies in the homeland, and their schooling therefore was entirely on the Western, mainly American, plan. While their Korean playmates were learning Korean, Japanese, and Chinese characters, the foreign children were learning English, French, and Western culture. By their teenage years, most Korea Kids still spoke a "children's Korean" and their education had diverged from that of their Korean friends. They never became familiar with the world of Korean thought and ideas.[2]

2. The language barrier was even more severe between Westerners and Japanese. "The great obstacle to cordial relations is undoubtedly the language barrier," wrote one British consular officer. "This does not exist where the local 'magistrate' or governor is a Corean but in most cases he is Japanese. The Japanese officials rarely learn Corean and, naturally enough, rarely speak English. In consequence the only means of intercourse are through an interpreter and the personal contact which would facilitate friendly relations is entirely missing. This is extremely

Nor did the view from the foreign compound reveal much about the world beyond Korea's shores. International telephone communication was unheard-of. Telegrams were costly and used only for the most urgent business.[3] An ordinary letter to America or Europe had to travel by ship, meaning that it took at least six weeks to get a reply. Hometown newspapers and magazines came months late if they arrived at all. Local news sources were of limited utility. English-language newspapers from Japan took a week to reach Korea and were of little interest. The government-run *Seoul Press* carried little more than train and movie schedules, the Chōsen Hotel guest list, snippets of political news about Japan, and only occasional international stories. Shortwave radios were outlawed in 1924 and the local radio station, JODK, was under strict Japanese control.[4] Thus much of Seoul's international communication was by hand-carried letter or word of mouth, transmitted during the rituals of departing and returning: the band of well-wishers at the railroad station bidding farewell to friends departing on their periodic furlough tucking notes and letters in the luggage, and the round of dinner debriefings for those returning. As a result, social life consisted of entertaining each other. Houseguests varied the monotony. National holidays were occasions to reach across lines in the missionary, business, and consular communities. And each year there were grand reunions at the annual meetings of the missions and at the foreign community's summer resorts.

At Home in Yŏnhi Village

One family that chose to live away from the compound environment was the Underwood family, headed in the 1920s by Horace Horton Under-

unfortunate as the Japanese line of approach towards problems of administration is in many cases very different from ours. Without a common language the Japanese official and the foreign missionary live each in a world of his own, neither understanding the point of view of the other." Consul-General Oswald White (Seoul), "Notes on a Tour of Southwest Corea," enclosed with White to Ambassador Sir John Tilley (Tokyo), July 15, 1929. Public Record Office file FO 262/1732.

3. Taking a lesson from consular practice, the missions and businesses in Seoul used standard codebooks to compress common phrases into economical code words such as "KAUDN," which meant "Wire instructions immediately," and "UQAHC," which meant "Please inform relatives."

4. The broadcast towers for JODK were erected in Chŏng-dong just outside the northeast corner of the British Consulate-General compound and had "the effect of practically cutting out concerts and other matter emanating from [short-wave] stations outside the [Japanese] Empire, a result which cannot have altogether been overlooked when the company was formed under official sanction." V.L.P. Foulke, "Annual Report of Affairs in Corea Other than Commercial for the Period January First to October Thirty-first 1927," enclosed with G.T. Paton (Seoul) to Tilley (Tokyo), January 9, 1928. Public Record Office file FO 262/1707.

wood, son of the pioneer missionary Horace Grant Underwood.[5] Born in Seoul in 1890, H.H. Underwood grew up within sight of Seoul's South Gate and was schooled at home by his parents. He then went to New York University where he graduated in 1912. In September of that year he returned to Seoul as a Presbyterian Mission "associate" to teach at the John D. Wells School (Kyŏngsin Boys' School). He taught English for a year at the newly founded Chōsen Christian College before having to return to the United States on emergency leave because of the death of his father, in the fall of 1916. In 1917 he went back to Seoul at his mother's request to care for her and, one suspects, to test his own ties to Korea. At this early stage of his life, he did not mean to make a career of missionary work. However, his affection for Korea, his respect for his parents' investment in the country, and his deepening involvement in Chōsen Christian College all worked to hold him in Seoul and point him to a life as Korea's first second-generation missionary.

Underwood was newly married when he arrived back in Seoul in 1917. His bride was Ethel Van Wagoner, who had been hired in 1912 to be the first full-time teacher at the newly opened Seoul Foreign School. Ethel was from Michigan, a graduate of Albion College, and the half-sister of Methodist missionary Carl Rufus. She came from a family with a shifting cast of stepparents, half-siblings, and relatives with whom she never formed close attachments. She was used to supporting herself, working as a housemaid during her teenage years in order to finance her education. She was a diligent worker and her employers helped her enter college where she studied to become a schoolteacher, one of the few careers open to independent women at the time. When the invitation came from halfway around the world to start a school for foreign children in Seoul, she accepted the challenge with characteristic grit and appetite for adventure. These qualities —intelligence, self-reliance, curiosity, and the wish to be of service— drew her to young Horace Underwood. In Seoul they began courting. In June 1916 they announced their engagement; and when Horace hurried back to America for his father's funeral later that year, Ethel followed. They were married in December at the Lafayette Avenue Presbyterian Church in Brooklyn.

5. Biographical information on H.H. Underwood is from his typed "Life Record, Horace Horton Underwood," in the papers of Horace G. Underwood, Seoul. The author is much indebted to Horace G. Underwood for his generous gifts of time and attention to the shaping of this book. Many of the stories and details about the Underwood family are from interviews and conversations with Dr. Underwood over a period of years between 1982 and 1997, particularly a series in May and June 1985, and from copies of a document that he wrote entitled "Reminiscences," that eventually formed the basis for his published autobiography. See Horace G. Underwood, *Korea in War, Revolution and Peace: The Recollections of Horace G. Underwood*, ed. and annotated by Michael J. Devine (Seoul: Yonsei University Press, 2001).

Horace and Ethel's first years in Seoul together were spent in Lillias Underwood's shadow as they shared her house in Imun-dong. Their first son—Horace Grant Underwood II, the third "Horace" in the succession[6]—was born there in October 1917. By the time Lillias Underwood died in 1921, Horace and Ethel both had grown committed to a future in Korea and had worked out an assignment with the Presbyterian Mission to teach at Chōsen Christian College as part of the Northern Presbyterians' commitment to provide personnel for the faculty. However, they needed more advanced credentials in order to qualify for faculty appointments, so they spent the next three years at New York University. They were awarded their degrees—a Ph.D. for Horace and an M.A. for Ethel—at commencement in 1925.

Part of the arrangement between the Underwoods and the Presbyterian Mission was the understanding that Horace and Ethel would not live on Presbyterian Mission property but on the their own eight-acre site adjacent to the Chōsen Christian College campus. They would use their own funds to build their own house, and while theoretically, as members of the mission, they could be assigned elsewhere in Korea, it was understood that their assignment to that one location would be permanent. This arrangement was both a blessing and a curse, for while it created a special status for the Underwoods and satisfied their commitments to the college, it also isolated them from the rest of the Presbyterian Mission in Seoul.

The house they built at Number 42 Yŏnhi Village (today's Yŏnhi-dong) was high on a hillside overlooking the farms of Yŏnhi Valley stretching southward to the Han River. In time, with three sons and a fourth on the way, Horace and Ethel needed a house of some size. Working with a design supplied by Brooklyn architect Mal Gray, a family friend, they hired a contractor and a small army of workers who completed the house just in time for occupancy by Christmas 1927. Though smaller than the Meiji-Baroque mansions of the former Korean royal family and the China Coast-style residence of the British consul-general, the house was the finest American house in prewar Korea. One end of the downstairs was a dining room and conservatory, which could, with squeezing, seat forty. The other end was a

6. The recurrence of the name "Horace" in four successive generations of Underwood men in Korea requires an explanation. The first was Horace Grant Underwood (1859-1916), the pioneer Presbyterian missionary who arrived in Korea in 1885 and later founded Chōsen Christian College (C.C.C.). The second was Horace Horton Underwood (1890-1951), born in Seoul, who returned as a missionary in 1912 and became president of C.C.C. in 1934. Horace Grant Underwood II (born in Seoul in 1917), spent his career at the present Yonsei University and is the father of Horace Horton Underwood II (born in Boulder, Colorado, in 1943), who served for most of his career on the Yonsei faculty and later was director of the Korean-American Educational (Fulbright) Commission in Seoul. The custom of naming first-born sons Horace ended in the fifth generation with an Underwood named Stephen.

600-square-foot, 5,000-volume library, which also served as the couple's study. One of Ethel's favorite outdoor features was the sunken garden with its honeysuckle-draped arbor, fishpond, and sundial. She enjoyed having family meals alfresco, on the lawn, in the sunken garden, or in the thatched Korean pavilion that she had built beside the path leading over the hill to the campus.[7]

The Palace of Heart's Delights

Grander than the Underwood house, however, was the house known as "Dilkusha," on the slope of Inwang Mountain near West Gate.[8] The Taylor brothers, Albert and Bill, the city's preeminent Western traders, owned Dilkusha. Until 1932, when he was offered the General Motors franchise in Manchuria, Bill Taylor was the senior partner in their trading firm in Hasegawa-cho (Sogong-dong) across the street from the Chōsen Hotel. After that A.W. ran "W.W. Taylor and Co.," and it was A.W. who built Dilkusha for his British-born wife Mary, their son Bruce, and Mary's sister Una Mouat-Biggs.

Dilkusha was Mary Taylor's treasure. The site's best feature was an enormous gingko tree, which dated back to the property's most famous owner, General Kwŏn Yul, hero of the 1593 Battle of Haengju against the invading Japanese. Another feature was the nearby Kuksadang center of Korean shamanist rituals where villagers and shamans gathered for kuts—as they still do—and the sounds of drums and chants rang through the darkness on many a night. Because of the presence of the newly rebuilt Kuksadang shrine,[9] spirits were thought to lurk everywhere on the mountainside—in the old tree, the ground around it, and the underworld beneath. Indeed, it was not easy to persuade Korean workmen to come up and build Dilkusha in the first place. The villagers nearby thought it no coincidence that a branch of the old gingko fell and nearly killed Una shortly after the family moved in, and that lightning hit Dilkusha two years later and burned it to the ground, necessitating a complete reconstruction.[10]

Mary Taylor was not daunted by these happenings. She used her home as a cultural center for Seoul's foreign community. As someone who had

7. Horace H. Underwood, "Ethel Van Wagoner Underwood" (typescript, 1949), pp. 4-5; Horace G. Underwood, "Reminiscences" (typescript, 1983), pp. 15 E-F.

8. Mary Linley Taylor (née Mary Mouat-Biggs) explained that she named the house "Dilkusha," meaning "Palace of Heart's Delight," after a place in India where one of her ancestors was said to have helped quell a mutiny. Her autobiography is *Chain of Amber* (Lewes, Sussex: The Book Guild, 1992).

9. The Kuksadang Shrine's original location was the west shoulder of Namsan, the site selected by the Japanese for the Chōsen Jingū, their main Shintō shrine, in 1925.

10. This is the dilapidated structure that now stands next to the gingko tree at No. 1 Haengch'ŏn-dong, nearly on top of the Sajik Tunnel in modern Seoul.

spent years in Shanghai as an actress, Mary asserted herself as the foreign community's queen of the arts, hosting script-readings over afternoon tea at Dilkusha for the Seoul Amateur Dramatic Club. When Seoul Foreign School staged its annual Shakespearean play, or the children of Seoul Union Church staged their annual Christmas pageant, the costumes were sewn under Mary Taylor's supervision at Dilkusha. Rare was the community play that did not find Mary Taylor backstage applying greasepaint.

Living in the Western Style

Most of Seoul's Westerners were Americans, but the British consul-general was, by common consent, the dean of the foreign community. The roster of British officials who served in Seoul was a virtual Who's Who of British diplomacy in the East: Sir Harry Parkes, W.B. Aston, Sir Claude MacDonald, Sir Walter Hillier, and J.N. Jordan, among others. The British consulate with its staff and imposing buildings, together with the neighboring Anglican mission with its bishop and pro-cathedral, constituted a substantial British presence in the heart of the city.[11] The British also hosted the Seoul foreign community's biggest social event, Empire Day, when the city's Britons—including Canadians and Australians—were pressed into hosting the other nationalities and the topmost officials of the Government-General on the consulate grounds. It was a proper celebration with tea and sandwiches and conversation for the adults, and games and snacks for the children. No disaster was allowed to interfere with Empire Day: consider the warehouse fire that roasted the consulate's supply of condensed milk on the eve of the festivities one year—burning it just well enough, as it turned out, for the cooks to make the best caramel ice cream that anyone could remember.[12]

Such resourcefulness was a requirement for Western life in Korea. Supply lines for many of the barest essentials stretched halfway around the globe. The simplest furnishing—a faucet handle or a brass drawer-pull or a window shade—might be impossible to replace. Clothes had to be bought months and years in advance, from catalogs, or made by tailors and dressmakers from catalog pictures. Westerners ate Western food, out of habit and for their health, so there was usually a vegetable garden next to the house and perhaps a fruit tree, all carefully controlled as to seed and fertilizer. Food preservation was primitive, often in iceboxes, later in kerosene-burning refrigerators. Much of the diet depended on home canning and food that was dried or bought in tins. People pooled their food orders and had large case-lots shipped in from Japan, Hong Kong, or America. Something as simple as a slice of toast at breakfast therefore became an in-

11. J.E. Hoare, *The British Embassy Compound, Seoul* (Seoul: Korean-British Society, 1984).

12. Horace G. Underwood, "Reminiscences," p. 21.

PYFS girls basketball team, P'yŏngyang, 1926.
Clark Collection.

ternational accomplishment: made with bread from home-ground Korean wheat flour, baked in a Japanese oven, toasted in an American toaster, and spread with Australian butter and English marmalade.

Eventually, suppliers in Seoul began to stock favorite food items. The leading store was E. D. Steward's, named for its Chinese proprietor who had assumed his English name during a prior career waiting tables on a British ship. "Steward's" store, located on Taihei-dōri (T'aep'yŏng-no), was a godsend for the foreign community, a cornucopia of such unKorean foods as Edam cheese, "KLIM" powdered whole milk (the brand being "MILK" spelled backwards), Kellogg's Corn Flakes, and Maxwell House coffee. Other stores took up the same business from time to time, but none endured like Steward's or enjoyed its reputation. Steward's sold house brands of staples such as coffee, along with locally produced "Morning Calm" foods from the Presbyterian Mission's experimental farm near P'yŏngyang and fresh vegetables from the Seventh Day Adventists' farm east of the city.

By the 1930s, the market infrastructure was such that many other Western necessities could be had in Seoul. Ilhan New made pharmaceuticals locally, in what became the Yuhan Chemical Company.[13] Woo Cho and You Shin Coal Companies sold coal. Stoves, hot water tanks, and plumbing and heating equipment could be had from Sugiyama Seishakushō Company in Takezoe-chō. J.H. Morris sold Coleman lamps. Rugs and mattresses could be ordered from the Anna Davis Industrial Shops on the Presbyterian com-

13. Ilhan New (Yu Ilhan) was a pioneer Korean-American businessman. His family was one of the first to be converted by Baptist missionaries at the turn of the century and he was given a Western education, first in Kearney, Nebraska, and then at the University of Michigan. His first business was the La Choy Food Products Company, which he founded in 1921. In 1926 in Korea, he founded the Yuhan Corporation, one of the country's pioneer companies, which grew into a leading pharmaceutical firm.

pound in P'yŏngyang. The Salvation Army made gentlemen's shirts for sale and the Chinese Gospel Building Association at No. 26 Chŏng-dong made furniture to order. With foresight, funds, a bilingual secretary as a go-between, and Korean cooks, amahs (nannies), washerwomen, and "outside men" one could maintain the Western style virtually anywhere in Korea.

Western children who grew up on the compounds led charmed lives. They were raised in protected environments, tended by servants, given educations, and nurtured by parents and neighbors who played the parts of "aunts" and "uncles." Korea Kids on any particular compound regarded themselves as virtual cousins and acted like an extended family. The compound was their neighborhood, which went together with other compounds to comprise an imaginary foreign hometown. A child could be born and raised as a native of this expatriate "town" without ever realizing that every moment spent there was borrowed time. Long before the term "third culture kid" was invented, Korea Kids had all the traits: the bonding with each other, the feeling of belonging nowhere, the longing to go home to a native place that existed mainly in the imagination, and the lifelong search for association—even marriage—with the rare souls who could understand their special upbringing.[14]

Pyeng Yang Foreign School[15] began in 1900 with the arrival of an 18-year-old schoolmarm named Louise O'Gilvy to teach the children of the Presbyterian Mission. Originally located in a small house below the Moffett family home, PYFS grew quickly and became a boarding school in 1913, promising the benefits of P'yŏngyang's wholesome missionary atmosphere to Western families across Korea and as far away as China. A two-story school building opened in 1925, an infirmary in 1929, a girls' dorm in 1930, and a gymnasium in 1931. By the mid-1930s PYFS had more than 115 students, many of them of them "China Flees" (or China "fleas"), boarding students whose parents sent them to P'yŏngyang, either to escape the fighting and antiforeignism in some parts of China, or because they preferred PYFS to more secular boarding schools in China.

14. So tight were the bonds among P'yŏngyang MK's, for example, that the alumni of Pyeng Yang Foreign School continued to hold periodic reunions in the United States for sixty years after the school was closed in 1940. The 1996 reunion in Montreat, North Carolina, drew 220 alumni and spouses and led to two groups returning to accompany shipments of medical supplies and to search for traces of the school in P'yŏngyang itself the following year. See John K. Wilson, comp., *PYFS*, a hand-assembled commemorative album prepared for presentation to North Korean hosts by the first PYFS alumni delegation to P'yŏngyang, January 1997.

15. Prewar missionaries spelled P'yŏngyang variously as "Ping Yang," "Pyeng-yang," or "Pyeng Yang," reflecting the use of "e" for the short Korean "ŏ" sound in early romanization systems. They also pronounced the name in special ways that are now archaic: i.e., "Ping Yang," reflecting the Chinese pronunciation, and "P-yang," a kind of nickname that reflected the regional dialect of South P'yŏng'an Province.

Pyeng Yang Foreign School student body, 1927. Clark Collection.

In Seoul, Western children attended Seoul Foreign School, founded in 1912 on property adjacent to Paejae Methodist Boys' School in Chŏng-dong. In 1923 the school moved to a compound at West Gate, which had been the home of the Plaisants, a family of French traders. Businessman J.H. Morris contributed an auditorium, which was built onto the Plaisant house as a second story, after which the building came to be known as "Morris Hall." Here the foreign community met for church services at four o'clock every Sunday afternoon.[16] Here, too, the school children presented their annual Shakespearean play, directed by Father Charles Hunt of the Anglican Mission with the assistance of Mary Taylor.

By the 1930s the staff of SFS included five teachers covering all grades. Admission was open to any English-speaking child and the students came from all sectors of the foreign community—unlike the larger Pyeng Yang Foreign School, whose students were almost entirely MK's.[17] The fierce rivalry that existed between the Seoul and P'yŏngyang schools usually went badly for SFS because it was so much smaller. However, there was one memorable occasion when the Seoul Foreign School baseball team, woefully behind in the early innings of a championship game, suddenly took the lead. PYFS Principal Ralph Reiner had already taken the trophy to the train station when SFS won the game. The triumphant Seoul team went en masse to the platform and confiscated the trophy—to cheers from the winners and boos from the losers.[18]

Events like these were significant when there were so few other entertainment. Missionaries belonged to the Seoul Union Club where they engaged in healthy pursuits.[19] Nonmissionaries joined the Seoul Club, housed in a Chŏng-dong building loaned by the former royal family, where they played cards and billiards and smoked and drank liquor. The two clubs' common ground was tennis, with annual tournaments for the Taylor Cup and the All-Korea Championship. Meanwhile, truly worldly people, including tourists and gold miners on one of their rare days off, had what

16. The hour was chosen to permit the missionary community to attend Korean church services at the traditional hour of 11 A.M. See Charles A. Sauer, *The Story of Seoul Union Church, 1886-1961* (Seoul: Seoul Union Church Diamond Anniversary Committee, 1961).

17. PYFS drew its students primarily from missionary families in northwestern Korea, but missionaries as far away as China chose to board their children at PYFS because of its religious atmosphere. There were also children from mining families at Unsan who had outgrown the little schoolhouse there, a few Russian children from around northern Korea, and children of American Corn Products Company workers in P'yŏngyang, which ran a sugar beet refinery and processing plant that turned Manchurian corn into syrup.

18. Horace H. Underwood II, *Seoul Foreign School, 1912-1978* (Seoul, 1978), passim.

19. Horace H. Underwood, *The Seoul Union: Fifty Years a Community Center, 1889-1939* (Seoul, 1939).

Chōsen Hotel, Seoul (built 1913). Behind: Hwanggung-u, part of the Korean imperial altar complex. Clark Collection.

could almost be called "night life" at the Chōsen Hotel. The hotel imported a 2,000-yen electric Victrola in March 1929, which added much to the atmosphere:

> Some say Seoul is slow [wrote the editor of the *Seoul Press*], but if one drops in some evening he or she will find the bar-room filled to capacity with old and young of both sexes indulging in the light fantastic to the tune of jazz music. With jazz music going at full blast and people dancing, the Chosen Hotel on Monday evening presented a very animated scene. Those who did not dance either played "snooker" or watched the dancers.[20]

Seoul as a Consular Post

When Korea became a Japanese protectorate in 1905, the foreign legations in Seoul were either closed or downgraded. The American Legation became a Consulate-General and remained so until 1942 when the last American representative in Japanese-occupied Korea, Harold Quarton, was repatriated in the early months of the Pacific War. During that period Seoul was not a top pick on the list of Foreign Service assignments. The post reports that were kept in Washington to tell new officers what to expect in Seoul were rather daunting. Health conditions were "unsanitary," though "one can survive with precautions." For recreation, prospective consuls were told there were the two foreigners' clubs, a golf club near the city, a music club, the Royal Asiatic Society, and hiking and hunting, but "practically nothing in the way of professional entertainment beyond a number of fourth-rate movies and an occasional visit from a traveling artist or a small troupe. Other entertainment is homemade and consists of amateur theatri-

20. *Seoul Press*, March 20, 1929, p. 2.

cals, concerts, parties of various kinds..." while "formal entertainments generally center around the visit of some notable persons, the visit of a foreign warship, national fete days, and the Governor-General."[21] Judging from this, it seemed important to arrive in Seoul with the lowest possible expectations—in hopes that things would actually turn out to be better.

As a branch of the American Embassy in Tokyo, the Consulate-General in Seoul had little to do with policy making. Over the years, however, American consular officials in Seoul were called upon to handle a number of delicate political problems. One was the alleged American involvement in the March First Independence Movement in 1919. Another was in 1924, when the U.S. Congress enacted the National Origins Immigration Act establishing quotas for immigrants from different parts of the world and pointedly excluding Japanese from immigration altogether on grounds of "unassimilability." The enactment of the overtly racist immigration bill in America, coming as it did after the Washington Conference when the United States had maneuvered, as the Japanese saw it, to limit their naval power to the Far East, and the Versailles Conference, where the United States had refused to accept the principle of racial equality, put American officials in the Japanese empire in an exceedingly awkward position. In Tokyo, before the end of the year, Ambassador Cyrus Woods resigned—ostensibly because of his mother's failing health but obviously because of his personal distress over the immigration bill—being replaced by Jacob Gould Schurman. The Japanese press carried stories speculating about the course of a future Japanese-American war, and an anti-American literature began to grow in Japan. Under the circumstances, American officials in Japan and its colonies had to think about possible Japanese retaliation against American citizens in their jurisdictions. In Korea, where the Saitō-era mood of conciliation prevailed, the Seoul Press took a long-suffering tone:

> Japanese—the great bulk of them—know perfectly well that the Americans dwelling amongst us are in no sense responsible for that unprovoked affront by their Government...and we would assure our American friends that the true sons of Dai Nippon are far too proud to demean themselves by venting their spite in any wrong and undeserved direction.[22]

Crises rarely touched the consular post in Seoul, however, where the routine work amounted to reporting on conditions in Korea and handling the occasional problems of American citizens. The officers stayed close to home and seldom ventured out on the railroad to any of the provincial towns, much less to remote American mission stations or the gold mines at Unsan. City-bound in Seoul, long-resident consuls such as Ransford Miller and Leo Bergholz enriched the information files of the State Department by passing on reports from the Government-General on everything from

21. U.S. State Department Post Report, Seoul, June 8, 1929 (125.8534).
22. *Seoul Press*, May 30, 1924, p. 2.

agriculture to zoology, dutifully recorded the births, marriages, and deaths of American citizens in Korea, mediated the occasional property dispute, and thus created the diplomatic variety of foreigners' wisdom about Korea.

American consular officials in Seoul were often skeptical about missionary work. They spent much time advising missionaries on legal matters relating to owning property and, on many occasions, on missionary work itself, some of which they regarded as faulty. For example, John K. Davies, the American consul-general in 1932, showed his opinion of both missionaries and Koreans in a report he wrote on Korean education, expressing his belief that Koreans were too backward to get much good out of the general education being offered by the Northern Presbyterians:

> Educational work is one feature of missionary activity, which, while strongly emphasized and theoretically highly commendable, is in some instances of very questionable benefit to anyone. The reason being the tendency in many cases to give to the sons and daughters of poverty-stricken coolies and peasants—simply because the parents have embraced Christianity—a type of high school or college education suitable for middle-class American children. The result, in a large percentage of such cases, is the creation of misfits who on the one hand are educated out of and beyond their natural environment and for whom, on the other, there do not exist in present-day Chosen opportunities for useful and gainful employment. Thus, instead of being an aid in meeting the actualities of the economic struggle, the type of education given has too often proven actually a handicap.

Davies thought vocational training was more appropriate, and he commended a trade school operated by the Southern Presbyterians in Sunch'ŏn:

> Boys are trained in brass work and…animal husbandry. Wages are credited to each pupil for his productive labor, payable upon graduation and then used to purchase equipment needed to enable him to carry on at his home the industry learned while acquiring an elementary education. For girls, courses are given in sericulture and silk weaving.…In this way students are given [enough to awaken] their minds, and yet not sufficient to unfit them for the environment in which their lives must be lived.…[23]

As Davies suggested, no curriculum would have satisfied everyone. Korean parents wanted their children to get educations that would prepare them to advance in modern society. This meant modern subjects like science and engineering along with traditional subjects such as history and government. Above all, the graduates needed to earn government certificates of graduation, the credential for jobs in the government including teaching, as well as in Japanese-run businesses. They kept pushing for

---

23. John K. Davies to SecState, March 14, 1932 (File 895,XX.) Davies's assessment of missionary schools seems harsh and in fact was wrong. Many mission schools taught vocational skills along with academics and religion.

more investment in the schools, higher standards, better teacher training, and more equipment. The missionaries, on the other hand, wanted to teach the gospel, recruit church members, and train a local pastorate, things that Korean Christian parents supported but did not think should comprise the sole purpose of their children's schools.

Although Seoul was definitely a backwater post for American consuls before World War II, several became quite comfortable and returned for repeated tours of service. One was Ransford Miller, who served in the 'teens. Another was Leo Bergholz, who became so involved in the 1919 Independence Movement. In the 1930s, William Langdon served several tours and became the State Department's top authority on Korea during World War II. Another, U. Alexis Johnson, a vice-consul in the late 1930s, made lifelong friends in Seoul and kept in touch with them for the rest of his life. But for others, like John Davies and his successor, O. Gaylord Marsh, Seoul was a post to be endured while waiting for something nearer the limelight.

Summertime in Korea

In summer, people left the city and headed for special foreigners' resorts. Two were beaches, one at Sorai on the west coast, and the other at Kalma, near Wŏnsan on the east coast. The resort at Sorai Beach,[24] founded at the turn of the century, was on a three-mile crescent facing south across

24. "Sorai" was the foreign community's romanization of the Korean name Solnae (pronounced "Sollae"), a colloquial name for the fishing hamlet over the hill from the small port of Kumip'o, in the Changyŏn District of Hwanghae Province. Sorai and Kumip'o are on the northern shore of the entrance to the bay named Taedong-man. The nearest village to appear on most maps of the area is Songch'on-ni.

In the distance lay the Sir James Hall group of islands: Paengnyŏng-do, which Westerners called by its translated name "White Wings," Taech'ŏng-do ("Big Blue"), and Soch'ŏng-do ("Little Blue"). These islands remained in the hands of the UN Command throughout the Korean War and after, and Paengnyŏng-do ("White Wings") was a base for covert military operations against North Korea.

One reached Sorai in the beginning via an intermittent coastal steamer that plied between Inch'ŏn, near Seoul, and Chinnamp'o, near P'yŏngyang, and which put in at Kumip'o. The unpleasantness of the trip enhanced Sorai's isolation. It also gave reason to go to Sorai for substantial periods—six weeks was not uncommon. By the late 1920s, it became possible to take the train to Changyŏn and travel by "public auto" to Sorai. The road was also good enough by then for vacationers to drive their own cars.

The Presbyterians were drawn to Sorai village at first because it was the home of Sŏ Sangyun (Suh Sang-yoon), an early Christian who had been converted in Manchuria by the Scottish missionary John Ross. Sŏ Sangyun was one of the first Korean Christians to welcome Horace G. Underwood, Samuel A. Moffett, James S. Gale, and other Presbyterian pioneers as they started work in Korea. He distinguished himself as their language teacher, translator, and advisor, and was of inestimable value as a companion on their exploratory trips into the Korean hinterland.

(Top) Sorai Beach, circa 1930. Clark Collection.
(Bottom) Fishing boats below Sorai Point, 1930. Clark Collection.

Taedong Bay toward the Ongjin Peninsula. By the 1930s, there were more than fifty private cabins, a four-unit lodge for visitors, an auditorium, dispensary, bakery, a summertime branch of E.D. Steward's general store, and houses for Korean servants, without whom the entire project would have been impossible. Since the purpose of the place was recreation and renewal, there was a busy schedule of tennis, swimming, miniature golf, and volleyball during the day, and church services and Bible studies throughout the week. A weekly highlight was the Sunday vesper service atop the point watching the sun set between the outer islands.

Wŏnsan Beach, across the country, was established by Methodist and Canadian missionaries stationed in the northeast. Seoulites preferred Wŏnsan Beach because it was just seven hours away by rail. Business families

(Top) View from Sorai Point, 1930. Clark Collection.
(Bottom) Sorai Beach cabins, 1930. Clark Collection.

like the Taylors, for example, lived there in the summers while the men commuted on weekends. Apart from the provisions supplied by the redoubtable E.D. Steward, Wŏnsan Beach's foreigners enjoyed amenities not available at Sorai: an eighteen-hole golf course, pure fresh water, a traveling market of Korean women who delivered fresh seafood and vegetables to the door, and daily deliveries of ice. The ocean itself was more entertaining than at Sorai, with friendly harbor seals, diving women from Cheju Island, and passing ships of every description—including, by the mid 1930s, more and more warships.[25]

25. Edith M. Deming, "Wonsan Beach," *The Korea Missions Yearbook, 1928,* pp. 196-198. Robert Grierson, "Wonsan Beach in 1923," *The Korea Mission Field,* XIX:10 (October 1923), pp. 202-203.

The Underwood family had a cottage on the headland at Sorai Beach, a haven that they occupied for almost twenty summers. At Sorai, Horace Underwood pioneered boating with the *Black Duck*, a 22-foot sailboat made of Japanese cedarwood, equipped with brass fittings and an outboard motor from America and driven by a canvas sail that had been made-to-order for him in a mission girls' school. Underwood entertained readers of *Yachting* magazine in 1931 with the story of how the boat was built by Korean methods in Seoul, launched by a team of none-too-sober coolies, and then sailed 170 miles to Sorai over the rough water between the Han River estuary and the Sir James Hall Islands. The voyage involved more than on-the-job training in seaman-

Sorai Beach fashions, 1926. Clark Collection.

ship. A storm blew up and forced the crew—two men and four boys—to put in for safety at a shrimping village on Su'ŏp Island. There they attracted a large crowd. Shortly after going ashore Underwood heard shrieks from his sons and saw them being chased around the beach by "a naked sailor who looked like one of Captain Kidd's right hand men." He grabbed the hardwood tiller handle from the *Black Duck* and put the pursuer to flight. Then, in a show that he described as a "most valuable Oriental device by which it is possible to say the most abominable things about a man without giving him the opportunity to be insulted," he mounted a boulder and with his back to the crowd, proceeded "to address the wild sea waves and the setting sun" in his best oratorical Korean:

"Thirty and more years have I lived in this country, visiting all of the thirteen provinces and receiving uniformly courteous treatment from a people of ancient civilization, now to come to the Yellow Sea Province and the Island of Su'op and find it necessary to take a club to defend the lives of my innocent babes....These people looked like Koreans and spoke the Korean language but evidently they were not Koreans. Well, if a person suddenly found himself among savages it was necessary to defend himself. But as soon as the children were through with their bath I would weigh anchor and leave these inhospitable shores." (The Koreans are the soul of hospitality, so this was a most unkind cut.) "I didn't really mind standing guard, if necessary, though it was rather hard work struggling with wind and wave for hours and hours, but what really hurt was my heart. No, certainly, my heart would not stand the strain of a night in this place. I would go somewhere where the old cordial relations between Koreans and myself, a stranger in a strange land, could be re-established. As for the particular creature who has done this thing" (he was shivering behind a rock in easy hearing), "he looked like a human being, but I found it hard to believe. Least of all could I believe that he was a Korean, for all Koreans I have met are courteous, and hospitable. Probably he had no parents or they were beyond description." (Filial piety is the virtue of virtues in Korea and all the East.) "Certainly that must be it; he was a barbarian from some barbarous isle; a man without either parents or children or he would not have tried to drown little children or harrow a father's heart by attacking them before his very eyes," etc. etc.[26]

With this, villagers inviting them to stay surrounded the crew of the *Black Duck*. Tokens were exchanged, and all was well. Three days later, back on the sea after many hours of adventure and moments of sheer terror in the tidal rips of Taedong Bay, they sighted Sorai Beach. After stopping for a quick swim and changing into clean clothes, "all available bunting was got out and about 9:30 a.m., July 10th, a very gay Black Duck dropped anchor in our own little harbor with most of the small summer colony down to greet her and her abnormally clean crew."[27]

Trekking in the Ever-White Mountains

On the Sino-Korean border in the mountain range called Changpai-shan is the mountain known as "Paektu-san," (lit. "White Head Mountain"). Paektu-san holds a mystic significance for all Koreans. Though unimposing by Himalayan standards, it is awesome in its context: a volcanic peak 9,000 feet high topped by a very deep crater lake called "Ch'ŏn-ji" in Korean ("Heavenly Lake"). The lake feeds a minor tributary of the Songhua (Sungari) River to the north, and the Yalu and Tumen rivers flow out of springs on Paektu-san's slopes to the west and east, forming the border between Korea and Manchuria.[28] The mountain's mystique is partly spiritual. Koreans

26. Horace H. Underwood, "A Korean 'Black Duck,'" *Yachting*, L:6 (December 1931), pp. 57-58.
27. Ibid., p. 99.
28. The entire frontier area around Paektu-san was as fascinating to foreigners as it was to Koreans. Travelers like Canadian E.J.O. Fraser, a missionary returning from a trip to Manchuria in March 1932, explored the eastward-flowing Tumen near Musan: "The Tumen...is not wide up there, but it is rapid. However, in winter it freezes over and a lot of travel is done on the ice...and we found it practicable to ride on a sleigh down the river instead of walking over the hills on the rough roads for a long day's tramp. Starting about nine o'clock in the morning we drove down the winding river....I was a wonderful ride, as most of the way it was between walls of rock where the river in the course of centuries has worn down its bed, leaving

associate it with the birth of Tan'gun, the legendary founder of their race who was born of the union between Hwanŭng, son of the Creator of All Under Heaven, and a she-bear who was magically transformed into a beautiful woman.[29] Contemporary North Korea links the Kim Il-sung cult with the cult of Tan'gun by making the mountain the site of Kim Il-sung's guerrilla base camp during World War II. Kim's son and successor Kim Jong-il has inherited this connection via the story that he was born at the camp.[30]

In the 1930s there were two famous expeditions up Paektu-san by foreigners from Seoul. The first, known as the Boots-McMullin Expedition, went up the southeast slope from the narrow-gauge railhead at Musan in August 1929, taking five days before reaching the Heavenly Lake.[31] Refusing to be outdone, H.H. Underwood organized an expedition in 1931, approaching the mountain from Hyesanjin in north central Korea. The Underwood family took a folding canoe to paddle out on the lake and a 16mm movie camera to record the expedition. They spent two days exploring the crater and testing the depth of the lake, which Koreans claim is bottomless:

> We had a reel with 1420 feet of rope on it and at one place that all went out. I guess Dad was tired of reeling twelve to fourteen-hundred feet of rope: anyway, he let the wooden reel go and it kept on down out of sight in that beautifully clear water, so the lake must be at least 1450 feet deep.

> About an hour later, walking along the shore of the lake to the Sungari River exit, we came to a little hot-spring trickling out into the lake and there, in a circle of about three or four feet, the water was just tolerable so we three [Underwood's sons Horace G., John, and James] "swam" in the Lake of Heaven at Paek-tu-san.[32]

the perpendicular walls of stratified rock, showing the different deposits of volcanic masses in great detail. In some places the solid rock seemed to be still boiling, as the formation gave that appearance. It was a sight to delight the heart of a geologist." E.J.O. Fraser to A.E. Armstrong, April 18, 1932. UCCA 83.006C, Box 2, File 54.

29. For the legend of Tan'gun, translated from Kim Pusik's twelfth-century *Samguk sagi*, see Peter H. Lee, ed., *A Sourcebook of Korean Civilization*, vol. I (New York: Columbia University Press, 1993), pp. 6-7.

30. The historical evidence shows that the younger Kim was born in Russia, near Khabarovsk. See Dae-Sook Suh, *Kim Il-sung, the North Korean Leader* (New York: Columbia University Press, 1989), p. 51.

31. J. Earnest Fisher, "The Boots-McMullin Expedition to Paik Doo San," *The Korea Mission Field*, XXVI:10 (October 1930), pp. 209-214.

32. Horace G. Underwood, "Reminiscences" and interviews, May-June 1985. See also, Mrs. Horace H. Underwood, "Paik Tu San, 1931: The Ever-White Mountain," *The Korea Mission Field*, XXVI:10 (October 1931), pp. 201-204.

Hunting Boar on Yongmun Mountain

Horace Underwood's outings were methodically planned, since absolutely everything that was necessary to enjoy Korea in the Western style had to be packed and transported. He outdid himself on the Paektu-san trip, which was intended as a once-in-a-lifetime project, but he organized other expeditions on an annual basis, like the winter hunting trip to Yongmun-san, a mountain in Yangp'yŏng County southeast of Seoul. Each year after Christmas Underwood would collect his sons and hardier friends, a cook and a retainer or two, and a favorite Korean hunting companion named "Ma,"[33] and head for Yongmun-san. There, by long-standing arrangement, the party was given the use of a certain villager's house for ten days out of the year. Underwood's part of the bargain was to pay for an addition to the house. The villager's part was to help the American find guides and beaters and supplies for the hunt.

Upon arrival there were formalities. The village elders came with greetings and the hunters paid their respects in turn. Then came the passing-around of weapons for inspection[34] and the hunting reports: what game had been seen on the mountain, and where. Wild boar were the prime interest, though there were always deer. Leopards were reported some years but none was ever seen or shot. At length, prices were agreed upon for portering, tracking, and beating, and after a night's sleep and a hearty breakfast prepared by the Underwoods' cook, the party set out for the hunt. The Korean beaters would then trek through the snow in their straw sandals, walking a ragged line over rocks and ravines making noise to frighten the animals toward the hunters, who were waiting with shotguns, sitting still and slowly freezing in place. If half a day passed without any success a fire would be built and arguments would ensue about what was being done wrong. If the beaters were successful and the hunters hit their mark, it was cause for wild celebration. As his son "Horace G." later described it,

> Of course when the animals came out and the shooting started it repaid all the hours of walking and waiting. There was always the temptation to jump up and go see what was happening, even though you knew better—another might break your way. Finally when it was all over, if an animal had been shot

33. "One time as we were returning to camp after a hard day's hunt in which we had killed one small boar, we were passing through a village and someone yelled, 'How many did you kill?' Ma, who had a dry wit, said, 'If we had killed nine more we would have ten.'" J. Earnest Fisher, *Pioneers of Modern Korea* (Seoul: Christian Literature Society of Korea, 1977), p. 268.

34. The old Korean hunter used a shotgun, which tended to be too short-ranged for good effect against boar. Underwood and the other Americans who hunted with him favored the .401 Winchester, while the Underwood boys carried .351 Winchesters. (Note from Richard F. Underwood, April 1996.)

we all gathered around it to talk over all the exciting parts—when it first got up, how one beater broke a gut running to head it off from getting out to one side, how the first shots missed, how the false sounds of wind or mice had fooled the hunter. If it was a big animal—an over-250 pound pig—the hunt would break up for the day. If it was a small pig or a deer one of the beaters would be designated to take it back to the village and the hunt would go on. A big pig had to be pulled out....

The biggest boar Dad ever shot was…42 inches at the shoulder. The heaviest that any of the occidental community ever shot was one Dr. Jack Boots got, weighing about 600 pounds….Korean wild boar are not particularly vicious and they do not "attack on sight."…Maybe they have confidence in their size. Nevertheless, they do occasionally attack people and the second one I shot gored one of the beaters. The pig was already wounded—partly really hurt, partly stunned—and was resting half conscious when the beater came up under him and shouted. The pig reared up, used his tusks to slash the beater's leg in a long clean cut (a knife could not have done it cleaner) and ran on down the valley. We of course bandaged the man up and saw to his treatment and he had no permanent after-effects, but Dad said that in all his years of hunting that was the first time he had ever seen a boar gore a person.

Back in the village the animals were cleaned by lamplight. As the story continued,

[I]f it was a big boar it was a village project. The beaters and bearers and others in the "party" got first chance at the blood, then anybody known to be weak or sickly. The liver we would keep (soak it in salt water overnight to get the blood, etc. out of it) but the other organs, especially the gall, were prized by the villagers. To see the old chief beater in the flickering light of pine-knot torches with blood dripping down his beard might almost be enough to justify the old [missionary stories of cannibals].[35]

Hazards of the Automobile Age

By the 1930s, many of Korea's foreigners had motor vehicles, either imported or bought locally from the W.W. Taylor Company.[36] The roads, however, were unpaved outside the biggest cities and hardly designed for traffic. Any motor trip therefore was an adventure that could easily turn into a disaster. The commonest problems were flat tires and running out of fuel, and no one went anywhere without patching equipment, pumps, and extra gasoline. Hazards included washed-out bridges and fords that were

35. Horace G. Underwood, "Reminiscences" and interviews, May-June, 1985.
36. In all of Korea there were three private automobiles registered in 1917, 350 in 1927, and 450 in 1929 (*Seoul Press*, February 2, 1929, p. 2). In 1930 there were 3,481 cars of all kinds in Korea, official, private, company-owned, and "public;" i.e., taxis. Of these, 1,834, or 52.6 percent, were taxis (*Seoul Press*, November 29, 1930, p. 3). In 1993 there were 4,271,253 automobiles (sedans) of all types registered in South Korea. Yonhap News Agency, *Korea Annual 1994* (Seoul: Yonhap, 1994), p. 256.

deeper than they looked, for which purpose drivers also carried ropes and chains. Nearby farmers and their oxen often had to be persuaded to help pull mired cars out of paddies, and everyone knew the characteristic "Oi-sha! Oi-sha!" chant of Korean men as they pulled.

Koreans had little experience with cars in the 1920s. Village children thronged to see them as they passed. It was common for pedestrians in the road to walk along completely oblivious to a large motor vehicle blowing its horn only inches behind them. On straightaways between villages, the roughness of the roads was such that drivers had to keep veering back and forth in search of the smoother side of the "washboard"—if the road was wide enough to have two sides. Dust got into everything, and when it rained it seemed that the merest sprinkle made mud that was axle-deep.

The Japanese authorities, anxious to help foreigners cope with conditions on Korea's roads, once published a list of rules in a sort of English:

1. At the rise of the hand of the policeman, stop rapidly. Do not pass him or otherwise disrespect him.
2. When a passenger of the foot hove in sight tootle the horn trumpet to him melodiously at first. If he still obstacles your passage tootle with vigor and express by word of mouth the warning "Hi! Hi!"
3. Beware of the wandering horse that he shall not take fright as you pass him. Do not explosion the exhaust pipe. Go soothingly by him, or stop by the roadside till he pass away.
4. Give big space to the festive dog that make sport in the roadway. Avoid entanglement with your wheel spoke.
5. Go soothingly on the grease mud as there lurk the skid demon.
6. Press the brake of the foot as you roll around the corner to save the collapse.[37]

No amount of vigilance was enough, however, to keep everyone safe on the highway, and there were frequent accidents. The most serious road mishap to befall the foreign community was the car-train collision on March 26, 1919, just south of Suwŏn. The car was a Buick convertible just imported through Inch'ŏn by Paul Sackett Crane, a Southern Presbyterian missionary from Mokp'o. The accident occurred while Crane was on his way home with three fellow passengers from the Southern Presbyterian station at Kwangju, including Kwangju missionary Eugene Bell, who was at the wheel. The Buick was making its way south along the dry dirt road that served as the main Seoul-Pusan highway when it came to a crossing of the parallel tracks of the north-south railroad a few miles south of Suwŏn at the village of Pyŏngchŏm. A small hill blocked Bell's view of the tracks at that

37. "Japanese Auto Rules Published in Korea," in Clara Hedberg Bruen, *40 Years in Korea*, p. 368. One suspects that this list of rules is at least partly apocryphal; however, a version of it was circulated at the 1996 reunion of Pyeng Yang Foreign School alumni in Montreat, North Carolina, with sober attestations to its authenticity as a government-generated list of instructions.

point and he failed to see the oncoming express train when he decided to cross the rails. The train hit the rear half of the car sending the occupants flying, and Mr. Crane and Mrs. Bell were killed.[38] The victims lost their lives on Korea's prime highway, reminding everyone that motoring involved risks to life and limb as well as the virtual certainty of mechanical breakdown.

Foreign Roots in Honam

The Southern Presbyterian Mission, of which the Bells and Mr. Crane were a part, was the main missionary effort in southwestern Korea—the two provinces of North and South Chŏlla that together are known as the "Honam" area—beginning in 1892.[39] The "SPs" maintained mission stations in Mokp'o and Sunch'ŏn on the southwest coast, the two provincial capitals of Kwangju and Chŏnju, and the west coast port of Kunsan at the mouth of the Kŭm River. Each station had a residential compound for its missionary staff and their families, one or more schools for Korean children, and a medical facility. At Yŏsu, near Sunch'ŏn, the mission also ran a leprosarium. The Chŏlla provinces became SP territory in the same 1909 apportionment that assigned the northwest to the Northern Presbyterians and the P'yŏngyang area jointly to the Northern Presbyterians and Methodists.

The Southern Presbyterian Mission was founded by a group of seven American volunteers who arrived in Korea in 1892.[40] They began their work in Seoul as colleagues of the Northern Presbyterians who were already there, and their first residence was the former German ambassador's residence in Chŏng-dong, which the neighbors quickly christened "Dixie." They had arrived at a time of missionary exploration and expansion into the hinterland, and while the Northern Presbyterians were deciding to es-

---

38. Horace H. Underwood, "A Serious Automobile Accident," *The Korea Mission Field*, XV:5 (May 1919), pp. 100-102.

39. This is not to overlook the Catholic missionary presence in Honam, represented by the Irish Columbans with their station in Mokp'o and their seminary in Kwangju.

40. The group consisted of Lewis B. Tate, William Davis Reynolds, and William McCleery Junkin, and four women: Mattie Tate, Linnie Davis, Patsy Reynolds, and Mary Junkin, the latter two being new brides. Mattie Tate was Lewis Tate's sister, and Linnie Davis was the only one who did not have a long relationship with the others. Linnie Davis was the first to arrive, in 1892, since the others were delayed by health problems. Miss Davis married missionary William B. Harrison in 1898 and died in 1903. Mattie Tate remained single and spent forty-three years in Korea, retired in 1935, and died in 1940. She is sometimes confused with Mattie Ingold, a Southern Presbyterian doctor in Korea from 1897 to 1925, who married Lewis Tate in 1905.

tablish stations in Taegu, Andong, and P'yŏngyang, the Southern Presbyterians decided to establish themselves in the southwest.[41]

The Chŏlla Provinces—the Honam region[42]—comprise a unique area on the Korean peninsula. Isolated by the Sobaek mountain range that divides Honam from its rival region of Yŏngnam in the southeast (the provinces of North and South Kyŏngsang), Honam is rich in agriculture, with broad valleys and alluvial plains especially fine for growing rice. The intensive labor required for this kind of farming has shaped the economic and social structure of Honam over many generations, giving rise to a particularly feudal system that favored large landlords and reduced many farmers to tenancy and day labor. Alienation is a theme of life in Honam, and its history reflects both its isolation and its social disparities. Koreans in other parts of the country regard Honam people as bumpkins and worse, identifying their regional dialect as a sign of social stigma. As a result, Honam has been an area prone to rebellion, hard to control, and characterized by unruly behavior. The realities of life in Honam, along with the general pattern of discrimination against its people by other Koreans, has made for a self-fulfilling political pattern. It is a fertile ground for alternative religious and political ideologies. Since 1850 it has been the scene of spectacular upheavals: the Tonghak risings of the 1860s and 1890s, anti-Japanese uprisings in 1919 and 1929, leftist peasant unions and Communist-led agitation in the 1930s and '40s, a low-intensity guerrilla war in the 1950s, and the bloody Kwangju "democratization" movement against the South Korean military dictatorship in 1980. From 1970 through the 1990s, South Korea's leading opposition politician was Kim Dae Jung, a Honam native whose career gave voice to the anger of Honam for decades and whose election to the presidency of South Korea in 1997 was a triumph for the cause of human rights and a vindication for the people of the Korean southwest.[43]

41. The Junkins and Tates went to Chŏnju, the capital of North Chŏlla Province and the clan seat of the Korean former royal family, and established the mission's base of operations there in 1896. Lewis B. Tate and his sister Mattie were the first permanent missionaries assigned to the territory. For the early years of the Southern Presbyterian Mission see Martha Huntley, *To Start a Work*, passim.

42. The geographical term "Honam" can include the province of South Ch'ungch'ŏng, but here it is used to refer to the two provinces of North and South Chŏlla (created in 1896 from the traditional single province of Chŏlla). The names of Korea's provinces are based on their two main cities; hence "Chŏlla" is derived from the first syllable of Chŏnju plus the first syllable of Naju (in which case, under the rules of Korean pronunciation, the N sounds convert to L sounds).

43. Kim Dae Jung's winning of the Nobel Peace Prize in the year 2000 was related to his breakthrough meeting with North Korean leader Kim Jong-il, but he had been nominated for his human rights stance many times before, and his supporters regarded the prize as recognition in part for his long years of suffering during the struggle for democracy in South Korea.

The Southern Presbyterians in Honam witnessed these events and offered Christianity as an alternative ideology. They found many receptive listeners. As the mission grew, the number of converts increased, until there were more than seven thousand Presbyterians in Honam by 1915. By that time, most of the families commonly associated with the mission—the Bells, Lintons, Cranes, Prestons, Talmages, and Wilsons—had arrived on the scene. They cooperated in the work of the Korea-wide "Presbyterian Council," an administrative device that coordinated the work of the two Presbyterian missions from the United States with the work of the Australian and Canadian Presbyterians, spreading out for better effect and operating certain key projects-in-common, including the college and seminary in P'yŏngyang, and the college and medical school in Seoul.[44]

However, the Southern Presbyterians always identified first with the Honam area, a link that separated them from other Westerners in Korea. SP missionaries in Honam liked to refer to themselves in jest as *sigol-saram* ("country bumpkins") and enjoyed flaunting their Chŏlla/Dixie Korean accents. Their regional identification was more than a mere consequence of the 1909 territorial apportionment: it helped them maintain the best points of Southern culture within Korea. When they were old enough, children of the mission attended boarding school at Pyeng Yang Foreign School, and when they went back to America for college it was to campuses in the South. Those who returned as second-generation missionaries did so after attending conservative seminaries; and if they married, either in America or on the field, the spouse often was another child of the mission who could feel at home in Honam.

Most of Honam's Southern Presbyterian missionary families summered not at the north Korean beaches, with the Yankees, but much closer to home in their own retreat high in the Chiri mountain range. Their resort was provided for them by a South Carolina benefactor and consisted of twenty-five stone cottages four thousand feet above the steaming paddies of South Chŏlla. Anyone who could make the hike was welcome to come and enjoy "days sunshiny with nights cool and bracing." The hike could be finessed by hiring chair bearers from a platoon of coolies bonded by the camp management. Once at the campsite, families normally stayed the entire summer enjoying the hiking trails, tennis courts, the swimming pool, horseshoe pits, and entertainment nights in the campsite's stone auditorium. The children learned to collect wild flowers by the trails, and there

44. The Presbyterian denomination is by membership the largest Christian group in South Korea today, though it is comprised of more than fifty big and small sub-denominations. Many reasons are advanced to explain this fracturing, a common one being the example set by Western missionaries who themselves were unable to overcome such divisions as the legacy of the American Civil War.

are oldsters who still remember helping Florence Crane collect flowers for her book *Flowers and Folklore from Far Korea.*[45]

The Kwangju Rising of 1929

At Camp Graham on Chiri-san it was easy to forget the seething politics in the valleys below. The South Chŏlla capital of Kwangju, famous in the 1980s as the center of South Korea's democracy movement, earlier earned fame as the point of origin of an anti-Japanese uprising by Korean students in 1929. Students were the leaders of anti-Japanese resistance in Kwangju because Japanese educational authorities clearly discriminated against Korean schools in the city, giving them inferior facilities and teachers. When the Koreans had established a good-quality higher common school of their own, the Japanese took it over and made it a public institution. Their takeover of the school in 1923 laid the groundwork for endemic conflict between Korean and Japanese students in the city.

To compensate for their inferior schools, Korean students joined special study groups that were created by nationalists, some of them leftists, in which the discussion topics often had anti-Japanese themes. The police watched these groups and pressured their members. The students answered with strikes for decent treatment, for fairness from Japanese teachers in classrooms, and an end to insults by Japanese students.

On October 30, 1929, a group of commuting Japanese students molested a Korean girl student who was trying to pass through a turnstile at the Kwangju railroad station. When some Korean schoolboys rushed to defend her there was a general melee. Others rushed to join in and the fighting spread throughout the day in the city's streets and alleyways. Outbreaks continued into mid-November, by which time the Koreans were well enough organized to turn it into a political struggle, which they advertised with handbills calling for a general revolt against the Japanese.

The colonial police, afraid that the students were about to "run amok," as the *Seoul Press* put it, launched an investigation and began making arrests. The police put out the story that "a secret communistic society" called the Tŏksu-hoe was trying to exploit racial feelings to inflate the "tri-

---

45. "Chidi San: Camp E. C. Graham" (brochure, 6 pp. n.p., n.d.). Katherine Boyer Moore, conversation, Seoul, July 16, 1990. "The Summer in Karuizawa," *The Korea Mission Field*, X:8 (August 1914), pp. 231-232. Florence Hedleston Crane, *Flowers and Folklore from Far Korea* (Tokyo: Shiseido, 1936; repr. Seoul: Garden Club of Seoul, 1969). By the 1950s most of Camp Graham had been destroyed in the fighting that raged in the Chiri Mountains in the Korean War era and the Southern Presbyterians had to relocate their retreat. Their new Chiri encampment was much smaller and lacked many of the amenities of the earlier resort.

fling incident" at the turnstile into a lawless rampage. Anti-Japanese demonstrations broke out in the nearby towns of Mokp'o and Naju, and in December, students on the campus of Keijō Imperial University in Seoul began circulating manifestoes and distributing them to secondary schools in
the capital. Students "imbued with radicalist ideas" went on strike at several schools and began raising the forbidden shout of "*mansei*" to signify a
revival of the Independence Movement. Communists in secret societies
were said to the "wirepullers" manipulating the students, hoping to generate a nationwide alliance of students, peasants, and workers. The left-right
coalition New Korea Society (Sin'gan-hoe), which the *Seoul Press* interest-
ingly characterized as "consisting of Korean communists and movers for racial emancipation," met on December 11 to discuss boosting the movement, thereby giving the police an excuse to arrest some of its leaders.
There was a hiatus during the winter vacation, but in mid-January, when
the middle schools reopened, student demonstrations resumed across the
country, including students at mission schools. The police continued to
make arrests and to claim that the international communist movement was
behind the outbreaks.[46] Those arrested included mission school students,
some of whom spent time in prison or got their names put on blacklists so
they could not receive government-recognized diplomas.

During the Kwangju rebellion of 1929, the missionary community saw it
as their main job to keep their schools open and their students out of trouble with the law. As in 1919, they had little use for the colonial police but
they also saw their students as less than heroes struggling for independence. At the Speer School for Girls in Kwangju, Principal Florence Root
tried to keep her students off the streets.[47] When one of William Parker's
students was arrested for mimeographing handbills, "a grave offence for
which [he] had to be punished," Parker expressed regret for kicking him
out of school but thought he saw a more important issue at stake: "[The
young man] is a fine fellow, a good student, and quiet and well behaved,
but in the matter of mimeographing the handbills he was guilty before the
law, of course."[48] L.T. Newland went farther, essentially echoing the police
version of what had happened:

> The trigger finger of the Korean school boy is very nervous and goes off at the
> least provocation. Any excuse is enough to make him express his Bolshevistic
> spirit which has been stimulated by a constant stream of bootlegged theories

46. "Facts of Student Trouble with Koshū Affair as Centre," *Seoul Press*, February
3, 1930, pp. 3-4.
47. Florence Root, Dear Friends letter, February 15, 1930, Presbyterian Church
U.S.A., Department of History, Montreat, North Carolina, hereafter referred to as
PCUSA Montreat Archives.
48. William P. Parker, Dear Fellow Workers letter, May 2, 1930, PCUSA Montreat
Archives.

from Russia which like all bootlegged articles has the minimum amount of food and the maximum amount of poison....No wonder there is no stability to the Korean youth and strikes are as inevitable as sunshine.[49]

Merely being near the action did not mean that foreigners like Root, Parker, and Newland would fully understand the Kwangju rebellion, but they did understand that the Honam region was a political tinderbox and though they could not have foreseen the full extent of the terror that would plague the region in the 1940s, L.T. Newland could hear the rumbling discontent. He wrote that the bucolic Chŏlla countryside was "as Vesuvius' calm before the destruction of Pompeii," for "hidden under this surface [are] contending forces that augur but poorly for the peace of this land." In a Christmas letter to supporting churches he noted that "the Christ Child lived in much the same atmosphere," and he appealed for support to make the gospel the answer.

> Korean society is going to burst into flame sooner or later, and whether it becomes a destroying fire or a purifying cauterization depends on the leaders who will direct the outburst. I cannot insist too strongly on this fact: NOW is the time to bring Christ to Korea. If this easily-to-be-reached people can only be influenced by the Gospel of Christ then the future is safe, if not—![50]

Regional politics, a phenomenon much remarked-upon today, has ancient roots in Korean tradition. It is interesting to note that the Southern Presbyterians in Honam, though they were not sympathetic with Japanese rule, nonetheless disapproved of Korean confrontations with the colonial authorities however just the cause. Their stance is another example of the apolitical attitude of missionaries under Japanese rule. "The Work" came first and had to be protected at all costs. Korea's salvation would come in God's own time and not from political resistance.

49. L.T. Newland, My dear friends letter, December 17, 1929, PCUSA Montreat Archives.
50. Ibid. Throughout the Japanese colonial period there were plots, police raids, and newspaper reports of what came to be called "communist" agitation in Honam, especially in South Chŏlla Province. Farmers organized peasants' unions and operated "proletarian" schools that taught resistance against the relentless appropriation of their land by big owners and Japanese residents and land development companies. They demanded reduction of rents and better prices for their prime products of rice, cotton, and seaweed, and they organized boycotts against merchants. Their methods were technically legal though decried by Japanese authorities, and labeling them Communists enabled the police to arrest them for illegal political activity. See Gi-wook Shin, *Peasant Protest and Social Change in Colonial Korea* (Seattle: University of Washington Press, 1996). The fact that the consular corps in Korea was aware of this problem is seen in R.L Cowley (Seoul) to Ambassador Sir Robert Clive (Tokyo), September 22, 1934. Public Record Office file FO 262/1867.

Dr. Haysmeir and the Apple Thief

One afternoon in 1925 on the Seventh Day Adventist Mission compound in Sunan, the P'yŏngyang suburb that is now the location of the city's international airport, a 28-year-old American missionary doctor named C.A. Haysmeir spied a 12-year-old village boy in the hospital orchard stealing apples. The orchard was a source of sustenance not only for the SDA Mission but also for the hospital patients, and it had a fence around it and signs forbidding trespassing. However, at harvest time when the apples were too ripe to resist, village children often came over the fence to steal the forbidden fruit. On this particular occasion Dr. Haysmeir had prepared himself to teach the thieves a lesson. When he saw the boy he burst out of the building, caught him, and then hauled him back to the lab where he traced the Korean word "*tojok*" (for "thief") on the boy's cheek with caustic soda. As the chemical burned into the boy's skin Dr. Haysmeir lectured him about stealing. Then he let him go.

Immediately there was a public outcry. Dr. Haysmeir tried to explain that he had not meant to inflict any permanent damage. He said that he had expected the brand to fade "in a few weeks"—though it was still visible the following spring. Word of the incident spread to Seoul where the newspapers picked up the demand for Haysmeir's punishment. Civic groups joined in. The Bar Association passed a resolution demanding the doctor's deportation. "We don't like to be experimented on like animals," wrote a Korean in a letter to the editor of the *Seoul Press*.

The Seventh Day Adventist Mission put up a weak defense of Dr. Haysmeir, pointing to his otherwise spotless record as a doer of good. However, the next year government prosecutors took him to trial. In short order he was convicted, forced to pay two months' salary (¥620) to the boy's family, and sentenced to three months in prison. The sentence was suspended on appeal, giving the Seventh Day Adventist mission a chance to hustle Dr. Haysemeir out of the country.[51]

Koreans have retold versions of the Haysmeir story ever since it happened, in 1925, and it is still a staple of anti-Western discourse in South, and doubtless North, Korea. The incident was outrageous for many reasons, not least because of the doctor's self-righteousness and the disproportion of his punishment of the boy. Haysmeir broke the code of his own religion, but on second look, his actions were not much different from many other manifestations of Western superiority in the East, not only in Korea but wherever Westerners looked down on "natives" or thought them to be lesser human beings. One suspects that there was some surprise in the foreign community when the law came down on Haysmeir as it would

51. *Seoul Press*, July 1, 13, 18, 20, and 29, 1926.

have done in his own country—and resentment as well, for harming the reputation of "the Work" in Korea.

Foreigners in Korean Eyes

The writer Younghill Kang once described two kinds of missionary in Korea: the kind that was "educated and sincere," and the type "that cannot get any job in the West so he comes to the East where he can live cheaply and have a cook and a waiter and a gardener and cherish a superiority complex over the 'heathen.' He announces that the Lord has called him for service, but in reality the West has kicked him out for being unfit."[52]

The notion that Korea's foreign expatriates were rejects from home was nothing new with Younghill Kang. To Koreans, who shuddered at the thought of exile or estrangement from their personal circle of family and friends and who had little experience of foreign travel, the idea of going abroad was something that connoted trauma. The Korean language is full of references to the sadness of being far from home. Whatever missionaries said about their motives for being in Korea, the fact of their "exile" represented a choice that few Koreans would have made for themselves.[53]

Korean wonderment at Westerners surfaced in many forms. "There were many stories and jokes about missionaries," wrote Younghill Kang: "how they bowed down to their wives even on the street, just like the Japanese before their emperor (this was when they were tying the women's shoes), and how they hugged them down from carts just as obscene drunken men might do with geishas, and how these women were not even picked out and married legally to them by their fathers and mothers."[54] Their daily customs were jarringly different. Westerners laughed out loud without covering their mouths, wore shoes indoors, and mingled the sexes in unregulated ways. *Yangban*-class Koreans disdained them for their ignorance of

52. Younghill Kang, *The Grass Roof* (New York: Charles Scribner's Sons, 1931), pp. 323, 311. Not surprisingly, Younghill Kang's remarks about missionaries in *The Grass Roof* elicited bitter comments about his ingratitude from several Canadian missionaries who had helped him as a student and arranged for him to study in the West. William Scott to Younghill Kang, December 16, 1942, in UCCA 83.006C, Box 5, File 129, and Armstrong to Fraser, April 19, 1943, same box, file 130.

53. Within the Korean Christian community, however, the missionaries were able to put across the idea that in order to grow, a church had to send missionaries abroad as an expression of Christian outreach. The first Korean "missionary" was the Presbyterian Rev. Yi Kip'ung, who was sent to Cheju Island in 1907. Other missions followed, to Vladivostok (1909), Tokyo (1912), Chientao (1910), and Shantung (1912). Missions have been an important emphasis of Korea's Protestant denominations ever since. See Allen D. Clark, *A History of the Church in Korea* (Seoul: Christian Literature Society, 1972), pp. 174-178.

54. Kang, *The Grass Roof,* p. 223.

ye—the Confucian rules of right conduct. But mostly they were merely strange and even a little ridiculous. Younghill Kang recalled the first American he ever saw: a solemn missionary doctor dressed in white trousers that looked just like the typical Korean grandmother's underpants.

Household servants were a prime source of gossip about the foreigners' strange habits. They noted that Caucasians had poor eyesight since their eyes, though large, were pale colors and most of them, even children, had to wear glasses, a fact that offended some adult Koreans because glasses were a badge of age and learning and therefore inappropriate for children. Quantities of medicine were required to keep foreigners healthy, and the medicine was of dubious type and origin, such that an early rumor went around that the missionaries were kidnapping Korean children in order to use their organs for medicine.[55] They also needed special foods—meats and cheeses that had to be imported. The weird things that foreigners ate helped make them different, suspect, and even repulsive to Koreans, as the Canadian doctor Florence Murray discovered while trying to get her nurses to treat some Russian refugees at her clinic in Hamhŭng:

> The nurses didn't like to nurse Russian patients and I once had to reprimand them for not being kinder to one.
>
> "We can't stand the smell of them," they protested.
>
> "Smell!" I exclaimed. "They won't smell if you keep them clean."
>
> "All the Russians smell awful. We hate to go near them. They all smell like weasels."
>
> "Like weasels, do they? If foreigners smell, we must smell too. What do Dr. Martin and I smell like?" I demanded to know.
>
> This was embarrassing, but they finally admitted we smelled like cows. "Don't you drink milk and eat butter and cheese?" they pointed out. "Why wouldn't you smell like cows?"[56]

The distance between foreigners and Koreans turned up in things as ordinary as the sense of smell. Westerners responded to the aroma of morning coffee. Koreans responded to the aroma of pickled *kimch'i* in the making and the smoky smells of the Korean farmhouse. The other senses too

---

55. Lillias H. Underwood, *Fifteen Years among the Topknots* (Boston: American Tract Society, 1904), pp. 15-16. This story was similar to the one that touched off the Tientsin Massacre of 1870, which cost the lives of fourteen French citizens, ten of them nuns at an orphanage. A latter-day variant of the story is the anti-American novelist Chŏng Tosang's *Amerik'a Durim* (American Dream) (Seoul: Tosŏ ch'ulp'an Indong, 1990), in which a fictional American couple adopts a Korean orphan in order to use his heart in a transplant operation for their own ailing birth-child.

56. Florence J. Murray, M.D., *At the Foot of Dragon Hill* (New York: E. P. Dutton, 1975), p. 36.

were differently conditioned. For Koreans it was the feel of the planking on the porch that had been worn smooth by generations of bare feet. It was the sound of farmers singing in fields and *makkoli* houses and the clanging of the *yot* candyman's taffy scissors. Sounds meant feelings: scary feelings when a grandmother told ghost stories after dark; excited feelings when the neighborhood shaman conducted a kut; or feelings of dread as the village men rehearsed the chant for the next day's funeral procession. These were things that Westerners, if they encountered them at all, discovered only as adults and then only as Korean curiosities. It took extraordinary effort to learn how to respond to these basic things.

Another factor in the social distance between foreigners and Koreans was the fact that Westerners mostly dealt with Koreans who were in subordinate roles as employees, compradors, students, and protégés of various kinds. In most work contexts, the Westerner/Korean relationships simply fit the Koreans' own paradigms of teacher/student and *sŏnbae/hubae* (senior/junior) relations, with the foreigner invariably in the superior position.[57] This grated on the novelist Yi Kwangsu, who accused the missionaries of having a colonialist mindset.

> A real Christian, so called, treats learning with the greatest contempt, calling it "worldly knowledge." Arguing that the "worldly knowledge" weakens faith, he regards learning as a temptation of the devil and an enemy of the soul. Those who desire to acquire an education higher than that of a [mission] school or desire to go abroad for study, are considered to have already stepped inside the gates of hell. "Faith is all important. To learn ever so much—what is the use of it?" is the instruction which a real believer gives to his children. In church schools no attention is paid to natural science, geography or history—the essential subjects in a modern curriculum. Remember that the Koreans of today must seek learning as the thirsty seek water.[58]

Korean intellectuals saw the tendency to keep Korean Christians "simple in the faith" as nothing less than racist. After all, the missionaries themselves typically had learned the liberal arts at their own Christian colleges. The educator Paek Nakchun (L. George Paik) argued that without a similar kind of modern education, a Korean clergyman could not command the respect of his own countrymen or do an effective job of pastoring his congregation.[59] Looking back, Korean analysts have decried the anti-intellectualism of some of the missionaries, blaming their fundamentalism and pater-

---

57. Conversation with Professor Min Kyŏngbae, Yonsei University School of Theology, Seoul, May 1984.
58. Yi Kwang-su, "Defects of the Korean Church Today," trans. Yun Ch'i-ho, *The Korea Mission Field*, XIV:12 (December 1918), p. 254.
59. L. George Paik (Paek Nakchun), interview, Seoul, April 6, 1984; also see Paik's *The History of Protestant Missions in Korea, 1832-1910*, rev. ed. (Seoul: Yonsei University Press, 1970), p. 216.

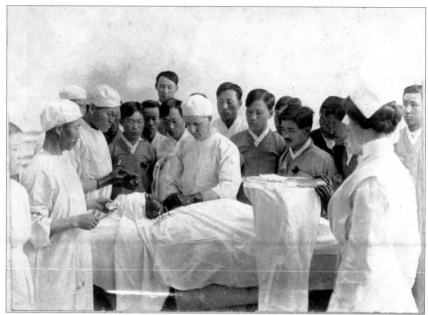

Teaching surgery techniques. Severance Union Medical College, Seoul, circa 1930.
Clark Collection.

nalism for the postwar tendency of Korean Christians to split hairs.[60] Some,
like Kim Kyosin, rejected the idea of Western denominations altogether,
following the example of the famous Japanese Christian Uchimura Kanzō
and his *mukyōkai* ("No Church") anti-institutional tradition.[61] Church historian David Suh (Sŏ Kwangsŏn) turned this critique into a missionary version of dependency theory, suggesting that the missionaries consciously
practiced a form of religious colonialism.[62] At the same time Suh expressed
his own ambivalence by noting the importance of the missionary effort in
setting the pace for the Korean church and cementing the American-Korean relationship:

> The Korean church is in large part an American success story. This sense of
> gratitude was later strengthened and stretched to cover the great event of the

60. Min Kyŏngbae, *Han'guk kidokkyohoesa* (Seoul: Taehan Kidokkyo Ch'ulp'ansa,
1983), pp. 410-419; Sung C. Chun [Chŏn Sŏngch'ŏn], *Schism and Unity in the
Protestant Churches of Korea* (Seoul: Christian Literature Society of Korea, 1979),
pp. 256-266 and passim.
61. See Chung Jun Ki, *Social Criticism of Uchimura Kanzo and Kim Kyo-Shin*
(Seoul: UBF Press, 1988).
62. David Kwang-sun Suh, "American Missionaries and a Hundred Years of Korean Protestantism," unpublished paper, 1982.

American victory over Japan and subsequent occupation of Korea in 1945. Korean Christians believe that the liberation of Korea from the Japanese and the maintenance of peace on the peninsula since the Korean War—and other things that have to do with the Americans—are and should be seen as a continuation of the American Protestant missionaries' first entry into the "hermit kingdom" a century ago.[63]

Antiforeign Student Strikes

Missionary-run schools were places where the tension between foreign and Korean attitudes worked themselves out. Foreigners invariably raised the money, founded the institutions, set the curriculum, and did the teaching, and then gradually turned the teaching, financing, and ultimately the administration, over to Korean successors who were, in many cases, their former students. However, there were often differences over the pace of this devolution, with Koreans wanting it speeded up. When the missionaries resisted, conflict was the typical result.

School administrators were sometimes caught off guard by outbreaks of student nationalism. They were not surprised when the nationalism was directed against the Japanese, but they were stunned when it was directed against them. It was understandable, for example, that Korean students should be angry when a Japanese anatomy professor told a class that skull measurements proved that Japanese were a superior race. However, it was a shock when students at Chōsen Christian College protested that Western professors

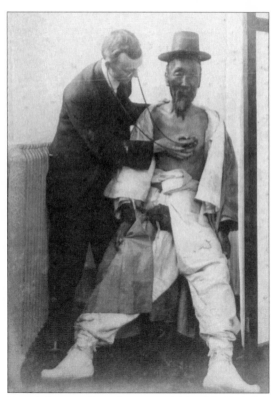

Examining a patient. Severance Union Medical College, Seoul, circa 1930. Clark Collection.

63. Ibid., pp. 43-44.

had the best faculty houses, Japanese the second best, and Korean professors the worst.

Sometimes the students accused the missionaries of enriching themselves at Koreans' expense. This objection seems to have been related to the impression that missionary life was luxurious—which no doubt it was to poor Korean students. Against such objections the missionaries were powerless to explain the reasons for living in the Western style and they were easy targets for charges that they were skimming from funds that had been intended by faraway donors for Korean recipients. The accusations hit hardest during hard times, for example, during the Great Depression when the Canadian Mission in northeastern Korea was having a hard time staying afloat. The missionaries indeed were taking pay cuts in order to keep their stations' church, school, and clinic functions going. Korean students on the northeast coast wondered aloud why the American Presbyterians in P'yŏngyang always seemed to have plenty of money for their schools.[64]

Missionary purposes sometimes elicited objections. In 1926 at the Canadians' Yŏngsaeng Academy for Boys in Wŏnsan, for example, a crisis developed when the mission decided to seek "designated school" registration status instead of asking the Saitō government to recognize the Academy as a more prestigious "Higher Common School." The mission's reason for choosing the "designated" category was that designated schools could teach religion while Higher Common Schools had to follow the regulation to exclude religion from the curriculum. The students, who wanted the most from their diplomas, called a strike and accused the missionaries of cheating them out of the more prestigious certification.[65]

Disciplinary action also sparked protests. One mission school freshman "infected with the Communistic, anti-Christian virus" wrote some scurrilous things about his teacher, a Korean Christian. The missionary principal, Edward Fraser, suspended the student for three months, whereupon his classmates disrupted the school's graduation ceremony. The school board, mostly missionaries, reacted by ordering the entire freshman class to apologize. After a few apologies and a few weeks of quiet, sophomores, juniors, and seniors started their own strike to demand dismissal of three especially unpopular teachers. The board suspended everyone for two weeks pending apologies. The students then got physical: one group prevented Mr. Fraser from boarding a train at the railroad station. Another group attacked the school building and beat up a teacher. Still others attacked the Frasers' coal deliveryman. Only a few students ever apologized as ordered, and in order to resume school the missionaries were obliged to back down. Fraser

64. For student critiques of missionaries and incidents of protests see O.R. Avison to Sidney Gulick, July 19, 1921, UCCA, 79.204C, Box 6, File 88, and L.L. Young to A.E. Armstrong, February 1, 1924, UCCA, 79.204C, Box 8, File 119.
65. William Scott to A.E. Armstrong, June 14, 1926. UCCA, 83.006C, Box 1, File 9.

tried to be philosophical. "This region has not much law in it," he wrote. "There is no general anti-foreign feeling, and the whole thing was not in any special way anti-foreign, but rather anti-Christian."[66]

British Diplomats and Korean Politics

As Ewha University historian Ku Dae-yeol has written, there was tension between Koreans and Britishers during the 1919 Independence Movement because of Anglo-Japanese alliance that had been in effect since 1902 and Britain's ostensible support for Japanese rule on the peninsula.[67] Though the alliance ended in 1922, Koreans continued to see England and Japan as collaborators thereafter. This was demonstrated in an incident that occurred in July 1929 in Shanghai, when the Korean independence leader Yŏ Unhyŏng was arrested by police of the International Settlement. Yŏ was a Christian, a youth leader among Korean exiles in China and a major figure in the Korean Provisional Government in Shanghai.[68] He had been traveling and giving speeches in Manila and elsewhere opposing British imperialism in Asia and Japanese rule in Korea, and on July 10, while watching a football match at the Shanghai racecourse, he was arrested by International Settlement police. He was arrested at the request of Japanese authorities in Shanghai, and under the rules of extraterritoriality that governed the International Settlement he was handed over to the Japanese police who charged him with plotting to overthrow the Government-General of Chōsen. At the time of his arrest, Yŏ claimed to be a Chinese national, but the authorities brushed this aside and after a few days in jail in Shanghai the Japanese transferred him to Nagasaki. British collusion in the arrest brought this angry threat in the form of a note delivered to the Consulate-General in Seoul:

TO THE BARBARIAN IMPERIALIST! You barbarian imperialists, that still persist in grinding down the weak and small countries, and the toiling masses of the world! Is it not your settled purpose to plunder the whole world draining it dry at whatever cost? We know that by your imperialism we have been reduced to the verge of death and that if it were but destroyed, we might live.

Hark! Is it not you that in Shanghai handed over to the dastardly clutches of the Japanese imperialists—for your common advantage—Ryo Woon Hyong who was working for the sake of the toiling masses and the weaker nations?

66. E.J.O. Fraser to A.E. Armstrong, May 9, 1927, UCCA, 83.006C, Box 1, File 20.
67. In Ku, *Korea under Colonialism,* pp. 243-246.
68. Yŏ Unhyŏng (1885-1947) was an alumnus of Paejae Methodist Boys' School in Seoul. He then worked for a time as an assistant to Charlie Clark in Seoul's Sŭng-dong Church and on Clark's itinerating trips to the countryside. He briefly considered a career in the ministry, for which he attended the Presbyterian Theological Seminary in P'yŏngyang, but did not graduate. See "Kwak Allyŏn sŏn'gyosa," in *Han'guk kyohoe inmulsa,* I (Seoul, 1975), pp. 199-200.

> This last outrage we cannot forgive, but, to avenge our wrongs, will give you baptism with bombs![69]

In Seoul, British Consul-General Oswald White was less disturbed by Yŏ Unhyŏng's anti-British speeches and the written threat of bombs than he was interested in the man and his case. He thought the Korean leader might have played a part in getting Japanese Prime Minister Hara Kei to liberalize the regime in Korea after 1919:

> After the Independence Movement of 1919, [Yŏ] went from Shanghai to Tokyo under a safe conduct in order to explain his views to the Japanese Government. On that occasion he had several interviews with the Prime Minister and it is possible that what he had to say may have been instrumental in causing the authorities to introduce a modern regime in this country. Since 1919 he has been living in the French Concession in Shanghai.[70]

However, Oswald emphasized the wrong part of the story by soft-pedaling the fact that Yŏ had been arrested in a third country and saying that he was being treated with consideration. "While being brought [to Seoul from Nagasaki] it was noticeable that the police officers did not treat him with the severity they are apt to mete out to political prisoners," wrote Oswald. "He was met by a number of friends and was allowed to converse at Seoul Station with his brother. He is [now] said to be 'under detention.'" This was an understatement. Yŏ spend the next three years in prison in Taejŏn.[71]

Studying Korea

Consul-General Oswald White's patchy understanding of the relationship between the Japanese and Korean political figures, while typical of the foreign community's limited comprehension of Korean affairs in general, was also good-hearted and eager to make the best of hard times. The same sincere impulses inspired groups of foreign residents to study and learn about Korean culture and thus, mostly unwittingly, to help Korean studies survive as a field. Their research emerged in the form of lectures at the monthly meetings of the Royal Asiatic Society of Great Britain and Ireland,

69. Letter received at the British Consulate in Seoul on August 21, 1929, "presumably from a Corean source but written in Japanese under the pseudonym Kimura Gi-ichi." Translation enclosed with report from Oswald White to Ambassador John Tilley (Tokyo), September 2, 1929. Public Record Office file FO 262/1732.

70. White to Tilley (Tokyo), July 22, 1929. Public Record Office file FO 262/1932.

71. Ibid.; Yi Hŭisŭng et al., Han'guk inmyŏng taesajŏn (Seoul: Shin'gu munhwasa, 1972), p. 464; Cumings, Korea's Place in the Sun, p. 191. Yŏ Unhyŏng was released in 1933, stayed in Korea, and took up a career in journalism, being chief of the Chung'ang Ilbo newspaper. At the end of the occupation, during the interval between Japan's surrender and the arrival of American military forces in Korea, Governor-General Abe Nobuyuki turned to Yŏ to organize an interim government (see chapter 14).

a scholarly organization with headquarters in London, which sponsored some of the best prewar Western scholarship on Asia through its branches in India, Japan, the China Coast, and wherever there were British residents. The Korea Branch of the R.A.S. in Seoul, with members from all English-speaking parts of the world, was founded in 1900. Its annual journal, called the *Transactions,* continues to the present. Among the best of the *Transactions* in the 1930s were articles by J.L. Boots and Horace H. Underwood on "Korean Weapons and Armor" and "Korean Boats and Ships."[72] Other significant studies included E.M. Cable's papers on Korean bells and on early American-Korean relations, the venerable Bishop Mark Trollope's "Corean Books and their Authors," and W.W. Taylor's down-to-earth "Korean Roads Past and Present."[73]

Westerners also served with Koreans and Japanese on the boards of organizations like the YMCA, YWCA, the Christian Literature Society, and the Korean Bible Society. They belonged to the Hanyang Lodge of the Masonic Order, the Seoul Rotary Club, the Royal Asiatic Society, the Chamber of Commerce, and the International Friendly Association, a club designed to promote good feelings between foreign residents and the government.[74] There were also English clubs where Korean students polished their language skills with foreigners. The "Good Life Society," for example, included Korean and foreign teachers who met to practice English by discussing current topics. As J. Earnest Fisher recalled, "If the Japanese Government-General authorities had known of our meetings and had heard some of our discussions, we might all have had to serve prison terms."[75] Some "Good Lifers" went on to very important positions: Pyŏn Yŏngt'ae, for example, served a term as prime minister in the 1950s under Syngman Rhee.[76]

72. John L. Boots, "Korean Weapons and Armor," *TKBRAS,*" XXIII, pt. 2 (December 1934), pp. 1-37, and Horace H. Underwood, "Korean Boats and Ships," *TKBRAS,* XXIII, pt. 1 (1934), pp. 1-99, reprinted as *Korean Boats and Ships* (Seoul: Yonsei University Press, 1979).

73. E.M. Cable, "Old Korean Bells," *TKBRAS,* XVI (1925), pp. 1-45, and "United States-Korean Relations, 1866-1871," *TKBRAS,* XXVIII (1938), pp. 1-230; Mark Napier Trollope, "Corean Books and their Authors," *TKBRAS,* XXI (1932), pp. 1-104; W.W. Taylor, "Korean Roads Past and Present, and Report on Investigations: Development and Trend of the Automotive Transportation in Chosen," *TKBRAS,* XV (1924), pp. 35-82. For more on the Royal Asiatic Society, see Lak-geoon George Paik, "Seventy Years of the Royal Asiatic Society in Korea," *TKBRAS,* XLVII (1972), pp. 25-39.

74. C. I. McLaren, "The International Friendly Association," *The Korea Mission Field,* XXXV:3 (March 1939), frontispiece and p. 63.

75. Fisher, *Pioneers of Modern Korea,* pp. 180-181.

76. In 1936 Pyŏn, who taught English at Seoul's Chung'ang High School, published a book of Korean stories in English that was reprinted in 1946 and again as Y.T. Pyun, *Tales from Korea* (Seoul: Shinjosha, 1956).

The language barrier, however, blocked access to the world of ideas. Speaking Korean was a matter of degree: everyone could speak a little and many could do very well in social and professional situations. But none of the Westerners in Korea had been educated in the Korean way and with the rarest exceptions they could not hold their own with educated Koreans on traditional subjects.[77] Such knowledge was not necessary to teach English or religion, nor was it relevant to technical or business matters. But the lack of it isolated Westerners from the intellectual life of their Korean associates.[78] They saw leading Christians like Yi Sangjae and Cho Mansik mainly in terms of their Christian affiliations. Nor did they keep up with the cultural renaissance being stimulated by more secular writers like Yi Kwangsu and Shin Ch'aeho; and they certainly paid no discernible attention to intellectuals from other traditions, such as the Buddhist leader Han Yong'un or the Ch'ŏndogyo leader Yi Chŏngnin.[79] Rather, the dialogue between missionaries and Koreans took place almost entirely over church matters, in the context of mission work.

There were certain environments where deep conversations did take place between foreigners and Koreans. One was the campus of Chōsen Christian College, where there was much dialogue between students and teachers and among the professors themselves. In 1931, out of a full-time faculty of thirty-one professors and instructors, nineteen were Korean, eight American, four Japanese, and one Canadian. There were also twelve part-time lecturers including four American faculty wives who taught music and English. Missionary and non-missionary faculties alike were professing Christians and most were well connected with church and missionary circles outside the campus. Both Yu Ŏkkyŏm, the dean, and L. George Paik, the head of the Literary [Humanities] Department, were on the YMCA board of directors.

77. One of these exceptions was James Scarth Gale, whose knowledge of Classical Chinese and Korean civilization made possible his history of Korea, later annotated and republished by Richard Rutt under the title *James Scarth Gale and his History of the Korean People*. Gale retired in 1928.

78. *The Korea Mission Field* often published a feature entitled "What Is Interesting the Korean Church," but it did not cover secular issues.

79. This generalization is based on perusal of letter files of the Northern and Southern Presbyterian Missions in Philadelphia and Montreat, North Carolina. Although missionaries regularly reported strikes and upheavals and rumors in their own mission organizations, the reports were on the order of news with little analysis or contextualization. The missed opportunities for intellectual exchange are suggested in chapters 4-6 of Kenneth Wells's *New God, New Nation: Protestants and Self-Reconstruction Nationalism in Korea, 1896-1937* (Honolulu: University of Hawaii Press, 1991), pp. 82-137.

PROFESSORS AND INSTRUCTORS, CHŌSEN CHRISTIAN COLLEGE, 1931[80]

Name	Degree	Subject
Oliver R. Avison	M.D., Toronto	President
Horace H. Underwood	Ph.D. New York Univ.	Vice-President
Yu Ŏkkyŏm	M.A., Tokyo	Imperial Dean
L. George Paik	Ph.D., Yale	Head, Literary
Yi Sunt'ak	M.A., Kyoto	Head, Business
Yi Ch'unho	M.A., Ohio State	Head, Sciences
J. Earnest Fisher	Ph.D., Columbia	Educ./English
Arthur L. Becker	Ph.D., Michigan	Physics/Math
Edward H. Miller	Ph.D., Columbia	Chem./English
Bliss W. Billings	M.A., DePauw	Hist./Bible/English
Harry H. Rhodes	M.A., Princeton	Bible/English
Keidarō Takahashi	Tokyo Univ. Law School	Morals/Ethics/
Paek Namsŏk	M.A., Emory	Psych./Educ./English
Paek Namun	M.A., Keijō Imp. U.,	Business
Keimon Kadowaki	B.E., Kyoto	Chem./Mech. Drawing
Ch'oe Hyŏnbae	M.A., Kyoto	Ethics/Korean/Educ.
Yi Wŏnch'ŏl	Ph.D., Michigan	Math/Astronomy
Shinji Nikaido	M.A., Tokyo Imp. U.	Japanese
Son Pongjo	M.A., Tokyo Imp. U.	Business
Kim Pongjip	M.S., Waseda	Physics/Engineering/Math
Hideo Kaiya	M.S., Tohoku	Math/Science
Hong Sŭngguk	B.A., Ohio State	English
Chŏng Inbo	[Classical education]	Chinese/Korean
Hyŏn "Rody" Chemyŏng	M.M., Gunn School, Chicago	Music
No Tonggyu	M.A., Kyoto	Economic Policy
Ch'oe Sunju	Ph.D., New York Univ.	Business
Ethel Underwood	M.A., New York Univ.	English
Yi Unyong	[Diplomas, Berlin & Vienna]	German
Gerald Corwin Speidel	M.S., Virginia	English
Chŏng Insŏ	[Tai Dong Law College]	Asian History
O Kyusin	[Chinese language school]	Chinese

80. Yonsei ch'angnip p'alsimnyŏn kinyŏm saŏp wiwŏnhoe, *Yonsei taehakkyo-sa* (Seoul: Yonsei University Press, 1969), pp. 350-351; Chosen Christian College, *Chosen Christian College Bulletin, 1914-1931: Annual Catalogue, 1931-32* (Seoul: Chosen Christian College, 1931), pp. 18-27; Horace H. Underwood, "Personnel," *The Korea Mission Field*, XXXIV:8 (August 1938), p. 163.

Chōsen Christian College Faculty and spouses at the Underwood House, Seoul, 1932. (Horace and Ethel Underwood, with Horace G., front row, second, third, and fourth from left) Harry A. Rhodes, *History of the Korea Mission, Presbyterian Church, U.S.A., 1884-1934* (Seoul: Chōsen Mission, Presbyterian Church, U.S.A., 1935), p. 422.

The International Education of L. George Paik

L. George Paik (Paek Nakchun) was born in 1895, the son of middle-income peasants in Ch'ŏngju, North P'yŏng'an Province, an area known for unsettled politics and a lively commercial economy based on traffic with Chinese merchants from across the Yalu River. As a child, Paik was impressed by manifestations of the modern world beyond Korea: the Japanese-built railroad that cut through the valley on its way across Asia to Europe; Chinese lamps that burned kerosene from shiny tins; new-style matches with phosphorous tips that replaced the old kind made of bamboo dipped in sulfur; and foreign people, namely gold miners from Unsan and missionaries from the nearby city of Sŏnch'ŏn who visited the local thatch-roofed church. Presbyterian missionary Stacy L. Roberts persuaded Paik to become a Christian, and Paik gave himself the Christian name "To-il" ("One way"), based on the first chapter of the Gospel of John.[81]

81. The passage of scripture that arrested Paik's attention in his session with Stacy Roberts was Philippians 4:13: "I can do all things through Christ who strengtheneth me." L. George Paik, interviews, January 19 and 26, 1984. This account of Paik's life also follows Paek Nakchun, "Naŭi salmŭl twe-torapomyŏ," in *Chilliwa Chayu ŭi Kisudŭl* (Seoul: Yonsei University Press, 1982), pp. 241-281, and Key S. Ryang, "Nak-chun Paek (1895-1985): His Life and Thought," *The Journal*

After being orphaned at the age of fourteen, Paik took his seventy wŏn inheritance (about $650) to the Hugh O'Neill Academy in Sŏnch'ŏn and asked the principal, George McCune, to admit him. McCune made Paik his protégé, employing him as a houseboy to earn his school fees and nick-naming him "Sosa" ("Little scholar"). In 1913 McCune sent Paik across the Yellow Sea to China for three years of further study at the missionary-run Anglo-Chinese College, where Paik's main business was learning English and Chinese. In 1916 he crossed the Pacific and enrolled in Park College, Parkville, Missouri, a school founded by George McCune's father-in-law, Cleland McAfee.

Park College was a place that could be trusted to give him a suitably con-servative religious education,[82] and later Paik referred to it as the "founda-tion" of his life and work and the source of many lifelong friends.[83] He spent six years there, first catching up with the American curriculum and then graduating with a B.A. in history in 1922. Graduate school came next: an M.A. in theology from Princeton Theological Seminary and then a Ph.D. in history from Yale. Issues of academic freedom were swirling in Paik's en-vironment at Yale, and he drank deeply of the new trends: James H. Robin-son's New History, the controversy between Charles A. Beard and Nicholas Murray Butler over America's involvement in World War I, and the emerg-ing interest in Asia that was being encouraged by his Yale mentor Kenneth Scott Latourette. But after exploring European and American political thought, he returned to his roots with his doctoral dissertation, a study of Protestant missions in Korea through the year 1910. He finished in 1927 and returned to Korea to take a faculty position at Chōsen Christian Col-lege in Seoul.

George Paik developed a Western "side" while studying in the United States, a manifestation of his personality that was different from the one that showed when he was thinking and speaking in Korean.[84] Paik claimed that his inner character was more American than Korean, less influenced by

of Modern Korean Studies, V (August 1993), pp. 42-95.
82. Park College was the model for the Union Christian College (Sungsil Col-lege) P'yŏngyang, with its combination of liberal arts studies, training for the reli-gious ministry, and work-study to teach discipline and self-support. Paik, *The His-tory of Protestant Missions in Korea, 1832-1910*, p. 308. It was at Park College that Paik first took the name "George," in honor of his missionary teacher George S. McCune.
83. This is clear from the files of private correspondence with Park College friends Jarvis Morris, Francis Bouquet, Constance Vulliamy, and "Prof" Teener in Paik's papers at Yonsei University.
84. This assertion is based on the writer's observation of differences between Paik's English and Korean writing, the body language he used toward Koreans and foreigners, and everyday manifestations as telephone manners, office-setting inter-actions with staff and visitors, both foreign and Korean, and interaction with family members.

traditional Neo-Confucianism than by the idealism of Lincoln and Wilson, the pragmatism of Franklin, and the intellectual iconoclasm of America's new social scientists. Yet his Korean side was quite traditional. Rituals, loyalties, networks, and protocol were still essential in Korea. Decades later, as president of Yonsei University, Paik showed his two "sides" differently. To a faculty faction that rose in rebellion against him in 1959-60, he was too paternal, even a dictator.[85] To his American associates he was resourceful, decisive, and even visionary. Though his Korean persona could be autocratic and even cruel toward Korean subordinates, his Western persona was genial, diplomatic, and brilliantly successful in cultivating foreign sources of support for the university.[86]

In the 1930s Paik became a department chairman and then a dean. Though lacking the seniority to become the college's president, Paik stood out as a leader. He fostered faculty research into Korean Studies—his most enduring contribution to the "cultural nationalist" response to Japanese rule. He joined the Suyang Tong'uhoe, a Protestant group dedicated to maintaining Korea's "self-reconstruction ideals,"[87] as a junior member. He also tried to open windows on Korean culture for the foreign community by lecturing and writing articles for the Royal Asiatic Society and helping others with studies on Korea, such as Horace Underwood's *Korean Boats and Ships.*

When he returned to Korea in 1927, Paik was taken in from the beginning by the city's Christian leadership: first by Methodist bishop Yang Chusam (J.S. Ryang) as a house guest, and then by Presbyterian missionaries John and Mabel Genso. It would have been harder to reestablish himself in Korea without them, for he was far from his home district and had no family and no old-boy network of schoolmates. His social standing derived entirely from his faculty position, his prestigious Western education, and his Christian church network. It was through Christian contacts, for example, that he met his future wife, Ch'oe Ikwŏn, a student at Ewha Womans College where he taught part-time. They were married in 1931.

85. This incident naturally pointed up parallels between Paik as the university president and missionary school principals of a previous generation, who were likewise accused of paternalism. The parallel is even more striking in light of the fact that after Paik's resignation in 1960, the interim president, Horace G. Underwood, grandson of the institution's founder, came under fire in the ongoing campus controversy. At one point, during a student demonstration, Underwood's own house on the campus was attacked with massive damage to furniture, etc. See Underwood, *Korea in War, Revolution and Peace,* pp. 244-246.

86. This assessment is based on many conversations, some of them taped, with present and former faculty members of Yonsei University both Korean and foreign (who invariably asked to remain anonymous); the author's own observations; and on papers in the Paik collection at the Yonsei University Library.

87. See Wells, *New God, New Nation,* esp. pp. 118-137.

George Paik family, circa 1940. Clark Collection.

Though close to foreigners like the McCunes and Gensos and admiring of them as individuals, Paik's graduate studies had made him generally critical of missionary paternalism. Though the Chōsen Christian College faculty was an oasis of intercultural collegiality, the missionary professors simply exercised too much control over budgets, plans, and personnel. A foreigner had to have great insight into the Korean social system in order to function effectively, and Paik fretted that the missionaries on campus were too naive. They "believed everything the Koreans told them, literally, whereas Koreans often told *relative* truths with all the background not clearly understood." Missionaries, on the other hand, had expectations and gave instructions that Koreans simply did not know how to follow. "Their mode of doing business was simply different," so the common modus operandi was simply to appear cooperative and work quietly behind their backs. One of the few foreigners who struck the proper balance in his dealings with Koreans, according to Paik, was Oliver R. Avison, the Chōsen Christian College president who hired Paik in 1927 and for whom Paik often translated. Avison was a medical man "not very interested in theology," who never learned Korean very well but knew how to pick trustworthy Koreans and delegate responsibility to them.[88]

88. Quotes and paraphrases from L. George Paik interview, Seoul, January 19, 1984. In a moment of surpassing courage, Ikwŏn actually snatched from the police

Americans in the Mind of Yun Ch'iho

However attractive the gospel might have been and however admirable the ideal Christian life, educated Koreans could not avoid being wounded by the outright racism displayed upon occasion by Westerners, particularly missionaries. The very inadvertence of the slights aggravated the injury. Seoul National University sociologist Kim Kyŏngdong, for example, remembers that his mother, a Christian deaconess and a person of some standing in her own community, sometimes was invited to help host social events on the nearby missionary compound. Normally, Kim liked to visit the compound and was intrigued by the big houses and strange people. However, on one occasion when his mother brought him along, he was shocked to see her relegated to the role of kitchen helper, essentially a servant to the foreign missionary women. Later he wrote, "I could not help feeling a chill in my heart when they treated us like servants, in spite of the friendly attitude they generally showed us."[89]

The dilemmas confronting educated Korean Christians are clear in the life of Yun Ch'iho. The son of a nineteenth-century Korean nobleman, Yun was born into the *yangban* class in 1864 and educated in the Confucian classics. In his youth, however, he had opportunities that put him in the middle of his country's first encounters with the modern world. In 1882 he toured Japan as a junior member of Korea's first overseas delegation and remained in Japan to study under the great Meiji-era intellectual Fukuzawa Yukichi. In 1883 he returned and took a job as translator to the first U.S. minister in Korea, Lucius Foote. In 1885 he went to Shanghai and enrolled at the Anglo-Chinese School in Shanghai under the mentorship of the renowned missionary educator Young J. Allen. Next he went to America and college studies, first at Vanderbilt University and then at Emory University in Atlanta. By that time he had been baptized into the Methodist church, beginning his life as a Christian.

In America, Yun Ch'iho was forced into the role of the deserving foreign student whose presence gave Americans a chance to congratulate themselves on the missionary effort. Yun resented this. It completely devalued his own cultured Korean background. Even worse, no one seemed to know, or care, that a "Corean" was different from a Chinese. To Americans Yun was just a generic "Oriental" from a faraway land that, though completely unknown, was assumed to be heathen and in need of "saving." Yun had a classical education and knew how to read and write four languages. He had knowledge of the world that was incomparably better than that of his classmates, yet they persisted in casting him in the role of noble savage.

the small Korean flag that Paik had treasured and kept with him from 1913 all through the years of study in America.

89. Kim Kyŏng-dong, "Korean Perceptions of America," in *Korea Briefing 1993*, ed. Donald N. Clark (Boulder, Colorado: Westview Press, 1993), p.163.

It made his blood boil to hear the language of white supremacy from American peers who were so blind to their own ignorance. Chinese immigration was a topic of national debate, and it cut him to hear Chinese characterized as "pernicious," "vile," "wicked," "degrading," "alien," "heathenish," "filthy," "immoral," etc. Once he attended a student debate on the subject where one of the speakers said, "Tell me rather to open the gates of the vilest dungeon and hug to my bosom the blackest criminal of the darkest deeds than to embrace these degraded wicked people [Chinese]."[90] Yun took this statement to heart. Completely alienated from his surroundings he wrote,

> when I contemplate the national humiliations and mortifications that have been and will be my lot to see–when I, in every turn of life's way, meet with the lacerating looks and words and acts due to my national badge, I feel weary of life. I do not and shall not court or seek death, but if it were to come now in natural course I shall not regret to part with a world so unkind to any but the strong.[91]

The dissonance between Yun Ch'iho's respect for the American system and his resentment of Americans as people was a major theme of the English-language diary that he faithfully kept for more than forty years. The entries for the years of his student life in the American South are filled with references to the subtle signs and slights by which he was forced to keep to his place. This was especially painful when it came to romantic attachments, for there seemed to be no hope that a white girl's parents would ever allow her to be courted, much less married, by an "oriental." Nor could an American bride ever be happy in Korea. Not only would she find it lonely, uncomfortable, and dangerous, but—in an interesting comment on racism as a two-edged sword—the groom's Korean family would never accept a foreign daughter-in-law. In his diary Yun speculated that her rejection would be worse than his own, in America.[92]

But for all his brooding about Americans and their hypocrisies Yun never lost his Christian faith. When he finished college he determined to return home to spread the Gospel. To this end he secured help from his mentors at Emory to found a mission of the Southern Methodist Church in Korea, with missionaries from the American South.[93] After returning home

90. *Yun Ch'iho Ilgi* [Yun Ch'iho's Diary], Vol. III (Seoul: Kuksa P'yŏnch'an wiwŏnhoe, 1983-1990), p. 95, hereafter referred to as "YCH." For Yun's life also see Koen DeCeuster, "From Modernization to Collaboration, the Dilemma of Korean Cultural Nationalism: The Case of Yun Ch'i-ho (1865-1945)," unpublished doctoral dissertation, Faculteit Letteren, Katholieke Universiteit Leuven, 1994.
91. YCH, III, 99.
92. YCH, III, 68-69.
93. Yun never served on the Southern Methodist payroll as a missionary. However, the Southern Methodist Church was one of the few to give regular missionary appointments to nationals of the countries where the work was being done. A

Yun Ch'iho's family, 1936: mother, wife, and twelve children. From Kim Yŏnghŭi, *Chwa'ong Yun Ch'iho sŏnsaeng yakchŏn* (Seoul, 1934), p. 242.

he was instrumental in helping the mission acquire property and the means to begin operations, and the new Methodist missionaries regarded him as their chief Korean benefactor. Through the 1890s he led several lives: as a government official, reformist intellectual, cofounder of the Independence Club (Tongnip hyŏphoe), and Christian youth leader. He used his family's fortune to build churches and schools and even founded his own Christian academy in Kaesŏng, following the example of his Shanghai mentor Young J. Allen by calling it the "Anglo-Korean School."

In 1910, when the Japanese annexed Korea, the new regime conferred titles on a number of Korean *yangban* and endowed them with generous pensions. Yun Ch'iho's father was honored posthumously in this manner, making Yun himself eligible for the title of "baron" in a specially invented colonial peerage. Titles were one of several types of Japanese bribes to the Korean ruling class and therefore a decided liability. Yun claimed to disdain

famous example in China is Charles Jones Soong, father of Soong Ching-ling (Mme. Sun Yat-sen) and Soong Mei-ling (Mme. Chiang Kai-shek), who became a Christian during his student days in North Carolina and was sent by the Southern Methodist Church to serve in Shanghai as a missionary. His work led to the founding of a Christian literature publishing house, and after he resigned from the mission to go into business for himself, his publishing house became a propaganda mill for the Nationalist Party (Kuomintang).

his "barony" though at times he put on the military-style regalia and appeared in public decorated with the badges of collaboration with Japan. However much Koreans might have disliked this display, Yun's American friends were much taken with their titled Korean friend and enjoyed referring to him as "Baron Yun."

Yun of course had always regarded himself as a nationalist, a voice crying in the wilderness to warn Koreans about what the outside world had in store for them. His life's work was the education of young Koreans through schools and associations such as the YMCA, in which he was a prime mover, to prepare them to defend their nation and its culture. His nationalist bona fides were further established when he went to prison in the 1911 Conspiracy Case, punished for allegedly plotting to assassinate the Japanese governor-general. However, chastened by his ordeal in prison, Yun emerged determined not to lose his future in pointless resistance against the overwhelming power of the Japanese colonial regime. In 1919, when courageous Korean religious leaders were standing up to the Japanese, Yun declined to be seen in the lead. Nor, as a wealthy landowner, did he choose to risk his family's security by supporting those who advocated armed resistance. Instead he poured his energies into Christian organizations, concentrating on his Anglo-Korean school, the Seoul YMCA, and the Korean Methodist Church. He also devoted much time to his children. He pursued his goals within the limits of Japanese rules, arguing that he was no good to anyone in prison. Like many others who took the same stance he seemed to be saying, "Japan is here to stay so let's do our best to preserve what we have."

Yun would have used his missionary connections as a lifeline to the outside world no matter what his inner feelings, but he also had authentic friendships in the missionary community and made himself available on numerous social and ceremonial occasions. His dazzling language skills were especially useful, as at the first commencement ceremony for Severance Union Medical College in 1908 when he gave separate speeches in English and Korean and then translated for the Chinese architect and the Japanese Resident-General Itō Hirōbumi. He was often on stage at school graduations, YMCA conventions, and church anniversaries, and he was frequently a guest in foreigners' homes.

At the time, few of Yun's missionary friends would have suspected that he was pouring out his considerable bitterness against them in his diary. Through the 1920s and '30s Western racism continued as a running theme as he scorned the missionaries for hypocrisy. Once, apparently forgetting that he had once lived with the Underwoods, he wrote that Americans would never allow a Korean to be an overnight guest.[94] Another night after having been slighted at dinner, he criticized his American hostess for showing "her vulgar origin and vixenish nature" when she "didn't address a single

94. YCH, IX, 93.

Yun Ch'iho, age 70 (1934). From Kim Yŏng-hŭi, *Chwa'ong Yun Ch'iho sŏnsaeng yakchŏn*, frontispiece.

word to [my companion] Kim and me during the two hours were there in spite of the fact that she knew we understood English."[95] He despaired of real friendship with foreigners, saying, "A group or class of men and women with consciousness of national or racial superiority can't very well mix with another group ...who are conscious of national or racial inferiority."[96]

The unwillingness of Westerners to follow Korean custom rankled Yun Ch'iho. One American woman sang at a funeral and "gave a solo in a tone and manner as if she were singing for a concert —entirely alien to the Oriental sentiment and spirit at such occasions."[97] The Salvation Army used annoying military metaphors for fighting sin, which he thought were "almost meaningless words to the Koreans who have been compelled to worship the pen—a brush—rather than the sword."[98] Not even H.H. Underwood measured up to Yun's expectations: "He spoke wonderfully well," wrote Yun in 1933 after hearing Underwood give an address. "Pity—the written version of his address is so far inferior to the spoken one."[99]

And the social distance between Korean men and foreign women continued as an item: for example, "As long as an American girl would blush to be seen to walk or dance with a Korean young man so long will it be useless to attempt any social mixing."[100] And on that rarest of occasions when he encountered a returning Korean student with his American bride he wrote, "I feel so sorry for the pretty American girl—for the humiliation of being the wife of Korean she will have to drain the cup of bitterness of the ostra-

95. YCH, IX, 154.
96. YCH, IX, 209.
97. YCH, IX, 248.
98. YCH, IX, 168.
99. YCH, IX, 139.
100. YCH, IX, 204.

cization [*sic*] of the foreign community in Korea."[101] He commented that any missionary who broke convention and actually got close to the Korean people would be shunned by his fellow Occidentals.[102]

Yun Ch'iho was an even harsher critic of his fellow-Koreans. Criticisms and lamentations about his countrymen fill the diary. Having roots in two worlds made it easy to find fault with both. This trait he shared with George Paik, but perhaps because Paik was a commoner and Yun was a *yangban*, the backwardness of Korea hurt Yun more. Paik seems to have adapted more readily to Western ways and complained less about foreign insensitivity. Yun in fact chided Paik for straying from Korean *ye* and acting like a foreigner. He saw it as naïve while Paik saw it as pragmatic. In Paik's later life—he died in 1985—his ability to get along with foreigners was an important element in his long and successful career.

101. YCH, IX, 222-223.
102. For example, after a farewell dinner for a missionary named Peters, who had "lived a real missionary life during the last 5 years, wearing Korean dress, eating Korean food and living Korean fashion," Yun wrote, "He has won the good will of the Korean people but is a black goat among his [American] nationals." YCH, X, 107.

-- 5 --

The Jerusalem of the East

By 1920 it seemed that Mabel Clark would never recover from early or-
deals in Korea. Since the loss of her first two sons she had languished
in a kind of quietude that resembled depression. At the age of forty her hair
had turned an ethereal white and she rarely went out of the house. Her
neighbors made the best of this by saying that she brought an "angelic presence" with her whenever she entered a room. She spoke when she was
spoken to and was never heard to complain. She remained technically on
assignment as a missionary and served in her own way by giving piano lessons in her own living room and occasionally taking charge of the littlest
children's Sunday School class at church. Charlie covered for her, insisting
on her standing as a full member of the mission, handling all her correspondence, and driving himself to do the work of two.

In 1906, broken in spirit and body himself after the death of Baby
Gordie, Charlie Clark had been ordered across the Yellow Sea to the Chinese resort of Chefoo, for an enforced rest. Charlie went of course, with
Mabel, but he was soon recalled to lend his Minneapolis builder's skills to a
construction emergency that had developed in Taegu. The newly built
Presbyterian Hospital building was about to collapse. The design had been
amateurish to start with, but to make it worse, supervising missionary
Woodbridge Johnson had fallen ill during the construction and had been
forced to go to Japan for medical attention. In his absence the contractors
created a monstrosity. Charlie and Mabel cut short their Chefoo vacation
and Charlie hurried to Taegu to take charge. Years later he recalled the
project:

> In building it, every possible crime had been committed. Sticky mud was
> used instead of lime, and, when the mud dried, it was no better than a flat

piece of board. Cross walls were not woven into the long side walls. Roof timbers were run through active chimney flues, etc. The mission sent me there to tear down the building and erect a new one, 33 feet by 50 feet, with an operating room projecting to the rear. We were given what materials we could salvage and $3,000 to complete the job, a story and a half high. I could get no contracts and had to do everything by day labor with Chinese masons, Japanese carpenters, and Korean coolies....

The old building had to be taken down carefully, brick by brick by hand and it was most hazardous. When done, we built kilns, dug up mud in our yard and burnt the necessary brick; dug up more mud, built a different kiln and burnt our heavy tile for the roof, all needed to supplement the salvaged materials. We sent ten miles out in the hills, bought a mountain, dug out limestone and burnt our own lime, and brought it in on men's backs as there were no roads. We bought a wooded mountain, cut the trees and brought those in on men's backs for rafters.

For water, we found a somewhat likely place 600 feet from the hospital but it was solid rock. We blasted down 18 feet and no sign of water. We set a man with a six-foot crowbar to drill down to see if there was water below. None in six feet. We lengthened the crowbar to twelve feet and drilled on. At ten feet the bar broke through into a stream of fine water and filled the hole 10 feet deep. The man had to get out for his life. We bricked the big 15-foot in diameter hole bringing it in to a small opening so that the Koreans could draw water with their buckets; then ran a pipe to the surface, put in a force pump run by hand, drove the water 600 feet on the level and up to the attic of the hospital, installed there a Montgomery Ward tank, and then I installed the whole plumbing plant with my own hands. That well, after 40 years, is still the only dependable water on the compound for our eight houses or for the nearby Korean village.

For the two buildings we brought flooring, doors, sash, glass, nails, and hardware from America. There is a big new hospital and dispensary now, but my hospital serves as a Home for Korean Nurses.[1]

The Taegu hospital project was Charlie's first test as the Presbyterian Mission's builder. Next came the assignment to oversee the building of his own house and eight others on the Presbyterian compound in Yŏnmotkol (Yŏn-dong) in Seoul. It was in the Clarks' new house that Mabel gave birth to their third son, Allen, in November 1908. Six years earlier, when Charlie and Mabel had left for their first eight-year term in Korea, the Crafts had fretted about how long it would be before they would see their future grandchildren. The deaths of Burton and Gordon confirmed their worst fears. Allen's birth raised the family's hopes; however, back in Chicago, first one and then the other of Mabel's parents died, as did her older brother.

1. Charles Allen Clark, "Memories of Sixty Years," unpublished memoir dated 1954 (mimeographed). The hospital in question was a forerunner of the Presbyterian Medical Center (Tongsan Pyŏngwŏn) in Taegu, now the Medical College of Keimyung University.

Charlie, Mabel, Allen, and Katherine Clark, 1920, Seoul. Clark Collection.

By the time the Clarks got home in 1910, only younger brother DeGray remained of Mabel's immediate family.

In Minneapolis, Charlie's family also had grown distant. Taking his "home assignment" seriously, Charlie left Mabel and Allen with relatives and traveled the country speaking and playing the part of visiting missionary in search of new recruits. At the age of 32 he enjoyed the honor with which he was received in his supporting churches and on the campus of his alma mater, Macalester College, where he was made an honorary Doctor of Divinity. But he was also eager to get back to the field. Even after a single term, Charlie felt that "home" had shifted to Korea and America was the place that he was only visiting.

When the Clarks returned from America, Allen was three years old. Mabel worried about him constantly and was terrified when he contracted typhoid the following year. It was a close call. Australian Mission doctor C.I. McLaren saved his life after it seemed that hope was gone, by giving him a risky veterinary injection of things that were not meant for humans. When he was six, Allen started attending Seoul Foreign School near West Gate. The Clarks' outside man took him back and forth on the Chongno streetcar line the first year, but in second grade he was sent by himself to wait on the corner, board the right trolley, get off at the right stop, and get in and out of school. Mabel was worried silly by this but Charlie insisted that their son needed to learn self-reliance. Mabel liked to walk with Allen on the mission compound and sometimes she would accompany Allen and the outside man on Allen's favorite trek, the half-mile through the alleys to nearby Ch'anggyŏngwŏn Park and the zoo that the Japanese colonial government had installed on the grounds of the old royal palace. Life in the Clarks' second term thus was altogether less stressful than it had been in the first. In 1919 Mabel bore a daughter, Katherine. In 1920 the family visited America on their second furlough.

During the 'teens, Charlie bought a Model-T Ford and invested in a little cabin at Sorai Beach for summer vacations. He also took up a part-time assignment teaching courses on the Old Testament and homiletics at the Presbyterian Theological Seminary in P'yŏngyang. This required extended absences from the family in Seoul, and in 1922, after their return from furlough, the Clarks moved to north Korea for good. They moved into a faculty house a short walk from the seminary and Allen started eighth grade at Pyeng Yang Foreign School across the way. Allen, however, took after his

Katherine, Charlie, and Mabel Clark, 1936, P'yŏngyang. Clark Collection.

mother, being very quiet, and Charlie worried that he needed bigger challenges. While not directly wanting to subvert his wife's influence over Allen, he continued trying to "make a man" out of him. He pushed him through the ranks of the Boy Scouts. In 1923 he took Allen and his best friend "Beekie" Bernheisel to explore Peking. And in 1924 he arranged for Allen to leave the unreal environment of the P'yŏngyang compound and finish high school in Minneapolis. Charlie constructed a vicarious adventure of his own planning an elaborate Grand Tour whereby Allen would travel with a group of America-bound missionary friends via Shanghai, Saigon, Singapore, India, Suez, Rome, Paris, and London. Allen made the last leg of the journey to Minneapolis on the train by himself, pausing in Chicago to see Mabel's brother DeGray and his wife Sophie.

Mabel herself was not to see Allen again for four long years. During that time she withdrew ever farther into her interior world. The P'yŏngyang missionary compound facilitated this by provided a caring community of friends who looked out for Katherine. Mabel always went to church on Sunday but during the week she was a homebody, seen only by Charlie, Katherine, Hakchongie the cook, and Hakchongie's wife, known by the Chinese nickname "Amah," who was Katherine's nanny. Mabel appears in photographs of compound life but seems always to have been in the background, alone or with Charlie but seldom with anyone else.

Charlie, by contrast, was relentless in his pursuit of multiple interests. In the 1920s he took up the cause of temperance, helping to promote the Korean chapter of the Women's Christian Temperance Union (WCTU) and writing polemics against alcohol. He learned Japanese well enough to take on an assignment in Japan itself, crossing back and forth to work with Korean congregations in the Kobe-Ōsaka-Kyōto region. His scholarly interests led to the steady output of texts and commentaries for seminary students, many of which appeared as articles in the seminary journal *Sinhak Chinam* (Theological Review). He wrote a novel based on his early experiences in Korea, a monograph on the importance of the Nevius Method in mission work, and a series of papers on traditional Korean religions that he eventually gave as lectures on furlough at Princeton Seminary and published under the title of *Religions of Old Korea*.[2] The religions book was an outgrowth of his encounters with Korean shamans, Buddhist monks and temples, and philosophical discussions with Korean scholars in a cultural environment that began with first trips into the interior in 1903 and continued for more than twenty-five years. It shows considerable appreciation for Korean religious traditions though it ends of course with a passage pointing to the Christian gospel as the solution for Korea's spiritual yearning.

By the mid-1930s Charlie Clark, having earned a Ph.D. at the University of Chicago in 1929, had become a senior professor at the Presbyterian Theological Seminary, with a network former students all across the country. There was great esprit de corps in the seminary student body and alumni, all of whom were members of a professional structure that was not managed by the Japanese. The seminarians liked to dress up for school in suits and ties and they practiced proudly for their future roles as social and spiritual leaders. The seminary published an American-style yearbook for each

2. Charles Allen Clark, *First Fruits in Korea* (New York: Fleming H. Revell, 1921), *The Korean Church and the Nevius Method* (New York: Fleming H. Revell, 1930), and *Religions of Old Korea* (New York: Fleming H. Revell, 1932). According to his biographer, Howard Howoo Lee, Charles A. Clark wrote 47 books, 42 of them in Korean and five in English, and more than 225 articles in English and Korean during his missionary career. The Korean works were done with the help of Korean secretaries and translators, two of whom went on to become famous figures in Korean politics: Yŏ Unhyŏng (Lyuh Woon-hyung), leader of the Korean People's Republic in 1945, and Ham Taeyŏng, vice president of the Republic of Korea from 1952 to 1956.

Charlie Clark and seminary students street preaching, P'yŏngyang, 1935. Clark Collection.

graduating class: the volume for 1937 was a typical souvenir of the new pastors' student days in class, on the basketball court, on outings to famous sights of P'yŏngyang and retreats in the Diamond Mountains. Naturally it also portrayed the faculty, with Charlie Clark front and center, splendidly turned out in his academic regalia.[3]

The American Colony in P'yŏngyang

By the 1920s, the Presbyterian Mission station in P'yŏngyang had become the most conspicuous Western installation on the Korean peninsula. The city, which had been called "pagan" and "filthy" by the earliest Western travelers thirty years earlier, had become a beloved hometown for more than a hundred foreigners, from pioneer missionaries to children in the dormitory at Pyeng Yang Foreign School. To the Presbyterians it was a new "Jerusalem,"[4] the queen city of Christianity in Korea. Some of the greatest

3. There was family significance to these faculty pictures, since beside Charlie Clark was Stacy L. Roberts, the seminary president, whose daughter Gene had married Allen Clark in 1933.

4. For example, Richard H. Baird wrote that "When the history of the Great Century of modern missionary activity is complete it may well be that Pyongyang Station in Korea will be found to have been the greatest mission station of that period." In *William M. Baird of Korea: A Profile* (Oakland, Calif.: family manuscript, 1968), p. 208. It is interesting to note that the postwar North Korean regime has reinvented P'yŏngyang as a holy city for ethnic Koreans worldwide. For a discussion see Ian Buruma, "Will the Wall Come Tumbling Down?" in the *New York Review of*

triumphs of the missionary effort were associated with P'yŏngyang. It had been a center of the Great Revival of 1907 that is said to have set the tone for Korean Protestantism for the rest of the century; and by 1925 it was the center of the fastest-growing Christian community in all of East Asia and, some said, the whole world.

Situated on a majestic S-curve of the Taedong River halfway between Seoul and the Manchurian border, P'yŏngyang had a distinguished history. Korea Kids at Pyeng Yang Foreign School grew up hearing that it had been founded in the time of Israel's King David by the Chinese nobleman Kija (Chinese: Ch'i-tzu), whose temple and tomb were among P'yŏngyang's prime historical sites and a favorite spot for picnics. The city wall with its loopholes paralleled the shining river for two and a half miles and then climbed the slopes of Peony Point (Moranbong) at the north end of the city before bending back to the Seven Star Gate (Ch'ilsŏng-mun) and the flats along Potong Stream. The rusting anchor chains of the 1860s American merchant ship *General Sherman* festooned the superstructure of the two-story Taedong Gate, P'yŏngyang's traditional front door. Across the old city to the northwest was the Potong Gate, P'yŏngyang's northern portal; and beyond that was the Presbyterian compound. With nearly a hundred men, women, and children, the P'yŏngyang Presbyterians outnumbered the city's Methodists and Catholics and completely overshadowed the city's foreign business contingent comprised of Russian merchants, a Portuguese trader and his family, and the American employees of the Corn Products Company's beet sugar refinery across the river.

The story of P'yŏngyang as a missionary station began in 1890, when the newly arrived Samuel A. Moffett paid a two-week visit to investigate the possibility of opening evangelistic work there. The following spring, Moffett and his colleague James Scarth Gale visited P'yŏngyang again while on a three-month exploratory journey by foot and horseback.[5] They held services in the city but found that people were still "suspicious of foreigners and afraid of Christian books"[6] because of the government's recently lifted prohibition against Christianity. P'yŏngyang remained impenetrable for several years, receiving occasional visits from Seoul-based missionaries who invariably found the local authorities inhospitable. The Presbyterian

Books, XLI:18 (November 3, 1994), p. 24.

5. This trek was something of a legend among the early missionaries. From February to April 1891, Moffett and Gale, accompanied by the Sorai Christian Sŏ Sangyun, explored the Korean north, holding meetings where Sŏ did the talking, and cultivating local officials wherever possible in hopes of furthering mission work. They practiced their language skills constantly, made contact with the Scottish missionaries in southern Manchuria, and returned via mountain roads across the peninsula to Hamhŭng and Wŏnsan before returning to Seoul. The fact that they survived the trip was remarkable in itself.

6. Samuel A. Moffett, *First Letters from Korea, 1890-1891* (Seoul: Presbyterian Theological Seminary Institute of Missions, 1975), p. 41.

Aerial view of P'yŏngyang and the Taedong River. Postcard. Clark Collection.

Mission assigned Samuel Moffett to P'yŏngyang as a full-time missionary in November 1893, and, after a rocky beginning that included attempts on his life by neighbors intent on killing the "foreign devil," he succeeded in buying property and founding a proper mission station in January 1895.

Forty years later, near the end of Moffett's distinguished career, the 120-acre Presbyterian campus in P'yŏngyang boasted a formidable array of modern institutions. These included Sungsil College (also called Union Christian College) and the Anna Davis Industrial Shops where Sungsil College students worked to pay their tuition;[7] the Lula Wells Industrial School for vocational training of abandoned wives and widows; the Presbyterian Theological Seminary training the denomination's pastorate for all Korea; Bible institutes for women and men in the laity; secondary academies for boys and girls; Pyeng Yang Foreign School (PYFS), the Union Christian Hospital, and the West Gate Presbyterian Church. Interspersed throughout the compound were Western-style residences, the homes of the missionar-

7. Sungsil College founder William M. Baird believed in the character-building value of labor. "As an Indiana farm boy," wrote his son Richard, "he was opposed to the Oriental idea of the long-robed scholar who could not be degraded by manual labor, who grew long fingernails to show that his hands had never been used for work." Baird, *William M. Baird of Korea*, p. 141. The work-study plan was modeled on Park College, Parkville, Missouri, which required that all students learn self-reliance and respect for labor by doing fieldwork, janitoring, or cooking and cleaning for several hours each day. A key difference is that roughly half of all Union Christian College students simply paid the fees and studied, while at Park College in Missouri the labor was a requirement, in effect a part of the curriculum.

Peony Point, P'yŏngyang. Government-General of Chōsen, *Annual Report on Administration of Chōsen, 1930* (Keijō: Government-General of Chōsen, 1931), p. 24.

ies themselves. Each day, hundreds of people, foreigners and Koreans, worked and studied in the various mission buildings. At intervals, hundreds more converged from the countryside to participate in special meetings, conventions, and church services. All year long, P'yŏngyang station teemed with energy; and in many years the entire Northern Presbyterian Mission converged on P'yŏngyang from the faraway stations of Taegu, Andong, Ch'ŏngju, and Seoul, and the nearer-by stations of Chaeryŏng, Sŏnch'ŏn, and Kanggye, to have their annual Mission Meeting and, incidentally, to admire the formidable successes of their P'yŏngyang brethren.

The vitality of the missionary establishment in P'yŏngyang, a medium-sized city of no more than 180,000, made the missionary campus a most conspicuous feature. For the missionaries, life revolved around "the Work," and everyone in sight was somehow related to it, whether as co-workers, servants, and employees, or potential converts. P'yŏngyang was different from Seoul, where there was social contact outside the missionary and church circles. It had fewer diversions, and people tended to talk to each other. The station's early arrivals had brought theological and cultural beliefs that were part of the revival sweeping American Protestantism in the late nineteenth century. These became the basis for their own teaching and example for the Koreans. And inasmuch as the missionary calling was the ultimate expression of those beliefs, they understood that their own work was of earthshaking importance. As one missionary put it, "Among the full-time professions, the missionary call was often viewed as

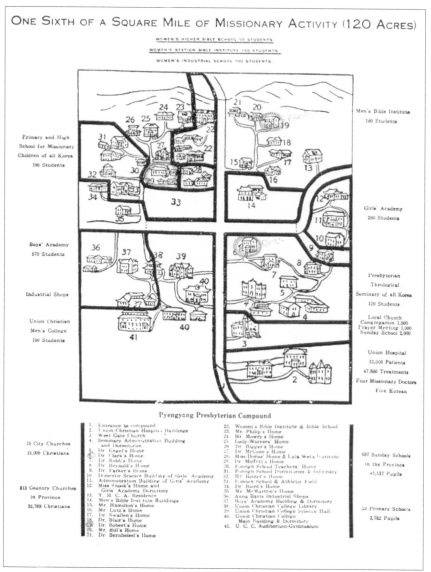

P'yŏngyang mission compound sketch map. Clark Collection.

the highest. This related in part to the degree of personal sacrifice: anyone who would leave home, family, friends, and country to go to a 'heathen' country to serve Christ was looked upon with a kind of holy awe usually reserved for saints."[8]

8. Everett N. Hunt Jr., *Protestant Pioneers in Korea* (Maryknoll, N.Y.: Orbis Books, 1980), p. 86. Also see the discussion in Ruth Compton Brouwer, *New*

The Presbyterian Compound skyline, P'yŏngyang, 1935. Clark Collection.

The "Nevius Plan" at Work

Across Korea, the Presbyterians' strategy was to establish churches and other Christian institutions that avoided dependence on foreign missionaries by training church leaders—pastors, deacons, school teachers, Sunday School teachers, women's club leaders, etc.—to run their own institutions as quickly as possible and to finance themselves through voluntary offerings and sacrificial giving. It put a tremendous emphasis on Bible Study—hence an emphasis on the ability to read *Han'gŭl*—and fervent and confessional prayer as daily manifestations of conversion, which was supposed to bring about a fundamental change in the way a new Christian lived. This meant renouncing old habits, including the *chesa*, the ancestral ritual that was the central rite of the Confucian family in Korea. Other renunciations included concubinage, opium, alcohol, and tobacco. New habits included a strict observance of Sunday as the "Lord's Day" (*chu-il*), a day free of worldly activities and devoted solely to worship and study.[9]

This prescription for Christian living grew out of a Presbyterian Mission retreat in June 1890. The lead speaker at the retreat, the Rev. John L. Nevius from the Presbyterian Mission in Shantung, China, exhorted the young missionaries in Korea to use discipline as a way to avoid the "rice Christians" phenomenon whereby new converts were motivated not by inner spiritual conviction as much as by the desire for advancement, money, jobs, or education. Along with this came an emphasis on founding small village churches and welcoming women into the church at all levels (except, of course, the

Women for God: Canadian Presbyterian Women and India Missions, 1876-1914 (Toronto: University of Toronto Press, 1990), especially pp. 76-78.

9. For example, in his handwritten diary for 1905 Charles Allen Clark decried the reluctance of new catechumens to part with their ancestors' memorial tablets, traditionally the objects of address, or "worship," in the *chesa*, the Confucian family's most solemn ancestral ritual. He insisted that new Christians should give them up before being baptized into the faith. On occasion he took charge of a household's ancestral tablets himself, and burned them. This was meant as a symbolic break with former beliefs, but one wonders if it was not understood by some Koreans as the missionary's own affirmation that the tablets contained some worrisome supernatural power.

pastorate). The Northern Presbyterians in Korea embraced the "Nevius Plan," as it came to be called, and church historians believe that it was the key to the institutional growth that made the Presbyterian denomination the largest Christian body in Korea from the beginning of the century.[10]

The Discreet Pride of the P'yŏngyang Team

Over the years, as the missionaries traveled country roads visiting the churches and schools in their districts, they developed a certain intimacy with the Korean northwest. Since most had joined the mission for life, "the Work" became the center of their existence and the valleys of northwest Korea became their home. As time passed, they acquired a certain expertise in things Korean, which they passed on to newcomers in the fashion of mentors. Younger missionaries learned to revere the older ones, who acquired unchallengeable authority within P'yŏngyang station and, to some extent, within the mission as a whole, based on their seniority and knowledge of the country and its language.[11] Newcomers were expected to listen; in fact, they were not even allowed to vote in mission meetings until they had been on the field long enough to pass a language exam.[12] During this stage

10. Charles Allen Clark, *The Nevius Plan of Mission Work in Korea* (Seoul: Christian Literature Society, 1937) and Helen S.C. Nevius, *The Life of John Livingston Nevius* (New York: Fleming H. Revell, 1895); also the thoughtful retrospective by G. Thompson Brown, "Samuel Moffett and the Nevius Plan," *Ch'odaebakjang Map'o Samyŏl paksa naehan paekchunyŏn kinyŏm kangyŏnhoe* (Centennial symposium commemorating Samuel A. Moffett's arrival in Korea) (Seoul: Presbyterian Theological Seminary, 1990), pp. 28-37.

11. To be sure, seniority was more important than skill in the language. Notwithstanding the texts that were written with the help of Korean language tutors, few foreigners—missionaries included—ever mastered all levels of educated Korean, spoken *and* written, instead settling for a practical level of skill that would enable them to explain lessons in a classroom, conduct simple negotiations, and deliver a speech or sermon. Most missionaries could read Korean and a little Chinese; a few could write as well as speak. This working level of Korean language ability was usually enough to carry on "the Work," but only a handful went beyond this standard to learn the classical language that opened the world of ideas. These exceptions (e.g., James Scarth Gale) invited criticism for spending too much time with the arcana of Korean culture and too little time on "the Work." The system therefore encouraged (1) devotion to "the Work" over devotion to "understanding Koreans"; (2) association with less-educated Koreans rather than with classically educated Koreans who might engage the foreigner in deeper dialogue; and, therefore, (3) a certain disinterest in what might be learned from Koreans. The author encountered a variation of this in Seoul in 1997 when he heard an American missionary say "I came to be a missionary and not to study about Korea!"

12. One byproduct of this rule was that a number of missionary women never got to vote in mission meetings. For a time, married women could not vote; then they were given the vote if they passed the language exam, like everyone else, but usually were so occupied with child rearing that they never were able to pass. Single

of their careers they were told what to think and how to work. There was little incentive to break the pattern or to challenge its assumptions. Instead, new missionaries learned many of their most useful lessons about Korea from their seniors within the mission rather than from Koreans.[13]

The seniority system had its advantages. The senior missionaries in P'yŏngyang were gifted leaders and planners whose skills had everything to do with the spectacular success of the Presbyterians as a mission. Their character and commitment inspired fierce loyalty in their understudies. Historian Martha Huntley has written of the loyalty and teamwork inspired by Samuel A. Moffett, in effect the "dean" of P'yŏngyang Station,[14] pointing to his own sacrifices, his traits of grace and humor, his ability to motivate others and willingness to share credit. These are effective leadership skills in any organization, and no doubt P'yŏngyang's success owed much to Moffett's gifts.[15]

The P'yŏngyang "team's" strict conservatism, however, sometimes led to conflicts with other missionaries. A prime area of disagreement was the Presbyterian Mission's educational policy. A working document entitled "Our Educational Policy" had been adopted by a majority vote of the mission in 1890, defining the purpose of missionary education as "the gospel for the heathen and education for the Christians." The mission agreed to support schools for the children of Christian parents, to train them as the church's next generation of leaders and to give them the social advantage of a modern education. The policy explicitly rejected "general education" as a means of attracting non-Christians to the atmosphere of Christian schools. As the paper's author put it, "The missionary teacher should be primarily a manufacturer of evangelists, and in so far as he has failed to do this he has failed as a missionary teacher, however successful he may be as an educator."[16]

This was the policy that was challenged in 1915 when the Government-General of Chōsen excluded religious instruction from the curriculum of any school that wanted its graduates' diplomas recognized by the government for purposes of future employment. At that time, the Northern Presbyterians had voted to close their schools rather than give up religious

women often passed the exam, but some of them were in clerical positions working with foreigners so much that they never used it, and therefore never got the vote.

13. The best source of information from Koreans was the language teachers who were assigned to new (mostly male) missionaries on the field. Women missionaries also depended on their "bible women" counterparts.

14. For Samuel A. Moffett, see Jong Hyeong Lee, "Samuel Austin Moffett: His Life and Work in the Development of the Presbyterian Church of Korea, 1890-1936" (unpublished Ph.D. diss., Union Theological Seminary, Richmond, Virginia, 1983).

15. Huntley, *To Start a Work*, pp. 391-398; William N. Blair, *Precious Memories of Dr. Samuel Moffett* (Duarte, California, n.d.); and remarks by Samuel H. Moffett in *Ch'odaehakjang Map'o Samyŏl paksa naehan paekchunyŏn kinyŏm kangyŏnhoe*, pp. 15-21.

16. William M. Baird, quoted in Huntley, *Caring, Growing, Changing*, p. 90.

The Presbyterian Missionaries of P'yŏngyang, 1936. Charles and Mabel Clark are sixth and seventh from the right in the back row. The author's maternal grandparents, Stacy and Evelyn Roberts, are fourth and fifth from the right in the middle row. Clark Collection.

Presbyterian Theological Seminary Building, P'yŏngyang. Postcard. Clark Collection.

instruction (a step that turned out to be unnecessary because of the subsequent liberalization of the rule under Governor-General Saitō). The vote came in the midst of a bitter dispute between "conservatives" in P'yŏngyang and "liberals" in Seoul over what kind of postsecondary education was appropriate in the mission's program of Christian schooling.

Personalities as well as principles clashed when the Seoul faction decided in 1912 to depart from mission policy and establish a government-recognized Christian college in the capital that would teach modern subjects and admit non-Christian students. Creating a separate college with a secular curriculum in Seoul threatened the Presbyterian Mission's dominant P'yŏngyang faction on many levels at once. To begin with, the P'yŏngyang team had doubts about attempting to cultivate Christian students in the "moral cesspool" of the capital, which one missionary likened to the red-light district of "South Clark Street, Chicago."[17] Secondly, straying into "secular education" looked like part of the trend toward "modernism" that was seen to be corrupting the entire Presbyterian denomination in America. Mission conservatives argued that a college that claimed to be Christian but had an essentially secular curriculum would actually foster skepticism toward the Bible, moral relativism vis-à-vis Korean culture and religious beliefs, and a preference for "modern" science over the unalterable truth of the Christian gospel. Such a college would attract non-Chris-

17. James E. Adams to Presbyterian Board of Foreign Missions, Joint Committee for Educational Work in Korea, letter dated January 29, 1913, and Joint Committee to the Educational Senate of the Korea Mission of the Presbyterian Church in the U.S.A., letter dated July 8, 1914, both in the Presbyterian Historical Society, Philadelphia, Record Group 140, Box 3, folder 5.

Astronomy students with their missionary professor. Yi Kyuhŏn, *Sajinŭro pon Tong-nip undong: Oech'imgwa t'ujaeng* (Seoul: Sŏmundang, 1987), p. 90.

tian students who would undermine the attempts of Christian students to live the godly life. Complying with government regulations and seeking government recognition as a secular institution completely undermined the mission's only valid reason for devoting funds to higher education, which was to have an educated native pastorate. The Seoul college promised to be an expensive undertaking that would rob P'yŏngyang's Union Christian College of funds for this primary purpose.

The Seoul faction, led by Horace G. Underwood, argued that by maintaining a single college exclusively for pastoral training in P'yŏngyang, the mission was neglecting its responsibility to reach the Korean upper crust in the capital. If the brightest young Koreans were so hungry for a modern education that they were willing to leave home, where there was as yet no college, in order to study in Japan, then the church in Korea should take the opportunity to offer instruction in modern subjects under a Christian faculty in the context of Christian college life. If these were to be Korea's future leaders in secular occupations, Underwood argued, it was important that they be offered Christian college educations. Severance Union Medical College, an institution that taught science, had already succeeded in attracting top Korean students to study medicine in preparation for careers in the Christian occupation of healing. Why not a college to train Korea's future Christian professionals in other areas as well?

The Seoul college proposal threatened the P'yŏngyang missionaries for political reasons as well. As a union institution run by a combination of the Presbyterian, Methodist, and Canadian missions, the new college would be beyond their control. This was clear from the way Horace Underwood was going about promoting his project. His brother John was a member of the Board of Foreign Missions in New York, and between them the Underwood brothers had many powerful friends in the homeland's church hierarchy. Having made a fortune in the typewriter business, John Underwood was dangling before the Board a designated gift of $25,000 of his own money to purchase the college campus in the Seoul suburb of Yŏnhi Village. He had re- cruited allies on the Presbyterian, Methodist, and Canadian mission boards in North America to form an interdenominational consortium that would oversee the Seoul college through an interdenominational Field Board of Managers that would answer to New York and not to the missions in Korea.

When Chōsen Christian College opened in 1915 as a *senmon gakkō* (Ko- rean: *chŏnmun hakkyo*; a kind of junior college under the Japanese sys- tem),[18] it seemed that the Northern Presbyterian Mission's majority faction in P'yŏngyang had been defeated in a power play by Horace and John Underwood. The Board of Foreign Missions had overridden their authority to vote and set policy for the Korea mission field. The "college question" thus became a struggle between the mission and the Board over field au- thority that was not settled until the Korea Mission actually brought an ac- tion against the Board of Foreign Missions on the floor of the General As- sembly of the Presbyterian Church in the U.S.A. Though the mission lost there too, the legacy of the argument remained in the consciousness of members of the Seoul and P'yŏngyang factions of the mission for many years, even after North Korea was closed to missionaries in the 1940s.[19]

The political aspect of the feud was exacerbated by the controversy within the church in America over "modernism," the allegedly corrupting tendency away from the literal interpretation of the Bible that even then was infiltrating the clergy through such doctrinally liberal institutions as Union Theological Seminary in New York and Princeton Theological Semi-

18. In 1915, a *senmon gakkō* was the highest level of education available to Kore- ans in Korea. It was equivalent to the last two years of high school and the first two years of college in the United States at the same time. The next-higher level was the Higher Common School (*kodŭng pot'ong hakkyo*) for ages 12-16, equivalent to the American grades seven through ten. Horace H. Underwood, *Modern Education in Korea* (New York: International Press, 1926), p. 41. A Korean student wishing to go on to higher studies had to leave Korea and study in Japan or some other country.

19. Of the Sungsil partisans, one, James E. Adams, had to resign from the mission under severe mental strain. Horace G. Underwood himself was so exhausted that his health broke and he died in 1916. Within the mission for two generations the descen- dants of the original contenders occasionally lined up on opposite sides of policy questions in ways that were reminiscent of the college question. Richard H. Baird, son of the P'yŏngyang pioneer and Sungsil founder William M. Baird, took the col- lege controversy seriously enough to set forth the P'yŏngyang faction's view in *Wil- liam M. Baird of Korea: a Profile*. Underwood's son Horace Horton Underwood de- voted his doctoral dissertation to the question of what kind of higher education was appropriate for Korea (Underwood, *Modern Education in Korea*). Underwood be- came vice president of Chōsen Christian College in 1926 and president in 1935.

nary. "Modernism" diluted faith by accommodating relativism, empiricism, naturalism (a code word for Darwin and evolution), and philosophy. The spread of modernism among American seminary students was of special concern to the traditionally conservative missionaries in Korea, among whom were many Princeton graduates concerned about the direction of their alma mater. They were determined to shelter their own pastoral candidates in P'yŏngyang and the Korean church in general from the worldly influences that were weakening the moral fiber of their own home church. The very language of the Underwood brothers' rationale for wanting a Christian college in Seoul thus triggered a battle in Korea that mirrored the war between modern culture and traditional theology in the United States.

The Maryknoll Mission and the Catholics of P'yŏngyang

The Catholic Church in Korea, older by a hundred years than the Protestant community, entered the twentieth century with a very different kind of history. Catholic missions in East Asia got their start in the 1500s when the Jesuit missionary Francis Xavier established a mission in Japan. The legendary Jesuit Father Matteo Ricci reached China in 1583 and devised a most effective approach to Chinese civilization. He bided his time learning the language of the educated elite of the late Ming dynasty and opened a dialogue with officials at the Imperial court based on his own mastery of the Confucian Classics and his respect for Chinese thought. In the teaching of the Neo-Confucians he discerned a Chinese comprehension of "God," framed in the Chinese language as the supreme arbiter of rightness and natural order. In his own life and writings he struggled to join the Western and Chinese concepts of God in a way that could serve as the basis for a Chinese branch of the Holy Catholic Church. Along these lines he was inclined to tolerate "ancestor worship," the central ritual of the Chinese patrilineal family, as one manifestation of God's provision for harmony and health among the living. He was not inclined to condemn Chinese practice or to call it heathen; rather, he was disposed to find common ground with it as a Christian and to understand how God meant for it to be included in his Divine Plan. Ricci set forth his understandings in a book, *Tien-chu shih-i* (Korean: *Ch'ŏnju sil'i*, The True Doctrine of the Lord of Heaven). This work was widely read by Chinese intellectuals and helped build mutual respect between them and Renaissance Westerners like Ricci. Throughout the seventeenth century, Jesuit missionaries, acting as astronomers and mathematicians in fields of keen interest to the Chinese court, were welcomed in Peking and treated as virtual members of the mandarinate in their own right.

The mutual admiration of the early Jesuits and the Chinese establishment, however, went sour when other Catholic orders started criticizing the Jesuits for tolerating the "idolatry" of ancestor worship. The Pope set-

134

Maryknoll Missioners, P'yŏngyang. Courtesy of the Catholic Foreign Mission Society of America.

tled this so-called Rites Controversy in 1715 with a decision that Christians could not engage in ancestor rituals, a decision that led directly to the out-lawing of Christianity by the Yung-cheng Emperor in 1722 and the expul-sion of almost all missionaries from China. Foreign Christians were permit-ted to remain only in Peking, under government supervision, tolerated only for their knowledge of the West, science in particular.

It was this remnant of Christianity in China that attracted the curiosity of a succession of Korean visitors to Peking in the late 1700s. The visitors were members of the embassies bearing tribute from the king of Korea to the emperor of China, Koreans who were permitted a certain amount of freedom to roam within the walls of the Chinese capital while their leaders engaged in official business in the Forbidden City. Here they discovered copies of Ricci's *The True Doctrine of the Lord of Heaven*, which they con-veyed back to Korea.

At the time, the Chosŏn dynasty had been ruling Korea for almost four hundred years, supported by the hereditary *yangban* aristocracy. Candi-dates from *yangban* families had a lock on positions in the bureaucracy, as in China the preferred route to status, and therefore to wealth and large-scale land ownership. Hereditary slaves and tenants supported the *yangban* class with labor on the land, while free commoners supported the state with taxes. Commoners with special skills or education per-formed specialized tasks and occupied a social rung called the *chung'in*, while offspring of the *yangban* by concubines lived as "*sŏja*" on the fringes of their fathers' respectability, their names marked with the character "*sŏ*," meaning essentially "illegitimate" in their official family genealogies. Eigh-teenth-century Korea had its glories—its art and literature represent the pinnacle of traditional Korean cultural expression—but within its social system there was plenty of grievance.

Traditional Korean society, so often painted as corrupt and benighted, was not without its internal correction mechanisms. One feature of the eighteenth century in Korea was the search for new ideas and the internally generated impetus for reform. The window on China via the annual tribute embassies was one source of new ideas, and it was through this opening that reformist Koreans of the lower *yangban* class found Christian meta-physics and the teachings of Matteo Ricci. Like China, the Korean govern-ment had outlawed Christianity, and so the travelers had to smuggle their newfound Christian literature back home in Chinese texts that they stud-ied in secret cells. These cells essayed Catholic ceremonies and evolved into underground congregations that attracted people of differing social backgrounds. Their brotherhoods were organized as secret societies like Chinese tongs, evolving a special way of life. In hidden mountain commu-nities they supported themselves with the materials at hand as *onggi* pot-ters, making earthenware pots in wood-fired kilns. Their liturgy, since it was invented on the spot, became an all-but-unrecognizable mélange of occult-seeming acts and incantations, all of which upset the authorities and brought on the vicious persecutions that nearly exterminated them in the nineteenth century.

The intellectual center of the early Catholic Church in Korea was in Seoul and its environs, and a number of educated men were part of its early history. In 1801 the Korean reform faction got caught up in a political controversy that led to a purge in which the court tried to exterminate the Catholics. Other persecutions followed, for example, in 1811, when the government found a letter that had been written by the survivors begging the pope to send military forces from the West to force the court to tolerate Christianity.[20]

Korean Catholics make much of their early history, revering their early martyrs and emphasizing the idea that the church was planted not by foreigners but by Koreans seeking religious truth and toleration on their own.[21] The missionary phase of Catholicism in Korea began in 1794 with the surreptitious arrival of the first foreign priest, a Chinese named Chou Wen-mu. Fr. Chou was killed in the 1801 persecution and there were no other foreign priests until 1836 when a contingent of three French fathers representing the Société des Missions Étrangères de Paris (MEP) snuck through a gap in the Ŭiju city wall and commenced work in disguise, taking full advantage, as the story goes, of the large Korean rain-hat, or *sakkat*, which kept their faces out of view. The French priests worked in northwestern Korea and south as far as Seoul until 1839 when they were caught and beheaded. In 1843 another French priest was caught and executed virtually upon arrival. Between 1850 and 1863 Bishop Simeon-François Berneux managed to set up a mission and a seminary, training Korean priests; but the persecution of 1866 wiped out Bishop Berneux, his mission, and most of the church.[22] Korean Christianity was moribund for about twenty years thereafter, until Korea's modern treaties with the West opened the

20. See Joseph Chang-mun Kim and John Jae-sun Chang, *Catholic Korea—Yesterday and Today* (Seoul: Catholic Korea Publishing Co., 1964).

21. This is not entirely true, since it can be shown that European Catholics visited and took an active interest in Korea in previous centuries, though they did not establish permanent missions there. See Joseph Ruiz de Medina, S.J., *The Catholic Church in Korea: Its Origins, 1566-1784*, trans. John Bridges, S.J. (Seoul: Royal Asiatic Society, Korea Branch, 1994).

22. The subversive character of Catholicism was reinforced in the view of the Korean government by the attempt of a group of Korean Catholics in 1811 to write the Pope for support, and again, in 1866 by an attempt to summon French military intervention. Both episodes are covered in Dallet, *Histoire de l'église de Corée*, Vol. I, pp. 251-268, and Vol. II, pp. 572-578. The circumstances of the 1811 episode are portrayed most effectively by the writer Hahn Moo-Sook in her historical novel *Mannam*, published in English translation as *Encounter* (Berkeley and Los Angeles: University of California Press, 1992).

way to missionary propagation. In the 1880s the Catholic effort resumed along with the beginnings of Protestant work in Korea.

The second century of Catholic Christianity in Korea began with the arrival of a series of bishops, outstanding among whom was Archbishop Gustav Charles-Marie Mutel, vicar apostolic of Seoul from 1890 to 1933. Archbishop Mutel built the great Myŏng-dong Cathedral in downtown Seoul, dedicated in 1895. The Sisters of St. Paul de Chartres arrived in 1888 to supplement the work of the Paris MEP Fathers with an effort to reach women; and in 1909 a mission of Benedictine monks from the Monastery of St. Ottillien in Germany founded a Korea mission. In 1911 Archbishop Mutel divided Korea into the two vicariates of Seoul and Taegu and in 1920 the northern vicariate was divided again, creating a northeastern district centered on Wŏnsan that was assigned to the Benedictines, and a district in the northwest into which the American church was invited. At the time there were around 90,000 Catholics in Korea, 3,700 of them in the P'yong-yang district, but no ordained Korean priests.

In May 1923 the first American Catholics arrived to relieve the French fathers in the northwest and to take over the job of making converts and cultivating candidates for the clergy. They were from the Catholic Foreign Mission Society of America, better known as "Maryknoll," named for the hilltop they called "Mary's knoll," near Ossining, New York, where the Society had its headquarters.

In 1923, the Catholic establishment in P'yŏngyang consisted of a one-acre compound with a gray-brick church seating three hundred on the polished floor and a red curtain down the middle to separate the women from the men during mass; a two-room, mud-walled convent housing three Korean nuns of the order of St. Paul de Chartres together with their Singer sewing machine, kitchen utensils, and all worldly possessions; a brick boys' school built for eighty but accommodating 185 students; two girls' schools, one mud and one brick, built for 120 but accommodating 240. "We were wondering how they did it," wrote one of the early Maryknollers, so the pastor explained:

> The class periods are short enough to allow the pupils to hold their breath, further space is secured by standing on one another's toes, and fat children are not admitted....We wondered who shoveled out the atmosphere after a winter session behind closed doors and windows. Yet these discomforts are not reckoned great, and there is a waiting list of over two hundred. What are they waiting for? Perhaps for us to build them a school.[23]

23. Quotations describing the Catholics' situation in P'yongyang are taken from "Diary from Fr. Byrne," dated May 8, 1923, in Mission Diaries, Korea, Box 1, Maryknoll Mission Archives, New York, hereafter referred to as "MDK."

The Maryknoll Mission in P'yŏngyang was a Spartan operation compared with the Presbyterian compound a mile across the valley.[24] The material disparity was part of the difference in the Koreans' mind between Protestantism and Catholicism that are distinguished (as in China and Japan) as different religions altogether. To this day the term "Christian" (*kidokkyo*) is compatible with "Protestant" (*kaeshinkyo*) but not with "Catholic" (*ch'ŏnjukyo*). Nonetheless, in this more ecumenical era it takes effort to reconstruct the distance that divided 1920s-era Protestant and Catholic missionaries in Korea. In P'yŏngyang, the Maryknoll newcomers were astonished by the visibility of their "separated brethren" and their rich resources. "Pyeng Yang is the most Protestant city I was ever in, in America or elsewhere," wrote one Maryknoller.[25] Old-time Catholic missionaries in Korea had explanations for the scale of Protestant success: "unlimited" funds—a million dollars a year versus $15,000 for the Catholics; more missionaries—542 Protestants versus 60 Catholics; more paid Korean clergy and catechists; indeed more of everything "in the service of error, [and] on the other [side] a scant budget and a scarcity of apostolic workers in the service of Truth." The Protestants were said to ask less of their converts: "It is not unusual to meet with Koreans, who are active and zealous Protestants but who still have concubines or engage in ancestor worship." And they hobnobbed with the upper and middle classes, taking advantage of the Korean thirst for education and putting schools above all else. The Protestants were Anglo-Saxons, argued one Catholic analyst in 1924, and therefore both idealistic and practical. And they had a political agenda:

> [T]heir fundamental aim is to educate the people, to instill into them their own mentality and thus to acquire an influence over them....It is easy to guess what advantages will be in the hands of those who are guiding this evolution at the present time. These advantages will be not only religious but also political and economic. The Anglo-Saxons, with their practical nature, are well aware of this.[26]

One of the Maryknollers' first experiences with sectarian strife in P'yŏngyang was a Seventh Day Adventist tent meeting organized to denounce the pope as the incarnation of the seven-headed beast referred to in the thirteenth chapter of the Book of Revelation. The organizers proclaimed their anti-Catholic theme on posters all over the city and mustered a large

24. One Maryknoller described the Presbyterian compound as "a vast oasis of green in a desert of tile roofs, with splendid churches, schools, and colleges. . . ." Some Catholics complained that the land had once been owned by a French priest but had been won by the Protestants through legal manipulation. "Now the two challenge comparison in the pagan mind, which can hardly be expected to hesitate in making a choice."

25. "Diary of Maryknoll in Peng Yang, August 1925 to March 1927," in MDK, Box 1.

26. *The Catholic Church in Korea* (Hong Kong: Imprimerie de la Société des Missions-Étrangéres, 1924), p. 97.

crowd. A delegation from the Young Men's Catholic Society also went, and as the speaker was making his point a young seminarian named Paul Kang, dressed in his cassock, arose to object. "A number of young pagans at the back of the hall" started chanting in support of Kang. Plainclothes police intervened and one was beaten up by the "young pagans" who subsequently fled. A "mild riot" ensued, during which Paul Kang tried to escape, his cassock flying, but was caught by the police who threw him in jail for disorderly conduct.[27]

So unwelcome were the Catholics among their "separated brethren" that they actually had trouble getting treatment at the Protestant-run Union Christian Hospital. "Father Kim and I have both tried to obtain treatment for minor sicknesses and have been repulsed," wrote one Maryknoller in 1927. "Perhaps it is better to say that the attitude is not 'general'; without a doubt it depends upon the individual person with which one comes in contact. Dr. Anderson practically threw out Fr. Kim and me when we went there for eye treatment; we went to the Government Hospital and received most courteous treatment, thorough, satisfactory, and efficient." The fathers also thought that Protestants were behind vandalism of their property. "In April [1926]," wrote the same missioner, "I went over and had an interview with Dr. Moffat [sic] who is in charge of Christian Union College here. After this interview the practice which had been common with the boys of the Protestant compound of breaking the windows in our church with stones ceased."[28]

Though Catholic and Protestant missionaries were wary of each other, their approaches to Korea had much in common. The first prefect apostolic of P'yŏngyang was Father Patrick Byrne, a sandy-haired Washingtonian who had a penchant for detective stories, played the fiddle, loved tennis, and kept dogs and a parrot. Byrne was a tireless traveler who was constantly on the road visiting country congregations. Like all foreigners who roamed the Korean countryside he suffered frequent bouts of illness, mainly dysentery, but his letters home told little of the hardships. Instead they were typically full of description, insight, and an especially sardonic humor for which he became famous at Maryknoll headquarters. Here was his early assessment of the Koreans' national costume:

> Nowhere else in the world is white so popular. The national flag should be a sheet. In America, 'tis true, the Palm Beach suit is quite au fait…; but here you find no snobby class distinctions. As a matter of fact, if the laundress be willing, why shouldn't a coal heaver enjoy his white in business hours as well as free?…As we saw this horde of whites…we wondered who had the contract for "Lux".…The answer came [when] we passed through our first Korean village.…In the village was a full session of the ladies "Knockers Club" kneeling

27. P.H. Cleary, MDK, July-December 1927.
28. Both comments in this paragraph are from "Diary of Maryknoll in Peng Yang, August 1925 to March 1927," in MDK, Box 1.

by the ever present brook or drain (it matters not) and with twelve-inch sticks belaboring helpless masses of soiled linen into a more contrite and purified state. The duration of such a session we dinna ken, but we have found that every day is wash day, and every trickle of water a potential tub. Moreover the ladies seem to like it. Perhaps because it enables them to give, with a stick, full vent to their feelings....

Before long Patrick Byrne became too busy with mission management to get very far with his language studies. He had to miss much of what went on around him and filter communication with Koreans through an interpreter. The result was, as a colleague put it, that "his rating of Korean intelligence was off—because of his failure to understand them or their failure to understand him."

But many Catholic missionaries did better. Lacking family distractions and living with Korean coworkers enabled the Maryknollers to develop levels of fluency that were rare among foreigners. The Catholics stressed written Korean and integrating Chinese characters, and newcomers were advised to spend their first five years studying the language with a paid tutor. The difficulty of the language caught some priests by surprise. "How many times in speaking at the seminaries when crossing America I said, 'Of all the Oriental languages Korean is the simplest,'" wrote one frustrated Maryknoller. "I don't know where I got that notion—perhaps the absence of tones. The fact is that Korean is admitted by all to be the most difficult."[29]

Under Byrne's leadership the Maryknoll Mission opened a chain of stations from P'yŏngyang, which remained the headquarters, to Yŏngyu (also called Op'a), near Ŭiju on the Yalu River, where the Catholic church and convent were the biggest structures in town. In Yongyu the missionaries set up a home for crippled adults, a kindergarten, an "industrial school" to teach sewing, and a home for the aged that included a number of "blind grannies." Maryknoll nuns founded a dispensary and established sodalities of young married women, teaching them singing, sewing, and recreational sports such as volleyball, and coaxing them into leadership roles as deaconesses for the congregation.[30]

Looking Back at Old P'yŏngyang

P'yŏngyang today is a most xenophobic city, the capital of the Democratic People's Republic of Korea (DPRK), a Stalinist "kingdom" that officially spurns religion. The visitor now sees a city rebuilt on the rubble of the Ko-

29. Letter from Fr. Donald V. Chisholm to Fr. Superior, September 27, 1927, in Mission Letters (Peng Yang and Chung Wha, 1927-1929), Maryknoll Mission Archives.
30. The various stations and installations of the P'yongyang diocese are discussed in detail in Ch'ŏnjukyo P'yŏngyang Kyogusa P'yŏnch'an Wiwŏnhoe, *Ch'ŏnjukyo P'yŏngyang Kyogusa* (Seoul: Pundo Ch'ulp'ansa, 1981), pp. 284-528.

rean War and is guided to museums and monuments that extol a new deity, the spirit of the late Great Leader Kim Il-sung. For visitors who knew the city before, there are precious few vestiges of P'yŏngyang when it was the Jerusalem of the East. The river still makes its majestic S-curve through the city. The Potong Gate is still there, though it has been repositioned. The anchor chains of the *General Sherman* hang in the Korean Central History Museum, and Kim Il-sung's grandfather is credited with having led the attack that destroyed it in 1866. It is possible to identify the street that bisected the Presbyterian Mission compound in the 1930s, but absolutely nothing remains on either side of it to suggest that there was once a large complex of red brick Western residences and school buildings on the site. Heavily guarded government office buildings fill the area and inquiries to the guards or passersby suggest that there has been an organized effort to forget that a colony of foreigners ever lived here. One P'yŏngyang-born graduate of the PYFS class of 1934 who visited in 1997 reported his delight at seeing the kind of magpies that used to nest in the poplar tree outside his bedroom window. Otherwise, for him as for the innumerable Koreans who knew P'yŏngyang before 1950, the environment of the ancient city exists only in remembering.

-- 6 --

The White Russians of Korea

White Russians were refugees from the Soviet regime, people who had lost everything in the Bolshevik revolution and hated the Red Russians who controlled their homeland. In Korea they were a mixed bag of former officials, merchants, landlords, and an odd variety of migrants—historical castaways who, unlike the other Caucasians in Korea, had arrived with nothing but what they could carry, stranded by history and forced to live by their wits and toil in whatever community would accept them. When the Bolsheviks reached the Vladivostok area in 1922, anticommunist Russians scattered into Manchuria, Korea, and China to live in Russian-speaking enclaves that were a familiar aspect of East Asian port life through World War Two. Korea, too, had its share of White Russians, mostly in Seoul, where several hundred of them supported themselves as shopkeepers and smugglers. Hardly a trace remains of them today, though the Orthodox Church that is now in the city's Map'o district serves as a museum of their presence in the country.

Seoul's small Russian community was a vestige of the contact that flourished between Korea and Russia around the turn of the twentieth century. Until 1905, Korea had a diplomatic relationship with Czarist Russia. It dated from 1860 when Russia won the "maritime province" of Siberia, the Manchurian seacoast that touches northeastern Korea along an 11-mile border at its southern end. Russo-Korean relations began with a treaty in 1884, and the first Russian Minister to Korea, Karl Waeber, took up residence in Seoul the following year. By 1890, the Russians had built an imposing legation building atop Chŏng-dong hill. By 1903 there stood next door a small but beautiful Orthodox Church and Mission, with Archmandrite Chrysanth Scetkovski at the head of a faithful congregation. A gate in the wall connected the legation and church compounds. Together they housed a handful of Russian business families as well as the priests and legation staff.

The period between 1895 and 1904 was the high water mark of Russian interest in Korea and it was the Russians, and not the British or Americans, who committed the most to blocking the expansion of Japan onto the Asian mainland. The completion of the Trans-Siberian Railroad had created vital interests in Manchuria and Korea, and Czarist diplomats worked hard to assert Russia's strategic position. Imperial Japan worked just as hard to do the same for itself. In 1902 the Japanese signed a formal alliance with Great Britain, agreeing to help block Russian expansion in the Far East. The period of Czarist ascendancy in Korea ended forever in 1904 when the Imperial Japanese Navy attacked the Russian squadron at Port Arthur. By the end of 1905, after its victory in the Russo-Japanese War, Japan had eliminated all her rivals for hegemony over the Korean peninsula. The Russian Legation in Seoul was reduced to a consulate-general, the Russian investors withdrew, and the Russian community in Seoul became an isolated collection of small merchants and clerics manning the Orthodox Mission.

Sergei and Natalya's Korean Odyssey

One of the Russian consuls was Sergei Tchirkine, a career diplomat who had started out as an Arabic specialist and had served in Persia and India before being assigned to Seoul in 1910-11. Korea was not where Tchirkine wanted to be, and he lost no time getting himself transferred to southwest Asia: first Bukhara, and then Tashkent, in the Russian protectorate of Turkestan. In Tashkent he met and married the beautiful Natalya Efremoff, daughter of the civil governor. Then came the Russian Revolution. The fall of the Czar rendered Sergei and his bride essentially stateless. As the Reds were entering Tashkent, the couple slipped away to India where they threw themselves on the mercy of the British.

Having reached India, the Tchirkines counted their assets. They had their health, good educations, enough of Natalya's jewelry to take care of emergencies, and friends in many places. One of these was a German in Seoul, someone with whom Sergei had often played billiards at the Seoul Club. An exchange of telegrams brought news that there was work to be had in Korea. With a British-paid ticket Sergei and Natalya sailed for Korea, and by the end of the year they were ensconced in an apartment on the Orthodox Church compound in Chŏng-dong. Sergei got a desk job at the Bank of Chōsen, then moved to the tourist bureau to handle foreign-language correspondence, and ended up teaching languages at Keijō Imperial University and Seoul Foreign School. The Tchirkines were an attractive couple and made many friends. Natalya set herself up as a beautician, selling an old diamond ring to pay for hairdressing lessons in Harbin. Her beauty parlor and Sergei's teaching financed a reasonably comfortable life.

In 1924 the birth of twins Vladimir and Cyril put an end to the beauty parlor and necessitated a shift. Thereafter Natalya worked at home as a dress-
maker and music teacher.[1]

Reds, Whites, and the Fall of Vladivostok

Japan did not recognize the Russian Socialist Federated Soviet Republic
(RSFSR) or accept Soviet consular representatives in the Japanese Empire
until 1925. Until then, the Russian legation and church compound in Seoul
continued as a Czarist outpost without a mother country, while its handful
of inhabitants supported themselves. However, shortly after the Russian
Revolution the number of Russians in Seoul began to grow. As the Red
Army fought its way east along the Trans-Siberian and the remnants of the
White Army retreated toward Vladivostok, the day of reckoning approached for the merchants, landlords, and former officials of the Russian
Far East. The decisive battles came in October 1922, as the Whites struggled to buy time for an orderly evacuation from areas in the Bolsheviks'
path. As the fighting intensified and panic increased, there were thousands
of casualties. At length the people around Vladivostok were told to take
what they could carry and put out to sea on anything that would float.
More than fifteen thousand men, women, and children set out on a motley
flotilla of gunboats, freighters, fishing boats, scows, and rafts heading
south along the coastline of the Primorsk region past the mouth of the
Tumen River to the Korean port of Wŏnsan. Of these, about half continued
on to Shanghai;[2] but seven thousand remained behind in Wŏnsan to spend
the winter in makeshift shelters provided by the Japanese.

The Government-General of Chōsen was unprepared to handle the human wave at Wŏnsan, and every charitable organization in the country was
asked to help. Red Cross officials and missionaries who visited Wŏnsan told
of the most wretched conditions in freezing winter weather. When the White
officers ordered the people to evacuate Vladivostok on October 22-23, they
gave no time for them to make arrangements and they had been forced to
sell their valuables at painful losses: a sable coat for a few yen, a French au-

1. This passage is based in part on interviews with Cyril Tchirkine, Hayward,
California, on September 28, 1989, and June 24, 1991; "Ataman (Hetman) of the
Don," sketch of the Efremoff family from *Russian Life* (San Francisco), translated
by Cyril Tchirkine; and Bruce Taylor, Santa Rosa, California, interview, August 8,
1989; and memoranda regarding the Tcherkine family sent to the author in November 2001.

2. At Woosung, near Shanghai, the Chinese authorities initially forbade the people to land. *The Times* (London), November 1, 1922, p. 9. Not all the refugees went
south. Many of them went inland, over the border to Hunchun and Lungchingtsun
in southeastern Manchuria, where the local Canadian missionaries witnessed their
miserable circumstances. See description in William Scott to A.E. Armstrong, letter,
January 8, 1923.

tomobile for 60 rubles. Some had boarded ship with nothing. The fortunate few carried jewelry, but many others grabbed other objects they
hoped to use to finance their resettlement. Some of their choices were
odd: one refugee brought her small dog, explaining that it was paralyzed
and had to wear diapers; another brought the curtains from his office.[3]
The ones who managed to flee with valuables were the ones who managed to buy passage onward to Shanghai. The more destitute refugees
were forced to stay in Wŏnsan through the winter. Men offered a day's
work for a cup of tea and some bread, but no one would hire them. Some
were too injured to even look for work, and in the harsh conditions others
got sick. Captain Andrei Tyulkin was so shell-shocked that he could hardly
function, and his thirteen year-old daughter Lola spent much of the winter
near death from typhus and malnutrition.[4] W.A. Noble, an American missionary, described the situation at the time:

> [H]ere are about 2,500 officers and soldiers on the ships in Wŏnsan harbor
> and on the shore and 2,800 other fugitives from the civilian population that
> include 1,600 women and children. There are about 2,000 of this number
> still remaining aboard ship. Eighty percent of these people are of the peasant
> class, and illiterate. Twenty per cent are educated, and represent a fine type
> of the Cossack people. The condition of those aboard ship can best be de-
> scribed by reading the tales of the slave ships of the early days of colonial
> American history. The people on shore are housed in the discarded customs
> go-downs. They are living on the concrete floors, and the only heat in the
> building comes from a small stove located in its center....During these many
> weeks they have been living in improvised camps, and aboard ship without
> means of ordinary comfort and sanitary privileges. They are therefore help-
> less victims of filth and vermin, while famine stares them in the face.[5]

Eventually spring came and the Wŏnsan refugees slowly dispersed.
Some scraped together enough money to get to Shanghai, Tientsin, or
Harbin, where they found work. Some migrated as far away as Mexico,
Brazil, and Chile. A few went back out to sea as pirates, terrorizing fishing
fleets in the waters off Vladivostok and northern Korea. Those who stayed
in Korea drifted to provincial towns where they opened little shops, usually selling clothing. Some went to work for the foreign mining concessions. In Seoul, the refugees struggled for survival. "They are preoccupied
at this moment with the insistent necessity of struggling to keep the wolf

    3. *New York Times*, October 31, 1922, p. 5; *The Times* (London), October 21,
1922, p. 10; Canfield F. Smith, *Vladivostok under Red and White Rule* (Seattle:
University of Washington Press, 1975), pp. 159-174; Florence Murray, *At the Foot of
Dragon Hill*, p. 35.
    4. *New York Times*, October 31, 1922, p. 5. Lola Tyulkin Neumann, San Fran-
cisco, telephone interview, June 19, 1991. Andrei Tyulkin died in Seoul in 1941 and
is buried in the Seoul Foreigners' Cemetery at Yanghwajin.
    5. W.A. Noble, "The Russian Refugees at Wonsan," *The Korea Mission Field*,
XVIII:11 (December 1922), pp. 277-278.

from the door," wrote the editor of the *Seoul Press* in 1925. Some went in for smuggling, bringing gold watches and jewelry back across the border from Harbin. Russian prostitutes appeared in the Nandaimon-dōri district. The circumstances bred conflict among the Russians themselves and between Russians and Koreans and Japanese over such things as overdue rent and debts. But there were also those who carved out legitimate livelihoods. The Sizransky family started a bakery in the Saitō Building in Nandaimon 4-chōme. The Goncharoff family opened a confectionery called "Flora," and sold desserts made of chocolate and bananas, pineapple, and cream. Russian tailor shops sprouted in Honmachi, while individuals worked at odd jobs in hotels and banks and freelanced as translators, teachers, and household servants.[6]

Until 1925, since there was no Soviet-Japanese agreement about property or diplomatic and consular representation, the White consuls Maximilian Hefftler and Aleksandr Troitzki continued living in the old Russian legation property. But then came the signing of a Russo-Japanese agreement restoring diplomatic ties in February 1925, and the Hefftlers and Troitzkis were forced to vacate the property.[7] With no way to return to Russia and no place else to go, they fell back on their own resources: the Hefftlers started a language school and Mrs. Troitzki, who was French and knew Parisian haute couture, set up a dress shop selling "Elegant summer gowns in crepe de chine, marquisette, crepon, marrocain, voile, etc., of latest fashions each of different design and colour."[8]

Meanwhile, Seoul prepared to receive the first consular officials from the new Soviet government. The arrival of the consul-general, Basil Charmanoff, was marked by an incident. His entourage checked into the Chōsen Hotel pending occupation of the consulate buildings, and the first night the delegation was in Seoul, Charmanoff's secretary entered the consul's room while he was in the bathtub, found his gun, started playing with it, and accidentally fired it into the wall. The sound of shots in the Russians'

---

6. Thomas J. Carter, "Wonsan," *The Korea Mission Field*, XX:3 (March 1924), p. 65; Yongsin Ak'ademi, p. 235-328 and passim. *Seoul Press*, May 24, 1924, p. 4; January 30, 1925, p. 2; April 15, 1925, p. 3; April 25, 1925, p. 2; and May 22, 1925, p. 3; Yi Kyu-tae, *Modern Transformation of Korea*, p. 105. Kim and Chung, *Catholic Korea—Yesterday and Today*, p. 500; and conversations with priests at the Orthodox Church, Seoul, in May and June 1984, and with Nina Belogolovy Jacobson, Fremont, California, July 1989.

7. Japan recognized the Soviet Union in 1925 but continued to express disdain for Bolshevism by such things as prohibiting Japanese citizens from singing the Internationale because of its references to communism and anti-imperialism. *Seoul Press*, January 27, 1927.

8. *Seoul Press*, May 28, 1926, p. 2. Maximilian Hefftler, the last White Russian consul in Seoul in 1925, remained in business until the war, during which he made his way to Switzerland and lived there until his death in the 1980s. Horace G. Underwood, interview, June 1990.

suite created consternation and a flurry of police activity in the hotel. The story was told many times, but except for a bad first impression of the Soviets there was no lasting damage. When the Red consulate-general opened officially on September 24, the foreign community turned out in force—all but the Americans, whose government was still withholding recognition of the Bolshevik regime.[9]

Shortly after that, Charmanoff announced an amnesty for the White Russians in his jurisdiction, offering Soviet citizenship and travel papers to any Russian resident who came in to apply before May 1, 1926. There were few takers. The Whites hated the Reds, and for the next twenty years there was icy distance between the small consular staff and other Seoul Russians, even those across the wall in the church compound. People thought it silly that the consulate set up loudspeakers to blare martial music across the Chŏng-dong landscape on Soviet holidays. The children picked up their parents' conflicts and there were rock fights over the wall between the Tchirkine twins and the son of a Soviet consul who lived inside the consulate compound. Nearly a hundred Russians lived in Seoul in the late 1920s, but hardly any of them were Reds.

Russians, Red Beards, and Koreans at Sidemi

In the 1920s word began circulating in Seoul of the improbable presence of a great Russian tiger hunter living in the Korean mountains near the Manchurian border. Those who visited the hunter's camp returned with tales of a Swiss Family Robinson-type settlement run by a White Russian exile named Yankovsky and peopled by his relatives and retainers. However, because the Yankovskys had little contact with other non-Russian foreigners in Korea, their story has always been shrouded in mystery.

The Yankovskys were refugees who had fled the Bolsheviks in 1922, abandoning their lands near Vladivostok and reestablishing themselves un-

9. Arthur Hyde Lay, the British consul-general in Seoul, reported that Charmanoff "speaks neither English nor French, though he understands them a little. His secretary and another member of his staff know some English, while the fourth man speaks Japanese fairly well. With the exception of the last named, none of them have apparently been out of Russia before, though it is understood that the vice consul (elsewhere characterized as a 'youngish and somewhat sinister-looking man') spent some time in Persia but in what capacity is not known. It is surprising and great contrast to the practice of the [Czarist] regime that a personnel so ill-equipped linguistically should have been appointed. Socially also they are ignorant of the proper usages as none of the wives of the members of the consulate-general have paid the necessary official consular calls. The Authorities are anxious as to the form the activities of the new Russian officials will take and are watching them closely." Arthur Hyde Lay, "Report on Affairs in Corea during 1925," enclosed with Lay to Sir Charles Eliott (Ambassador in Tokyo), January 7, 1926. Public Record Office, FO file 262/663.

der the protection of the Japanese colonial regime in Korea. Their camp, which they named "Novina," became renowned among White Russians all over the East as a resort that attracted wild game enthusiasts from as far away as Sweden. It was also a favorite with Russian theatre people in Harbin and Shanghai, and in the summer at peak season there were often more than a hundred guests and family members in residence at Novina.

The original clan patriarch, Mikhail Yanovich Yankovsky, was a Polish nobleman who had been arrested by the Russians in 1863 and exiled to the Far East in 1870. Russia had just acquired the coastal strip of Manchuria in the 1860 Treaty of Peking, and Yankovsky was one of the earliest European settlers to arrive there. Joining forces with a Finnish whaling captain named Fridolf Gek, he staked a claim to an 8,000-acre estate in the Primorsk Region across Amur Bay from Vladivostok. He named his place "Sidemi" ("The Seat") and started raising little sika deer, the spotted animals whose horns are so prized in Chinese medicine. To tend his herd he hired Koreans and Chinese workers, and as they harvested deer antlers year by year, Yankovsky became a very rich man.[10]

Yankovsky's natural enemies at Sidemi were wolves and *hung hu-tze,* "Red Beards," the forerunners of the bandit armies that plagued the region well into the twentieth century. Naturally, as he grew wealthy, he had to build up his defenses. A system of barriers and watchtowers across the neck of the Sidemi peninsula did little to deter wolves, which simply went around the barriers on chunks of ice. The Red Beards likewise proved resourceful and cruel. Once in the 1870s, when Sidemi was still struggling to survive, Mikhail Yankovsky and Fridolf Gek returned from a supply run to Vladivostok to find that the outlaws had murdered Gek's wife, servants, and three of his children and had kidnapped a fourth. In a fury, Yankovsky rousted a posse of Russians and Koreans and chased the Red Beards inland, exterminating what he thought to be their main band at their camp. Gek's fourth child, however, was never found. Shattered, the captain left the settlement and returned to whaling, never to be seen again.[11]

In time, new neighbors came to Sidemi. One was Yulius Ivanovich Bryner, later famous as a player in Russian development plans for the Korean-Manchurian border, the recipient of a lucrative Yalu River timber con-

10. In fact, several thousand deer descended from the original Yankovsky herd are still roaming the site, which is now known as the Bezverhovo peninsula. From *Sidemi* (Vladivostok: Krasnoye Znanie, 1991), a brochure commemorating the unveiling of a statue of Mikhail Yankovsky at Bezverhovo in September 1991 and a videotape of the visit of Victoria Yankovsky and her son Orr Chistiakoff to Bezverhovo for the ceremony.

11. Valery Yankovsky, *Potomki Nenun* (Four Eyes' Descendants) (Moscow: Sovremennik, 1986), 30-37.

cession in 1896.[12] There was a family tie: Yankovsky and Bryner were married to cousins who had grown up together in Irkutsk. Another neighbor was Mikhail Sheveler, a merchant who had made his fortune trading tea in Hankow, China, shipping camel-loads of it across the Gobi to Russia. As Yankovsky, Bryner, and Sheveler worked together, they hired more men to help guard the land and tend the herd—men who came to be known as "Yankovsky's subjects."[13] Yankovsky turned his "subjects" into a private army, recruiting exclusively Koreans—whom he believed he could trust —to search out and destroy the Red Beards.[14] His own Red Beard-hunting skills were such that his subjects nicknamed him *"Chetire glaza"* ("Four Eyes") for the extra pair of eyes he seemed to have for seeking out the bandits. Yankovsky's children remembered being called *"nenun-ŭi aidŭl"* ("Four Eyes' kids") by the Korean employees."[15]

At Sidemi the Yankovskys had three sons, Yuri, Yan, and Paul, and they made sure that the boys got the equivalent of an upper-class Russian education. The peninsula, of course, was a nature laboratory, and the boys grew up with a deep appreciation for the land and its wildlife. Their father set the example, carefully collecting specimens of rare fauna and getting the

12. Andrew Malozemoff, *Russian Far Eastern Policy, 1881-1904* (New York: Octagon Books, 1977), p. 89 and passim. Ian Nish, *The Origins of the Russo-Japanese War* (London: Longman, 1985), pp. 155, 169; *The Korean Repository*, III (1896), p. 380.

Yulius Ivanovich Bryner (1849-1920), born in Switzerland and originally named Jules Johann Bryner, migrated to East Asia aboard a pirate vessel in the 1860s and worked for an English businessman in Yokohama before going into business for himself. After moving to Vladivostok and marrying Natalia Kurkutova, said to have been "the daughter of a Mongolian prince," he took the Russian name Yuli and made his fortune in the Vladivostok area. One of his residences was at Sidemi. One of his businesses was a timber concession on the Tumen River, granted by King Kojong at the urging of Russian Minister Karl Waeber in 1896. In 1898, Bryner sold the concession to the Russian government, and it was lost to the Japanese in the Russo-Japanese War. Yulius and Natalya Bryner had six children. Their son Boris was the father of actor Yul Brynner (1920-1985), who was noted for his "Oriental" roles, notably in Rogers and Hammerstein's *The King and I* on Broadway and in the movies. Rock Brynner, *Yul: The Man who Would Be King* (New York: Simon and Schuster, 1989), pp. 18-22.

13. Not everyone had fond memories of the fief at Sidemi. Mikhail Yankovsky's relationship with the locals is portrayed as feudal and exploitative in the Korean novel *Ma'ŭl saramdŭl* (Village People), by Myŏng Chŏl, published in *Lenin kich'i*, the Korean newspaper of Alma Ata (Alamaty), Kazakhstan, in installments (September 30 through October 3, 1980).

14. For a laudatory account of Koreans in the Ussuri area see Isabella Bird Bishop, "Koreans in Russian Manchuria," *The Korean Repository*, IV (1897), pp. 41-44.

15. Sten Bergman, *In Korean Wilds and Villages*, trans. Frederic Whyte (London: John Gifford, 1938), p. 133. Victoria Yankovsky, interview, Healdsburg, California, August 16, 1989.

Yankovsky name attached to previously undiscovered varieties such as the swan *Cygnus jankowskii*, the bunting *Emberiza jankowskii*, and the beetle *Captolabrus jankowskii*, among other regional flora and fauna.[16]

In 1900 the Yankovskys won a contract to raise horses for the Russian army in Vladivostok. Mikhail set out by rail and dog-sled to Omsk to buy a herd of horses. Oldest son Yuri ("George" in English) was dispatched to America to learn horse-breeding, first in Texas and then at the Golden Gate Fields stables in Berkeley, California. In Berkeley, George got interested in horse racing, and at the end of his stay he bought four horses for a new racing venture at the family's stable in Vladivostok.[17]

The Yankovskys' business diversification continued with a mink farm and a small ship repair facility on "Bryner's Point" at Sidemi. Mikhail, meanwhile, began to suffer increasingly from arthritis. In 1907 he retired to the healing waters of the Crimea where he died in 1912, leaving his various business interests to his sons. George meanwhile married the girl next door, Margarita ("Daisy") Shevelev, in an elegant Vladivostok church wedding. The moneymaking continued with government contracts, and the Yankovskys entered the shipping business with a tugboat and string of barges purchased in order to haul sand for a Vladivostok city beach.

By 1917, George and Daisy had two daughters and three sons and their businesses had gone international: the Japanese colonial government in Korea was buying their horses. But then came the Russian Revolution. At first the Bolsheviks were nothing but a distant rumble, but then they started coming east. By 1922, the landlords of the Primorsk region knew their days were numbered, and they made plans to pull out. At Sidemi, the Yankovsky family also got ready to pull up stakes. Hoping that their exile would be temporary, George dispatched one of his brothers to the Korean port of Ch'ŏngjin to buy a house and a place to keep the animals. But then Vladivostok's defenses suddenly collapsed and the orderly retreat became a sudden flight. Towing barges laden with family members, servants, retainers, horses, and deer, George captained the tugboat from Sidemi to Ch'ŏngjin, in time to spend the winter in a tiny mud-walled Korean farmhouse.

16. Richard Howard and Alick Moore, *A Complete Checklist of the Birds of the World* (Oxford: Oxford University Press, 1980), p. 536; Michael Gore and Won Pyong-oh, *The Birds of Korea* (Seoul: Royal Asiatic Society, 1969), p. 421; Willard Price, "Jap Rule in the Hermit Nation," *The National Geographic Magazine*, LXXXVIII:4 (October 1945), p. 432; conversations with Victoria and Muza Yankovsky, Healdsburg, California, August 16, 1989 and June 24, 1991. There is also a 15-kopeck USSR stamp issued in 1981 with the bird *Ovsranka Yankovskovo*.

17. Victoria Yankovsky, interview, Santa Rosa, California, December 19, 1992. The Yankovskys enjoyed telling about the look on the stable owner's face when the presumably impoverished George plunked down cash for the four fine horses.

The Mighty Hunter at Novina

Reestablishing the Yankovskys in Korea was no small task. To meet expenses, they sold off some of their animals and experimented with various small businesses. An attempt to break into the transportation business failed when local carters went to the authorities to object to the competition. A try at herring fishing in the Sea of Japan brought protests from the local fishermen. To cut costs Yankovsky furloughed many of his "subjects," sending them to Shanghai and Harbin and inland to find jobs.

Meanwhile the Yankovskys themselves found opportunities in the hinterland. Here were the foothills of Paektu-san, Korea's sacred mountain, covered with forests that were rich in game animals including deer for horn and venison and boar for pork. In 1926, Yankovsky closed a deal with the Japanese army to supply meat for the troops, and with this much steady income assured, he set up his hunting headquarters on a site twelve miles above the town of Chu'ŭl on a horseshoe bend of the rushing Chu'ŭl River, the spot he named "Novina," the "New Place." Novina lasted nineteen years from 1926 to 1945, during which the Yankovskys supported themselves by farming, animal breeding, hunting, and selling game, and opening their colony as a resort. As they built cabins along the river they built their clientele by word of mouth, using family connections to bring in Russian expatriates from Shanghai.

George Yankovsky and trophies at Novina. Courtesy of Victoria Yankovsky.

As time passed, Novina came to depend on tourists who came for the coolness and the enchantment of the Paektu-san foothills. Yankovsky and his children organized treks up the mountain in the summer and hunting expeditions in the fall and winter. The area was renowned for the Manchurian tiger,;and George relished his reputation as "Asia's Mighty Tiger Hunter." On a cliff above the river George built the family's main house, an interesting building constructed around the trunk of a great tree that appeared to hold it in place. Above this he built a "Tower of the Ancestors," a partial replica of Sidemi, and next to this a lodge that was partly in a cave used by the family as a

The Yankovsky family and guests before the Tower of the Russias, Novina, circa 1937. Courtesy of Victoria Yankovsky.

Great Hall. Below, he stretched a chain bridge across the Chu'ŭl River, and farther down he built a row of huts for his servants and farmhands. There were orchards for apples and pears, fields for vegetables, and hives for honey, all tended by Novina's Korean workers, while the mountain forests furnished abundant venison, pork, and pheasant. Evenings at Novina featured dinners with as many as twenty people seated at the dining table, followed by vodka and storytelling by the fireplace in the cave.[18]

18. See Yankovsky's autobiography, originally published in Harbin: Yura Mikhailovich Yankovsky, *Polveka Okhoti n Tigrov* (Half a Century of Hunting Tigers), reprint, Series Arsenevskaya Biblioteka (Vladivostok: Ussuri, 1990). For details of life at Novina the author is grateful to Michael Hintze, of Sydney, Australia, for his English-language translation of Valery Yankovsky's memoir entitled *From the Crusades to Gulag and Beyond,* 2d. ed. (Sydney: private print, 2001), and to Cyril Tchirkine for making a copy of the translation available.

Sunday services also took place there,[19] and plays in the summer tourist season. Many of the visitors were show people from Shanghai who liked to amuse themselves by staging productions at Novina.[20] In fact, Novina's reputation for theatre is what attracted the former Shanghai actress Mary Linley Taylor, one of the camp's few non-Russian visitors from Seoul.

Mary Taylor learned of Novina by accident, through her friend Natalya Tchirkine. She was visiting the Tchirkines' one day for tea, when a lithe Russian teenager entered the room in soft leather slippers, dressed in a soft leather "Indian" smock and wearing tiger-tooth earrings. The girl seemed shy, even mysterious, and spoke only broken English, so Natalya had to interpret. She was "Ora," or Victoria, the second daughter of the famous tiger hunter George Yankovsky at Novina. Mary sat raptly as she heard the family's story for the first time. By the end of the visit she had vowed to visit and had gotten a promise from Victoria to get her an invitation. Before long she was on the train to the tiny station at Chu'ŭl to be met by a Yankovsky car for the trip up the valley to the campsite. On this and subsequent visits, Mary Taylor collected enough Yankovsky lore to write a book with fairy-tale overtones:

> If one believed [the Korean rumors], one must also believe that this was not only a family of fabulous hunters, but that they lived in a castle which was only prevented from sliding into an abyss by one great tree that supported it. This castle, it was said, had a high tower, in which a gruesome dragon was kept prisoner, because he had fallen in love with the hunter's beautiful daughter. One only had to hear his woeful bellowings to know that this was true! Hearsay also had it that the Hunter-in-chief had saved his wife's life by cutting out her appendix with his hunting knife, and it was also said that this family lived solely on tiger steak and vodka! But, said the informants, the most astonishing thing of all was that the Japanese allowed such barbarians to remain in the country, and even let them fly the "Flag of all the Russias."[21]

For the real-life people at Novina, however, life was less a fairy tale than a test of character. At first the Yankovskys' five children—Muza, Victoria, Valery, Arsenii, and Yuri—were tutored by a "home gymnasium" teacher from Harbin. Muza, the eldest, turned eighteen during the first year at Novina when there were no parties, plays, music, or eligible boys. Two

---

19. Yankovsky's priest was from the Russian Orthodox Diocese in Harbin. This sparked a territorial objection from the church in Seoul, in whose territory Novina was located. Yankovsky responded by declaring Novina independent of *all* church authority. Victoria Yankovsky, interview, Healdsburg, California, August, 1989.

20. Victor Petrov, *Shanhai na Vampu* ("Shanghai on the Huangpu")(Washington, D.C.: Russkovo Amerikanskovo Istorichenskovo Obshchestva [Russian-American Historical Society], 1985), p. 85.

21. Mary Linley Taylor, *The Tiger's Claw: The Life Story of East Asia's Mighty Hunter* (London: Burke, 1956), pp. 23-24.

years later, shortly after a feckless Japanese frightened her with a clumsy marriage proposal, the family decided to send her to live with her maternal relatives in Shanghai, where there were eligible Russian boys.[22]

Victoria, two years younger than Muza, was the child who seemed to embrace life at Novina with the greatest gusto. Victoria was the tomboy, the one who pleased her father by learning how to track animals in the mountains as well as any of the Korean guides and shoot as straight as any of the Yankovsky men. In her twenties she affected her "Tarzanka" style with Indian dresses and a trademark headband, jewelry made from tiger's teeth, or, when it was warm enough, daring two-piece outfits like the one in the treasured 1932 snapshot where she stands

Victoria Yankovsky in summer hunting attire, Novina, 1932. Courtesy of Victoria Yankovsky, 1989.

with a rifle by her side. "Tarzanka's" personal deity was Pan, the god of nature, and when her father built a little Korean house for her to live in by herself on the riverbank, she installed a shrine containing a statue of Pan playing his flute. As a teenager she spent many hours in her hut writing poems and burning incense before the statue, and people who visited Novina as children recall sneaking up on Victoria's hut to listen to her chanting her mantra and reading poems to herself.[23]

Novina continued with its cast of characters until 1945, profiting from George Yankovsky's good relations with the Japanese. In the late 1930s, even as other foreigners in Korea were being kept away from the seashore and having their cameras, maps, and radios confiscated, the Yankovskys were allowed to open a branch resort on the ocean near Novina.[24] Wartime

22. Muza Yankovsky, interview, Healdsburg, California, August 16, 1989, and Harriet Sergeant, *Shanghai: Collision Point of Cultures, 1918-1939* (New York: Crown Publishers, 1990), 43-45.

23. Cyril Tchirkine, June 26, 1991. Victoria Yankovsky later published some of these poems together with others from other phases of her life under the title *Po stranam rasseyaniya* (Through the Lands of Exiles)(New York: Am-izdat, 1977).

24. The resort was named "Lukomorie," or "Bow-and-Arrow," from a reference in Pushkin's *Luslan and Ludmilla*. The Japanese name for the spot was "Ryuken," which the Yankovskys thought sounded roughly similar.

travel restrictions kept it from developing into anything more than a beach house for Novina's own residents, and the Yankovskys had to give it up after Pearl Harbor. They continued to do business at Novina, however, supplying meat and produce to the Japanese. This was a short-term blessing but also a long-term curse, for when the Soviet Red Army occupied North Korea after the war, the Yankovskys had to face the consequences of being not only anticommunist White Russians but also wartime collaborators with the Japanese.

-- 7 --

Life and Death on the Manchurian Frontier

In 1931, Army General Ugaki Kazushige replaced Admiral Saitō Makoto as governor-general of Chōsen. Ugaki's five-year tenure brought the remilitarization of colonial rule in Korea, a development that was related to Japan's takeover of Manchuria in 1931-32. The creation of the puppet state of Manchukuo was a key part of Japan's expansion onto the Asian mainland in the 1930s, and the Tokyo government was determined to let nothing threaten its hold on its new possession. As a result, beginning in 1932, Korea became a staging area for Japan's economic and military exploitation of the mainland. Like Japan itself, Korea became militarized over the course of the 1930s, and there was correspondingly less toleration for dissent, foreign ideas, and foreign people.

The large number of Koreans living in Manchuria made it easier for Japan to justify its expansion beyond the Korean border. In Chientao alone there were about 400,000 Koreans in 1930, comprising 80 percent of the population.[1] This sizable community was the result of a combination of historical and political factors. The border between Chientao and Hamgyŏng Province had always been porous, with merchants and migrants freely crossing the Tumen River for decades. Japanese occupation authorities in Korea had encouraged migration to Chientao and beyond to help colonize the area and establish a Japanese presence there; and displaced sharecroppers and impoverished migrants from southern Korea had trekked there in search of jobs and land. Manchuria historically had not been part of the Chinese empire. It was the homeland of the Jurchen people, ancestors of the Manchus, and when the Manchus conquered China

1. Government-General of Chōsen, *Annual Report on Administration of Chōsen, 1930* (Keijō: Government-General of Chōsen, 1931), p. 16; also *Seoul Press*, October 11, 1930, p. 3.

proper and established the Ch'ing dynasty in 1644, they decreed the preservation of their homeland in its pristine, lightly populated state. It remained lightly populated, undeveloped, and essentially undefended until the late nineteenth century when it became the object of rivalry between the Russians and Japanese. Between 1890 and 1911 the Ch'ing Empire tried belatedly to establish enough of a Chinese and Manchu presence in Manchuria to preempt a takeover by either the Russians or the Japanese. This brought about an infusion of rootless Chinese in search of opportunity, creating a wild frontier atmosphere. In the 1890s, the Russians contributed to this by beginning railroads through Manchuria with key terminals in the Russianized towns of Harbin and Port Arthur. In 1905 the Japanese evicted the Russians and continued the development of Manchuria through two instruments: the South Manchurian Railway Company, a quasi-governmental agency that ruled the right-of-way between Port Arthur and Harbin, and the Kwantung Army, a field force headquartered on the Kwantung Peninsula in Dairen. The job of the Kwantung Army was to protect the South Manchurian Railway and other Japanese interests in Manchuria. Its historical importance was as a spearhead for Japan as it reached for hegemony over all of northeast Asia in the 1930s.

Two indigenous forces slowed the Japanese thrust into Manchuria. One was the Manchurian army of the warlord Chang Tso-lin that had evolved into a force loosely allied with the Republic of China under Chiang Kai-shek by the time the Kwantung Army assassinated Chang Tso-lin in 1928. The other was an assortment of private armies, some of them not much better than criminal gangs. These derived from the ancient tradition of secret societies, from village self-defense forces, from drug lords fighting to protect turf, and from the turn-of-the-century Russian "Red Beards" (the *hung hu-tzu*).

Once Japan had displaced Russia in Manchuria and established its protectorate over Korea, it set about merging its continental holdings via a process that extended into the 1930s. In Chientao, where Korean farmers had freely crossed over to work the rich alluvial soil of the Tumen River valley, the Japanese set up a branch of the Government-General of Chōsen, complete with the military forces that later became involved in the notorious "Chientao Incident" of 1920 (see chapter 3). The Japanese were there to protect imperial interests in the area including Koreans who were imperial subjects; but they were also there to show the Japanese flag. When Japanese outposts were attacked, as in 1920 by Koreans, in 1923 by Chinese, and in the 1930s by partisans of the Korean Communist Kim Il-sung, they responded with repression, contributing to a self-perpetuating cycle of violence and suffering.

During the 1920s, the Japanese intentionally blurred the boundary between Manchuria and Korea, the better to promote their expansion. Japanese scholarship focused on the origins of the Korean people and their southward migrations from Manchuria, along with the histories of the early Korean kingdoms that owned territory north and south of the Yalu River. Koreans were encouraged to settle in Chientao and beyond, as far as Harbin. Coincidentally, Chinese workers and settlers also moved into Korea with relative ease, and many of Korea's cities had significant Chinese minorities in recognizable Chinatowns.

By 1930 more than six hundred thousand Koreans were living in Manchuria, and they comprised a unique field for Western missionary work. The Canadian Presbyterian Mission in Korea had "annexed" Chientao when they opened their station in Lungchingtsun shortly after the annexation to serve the Korean population there. They had witnessed Japanese retribution against Koreans there during the Independence Movement. In an area saturated with political ideologies ranging from traditional Confucian to nationalist and ultraleftist, the Canadians faced the challenge of supporting a community of Korean Christians who were in an ideological competition with everyone from cultural xenophobes to communists.

Terror in Chientao

The Canadians were directly affected by the political trouble simmering in Chientao during the 1920s. Arsonists set fire to their Bible Institute at Lungchingtsun. Were they "communists"? The missionaries doubted it.[2] They prayed for an end to the violence, longing for the kind of peace that seemed so much better suited to the rich, even polychromatic, landscape once described by Duncan MacRae:

> It stirs one's heart to look out over those great rolling hills and mountains of "the land in between" (Chientao). The hills and mountains are now coloured with red, orange, green, yellow, gold, and black with ripened crops of white rice and black rice, golden millet and red millet, green beans, yellow beans, white beans, black beans, green flax, red pepper, green tobacco and red sorghum, golden wheat, and yellow corn. Anywhere, everywhere, on the beautiful plains, the deep valleys, over the rolling hills up the crest of the mountain peaks, this is to be seen, and towering over all, oats, potatoes, and turnips crown the summits of the mountain ranges. The heads of a golden harvest droop heavily with one of the richest crops that has rewarded the "hardy hands of toil" for many years.[3]

2. "'Blame Russia' is the easy way to account for everything nowadays." D.A. Macdonald to A.E. Armstrong, December 9, 1930. UCCA, 83.006C, box 2, file 40.

3. Duncan MacRae to A.E. Armstrong, September 24, 1930. UCCA, 83.006C, Box 2, File 44. Much of the following material is from this handwritten 17-page letter that is an eyewitness account of conditions in Manchuria. The letter is reprinted in Dae-Sook Suh and Edward J. Shultz, eds., *Koreans in China*, Papers of the Center for Korean Studies, No. 16 (Honolulu: University of Hawaii Press, 1990), pp. 166-173.

But if the land was so fruitful, why was there such discontent? Because "the moneylender 'croucheth at the door' and the official squeezes must be paid," wrote MacRae. "Anxiety in many homes, for loved ones are in prison; sorrow in other homes, for breadwinners have been shot. Others are missing and they know not where they have gone. Homes are deserted. The rice pot is cold in the kitchen and the doors are left open."

The innocent crops described by MacRae were not, however, the prime commodity in Manchuria at the time. Manchuria was experiencing opium fever. The open lands were perfect for poppy growing. Vast profits awaited anyone able to harvest and export opium from southern Manchuria, profits that could fund a private army with plenty to spare. In the twenties and thirties, Chientao, the area most populated by Koreans, was experiencing an "opium rush" comparable to a gold rush, with all its attendant claim-jumping and general mayhem.[4]

The nominal ruler of Manchuria, the warlord Chang Tso-lin's son and heir Chang Hsueh-liang, aka the "Young Marshal," was powerless against the heavily armed lords of the countryside around Chientao. The odds against making an honest living were formidable in an area infested with bloodthirsty local warlord troops, apolitical *hung hu-tzu*, highly political communists, and shiploads of penniless Chinese vagrants from Shantung coming in through Dairen in search of work. Survival required belonging to a protector. Korean farmers were tenants renting from landlords who were protected by warlords getting rich on the opium trade. Until the Japanese Kwantung Army established control over Chientao in the mid-thirties, people had little choice but to pay them tribute. Communists, on the other hand, rightly decried the exploitative conditions of life in Manchuria. Seeking armed struggle they recruited from among the farmers, and to motivate the recruitment they used violence too.

It took fortitude to live peacefully in the harsh conditions that obtained in Chientao. Local people were chronically in debt, victimized by moneylenders who charged compound interest in excess of 50 percent per month. A farmer borrowing money in the spring would face an impossibly high debt by the time of the fall harvest. Or, alternatively, if he promised to repay the loan with part of his crop, say beans, the lender would set an artificially low price on his beans as part of the contract and he would end up spending most of his crop just to pay the debt.

The law was no help. The local Chinese police were supposed to keep order, but they were only paid four dollars a month and so every transaction required a payment of "customary fees" called "squeeze." To generate squeeze, the police invented reasons to detain people. Even when there was a legitimate charge and the accused was acquitted in court, he re-

4. Owen Lattimore, *Manchuria, Cradle of Conflict* (New York: Macmillan, 1932), pp. 187-197.

mained in detention until the "customary fees" were paid. The Chientao Koreans said they preferred the Japanese: at least if you were acquitted in their courts you got out of jail.

The Chinese landlords were relentless in their pursuit of their mortal enemy, the communists. Wherever the communists visited in search of food and funds the Chinese police were sure to follow, taking villagers to the prison at Lungchingtsun for interrogation. One example:

> I am very sorry to say that Mr. Hong and Mr. Yu Tai Song have been accused of complicity with the Communists and have been in the Kookjaga [Lung-chingtsun] jail for the past five months. In truth these men have no slightest concern with Communism but had some slight differences with two members of [their village] police force....The police arrested them and searched their houses and the church. In Yu's house they found a book with some extracts from a writing by Mr. Chung In Kwa [Chŏng In'gwa, a Sunday School secretary in Seoul] in which the word "communism" was found....

> They found in Mr. Hong's drawer a letter addressed to "The Chosen School" in which was a note concerning the death of a Communist. The letter was not addressed to Mr. Hong at all and as there are three Korean schools in the town, how could they know which one it was for?[5]

Woes multiplied when people took any kind of action in their own behalf.

> A well-to-do Korean family in the country was suspected of giving information to the police, in regard to demands that had been made on them for money by Communists. Some of them were arrested, not long after. One night a visit was made to this home by friends of those arrested. One son was shot and killed.

> The family moved in to Lungchingtsun for safety. Here again one night two men came to the home demanding money. While the wife was conducting the men to the room occupied by her husband, one of the men noticed a Japanese policeman in the yard. Immediately shooting began. The two robbers were killed. One was recognized as one of two bandits who killed three Japanese on the train, when trying to rob [an official] who was carrying money to the Chief Commissioner of Customs at Lungchingtsun.

> This last episode in the home was too much for them, so they decided to sell out and move back to Korea. The mother and son went to the country home to gather up their belongings. The first night there, friends of the dead robbers visited the home and shot mother and son, killing them both.[6]

5. Yi Syung Kuk to E.J.O. Fraser, October 27, 1930. UCCA, 83.006C, Box 2, File 44. The documents in question were in mixed Chinese and Korean script, with the Chinese police only able to make out the characters for such nouns as "Communism," while they could only presume what the Korean script meant.
6. Duncan MacRae to A.E. Armstrong, September 24, 1930. UCCA, 83.006C, Box 2, File 44.

The only organized political ideology in the area was the local form of communism. Christians and communists were outraged by many of the same things, but they differed in their solutions to problems. The Christians were reformers whose proposed changes were too slow for the communists, who wanted radical action. The communists galled the Christians by coming into towns from their "revolutionary bases" to take over meetings, often in the Christians' own churches, and giving speeches claiming that violent revolution was the only answer. The Canadian missionaries liked to tell the story of a young communist who was heard haranguing a crowd with an attack on the reformers. "Even the Christian church, what is it doing for us?" He demanded. And a passing Korean clergyman shouted back, "What is the Christian church doing? In this city we have four churches giving instruction and teaching, a kindergarten, a night school for girls, a hospital giving treatment to rich and poor, two high schools where 2,000 are enrolled who would not otherwise get an education, an old ladies' home, and a YMCA. The Christian population of this city is only about 1/20 of the entire population. What is the other 19/20 doing?"[7]

The Wanpaoshan Incident

The political cacophony in Manchuria was heard in Korea as Japanese-controlled newspapers carried stories throughout the 1920s about Chinese attacks on Koreans beyond the border. The incidents grew more frequent as the Government-General encouraged Koreans to penetrate farther north, giving them cash grants to develop land, particularly land for rice to be exported to Japan. By 1928 there were half-a-million Koreans in the Harbin-Tsitsihar region, a few of them deportees or refugees from Russia, but most of them migrants from Korea, especially the southwestern Chŏlla provinces. These were harassed, taxed, kidnapped, and even killed by local Chinese and police and had to take up weapons to defend themselves. The terms of their leases on farmland were reportedly disadvantageous—rarely exceeding three years—meaning that Manchurian landlords were using the Koreans to do the hard work of reclaiming the land and getting it into cultivation, and then taking it back.[8] Meanwhile, Chinese migrant workers entered Korea every spring to earn money as day laborers: 25,000 of them

---

7. William Scott, Report, March 26, 1938. UCCA, 83.006C, Box 4, File 97.

8. See discussion of how the Chinese in Manchuria "abused and dispossessed Korean farmers, [turning them] out of the marshlands which they have rented and converted into fertile rice fields at the termination of the very short lease, rarely exceeding three years." Consul-General F.E. Wilkinson (Mukden) to Ambassador Miles W. Lampson (Peking), dispatch # 51, December 20, 1927, Public Record Office file FO 262/1688 (1927).

in 1928, and 30,000 by the middle of 1929.[9] Many of these returned home after the harvest but some remained, and Chinatowns developed in Korea's major cities. By 1930, the ethnic Chinese population within Korea was officially numbered at 67,797.[10]

Chinese in Korea became targets of reprisals whenever there was news of trouble involving Korean settlers in Manchuria. In November 1927, news that Chinese police were removing Korean settlers from their lands in Manchuria sparked three weeks of attacks on Chinese living in Korea.[11] In July 1931, there was a climactic confrontation between Korean farmers in northern Manchuria and local Chinese over water rights and the building of an irrigation ditch near the town of Wanpaoshan in the vicinity of Changchun. The fields' owners had attacked Koreans digging the ditch across some neighboring fields without permission. It seemed that Japanese intentionally exaggerated reports of the incident reaching Korea in an attempt to inflame the Koreans. The news touched off a wave of reprisals against Chinese people and neighborhoods in towns within Korea. In P'yŏngyang, a Korean mob laid waste to the Chinese business quarter, burning and looting the shops and covering the street with Chinese belongings. The riot broke out suddenly and the Westerners feared that it was a general outbreak against all foreigners. Some fled in cars. Others stayed behind barricaded doors as the mob approached the Presbyterian compound in search, not of Westerners but of the compound's Chinese gardeners.[12] From his front porch, Charlie Clark observed the riot that threatened the Presbyterian compound.

> Monday evening the mob came out of the city towards our compound at about 11 p.m. My Korean friends tell me that at about 11 men began running from house to house throughout the city beating on the doors with clubs and demanding that at least one man from each house come out to swell the mob. Most houses responded from curiosity as much as from anything else, and the mob grew and grew. The new Matsunaga-dori between the two halves of our Presbyterian compound is 72 feet wide. The mob passed through that and from 11 to 3 a.m. a large part of the mob just stayed there and yelled. The leaders went on out beyond where there were perhaps 20 thatched houses of Chinese market gardeners. These houses they set fire to and of course that still further inflamed the mob.

9. *Seoul Press*, June 29, 1929, p. 2; July 3, 1929, p. 2; August 18, 1929, p. 2; August 22, 1929, p. 2; February 23, 1930, p. 2; September 13, 1930, p. 2.
10. Government-General of Chōsen, *Annual Report on Administration of Chōsen, 1930*, p. 13.
11. *Seoul Press*, July 7, 1931, p. 2.
12. These "gardeners" were Chinese truck farmers working little patches of land up by the compound. They were murdered with great brutality. For example: "...another Chinese was held 'spread-eagled' on the ground by several Koreans while another went and brought a heavy earthenware jar which he dropped upon the victim's head." Davis to SecState, July 8, 1931 (895.4016/18).

One half of our compound had no gate in front of it and the people in the houses nearest that gateway, the Lutzes, Hamiltons and three [business] families deserted their houses about 1 a.m. and took refuge at Bernheisel's, the furthest house from the gate. The thing of interest in all this... is that apparently there were no police, gendarmes, or soldiers anywhere around those eight American residences or the other 13 residences near by. It was only the mercy of the Lord that brought it about that some drunken communist did not call attention to those dwellings and to the fact that there had been no loot available that night....If one such shout had gone up those houses and all the rest of our dwellings might have been cleaned out as were the Chinese houses....Apparently the leaders of the mob knew the exact location of every Chinese in town. The blue clothes of the Chinese betrayed them everywhere, so many of the Chinese stripped them off and went naked to avoid notice....One Chinese doctor who has always worn the white Korean clothes presumed on that and did not flee, but the rioters knew his house and he was killed so I was told.[13]

The vulnerability of missionaries in any such disturbance was a serious worry. Though anti-Western violence was rare in Korea, it was a fact of life in nearby China. Barely thirty years had passed since the Boxers murdered scores of Westerners, including missionaries, in China's Shantung Province across the Yellow Sea. More recently, in 1927, Chinese Nationalist troops had abused foreigners during their Northern Expedition and had actually murdered an American administrator at Nanking University.[14] More than a hundred China missionaries had fled to Korea for safety during the outbreaks, their housing and care being arranged by a special relief committee.[15] Nothing comparable had occurred in Korea itself since the massacre of Catholics in 1866, but neither had there been anything like the anti-Chinese rampage that followed the Wanpaoshan Incident in 1931. Especially distressing was the way the Japanese police stood by and seemed entirely too willing to let the enraged Koreans take care of the colony's troublesome Chinese minority problem. As they stood powerless to help the hapless Chinese, the missionaries wondered whether the police would be any more willing to defend them if the mob turned anti-Western.[16] Knowing

13. Charles Allen Clark to U.S. Consul-General C. H. Stephan (Seoul), July 15, 1931, enclosed with Stephan to SecState, July 31, 1931 (895.4016/25).

14. Kenneth Scott Latourette, *A History of Christian Missions in China* (London: Society for Promoting Christian Knowledge, 1929), pp. 815-821. In the Nanking Incident, advancing Kuomintang troops deliberately looted missionary compounds as they entered the city in March 1927, and killed Nanking University vice-president John E. Williams in front of his own home. See Paul A. Varg, *Missionaries, Chinese, and Diplomats* (New York: Octagon Books, 1977), pp. 180-193.

15. The refugees numbered one hundred Americans and two Britishers. V.L.P. Foulke, "Annual Report . . . 1927," enclosed with G.T. Paton to Ambassador John Tilley, January 9, 1928, Public Record Office, file FO 262/1707.

16. Elsewhere, where the anti-Chinese attacks were smaller, missionaries did intervene to shield the intended victims. In Seoul, for example, the Australian doctor

how the Japanese felt about alleged missionary involvement in the 1919 Independence Movement, might it not be tempting to allow angry Koreans to rid the colony of Americans and Europeans as well? Looking at the wreckage of P'yŏngyang's Chinatown it seemed that such a thing could happen. The foreigners' favorite Chinese tailor shop, Taion and Co., had been sacked, and bolts of Taion's finest cloth hung from the light poles and lay trampled in the street. Taion's manager, P.C. Yang, was in hiding, and the Chinese who could pull up stakes were leaving the country in droves.[17]

Most of P'yŏngyang's Americans missed the Wanpaoshan riots because they were away at Sorai Beach. PYFS too was on summer vacation. But the fighting that continued all summer between Koreans and Chinese was of direct concern to the missions—the Canadians, Methodists, and Northern Presbyterians—that had missionaries in Manchuria. The Canadians insisted they were safe enough at Lungchingtsun because of the Japanese Army's control of the town itself; but farther west, nearer to Mukden, there were attacks on Japanese and Koreans. At Hsinpin, a Northern Presbyterian Mission station 85 miles due east of Mukden (now known as Shenyang), things were much more dangerous. The local Chinese general was violently anti-Japanese and had sworn to fight them to the bitter end. Hsinpin was isolated: it lay fifty miles from the nearest railroad, the only mail service was a monthly run-of-the-gauntlet from Mukden, and the only source

---

C. I. McLaren took in about ten Chinese—one with a nasty head wound—on July 3 and held off an angry mob of Koreans who claimed they had murdered three Korean girls, long enough to summon the police to take charge. John K. Davis to SecState, July 9, 1931 (895.4016/18). And at Sorai Beach, the foreign resort community closed ranks around Chinese grocer "E.D. Steward" who was operating a summertime concession. The Underwoods gassed up the engine on the *Black Duck* to spirit the Chinese out to sea if the need arose. In the end, a group of American teenagers borrowed one of the missionaries' cars and drove Steward inland to the railroad and transportation home to Seoul. Fran Lampe Peterson, interview, Seoul, May 9, 1990. Bruce Found, letter to the author, July 24, 1991. Also, statement of Miss Margaret Best, Presbyterian missionary from P'yŏngyang, at the American Legation, Peking, enclosed with Johnson to SecState, August 14, 1931 (895.4016/30).

   17. P.C. Yang, Taion's Chinese manager, suffered the deaths of two daughters not long after the Wanpaoshan Incident, deaths he attributed to fright from the riots. He left Korea not long after that, leaving the management of the tailor shop in the hands of missionary son George McAfee McCune who used Sungsil College students to help make and deliver the goods. William P. Parker, letter to "Fellow Workers," August 31, 1931, MCD Letters, Presbyterian Church (U.S.A.), Department of History, Montreat, North Carolina.

   By July 10, four thousand Chinese had fled Korea across the Yalu at Sinuiju/ Antung and one thousand more left Inch'ŏn aboard ship. *Seoul Press*, July 10, 1931, p. 2; July 11, 1931, p. 2. Thousands more left by rail and ship during the months that followed.

of news was the short wave radio through which there crackled a nightly English-language broadcast from Paris.[18]

A Bullet at Midnight

Two months after the Wanpaoshan Incident, on September 18, 1931, Japan's Kwantung Army staged an explosion on the South Manchurian Railway south of Mukden, accused local Chinese troops of sabotage, and used the incident as the excuse for a general takeover of Manchuria. Though their assault was a violation of the League of Nations Covenant and the Kellogg-Briand Pact, the Japanese claimed they were doing the world a favor by imposing order on the lawless Manchurian region. Eventually they turned Manchuria into the puppet state of "Manchukuo"; however, in 1932 they had not yet asserted control over every part of Manchuria, and the Hsinpin area was one that was still being contested. As fighting continually ebbed and flowed around them, the Hsinpin Presbyterian missionaries in their brick houses minimized the danger, at least from the people of their town. They had long since taken basic precautions. The two American couples, the W.T. Cooks and the Lloyd Hendersons, had steel shutters on their windows to protect against stray bullets at night. Maud Cook and Helen Henderson spent their time close to home while only the men went out, accompanied by their Korean and Chinese coworkers. Their job was to canvass the area, traveling miserable tracks passable only by mule-powered wooden Chinese carts, to visit villages where there were Korean churches. Cart travel along the ruts was slow and uncomfortable, and it made the riders tempting targets for small-time holdup artists bent on stealing a little cash.

Presbyterian missionary Lloyd Henderson sometimes wrote about his experiences on the back roads of Manchuria. In May 1932, for example, he had an adventure. Coming home from a trip he ran into a gang of bandits who called themselves the Big Sword Society.[19] The Big Swords had taken temporary possession of Hsinpin town, and in order to get home Henderson had to coax his carter, his Chinese servant, his Korean cook, and his

18. E.J.O. Fraser to A.E. Armstrong, December 6, 1932. UCCA, 83.006C, Box 2, File 54.

19. The Big Swords (Ta-tao hui) were a semireligious secret society related to the Red Spears, who were descended from the turn-of-the-century Boxers. They had been invited by Tunghua-area landowners to come up and help protect them from bandits. When they became a power in the area, the warlord government in Mukden outlawed them and sent troops to suppress them. The battles swept back and forth through Hsinpin, among other places, and when the Japanese Kwantung Army took over Manchuria in 1931-32, it inherited the task of suppressing the Big Swords. See Chong-Sik Lee, *Revolutionary Struggle in Manchuria*, pp. 73-74.

team of mules through the line of battle between warlord troops from Mukden and the Big Swords at his destination. By spending the last night on the road in an abandoned inn at Yungling, fifteen miles west of Hsinpin, and getting up at daybreak before the combatants awoke to fight, the Henderson party made Hsinpin by noon. The battle followed them into town later in the day. As the Big Swords pulled out of Hsinpin, "the manager of [Hsinpin's] largest shop was shot and killed by an angry robber who had demanded a saddle and been refused," wrote Henderson. "One Korean shop lost thirty pairs of Korean shoes taken by the robber-soldiers as they ran. The mission hospital has ministered to about twenty wounded warriors carried in from the battle at Yungling. Besides the wounded it would be hard to tell how many non-combatants have sought shelter in the hospital at night....Our hearts are full of thanksgiving that our Father keeps us safe in the storm."[20]

After eleven years in Manchuria, Lloyd Henderson knew about the risks he took whenever he left the safety of the Hsinpin Presbyterian compound. In the summer of 1932 it was agreed that his wife Helen should take the two children and go by cart and train to Sŏnch'ŏn, in Korea, to wait out the fighting. Henderson was alone for several weeks, and in September he decided to pay his family a visit. He set out in the cart once more from Hsinpin, heading west to the railroad station at Tunghua. The fighting up ahead on this occasion was between the Big Swords and the Japanese Army battling eastward from Mukden to conquer the Hsinpin area. Again he coaxed his carter, servant, cook, and mules along the rutted clay, flying the Stars and Stripes for whatever protection it might afford as they passed through the Big Swords' lines and then, a short while later, through lines of Japanese. Well beyond the battlefront they put up for the night in a deserted village. Around midnight a Japanese patrol woke them there and ordered them to backtrack to the detachment's encampment at the town of Malientun, where it was said they would be safer. Henderson objected, since he wanted to get to the railroad the next day, but the Japanese soldiers insisted—and the officer in charge reportedly drew his revolver and fired around Henderson's feet.[21] Thus persuaded, the party started back under army escort toward Malientun until they got to a narrow cut through a hill. There in the pitch-blackness sometime after midnight they ran into an ambush. For a minute, bullets flew in all directions, but only one caused any damage: the one that entered Lloyd Henderson's mouth and exited through the base of his brain, killing him instantly.[22]

20. L.P. Henderson, "The Big Swords in Hsinpin, Manchuria," *The Korea Mission Field*, XXVIII:7 (July 1932), p. 142.

21. As reported in Tokyo and carried in the *New York Sun* and quoted in H.T. Owens (Seoul) to German Ambassador (Washington), November 26, 1932. UCCA, 83.006C, Box 2, File 57.

22. Harold H. Henderson, letter to his mother, October 23, 1932.

Lloyd Henderson was only one of thousands who died during the violence in Manchuria that year—and not the first missionary. In June, a German Benedictine priest had been bayoneted and shot by Japanese soldiers —reportedly for refusing to dismount from his horse to show his papers to a local sentry.[23] In Korea, the Presbyterian Mission rallied around. Lloyd Henderson's brother Harold, serving in Taegu, rushed to Sŏnch'ŏn to comfort the widowed Helen and her two children, as the mission met for the funeral on October 24. Meanwhile, Japanese authorities blamed Lloyd Henderson's death on Manchurian *hung hu-tze* and Koreans blamed it on the Japanese. But no one had seen who fired the fatal shot and the Japanese had followed their practice of cremating the body within two days, before investigators could reach the scene from the American consulate in Mukden.[24]

When the Japanese finally got control of southern Manchuria they established a fearsome military presence. Control radiated from the railroads by which the Japanese connected the northeastern seacoast of Korea with the network of Japanese rail lines in Manchuria. It took full military trains with armored cars and engines to keep the railways open and even then the raids dropped off only gradually.[25] By 1933, the consensus in Chientao was that the bandit problem was under control but that the Communist menace was continuing. The Japanese Army organized Korean communities into "self-protection corps" that were supposed to collect intelligence on Korean communists operating in the area. Where raids were especially troublesome the Japanese provided the Korean corps with weapons.[26]

The Canadian missionaries in Chientao saw this imposition of Japanese control as a benefit to everyone, especially the Koreans, simply because it put an end to the awful chaos of the preceding period. Donald Black put it this way:

23. H. T. Owens to German Ambassador, November 26, 1932, UCCA, 83.006C, Box 2, File 57.
24. The Japanese liked to blame the *hung hu-tze* for unexplained deaths in their jurisdiction. For example, in 1921 a Korean reporter from Seoul who was investigating a Japanese massacre near Lungchingtsun in 1921 became upset and lodged a protest with the local Japanese army unit. Soon thereafter Japanese soldiers "escorted" him out of the area and he was "murdered by Hunghutze" in the process. Stanley Haviland Martin (Lungchingtsun) to A.E. Armstrong (Toronto), February 4, 1921. UCCA, 79.204C, Box 6, File 83. After Lloyd Henderson's murder, the Japanese Army sent a message to W.T. Cook in Hsinpin asking permission to cremate the body. Cook replied that the body should not be cremated under any circumstances but that it should be brought to Hsinpin for burial. The army cremated the body anyway. (H.T. Owens to German Ambassador, November 26, 1932.)
25. Donald M. Black (Lungchingtsun) to A.E. Armstrong, October 15, 1933. UCCA, 83.006C, Box 2, File 61.
26. George F. Bruce (Lungchingtsun) to A.E. Armstrong, January 17, 1933 and October 1, 1933. UCCA, 83.006C, Box 2, File 62.

I think that it is pretty well conceded that Japan is in Manchuria to stay. In fact her withdrawal now could mean nothing but anarchy and disorder far greater even than that which has existed. The common people will undoubtedly benefit from Japanese rule and the law and order which will eventually result. [Their] prosperity is, of course, to the interest of the Japanese, for Japanese will never come in any appreciable numbers for agricultural work in the cold Manchurian climate. The Korean population certainly stands to gain considerably by the change for they were previously used to no small extent as innocent agents of Japanese penetration and, as such, were disliked and persecuted by the Chinese. Now they will have equal citizenship. Further, the Japanese have created employment for a good many educated Koreans in connection with the new government offices that have been set up.[27]

27. Donald M. Black (Lungchingtsun) to A.E. Armstrong, October 15, 1933. UCCA, 83.006C, Box 2, File 61.

-- 8 --

Western Women in the Land
of the Morning Calm

Women were a major part of the Western presence in early twentieth-century Korea. Though they were far from having equal rights with men in their own homelands, they made significant gains for Korean women and for themselves through their work in Korea. Missionary women, though never ordained themselves, were important in "women's evangelism"—the contacting and teaching of Korean girls and women in homes, schools, and churches throughout the country. In education and medicine also, where they served as doctors, nurses, and teachers, female missionaries were a main ingredient of the success of Christianity in Korea.

Certain church denominations in America had separate boards for missionary women overseas that supported special women's projects. The Ewha School for Girls in Seoul, for example, was supported by the Women's Board of the Methodist Episcopal Church. Methodist missionary couples were therefore under two Boards at once, with their salaries and project funds coming from separate sources. The Northern and Southern Presbyterians, on the other hand, appointed single men, single women, and married couples together under single administrative structures. The difference was that married women were cast in a supporting role, could not always vote in mission matters, and were paid jointly with their husbands as a couple, with supplementary allowances for children.

The need for women missionaries in Korea was clear from the fact that males, and especially foreign males, were barred from contact with respectable Korean women. Horace Allen, the first Protestant missionary doctor, found that under no circumstances could he treat female patients. When he founded his clinic in 1885, he had to borrow palace women,

Sewing circle, Ch'ŏngju, Korea, 1939. Clark Collection.

kisaeng entertainers actually, to be "nurses" to assist in the treatment of women. Lillias Horton, M.D., the first woman doctor in Korea, was recruited to work with women explicitly because of this cultural taboo.[1]

Mothers and Daughters: Susan and Lilian Ross

Northern Presbyterians Cyril and Susan Ross were a typical missionary couple. Like many Americans of his generation, Cyril Ross was an immigrant, born and educated in Scotland before his family moved to Canada and then to the United States. He earned degrees at Park College and eventually at Princeton Theological Seminary, schools that emphasized missionary training and had alumni in Korea. Susan Shank Ross was an Illinois native who earned her medical degree at Northwestern in 1896. In 1897 she volunteered for service with the Presbyterian Board of Foreign Missions and was assigned to the newly opened field of Korea. Eleven days before she sailed she married Cyril Ross, who was by then a fellow missionary-designate.

1. One of Lillias Horton Underwood's first patients was Queen Min, who had been getting medical attention by means to a cord tied to her wrist and passed to a male doctor in another room, and alternately by direct examination of her tongue, which "was protruded through a slit in a screen for the [male] physician's observation." Lillias H. Underwood, *Fifteen Years among the Topknots* (Boston: American Tract Society, 1904), p. 25.

In Korea, the Rosses were first stationed in Pusan, where their main business was language study. Cyril tried out Korean phrases with his teacher on short trips to nearby villages while Susan practiced her Korean in the station clinic, treating women patients. It was not long before the Rosses had begun to learn the price for volunteering to serve in Korea. Their first child, Dewy, born in Pusan in 1897, died suddenly while the family was visiting Seoul the following year. As she awaited the birth of her second child in the summer of 1900, Susan looked back upon their loss and the empathy it had generated:

> It has been a comfort in our sorrow to know that friends at home have been with us in prayer and sympathy. Our Korean friends seemed to come nearer to us, in that time, than ever before. It seems to me that the real soul is alike in us all, though scarcely anything else is. The day when we came back to our lonely home, the Koreans came in one after another, all day, to tell us of their sympathy and their prayers for us. Some who had loved the little baby wept when they spoke of him. As they came and went, I felt that all the differences of complexion and feature, of physical and mental habits, were but the merest incidental circumstances and the people themselves are exactly like us. I had felt this before when some of our people had themselves been in sorrow.[2]

The Rosses' second child, Lilian, was born in Pusan in November 1900. By then, Susan had become accustomed to making the 100-mile journey to Taegu to work as the women's doctor in the Presbyterian hospital there, and in the spring of 1900 baby Lilian went with her. "It has been a nice opportunity to see the work in a new inland station," wrote Susan.

> Miss Nourse, with whom I have been staying, and Mrs. Adams receive Korean women who call and Mrs. Adams has a class which meets every Wednesday afternoon while Miss Nourse meets with and teaches women who come in, on Sunday morning especially. There are as yet no women who are even catechumens, but there are six in Mrs. Adams' class who are interested and say they believe.[3]

In 1902, the Rosses were sent to join the newly opened mission station at Sŏnch'ŏn. Cyril started "itinerating" to nearby villages visiting the homes of students in the Sŏnch'ŏn Presbyterian boys' school, seeking out parents for possible conversion to Christianity. As the students' families became Christians and started little house churches, they invited relatives and neighbors to join, increasing the Christian community in the Sŏnch'ŏn ter-

---

2. Quoted in correspondence between Eileen F. Moffett and Lilian Ross, November 4, 1990, in the papers of Lilian Ross. Eventually the Rosses lost three of their five children. Son Willard, born in 1904, died of diphtheria in 1912 and son Lawrence, born in 1907, died of vaccination poisoning in 1908. Son Albert, born in Nagasaki in 1902, survived, as did Lilian (1900-1993).

3. Ibid.

Susan Ross, M.D., and her daughter, Lilian, 1902.
Clark Collection.

ritory from 677 to 4,039 between 1902 and 1907. The boys' and girls' academies on the Sŏnch'ŏn mission compound became important regional institutions along with the Presbyterian clinic run by Drs. Alfred Sharrocks and Susan Ross, the men's and women's physicians. When she was not seeing patients, Susan Ross ran a class in her living room for women who wanted to join the church, taught hygiene at the girls' academy and paid visits of her own to women in homes throughout the city—dropping in unannounced to talk on the women's porches and invite them to church or to communicant classes. Like all other women missionaries, Susan Ross did not go calling alone: she was always accompanied by a Korean companion known as a *yŏchŏndosa*, or "biblewoman." Biblewomen were workers paid by the mission to act as assistants to missionary women doing evangelistic work. Some did double duty as the missionaries' language teachers, accompanying them whenever they went out on what amounted to language laboratory sessions in public. Some Biblewomen were students, or former students; others were deaconesses in the local church; others were simply Christian women who applied for positions as Biblewomen in an employment climate that otherwise offered them very little chance to earn an income. The foreign women depended on them and respected them both for their dedication as Christians and for their strength as women.[4]

4. *Yŏchŏndosa* were usually "independent" women, either widows of elders or pastors or mothers of grown children. In Korean churches their status was higher than *chibsa* (unpaid volunteer deaconesses), who took care of housekeeping and informal congregation-tending. *Yŏchŏndosa* were educated, usually with an elementary education plus coursework in the Bible Institute (for which see below), where they learned how to tell Bible stories, teach, and do rudimentary counseling. They functioned as pastors' assistants on home visits, meeting with the women of

第七回山西女傳道聯合會
1936, 8, 28日 旅楚山

優勝

Olga Johnson, Lilian Ross, and biblewomen at retreat, 1937. Clark Collection.

Biblewomen were major sources of cultural information for the missionaries and often spared them from embarrassing failures. Once, for example, Susan Ross wanted to do some calling on women in "unbelieving
homes." "The Biblewoman told me the women in such homes would be so
embarrassed by [my] coming upon them in the dishabille to which they let
themselves down in August heat that I could do them no good. So we

the house and giving Bible lessons in the villages. They were respected for their education and human concern and they did much to enhance the identification of
women with Christianity. It was this established role in the Korean church that they
transferred over into the function of missionary companion. And when serving
alongside missionaries they were more often paid with mission funds or money
from the individual missionary's own salary, whereas when they assisted Korean
pastors they were usually not on salary.

The English term "biblewoman" also covered female *kwŏnsa,* a slightly
higher level of church worker in a category invented after World War II for women
church leaders who could not be elders because they were female. Nowadays, however, women hold many important positions in churches, some of them salaried,
and they do everything except administer the sacraments and preach formally from
the pulpit. (This information is distilled from observation, conversations with Korean pastors, Korean church workers, former missionaries, and archival sources
such as Charles Allen Clark's obituary of Biblewoman Oh Chan Il entitled "A Christian of Fiery Zeal" [June 5, 1941] in the author's possession.)

waited for cooler weather," she continued, and "We had some good times calling until the weather grew cold and the women went into their houses and shut their doors. After that we could still call where we knew the people but it was not so easy to approach perfect strangers as it had been when we would find the women in their yards or sitting in their open doorways.[5]

Susan Ross and her biblewomen conducted classes for village women in Sŏnch'ŏn, teaching them how to read and understand the Bible and encouraging them to develop leadership skills. The biblewomen helped her attract local women to the "mothers clubs" ("ŏmoni-hoe") that she started in order to teach better maternal and child health. Dr. Ross's concerns in this work reflected an interesting blend of Calvinism and modern science. "So many children are fed whatever they want whenever they want it," she wrote, echoing a common Western criticism. "No system at all, not only digestion suffers, but when such practices are carried to extreme, disobedience and lack of self-control are the result." She was not the first or the last Westerner to comment disapprovingly on the freedom permitted Korean toddlers, but she was just as quick to acknowledge the futility of many Western remedies for what ailed the local population. Once she returned from a trip to Seoul full of ideas, charts, posters, recipes for a milk substitute made of beans, and a substitute for orange juice made from cabbage. "Some of the mothers know and put into practice already some of the modern ideas of child hygiene," she wrote. "Babies are very much better taken care of now than when we first came to town. Still the most willing mother has so little with which to do that it is small wonder if she sometimes grows tired of hearing foreigners who have all the milk, soap, clean clothes, orange juice, etc... tell her how to do things. She would be glad to do so also if only she could." [6]

As younger missionaries arrived to staff the Sŏnch'ŏn clinic, Susan Ross devoted increasing amounts of time to teaching in the girls' academy and the Women's Bible Institute. The "BI" classes were short courses on the Bible aimed at non-Christians who were recruited by the biblewomen who promoted them as chances to attend school—a rare privilege for ordinary Korean village women. Some classes were more advanced and aimed at leadership training for church women. Hundreds of women turned out for sessions of Sŏnch'ŏn's Bible Institute. Some failed the courses and simply returned to try again. Susan Ross sympathized with women who were ill prepared for school by life in rural Korea. As she once observed, "Minds

5. "Personal Narrative of (Mrs. Cyril) Susan Ross, Year 1929-1930," in the papers of Lilian Ross.
6. Material in this paragraph is from the memorial minute for Mrs. Cyril Ross, M.D., adopted by the Presbyterian Board of Foreign Missions, June 22, 1954, in the papers of Lilian Ross.

that have not only been untrained but have been dulled by grief are slow in awakening."[7]

Dr. Ross also devoted much of her time to her children, Lilian and Albert, who grew up in a mission station that was full of foreign and Korean playmates. The Sŏnch'ŏn missionaries were a fertile lot, and the mothers had much child care to occupy them, even with the help of Korean *amah*s. They took turns home-schooling the compound's children through the early grades, while the older children went to boarding school in P'yŏng-yang. In 1918 the Rosses' neighbors included the George McCunes (four children), the Stacy Robertses (five), the Alfred Sharrockses (four), the Henry Lampes (eight), and the Norman Whittemores (one), for a total of twenty-four children under eighteen. In that year, Lilian Ross graduated from Pyeng Yang Foreign School and was sent to her father's alma mater, Park College, in Parkville, Missouri.

Studies at Park, and later Huron Colleges, and graduate work at Biblical Seminary in New York prepared Lilian Ross to return to Korea as a missionary in her own right. No doubt there was an element of "going home" in her decision to apply to the Presbyterian Board for service in the country where she had grown up; yet as with other second-generationers who were returning to Korea in the 1920s, it was thought that her experience with the language and gladness to serve in the land of her birth were important indicators of effectiveness as a missionary so she was welcomed home not only as a daughter of the mission but as a valuable mission asset.

As a teacher, Lilian was eager to get started gathering classes of women and children to learn the Bible through storytelling. In the United States she had studied teaching methods, including storytelling via simple visual media such as the flannel graph, a plain flannel-covered easel on which colored flannel cutouts of Bible story characters and all the other elements of scenery for storytelling could be stuck and moved around as the story continued. In Korea the Presbyterian Mission assigned her to general evangelism in the provincial town of Kanggye.

Kanggye was a regional center of eighteen thousand inhabitants, accessible via a railroad spur that ran from Sinanju on the west coast up through the mountains to the Yalu River. It was an ancient walled frontier town, an erstwhile fortress that had recently been transformed into a regional base of operations by the Japanese colonial regime. In the mid-1930s the Japanese upgraded the railroad connections in keeping with their plans to open more access points between Korea and Manchuria, for which reason there was a significant increase in the Japanese population. The Presbyterian Mission compound commanded a view of the valley junction in which Kanggye was nestled, and from her bedroom window Lilian could look out

7. "Personal Narrative of (Mrs. Cyril) Susan Ross, Year 1929-1930."

Lilian Ross and Olga Johnson and their biblewomen, Kanggye, North Korea, 1937. Clark Collection.

on the woods nearby, the terraced fields in the valley beyond, and a distant range of mountains that were covered with snow in winter.

The Kanggye mission compound had its own garden plots, and Lilian spent much time watching the weather and tending her household economy. Winters in Kanggye were so cold that it took hours to warm up the house in the morning; and on some days Lilian simply stayed in bed reading until it was possible to function. Summers were milder, but the Korean rainy season made things soggy and sometimes dangerous. "The river is flooded," she wrote one July day in 1937, "carrying away pigs and houses and covering fields. What the drought did not destroy the floods aim to ruin. The ceiling is leaking in our dining room; plaster is falling. There has been a lot of sickness this summer and not a few deaths among our church families."[8]

In most years, however, the Kanggye valley was rich with the fruits and vegetables that ripened through the spring and summer months. Lilian spent much time tending the garden.

> Our grapes are huge but it is some time before they will ripen. Some sunny day I might check the disease started among them. I shall pick them over a little tomorrow. Have already canned quite a little tomatoes. We pick and ripen [them] on the sun porch to reduce loss by decay. I want to put up plenty. Shall serve for dessert fruit this winter, for salad or vegetable, or for appetizers. If plums and grapes fail, strawberries and tomatoes will be my stock of fruit! Sometimes I'll be reckless and buy apples or pumalo [pomelo?]. (Never fear, stingy Scotchman that I be, I always live on the fat of the land.) Have had watermelon, peaches, apples—and not failed for meat either.[9]

Every two or three days, Lilian took sheets of onionskin paper and hand-wrote letters to her parents, beginning them in *Han'gŭl* script with Dear "abu" or "ŏmma," childhood forms of the Korean words for father and mother. The letters were cathartic for her to write and a joy for the Rosses to receive and file, so that they constitute a diary of Lilian's early ca-

8. Lilian Ross, letter to her family, July 30, 1937.
9. Lilian Ross to Cyril Ross, August 17, 1941.

reer on the mission field. Between the lines, as Lilian wrote of happiness when new missionaries were assigned to Kanggye and particularly when women were assigned to terms as "companion" missionaries in the single ladies' house on the compound, one detects suggestions of loneliness. However, her expressions seem never to have transgressed family propriety by mentioning a longing for romance or a fear of spinsterhood. Women missionaries were free to have relationships and marry, but in Lilian Ross's case one senses a renunciation something like that of a Catholic nun. Her letters tell of small pleasures such as working in her garden, receiving visits from old friends, and small deeds for others like sewing a sleep outfit for a

Lilian Ross's student and daughter, with daughter's baby. Clark Collection.

new baby in the neighborhood. They reveal her struggle to upgrade her childhood Korean as she worked with a tutor to learn the proper forms of address for use by a mature woman. This was a matter of polish for second-generation missionaries who were quite confident in their ability to speak street Korean but needed a more dignified vocabulary to function effectively as a teacher and command respect from Korean peers and students. Perhaps as important was the fact that passing the second-year-level exam in Korean would qualify her to vote on mission matters.

Lilian Ross easily found women who needed her attention. Kanggye too had a Bible Institute that offered classes for men and women in the slack season for farming. Her women's Bible Institute alumnae formed her network of contacts in the surrounding villages and provided her with welcoming places to visit when she went out to conduct classes at village churches, welcomes that she reciprocated when they came calling in Kanggye. At home she also opened her living room to classes for the town's working women, the castaways and runaways who worked in restaurants, bars, and coffee shops and often engaged in prostitution. These were women who routinely endured degrading abuse, and on their rare days off Lilian Ross tried to give them a warm environment in which they could talk and sing and regain some dignity through study.

> Tomorrow I am hoping to have a group of cafe girls. The Jap. keeper is not sending his girls (only 3 of 12 are Korean) but the [Korean] keeper said he would. He is reported to have said, "And does the foreigner consider us as folks? Then invite us!" We shall see what happens. Then next I want to return

to the *kisaeng* house where Ch'anghi was and where I have called several times, and see if I can have them come for a party. How else can one get on the inside? There is so much to be done and so little being tried for these neediest ones. I love to have more folks to love, with music, flowers, and books, but most of all our Savior to share with eager ones—His lambs and sheep for whom I too am responsible. Just how could I not be happy![10]

One of her forays into social work with young working women was her class for "bus girls," the undereducated teenagers who operated the doors and collected the fares on public autos and buses. Bus girls worked cruel hours, often starting work in the freezing predawn and staying on their vehicles with little time for rest or food, until the last run in the evening. They answered to several "bosses" at once: the drivers, their supervisors, and the customers, and they suffered considerable psychological and physical abuse. Lilian Ross considered them prime candidates for evangelism, and despite the hardships of their working days they were still endearing as teenagers:

> Yesterday evening the bus girls came to play. Of the nine, three have had some church training. When I led in prayer one of the youngsters started giggling and that started one or two more. The others called them down. (One of the girls came today and said the one who started giggling said she was sorry and that she did badly and that she wanted to be a Christian after this.) While we ate I said each one of us should do a stunt. One girl had brought her hymnbook and so the stunts consisted of hymn singing. I told them the story of the boy who had to pay store price for the boat that he himself had made and lost and found on sale—and ended up "Ye are bought with a price." The girls asked one of their number to lead in prayer before they left. We had a good time getting acquainted and playing games. They seldom have time off to go to church working on Sunday. They are a responsive bunch well worth some effort and help....The child who came back today said she was leaving the bus work, no future to it, unable to be a Christian. She hoped there would be some opening at our hospital which there isn't.[11]

The hardships of working-class Korean women were revealed a little differently in another letter about a recent Bible Institute graduate.

> Her younger daughter (17 years) was sold to a *yorichip* (roadside restaurant) by her husband. She did not know any better than to go and did not even notify her mother for some months. Now she is kept here in town. She has been spending her spare time weeping at her mother's. The mother is distracted. The price of the girl has gone from ¥100, which the husband received, to ¥230. The police doctor [has] sent her to the hospital and already the price is ¥240. [I received] ¥60 from the US recently. The mother thinks she can raise ¥60 by selling her sewing machine. I do not have the [funds] even to advance [the rest].[12]

10. Lilian Ross to Susan Ross, January 12, 1938.
11. Ibid.
12. Lilian Ross, letter to her family, July 30, 1937.

"Miss Florence" and the Speer School

In 1927, the same year that Lilian Ross began her work in Kanggye, the Southern Presbyterian Mission acquired a single missionary named Florence Root for similar work with women in Kwangju, far to the southwest. From the beginning, the Southern Presbyterians had emphasized girls' education and women's evangelism, and by 1927 women comprised fully 60 percent of the Honam Protestant community. The mission employed many single women who were renowned for braving weather, distance, bad food, and illness, to hold classes for country women in tiny *anpang*, the "inner rooms" of farmhouses that sequestered the women of the region and isolated them from education and mental exercise. Elise Shepping, to name a single example, started a school for girls, founded the first Korean branch of the WCTU, and created a chain of dozens of "auxiliaries," or "circles," for women to meet and practice reading the Bible, teaching each other without male interference. When Florence Root arrived in Honam, she quickly found her place in this formidable succession.

Born in 1893 in Oswego County, New York, "Miss Florence" attended Smith College, taught in public schools in upstate New York, and did office work as a secretary and a bookkeeper before she decided to volunteer for missionary work in Korea. After a period of language study she was assigned to the Speer School for Girls in Kwangju, where she taught English and Bible and soon became the principal.

One of Florence Root's first letters home included this assessment of what the Christian gospel could do for rural Koreans, particularly women.

> To the skeptics and others who feel that the missionaries are forcing an undesired and unneeded religion on non-Christian people I would like to say, "Come with me to these villages I have just visited, and let me show you how the Christian stands head and shoulders above his non-Christian brothers in the community. One little village called White Stone, straggling along beside a clear mountain stream, in one of the most picturesque places I have seen, was almost entirely heathen. But there was a seventeen-year-old Christian girl who had attended our mission school for girls in Chunju [Chŏnju] for several years. Her clothes were clean, she herself was neat and clean and alert—a marked contrast to the passiveness and slovenliness of most of the women there. This contrast prevails in greater or less degree wherever one finds Christians and non-believers together."[13]

Kwangju, Korea was a long way from Florence Root's native New York, but she lost no time becoming thoroughly countrified in the Southern Presbyterian territory. Before the end of her first term in Korea she already looked on Seoul as a Mecca of civilization "with its wide streets, beautiful stores and hurrying automobiles and streetcars." However, Korea was al-

13. Florence Root, "Dear Friends" letter, November 4, 1927, in the Presbyterian Church (U.S.A.), Department of History, Montreat, North Carolina.

ways playing tricks on foreigners. One day, sated with shopping and good food from Seoul, as she was waiting for her train in the city's new baroque railway station, a pair of middle-aged males opened their parcels and held up sets of brand-new long johns.

> They were very much pleased with the appearance of these garments, and—apparently not content to wait until they got home—proceeded to disrobe, completely, e'en down to nature, don the new purchases, reclothe themselves and go on their way rejoicing to catch their train. All this in absolute unconcern and unconsciousness of their surroundings, and in the main waiting room of a railway station that would do credit to one of our American cities![14]

Like Lilian Ross and other single women missionaries in Korea, Florence Root shared a home with other unmarried women in what was referred to in most locations as the "ladies' house" but in Southern Presbyterian territory was called the "saxie house," using the colloquial term for "maiden" or "bride." Normally in Korea a "saxie" (*ssaeksi*) was someone young and marriageable, ready to become a faithful wife, filial daughter-in-law, and a bearer of sons. In the daily speech of missionaries, the term "saxie" attached to single women missionaries with a certain irony since missionary saxies were likely to remain unmarried and were established in careers where they often had considerable autonomy. It derived from the colloquial speech of Koreans, particularly servants, who had no other word to fit the situation.[15] Indeed, the combined strangeness of being foreign, female, and single occasioned much comment, often within earshot. Florence Root told this anecdote in the same letter as the one above:

> I overheard two women in the hospital talking about me the other day. One said to the other: "Look at that foreign woman—do you suppose she is a Big Baby?" The other one who knows me well replied, "Yes." "How many rice cakes has she eaten?" (being interpreted, how old is she?) "You must not ask that: American ladies don't like to answer that question."

> A Big Baby is a daughter who is in her middle teens or above who has not yet married. In the old days, it was not necessary to ask that question among Koreans at all, because no unmarried girl could wear her hair done up, but had to wear it in a braid down her back. But now that girls are going to school and on to higher schools the custom has changed so that even some of our high school girls who are older than the majority wear their hair up, and no questions asked.

14. Florence Root, "Dear Friends" letter, November 26, 1933, in the Presbyterian Church (U.S.A.), Department of History, Montreat, North Carolina.
15. Both single and married male and female missionaries apparently without any insulting connotations used the term "saxie." It seems better than some of the English euphemisms that were attempted, such as "unclaimed blessings," a term used in the author's hearing during a meeting of missionaries, including single women, as recently as 1968.

Florence Root's blond-ish hair was kept in a long braid that she coiled around her head in a fashion statement that helped define her as a special case. Passersby and students soon learned that her Korean was too good to allow them to make rude comments where she could overhear them. Like her contemporary Lilian Ross, as her command of the language progressed she was able to learn more about the condition and needs of Korean women in general. It seemed urgently necessary not only to teach girls via an organized curriculum in the Speer School but also to offer adult education that would lift mothers and grandmothers out of illiteracy and, it was hoped, to a knowledge of the gospel. During winter breaks she taught women's classes in the winter "Bible Institute," the Korea-wide effort of Presbyterians to provide ordinary country people with a two-week series of lay people's classes in *Han'gŭl* literacy and Bible study during the slack season for farming. The Bible Institutes were fun partly because they involved music, singing, and scripture memorization games and contests, and the job forced Florence to sharpen her musical skills.

Cultivating Modern Womanhood at Ewha

Florence Root was never prouder than when her Speer girls went on to college, often in Seoul at the Methodist Ewha Womans College (now Ewha Womans University). Ewha was a project of the women's division of the American Methodist Episcopal Church and the flagship institution of the entire pan-denominational effort in women's education. It was founded in June 1886 by Mary F.B. Scranton, who began with a single pupil, a child found lying against the city wall with her mother who was suffering from typhus. The mother, once recovered, briefly pulled her out of Scranton's school for fear that she was going to be kidnapped to America. Such was the fear of foreigners and indifference toward education for lower-class girls in Korea. The school's founder, Mary Scranton, then recruited a second student who happened to be an orphan. Within a year she had seven students. The Protestant effort in girls' education was under way. By 1935, in all of Korea there were twenty-three thousand girls in Protestant mission and church schools, and thousands of adult women had been taught to read in Sunday Schools and Bible Institutes.

Mary Fletcher Benton Scranton, a 52-year-old widow from Belchertown, Massachusetts, arrived in Korea in 1885 with her son William, a pioneer Methodist missionary. Not being a formally appointed missionary herself, Mary Scranton's school soon was taken over as a regular mission project by the Women's Board of the Methodist Church, which has retained an interest in it ever since. The early faculty of Ewha were all women appointed directly by the Women's Board to teach in what was not yet a college but a middle and high school—advanced enough for turn-of-the-century Korea. It was located in Chŏng-dong, on property still occupied by Ewha Girls'

Ewha Girls School Students, circa 1910. Clark Collection

High School, until 1935 when the present campus in Sinch'on was dedicated. That dedication was a triumph of missionary planning and effort as well as the result of substantial gifts from leading Methodist laywomen in the United States. Mrs. Philip Gray of Detroit and her two daughters bought the land for $30,000. Mrs. Henry Pfeiffer of New York, who wanted to be first with the gift for the land, had to settle for Pfeiffer Hall, the donation for which brought her accumulated gifts to the $50,000 mark, later supplemented by an additional $104,000.

Missionary educators did the daily work of building Ewha, and the bonds that were forged between foreign and Korean women and between foreign teachers and their Korean students are clearly visible in every aspect of the school's history. Jeannette Walter, a teacher at Ewha from 1911 to 1926, spent her middle years in the school's family of missionaries, workers, and students. Her life revolved around the Chŏng-dong campus and the faculty house with "Sunamie" the cook, "Ye Subang" the outside man, and "Pedro" the houseboy. Ewha had many dormitory students, and Walter was the dorm supervisor with duties that included room inspections and bed checks. Student health was her concern, and it was her job to nurse the girls when they had the flu and to organize medicine-taking sessions to fight parasites.

Jeannette Walter taught English and never learned Korean well enough to get acquainted with her students on a level that would have opened up their home experiences or their attitudes toward the political turmoil then affecting the city's new student culture. Instead she expressed her feelings in maternal ways, finding much fulfillment in the girls academic successes and their development as young Christians. The curious dissonance between her orientation and theirs is seen in her account of how Ewha girls tried to join the student demonstrations during the March 1 Independence Movement in 1919.

> At Ewha...the big gate was bolted, but when the girls, enmasse, ordered it to be opened, the gateman opened it. Miss Frey [the principal] stood there with arms outstretched and announced, "Well, girls, you will go over my dead body." Some went back to their rooms, but others were taken to prison from the streets. In a few days we dismissed school and sent the girls to their homes, where many became leaders in their own communities. Induk Pak and Julia Syn, two of our teachers, were in prison for long terms.
>   Months afterward, Yu Kwansoon, a little sixteen-year-old girl, died in prison. We had her body brought back to the school, and the girls prepared cotton garments for her burial. Then, during the night hours, they decided that she was a real heroine and they hunted up silk materials and re-dressed her in silk. We were allowed to have a quiet service at the church with only her classmates present. They all wanted to walk to the cemetery, but there was no permit for that, and I thought I was going to have trouble. Then Helen [Kim] told them that she would go with me to the gravesite as their representative and home-room teacher, so we went, and that incident ended quietly. But Yu Kwansoon has not been forgotten. Much later, when Korea was free, a movie was made about her life....I was featured in the picture [played by a later missionary, Emma Wilson]. However, when I was in Korea in 1959, I was interviewed by a group from Kwansoon's school, and I assured them on tape that her body was not mutilated. I had dressed her for burial. [16]

Among Walter's junior colleagues at Ewha were two who forged a particularly significant relationship: Alice Appenzeller, the president of Ewha during the thirties, and her Korean understudy, Helen Kim (Kim Hwallan). Kim was born in 1899, the daughter of a Chemulp'o businessman. Her mother was persuaded to become a Christian by a Methodist Biblewoman, following which her parents adopted the revolutionary idea of sending their daughters to school as well as their sons. Helen was one of the first students to go all the way through Ewha, beginning in 1907 and graduating from the college in 1918. In 1922 she entered Ohio Wesleyan University, earned a B.A. in 1924, and then went on for an M.A. in Philosophy at Boston University before returning to join the Ewha faculty in 1925.

Alice Appenzeller, meanwhile, had been accruing her own seniority. Born in 1885 and commonly referred to by the other missionaries as "the first white child born in Korea," Appenzeller returned to the United States

16. Jeannette Walter, *Aunt Jean* (Boulder, Colo.: Johnson Publishing Company, 1968), pp. 142-143.

with her mother when her father, Henry Gerhardt Appenzeller, died in a ferryboat mishap in 1902. Twenty years later, after her education at Welles-ley College and Columbia University, she returned to Seoul to become principal of Ewha. Three years after that, Helen Kim joined her there and began rising as Appenzeller's understudy. Kim's prominence as a leader of the Korean women's movement was established early on when she helped found the Korean YWCA. However, she also acquired detractors who ex-ploited the tension created by her obvious ambition to succeed Alice Appenzeller as president of Ewha. In 1933 a Korean acquaintance wrote, "I gather that the gradual estrangement between Miss Appenzeller and Miss Kim Helen has taken a definite shape and form. Miss A. indignantly said to a Korean friend that K.H. [Helen Kim] would be glad if [Appenzeller] dropped out and that [Appenzeller] after having worked so hard for Ewha College, wouldn't play a figurehead."[17]

To almost everyone in the foreign community the Appenzeller-Kim pair-ing seemed ideal, the embodiment of what was intended in the missionary effort: well-developed institutions, a trained Korean leadership, and a mis-sionary withdrawal. But when Kim's ambition surfaced in the mid-1930s, Alice Appenzeller was in her forties—much too young to retire or be kicked upstairs. Kim, on the other hand, was no younger than many of the missionaries when they arrived on the field to manage comparable enter-prises—and she knew in her heart that she was much better prepared than they. She had plans for Ewha: she wanted to add a women's medical de-partment.[18] She was thinking ahead about the terms of a possible merger with Chōsen Christian College.[19] Appenzeller, a conservative like most mis-sionaries, thought the Ewha enterprise overextended already; but Helen Kim thought "the Lord will provide."[20] Though the pressure from Kim may have helped keep Ewha moving, it was personally unpleasant for Alice Appenzeller.[21] In 1939, finally, the Japanese settled the matter by forcing all missionary school administrators to resign, and Appenzeller was able to make the gracious gesture of nominating Helen Kim to be Ewha's new president. As she capitulated she quoted Shakespeare's *Twelfth Night* to Kim: "'Some are born great, some achieve greatness, and some have great-ness thrust upon them.' You are in the third category. You will have to take the presidency whether you like it or not."[22]

17. *Yun Ch'iho Ilgi* (YCH), Vol. X. p. 177.
18. Ibid., p. 184.
19. L. George Paik, Interview, Seoul, March 16, 1984.
20. YCH, X, 186.
21. For example see YCH, X, 208-209; 272; 310; 320-321; 340; 347; 349-352; 388; 391; and XI, 67 and 131.
22. Helen Kim, *Grace Sufficient* (Nashville, Tenn.: The Upper Room, 1964), p. 93.

A Missionary in Her Own Country

A bond of a similar kind in the Catholic church was the relationship between foreign and Korean nuns, a bond enhanced through communal living and daily rituals, and by the Catholic missions' policy of integrating religious orders.

At the Maryknoll convent in P'yŏngyang, two of the fifteen nuns in 1930 were Korean, officially part of the Maryknoll Congregation and vested with the responsibility for leading the Korean sisterhood. One of them was Chang Chŏng'ŏn, otherwise known as Sister Mary Agneta Chang, known to history as the sister of John M. Chang (Chang Myŏn), sometime ambassador, vice-president, and prime minister of the Republic of Korea from 1960 to 1961. John, Mary, and their siblings Louis, Cunegunda, and Martha were the children of Leo and Lucia Chang, the descendants of two nineteenth-century Catholic martyrs. Leo Chang made his living as a comprador for foreign trading firms in Inch'ŏn and Seoul and sent his children to Catholic schools. In 1913, the year the family moved into a new house in Seoul's Hyehwa-dong neighborhood, Mary Chang made her first communion and started attending the nearby parish church of St. Benedict, the center of the German Benedictine Mission. During the week she went to a school run by the French Sisters of Saint Paul de Chartres where she acquired her multilingual Western education. The crowning event of her model Catholic upbringing was her confirmation in Seoul's great Myŏng-dong Cathedral by the patriarch of the regenerated Korean church, Archbishop Gustave Charles-Marie Mutel.

Not long after her two brothers began studying in America at Manhattan College, Mary Chang and her sister Cunegunda began their religious careers at a convent in Seattle, studying religion and serving in a "home for Japanese children" because they knew Japanese. In 1922, when Mary was seventeen, the sisters entered the Maryknoll novitiate at the "motherhouse" in Ossining, New York. There the way of life involved poverty, manual labor, and a rigorous schedule of study and prayer. The Chang sisters, though Catholics, had been reared in a Confucian culture that taught them stoicism in such circumstances, and the American novices quickly learned to admire them for their discipline. Eventually they were received into the Congregation, Mary with the name Sister Mary Agneta, and Cunegunda with the name Sister Mary Clara.[23]

In 1925 Sister Mary Agneta—alone by that time because Cunegunda had left the order—was assigned to return to Korea as a Maryknoll missionary Sister. Her first assignment was at the new Maryknoll station in Ŭiju, teach-

23. This account of Sister Mary Agneta Chang follows Sr. M. Gabriella Mulherin, M.M., "Flower of the Martyrs," typescript biography in the Maryknoll Mission Archives, New York.

ing religion in the mission school, visiting the sick, and helping the American Sisters learn Korean. As the only Korean among the Maryknoll Sisters, it fell to Sister Mary Agneta to explain her country to the Americans. She was also the most likely candidate for the new work of training a community of Korean nuns to be attached to the Maryknoll prefecture. To prepare for this she went to Tokyo for further study between 1932 and 1935.

It was during breaks from her training in Tokyo and in the early years of training the Korean sisterhood that she learned to treasure being a Maryknoller. "Our school is closed…and I am now enjoying the happiness of being with the Sisters again," she wrote one Sunday in 1931. Needless to say, how wonderful it seems to be in our own community after being away even for a short time.…Sister Richard is trying to make me fat!" Like all the Maryknoll nuns, Sister Mary Agneta was required to write a journal made of letters addressed to Mother Mary Joseph Rogers, the superior of the Maryknoll Sisters in New York. Mary Agneta's letters glow with not-necessarily-contrived happiness. "I really love my work—I mean my life, Mother," she wrote in 1938 during a stint teaching novices in Yŏngyu near Ŭiju. "I am preparing some things for their classes. One of them is translating our vow book—Cotel's. In helping Sister Sylvester and in preparing the classes and spiritual talks, I realize what a privilege it is, and I feel as though I am having my own novitiate again."

One of Mary Agneta's closest friends was Sister Mary Gabriella Mulherin, with whom she shared many interests besides the work: they read the same books, shared opinions about trends in the church, and had a special sympathy for each other as women and sisters. Sister Gabriella thought Mary Agneta was like the proverbial bamboo plant, fragile-seeming but able to withstand fierce gales. That assessment was to prove prophetic in the two wars that separated the Maryknollers from Korea and left Agneta in charge of the work—a duty for which she ultimately gave her life in 1950.

A Blue-Eyed Daughter-in-Law

Marriages between Koreans and foreigners were not unheard-of, but they were rare. One instance—famous because the bride wrote a book with the matter-of-fact title I Married a Korean—was the union of the American-educated Methodist student David Chuhwang Kim and his Drew University classmate Agnes Davis. The wedding took place in Korea in 1934 after a number of American missionary women had attempted to dissuade the bride upon her arrival in Seoul. Agnes Davis was troubled by the attitudes that she encountered in the expatriate community, not only because they were so racist but also because she needed to be accepted by the missionary women in Seoul who were her natural social set. There were the direst predictions of a life of slavery under a domineering mother-in-law, the type of mother-in-law that the missionary wives said was typical.

Once she went through with the marriage, however, Davis had a very different experience. She grew into a close relationship with David's mother, whom she called "O-man-ee" (ŏmoni, "mother"). In her memoir she recalled learning from "O-man-ee" the work of a Korean wife: how to fire the ŏndol floor, how to grind grain, how to make kimch'i, tubu (tofu), ttŏk, and myriad side dishes for the table, how to spin cotton and silk, how to design and make Korean clothes and how to wash and starch and iron them by beating them with sticks. Seated across from "O-man-ee" she learned the intricate rhythms of the ironing sticks—rhythms that also taught her something deeper about the love and intimacy between women and their families. "O-man-ee" was not just slaving endlessly at housework: she was smart and tender and endlessly resourceful, someone not to be pitied but to be admired.

The final chapter of Agnes Davis's book, which was published in 1943, was entitled: "Would I Do it Again?" On this she equivocated: there were ways she felt she had held David back because she was a foreigner. And there were stressful times during which Agnes's own American-bred unwillingness always to keep to second place threatened the marriage. But her respect for "O-man-ee" pulled her through. "O-man-ee had learned more perfectly than anyone I ever knew the secret of losing her life to find it," wrote Agnes. "Her energies were not wasted in anger or vain regrets or desire for what she could not have. The only time she was not up and doing more than her share of the load of work was when she was too sick to lift her head from her pillow."[24]

24. Agnes Davis Kim, *I Married a Korean* (New York: John Day, 1943), pp. 228-229.

— 9 —

General Minami and the Iron Fist

Japan began mobilizing the Korean people for war on August 26, 1936, the day Army General Minami Jirō arrived to take the reins as governor-general of Chōsen. Everything about General Minami suggested the hard line. All of his experience was military. He had served in Korea before, as commander of the Chōsen Army, in Japan as war minister, and later in Manchuria, as commander-in-chief of the Kwantung Army and ambassador to Manchukuo—meaning that he pulled the strings of Emperor Henry Pu-yi's puppet government. Minami was no friend of Western business: that much was clear from the way he had nationalized the oil industry in Manchuria.[1] He had also made life difficult for Chinese employees of Western businesses and missionary organizations in Manchuria by arresting many of them as security risks. So the news of Minami's assignment to Korea was greeted with foreboding in Seoul. Nor was there cheer over the appointment of Minami's faithful henchman in Manchuria, Ono Rokuichirō, to the number two spot as civil governor.

From the start, Minami was all business, right down to his daily habit of wearing his uniform to the office, a thing not seen since the days of General Hasegawa in 1919.[2] As one Korean writer glumly expressed it, Minami was used to "wielding power like a viceroy in Manchukuo where the military is all-powerful, militaristic absolutism prevails, personal rights and public expressions are prohibited, and newspapers and magazines are official organs or they could not exist."[3]

1. U. Alexis Johnson, "Present Position and Future Prospects of American Oil Firms Operating in Chosen," January 26, 1938 (895.6363/13).
2. Andrew W. Edson (Seoul) to SecState, September 1, 1936 (891.001/23).
3. "The Chōsen and Manshu," quoted in Edson to Erle R. Dicker, chargé d'affaires, Tokyo, September 29, 1936 (895.01/45).

Government-General of Chōsen Building, Seoul, 1926-1945 (demolished 1996). Postcard. Clark Collection.

For a while there were some who refused to be intimidated by Minami's dreadful reputation. The Seoul newspaper *Tong'a Ilbo* proposed an agenda in an August 23 editorial: flood control measures, more and better schools for Korean children, policies to reverse concentration of wealth at the expense of small businesses, and more freedom of expression. The editorial was especially bold in mentioning "too strict control of speech and public meetings" in Korea and warned that too much control might put the people "in a desperate mood" and perhaps "give rise to reactionary movements."[4] On August 25, the day before Minami's arrival, the paper had published a wire photo of the Korean marathoner Son Kijŏng receiving his gold medal at the Olympic Games in Berlin. Son, though a Korean, had participated in the games on the Japanese team under the Japanese named "Kitei Son" and was shown wearing a shirt emblazoned with the *hinomaru*, or Rising Sun. The *Tong'a Ilbo* referred to him by his Korean name, however, and altered the *hinomaru* to look like the Korean *taegŭk*, or yin-yang, symbol. The altered picture is what General Minami saw on the 26th, and on the 27th he ordered the newspaper suspended for nine months for its "resistance to the national efforts…for the unification of Japan and Chōsen."[5] Thus began the Minami era in colonial Korea.

4. Ibid.
5. Ibid. The story of the closure of the *Tong'a Ilbo* is found in Choong Soon Kim, *A Korean Nationalist Entrepreneur: A Life History of Kim Songsu, 1891-1955* (Albany: State University of New York Press, 1998), pp. 95-96.

As governor-general of Chōsen, Minami Jirō did not need the *Tong'a Ilbo* to tell him what to do. He had his own five-point program:[6]

1. Manifestation of the National Polity (the *kokutai*), including enforcing Shintō rites, displaying the flag, singing the national anthem, and using the Japanese language.

2. Unification of Chōsen and Manchukuo, including propaganda about Manchukuo, development of trade with Manchukuo, and Korean emigration to Manchukuo.

3. Development of Culture and Education, including "cultivating national character," and "improving the character of educators."

4. Equal Development of Agriculture and Industry, including better land use, increased production of food and manufactures.

5. Reform of General Administrative Affairs, including "improvement of private life of government and public officials," "reform of old practices," and "simplification" of business.

In the Governor-General's Garden

Japan's authority in Korea was on display on the evening of February 24, 1937, when the colony's ruling elite gathered in the ballroom of the Chōsen Hotel in downtown Seoul to celebrate the thirty-second anniversary of Rotary International.[7] The Keijō Rotary Club[8] was Seoul's most elite civic organization, and it was no accident that the party reflected modern Japanese urban culture down to the smallest detail. General Minami had to be away in Tokyo, but he was represented at the head table by his wife Kakuko. With her were Koisō Kuniaki, commanding general of the Chōsen Army,[9] Mayor Yoshikuni Kanja, chemical tycoon Noguchi Jun,[10] and Mitsukoshi Department Store manager Miwa Kunitarō, acting as master

6. "Five Basic Administrative Policies of Governor-General Minami," enclosed with O. Gaylord Marsh (Seoul) to SecState, July 28, 1937 (895.01/66).

7. This account follows an article that appeared in *The Seoul Press*, February 25, 1937, p. 3.

8. "Keijō" was the Japanese rendering of the Chinese-based Korean name "Kyŏngsŏng," one of the common names for Seoul. The name means "capitalcity," and since it can be expressed in Chinese characters it is useful to speakers of Chinese and Japanese as well as Korean. The name "Seoul," which was in use in the last days of the Choson dynasty, likewise means "capital," but because it is a native Korean word that is written in the Korean phonetic *Han'gŭl* alphabet, the Japanese preferred the name Kyŏngsŏng, which they pronounced Keijō." Today, the Japanese use "Seoul" and write it as "Sō-ru" in their *katakana* phonetic script.

9. Koisō Kuniaki eventually became governor-general of Chōsen during World War II and finally prime minister of Japan, succeeding General Tōjō Hideki in 1944.

10. For Noguchi Jun and his industrial development activities as "entrepreneurial king of the peninsula," see Barbara Molony, "Japan's Strategic Investment in High Technology in Colonial Korea, 1925-1945: The Role of Noguchi Jun," *The Journal of Modern Korean Studies*, IV (May 1990), pp. 78-93.

Nandaimon-dōri 3-chome (today's Namdaemun-no 3-ga), with the Bank of Chōsen and the Central Post Office. Postcard, Clark Collection.

of ceremonies. Foreigners present included British Consul-General Gerald Phipps and American Consul-General Gaylord Marsh, as well as leading traders such as James H. Morris. The only Koreans in the room were related in some way to the colonial government, such as Frank Kim, editor of the government's English-language newspaper, *The Seoul Press*.

Among the modern structures in downtown Seoul the Chōsen Hotel occupied a certain pride of place. Built by the Japanese-owned Chōsen Railway System in 1913, it was one of the jewels in a system of luxury hotels situated at intervals along the routes connecting Japan with its far-flung holdings on the mainland as far as the Siberian border. The hotel was only four stories tall, but that was enough to loom over the Seoul cityscape, where most buildings were still one-story Korean houses, many of them with thatched roofs. Indeed, the city itself was a metaphor for the colonial experience, the hard lines of its Japanese-built concrete-and-stone structures overpowering the mud-walled Korean dwellings.

The Rotary guests were from the class that built and occupied those rigid buildings, the operators of the biggest enterprises Korea had ever seen but from which Koreans themselves were generally excluded. The prevalence of Japanese among them meant that the party looked approximately like a Rotary party in Japan would have looked. Before they entered the Chōsen ballroom, the guests were invited to improvise designs with brush-and-ink on souvenir *raku* bowls that could be fired and made ready to be taken home by the end of the party. Inside the ballroom the decor was all cherry blossoms, with paper lanterns around the room for atmosphere.

Each table was labeled with the name of a Japanese city, and the guests found their seats by locating the table with the city name printed on their invitations. The festivities began with the singing of the Japanese national anthem, *Kimigayo* ("The Reign of Our Lord"), and then the Rotary Song in English and Japanese (but not Korean). Next came the banquet during which there were speeches and toasts, followed by a lottery drawing and a music and dance program. Members of the Keijō Philharmonic provided accompaniment for pop song singing, a *shakuhachi* flute solo, and a *nagauta* song rendition by Mr. Miwa of Mitsukoshi's. At the end of the party the assembled guests rose to give three rousing "banzai" cheers for Rotary.

The Rotarians were well aware of their own power. They ran the banking industry, insurance, trade, mining, fossil fuels, chemicals, electricity, textiles, and transportation industries in Korea. They controlled publishing, education, and religion, and ran the Keijō Chamber of Commerce. Agriculture remained the province of Koreans despite Japanese efforts to take it over also; but even then, the best of Korea's lands fed the Japanese home islands and not Korea. Korean landlords sometimes invested in industry, but they were hard pressed by the richer Japanese. In Keijō, no Korean who wanted to rise in his profession could do so without compromising with the Japanese at some level.[11] This invariably invited criticism from fellow Koreans: a case in point was Pak Hŭngsik, the owner of Hwasin Department Store, who was widely resented as a collaborator. Also suspect was the Kim family of Koch'ang, founders of Keijō Spinning and Weaving, the *Tong'a Ilbo* newspaper, and Posŏng College (later Korea University).[12] But that was Korea in 1937: the players played by Japanese rules.

In that year, the city they called "Keijō" had a population of 706,396. Twenty percent of the population were Japanese, but they were the top twenty.[13] Downtown, the biggest single object was the Japanese Govern-

11. Recent Western scholarship on Korean business under Japanese rule includes Carter J. Eckert, *Offspring of Empire: The Koch'ang Kims and the Colonial Origins of Korean Capitalism, 1876-1945* (Seattle: University of Washington Press, 1991); Dennis McNamara, "The Keishō and the Korean Business Elite," *Journal of Asian Studies*, XLVIII (May 1989), pp. 310-323, and *State and Society in Colonial Korea* (Cambridge: Cambridge University Press, 1990); Karl Moskowitz, "Current Assets: The Employees of Japanese Banks in Colonial Korea" (Ph.D. diss., Harvard University, 1979); and Kim, *A Korean Nationalist Entrepreneur*.

12. See Bruce Cumings, "The Legacy of Japanese Colonialism in Korea," in *The Japanese Colonial Empire, 1895-1945*, ed. Ramon H. Myers and Mark R. Peattie (Princeton: Princeton University Press, 1984), pp. 478-496, and Cumings, *The Origins of the Korean War*. Vol. I, pp. 17-25 and 39-67.

13. In 1937, the total population of Korea was 23,898,000. Out of Seoul's population of 706,396, Koreans numbered 572,774. There were 131,128 Japanese, 2,114 Chinese and Manchus, and 486 Westerners. Of the Westerners, 238 were Americans. There were 104 Russians (92 "White" and 12 "Red'"), 88 British

ment-General building occupying the city's prime spot at the foot of Pugak Mountain. One did not have to be Korean to sense the meaning of this structure with its anthropomorphic features: the metal-clad dome with its pillared finial, the vertical windows of the cupola, and the broad wings to east and west culminating in heavy granite epaulets. Nor could one mistake the symbolism of the site. The Japanese had planted their headquarters in the foreground of the Kyŏngbok Palace, Seoul's miniature version of Peking's Forbidden City. They had leveled the front third of the royal palace grounds, relocated the palace's elegant gate, and removed the buildings and the exquisite marble bridges that lined the approaches to the main throne hall. In this clearing they had constructed their own vast building, designing it around two courtyards so that it formed the character for "nichi" ("sun"), the first half of the word "Nippon" ("Japan"). To be sure, the royal throne hall remained intact behind it, but the sheer mass of the Japanese Government-General building diminished it and robbed it of its majesty.[14] In his conference room on the second floor, the governor-general could swivel his chair and gaze down into the Kyŏngbok Palace as if it were his private garden. And from the boulevard that once had swept grandly toward the palace gate one saw nothing but the great Japanese building. The only thing that recalled the palace gate and the remaining buildings hidden by the colonial headquarters was the pair of *haet'ae*, stat-

subjects (including Canadians and Australians), plus 26 French, 4 Swedes, 20 Germans, 4 Poles, and 2 Czechs.

Among Westerners in Seoul, Protestant missionaries from the United States and their families were the most numerous, with 91 Methodists, 56 Northern Presbyterians, and 31 Seventh Day Adventists. Other Protestants included Anglicans, Canadian and Australian Presbyterians, and British and Swedish Salvation Army officers.

The Catholic missionary community was composed primarily of French priests and nuns, though there were Irish, German, and American Catholics in other parts of the country.

14. To add insult to injury, the Japanese positioned the Government-General Building slightly out of alignment with the vital north-south axis of the palace. The new building was oriented five degrees off center toward the southeast. This was not apparent to onlookers while the building stood, but it created an expensive nuisance for the Koreans when they tore it down in the 1990s and started restoring the Kyŏngbok Palace to its nineteenth-century glory. The palace's main gate (Kwanghwamun, or "Gate of Transforming Light") had been removed by the Japanese during construction of the Government-General Building and repositioned in the east wall of the grounds in 1926, where it stood until being returned to its original site by President Park Chung-hee in 1969. In 1969 the rebuilt Kwanghwamun was centered on the Government-General Building (then called the "capitol" or *Chungangch'ŏng*) rather than on the palace behind; when the old capitol was removed, the gate was revealed to be out of line with the central axis of the palace running not through the center arch but through the secondary arch to the west. The government was then faced with the problem of whether to dismantle the gate with its elaborate concrete and stonework, or leave it out of line.

ues of the mythical Chinese beast that protects against fire, that originally
had stood before the palace gate but were not retained as ornaments in the
lawn of the Government-General Building.[15]

The Government-General Building dominated the downtown as it gazed
upon the other symbols of Japanese power: the broadcast towers of radio
station JODK near the Kwanghwamun Crossing which the Japanese called
"Kōkamon"; Citizen's Hall, with its clock tower on Taihei-dōri (T'aep'-
yŏng-no), the Keijō City Hall, and the Mitsui Building at Koganemachi-
iriguchi (Ŭlchiro-ipku);[16] the Chōsen Hotel in Hasegawa-chō (Sogong-
dong); and beyond, around what was then the city's main square, the Bank
of Chōsen, the Keijō Main Post Office, the Mitsukoshi Department Store
(later the Shinsegye), and the Dai-ichi (Che'il) Bank.

In 1937, the year Japan went to war in Asia, Keijō was enjoying a spate of
urban construction. A granite museum building had just opened in Tŏksu
Palace. The Chōsen Building[17] was going up across the street from Mitsui
to serve as an office building and hotel. Around the block on Nandaimon-dōri, the Chōjiya Department Store (today's Midop'a) was going up.
Beyond this in Meiji-chō (today's Myŏng-dong), fashionable people attended concerts in the new Meiji-za Theater (the postwar National Theater). East beyond the Cathedral of the Immaculate Conception of St. Mary
were two new movie houses, the Kogane-za (today's Kukdo) and the
Wakakusa Gekijō (the Scala).[18] Nandaimon-dōri was the main avenue of
Japanese Keijō, running between the Chongno Bell intersection and the
Keijō Railroad Station. Along it ran a streetcar line, and the byways on either side were lined with Japanese banks, stores, and businesses of every
description. To top it all off was the ultimate symbol of Japanese cultural
dominance: the Chōsen Shrine, the symbolic headquarters of the Japanese
Shintō religion in Korea, on the shoulder of Nanzan (Korean: Namsan),
Keijō's South Mountain.[19] Other monuments had also sprung up to com-

15. For a concise history of the Government-General Building, see Chŏng Unhyŏn, *Sŏul sinae ilche yusan tapsagi* (A Survey of Japanese Colonial Properties in
Seoul) (Seoul: Hanŭl, 1995), pp. 15-77.
16. The Mitsui Building housed the American Embassy from the Korean War until the mid-1960s. Subsequently it housed the U.S. Information Service's American
Cultural Center until 1992, when it was turned over to the Seoul City government.
17. This was later the Bando Hotel, on the site of today's Lotte Hotel. The builder
was Noguchi Jun of the Chōsen Fertilizer Company.
18. Seoul's movie houses showed a combination of Japanese and Western movies. Among the features in 1937 were "Poor Little Rich Girl," with Shirley Temple,
"Le Vagabond Bien-Aimé," with Maurice Chevalier, and "The Jungle Princess," with
Dorothy Lamour.
19. Seoul's other main Shintō establishments included shrines to the spirits of
prime figures in the conquest of Korea, among them Itō Hirobumi, the Japanese
statesman who was Korea's first Japanese ruler from 1905 until his assassination
in 1909 by the Korean An Chunggŭn. Another was General Nogi Maresuke, the

memorate Japanese heroes like the "Three Human Bombs," who gave their lives trying to save their superiors from an attack by Koreans in Shanghai.[20] All these things emphasized Japan's imperial possession of Korea, a fact that everyone was required to accept.

Rumblings from the "China Incident"

Then came the night of July 7, 1937, when Japanese forces maneuvering near Peking touched off the "China Incident." It was of course no mere "incident." It was an onslaught that led directly to the Pacific War. In the beginning, however, Japan's aims were limited. The objective was to break the Nationalist government of Chiang Kai-shek's Kuomintang Party and force him, or his successor, to marry China to Japan's plan for a "Greater East Asia Co-Prosperity Sphere," a Japanese-controlled commonwealth that would end Western colonialism in East Asia and subject Japan's neighbors to its benign direction.

When news of the hostilities reached Korea, the number one topic of conversation was whether the Chinese Nationalists would surrender. The Japanese Army controlled all news and information reaching Korea, and it was impossible to know how long it would take for the military situation in China to be resolved. Without short-wave radios and with newspapers under strict censorship, word of mouth became a primary news source. When the government shut down the *Seoul Press*, the Western community fell under an almost total news blackout.[21]

military hero of the Russo-Japanese War of 1904-05. For descriptions of main shrines in the city, see Chŏng Unhyŏn, pp. 84-102. In a historical turnabout, a statue of Itō's assassin, An Chunggŭn, now stands on the former site of the Chōsen Shrine on Nam-san.

20. In this incident, the Korean Yun Ponggil threw a bomb at a group of Japanese officials, who had gathered to celebrate Emperor Hirohito's birthday in Hung-k'ou Park, Shanghai, on April 29, 1932. He succeeded in killing and wounding several important Japanese diplomats. Among the wounded was Nomura Kichisaburō, later famous as Japan's ambassador to the United States at the time of the attack on Pearl Harbor in 1941. Another was Shigemitsu Mamoru, later Japan's foreign minister, whose injuries from Yun's 1932 bombing in Shanghai caused him to limp and use a cane as he went aboard the USS *Missouri* to sign the Japanese surrender in September 1945.

21. The *Seoul Press* had been slipping into a wartime propaganda mode as it was, devoting much space to such things as anti-Bolshevik speeches by Joseph Goebbels. When editor Frank Kim fell ill and died in the spring of 1937, the Government-General took the opportunity to close the paper for good, explaining that there was no longer any need for it since the foreigners in Korea were doing such a good job of learning the "national language," i.e., Japanese. English-language newspaper readers after that were forced to wait several days for the *Japan Advertiser* and the *Nippon Times* to come from Japan.

And so the people of Keijō continued their routines. In March, the city hosted General Tōjō Hideki, commander-in-chief of the Kwantung Army, Japan's military force in Manchuria. In April, a Hollywood cosmetician named Mildred Maitland came to town to give free makeovers in the Max Factor exhibit at Pak Hŭngsik's Hwasin Department Store. The Dutch diplomat and mystery writer R.H. Van Gulik stopped over for several days. A Japanese-American baseball team from Alameda, California, visited to play some exhibition games in Keijō Stadium. The British community, which usually celebrated Queen Victoria's Birthday on May 24 with a party on consulate grounds, shifted the celebration to May 12, coronation day for King George and his Queen Elizabeth.[22] Helen Keller visited in June and spoke several times before continuing on to China. And at Chōsen Christian College, two American graduate students named George McCune and Edwin O. Reischauer were hard at work with the help of Korean linguists on the faculty inventing a new romanization system for writing Korean in the Western alphabet.[23]

The year 1937, however, opened a new and traumatic chapter in the colonial ordeal of the Korean people. Japan started turning Korea into a stag-

22. Coronation Day in Seoul began with services at the Anglican Cathedral of St. Mary and St. Nicholas, followed by a luncheon for honored guests at the British Consulate. In the afternoon there was a reception at the Seoul Club for the rest of the foreign community, after which the Britishers returned to their compound for tea. Around suppertime they gathered around a radio to listen to a special broadcast of the coronation ceremonies in Westminster Abbey, relayed from London. The day ended with time around the piano singing British songs.

23. McCune and his wife, Evelyn, were spending the summer with Evelyn's parents, who taught at the college. Reischauer and his wife, Adrienne, were on their way to Peking for his doctoral research when the Marco Polo Bridge Incident interrupted their trip and forced them to stay in Korea awaiting travel clearance. To pass the time, Reischauer turned to learning about Korea and immediately ran into the lack of a standard system for romanizing the Korean language. Romanization systems were on everyone's mind at the time, because the Japanese had just instituted a new system for transliterating Japanese that turned "Chōsen" into "Tyosen," for example, and "Prince Chichibu" into "Prince Titibu," among other oddities.

When Reischauer found that "Mac" McCune was also frustrated by the same problem, the two young scholars sat down with Chōsen Christian College linguists Ch'oe Hyŏnbae, Chŏng Insŏp, and Kim Sŏn'gi, and invented the McCune-Reischauer System for romanizing Korean. This system was adopted during World War II by the U.S. government and subsequently, in modified form, by the South Korean government in Seoul.

McCune and Reischauer both served in the U.S. government during the war, and both became noted East Asia scholars. McCune founded the field of Korean Studies in the United States at the University of California at Berkeley, but unfortunately died when he was only forty, in 1948. Reischauer became "dean" of Japanese Studies in the United States, serving on the Harvard faculty for nearly forty years. In the 1960s he served as U.S. ambassador to Japan under presidents John F. Kennedy and Lyndon B. Johnson.

ing area for the war effort on the mainland, mobilizing the Korean people under the policy of *naisen ittai* ("Unity of the homeland and Korea"). As loyal subjects of the emperor,[24] the Koreans eventually would be forced to give up most vestiges of their national identity, their Korean language, their traditional associations, and even their own Korean names. In return they were offered the privilege of labor service in Japan, military and police service under the Japanese flag, and the role of worshippers at ceremonies honoring Japan's Shintō deities. During these humiliations the Korean people found few friends or sympathizers beyond their own shores. Their own efforts at armed resistance—the citizen militias, guerrilla fighters, saboteurs, and assassins—had failed to shake Japan's grip on their land. Popular resistance in the streets had also failed, notably the nationwide Independence Movement of 1919 and the occasional outbursts of the 1920s and '30s. The war in China now pointed them to an even bleaker future, both as victims of Japanese imperialism and as collaborators in its advance.

Though Koreans were not allowed in the Japanese armed forces at first, as the China Incident unfolded in 1937-38, Japan's population of 69 million proved insufficient to supply the military's manpower needs.[25] Thus in February 1938, shortly after the Rape of Nanking and the Imperial Japanese Army's failure to force the Chinese Nationalists to surrender, Koreans were offered the privilege of volunteering for service in the Chōsen Army. The Japanese, with telling caution, made it a pilot program at first, taking 406 recruits in April and just under 3,000 out of 825,000 eligible by the end of the year. The recruits were given six months of training that included "moral lessons," Japanese language, and Japanese studies.[26] Though they hoped to expand the program, their initial caution was aimed at finding and training only the most dedicated Korean collaborators.[27]

Giving Koreans the chance to serve in the Japanese military was only one of General Minami's ways of making them better imperial subjects. In March 1938, through the New Korean Education Ordinance, he decreed that not only would Japanese be the only language used in schools but that schoolchildren thenceforth would be punished for speaking Korean anywhere, even at home. The government would redouble efforts to teach Japanese to adults.[28]

24. Edward I-te Chen, "The Attempt to Integrate the Empire," in *The Japanese Colonial Empire, 1895-1945*, ed. Ramon H. Myers and Mark R. Peattie (Princeton: Princeton University Press, 1984), p. 246.

25. Chong-Sik Lee, *Japan and Korea: the Political Dimension* (Stanford: Hoover Institution Press, 1985), p. 7.

26. Marsh to Grew, March 4, 1938 (895.20/1).

27. Gregory Henderson, *Korea: The Politics of the Vortex* (Cambridge, Mass.: Harvard University Press, 1968).

28. Children, being more adaptable, generally switched back and forth between Korean and Japanese with ease. "I remember. . .primary students coming out of the gate of the school across from J.H. Morris, switching to Korean in mid-sentence as

In July 1938, the regime established the Korean branch of the "Movement for the General Mobilization of the National Spirit." Koreans were organized into patriotic groups (*aikokuhan*) along lines familiar to all East Asians[29] but organized now to improve surveillance of the population for the Japanese war effort. Each patriotic group (*han*) was made up of several households. Several *han* made a *kumi*, or "team," and several teams made a *chō*, or neighborhood. Patriotic groups kept track of members and their actions, employing peer pressure and mutual responsibility to enforce tax laws, wartime rationing, and the panoply of rules regulating daily life. People marched to the Shintō shrines together according to patriotic group, to bow and show spiritual unity with their overlords.[30]

As Japan ravaged China's cities, the Korean people suffered ever-greater hardships. Minami's regime had one main purpose: to support the war. This meant energetic production efforts, not only in "legitimate" business and industry but also in shadier areas. Under Minami, officially sanctioned opium production increased dramatically in Korea. Most of it was controlled and exported for "medicinal" sale in Manchukuo;[31] but some inevitably went astray and combined with unregulated opium to help accelerate the addiction rate in Korea.

If the state-sponsored opium trade was a cynical exploitation of the Korean people, it was just one part of the pattern of using the colony and its people to do the most objectionable jobs in the Japanese economy. The transfer of Korean laborers to Japan—the men to work in coal mines, the women to work in textile factories—was a phenomenon of historic importance since it created the long-suffering Korean minority in Japan. The terms of employment for these workers were inhumane to say the least, in-

they came through." Horace G. Underwood, note to the author, March 1990.

29. The principle was similar to the ancient *li-chia* and *pao-chia* systems of the Chinese and the five-household *gonin gumi* system of Tokugawa Japan. The five-household responsibility system is still in use in North Korea today.

30. Lee, *The Politics of Korean Nationalism*, p. 264. This was the social system into which all Koreans had become ensnared when the Presbyterian General Assembly, for example, was forced without debate to affirm the government's position on the Shintō worship issue. No Korean delegate at the Assembly could have escaped retribution for doing otherwise and, with the patriotic groups in place, each delegate's family was held responsible for his actions.

31. There had already been a vast increase in opium production in Manchukuo: "From before the Mukden Incident drugs were being sold widely by so-called pawn brokers in every village, acting as vendors of opium *and* as spies. Now [1936] licensed stores have been added in the larger centers, and last winter many addicts froze to death in the streets of the new capital [Hsinking/Changchun] itself. Meanwhile on Wumalu Road [in Hsinking] where the Irish Presbyterian Mission has a church, schools and hospital, twenty-three brothels have been opened with Japanese clerks, etc. Such are the moral liabilities of imperialism." L. S. Albright (Canadian Mission in Japan), "Extract from Report on 'A Summer Visit to Korea,'" UCCA, 83.006C, Box 3, File 86.

volving deception at recruitment, brutal living and working conditions, and discriminatory pay. The entrapment of young Korean women in Japanese factory dormitories was tantamount to slavery; however, even that was not as bad as their entrapment in Japanese army brothels to function as sexual "comfort women" (*ianfu*; Korean *wi'anbu*) for the troops.

"Comfort women" were an aspect of the Japanese labor pattern that developed with the advance of the Japanese war in China. It involved the conscription of men and women as laborers in support of fighting units. Female laborers cooked and did laundry for the soldiers, and many also were forced to endure what amounted to gang rape.[32] The recruitment of Korean girls to be members of what the Japanese euphemized as the *jōshi teishintai*, the "women's self-offering corps," was an unspeakable humiliation for their families and society.[33] Wartime censorship helped keep the secret of the girls' degradation. It also

"Golden Hairpin Society." Korean women donate their jewelry to the Japanese war effort, 1938. Government-General of Tyosen, *Annual Report on Administration of Tyosen, 1937-38* (Keizyo: Government-General of Tyosen, 1938), p. 116.

32. On "comfort women" see *positions: east asia cultures critique*, V (June 1997), "Special Issue on Comfort Women," ed. Chungmoo Choi; and Keith Howard, comp., *True Stories of the Korean Comfort Women* (London: Cassell, 1995).

33. As the world was shown during the early phases of "ethnic cleansing" by Bosnian Serbs in the former Yugoslavia, the act of rape by soldiers is directed as much against the men of a conquered society as the women who actually endure the assault, because it is intended to prove that the men cannot protect their women. See the discussion by Cynthia Enloe in *The Morning After: Sexual Politics at the End of the Cold War* (Berkeley and Los Angeles: University of California Press, 1993), pp. 239-244. And as Chungmoo Choi points out, in Korean society the degradation of the military comfort women led to the even more devastating rejection by their own families, especially male relatives who, in some cases, they had offered themselves to protect; see Chungmoo Choi, "Korean Women in a Culture of Inequality," *Korea Briefing 1992,* ed. Donald N. Clark (Boulder, Colo.: Westview Press, 1992), p. 104.

enforced silence among the few Westerners who were aware of *teishintai* recruitment. One of these was Ethel Underwood, who wrote an unpublished memorandum about it entitled "The Darkest Blot in Korea" in 1942. In her view, recruitment for military brothels was an extension of the established business of prostitution that preyed on girls from poor Japanese families as well as from Korea:

> Agents deliver the girl to the crowded dormitory of the employment agency. From here they are sold and resold to factories, hotels, inns, and private homes. The younger girls are taught how to serve food and drink, how to dress and comb up their hair, then they are sold to "cafes" or "drink houses," [and] resold at rising prices until the original 100 yen becomes 200 yen, 300 yen, or sometimes 1,000 yen or more. Girls who from their infancy have learned submission to men are now taught to please them. At any stage from the mother's door to the third or fourth sale the girl may be raped, "broken in," "prepared," for commercialized vice. The totals are appalling. During the one month of March 1940, 1,500 Korean girls around the age of fourteen were taken through the one port of Antung into Manchuria and northern China. Parties of ten to twenty little pre-adolescent girls were constantly seen being taken to the police stations for identification, for travel permits, medical examinations, [etc.]. Older girls are not wanted. "They fight too much if they are not broken in before puberty." Police regulations make the tracing of girls difficult....
>
> Sometimes a tearful mother goes on a journey and returns with a pitiful little body, sick and defeated, disillusioned and disgraced. More often nothing is ever heard of the little girl. But the dives of Mukden, Peking, Shanghai, and the barracks of Nanking, Hong Kong, and now Manila have competent doctors to throw out any girl dangerously diseased. Koreans hear, shudder, and are ashamed. They revile and hate their rulers and despise them. Thousands of Korean leaders from schools and churches, from newspapers and farms [who have been] thrown into jails these last few years report that the only conversation of the police force is of drink, and of the lustful delights of girls from inns and cafes, and from the registered brothels. Brutal by day and bestial by night, the policeman is both hated and despised.[34]

Putting an End to Western Business

A regime that was not above drafting women as sex slaves and dabbling in the opium trade was hardly likely to care much about the concerns of Korea's Western residents. In Seoul, relations between the foreign community and the Government-General grew strained. Instead of trying to work things out, the regime increased pressure on the Westerners and started curbing their ability to do business. An early instance was the pressure put on Western oil companies, which were ordered to keep six months re-

34. Ethel Van Wagoner Underwood, "The Darkest Blot in Korea," unpublished report enclosed in letter to J.L. Hooper, October 8, 1942, Presbyterian Historical Society.

serves on hand in Korea, to sell only enough to meet set quotas of gasoline, kerosene, and heating oil, and to use only Japanese tankers to bring petroleum into the country. This was a hardship for the foreign oil companies operating in the peninsula—Standard-Vacuum, Caltex, and Rising Sun Petroleum, which was a subsidiary of Royal Dutch Shell. All three supplied Korea from company tanks in China, with Caltex delivering in specially designed ships. Standard Oil built some tanks in Korea in an effort to comply, but it was soon clear that the real purpose of the new rules was simply to eliminate foreign competition. In July 1936, as the Western companies' operations were being limited, the Japanese-owned Chōsen Petroleum Company opened its new refinery at Wonsan, taking over the share of the market that the Westerners were having to give up.[35]

Minami's hard line affected individual Westerners too, as police surveillance became an everyday reality. Early in his regime, Minami ordered the expansion of the foreign affairs police, especially around Seoul and in the northeast, where ports were being developed at Chŏngjin and Najin—ports through which military cargoes were passing into Manchuria. Security was one reason for the stepped-up surveillance of foreigners, but harassment was another. There were new rules prohibiting picture-taking near anything remotely connected with industry or the military, including bridges, the seashore, and mountain tops. Foreigners were forbidden to buy land near certain beaches, tunnels, and bridges, and some of their property was confiscated. The 1937 summer season at Wŏnsan Beach proved to be the resort's last, for example, after a vacationer took his sailboat too close to the ship channel, which had been declared a restricted military area. The government commandeered the resort and furnished a new site sixty miles farther south at Hwajinp'o, compensating the owners and letting them rebuild their cottages at the new location.[36]

Soon after Minami's arrival, the Government-General started looking for ways to force Westerners out of the colony. Surveillance intensified, and detectives diligently sought to catch violations that could be used as reasons for deportation. Longtime businessman Paul Plaisant, for example, kept selling French wine in Seoul long after the importation of wine was prohibited. Where was he getting it? A search of the Plaisant premises

---

35. This, of course, is much the same situation the oil companies faced in Manchuria during General Minami's "ambassadorship" there, and no one was much surprised.

36. The beach at Hwajinp'o was rocky and inferior to the one at Wŏnsan, but there was a fine inland lake affording views of the water in both directions. Owners whose cottages could not be moved were paid enough to build new ones at the new resort. Sherwood Hall, M.D., *With Stethoscope in Asia: Korea* (McLean, Va.: MCL Associates, 1978), pp. 517-518. Hwajinp'o, near the town of Kojin above Sokcho near the Demilitarized Zone (DMZ), is the only one of the prewar beach resorts within South Korean jurisdiction.

turned up a private winery and a press for printing labels. In trouble and embarrassed, Plaisant struck a deal: he would not be prosecuted if he made a 5,000-yen contribution to the Japanese Army and left Korea. Shortly thereafter the Plaisants, one of Korea's oldest foreign business families, moved to Shanghai.[37]

Deporting a single businessman was easier than finding pretexts to get rid of Korea's numerous foreign missionaries, whom the Minami regime regarded as agents of sedition but whose work was protected by many years of law and custom.[38] Detectives were ordered to redouble their efforts to find infractions. Plainclothesmen shadowed foreigners everywhere, even in the remote interior. They listened in on classes and church services in hopes of catching foreigners inciting Koreans to rebellion. They visited foreign homes in search of pernicious books and magazines from abroad. They demanded inventories of cameras, typewriters, and especially radios—anything that could be construed as spy equipment. All meetings had to be reported in advance, with lists of who was going to attend and what was going to be discussed. It became routine to detain Koreans who visited foreigners. The effect, of course, was to deter all but the most essential contact.

Cracking Down on Christians

Koreans with foreign connections were easy targets for the Japanese as were all intellectuals involved in Korean "self-strengthening" societies. "Self-strengthening" had been an important concept in the minds of late nineteenth-century Chinese intellectuals as they struggled to organize resistance against Western imperialism and the humiliating terms of the treaties forced on the Ch'ing empire by gunboat diplomacy. Twentieth-century Korean intellectuals, most of whom were familiar with the ideas of Chinese opponents of foreign domination, appropriated "self-strengthening" (*chagang* in Korean), and used it as a code word for building up Korea's ability to win its independence from Japan. The early nationalists Chang Chiyŏn and Yun Hyojŏng, for example, started a club called the Taehan Chagang-hoe (Korean Self-Strengthening Society), its ideology an eclectic mix of eighteenth-century Korean *Silhak* reform thought, Social Darwinism, ideas from the French Enlightenment, and Christianity. It ran afoul of the Japanese authorities during the Protectorate period, when it organized protests against the removal of Emperor Kojong following the ill-fated Hague Conference appeal in 1907.

37. Cyril Tchirkine, interview, Hayward, California, June 24, 1991.
38. An analogy would be the attitude of Americans toward the German-American Bund in the United States around the same time. Americans who joined the Bund were regarded as security risks, while Koreans who became Christians were security risks to the Minami regime.

"Self-strengthening" remained an ideal in the minds of reformers throughout the Japanese period, with Yun Ch'iho being a prime example of one who accepted Japanese rule in the short run but strove to make Koreans "worthy" of independence in the long run through self-improvement. In fact, he was once president of the Self-Strengthening Society and probably would have continued to lend his considerable talents to the *chagang* movement publicly if he had not been jailed in the 1911 Conspiracy Case and tried to stay out of trouble after his 1913 release. The latter-day self-strengtheners were in the tradition of the "cultural nationalists"; reformers who envisioned eventual independence but preferred education and self-cultivation to revolt or popular revolution. They tended to be educated, conservative, often businessmen or landowners, and often members of one of Korea's "newer" religions, namely Ch'ŏndokyo and Christianity.

The "cultural nationalists" carried forward the self-strengthening movement, organizing clubs and societies around core memberships of intellectuals and religious believers. The Suyang Tong'u-hoe, for example, published a magazine that advocated national consciousness, something that would have been allowed under Governor General Saitō and even under General Ugaki, but was ruled off limits by the Minami regime. Most members of the Suyang Tong'uhoe were Christians, many of them being linked to the YMCA, and many of these were Presbyterians from northwestern Korea who had histories going back to the Independence Movement and even the 1911 Conspiracy Case. Some of the funds for the Suyang Tong'uhoe came from the Los Angeles-based Hŭngsadan (Society for Fostering Activists), founded by the nationalist An Ch'angho, a Christian organization that envisioned a Korea true to its heritage and able to protect itself.[39]

Idealism was also the attraction of a similar organization called the Hŭng'ŏp Kurakbu (Industry Promotion Club), a group that included George Paik and met to promote Korean historical and cultural studies and to foster economic independence from Japan. Its members were primarily Christian, being associated with the YMCA as well as the Methodist Church. The Industry Promotion Club's founder was Hugh Cynn (Shin Hŭng'u), a Methodist youth leader who had returned from a church conference in Hawaii full of enthusiasm for the ideas of the Hawaii-based Tongjihoe, Syngman Rhee's group of overseas Koreans. The Club called itself "revolutionary" and was organized as a secret society, however innocuous its actual program.

As soon as Minami Jirō became governor-general, however, he ordered the police into action against the cultural nationalists. In 1937-38, the po-

---

39. Kenneth Wells discusses the ideals of the Hŭngsadan and the Suyang Tong'u-hoe in detail, in *New God, New Nation* (Honolulu: University of Hawaii Press, 1990), pp. 120-127.

lice raided offices of the Suyang Tong'uhoe in Seoul, P'yŏngyang, Sŏnch'ŏn, and Anak, arresting a total of 181 members for breaches of the Peace
Preservation Law. The political nature of the arrests can be seen in the fact
that only forty-nine of those arrested, most of them Presbyterian Christians, were ever tried, and that after four years of incarceration during ap-
peals they were finally released for lack of evidence.[40]

The Japanese also descended on the Chōsen Christian College faculty
and arrested those who belonged to the Suyang Tong'uhoe, the Chindan
Hakhoe historical society, the Korean Language Society (Han'gŭl Hakhoe),
and the Industry Promotion Club (Hŭngŏp Kurakbu). The attack on the Industry Promotion Club, which began in March 1938 with a roundup of Korean economists including members of the C.C.C. faculty, turned up a club
manifesto written in "revolutionary" language. The police then went after
all the club's members, carrying on house searches and terrorizing families
in addition to arresting individuals. Yun Ch'iho and Hugh Cynn were arrested. So were Chōsen Christian College vice-president Yu Ŏkkyŏm and
many of the remaining Korean faculty including Ch'oe Hyŏnbae and Yi
Ch'unho, both prominent "cultural nationalists." They were held for investigation of their "anti-Japanese" activities and subjected to physical abuse
to elicit confessions about their alleged collaboration with foreign spies, after which they were released under suspended indictments but forbidden
to return to work.[41] Eventually they were forced to sign confessions and
apologies for subversive activity, supporting independence and the overseas leader Syngman Rhee.

George Paik escaped the roundup by happening to be in the United
States attending the General Assembly meeting of the Presbyterian Church.
To help keep him out of prison, the president of Park College invited him
to stay in America and teach Bible and international relations for a year until things cooled down in Korea. While he was away, police ransacked his
house and intimidated his wife who tried as best she could to hide or destroy the family's most damning links to Korean nationalism and Western
influence.[42] Without much hope for the future he returned to Seoul in
1939. Shortly thereafter, the authorities also forced him to resign from the
Chōsen Christian College faculty.

40. Koen DeCeuster, "From Modernization to Collaboration, the Dilemma of Korean Cultural Nationalism," pp. 430-431.
41. L. George Paik, interview, Seoul, December 23, 1983. Yi Manyŏl, pp. 263-
264, Horace H. Underwood, statement enclosed with Harold B. Quarton to Grew,
August 18, 1942 (395.1163/119), and Yonsei taehakkyo ch'angnip p'alsim nyŏn
kinyŏm saŏp wiwŏnhoe, *Yonsei taehakkyosa*, (Seoul: Yonsei University Press,
1969), pp. 388-390.
42. L. George Paik, interview, Seoul, March 16, 1984. The flag, with note attached telling the story, is in Paik's papers in the Yonsei University Library.

Altogether, 126,626 persons were arrested or subjected to political harassment by the Japanese in the single year 1938.[43] Events seemed to have
turned a corner, and Westerners living in Korea found themselves contem-
plating new dangers, not only for themselves but also for their Korean associates. The Christian and foreign links of the Industry Promotion Club
had been central to the case against it, and the Minami regime clearly made
the point that it was dangerous for Koreans to get too close to Westerners
and their ideas.[44]

43. Henderson, *Korea: The Politics of the Vortex*, p. 103.
44. Yi Manyŏl, *Chonggyo kyoyuk t'ujaeng* (Seoul: Minjok Munhwa Hyophoe,
1981), p. 263; Wells, *New God, New Nation,* passim, especially pp. 160-161;
DeCeuster, "From Modernization to Collaboration," pp. 433-435.

-- 10 --

Render unto Caesar the Things
That Are Caesar's

In 1936, the U.S. State Department assigned a new consul-general to the post in Seoul. He was O. Gaylord Marsh of Buchanan, Michigan, a veteran of thirty-one years in the federal bureaucracy. By the time he reached Korea, Gaylord Marsh, 57, had had many years of practice cultivating a style that would satisfy his superiors and ingratiate himself with his host country counterparts. Bald with grey on the fringes, of medium height and weight, bland and bespectacled, he was the very model of a foreign service officer.

Marsh's orders told him to report for service under the American ambassador to Japan, at the consular post called Seoul, also known as Keijō. Marsh knew that Korea, now called Chōsen, was a colonial acquisition of Japan. He was also aware that Korean malcontents had been known to demand American intervention to help them regain their independence. But that was in the past. The United States recognized Japan's sovereignty and his job as consul-general was to represent his government in Chōsen.

Consular work had been Gaylord Marsh's profession, but he enjoyed some of its routines more than others. He did not enjoy fixing the damage done by his thoughtless countrymen abroad—the stranded tourists, the drunken sailors, the bankrupt businessmen, and the whining missionaries. Invariably after receiving his help they showed an annoying lack of gratitude. Marsh's ideal consular post would have been one where all the American residents obeyed the local laws, stayed out of trouble, and got along with local officials. It also helped if the local officials could speak English and were eager to further American interests. Marsh noted that Keijō did not seem to be such a place.

Gaylord Marsh had seen duty previously in the Philippines, Canada, Uruguay, France, and Guatemala. Guatemala had been his favorite. American interests there were self-sustaining and the United Fruit Company, which virtually ran Guatemala through the regime of Jorge "Tata" Ubico, suffered little interference. Marsh thus had much time to himself. He kept a vegetable garden in the rich volcanic soil, importing seeds via the diplomatic pouch. He started a collection of tropical fish. He went boating in the bays of the Caribbean coast and deep-sea fishing in the Pacific. The American business circle made him one of their own. The local manager of the United Fruit Company took him sightseeing up through southern Mexico. Even New Orleans was on his beat: the year 1934 took him there for an international conference on smuggling. Marsh expected to miss Guatemala very much at his next post in the Orient.

One thing Gaylord Marsh was looking forward to in Seoul was married life. After years as a divorced man, he had courted his childhood sweetheart Ruth Ellsworth via the mails, and when his orders came to proceed to Seoul, the couple arranged to be married in San Francisco. After a quick ceremony on December 13, they boarded the S.S. *Empress of Russia* for a honeymoon cruise to Imperial Japan.

Inevitably, perhaps, the Marshes' first days in Korea were not auspicious. The consul-general's official residence—Lucius Foote's old Korean house with patchwork improvements—was undergoing renovations. One room was entirely filled with the personal effects of the late consul Ransford Miller. The Marshes' own things, meanwhile, were stuck in San Francisco because of a dockworkers' strike. Their furniture sat for months in a waterfront warehouse, warping in Guatemalan green-lumber crates. The Marshes had a hard time keeping up their spirits. Gaylord missed the tropics. Nothing in Korea seemed as good. People noticed the faraway look in his eye when he told stories of travels in the Yucatan. On one occasion he gave an elaborate lecture on the conquest of yellow fever by the Army Medical Corps in Panama, attempting to link it to Korea by pointing out that Walter Reed had had a Japanese doctor named Noguchi on his staff. After one particularly lyrical description of his previous post, one of the listeners jokingly referred to him as "Guatemala Marsh," someone else picked it up, and the nickname stuck.

Spring came, and brilliant yellow forsythia bloomed along the consulate compound's pathways, inspiring the Marshes to get involved in what passed for Seoul's social scene. They joined the Seoul Club and the Anglican Church. Ruth joined the Women's Club of Seoul and got her husband to lecture on tropical gardens. Gaylord Marsh himself joined the International Friendly Association, the Royal Asiatic Society, and the Seoul Rotary Club. The consul-general was at his genial best on holidays: raising toasts to King George on his birthday, to Governor-General Minami on Japanese Foundation Day, and to Emperor Hirohito on any occasion at all. He put cherry candies by every plate at the Rotary luncheon on George Washington's birthday. And he liked to host the American community's traditional Fourth of July garden party.

Part of Marsh's job was to cultivate Governor-General Minami who was not known for friendliness toward Americans. One of Marsh's early diplomatic coups came because of his wife's talents as an artist. Minami was known to have noticed that Ruth was a painter, and Marsh seized the opportunity to send him one of her works, a Korean village scene. The governor-general responded with a specimen of his own calligraphy reproduced in mother-of-pearl set in lacquer. Marsh documented this success in a dispatch to the State Department, complete with photographs of the art works that had been exchanged.[1]

Although Ruth Marsh liked to paint Korean scenery, her husband displayed little interest in Korea as such. Korean things seemed anachronistic to him, reminders of a past that should be forgotten. He was annoyed at the way longtime American residents kept the memory of Korea alive, for example, by using old Korean names for things. Korean place names were written in Chinese characters and had different pronunciations in Korean, Japanese, and Chinese. The country was "Chosŏn" to a Korean and "Chō-sen" to a Japanese. The capital city was "Kyŏngsŏng" to a Korean and "Keijō" to a Japanese. Pronouncing things in the Japanese way, or using Japanese names for streets and places, connoted acceptance of the colonial regime.[2] Old-timers knew that calling the city "Seoul" or "Kyŏngsŏng" meant they were taking sides with the Koreans.

In Gaylord Marsh's opinion, Americans had no business calling Seoul anything but "Keijō." P'yŏngyang, too, should be "Heijō," Japanese-style. To set an example, he threw away the consulate's supply of stationery that said "Seoul" on the letterhead and replaced it with new paper that said "Keijō." He also initiated a change in Washington, advising the government to use only Japanese designations for places in Korea.[3] Thus did the new American representative make it plain that he would not be a friend of Ko-

1. Marsh to SecState, April 20, 1937, and memo from Division of Research and Publication (895.014/2). Ruth Marsh may have been consciously imitating Alice Grew, the wife of Ambassador Joseph C. Grew in Tokyo, who had distinguished herself by painting delicate Japanese scenes in water colors and giving them away. Rena Krasno, *That Last Glorious Summer, 1939—Shanghai-Japan* (Hong Kong: Old China Hand Press, 2001), p. 25.

2. Two examples: The Japanese named one of the main streets "Takezoe-chō" after an 1880s Japanese ambassador to Korea, and another "Hasegawa-chō" after the Japanese governor-general who suppressed the Korean Independence Movement in 1919, something comparable to renaming Atlanta's Peachtree Street "Sherman Avenue."

3. Marsh to SecState, April 20, 1937, and memo from Division of Research and Publication (895.014/2).

rean independence, or of any American who took a public stand against Japanese rule in the colony.

The Problem of the Shintō Shrines

To the missionaries in Gaylord Marsh's jurisdiction, things were not so simple. Though they had sublimated their Korean sympathies for fear of endangering their work, their long years in country had given them a paternal interest in Koreans, especially Christians, that was nonpolitical on the surface but anti-Japanese underneath—just the kind of stance that Marsh considered inappropriate for Americans abroad. Nowhere was this special interest more evident than in the Presbyterian Mission station at P'yŏngyang.

By the mid-1930s, P'yŏngyang had become the citadel of Christianity in Korea. There were thirty churches, both Protestant and Catholic, for an urban population of about 200,000, and a hundred more churches within a day's drive.[4] Credit for what had been accomplished in the first half-century of missionary work belonged largely to the pioneer generation that included Samuel Moffett, William Baird, George McCune, and William Swallen. Altogether, these old-timers, their wives, and the forty-three continuing members of Presbyterian station at P'yŏngyang had accumulated 1,003 years of experience in Korea. Seven of them had spent more than thirty years on the field, fifteen more had been there for at least twenty, nine more had served more than a decade, only seven had been in Korea for less than that. The P'yŏngyang team had much to be proud of. It also had much to defend. This sense of personal investment in "the Work" combined with sympathy for the Koreans and distaste for the Japanese proved to be a recipe for trouble in the 1930s when the colonial regime began mobilizing the Koreans for war. The occasion for the conflict was the Japanese decision to force Koreans, as subjects of the emperor, to perform obeisances resembling acts of worship at Japanese Shintō shrines.

The opening shots in the confrontation over Shintō rites were fired in November 1935 when government education authorities in P'yŏngyang called a conference of the city's school principals. Veteran missionaries George McCune and Velma Snook, as heads of the P'yŏngyang Presbyterian boys' and girls' academies, were among those summoned to attend, as was Father Joseph Connors of the Catholic mission school. But because the first item on the conference agenda was a ceremony at the city's main Shintō shrine to honor the spirits of Japan's national ancestors and war dead, the three missionaries refused to appear. They explained that as Christians they could not participate in religious rituals of other faiths. To

---

4. Rhodes, I, pp. 88-91, and Government-General of Tyosen, *Annual Report on Administration of Tyosen, 1937-38* (Keizyo [Seoul], 1938), p. 14.

Chōsen Shrine, South Mountain, Seoul, circa 1930. Government-General of Chō-sen, *Annual Report on Administration of Chōsen, 1932-33* (Keijō: Government-General of Chōsen, 1933), frontispiece.

the Japanese, however (and to watching Koreans), their stand was a challenge to the authority of the Japanese government, and it required a response.

The Shintō shrine conflict was not about missionaries, of course, but about the attitude of Korean Christians toward the Japanese colonial regime. As Japanese politics veered to the right in the 1930s, participation in Shintō rites became a test of loyalty to the emperor. Outwardly, the ceremonies consisted of little more than simple bowing, but inwardly they were highly symbolic. The spirits being worshipped were those of Japanese ancestors and war heroes. Shintō rites affirmed Japanese-ness, and Koreans gave up something of their Korean-ness every time they bowed. Perhaps Shintō would have been more palatable to the Koreans if the Japanese had made more of an effort to present it as a common tradition.[5] But instead, they transferred their state cult to Korea intact. In 1935, under the policy of *naisen ittai* ("Unity of the homeland and Korea"), the Japanese began forcing Shintō worship on all Japanese citizens, making it a symbol of cultural genocide for the Koreans.

5. Attempts to make a case for common ancestors for the Korean and Japanese people were made, even by such reputable Koreans as Ch'oe Namsŏn, drafter of the 1919 Declaration of Independence and acting, presumably, on Japanese instructions, to promote their *naisen ittai* policy. YCH, pp. 528-529.

Torii Gate, Chōsen Shrine, South Mountain, Seoul, circa 1938. Postcard. Clark Collection.

Korean Christians who refused Shintō worship did so on religious and constitutional grounds. They pointed to the First and Second Commandments in the Bible and the guarantees of religious freedom in the Meiji Constitution. The Japanese government argued, however, that the rites were not religious but patriotic—merely "reverence for ancestors"—a concept familiar to the Confucian Koreans. They equated bowing at shrines with standing at attention during the singing of the national anthem. But everyone knew that it was more than that. Forcing Koreans to accept Japan's national myths was a matter of colonial power.

Foreigners themselves were not required to bow at the shrines. The missionaries were personally required to bow, however, in their capacity as school officials along with their students. The immediate issue, therefore, was one of example: whether Christian teachers should set an example of bowing to heathen spirits. The substance of the ritual connoted communion with the spirits. It was up to the individual to decide whether this was a "religious" or "patriotic" act. If it was religious, as the Presbyterian conservatives in P'yŏngyang believed it to be, they had no right to lead their students into error. On the other hand, if they refused and the students followed their example, they would be leading them to break the law, for which the students would be punished.

Christianity had confronted Shintō before, in turn-of-the-century Japan. There, the Japanese Christian church had accepted the government's distinction between "State Shintō" and "Sect Shintō," making no objection to Christian participation in "State Shintō" rituals. At the time, the flush of victories over China and Russia had created a mood of nationalism in Japan that made it dangerous to oppose the state or its myths; and so the church fell back on the Japanese tradition of syncretism, living with State Shintō as it had accepted the Confucian notions of loyalty and filial piety. Christians went to the shrines feeling no great conflict. Nor was the foreign missionary community in Japan troubled by it. The Catholics, whose eighteenth-century predecessors had been expelled from fields all over East Asia for opposing ancestor worship in the Rites Controversy, accepted it. So did the newcomers—including the American Presbyterians and Methodists.

The Japanese had expected the same attitude on the part of the Christian church in Korea, and when Shinto was first imported to Korea in the form of shrines for the use of Japanese residents, there had been little cause for conflict. But then in the 1920s, the colonial regime began giving Shintō a much higher profile. As part of its massive public buildings program, the Government-General cleared a prominent spot on Seoul's South Mountain and erected an imposing headquarters shrine for the colony.[6] Elaborate Shintō rituals that were manifestly religious marked the opening of the Chōsen Shrine in October 1925. Sacred *mitamashiro*, or symbols, of the Sun Goddess and the Meiji Emperor—including one of the emperor's swords—were conveyed to Pusan on a naval destroyer and thence by rail to Seoul Station. A motorcade carried the *mitamashiro* up the slope to the shrine to be installed by twenty-five white-gloved young men in a solemn sunset ceremony. For twenty years thereafter the Chōsen Shrine overlooked the city of Seoul from its height on the mountain. People climbed the granite steps from South Gate to bow at the shrine every day, and important visitors always were taken there to pay respects. Each spring there was a ceremony there to pray for a bountiful harvest. And it also served an educational purpose: like other shrines in Korea the Chōsen Shrine published morals texts for young people.[7]

P'yŏngyang (or "Heijō," as it was called in Japanese) also acquired a shrine. Like the Chōsen Shrine in Seoul, the Heijō Shrine in P'yŏngyang was originally built to serve the city's Japanese residents and was merely a Japanese symbol to the Koreans, few of whom had anything to do with it. But then came the 1930s, the arrival of a more rigid regime in Korea under Governor-General Ugaki Kazushige, the Japanese takeover of Manchuria, and the implementation of Japan's assimilation program for the Koreans.

6. The location of the shrine is an interesting case of the use of "sacred space." To build the Chōsen Shrine the Japanese removed from the location a shamanist shrine that had stood for centuries—the Kuksadang, and put it on Inwang mountain across the valley (near the Taylor family's "Dilkusha"). To carry the symbolism further, when the Japanese were removed from Korea in 1945-46, the site was used temporarily for the Presbyterian Theological Seminary and Easter sunrise services were held on the grounds. Over the years since then the site has been been home to a succession structures including a huge statue of Syngman Rhee, the National Assembly Library, and a Children's memorial hall in memory of Yuk Yŏngsu (Madame Park Chung-hee), who was killed by an assassin in 1974.

7. *Seoul Press*, October 13, 15, 17, and November 5, 1925, and March 14, 1926.

In 1935, when the foreign missionaries refused to be part of the education director's conference in P'yŏngyang, they were given the choice of conforming or resigning their principalships. Presbyterians George McCune and Velma Snook resigned. Father Connors signed an agreement to obey orders—with the written reservation "in all things that pertain to civil matters." Soon after, the Heijō Shrine was the site of another, especially meaningful demonstration of Japanese power over the Koreans, one that fused religious and political resistance. The city organized a children's lantern parade and shrine ceremony to commemorate the naming of Crown Prince Akihito. Mission school students marched in the parade but obeyed their Christian teachers when told not to bow when they got to the shrine. The lantern ceremony for the little prince therefore marked the Christians of P'yŏngyang in general as disloyal.

Not all Western missionaries in Korea saw the Shintō issue the same way. Though they were troubled by the ramifications of Shintō worship in Korea, the Catholics followed the example of the Catholic Church in Japan proper and called the rituals patriotic. This was the *official* position; however one priest, Monsignor John Morris, openly refused to accept the distinction between "State" and "Sect" Shintō and had to be removed by his superiors.[8] The same divergence of views afflicted the Protestants,[9] but the issue affected the P'yŏngyang Presbyterians most dramatically because of their numbers, their visibility in the most "Christian" part of the country, and their conservative theology. Sticking to principle, they declared that Christians should oppose Shintō worship and that if the church as an organization was forced to compromise, each believer as an individual, whether Korean or foreign, should take a personal stand against Shintō at all costs.

And the costs started adding up. Early in 1936 the Government-General announced that it would not recognize diplomas from schools that neglected Shintō rituals, thereby barring their graduates from government jobs, including teaching. The regime also began revoking the licenses of missionary school principals, replacing them with Koreans. Some who wanted more independence for the Korean church welcomed this. A result

8. Father Morris was ordered to resign in 1936 by the Superior General of Maryknoll, Fr. James E. Walsh, after consultation with various Maryknoll leaders in East Asia, in the interest of restoring harmony to the P'yŏngyang diocese. See Jung Soon Lee and Tae Ho Lee, *Father John E. Morris, M.M.* (Seoul: Sisters of Our Lady of Perpetual Help, 1994), especially Part IV.

9. William Scott, a leader of the Canadian Mission, found little to object to. After watching one of the rituals he wrote, "It was a very simple service, and there was nothing that one could object to. The mode of expressing their respect to the departed may differ from ours, though much simpler than the Roman Catholic ceremonies. There is no idol on the altar, no incense is burned, a simple prayer is said, the hands clapped twice, all bow respectfully, and the ceremony ends." William Scott to A.E. Armstrong, December 13, 1936. UCCA, 83.006C, Box 3, File 86.

is that a rift began to develop within the Korean church between pro-missionary and anti-missionary factions.

Had these things happened later, after Japan had gone to war in China, the colonial administration in Korea would not have tolerated such an open challenge from outsiders. But in the winter of 1935, before General Minami arrived and imposed his wartime hard line, the Ugaki regime was still trying to maintain pretenses of courtesy, custom, and law. Under the property laws, private schools were "owned" by "founders," and "founder" status carried with it almost absolute authority to dispose of the schools, to hire and fire staff, collect, invest, and spend funds, and buy and sell property. The official "founder" of all three Presbyterian schools in P'yŏngyang —Union Christian College, Sungsil Boys' Academy, and Sung'ŭi Girls' Academy—was the venerable Samuel Moffett, retired at age 70 but staying on expressly as the "owner" of the properties in order to forestall the complications that were likely to arise from trying to transfer them to a successor. Moffett, for his part, was personally opposed to any kind of Shintō practice in the mission schools.

In 1936, the P'yŏngyang Presbyterians reaffirmed their stance against participating in Shintō rituals. If the government forced them to do so as part of the educational program, they would close their mission schools. This immediately brought objections from the some of the students' families. The Christian parents accused Moffett and the missionaries of risking their children's educations just to make a political point in a contest they could not win. The families were especially upset by the missionaries' assertion that they were acting in the students' best interests by closing the schools in order to protect them from the heresy of Shintō. Some said that were being subjected to two kinds of colonialism simultaneously, the Japanese and the American.

But there was also a Korean faction that supported the missionaries. When the government forced George McCune to resign as president of Sungsil College and replaced him with a Korean faculty member more amenable to the government position, a "Moffett faction" of about two hundred students began boycotting classes and demanding a return to missionary control.[10] Tensions rose and there were angry words. The head of the local Japanese Army Reservists' Association visited the new Korean college president and warned him "that the temper of [the reservists in P'yŏngyang] was dangerous and that undue protraction of a settlement of

10. The British consul-general said of this group, "There is at the same time reason to believe that a section of the Korean church members is backing the Heijō missionaries in their stand against the Japanese authorities for ulterior political reasons of their own with which religion has nothing to do." Gerald H. Phipps to the British ambassador in Tokyo, November 6, 1936. Public Record Office file FO 262/1944.

the shrine question might lead even to a massacre of Christians."[11] To move the matter along, the next day the students and faculty of the college "under official pressure and intimidation" passed resolutions demanding that management of all the mission schools be transferred to Koreans.

As they found themselves caught in the crossfire, the P'yŏngyang missionaries again felt their vulnerability in colonial Korea. They recalled their helplessness when the police had stood by and let the rowdies of the city massacre P'yŏngyang's Chinese during the 1931 Wanpaoshan Incident. Could such a thing happen again? People discussed evacuating all Americans from the city. George McCune and Samuel Moffett hurried to Seoul to ask for protection from the "growing unruliness of the students,"[12] and there was relief when Consul Bill Langdon arranged to have a detachment of *kempeitai* gendarmes assigned to reinforce the compound's normal police detail.[13]

In a state of high excitement, the Northern Presbyterian Mission assembled in P'yŏngyang for its annual meeting. The conservative majority, true to its long-held position that education devoid of Christian content was not the business of the mission, voted to close all eight of the mission's schools, shutting out 2,587 students. The mission's decision also closed schools in Seoul and Taegu, where there had been no trouble, and it affected other missions through union projects such as Chōsen Christian College and Severance Union Medical College—which could not be maintained by the other cooperating missions without Northern Presbyterian support.[14] But pulling out of "secular" education proved more difficult

11. Langdon to Grew, February 28, 1936 (395.1163/28). The reservists' threat was not to be taken lightly. On the Japanese island of Tanegashima, where island Catholics were resisting worship at the shrines, the local Japanese reservists and veterans attacked churches and actually burned one down. The French missionary priests on the island were forced to evacuate. The veterans augmented police efforts to enforce Shintō worship on other islands where Japanese sovereignty was weak, such as Ōshima and Okinawa. Ibid.

12. Some of the local people were angry enough with the missionaries to threaten "violence similar to the anti-Chinese [Wanpaoshan] riots of July, 1931," as stated in a letter received by Eli Mowry, which was seen by American Vice-Consul Ralph Cory during his visit to P'yŏngyang in May 1937. "Mission School—Shrine Question in Chōsen" (395.1163/52).

13. Langdon was in a difficult position. His duty was to bring the missionaries to a modus vivendi with the Japanese, but his private view was that the Japanese position was untenable. "Regardless of official declarations," he wrote, "the Shintō ritual, with its exorcism, incantations, incense-burning, offerings, and prostrations, is definitely a religious office, and to be compelled to participate in it appears to believers in Jehovah nothing less than a denial of . . . religious liberty. . . if not actual religious persecution." Langdon to Neville (Tokyo), December 10, 1935 (395. 1163/21).

14. Harry A. Rhodes and Archibald Campbell, eds., *History of the Korea Mission of the Presbyterian Church in the U.S.A.*, Vol. II, 1935-1959 (New York: United

than anticipated. A group of Korean Christians offered half a million yen for the mission's schools in P'yŏngyang. When the missionaries refused to sell, saying that the buyers would use the property in an "un-Christian" manner (i.e, by letting the students attend the shrines), the Koreans tried to scare them into selling. A newspaper article in the *Mae'il Sinbo* of June 17 noted that the public in P'yŏngyang was ready to "raise movements" if the mission did not agree to sell.[15] Opposition also sprouted in Taegu, where a group of leading Christians published a statement suggesting that the missionaries go home: "We feel that missionaries who [are refusing to sell the schools] do not show a Christian spirit and that no mutual benefit to them or us will be served by their continued service in Korea."[16] Many Korean Christians thought that it should be permissible to go the shrines and stand still, or bow with "mental reservations."[17] But to the missionaries it was a matter of principle on which a public stand should be taken. The consequences of taking such a stand, of course, were likely to be different for Koreans and foreigners.

Rendering unto Caesar the Things That Are Caesar's

In Seoul, Horace H. Underwood rued his mission's school decision. Underwood was unhappy about Japanese pressure on the Korean church, but he was willing to "render unto Caesar the things that are Caesar's and unto God the things that are God's" (Mark 12:17). Japan was the ruler in Korea, and it was within Japan's rights to require patriotic observances of all citizens. As to whether Christians should bow at Shintō shrines, that was a matter of conscience and not something that American missionaries should decide for Koreans. What sense did it make, he wondered, to oppose Japan in a losing battle that would cripple the church and threaten the achievements of a half-century of mission work?

Presbyterian Church in the U.S.A., 1964), pp. 8-12. Also, Enclosure No. 2, Andrew Edson to SecState, August 14, 1936 (395.1163/39).
15. Marsh to SecState, June 19, 1937 (395.1163/61). The following is typical, signed by some of the country's leading Christians including Yun Ch'iho, Yang Chusam, Kim Chŏng'u, Helen Kim, Oh Kungsŏn, Ham Taeyŏng, and 77 others.
  PETITION TO THE NORTHERN PRESBYTERIAN MISSION
  I believe that Christians may properly conduct Christian schools under the conditions now maintaining [*sic*] in Korea, and I sincerely hope that the Northern Presbyterian Mission will continue to carry on educational work in Korea.
[Presbyterian Historical Society, Philadelphia, Record Group 140, Box 12, File 23.]
16. Signed by Paek Namche, Kim Chŏng'o, and seven others. Presbyterian Historical Society, Philadelphia, Record Group 140, Box 15, File 13.
17. These reservations could be very subtle, as in the case of those who bent over to inspect their shoes or tie their laces.

For Underwood, the vote to close the schools had been a personal disaster, forcing him to choose between obeying the mission and continuing work at Chōsen Christian College—a choice much like the one his father had faced during the debate over the original decision to start a college in Seoul in 1912-1915. What more appropriate course than to fight back the way his father had fought two decades earlier, with persuasion, logic, family money, and the support of the Board in New York?

The lights burned late into the night as Horace and Ethel together wrote letters home about the mission's decision to undercut their college. They used the political argument about Japan's sovereignty in Korea. They used the biblical argument about rendering unto Caesar. They used the social and educational arguments about hurting the Christian students and their families. They mustered letters of support from the college's Board of Managers, a resolution expressing "grief" from the college faculty, and a letter from Severance Union Medical College President Oh Kungsŏn saying, "I think some of the missionaries have failed to understand the psychology of the Korean people." And in personal letters to Presbyterian Board Secretary Charles T. Leber, Underwood threatened to resign from the mission and stay on, diverting his family's financial support from the mission to the college.[18]

The Underwoods' letters had their desired effect. In New York, the members of the interdenominational Cooperating Board for Higher Education in Chōsen (CBCHEC) questioned the right of the Northern Presbyterian Mission in Korea to walk away from its commitment to the two union colleges in Seoul and leave the the full burden of support with the other supporting missions.[19] The Presbyterian Board of Foreign Missions then stepped in and ordered its Korea mission to continue supporting the Seoul colleges at least until 1941. The Board also took the opportunity to order the mission to sell school properties to local Christians regardless of

18. See Presbyterian Historical Society, RG 140, Box 15, File 13, for faculty and Board letters, and letters: Underwood to Leber, June 28, 1938, and M.L. Swinehart to Leber (undated).

19. The Cooperating Board for Christian Higher Education in Chōsen was the church consortium created after the "college question" controversy to raise funds and hold the endowment for Korea's two union efforts, Chōsen Christian College and Severance Union Medical College. Though the CBCHEC was a useful administrative device, it further separated Chōsen Christian College from the Presbyterian Mission in Korea and unavoidably contributed to the isolation of the Underwood family in Seoul who answered, in effect, to two boards instead of one while Horace H. Underwood was president of Chōsen Christian College. See PHS, RG 140, Box 15, File 13 for C.C.C. faculty and Board resolutions, and letters: Underwood to Leber, June 28, 1938; Ernest Hall (CBCHEC, New York) to Leber, January 20, 1938; J.L. Hooper to George Sutherland (Methodist Board, New York), April 22, 1939; A.E. Armstrong (Toronto) to Hall, November 30, 1938.

their stand on shrine worship, overruling the conservative majority on that point as well.[20]

While the missionaries argued with their headquarters in America, the Presbyterian Church of Korea (PCK) came under unbearable pressure to surrender on the shrine issue. When the denomination convened its annual General Assembly in P'yŏngyang in September 1938, the police summoned each of the Korean delegates and instructed each one to support a resolution endorsing Shintō worship. Those who refused were arrested. The foreign missionary delegates were also ordered to stay out of the debate. When the Assembly met, the police forced the moderator to call the vote without permitting anyone to vote "nay"; and when a group of missionaries stood up to object, arguing that the vote was illegal under Robert's Rules of Order because the "nays" had not been called for, plainclothesmen hustled them out of the hall.

The Korean delegates' vote to accept Shintō worship triggered a highly judgmental response from the foreigners at the Assembly meeting: the missionaries caucused and decided to resign en masse from the Korean church. They declared that they could not associate with a church that had compromised on Shintō worship. Horace Underwood, however, saw this renunciation as unnecessarily cruel and completely self-defeating. It robbed the church of key people at a critical time. As he put it in a dissenting report: "[E]ach of these men [the missionaries] probably averaged at least 25 groups or churches placed under his charge...that is 50,000 people or nearly one-quarter of the Presbyterian Church in Korea. The ecclesiastical care and spiritual training of 50,000 has suddenly been thrown upon the shoulders of the [Korean pastorate]."[21]

20. This was a difficult decision because the mission had been overruled once before on the "college question" in the 1910s and had challenged the Board in public on the floor of the General Assembly of the Presbyterian Church in the U.S.A. The Board had prevailed at that time but it had also been told to let the mission have autonomy in matters of field policy thereafter. In 1938, the Board's step raised the issue of field autonomy again. Several members of the mission resigned blaming "modernists" in New York for being untrue to the faith. See W.H. Chisholm, "Dear Friends" letter, April 11, 1940. PHS, RG 140, Box 18, File 1. Mission conservatives also took the extraordinary step of mustering a delegation of missionaries on furlough to go to the Board offices in New York to demand once again that issues of field policy be left to the mission. The delegation's formal protest was in the process of being handled in 1940-41 when the war overtook the situation and the mission pulled out of Korea altogether.

21. Horace H. Underwood, "Christian Missions in Chōsen in 1939," in the *Japan Christian Yearbook, 1940*, ed. Charles W. Iglehart (Tokyo: Christian Literature Society, 1940), p. 205.

Consuls versus Missionaries

The outgoing consul-general Andrew Edson attended the Northern Presbyterians' 1936 annual meeting in P'yŏngyang, saw for himself how closely they were being pressed by the police, and showed some appreciation for their dilemma. But when Gaylord Marsh arrived to take Edson's place, he was "astounded" at the missionaries' opposition to orders from the Japanese regime and their contrariness over the school closing issue. His first encounter with the issue was in September 1937, when students in Kwangju at the Speer School for Girls went on strike against the school's missionary management over the Southern Presbyterian Mission's decision to follow the example of the Northern mission and close their schools. Principal Florence Root was a hard-liner on the Shintō issue and absolutely forbade her girls to obey the government's order to bow at the shrines. At the time, the local authorities in Kwangju had allowed the issue to slide. However, when the new school term began, the Speer girls were ordered to the city's Shintō shrine for a back-to-school ceremony. Miss Florence ordered them not to go and stood in the schoolhouse door to block their way out. Police soon arrived with an order to close the school. Several Korean teachers were taken in for questioning. There followed a protest demonstration against the missionaries, in which one foreigner was briefly taken hostage. Florence Root herself was subjected to death threats, though she remained firm in her own conviction that the Japanese were entirely in the wrong and that it was they who had made Christian schooling impossible. "It nearly broke my heart," she wrote, "as the children of our Speer School stood this morning in front of the building to receive instructions from the educational office about going to another school, to tell them good-bye, knowing that they would never be my children again."[22]

To Gaylord Marsh, though, it was Miss Florence who was being unreasonable. The missionaries, he reported, were "disposed to assume the role of martyrs, and are afflicted with an extraordinary conditions of 'nerves.'" Nor could he understand why the Presbyterians, North and South, were

22. Many of the nine hundreds students at the Speer School were able to enroll in government schools when they agreed to follow orders about Shintō worship. Of the teachers who were thrown out of work by the closure, four agreed to obey the government and were employed immediately to teach their former Speer pupils in government schools. Two teachers publicly refused to keep teaching under the circumstances and a number of others retired. "We are sad at heart to think of those whose faith was not strong enough to keep them, but when we realize that the seven teachers who stayed at home will never get another permit to teach under the present regime, we can but honor them the more for their courage. Obedience to their Lord's commands meant real sacrifices on their part." Florence Root, "Dear Friends" letter from Kwangju, begun on September 7 and mailed on November 18, 1937. Presbyterian Church, U.S.A. archives, Montreat, North Carolina.

being so stubborn when the Methodists, Catholics, Seventh Day Adventists, and Congregationalists had no such scruples about attending shrine ceremonies. He pointed out that the Government-General was actually rewarding the Methodists with privileges that it withheld from the Presbyterians—all they had to do was go along.[23] He drew his own conclusions:

> There seems to be no doubt that there is a Korean nationalistic element connected with certain mission stations that is eager to use...the Christian churches and schools to further their nationalist aspirations and to oppose the Japanese....Some of the missionaries are perhaps lending themselves to that purpose, a few willingly by reason of a prejudgment formed long years ago and others by fear of violence from their adherents of nationalistic sentiments.[24]

But Miss Florence's actions in Kwangju paled beside the offenses of the Northern Presbyterians in P'yŏngyang. "Some of the older missionaries who served under the [former] Korean government," wrote Marsh, "have difficulty in reconciling themselves to the fact that Korea was occupied by Japan, notwithstanding the fact that the occupation has the recognition of all governments of the world. And that attitude, which is sensed by the Japanese with what seems to me to be extraordinary toleration, makes the problem more difficult."[25] Marsh minced no words about the individuals involved. Of George McCune (whom he had never met) he wrote,

> Dr. McCune is stated, by those who know him, to be careless in utterances, incomplete in expression, sensational in statement, and grotesque in manner and gesture, he often throwing off his coat and suspenders, being tactless in criticisms of the Japanese, and being known among the Koreans as the "undo bokushi," or the Athletic Preacher....He is persona non grata to the educational authorities; and he is on prolonged furlough in the United States to the gratification of the press, to the satisfaction of the Japanese officials, to the peace of mind of his fellow missionaries, and to his own "face saving" with his Korean followers....[26]

As a Western diplomat in the age of empire, Gaylord Marsh can hardly have been expected to side with upstart Koreans against the Japanese, or with Americans who incited them to resist the dictates of the colonial re-

23. U.S. National Archives and Records Service, Record Group 84: General Records of the Department of State, Marsh to Grew, February 10, 1939 (360.Methodist Mission in Chosen).

24. Marsh to SecState, April 20, 1937 (395.1163/50).

25. Marsh to SecState, September 24, 1937 (395.1163/70).

26. Marsh to SecState, March 8, 1937 (395.1163/48), responding to a report from Washington that Dr. McCune had visited the State Department to share his views on the Shintō issue. The use of the term "undō bokushi" in Japanese (rather than the equivalent Korean "undong moksa," which is what the Koreans would have called McCune) is a clue to where Marsh was getting his information.

gime. One of his duties was to exhort American citizens in his jurisdiction to obey the laws of the land where they lived.[27] This duty was balanced, however, by Marsh's obligation to protect the interests of the United States and its citizens in Korea, and to help resolve conflicts between the government and the lawful interests of Americans, including property, livelihood, legal rights under the Meiji Constitution, and human rights. Early on in his tenure as consul-general, Marsh apparently made up his mind that Americans had no right to support the cause of Korean independence or any idea that undermined imperial Japanese rule in the colony. Thus he was adamant that Americans respect Japanese authority.[28] He clearly regarded as trivial the ethical and religious dilemmas of the missionaries in the shrine controversy. Thus it is no surprise that a fact-finding trip to P'yŏngyang did nothing to enhance his objectivity: the weather was depressing, his choice of transportation—a car instead of the comfortable train—was a mistake, and the missionaries he met in P'yŏngyang were simply not his sort.[29] He returned to Seoul with a sense of trouble to come.

27. For example, Marsh was astonished that members of the foreign community still had short-wave radios more than twelve years after the 1924 ordinance outlawing their possession by private citizens. Insisting that they turn them in, he circulated a warning that he would do nothing to defend any American who was punished for violating the regulation. Marsh to Grew, March 12, 1937 (895.76/4).

28. Marsh's quickness to side with the Japanese actually got him in trouble once during the *Panay* incident, when he accepted 10 yen in condolence money from a Japanese official in Seoul after the Japanese had sunk an American naval ship in the Yangtze River. At the time, the U.S. government was holding out for somewhat more meaningful gestures on the part of the Japanese and Ambassador Grew was most annoyed with Marsh for having made his own foreign policy. Grew to Marsh, January 11, 1938, in National Archives and Records Service *Panay* file, Suitland, Maryland (310.PANAY).

29. The trip did, however, afford him the authentic Korean experiences of crossing the Imjin River on a wooden ferry and stopping off to watch a shaman's *kut* at a farmhouse. Marsh to SecState, June 1, 1938 (123M 351/481).

-- 11 --

The Rise and Fall of the
Oriental Consolidated Mining Company

Until 1900, the few people in the West who had ever heard of Korea or could locate it on a map might have known one "historic" fact about it: that it had gold. A thousand years earlier, Arab traders had said that in the "land of Sila," east of China, there was a country rich in gold.[1] Chinese sources as early as Han times (206 B.C.- A.D. 220) had recorded reports of gold on the peninsula. The Korean kingdom of Koryŏ (A.D. 918-1392) had sent tribute gold to the Chinese court and by late Koryŏ, the Chinese were demanding specific amounts of gold each year, and the provision of gold, along with silver, horses, and other specified commodities, was a basic requirement of Korea's tributary relationship with the Chinese emperor.

Given its intrinsic value and its strategic significance in the Chinese tributary trade, the Korean court naturally placed special emphasis on mining gold. Gold-producing areas were reserved as royal lands. Contractors were assigned to supervise the extraction, collection, and proper remission of gold to the court. Out of their commissions they hired workers and bore all the costs of the operations and functioned, in effect, as concessionaires, somewhat like the Western concessionaires who came later.

The Korean government's monopoly on gold mining turned into a political problem during the late Chosŏn period (1392-1910). In 1811, when the rebel Hong Kyŏngnae raised the standard of revolt in north P'yŏng'an Province in one of the most serious regional uprisings of the entire dynasty, he began by inciting gold miners to set up a separate kingdom, and for many years after the Hong revolt was crushed, the area's miners continued to harbor grievances against outsiders in general and the Seoul govern-

1. Pak, *Sŏyang'ini pon Chŏson*, p. 16.

ment in particular. This fact no doubt contributed to the labor troubles experienced by the Western gold mining concessionaires who arrived at Unsan in the late 1890s.

Throughout the Chosŏn period, however, Korean gold mining continued using primitive methods. There was little systematic prospecting or digging for underground sources; rather it was placer mining in streams that were known to turn up gold nuggets in their sediment. Much gold was overlooked, lost, or pilfered in the process of being collected for the royal treasury; and so in the 1880s, King Kojong's court decided to modernize the royal mining operation and make it more profitable. In 1889 the Korean government imported ten ore grinding machines (called "stamps") from California and delivered them to the prime producing district of Unsan, about 120 kilometers north of P'yŏngyang. The local workers, however, lacked the skill to operate them, so at first they simply sat near the town of Pukchin and were not put into operation.

Westerners, meanwhile, began to act on the ancient rumors of gold in the Korean hills. Hong Kong's Jardine, Matheson and Company won permission to start prospecting in 1885, but the "Great Company," as Jardine's was known, was discouraged by the remoteness of the most promising sites and the vast expense of having to provide roads and other elemental items of infrastructure.[2] To be sure, Jardine's had better bets elsewhere; but there were others who were willing to take the risks. In the 1890s, their ambitions merged with King Kojong's desire to boost gold production and U.S. Legation Secretary Horace Allen's emergence as a promoter of American involvement in Korea. Allen wanted to attract American business to the peninsula in hopes that the U.S. government would feel sufficiently involved to protect Korea from Japanese aggression.[3]

Dollar Diplomacy and Korean Gold

Horace Allen made much of the profit potential in Korean gold mining, yet even the most adventurous Yankee entrepreneurs were reluctant to take on the frightful up-front costs involved in starting operations. To entice the first American investor, Secretary Allen had to persuade King Kojong to offer the most generous terms. The investor turned out to be James Morse of the American Trading Company in Yokohama,[4] whom Allen persuaded to

2. *The Mining Journal* (London), October 23, 1909, p. 121, quoted in Edwin W. Mills, "Gold Mining in Korea," *TKBRAS*, VII:1 (1916), p. 23.
3. Horace N. Allen, *Things Korean* (New York: Fleming H. Revell, 1908), pp. 231-232.
4. For the American Trading Company in Korea, see Harold F. Cook, *Pioneer American Businessman in Korea: The Life and Times of Walter Davis Townsend* (Seoul: Royal Asiatic Society, 1981).

take two concessions: one for a relatively sure railroad, and one for Korea's most promising gold mining concession in Unsan County in north Korea.

Under the terms of the proposed Unsan lease, Morse was to have exclusive rights to mine gold in a 200-square-mile area for twenty-five years. He would pay no property or income taxes, nor would there be customs duties on imported equipment or export taxes on the product—pure gold—as it was shipped out of Korea to the world market. The government even gave up the right to inspect Morse's books.[5] The terms further entitled Morse to exploit the environment. He was given the right to cut whatever timber he needed from the mountain forests around Unsan, to build roads and railroads wherever he saw fit, and to maintain company guards and stock weapons to protect his company's operations. When it came to labor, he had the right to make the local residents stop working the streams and to convert them from freelance placer miners to company employees—to "teach the Korean miners modern methods," as the agreement put it—and to import Chinese workers from across the Manchurian border if the labor supply ran short. Morse's part of the bargain was simple: Get the operation started within one year, and pay the king a quarter of the concession's profits annually thereafter.

The catch was the one-year deadline. To begin with, Morse was short of cash. He went to the United States in search of partners for the venture and came up empty. So he tried Shanghai, and there he found a bankrupt Seattle businessman named Leigh S. J. Hunt traveling a step ahead of his creditors and looking for a high-gain investment in the East.[6] Hunt was broke but he had rich friends. When he heard about Unsan, Hunt cabled New York financier J. Sloat Fassett[7] and persuaded him to put up $100,000. Then he went to Seoul, and with the one-year deadline fast approaching, he persuaded King Kojong to grant a six-month extension.

Leigh Hunt's Korean Bonanza

By the summer of 1897 Leigh Hunt had become the key player in Morse's operation and prospecting was in full swing. The two men differed, however, over long-term prospects. Morse's engineer, Henry Collbran, was pessimistic, calling the whole thing a wildcat venture not worth an addi-

5. Harrington, *God, Mammon, and the Japanese*, p. 156.

6. Hunt was a former president of Iowa Agricultural College (today's Iowa State), and then owner of the Seattle *Post Intelligencer*. He had gone more than a million dollars in debt over schemes to develop the city of Seattle and had been ruined by the Panic of '93. See Laurence B. Rand, *High Stakes: The Life and Times of Leigh S.J. Hunt* (New York: Peter Lang Publishing, 1989).

7. Jacob Sloat Fassett of Elmira, New York, was a politician, a member of the New York Senate, 1884-1892, a Republican nominee for governor of New York in 1891, and congressman in the 59th, 60th, and 61st Congresses. He died in 1924 enroute home from a trip to the Far East.

tional dime. Hunt and his engineer, James Duff, thought they had evidence of rich underground deposits at the town of Pukchin, in Unsan County. While they argued over the omens there were problems with the local people. The freelance miners were not about to give up panning for gold in their crystalline streams in order to go down into filthy tunnels to dig out gold ore for the foreigners. County officials, aware that the king was a quarter-owner of the venture, tried to intercede, but with little success. These were tense times, and Hunt and his men carried revolvers and bandoliers of ammunition everywhere they went.

The first clash came at Chiribalbi (or Nidap; called "Chittabalbie" by the foreigners), the site of Hunt's first mining installation.[8] There a crowd of three thousand hostile Koreans armed with stones demanded that Hunt lease the concession back to them. Hunt, with his Winchester rifle strapped across his chest and a revolver on each hip, decided on a show of force. He threatened to shoot a Korean—beginning with the mayor of Pukchin—for every stone that was thrown. A skyward blaze of gunfire succeeded in dispersing the crowd for the time being.[9]

But the trouble continued. A strike ensued, which the Koreans tried to enforce with death threats, again raising fears that the Americans would miss the king's deadline for starting production. Hunt therefore invited the provincial governor to Unsan for a discussion. The governor, a central government appointee, readily endorsed Hunt's proposed wage scale of 25 cents per day and ordered the miners to work. He apologized to Hunt for the disturbance, and Hunt thanked him with a gold watch and a bottle of French brandy.

Though the miners grudgingly went to work, they continued panning for gold on the tract. Hunt called this stealing and he summoned the police. When the police refused to make arrests, Hunt formed a posse of Americans to shoot anyone caught collecting nuggets anywhere on the property. Before long there were casualties: one Korean killed and seven wounded. The Unsan magistrate objected. He claimed that the dead man had been an innocent farmer and he urged the people of Unsan to rise up against the foreigners. In Seoul, Foreign Minister Pak Chesun declared that the Americans were not entitled to commit murder to protect their concession. Once again Horace Allen, by then U.S. minister to Korea, got involved, persuading Leigh Hunt to apologize and offer jobs to the dead man's relatives by way of compensation.

8. The place names used by the Westerners were based on the local colloquial usage. Proper names for the mining sites and their proper Korean names with Chinese characters were: "Chittabalbie" (Ch.:泥踏 Nidap); "Tabowie" (Ch.:大岩 Tae'am); "Taracol" (Ch.: 橋洞 Kyodong); "Maibong" (Ch.: 每峰 Maebong); "Candlestick" [East and West](Ch.燭臺峰 Ch'oktaebong); and "Tulmichung" (Ch.: 楠亭 Namjong).

9. Rand, *High Stakes*, p. 99.

The labor troubles eventually soured James Morse on the Unsan venture and he was only too happy to sell out to Leigh Hunt and Sloat Fassett for $70,000 in August 1897. Fassett went back to America to raise more money and to get the venture incorporated, a legal process from which it emerged as the Oriental Consolidated Mining Company, Inc., of West Virginia.[10] Hunt stayed on to deal with the locals and to do his best to meet the deadline despite shortages of equipment and money to build the tunnels, roads, and railroads that would make Unsan a paying proposition.

King Kojong continued to demand results by the deadline, and the first profits from the first mine at Chittabalbie had to be diverted to pay him his share, leaving little for reinvestment. In fact that was the main problem with the whole concession: it was designed to generate cash for the king instead of long-term production. So in 1899 Hunt and Fassett decided to deal with Kojong the way they had handled James Morse: they offered to buy him out for a lump sum. The monarch, in need of cash as always, agreed to sell them his quarter-share of income for $100,000 plus an annual royalty of $12,500, extending the lease to 1924 in the bargain. In 1900 they prevailed on him to add fifteen years to the lease for an additional $12,500, taking it to 1939 with an option to extend it again to 1954. The result was that Hunt and Fassett paid less than a quarter-million dollars for a 40-year, tax-free gold mining concession, complete with its own supplies of labor, timber, and water.

Meanwhile, the "modern methods" that the company had promised to teach the Korean mine workers turned out to be a disappointment. As Leigh Hunt's biographer described it,

> Natives worked twelve-hour shifts in narrow mine shafts, naked because of the heat and humidity. Scurrying rats stole their food, even when miners hung it from spikes. Cave-ins, machine-related accidents, and dynamite explosions were commonplace. When miners were brought out of the shafts, they sat on top of ore cars and were hoisted by a headframe. They had to rely on the headframe operator's wits to stop each car in time to prevent them from being dumped into a rock crusher along with its ore.[11]

The miners focused their bitterness on their foreign bosses and actually killed one of their foreign foremen, an Englishman named T.D. Bland. Bland had believed that liquor was the cause of the company's labor troubles and had tried to discourage its consumption. Late one night he broke up a miners' party and threw away their liquor. After he had gone to bed, the revelers entered his tent, hacked him to death, and looted his possessions including rifles and cash.

---

10. See ibid., passim; also Spencer J. Palmer, "American Gold Mining in Korea's Unsan District," *Pacific Historical Review*, XXXI:4 (November 1962), pp. 379-391.
11. Rand, *High Stakes* , pp. 146-147.

Tabowie Gold Mine Mill, Unsan. Oriental Consolidated Mining Company.
Courtesy of Gordon Chapman and Paul Fleck.

Leigh Hunt and the OCMC responded to Bland's murder with an investigation that led to the "arrest" of the mayor of the town of Pukchin and demands that the Korean government in Seoul outlaw the use of liquor on
the Unsan concession. The Americans got the mayor to reveal the names of
the murderers by putting him on a rack and using wooden levers to pry his
legs apart until he talked. The government in Seoul, however, was unmoved. Foreign Minister Pak Chesun refused to declare Unsan dry, a thing
he said was "unheard of" in Korea.

Once the Unsan concession was American land, in effect, the gold became American gold. American engineers discovered one- and two-mile
long veins of ore in the mountains, and during the first eleven months of
1899 the Chittabalbie Mine alone yielded $340,000, enough to pay off the
king and push ahead with other mines around the site. Heavily guarded
wagon trains began carrying the bullion out to Unsan's inland river port,
where flat-bottomed riverboats carried it to Anju on the Ch'ŏngch'ŏn River
to be loaded on company schooners for the trip to Chinnamp'o, the
OCMC's trading port.

In January 1901 Leigh Hunt and J. Sloat Fassett reorganized the OCMC.
The much-enlarged company was now worth $5 million and included partners like William Randolph Hearst, Darius O. Mills, and James B. Haggin of
California, and William L. Bull of New York, as well as several London investors. Hunt and Fassett retained substantial interest *and* realized about $2
million each.[12] For Hunt there came a triumphant moment. After having

12. Laurance B. Rand III, "American Venture Capitalism in the Former Korean
Empire: Leigh S.J. Hunt and the Unsan Gold Mines" (paper presented at the Columbia University Seminar on Korea, May 1984), p. 43. For the links among the
OCMC's buyers and purchasers see Cumings, *The Origins of the Korean War*, Vol.

left Seattle a pauper in 1894, in 1901 he went back and gave a dinner for his creditors, a party that was described in a local newspaper: "At the end of what was probably the finest dinner ever served in this city up to that time, Mr. Hunt made a little speech and delivered to each of his guests an envelope containing a check for the amount of his debt, with interest added."[13]

The Heyday of Gold Mining in Korea

By 1903 the Unsan concession was booming. Seventy Westerners, seven hundred Chinese, and more than two thousand Koreans were on the payroll. Eight mines, three cyanide plants, and five mills were processing ore at a rate of more than 200,000 tons per year. In 1903 alone, the take was $750,000, more than triple what Hunt and Fassett had paid for the concession between 1897 and 1900, and the stockholders gotten their first dividend of 12.5 percent.[14]

When Japan established her protectorate over Korea in 1905, the new resident-general Itō Hirōbumi took over the job of supervising mining operations from the Korean Household Ministry (Kungnaebu) and put it under the newly formed, Japanese-controlled, bureaucracy. The government studied the agreements by which foreign firms were doing business in the mining sector and subjected several of them to ruinous intervention. For example, an error in the maps and survey documents of an American-owned copper mine at Kapsan caused its owners to lose their exclusive timber rights, and the company was forced to sell.[15]

II: *The Roaring of the Cataract, 1947-1950* (Princeton: Princeton University Press, 1990), pp. 141-144, 801.

13. *Seattle Argus*, January 8, 1934, quoted in Rand, p. 2. Hunt dealt similarly with creditors in Eton Township and Whitley County, his Indiana home, paying longstanding debts and endowing the local public library with a start-up fund of $14,000.

14. Harrington, *God, Mammon, and the Japanese*, p. 26.

15. Without access to timber, sometimes beyond the boundaries of their leaseholds, foreign firms were hard pressed to construct their tunnels and railroads. The quality of the timber in the Manchurian border region made it a political problem. Large trees two feet in diameter and two hundred feet high were common in the area, and it was estimated that one large mine required all the timber for a radius of twenty miles. D.M. Tomlinson (Kapsan mine) to general manager, Kapsan Mining Co. (Seoul), August 28, 1910. Access to Korean timber was one of the Russians' keenest interests in Korea and was one of the factors leading up to the Russo-Japanese War.

The firm at Kapsan was the American-owned Collbran and Bostwick (C&B) copper mine. In 1910 Collbran and Bostwick found tree-cutters from the Government-General's Forest Bureau taking lumber out of forests adjacent to the mine, forests that the company believed were part of its concession. When they protested, Collbran-Bostwick quickly got entangled in red tape. County officials examining their timber concession documents claimed that there was an error: there was no

The two main Western gold mining concessions at Unsan and Taeyu-dong (see below), however, survived the change in regimes. One reason was the careful language of their leases. Another was their cultivation of good relations with the Japanese authorities. The American Mines at Unsan kept an office in Seoul to maintain contact with the government, an astute provision that helped them keep their mineral *and* timber rights until they sold out in 1939.[16] The Japanese willingness to assume the Korean government's part of the bargain in these operations helped make the takeover of Korea easier for the Western residents to accept.

By 1915, Unsan was producing at an annual rate of nearly 3 million tons of ore worth $1.875 million. Twenty-five million dollars worth of ore had been processed since the beginning, in 1897, and the stockholders had been paid half again as much as they put into the venture. Best of all, the Japanese annexation in 1910 did not alter the terms of the company's concession. The new colonial government agreed to honor existing agreements between the Korean government and foreign businesses.[17] So the Oriental Consolidated prospered with its tax-free advantages, cheap and plentiful Korean and Chinese labor, and tax-free access to the world market. A year after the annexation it was exporting bullion at a monthly rate of $130,000.

Meanwhile, other foreigners also got into gold mining. Three other ventures enjoyed long-term success: Taeyudong, in the county of Ch'angsŏng just north of Unsan; Su'an, in Hwanghae Province; and Chiksan, in South Ch'ungch'ŏng Province. Taeyudong, known to the foreign community as the "French Mines," was a 1901 concession to a Frenchman named Saltarel, who contracted development of the mine to another Frenchman named

such place on the map as the district where the concession was located. The place names, it turned out, had been changed. When the company asked to have the names on the documents updated, there was much hemming and hawing. Department of State, documents relating to the Collbran-Bostwick Development Co. Kapsan Concession, file date June 6, 1913 (895.63C68).

16. Alf Welhaven, the Norwegian general manager of the Unsan concession, used the liaison office to good effect in other ways as well, for example, getting daily mail delivery and telephone and telegraph lines long before other remote mountain regions got them. *Seoul Press*, January 11, 1911, p. 2. For the story of the lease extension see Matsunaga Takekichi, chief of the Foreign Affairs Section of the Government-General, to U.S. Consul General Ransford Miller, April 21, 1921 (895.6171/74 1/2).

17. George H. Scidmore (Seoul), to SecState: "Mining Rights of Foreigners in Chosen," December 15, 1910 (895.63/1). The terms could have been changed if the Japanese had discovered errors in the company's dealings with the Korean government, but they found none. The only fault ever found—the failure of the Korean foreign ministry to countersign along with the Imperial Household Department—had already been corrected in 1900.

Emile Martel. Martel, who had come to Korea in 1898,[18] bought up some abandoned equipment left over from an earlier German venture at Sŏnch'ŏn, started it up in Taeyudong, and kept it going from 1911 to 1937.[19] In their first three years the French Mines rang up bullion sales of $700,000.

The Su'an and Chiksan concessions were shorter lived, but they too produced respectable profits. In 1915 they produced nearly a million dollars worth of gold ore—less than Unsan, but still significant. Like Taeyudong, Su'an and Chiksan were multinational. Su'an was owned by a British syndicate (The Korea Syndicate, Inc., of London) and operated by American investors William H. Collbran and H.R. Bostwick through their Seoul Mining Company. Collbran and Bostwick leased the Su'an concession in 1907, started produc-

Working in a mineshaft at Unsan Oriental Consolidated Mining Company. Courtesy of Gordon Chapman and Paul Fleck.

tion in 1909, doubled their mill capacity by 1911, opened a second mine shortly thereafter, and increased capacity even further with new milling machines in 1915, bringing the concession's yearly output to $700,000. In the first six years of operation, the company produced $3,283,122 worth of gold and paid accumulated dividends of 275 percent. Indeed, for a while it seemed that Su'an might outdo Unsan. But then the ore started running out and the operators shut the mine down in 1924.

18. Martel was one of the longest-resident adult Westerners in the history of the foreign community, arriving in 1898 and passing away in 1949.

19. There was nothing particularly French about the "French Mines." A London syndicate controlled them most of the time, blocks of shares changed hands frequently, and the foreign employees frequently switched jobs among the various Western mining companies in Korea. In fact, Britishers predominated at the French Mines, and they were close enough to Unsan to share life with the English-speaking American community life there. People in Seoul usually thought of them as a single operation. See documents in Public Record Office file FO 262/1663 et seq.

The Chiksan concession was originally granted in 1900 to the Japanese partnership of Shibusawa and Asano, but it did not become a paying proposition until the American-owned Chiksan Mining Company took it over in 1911. By 1915 the Americans were coaxing nearly a half a million dollars worth of gold per year out of the ground at Chiksan. Though less profitable than Unsan and Su'an, Chiksan continued to make money until the 1920s, when the good ore began running out, though there was still enough to keep up the business until 1940.[20]

"Nodaji"

The Oriental Consolidated Mining Company's headquarters camp at Pukchin evolved from "primitive" to "comfortable" by 1930. In the beginning, when the American engineers lived in mud-walled dwellings with furniture made of old crates and cut-up kerosene drums, the winters seemed especially harsh.[21] But year by year the quality of life improved. A motor vehicle road connected Pukchin with the outside world. A narrow-gauge railroad system connected the mining valley with the surrounding timberland and eventually linked the company to the standard-gauge Korean railroad system. Wood-fired steam power ran the company's equipment at first; then came kerosene; and then, when operations expanded and the mines went deeper underground, a hydroelectric power network: nearly a million dollars' worth of reservoirs, dams, generators, and lines, supplemented by a diesel backup system, making for the most reliable power supply in the country at the time.

Since Unsan was gold country, there was always plenty of money around. The Koreans used their copper cash in the beginning, little coins with holes for making cash "strings," multiples of which were required for even the cheapest purchases and carloads of which were required to meet the payroll. After 1905 it was silver yen and Mexican dollars, the common currency of the China Coast. And there was the gold itself. Bullion boxes bore the words "No touch"; and in fact, the frequently shouted words "No touchee!" were so well known at Unsan that soon they became part of the language. Even today, "nodaji" is a Korean word meaning gold (or any bonanza).

20. For more on the Collbran and Bostwick enterprises in Korea see *The Korea Review*, VI (1906), 83-87. Other developers tried their luck. American businessman James H. Morris started up the Chōsen Mining Company in 1911 and went prospecting in Yongbyon, in North Pyŏng'an Province, finding enough gold to justify the effort. Others made money briefly and still others failed completely. But the luckiest ones—Hunt, Fassett, Martel, Collbran, Bostwick, and Morris—struck it rich.

21. Telephone interview with Paul Deal, son of OCMC miner Frederick W. Deal, July 26, 1989, in Columbia City, Indiana.

Guns also continued to be part of the OCMC operation—to guard the cash and bullion as well as to keep the workers in line—and the company maintained a certain level of combat readiness at all times. Armed guards rode the wagons that carried the bullion out to the railroad, and holdups were all but unknown. There was one very serious incident, however, in October 1916, when a pair of wagons bringing 80,000 yen in paper money from Mochu-ri station was ambushed. The Norwegian Fin Welhaven, brother of OCMC manager Alf Welhaven, was killed along with one of the Japanese guards and a Chinese driver. Two other Westerners were wounded, as was the other Chinese driver, while the remaining Japanese guard drove the attackers off all by himself.[22] After that the company stepped up security and got the Japanese colonial government to station more gendarmes in the area. In December, the company newspaper compared the new arrangements for guarding bullion wagons to those of the rear guard of a Mexican expeditionary force, with five Europeans and five Japanese armed with the best make of rifles carrying ammunition enough "to wreck the forts of Verdun."[23]

Like the Welhaven brothers, many of the foreigners at Unsan were from Europe; but of the Americans, the largest contingent came from a single area of the United States, Whitley County, Indiana, the original home of Leigh S.J. Hunt. When the Unsan concession started to look like a success, Hunt sent for his brothers, James and Fred; and they in turn recruited friends from Whitley County for positions as foremen and straw bosses at Unsan.

The American boys did well: for example, one group, which went out in 1901 on a standard three-year contract of transportation, housing, and $33.33 per month, was being paid double by the end of the year. Several stayed on; Joseph B. Lower was a mine foreman and sometime manager until OCMC sold out in 1939, and S.P. ("Pete") Clapham was still in the Korean mining business at Chiksan in 1940.[24] Joe Lower returned to Whitley County for his bride, Elsie Schumaker, in 1906, and the couple raised their daughters Rachel and Katherine at Unsan before sending them to boarding school at Punahou in Honolulu. Joe's sister Mable was the first schoolteacher at Unsan, married a miner named Clement Bridge, and raised two children there before returning home. The Lowers' niece Madge Schu-

22. The incident is recounted in Ransford Miller to Post Wheeler, American chargé d'affaires in Tokyo, October 9, 1916 (895.68/5). The heroism of the Japanese guard is said to have been "greatly exaggerated" by the local Japanese press. Miller to Wheeler, October 19, 1916 (895.63/6).

23. Palmer, "American Gold Mining in Korea's Unsan District," p. 388, quoting the *Unsan See-saw*, I (December 22, 1916), p. 1.

24. Edwin Meitzler, "Boy from Etna Gained World Fame and Fortune," *Bulletin of the Whitley County Historical Society* (February 1976), p. 8; and conversation with Helen Clapham Stinnett, El Paso, Texas, June 1991.

maker also came out to teach school and married mining engineer Howard Woodham. Whitley County native Soldon Blain found a Japanese wife during his years in Korea and eventually brought her back to Indiana with their sons James and John. So in a sense Unsan internationalized Whitley County the way rural Indiana briefly internationalized Unsan.[25]

As American families began settling at Pukchin, the company's main encampment, a foreign frontier town sprang up. By 1910 there were real houses with doors and windows and furnaces. The schoolhouse was in operation and there were other amenities as well, such as a chapel, club, library, tennis courts, and playgrounds for the children. Wives had "a beautiful life, with parties and servants, and lots of free time." Alongside the constant din of the mills mothers read to their children and taught them crafts and sewing. Amusements included ball games, dances, card parties, dinner parties back and forth, and even weekly movies in the 1920s, when the company imported a projector. Little things could mean a lot: when a miner returned from a weekend in Seoul with a new 78-rpm record of Fred Astaire singing "Night and Day," the community gathered in the clubhouse to hear it played over and over on the gramophone and "nearly wore it out the first day."[26]

The reliable electrical supply helped make life comfortable even as it powered the noisy machines that ground the ore into powder. In fact, the mills stopped only one day a year, the Fourth of July, when the whole town took a holiday to indulge in the Indiana pursuits of picnicking and baseball. There was an occasional visitor: Herbert Hoover is said to have visited once—and to have left without paying his bar tab at the club.[27] Otherwise it was shifts of round-the-clock production with individual staffers getting a complete day off (a "change day") once every two weeks.

Single men lived in bachelors' quarters. Like all the foreigners at Unsan they were provided for by Chinese and Korean servants who spoke some English, kept house, boiled the water, washed the vegetables from the

25. Cleon Fleck, "Happy Trio Thrilled to Seek Adventure in Korean Goldmines," *Bulletin of the Whitley County Historical Society*, XXI:6 (December 1983), pp. 15-22.

26. Among the dozen-odd students at the Pukchin school in a given year one would find Americans, Norwegians, Canadians, Germans, and a Russian or two. The school did not go past the eighth grade, and all eight grades were seldom taught in the same year. Nearby options for older children included foreign boarding schools at P'yŏngyang, Kobe, and Shanghai, as well as American schools in Peking, Seoul, and Tokyo. Madge Schumaker Woodham, "Brave Girl Sailed to Korea to Teach School," *The Bulletin of the Whitley County Historical Society*, XXI:6 (December 1983), pp. 23-25; Katherine Hatfield, quoted in Fleck, "Happy Trio," pp. 20-21. Gordon Chapman, interview with Paul Fleck, Columbia City, Indiana, December 24, 1991; and Eugenia Roberts Clark, conversation, Duarte, California, August 6, 1989.

27. Cumings, *The Origins of the Korean War*, Vol. II, p. 142.

company gardens, and put food on the table; yet it was a lonely existence whose chief benefit was in saving their pay to accumulate back home. Female companionship was hard to come by. The Russian girls who visited from nearby settlements—daughters of the odd Russian refugee or relatives of some of the Russians who worked at Unsan—were always welcome. Missionaries, notably single teachers from the foreign school in P'yŏngyang, often were invited. Otherwise, social life outside the OCMC "family" was something to be pursued on those rare occasions when the men could manage more than a 24-hour "change day" and could set their sights on Seoul and the Chōsen Hotel.[28]

Every OCMC worker represented a significant investment that had to be protected. The company had learned that epidemics could be costly and inconvenient in 1911, when a cholera epidemic swept the mines and completely disrupted operations. Though the foreign community was spared, the dead were everywhere in the mines, and with the Korean and Chinese workers refusing to go underground to retrieve the bodies, it was the Americans and Europeans who did the grisly work of reburying the dead.[29] Not that the foreigners were immortal. Over the years a fair number of them were buried in the Unsan community cemetery or in P'yŏngyang or Seoul.

To ward off any more such disasters, the company put a premium on top-notch health care at the mines. To keep the foreign staff healthy there was a full-time foreign doctor and nurse at a company dispensary that was equipped with imported drugs and medical equipment. The dispensary also served the Korean and Chinese miners and their families. Villagers from outside Unsan were accommodated on a space-available basis. Foreigners from elsewhere in Korea also came, for the OCMC's special import rights and reliable electricity supply helped make the clinic one of the best-equipped medical facilities in the country.[30]

Life in the mining concessions continued in a very different style, of course, for the Koreans and Chinese who worked for the foreign companies. The miners' settlements in Unsan were squalid shanty towns wedged into steep valleys with few amenities. None of the mines would have made money at all if the company had not been able to make local men go thou-

28. Mining families got special rates of $10 per night. Jon Carter Covell, *On Center Stage for Seventy Years* (Seoul: Hollym Corp., 1984), pp. 29, 31-32; Lee Misook, "Cheesman Enjoyed Mining Life," *Korea Times* (Seoul) (September 16, 1982), p. 4.

29. Paul Deal, Columbia City, Indiana, telephone conversation, July 26, 1989; Post Wheeler (Tokyo) to SecState, October 12, 1916 and enclosures (895.68/5); Seoul Mining Co., *Director's Report and Statement of Accounts for the Year Ended December 31st, 1922*, p. 16.

30. Sherwood Hall, *With Stethoscope in Asia: Korea* (McLean, Va.: MCL Associates, 1978), pp. 373-380.

sands of feet down into the ground to work, naked, in the dark, dust, and heat of the shafts. Notwithstanding the occasional provision for the workers' benefit, such as Unsan's clinic, the work of digging mine shafts, cutting trees and placing timbers, blasting, digging ore, and hauling it up thousands of yards of tunnel works was difficult, dangerous, and sometimes even fatal. The companies argued that their workers at least had jobs and were learning modern skills, but this was scant compensation for backbreaking work that paid only pennies a day.

Sunset for the Oriental Consolidated

By 1935, the Oriental Consolidated Mining Company's gold concession at Unsan had far exceeded expectations. It had paid its stockholders a total of $14.3 million in dividends, an average of $446,000 per year since 1903, all the while paying no more than the annual royalty of 25,000 yen ($12,500) to the government, a payment that worked out to a rate of 2.8 percent in lieu of taxes under an arrangement due to continue until 1954.[31]

Like the oilmen and the missionaries, the gold miners also felt General Minami tightening the Japanese noose. The colonial regime had not challenged the OCMC's right to continue operations in north Korea because the company was using the most advanced mining methods to extract the maximum amount of gold ore, which, by the 1930s, was being bought by the Tokyo government. In theory, the company continued to be entitled to sell its bullion on the world market, but in 1931, the Imperial Government had prohibited all gold exports from the empire and made itself the sole legal buyer. It then had set the price for gold at a level below the world market price. Being forced to sell to the Japanese at an artificially low price cost the OCMC much of its profits and the company raised objections.[32] OCMC officials argued that the lost profits amounted to a tax in violation of the company's original charter that strictly limited what had to be paid to the government. The Japanese, however, ignored the argument.

31. The OCMC pointed out that it generated indirect tax revenue by employing three hundred miners and laborers and providing a living for an estimated twelve thousand people in the Unsan district. It also paid taxes in the United States: in 1937 its corporate tax was "about $135,000, in addition to several times that amount received by reason of the tax on salaries and on profits distributed to individual stockholders." Lewis Henry to Stanley Hornbeck, May 12, 1938 (895.63 OR/68).

32. In 1937 the Oriental Consolidated estimated that it had lost $1.7 million by having to sell to the Japanese government. Oriental Consolidated Mining Company, *Annual Report, 1933*, enclosed with J.B. Lower, Oriental Consolidated Mining Company, to Ambassador Grew, April 6, 1934 (895.63 OR/40). Lewis Henry, president, Oriental Consolidated Mining Company, to Stanley K. Hornbeck, Department of State, May 12, 1938 (895.63 OR4/68).

In 1934, the Ugaki regime ordered the company's employees to start paying income taxes. Once again OCMC officials pointed to the concession agreement noting that since the government had no right to inspect the company's books, there was no basis on which to figure income taxes. This protest too proved untenable: even the American Embassy in Tokyo advised the company to drop it, since the United States made all foreigners, including Japanese, pay taxes. The embassy's view was that the extraterritorial tax exemption that the OCMC had obtained from the defunct Korean government was now an unenforceable anachronism.[33] For a while there were negotiations about "voluntary" reporting of payroll figures, but these went nowhere and the company was forced to open its books.[34]

The Oriental Consolidated suffered a third setback in the winter of 1936 when the Unsan police began stopping company vehicles from exiting the OCMC concession. No taxes had been paid on the vehicles, said the police, which meant that they could not be driven off company land. This prevented the Oriental Consolidated from using its vehicles to transport supplies from the railroad at Anju or the port at Chinnamp'o. At first the company tried to rent Korean trucks, but these were too small to haul the big machinery. When the OCMC was refused permission to send its tractor-trailer rig to Chinnamp'o to pick up a new generator, it was forced to buy and pay tax on two Japanese trucks to do the job.

The Oriental Consolidated's truck tax problem was Gaylord Marsh's first Japanese-American business conflict when he arrived in Korea as the new U.S. consul-general. Having reviewed the company's remarkable history, Marsh made no secret of his belief that the company had been living a charmed life. He agreed with the Government-General that the Oriental Consolidated had been abusing its tax-free status, that its trucks had been competing unfairly with local truckers, and that it was not being harassed. He reported to Ambassador Joseph Grew in Tokyo that the OCMC was being unreasonable, and that he thought that if the company would only drop its outlandish claims of tax immunity, all would be well.[35]

But Marsh was mistaken. By late 1937, the Government-General of Chōsen was well on its way to ending the Open Door era in Korea. In 1937, it persuaded the owners of the "French Mines" at Taeyudong to sell out to the Japan Mining Company (Nihon Kōgyō K.K.) for 15 million yen (about $7 million), the equivalent of three years' output.[36] Though the Oriental Consolidated's owners and managers had thought that they could survive

33. Edwin L. Neville (Tokyo) to SecState, October 2, 1934 (895.63 OR4/63).
34. Tanaka Takeō, Department of Finance, Government-General of Chōsen, to Consul-General John K. Davis (Seoul), May 10, 1935 (895.63 OR4/47) and Tanaka to Consul-General William R. Langdon (Seoul), October 19, 1935 (895.63 OR4/53).
35. O. Gaylord Marsh (Seoul) to Grew, June 27, 1937 (895.63 OR4/62).
36. *Seoul Press*, May 28, 1937, p. 2. A single Swedish technician was the only Westerner at Taeyudong a year later.

that year, the company made an unfortunate technical mistake that marked the beginning of its own end. While the OCMC was fighting the government over its tax status, a company agent at Chinnamp'o got careless and obeyed a demand for 142.56 yen (approximately $90) of import tax on a shipment of gasoline. This set a precedent, and the Chinnamp'o customs office began demanding import taxes on other company shipments and impounding the goods when the payments were not made. There was another round of protests. Assistant Manager Melvin Arick appealed directly to the colonial Finance Bureau in Seoul, only to be told that the goods were not being "taxed" but rather "import controlled." Bureau officials said that they needed to be sure that the OCMC was not importing wartime contraband. More ominously, they asked how the company was paying for imports from abroad when it had no legal way to export hard currency out of the empire. There would have to be an investigation, said the Japanese, and in the meantime the Oriental Consolidated should get used to applying for permits to import everything.[37]

Arick was furious, not only with the Japanese but with Gaylord Marsh who seemed to have abdicated his duty to protect his company's interests. However, by that time it was 1938. Japan had launched its invasion of China and was openly calling for an end to Western imperialism in the "Greater East Asia Co-Prosperity Sphere," and the authorities in Korea were in no mood to let an American company continue to exploit the empire's gold resources.

The Unsan mines limped along for another year in legal limbo with company officers glumly applying for every kind of permit. They had to get permission to import medical supplies, shovels, wire, rope, iron pipe, belting, jackhammer parts, drill parts, padlocks, and a host of daily necessities. To mine and refine gold the Oriental Consolidated required large quantities of chemicals, which had to be ordered far in advance. By the end of 1938 the company was critically short of pentazol xanthate, a flotation reagent without which the gold ore simply could not be processed. In January 1939 the company wired Gaylord Marsh in Seoul that it would have to shut down if it could not get delivery of a shipment of pentazol xanthate that had been held for months in a Chinnamp'o customs warehouse. Marsh of course had no leverage, and without the chemical the OCMC had to cut production.[38] In August 1939, Nihon Kōgyō K.K. (the Japan Mining Co.)

37. Melvin Arick (Unsan) to Mizuto Naomasa, Director, Finance Department of the Government-General of Chōsen, December 11, 1937; Arick to Muzuto, December 16, 1937; Arick to Marsh, January 18, 1938; Arick to Marsh, February 9, 1938; Matsuzawa Tatsuō, Director, Foreign Affairs Department, Government-General of Chōsen, to Marsh, April 5, 1938 (895.63 OR4/64-66).

38. Arick to Marsh, January 30, 1939, and Oriental Consolidated Mining Company to Hozumi Shinrokurō, Director, Industrial Department, Government-General of Chōsen, January 19, 1939 (895.63 OR4/66).

stepped in as it had with the Taeyudong mines in 1937 and made an offer of $8,174,500 for the OCMC's Unsan concession. The directors readily agreed to sell.[39]

Through the autumn of 1939, the Oriental Consolidated packed up and its foreign employees started leaving. Only one, geologist Pitt Hyde, stayed on the site to work with the new owners. The others went to other kinds of work within Korea, or to jobs in the Philippines, or back home to Whitley County, Indiana. Gaylord Marsh officially rang down the curtain in a cheery retrospective that would have pleased the Japanese though not the Koreans:

> This sale and transfer mark the close of an interesting chapter in American enterprise abroad—a hurried though profitable forty-four years from the entry of pioneer American gold miners into an obscure and undeveloped Oriental land just out of seclusion down to the sophisticated though bewildered present wherein the East is more like the West, but wherein neither is in agreement regarding the true worth of gold—nor forsooth of that which is golden. But Chosen benefited, and American enterprise received its reward. The change was inevitable; and it is a satisfaction to know that this American enterprise was initiated and terminated by fair dealing between men on relatively equal terms. There can be, therefore, no regrets.[40]

The Oriental Consolidated's forty years at Unsan were a resounding success for the company's stockholders. King Kojong may have been drawn into signing the original lease under false pretenses: aware that he was giving generous terms to James Morse and Leigh Hunt but believing that the concession would help persuade the American government to keep its promise in the treaty of 1882 to shelter Korea in case of encroachment by Japan or some other imperialist power.[41] He had been encouraged to believe this by U.S. Minister Horace Allen, who also thought that economic

39. *New York Times*, August 5, 1939; Oriental Consolidated Mining Company Board of Directors letter to stockholders, July 14, 1939 (895.63 OR4/74). Nihon Kōgyō was to pay $2,227,000 as a first installment, with the balance payable on a schedule through August 31, 1943. In 1940, however, the OCMC directors offered Nihon Kōgyō a 25 percent reduction on the balance if they would pay it off at once. NKK accepted the offer and the stockholders were spared the losses that otherwise would have followed the outbreak of the Pacific War. Spencer J. Palmer, "American Gold Mining in Korea's Unsan District," p. 390.

40. Marsh to SecState, September 16, 1939 (895.63 OR4/47). In the late 1980s the Japanese revived their interest in Unsan by means of a syndicate that began working the site with an investment of $750,000. "Total expected investment, largely involving Japan's best mining equipment, may reach $50 million." *Pacific Century*, I:11 (December 1986), p. 2.

41. Yi Paeyŏng, *Han'guk kŭndae kwang'ŏp chimnyaksa yŏn'gu* (Seoul: Ilchogak, 1989), especially pp. 242-244, and Yi Paeyong, *Ku Hanmal Miguk-ŭi Unsan Kŭmgwang Ch'aegŭlgwŏn hoetŭk-e taehayŏ* (thesis, Ewha Womans University, History Department, 1970), passim.

stakes in Korea would attract governmental protection. This belief, of course, turned out to be wishful thinking.

Even so, during forty years of operations at Unsan, the Oriental Consolidated enriched its overseas stockholders by controlling—some might say virtually enslaving—the workers of Unsan county, completely dominating their lives and environment. The company even tinkered with the demographics of Unsan by importing thousands of Chinese laborers to augment the sullen Korean work force. Naturally enough, Koreans now recall the foreign mining concessions not as models of international development but with shame. They feel that the Americans and Japanese connived to force the Korean workers to steal from themselves.[42]

42. For example, take the 1911 labor disturbance not far from Unsan at the "French mines" in Taeyudong. Mine manager Emile Martel had found it necessary to fire his labor contractor, the individual who recruited and supervised his local workers, but when he brought in a replacement, his workers walked off the job. The replacement upped the wages, and some of the strikers went back, bringing on the wrath of the strikers, who attacked them. Martel had to send to Unsan for help, whereupon the Oriental Consolidated sent him a machine-gun crew pending arrival of the Japanese gendarmerie. As a result of this exemplary international cooperation, the miners were forced to accept Martel's terms. *Seoul Press*, December 9, 1911, p. 3, and December 16 and 17, 1911, pp. 2. For other commentary on the mines, see Yi Kyu-tae, "Rulers Discouraged Korean Gold Mining, Feared Foreign Exploitation of Resources," *Korea Herald,* February 8, 1970, p. 4.

-- 12 --

The Winds of War

Japanese aggression in China created a unique opportunity for some of the more adventuresome Westerners in Korea—to multiply cash in the Peking currency market. This remarkable system was the result of Japan's efforts to wreck the Chinese Nationalist currency, or yuan. Japan wanted yuan holders to dump their Chinese money in favor of other, preferably Japanese, currencies. To encourage this they had their Japanese-owned banks in North China buy yuan and sell Japanese money at phony exchange rates. For the colonial Korean yen, issued by the Bank of Chōsen in Seoul, the Japanese set an artificial exchange rate in Peking of 1 Korean *yen* for 1 Chinese yuan, even though the Korean money was worth less than a third of the yuan on the open market.

Foreigners in Korea made money off this system because the Government-General of Chōsen allowed them to carry up to US$125 in cash whenever they left the colony. Within Korea, this amount of American money was worth 500 Korean yen at the legal exchange rate. However, in Peking, the same $125 could be traded on the street for as much as 1,625 Chinese yuan. Americans began taking their $125 traveling allowances to Peking and trading their greenbacks for 1,625 Chinese yuan, then taking the Chinese money to a Japanese bank and trading it back at the artificial Japanese exchange rate for 1,625 Korean yen, an amount more than three times what they could have obtained for their $125 in Seoul.[1]

Though short-lived, it was a neat trick. People financed family vacations and honeymoons with the profit. Presbyterian missionary Henry Lampe gave his teenage children a train ticket and fifty dollars each and sent them to Peking where they enjoyed an educational tour, bought gifts and an-

1. For a discussion of Japanese attempts to break the Chinese *fapi* yuan in north China, see Arthur N. Young, *China and the Helping Hand* (Cambridge, Mass.: Harvard University Press, 1963), pp. 65-69.

tiques, and came back with more cash than they had had in the beginning. One enterprising American student who lived in Shanghai but attended school in Seoul made a business of charging a five percent commission for shuttling cash back and forth during vacations.[2] The Japanese were aware of the foreign community's transactions in China, but they were slow to interfere because they did not want to call attention to the thing that made the system work—the relative worthlessness of the colonial Korean currency. Instead they winked at a certain amount of the trading as long as it was, in their words, "for commercial transactions or other actual need."[3]

American "Korea Kids" were not the only ones to take advantage of the chance to triple the yield of their scarce depression-era dollars. It was only a matter of time before adults got caught abusing the system. In 1939, Ada B. Hall, the treasurer of the Methodist Mission, was arrested for trading $3,311.74 at the National City Bank of Peking for the Korean *yen* equivalent of $11,788.78. The authorities accepted her plea that she had done it for her charitable organization and not for herself, and they levied a fine for the amount of her profit. But being able to catch foreigners breaking the law gave the Japanese a new lever and in 1940, when the colonial regime was well on its way to forcing all Westerners out of Korea, the penalties suddenly turned harsh. Four Peking-bound Americans who were arrested with more than the allowed dollar limit were arrested, tried, convicted, and given the choice of going to prison or leaving Korea for good.[4]

The crackdown on currency trading was in the spirit of Japan's pressure on Westerners in general. Many kinds of regulations and police intimidation became normal in General Minami's Korea. The case of Dr. Sherwood Hall in 1938-39 is a good example. Hall was a Methodist doctor, the leading TB specialist in the country and the operator of a sanitarium in Haeju. His crime was to take his U.S. dollar checkbook in his briefcase on a trip to China. Japanese detectives construed this as tantamount to exporting the entire balance of his account, even though his bank was in the United States.[5]

2. Frances Lampe Peterson, interview, Seoul, May 8, 1990; Horace G. Underwood, interviews, Seoul, May-June, 1985; J. Elmer Kilbourne, interview, Taech'ŏn Beach, Korea, July 28, 1990.

3. The "commercial transactions or actual need" phraseology was part of the judgment against S.P. Clapham, a retired American gold miner living in P'yŏngyang, who was convicted in 1939 of cashing $120 in pension checks in Peking and remitting the proceeds in the form of "Manchoukuoan yuan" to Korea "without the necessity of commercial transactions or actual need." He was given a choice between three hundred days at hard labor or a 1,200 yen fine. U. Alexis Johnson to SecState, April 5, 1940 (395.112.1).

4. U. Alexis Johnson to SecState, March 18, 1940 (395.112/1).

5. Charles A. Sauer, "The Situation in Korea, May 1941," undated circular to former Korea missionaries in the archives of the Korea Methodist Mission, Drew University, p. 6. Sherwood Hall was no relation to Ada Hall.

The police had been watching Dr. Hall. The previous summer they had raided his beach cottage at Wŏnsan and had confiscated a house guest's contraband short-wave radio. This had marked him for special surveillance and it was in this vulnerable condition that he tried to leave the colony with his checkbook.

Confined to home pending trial, Hall gamely carried on. In the autumn of 1940 he started printing his annual stock of Christmas seals, the decorative stamps that he had been using to raise funds ever since 1932. Church people all over the country bought the seals, which were issued as a series. Each year's issue bore a winter scene with a Christmas theme and the number of the year. This time Hall chose a snow scene painted by artist Elizabeth Keith[6] and had thousands of sheets printed up with the legend "1940-41." The trouble was that the Japanese had decreed the use of the Japanese Imperial calendar for public use in Korea. Indeed, 1940 was a special year—the 2600th anniversary of the legendary founding of the Japanese Empire by Jimmu Tennō. The police abruptly demanded that the entire batch of Christmas seals be reprinted either with the year "2600" or the year "Showa 15."[7]

Sherwood Hall, in a dudgeon over having to print the seals twice, refused to let them be used as a reminder of Japanese rule and argued the authorities to a compromise: the seals would say "Ninth Year," referring to the beginning of the seal series in 1932.[8] Soon thereafter a judgment was rendered in the case of Hall's currency transgression and he was ordered to pay a fine of 5,000 yen. This amount was returned to him, in effect, in a most ironic way. At the end of December the government announced a list of worthy individuals and charitable institutions throughout the empire that were to receive special recognition. One of the institutions was the Methodist TB sanitarium in Haeju run by Sherwood Hall. With the recognition came a gift of 5,000 yen, the exact amount of his fine.[9]

6. The Scottish-born Elizabeth Keith was known in the 1930s as a Western expert on Japanese wood block printing techniques and she designed a number of Korean scenes that are now very valuable; some of them appear in English-language books about Korea. A student of print master Watanabe Shosaburō, Keith traveled in Japan, China, Korea, and the Philippines studying and creating.

7. The Japanese normally used the Western calendar along with their preferred system of numbering years according to the reigning emperor's years on the throne—by which 1940 was the fifteenth year of the reign of the Emperor Shōwa (Hirohito).

8. Hall, *With Stethoscope in Asia: Korea*, pp. 574-575.

9. Ibid., p. 581; Sherwood and Marian Hall, "Dear Friends" letter, December 13, 1940.

Easter Morning Showdown

While the Japanese Imperial Army fought in China to rid East Asia of Western imperialism and Soviet communism, the Government-General of Chōsen set about making Korean organizations sever their foreign ties. In 1938, the Korean YMCA and YWCA had to break with their international headquarters in the United States and become part of Japanese Y organizations. The missionary-led Korea Sunday School Association dissolved itself rather than do as the Y's had done. The WCTU, the Presbyterian Christian Endeavor youth organization, and even the Korean National Christian Council all were required to rewrite their charters to exclude foreigners and become branches of organizations in Japan.[10]

In the autumn of 1940 the Methodist Bishop in Tokyo, following orders from the Japanese government, restructured the Korean Methodist Church to be a *kyodan*, or "church federation," moving toward the eventual amalgamation of all Christian organizations into a single national church that would support Japan's Greater East Asia Co-Prosperity Sphere. The *kyodan*'s leaders said that a united church would be better able to fight the perfidious ideologies of individualism, liberalism, and communism and uphold the Imperial Way (*kōdō*) by attendance at Shintō shrine ceremonies, encourage Christians to volunteer for military service, and do without foreigners in positions of leadership.[11] With the reorganization, the role of missionaries in Korea reached the vanishing point except as holders of titles to mission land and buildings.[12]

Mission institutions in Korea were also transferred from foreign to Korean management. Horace Underwood managed to keep Chōsen Christian College under Christian management by arranging for the aged Yun Ch'iho to be appointed president, an American-educated Japanese Christian named Matsumoto Teru to be brought over from Aoyama Gakuin, the Presbyterian college in Tokyo, to serve as vice president, and for himself to remain on the faculty and Board of Managers.[13] Nearby, at Ewha Womans Col-

10. Sauer, "The Situation in Korea," pp. 83-85.
11. Chong Chunsu, "Reform Plan for the Korean Methodist Church," October 2, 1940, "Exhibit A" of *Church and Mission in Korea*, a report by Bishop James C. Baker and Dr. R.E. Diffendorfer to the Board of Missions and Church Extension of the Methodist Church, January 1941.
12. "The Korea Methodist News Service," newsletter dated October 2, 1940; Charles A. Sauer, "The Situation in Korea." Almost immediately, however, Korean church leaders began renting out Mission-owned property. C.A. Sauer to R. E. Diffendorfer, March 7, 1941.
13. Statement by Horace H. Underwood, enclosed in Harold B. Quarton to Grew, August 28, 1942 (395.1163/119), Horace H. Underwood, "Coming Over to Help You," *The Korea Mission Field*, XXXVI:3 (March 1940), and "A Korean College Carrries On," *Presbyterian Tribune* (October 1943), pp. 9-11.

lege, Alice Appenzeller stepped aside in favor of her protégé Helen Kim, and at the Methodist seminary "Fritz" Pyun took the reins from Bliss Billings.

On the Presbyterian compound in P'yŏngyang, however, the transitions were not so smooth. Japanese pressure, aggravated by differences among the missionaries themselves over the Shintō shrine question, had hardened the most conservative individuals in their determination to make a show of resistance, ostensibly in place of their silenced Korean followers. The basis for their position was the fact that a delegation of Korean pastors had come to them just before being silenced by the Japanese police in 1938 and had begged the American missionaries to resist on their behalf.[14] Accordingly, the P'yŏngyang Presbyterians, together with their most determined Korean associates, dug in to fight Japanese interference to the bitter end.

One arena for this last-ditch resistance was the Sanjŏng-hyŏn Presbyterian Church in P'yŏngyang, whose missionary liaison work had been performed for years by Charles and Helen Bernheisel. In the late 1930s, the Sanjŏng-hyŏn Church was subjected to police pressure because its pastor, Chu Kich'ŏl, was the leader of a Christian faction that refused against all odds to bow at the Shintō shrines. When the Presbyterian General Assembly accepted Shintō worship in 1938, the authorities arranged to have Reverend Chu removed from his pulpit and there was a confrontation.[15] Dr. Bernheisel tried to defend Chu but was physically restrained by plainclothesmen while the pastor himself was arrested. Subsequently Bernheisel took over as acting pastor of the Sanjŏng-hyŏn Church on the assumption that a foreigner was better able to keep the faith publicly than a Korean. His wife Helen took over as Sunday School superintendent.

After thirty-nine years in Korea the Bernheisels had a considerable following among P'yŏngyang's Christians. This made it all the more imperative for the Japanese to answer their public challenge. The authorities' first move was to dismiss the Sanjŏng-hyŏn Church's board of elders. In their place they appointed a slate of their own pro-Shintō elders—backsliders, in Bernheisel's opinion—who could be depended on to oust the missionary pastor. Sunday after Sunday, despite police orders, Bernheisel postponed the installation of these new elders, keeping charge of the church himself and presiding alone at services.

The police decided to install the pro-Shintō elders, by force if necessary, on Easter Sunday, 1940. To prevent Dr. Bernheisel and his supporters from

14. William N. Blair, *Gold in Korea* (New York: Presbyterian Church in the U.S.A., 1946), p. 98.

15. This was done by a 49-1 vote in P'yŏngyang Presbytery. The lone dissenter was jailed for eighteen days. Charles L. Bernheisel, "Recent Events in Pyengyang (Heijō), Chosen," report dated March 26, 1940. Presbyterian Historical Society Record Group 140, Box 18, File 1.

interfering they threw a cordon around the church before the service and refused to let them enter. Helen Bernheisel, however, was already inside. She mustered the 600-member Sunday School for a non-stop singing of the rousing martyrs' hymn "A Mighty Fortress Is Our God." There was an awkward standoff as the police pondered what to do. Finally, with their new elders in tow, they forced their way into the church, charged the podium, and ordered the congregation to stop singing. When the singing continued, the officers fanned out through the audience snatching away hymn books and using them to swat parishioners at random. Finally they physically removed the 67-year old Mrs. Bernheisel from her pew and deposited her outside on the front steps, according to her official complaint, inflicting bruises, a sprained shoulder, and "a severe nervous shock" on her in the process.[16]

Outraged at the manhandling of the venerable Mrs. Bernheisel, the P'yŏngyang missionaries filed a protest with the U.S. Consul-General O. Gaylord Marsh. Some of their neighbors praised the Bernheisels for their principled stand, while others regarded it as futile and ultimately demoralizing to the purposes of the church. Their words and opinions made little difference, however, to the Koreans involved. By nightfall the police had arrested Reverend Chu's wife and the remaining members of the Chu-Bernheisel faction and the church building had been padlocked.[17]

In Defense of American Property

Charlie Clark was beginning his fourth decade in Korea when the Shintō shrine crisis arose in P'yŏngyang. He was not himself the most anti-Japanese of missionaries, having worked in Japan for periods in the 1920s. He had also made a sincere effort to learn Japanese and to live within the regulations imposed by the colonial regime. But in his studies of Asian religions he had learned a great deal about Shintō and he was opposed to it for the same reasons that he opposed basic Korean shamanism. Unlike Buddhism, for which he had some respect as a scholar, shamanism and Japanese

16. U. Alexis Johnson to SecState, March 18, 1940 (395.112/1) and Bernheisel, "Recent Events in Pyengyang." The Japanese version of the incident was that there had been disorder among the members of the Sanjŏng-hyŏn Church because of a dispute among Christian leaders; that Mrs. Bernheisel had "paid no attention to the orders of those in charge to stop [singing]," whereupon "the police who were present kindly and politely urged her, the same as they urged the other persons connected with the affair, to leave." "The fact is," wrote Matsuzawa Tatsuō, Director of the Foreign Affairs Department of the Government-General, in reply to Consul Alex Johnson, "that she was absolutely not mistreated nor injured in any way."

17. Chu Kich'ŏl was in prison from August 1939 until April 1940, just after the incident, and then he was rearrested in August and died in prison. See biographical note in Allen D. Clark, *A History of the Church in Korea* (Seoul: Christian Literature Society, 1972), pp. 452-457.

Shintō were both distractions from the theological issues that he liked best. He saw them as the preoccupations of poor and ignorant people who did not know enough to question superstition and were easily gulled into turning their hard-earned savings over to unscrupulous cult leaders. However, in the case of shamanism he conceded that it was a home-grown religion at least. Shintō, on the other hand, was an imported animism that had absolutely nothing to offer the Koreans. He was therefore offended when the colonial government began pushing Shintō rites on the Koreans. He looked to educated Christians to help block the trend. In this, of course, he was disappointed.[18]

The Presbyterian Seminary in P'yŏngyang had been thrown into an uproar by the missionaries' 1938 decision to separate itself from the Presbyterian Church of Korea because of the Korean General Assembly's vote-under-duress to permit Shintō worship. A few missionaries had thought that because the seminary was a wholly religious institution it might be able to keep functioning, but that hope was dashed in 1939 when Japanese officials forbade the starting of a new school year without a permit that could only be obtained by promising to let the students participate in Shintō ceremonies. The Americans therefore "postponed" the 1939 school year, leaving the students in limbo. One group of students started a rump seminary of their own off campus. In mid-1940 they went to acting seminary president Charles Allen Clark to demand use of the closed seminary buildings.

Charlie Clark was the mission official who had closed the seminary in 1939, and when the students made their demands and occupied the seminary dormitories, it was Clark who cut off their electricity and water in an attempt to force them to vacate the premises. When this failed to dislodge the demonstrators he appealed to Consul-General Gaylord Marsh in Seoul for official protection, pointing out that the students had seized American-owned property. He argued that a dangerous precedent was being set for American property all over Korea.

Gaylord Marsh, however, saw the incident as a satisfying comeuppance for the P'yŏngyang missionaries who had been so rigid in their stance on the Shintō issue. He took the dormitory occupation as a chance to toy with Charlie Clark. He wrote back professing to be mystified. Why not just let the students bow at the shrines, reopen the seminary, and get on with normal business? Marsh's response offended Charlie Clark, who countered with an emotional and theological argument ending with the statement, "If our Christian forefathers had accepted your opinion," he objected, "would there be any Christian Church in the world today? I surely do not believe that [the students] or anyone else can say that they bear no responsibility

18. Clark, *Religions of Old Korea*, pp. 129-130; 218.

(moral) when they violate their own consciences and bow to other gods."[19]

Marsh considered himself a decent Christian but he was not much interested in Clark's reasoning. He tried a legal tack. Why not sue to recover the property in court? Clark was so put out by this that he went over Marsh's head to Ambassador Joseph Grew in Tokyo. He explained to Grew that Marsh's idea of a lawsuit was unworkable "as our religion forbids Christians going to suit before heathen courts" and he appealed again for official protection from the students.[20] Ambassador Grew naturally consulted first with Gaylord Marsh, who was angry to learn that Charlie Clark had gone over his head to his boss. "Truly, many of these Northern Presbyterian missionaries are childlike in business matters," he fumed. "They often choose their words badly, and they like to receive contributions and protection with but little unity and only partial worldly allegiance in return."[21]

Charlie Clark, meanwhile, decided that he had no choice but to bend and let his students have the dormitories. At first when they occupied their rooms, he wrote, "I went personally and forbade it, and was told that 'even tho they had to hit me to get possession of the dormitories they were going into them.' Stealing our buildings was sin enough for a group of theological students. I did not want to let them incur the additional shame of beating up a teacher old enough to be their grandfather, so I've stayed away from there."[22] When U.S. Vice-Consul Arthur Emmons visited P'yŏngyang some months later he reported that the students, "many of whom appeared to be on reasonably friendly terms with Dr. Clark," were living in the dorms using the electricity and water lines free of charge.[23]

Spies, Solitude, and the Quality of Life

By the middle of 1940, living conditions in Korea were growing grimmer by the month. The war in China was diverting everything from the consumer economy. Sugar was rationed along with butter, flour, meat, and eggs. As winter approached, there was no coal to be had, and residents were forced to scrape their coal bins and stockpile wood whenever they could find it. No foreign goods were to be found in the stores, nor could

19. Charles Allen Clark to Marsh, September 13, 1940. National Archives and Record Service, Suitland, Md., Record Group 84, General Records, Tokyo, Japan, 1940, Box 120.

20. C.A. Clark to Grew, October 18, 1940, in ibid.

21. Marsh to Grew, October 30, 1940, in ibid.

22. C.A. Clark to Grew, October 1, 1940, in ibid.

23. Enclosure, "Visit of Vice Consul, Keijō, to Seized Presbyterian Property in Heijō, Chōsen, by Vice Consul Arthur B. Emmons, III, January 25, 1941." National Archives and Record Service, Suitland, RG 86, General Records—Tokyo, 1941, box 148.

they be ordered because of the currency restrictions. Hospitals especially felt the lack of imported supplies, but there was no bending the rules for them. In fact, the "China Incident" seemed to be diverting even the simplest Japanese-produced medicines: alcohol, aspirin, cod liver oil, quinine, and iodine. Ironically, opium derivatives were also impossible to get even though, as Stanley Martin wrote, "the Japanese are *debauching* the whole China coast with opium derivatives."[24] The medical risks of keeping families in Korea were obvious. "Surely Korea is no place for women and children," wrote one American, "and hardly a fit place for the stronger sex."[25]

The kindest thing a Westerner could do for his Korean friends in 1940 was to avoid them. Police surveillance was intense, and many foreigners had full-time detectives assigned to report on their every move. These detectives made themselves conspicuous at the gates of foreigners' houses explicitly to discourage Koreans from coming to visit. P'yŏngyang missionary Francis Kinsler had given up trying to visiting Korean churches in his jurisdiction in 1939; in 1940 even his former students stopped dropping by to visit him at home. His Korean secretary came in stealth, at night, via the back door.[26] Some of the most heavily guarded missionaries found that their only remaining "ministry" was at home, to the household servants and the Japanese detectives themselves. Taegu missionary Bill Lyon invited his English-speaking detective in out of the cold and let him sit in the living room spending days leafing through old issues of *National Geographic*.[27] It was more trouble than it was worth to "lose" one's detective, moreover, since one always had to return home, and detectives whose charges had temporarily eluded them were required to redeem themselves by conducting extra interrogations and filing extra reports. In fact it became practical to think of one's detective as a parole officer, checking in regularly with him to avoid extra trouble.

By the end of 1940, venturing out was such a problem that foreigners in Korea simply reorganized their lives around things that could be done at home. The loneliness—and pointlessness—of their existence was well expressed by Father Charles Hunt of the Anglican Mission, describing his last weeks in Ch'ŏngju:

24. Stanley Haviland Martin to A.E. Armstrong, April 21, 1940. UCCA, 83.006C, Box 4, File 111.

25. E.M. Cable to J.L. Hooper, November 16, 1940. National Archives and Record Service, Suitland, Md., Record Group 84, General Records, Tokyo, Japan, 1940, Box 120.

26. Francis Kinsler, interview, Duarte, California, May 28, 1987.

27. Lyon eventually left Korea, at which time he donated his desk to the detective, whose name was Shimamura. In Tokyo after the war, Mr. Lyon and his wife were on their way to a movie and stopped at a *koban* to ask directions of the neighborhood police. Much to their astonishment Mr. Shimamura emerged from a back room—to surprised greetings and an embrace. William B. Lyon, interview, Duarte, California, May 29, 1987.

Towards the end of the summer it became impossible for me to preach or teach in public and I was left completely alone at the top of the hill and apart from church services. I saw no one and no one came to see me. Surrounded by a forest of trees I had for my companions the golden oriole—a glorious bird that sang from June to mid-September even through the endless rain of summer, one chipmunk, a golden necked pheasant, and a very small mouse in my room. Occasionally a snake would cross my path on the hill, but looking out over the town I felt it to be utterly unfriendly and could recall no kindness of any kind except perhaps that of a Corean man who sold me scraps of chicken that kept me alive. When I left to go to Seoul...a detective accompanied me to the railway station, and I was not allowed to say good-bye to the few Christian folk, nor to my servant, or church workers.[28]

28. "(U)SPG Report from Father [Charles] Hunt," March 12, 1941, as hand-copied in the papers of Josephine Roberts.

-- 13 --

Living Dangerously in Chōsen

"Now you are old, why do you go away at all? Stay here altogether and we will give you a grand funeral!"[1]

On September 12, 1940, U.S. Ambassador Joseph Grew cabled Washington from Tokyo with his famous "green light message," switching his support to the hard-liners in the U.S. government who wanted to punish Japan for its aggression on the Asian mainland. Yet punishment was hardly advisable as long as thousands of American civilians, all potential hostages, were living in the Japanese Empire. It was time to put out the signal that war was getting closer by evacuating "non essential" American civilians from East Asia. The number to be evacuated from China, Japan, and Korea was estimated at over a thousand, making it necessary to charter several passenger ships to make the rounds and pick them up. The SS *Washington* was sent to Shanghai, the SS *Monterey* to Shanghai and Yokohama, and the SS *Mariposa* to Shanghai and Ch'inhuangtao in northeast China, Jinsen (Inch'ŏn) in Korea, and Kobe, Japan.

The State Department's evacuation order went out to embassies and consulates during the second week of October. When it reached Seoul, Consul-General Gaylord Marsh quickly wrote up a notice and passed it to American community leaders for distribution. It read:

1. Remark by Korean friend to Dr. Anne Borrow at the Anglican Hospital in Yōju, upon being told of the missionary evacuation in 1940. "Report of Dr. Anne Borrow, missionary at Yōju in the diocese of Korea for the period April 1940-November 1940," in the papers of Anglican missionary Josephine Roberts.

250

Confidential

Owing to an abnormal situation in the Far East interfering with proper cultural, business and other activities of American citizens, and to adverse effects on living conditions, the Department of State in Washington has come to the conclusion that *control of passports* [emphasis added] should be exercised and the withdrawal, to the United States, of American citizens should be suggested, such steps being similar to those taken for some time past in disturbed areas in Europe. Withdrawal applies especially to women and children as well as to those men whose presence in the future is not deemed to be urgent or indispensable. The advisability is indicated of utilizing available transportation while still open, it not being possible to guarantee that transportation will indefinitely continue to be available.[2]

Marsh's "control of passports" phrase was pure bluff. He had no legal power to order anyone to leave Korea. However, the American community reacted with something bordering on panic. An immediate casualty was Pyeng Yang Foreign School. At the time, PYFS was one of the best international boarding schools in Asia with a history of more than forty years. It had started the 1940-41 school year in September with new teachers from the United States and 105 students, 55 of them from outside Korea, and everything had functioned normally through the middle of October. But over the weekend of November 1, PYFS simply ceased to exist. When the evacuation order came from Consul-General Marsh, the school board held an emergency session and voted to suspend classes without delay. The boarding students were put on trains within hours, and three days later, on Tuesday, November 4, the school closed forever.[3]

The PYFS boarding students from China were especially hard hit by the school closing. Some of their U.S. passports bore the notation "Not valid for travel to China" and therefore required a special consular endorsement. The school staff found three such students, Virginia Bell and Jack and Tommy Bridgman. Carrying his brother's passport senior Tommy Bridgman took the train to Seoul on Sunday, together with freshman Virginia Bell. The pair checked in to Mrs. Kumabe's Guest House and got up early Monday morning to go to the consulate. As Virginia tells it, "I will never forget O. Gaylord Marsh for he was still under the influence of a party from the night before. We stood before him while he blessed us out for 'eloping, disgracing our parents and the school' and anything else he could think of. He took our passports and refused to give them back until we were vouched for by Mr. Hamilton later in the day." The students

2. The document continued: "You are requested to notify all members of your station to give due attention hereto, and you should avoid any false interpretation of this notice, you being assured that there is not cause for alarm." Copy enclosed with Marsh to SecState, November 20, 1940 (390.1115A/305).

3. Ralph O. Reiner, comp., *The Master Kulsi,* a special summary edition of the Pyeng Yang Foreign School Yearbook (New York: private print, 1943), p. 24.

missed the afternoon train back to P'yŏngyang that would have given them time to collect their baggage from the dormitory. They had to take the evening train and friends had to bring their suitcases down to the station and hand them in through the window when the train paused on its way north to the Manchurian border.[4]

The withdrawal of American civilians from Korea touched off withdrawals by British subjects also, including Canadians and Australians who were essential to the Protestant missionary effort. In Seoul, Horace and Ethel Underwood were appalled by the stampede. After fighting off the Presbyterian Mission's attempts to remove them from Chōsen Christian College, they were in no mood to obey the consul-general's alleged order. Horace was angry at the way Gaylord Marsh had frightened the expatriate community. He wrote,

> I do not think that an American agent has a right to refuse such protection as he can give to an American citizen who is carrying out his lawful occasions in a country with which the United States is at peace. However, this *threat* has alarmed a number who, I think, might otherwise have stayed....I fully realize that staying on may involve very considerable embarrassment and possibly even danger, but having as a child seen some of the periods through which the missionaries continued steadfast at their work, I am at a loss to understand the present hysterical panic.[5]

Many realized that they might be leaving Korea forever. In conditions short of war they did not want to liquidate fifty years of work, and the older people were shocked to think that they were suddenly facing retirement. Pulling out also meant leaving Korean friends behind in an ominous situation, perhaps never to be seen again. There was much soul searching. Some saw the evacuation as a providential part of the oncoming war that would be God's punishment for Japan's militarists. Australian missionary C.I. McLaren wrote, "[If Japan rejects the Gospel] then we are not only free, but enjoined to depart (Matthew 10:14-15; Luke 21:20) and God's processes of judgment must overtake the Empire."[6] Others criticized the Koreans themselves, speaking of the disaster as punishment for Koreans who had surrendered to Shintō worship.[7] Such ideas shocked the mission-

4. Virginia Bell Somerville, interview, August 15, 1995, Montreat, North Carolina, and correspondence, November 19, 2002.
5. H.H. Underwood to J.L. Hooper, October 14, 1940.
6. Charles I. McLaren, paper analyzing the motives of departing missionaries, RG 140, Box 16, Folder 23, Presbyterian Historical Society. The Australian Presbyterian Mission left at the same time.
7. As Henry Lampe once put it, "The majority [of the Presbyterian Mission] say [the Korean church leaders who have accepted Shintō worship] should be treated as sinners and until they repent, we can have no official relations with them." Lampe to J.L. Hooper, June 6, 1940, RG 140, Box 16, Folder 23, Presbyterian Historical Society, Philadelphia.

aries who wanted to stay. Ethel Underwood was bitter about the way some of her fellow-missionaries were abandoning the Koreans:

> the self-satisfied leaders now call their own pupils "apostate." Their own trained leaders, trained by themselves are condemned en masse on their first test of independent thinking. Not only are they blamed but blocked in every effort to separate patriotism from religion—those former leaders, I cannot understand, nor do I have to understand.[8]

The evacuation itself was a matter of logistics, including finances. The mission boards agreed to pay for passage on the *Mariposa,* even though the fares on the evacuation ship were more than double the normal trans-Pacific tariff. Those remaining were warned that they did so at their own risk and that it might be very difficult and certainly more expensive to get out later on. As it was, the rates on the *Mariposa* troubled the more frugal missionaries who responded by demanding "emergency accommodations," the cheapest category of passage that literally meant cots in the hallways. The State Department, which had fronted a small fortune on the evacuation, started worrying about the number of unsold cabins and pressured its consuls to sell the cabins before resorting to "emergency accommodations." This made Gaylord Marsh a kind of salesman, having to talk people into buying more expensive cabin space.[9] Hating this, Marsh criticized the State Department for sending such a luxurious ship. In an angry telegram he wrote,

OVER ONE HUNDRED MISSIONARIES POSITIVELY DECLINE TO PAY MORE THAN TWO HUNDRED FORTY DOLLARS FOR PASSAGE ON MARIPOSA. MANAGEMENT OF THIS PROJECT HAS BEEN DISGUSTING. CAN YOU DO ANYTHING? TIME IS SHORT NOW.[10]

8. Ethel Underwood to J.L. Hooper, November 15, 1940. Charles McLaren agreed, pointing to the irony of the missionaries' trying to construe their departure as a "protest" against the Korean church's attitude: "[T]his protest is made nugatory by [turning over church properties and leadership] to the Korean leaders chiefly responsible for the de-Christianizing of the church. . . ." McLaren, paper analyzing the motives of departing missionaries.
9. Like the *Monterey* and the *Washington,* the Matson Lines' S.S. *Mariposa* was a luxury liner with all-day food service, sports and recreation facilities, and a dance band—hardly the natural choice for an emergency evacuation. To finance the voyage the U.S. government had to put up "several hundred thousand dollars" in anticipation of filling the ship with evacuees willing to pay "rates equal to those for similar accommodations on regularly operated ships in the trans-Pacific passenger trade." Tickets on the *Mariposa* ranged from $275 to $400 whereas the ordinary transpacific fare from Kobe to the West Coast was $150. On the other hand, the *Mariposa* was sailing from Inch'ŏn, sparing the passengers the usual expense of crossing over to Japan to catch the boat, and passengers embarking at Inch'ŏn could carry considerably more baggage than might be possible later on in an emergency evacuation.
10. Marsh's tone wounded his colleague Samuel Sokobin, the American consul in Kobe who had been orchestrating the thankless task of getting American citizens out of ports all across the Far East. Ambassador Joseph Grew was sufficiently

The evacuation "order" caused consternation in Japan. In Tokyo, the *Japan Advertiser* gave the official Japanese view that "Evacuation in principle is all wrong and a retrograde move. Even at the cost of some personal and temporary difficulties it should be stopped, if not by governments, as far as possible by individuals."[11] A columnist in the *Miyako* described the U.S. government as "trembling at phantoms" while the Tokyo *Nichi Nichi* said that the evacuation was one of a series of moves meant to intimidate Japan and wondered what subsequent moves might be. Other Japanese papers welcomed the withdrawal as a chance to move in on American privileges and markets in China and Korea. While expressing amazement that Washington could think its citizens in danger, the departure of American and British "fifth columnists" was seen as a boon to the future of the Greater East Asia Co-Prosperity Sphere.[12]

On November 15, 1940, the *Mariposa* crossed the Yellow Sea and anchored at Inch'ŏn. The 291 Americans who had boarded previously at Shanghai and Ch'inhuangtao soon got a taste of life under the Minami regime when they were mustered on deck to be questioned by "health officers" while a search for contraband went on below. None was found, but

irritated to order a staffer to Seoul to check on Marsh's mental state. Marsh explained that he had meant to characterize the shipping companies' handling of the tickets as "disgusting" and certainly not the work of the esteemed State Department. He also was "disgusted" at the way the missionaries were waffling about whether to leave, and how much to pay. Grew's man in Seoul attributed Marsh's outburst to stress: "He himself says that at times his patience has been tried by the attitude of a certain type of missionary who regards all official advice as unwarranted interference or coercion....I may mention that Mr. Marsh has been under considerable nervous strain in connection with the work of evacuating en masse a large number of American citizens and that he is normally a man of somewhat irascible temper and forthright nature. He is, however, an officer of long experience and mature judgment who would not be likely to make irresponsible statements or to take unconsidered actions." "Memorandum of Conversation re Withdrawal of Presbyterian Missionaries from Korea between J.L. Hooper and George Atcheson," November 7, 1940 (390.1115A/280); telegram, Cordell Hull to Marsh, November 9, 1940 (390. 1115A/211B); telegram, Marsh to SecState, November 11, 1940 (390. 1115A/201); Joseph Davies to G.H. Helmbold, November 12, 1940 (390.1115A/ 254B); Breckenridge Long to A.L. Warnshuis, November 13, 1940 (FW 390.1115A/ 201); John H. Reisner to secretaries of Mission Boards having work in East Asia, November 15, 1940 (FW 390.1115A/201); Marsh to SecState, November 23, 1940 (390.1115A/308); Telegram, Grew to SecState, December 2, 1940 (390.1115A/ 265); Samuel Sokobin to SecState, October 28, 1940 (390.1115A/241). Turner to Grew, report on O. Gaylord Marsh, quoted in Grew to SecState, telegram, December 2, 1940 (390.1115A/265).

11. *Japan Advertiser* (Tokyo), October 29, 1940, enclosed with Grew to SecState, November 1, 1940 (390.1115A/242). The *Advertiser,* which earlier had been American-owned, by 1940 had moved from Kobe to Tokyo and, in the words of Ambassador Grew, was "virtually an organ of the Foreign Office."

12. Ibid.

the officers did discover a passenger passed out in her cabin. Refusing to believe that she was merely drunk, they set off on a search for narcotics. When one of the officers unaccountably lost his sword, an additional search for the sword became necessary, and only after it was found were the passengers allowed back to their cabins.[13]

For the Americans on shore, the next morning brought Evacuation Day. From all parts of Seoul by car, Korean *kuruma* cart, and on foot, more than two hundred Americans converged on the railroad station for the 22-mile trip to Inch'ŏn. Porters carried trunks on *chigye* A-frames, enough to create a mountain of baggage on the platform.[14] Korean friends braved police surveillance to come and say good-bye, and there were enough empty seats on the special evacuation train to permit many of them to travel all the way to Inch'ŏn for their last farewells. Gaylord Marsh described the scene when they arrived at the port:

> The officials of the city...tried to have the Americans march in five columns from the station to the wharf, but columns were quickly broken with many a joke [about being the "Fifth Column," etc.]....The chief of the Jinsen [Inch'ŏn] police kindly placed chairs on the wharf for the comfort of the Americans; but in a speech he unnecessarily warned against taking photographs, making soundings, measuring tides, surveying atmospheric conditions, upsetting the tender by crowding to one side, and other acts in contravention of laws and regulations principally governing fortified areas like Jinsen. Customs inspection was unnecessarily thorough, but no duty was charged, no fines imposed, and no significant confiscations were made.[15] A few of the two or three thousand trunks were broken, the contents of a few trunks were

13. Sailing and port directions, Gerald H. Helmbold, U.S. Maritime Commission, to Brandt, November 13, 1940 (390.1115A/255). Mrs. R.L. Smyth to SecState, December 31, 1940 (390.1115A/380).

14. The Southern Presbyterian Boyer family from Chŏnju walked the whole way from the Chōsen Hotel, seven members in all, each one carrying a suitcase and her mother carrying 3-year-old Helen. Katherine Boyer Moore, interview, Seoul, January 25, 1990.

15. Here Marsh was being unduly generous to the Japanese. Mrs. Arthur Emmons, wife of the American vice-consul, told a different story. "When they reached the pier, although the Consulate-General at Keijō had been assured there would be only a perfunctory examination, the passengers were delayed while only one customs officer at first (later an assistant joined him) proceeded to go through their baggage with the utmost care, looking in pockets and taking out each article and examining it. The. . .examination took many hours. . . .As there is reportedly a ban on the taking of photographs out of Korea, the customs officers tore up photographs belonging to the passengers, including their family and other personal photographs. Mrs. Emmons, traveling with a diplomatic passport, had her baggage examined as minutely as the other passengers, although none of her photographs were destroyed." "Memorandum by Mrs. R.L. Smyth, Wife of First Secretary Smyth at Peiping," December 31, 1940 (390.1115A/380). Katherine Boyer Moore recalls that evacuees had to declare gold fillings and eyeglasses rims as gold export items. Conversation, Seoul, July 16, 1990.

The S.S. *Mariposa*. Postcard. Clark Collection.

trampled with muddy feet, and the transfer fee on baggage from station to wharf had to be raised to a not unreasonable amount by reason of error in the original estimate.[16]

At mid-afternoon, the 219 Korea evacuees were ferried out to where the *Mariposa* lay at anchor. As they rounded the stern of the ship, on which was painted a huge American flag, Alice Appenzeller thought about her father. Henry Gerhard Appenzeller had landed here at Chemulp'o, as it was then known, on Easter Sunday 1885 to begin the work of the Methodist Episcopal Mission. In the fifty-five years of work since then, hundreds of American Methodists had founded churches, schools, and hospitals across Korea. Some, like her father himself, had given their lives in the work. Now, after all that effort, what would be left if war came to Korea?[17] As E. Wade Koons put it,

> No vessel ever left Jinsen with such a freight as the *Mariposa* carried. Children leaving their parents, wives parted from their husbands, friends who thru hard years have been closer than brothers separating perhaps never to meet again, unfinished plans, abandoned projects, cherished work left with little hope that it will be carried on—God only can count the sorrow hidden behind those resolute smiles.[18]

Meanwhile, "a group of sad-faced Korean Christians and friends and servants lingered to a late hour in Inch'ŏn to have a last look and a last

16. Marsh to SecState, November 20, 1940 (390.1115A/305).

17. Alice Appenzeller, "Dear Friends" circular, June 6, 1941, in the archives of the Korea Methodist Mission, Drew University.

18. E.W. Koons, "The Mariposa Comes to Jinsen," *The Korea Mission Field*, XXXVI:12 (December 1940), p. 201.

good-bye, notwithstanding the fact that they were photographed by the official photographer for what purpose they did not know."[19]

Toward dusk, the *Mariposa* weighed anchor and headed for the open sea, the Americans aboard feeling reassured by a rumor that the cruiser USS *Augusta* was out in the darkness standing watch. Life on the *Mariposa* then took shape as people settled into their cabins. The ship was not full, so the captain did away with the class system—after making sure that the Foreign Service families had the best cabins. The crew organized games and parties for the 196 children on board. Religious services were organized and a room was set aside for daily meditation. And there were the ship's usual amusements: tea dances, movies, and band concerts. On Thanksgiving Day there was a turkey feast. In fact, everything wonderful about America seemed to be contained on the *Mariposa*. "The *Mariposa* is a little bit of Heaven," wrote one evacuee. A tea dance menu carefully preserved by another bore the notation "This boat is a luxury ship, and no mistake—everything about it is superb."[20]

But there was no escaping the regret. During one shipboard concert, the band played the passage from Donizetti's *Lucia di Lamermoor* that Korean Christians long had used as the tune for their patriotic hymn "Samch'ŏllibando" ("Our three-thousand *li* peninsula") and it brought on tears.[21] The passengers tried to reassure each other that they had done the right thing. They rehearsed what they would say to supporters back home who would ask them why there had been an evacuation when the United States and Japan were still at peace. One group drafted a statement giving five reasons: (1) the Japanese attitude that missionaries were really spies, (2) the danger of being trapped if war broke out, (3) the wedge that had been driven between missionaries and Korean Christians, (4) the new limits on religious freedom, and (5) the danger that Koreans faced if they associated with foreigners. The document closed with this:

> It is tragic to leave. It is terrible to have to remain. The issue of it all is not in the Orient alone, but in Europe and America, a world issue. In the faith that God has "some better thing" for his Church in these troubled lands we return, praying that He may again send us forth to make a new and better world, upon which the Sun of Righteousness shall arise with healing in his Wings.[22]

19. Ibid.

20. Mrs. R.L Smyth, December 31, 1940; Koons, "The Mariposa Comes to Jinsen," p. 201; menu enclosed with Henry Lampe to J.L. Hooper, November 25, 1940; and Bliss W. Billings to Frank T. Cartwright, December 3, 1940.

21. Richard H. Baird, interview, May 27, 1987. The hymn *Samch'ŏllibando Kŭmsugangsan* is still sung as a patriotic hymn especially around the anniversary of liberation from Japan, August 15.

22. "A Brief Summary of the Factors Presented by Evacuees on Board the S.S. *Mariposa* as their reasons for Returning Home" (November 25, 1940), enclosed

Prelude to Pearl Harbor

Three-fourths of the American residents in Korea were out of the country by the end of 1940. Those remaining included business owners like the A.W. Taylors, foreign employees of companies such as Standard Oil and Ilhan New Pharmaceuticals, the consular community, and a few missionaries, notably the Catholics and the Northern Presbyterians, who had made the evacuation voluntary.[23] All those remaining were subjected to stepped-up Japanese pressure. In November 1940, Edna Lawrence, a Northern Presbyterian Mission nurse, was arrested on charges of being a communist agent —charges that were dropped when it became obvious that her male accuser was making the allegations because she had spurned his romantic attentions. In January 1941, Ch'ŏngju Presbyterians DeWitt Lowe and Otto DeCamp were arrested for desecrating Shintō *kamidana*, little house shrines that they found in their Korean servants' quarters on the mission compound. Local authorities had decreed that every Korean house in Ch'ŏngju should have a *kamidana*, confronting the American missionaries with idolatry on their very doorstep. Lowe and DeCamp removed the shrines and burned some of the sacred papers associated with them, allegedly saying that they would help alleviate the local fuel shortage.[24] The Japanese were not amused. The two Americans were arrested and jailed in the city of Taejŏn pending trial, and when the Presbyterian Mission's Japanese lawyers failed to fend off a conviction they were sentenced to ten months in prison.[25]

with R.E. Diffendorfer to Department of State, December 10, 1940 (395.116 M56/7).

23. The remaining Presbyterians represented the liberal/conservative, Seoul/ P'yŏngyang spectrum of views within the mission. As one said to Methodist Board secretary Frank Cartwright, "I think in our Northern Presbyterian group because of the split in sentiment each side was unwilling to leave for fear that the representatives of the other side would be swinging things in the wrong direction in their absence." Frank T. Cartwright to James Moore, January 10, 1941.

24. Japanese Ambassador Nomura Kichisaburō told American authorities in Washington "...that DeCamp and Lowe were disrespectful and jocular in their attitude in removing the *kamidana* and said that in view of the shortage of fuel they would no doubt make good fire wood;..." Memorandum of Conversation, Calvert Coville (Far East Division, Department of State) with Presbyterian Board Secretaries John Hooper and Charles Leber, April 23, 1941, in the Presbyterian Historical Society, Philadelphia. Also see Marsh to Grew, "God Shelves on American Mission Property in Chosen," January 31, 1941 (390.115A). Otto DeCamp always denied that either of them had said anything of the sort. Interview, Duarte, California, July 21, 1983.

25. The sentences were handed down in April 1941. J. L. Hooper to Calvert Coville (Far East Division, Department of State), February 22, 1941; E.H. Miller to Hooper, March 22, 1941; and H.E. Blair to Hooper, April 11, 1941, Presbyterian Historical Society, Philadelphia.

In February, a group of Protestant women organized their annual observance of the International Women's Day of Prayer, scheduled for February 28, 1941, day prior to the anniversary of the Korean Independence Movement. The police were especially jittery; however, Alice Butts, the organizer, did not consult them about the printed program. Instead she took the international committee's suggested order of worship and came up with the following:[26]

ORDER OF WORSHIP

Opening Hymn	"All Hail the Power of Jesus' Name"
Scriptures	Daniel 4:3. "His Kingdom is an everlasting kingdom, and his dominion is from generation to generation." Psalm 22:27-28. "For the Kingdom is the Lord's and He is governor among the nations." Revelation 11:15. "Then the seventh angel blew his trumpet, and there were loud voices in heaven, saying, 'The kingdom of the world has become the kingdom of our Lord and of his Christ, and he shall reign for ever and ever.'"
Confession	"We must confess that for the interests of our own country we afflict other countries...making war against other nations for our own gain...."
Sermon, prayers, etc.	
Closing Hymn	"Must Jesus Bear the Cross Alone?"
Closing Scripture	Revelation 21:1-4. "And God himself shall be with them; He will wipe away every tear from their eyes, and death shall be no more, neither shall there be mourning nor crying nor pain any more, for the former things have passed away."

Miss Butts then had fifteen thousand copies of the program printed up and distributed across northern Korea. The women's prayer services took place on February 28 and the independence movement anniversary passed without incident on March 1; but on March 2 the police came to arrest Miss Butts on charges of circulating seditious literature. Nineteen of her alleged accomplices, including Ethel Underwood, Lilian Ross, and Charlie Clark, were also arrested over the next several weeks.

The Japanese press in Korea used the opportunity to attack missionary "subversion" once again, accusing the detainees of an "anti-war plot" and of "craftily arousing anti-war and anti-state ideas" among the Koreans. The printed program had been "exceedingly seditious," grumbled the *Mae'il Sinbo*, the government's Korean-language paper. "The people in general should take care

26. Program enclosed in Herbert E. Blair to J.L. Hooper, October 8, 1941, RG 140, Presbyterian Historical Society.

not to commit un-national crimes unwittingly, and at the same time they should strengthen the consciousness of their being Imperial subjects and whole-heartedly render service for the state behind the gun."[27]

American officials were appalled by the missionaries' poor sense. In New York, Methodist Board Secretary George Sutherland said, "Phrases of this kind in printed documents circulated in any country in wartime would be questionable."[28] And in Seoul, Consul-General Gaylord Marsh was predictably livid. On March 4 he fired a cablegram to Ambassador Grew in Tokyo:[29]

I SUGGEST THE PRESBYTERIAN MISSION, NEW YORK CITY, BE URGED TO WITHDRAW ALL UNESSENTIAL, MILITANT, AND INDISCREET MISSIONARIES FROM THIS FIELD....WE CANNOT AFFORD TO HAVE TO DEFEND INDIVIDUAL INDISCRETION NOR SUPPORT SELF-APPOINTED CANDIDATES FOR INTERNATIONAL MARTYRDOM.

Most of the arrested in the World Day of Prayer case were held for only a few days, though they were often brought back later for interrogation. In Kanggye, the police repeatedly summoned Lilian Ross for questioning in the middle of the night. The interrogation was never abusive and in fact took on a ritual quality. The sessions were not much more than conversations, and an hour or two later, when they were over, she would be given a choice between spending the rest of the night in jail and going home to her own bed. She always chose to go home, and on the way she would pass the town's roving night watchman. "Oh, it's you!" he would say. "Are they through questioning you for the night?"

"Yes," Lilian would answer.

"Good," he would say. "Have a good sleep."[30]

In July, the Presbyterian Mission and the colonial government worked out a compromise whereby the missionaries in the case would confess, apologize for breaking the law, and leave Korea forthwith.[31] In Taejŏn,

27. Enclosed with Marsh to Grew, April 1, 1941 (395.1121/22).

28. George Sutherland, memorandum for the file, August 8, 1941.

29. Marsh to Grew, March 4, 1941, quoted in Grew to SecState, March 5, 1941 (390.1115A/400). In a follow-up report he described to Grew the careless language used by the missionaries in "the prayer circular with its several statements so well understood in Christendom and so open to misinterpretation by intention or lack of comprehension" and explained how the Japanese authorities must have resented "the activity of strong-minded missionary women who contrast so greatly with the present Japanese conception of a woman's lack of any place in affairs in general." Marsh to Grew, April 1, 1941. This was Marsh's official report on the matter, less colorful than an earlier telegram to Grew in which he said THIS CONSULATE GENERAL REGARDS HER [Miss Butts] AS HAVING BEEN STUPID AND INDISCREET. Marsh to Grew, quoted in Grew to SecState, March 11, 1941.

30. Lilian Ross, interview, Duarte, California, May 26, 1987.

31. The text of the confession was as follows: "In connection with the International Women's Prayer Meeting I apologize for having acted in violation of the

DeWitt Lowe and Otto DeCamp were also given a way out in the *kamidana* case: a two-year stay of sentence with permission to leave the country. Both settlements were deportations, in effect, and the Americans involved lost no time getting out. After having refused repatriation on the *Mariposa* —though he had sent Mabel home on the ship along with his son Allen and his family—Charlie Clark accepted that he ought to go with the group that was headed for America via Shanghai. Some, like Lilian Ross, volunteered for transfer to the Philippines. By the end of November 1941, only twenty-four Protestant missionary men, women, and children remained in Korea, among them six members of the Underwood family.

Earlier that year, in March, the last Canadians at Lungchingtsun had been ordered to leave Chientao. Ironically, when they left they believed that the Korean Christian community was in the best shape it had ever been. The East Hill Church had its own missionaries visiting country churches all across the region, and the Ŭnjin School had a team of students running a Sunday School in a neighboring town. Trusted Korean associates had taken over St. Andrew's Hospital, the school, and the night schools for adults. But these encouraging signs only lasted a few months. By November, the Japanese Army had taken over the Canadian Mission compound and turned it into a military base, and St. Andrew's had become a military hospital.[32]

In Seoul, Ethel Underwood had spent the year keeping up a façade of normalcy. In January her husband had been forced to resign as president of Chōsen Christian College. In March she herself had been arrested as a member of the Women's Day of Prayer Committee. But with few other interruptions she and Horace both continued teaching at the college. Eldest son Horace Grant ("Young Horace") was back after graduating from Hamilton, teaching English as a volunteer on a family allowance. The two youngest children, Dick and Grace, commuted by train each day to Seoul Foreign School where they were a significant percentage of the student body.

There was even time for romance. The Henry Davidsons' daughter Joan had returned from her schooling in England to start a secretarial job with the British consulate. She and Young Horace soon began spending time together and by February they were ready to announce their engagement. The wedding took place in July 1941 at Seoul's Anglican cathedral, fol-

Chōsen Pernicious Papers Temporary Control Ordinance.' I have now received generous treatment with special consideration and a kind admonition for the future, for which I am highly grateful. I therefore respectfully pledge myself not only to desist henceforth from doing such improper things, but also to return to my country immediately."

32. Donald M. Black to A.E. Armstrong, May 1, 1940 (UCCA, 83.006C, Box 4, File 109); George Bruce to A.E. Armstrong, December 22, 1940 (UCCA, 83.006, Box 4, File 110); unsigned "Report on a Trip to Northern Stations, May, 1941," (UCCA, 83.006C, Box 5, File 116).

lowed by receptions at the Seoul Union Club and at the Myŏngwŏlgwan Korean restaurant in Insa-dong. The newlyweds honeymooned in Peking, returning to join the Underwood family for the rest of the summer at Sorai Beach. The trip back to Korea was a study in wartime aggravations. They were stopped at the border because Joan was carrying a diplomatic passport even though she had quit her job at the consulate. This obstacle was eliminated when one of the border officials turned out to be a Chōsen Christian College graduate. However, the delay caused them to miss their reserved-seat train, and they had to travel to Changyŏn sitting on their suitcases in the aisle. At Changyŏn the police confiscated a pair of Joan's earrings because they were decorated with a *yang-yin* motif that the Japanese decided was a *taegŭk* symbol from the forbidden Korean flag.[33]

At Sorai Beach, Ethel Underwood tried to keep up everyone's spirits. On a postcard to Board Secretary J.L. Hooper in New York she wrote, "Life is grand—Sixty are enjoying the summer here."[34] But by summer's end even Ethel was willing to admit that things were rough. The ride home was emblematic of how far things had gone wrong. The Underwoods had a 1938 Chrysler convertible that they had bought with delight at its red leather upholstery but had been forced to reupholster because red was said to be the emperor's color. When it came time to drive back to Seoul at the end of the season, the Changyŏn district police first ordered them to leave the car at the beach to prevent them from wandering unsupervised in military areas. Permission was finally granted on condition that a policeman ride with them in the car. Soon after they started—the four adults, two children, family cook, and policeman—the Chrysler's clutch stuck. The policeman insisted that they keep driving anyway; and though the clutch eventually shook loose, it was a most harrowing trip. When they got home they found their neighbors were keeping their suitcases packed, and that the oncoming war was Topic A.

Pearl Harbor Day in Korea

At the Maryknoll Mission in P'yŏngyang, the Catholics watched the Protestants' rush to board the *Mariposa*. As American citizens they too felt pressured to evacuate by Gaylord Marsh, but as single workers without families they were not as vulnerable to the suggestion of danger, nor did they believe that the United States and Japan were about to go to war. Their work was intensely local—kindergartens, old people's homes, middle schools, music lessons, and small congregations—and they were well known to the local authorities who did not seem to threaten them. News of the war in China did not affect them much, and rumors of a war looming between Ja-

---

33. Horace G. Underwood, interviews, May-June, 1985.
34. Ethel V. Underwood to J.L. Hooper, postcard, July 30, 1941.

pan and the United States seemed far-fetched. In August 1941 the nuns at Ŭiju on the Manchurian border were ordered indoors for two weeks, presumably to keep them from observing troop movements, but that was understandable, and from September to December they were allowed to work in much their normal fashion.[35]

News of the Japanese attack on Pearl Harbor reached Korea in the morning of Monday, December 8, 1941, Korea time. The houseboy brought the news to Sisters Mary Gabriella and Loretta Rose at the Maryknoll convent in Ŭiju. They were in the midst of a feast day celebration that immediately developed into a bonfire for mission financial records and documents. Next door, Father Gervis Coxen was taken to the police station and told to pass the word that the Japanese had nothing personal against the Maryknollers and they should simply keep to their quarters. However, by midnight there were new orders: the police came to take the mission's three priests away. The Sisters watched from an upper window of the convent, then went together to the chapel to recite Psalm 90: "Lord, thou hast been our dwelling place in all generations. Before the mountains were brought forth, or ever thou hadst formed the earth and the world, even from everlasting to everlasting, thou art God."

Down south in Kwangju, the handful of Southern Presbyterians had a visit from the police, who told them that Japan had demolished the American fleet at Pearl Harbor and war had been declared. They ordered the missionaries to keep off the streets but assured them that they would be safe on the Presbyterian compound. However, later in the day they came again, this time to arrest senior missionary J.V.N. Talmage and take him to the city jail for 121 days of detention in a 6-by-10-foot cell. The three remaining missionaries, Talmage's wife Eliza, Mary Dodson, and Florence Root, were kept under house arrest in the "saxie house" wondering about Dr. Talmage's fate. They were not to see him again until April 9.[36]

In the Russian Orthodox Church compound in Seoul, Vladimir and Cyril Tchirkine had gone to bed Sunday night dreading the exam that was scheduled for Monday morning, December 8, in Aline Phipps' English class at Seoul Foreign School. In the morning they walked around the corner into the schoolyard and were surprised to find no one there. What had happened? Was it somehow still Sunday? Did it mean that Mrs. Phipps would cancel her test?

While the Tchirkine twins puzzled over their deliverance from their English test, Mrs. Phipps herself was at home on the British consulate compound. The Phippses had been awakened that morning by a phone call from Ethel Underwood telling of the attack on Pearl Harbor. Before long,

35. Sister Mary Gabriella Mulherin, M.M., to Mother Mary Joseph Rogers, M.M., August 28, 1942, Sisters Letters, Maryknoll Mission Archives.
36. Florence Root, "Dear Friends" letter, September 11, 1942, in the Presbyterian Church, U.S.A., Department of History, Montreat, North Carolina.

police at the gate were delivering an order to Consul-General Gerald Phipps to report to the Foreign Affairs Bureau at 2:30 P.M. In the meantime, the British staff were not to use the telegraph or try to leave the compound, which was to be guarded by a truckload of gendarmes. The Phippses spent the morning burning papers, and in the afternoon Mr. Phipps reported to the Government-General building as ordered, to be told that Japan and Great Britain were officially at war. Plainclothesmen then descended on the British compound to enforce house arrest, beginning with a thorough search during which the British staff were made to stand, shivering, in the garden. The police took the radio, cutting off their contact with the outside world, and by 5:30 P.M., after a "harrowing afternoon," the compound had become a prison. "We are in an impenetrable fog," wrote Aline Phipps in her diary, "where we hear no one nor make ourselves heard." "The militarists," she added, "have had their way and will lead this country through a time of terrible misery and suffering."[37]

At Dilkusha, A.W. and Mary Taylor also spent the morning burning papers from A.W.'s occasional side job as an Associated Press reporter—since by 1941 the Japanese considered all journalists to be spies. At Chōsen Christian College, the Underwood family spent the time consolidating supplies. They put the top down on their Chrysler convertible and used it to move Young Horace and Joan back to the parents' house, starting with their personal effects and ending with their coal, which was added to the family's supply in the Underwood House basement.

Horace Underwood was still hauling coal at around 2:30 P.M. when the gendarmes came to arrest him. They drove him to the military police interrogation center on Namsan, where he was grilled about his ties with the American consulate and his possession of cameras, radios, and foreign exchange. There was much snickering about how much liquor he had stashed at home and how many Korean women he had slept with over the years; but there was no physical abuse, and within a few days he found himself in an makeshift concentration camp: an empty classroom of the Methodist Theological Seminary in Naengch'ŏn-dong where he was reunited with Young Horace and a handful of other Seoul expatriates.[38]

Elsewhere in the city, Presbyterian missionaries Ralph Reiner, E.H. Miller, Wade Koons, and Bill Kerr were interrogated about their alleged crimes, which ranged from embezzlement to espionage. Their bouts with the police were particularly rough, since the interrogators had the hardest time establishing the link between them and the American consulate. During one especially nasty session they were subjected to the dreaded "water

37. Aline Phipps, Diary, December 8, 1941, and Joyce Phipps Taylor, interview, Santa Rosa, California, August 10, 1989.

38. By December, 1941, the Korean leaders of the Methodist church had been forced to rent the seminary property in Naengch'ŏn Dong to the police as a parole school, hence its appropriation as a detention center in 1942.

cure" and beaten with rubber hoses. The 70-year-old Miller told of being beaten so severely over the head that, though he was never hit below the ears, he was black and blue down onto his chest.[39]

Eventually the seminary inmates numbered fourteen, half of them non-missionaries.[40] The room was uncomfortably cold in mid-winter and the guards sometimes used insulting language, but the officer in charge, a Korean missionary school graduate, was considerate and appeared to want to make things tolerable. The prisoners slept on cots, were always escorted to the toilet, and were taken outside twice a day for exercise. During these exercise periods, A.W. Taylor could see his wife Mary watching from Dilkusha across the valley, even though neither one dared signal to the other. Families were allowed to send blankets and cooked food, some of it still hot in thermos containers and some that they warmed on electric hotplates. Although all incoming and outgoing items were searched, the Underwoods learned how to pass notes back and forth by hiding them inside the thermos casing.

Back at the Underwood House, Ethel, Joan, and teenagers Dick and Grace adjusted to life under house arrest. The evening before the Pearl Harbor raid there had been a black-tie dinner for Seoul's few remaining foreign residents, to celebrate Horace and Ethel's twenty-fifth wedding anniversary. Of the male guests, only the septuagenarian Henry Davidson had escaped arrest on December 8—exempt because of his 1911 decoration for meritorious service to the Japanese government.[41] At the Underwood House there were frequent police visits and searches for "incriminating evidence," opportunities for harassment during which the family lost, among

39. The water cure, as described by Reiner, involved being trussed into the fetal position with ropes and then being rolled onto his back and shoulders with his feet up in the air, while cold water from teakettles was poured into his mouth and nose. Both the water cure and the beatings were conducted by a Korean named Song Kapchin (Japanese name: Morita), who was caught and tried after the war for torturing the three American missionaries in 1942. Song/Morita got ten years at hard labor. "Subject: U.S. vs. Kapchin Song," Supreme Commander for the Allies Powers, GHQ Legal Section, Informational Summary No. 202, 23 January 1948 (File 014.13), Presbyterian Historical Society.

40. The seven were American businessmen A.W. Taylor and Archibald C. Biddle (of the American Trading Company and the Hongkong and Shanghai Bank, married to a Japanese); Canadian businessman Alexander McFarlane (married to a Japanese); Russians Maximilian Hefftler (the last Czarist consul, later a Seoul businessman and sometime Ilhan New Pharmaceuticals employee), and M. Svensitsky (Standard Oil employee); Hungarian D. Barat (a chemist with Ilhan New); and one woman, Astrid Pedersen, a Norwegian-Japanese employee of Standard Oil. Horace G. Underwood, interviews, May-June 1985 and June 1990, and Bruce Taylor, interview, August 10, 1989.

41. Davidson had been given an official pair of gold cufflinks and a citation for his service with the Korean Customs Service when he resigned in 1911 to go to work for J.H. Morris. Seoul Press, November 21, 1911, p. 3.

Seoul Western internees after Pearl Harbor, 1941-42. Courtesy of
Horace G. Underwood.

other things, several cameras and thousands of feet of home movies. The
military police even staged a search on Christmas Day—something that
Ethel decided to turn into an occasion. She explained the family's Christmas dinner tradition to the surprised gendarmes and then, since no other
guests were available, she sat them down and served them lunch.

On compounds elsewhere in the city, other foreign spouses likewise endured house arrest. Floy Koons, confined on the Presbyterian Mission
compound near East Gate, was allowed to have her Korean cook and *amah*
by day but spent her nights alone. At Dilkusha, Mary Taylor stationed her
Korean gardener downstairs at night while she slept in the bedroom with
her two German Shepherds. The military police visited all the wives on
Christmas Day. Mary Taylor's visitors gave her a note with news, which later
proved to be spurious, that her only son Bruce had been killed at Pearl Har-

bor. Floy Koons, on the other hand, got an apology from one of her Christmas raiders: "I know this is your Christmas," he said. "I am sorry to have to do this."[42]

Weeks passed. Family visits were permitted on January 29, the day Astrid Pederson and Messrs. Barat and Hefftler were released. In February they were allowed to receive Japanese newspapers and books from home, and someone sent a Parcheesi board. On the day of the second family visit, March 3, McFarlane and Biddle were released, and on March 6, A.W. Taylor was sent home to Dilkusha, leaving the six missionaries. Restrictions on the families also were eased. Visitors began coming to the Underwoods. A former student offered funds. A Japanese professor from C.C.C. brought coffee, butter, and eggs. Other friends came with rice and staples. Joan was allowed to move in with her parents so she could help take care of her father, who had contracted pneumonia. Ethel Underwood, meanwhile, pushed for more normal conditions for her children. When Dick and Grace came due for visits to their German dentist, she got them permission to ride the streetcar downtown by pointing out to the police that their German ally needed the income. The same tactic succeeded with Grace's music lessons, which were taken from a Japanese teacher. Eventually the Underwood children found it possible to roam around the city freely, as long as they let the police know where they were at all times.

Up north in the Maryknoll convent at Ŭiju, the Sisters remained under house arrest. In December the police had ordered them to estimate how much food they had in storage and they had unthinkingly said enough for a year and a half. Now as the supply dwindled, showing much less than that, the Japanese scolded and verbally abused Sister Gabriella Mulherin, who was in charge, for excessive consumption when the country was under strict food rationing. In fact the Sisters had overestimated their food reserves and were running low. Sister Agneta Chang had to smuggle them sugar, canned goods, milk, flour, and cereal from the outside. They were wiser with their cash. They only reported half of it and had enough hidden away to buy supplies secretly.[43]

The Pearl Harbor aftermath went worse for others. Sister Elenita Barry, a 34-year-old nun in Chinnamp'o renowned for her touch with the violin, was arrested on December 8 and taken with her coworker Sister Gregoria Fogarty to the police station. The Japanese police released Sister Gregoria but kept Sister Elenita to be searched. They stripped her to her tunic and manhandled her. "In order to make sure I wasn't concealing anything they lifted up my tunic and started to feel me all around. In my embarrassment I turned around and found two cells full of men prisoners watching me.

42. Alice Appenzeller, "Gripsholm Supplement" letter to friends, August 31, 1942.

43. Mulherin to Rogers, Personal Narratives of WWII.

268 Living Dangerously in Korea

Most of them were decent, but a few were quite rude." Then she was put
into a freezing cell with no furniture where she had to sleep on the concrete floor every night for two weeks. In a memorandum about the experience Sister Elenita continued,

> Every morning, along with the other prisoners, I was examined to see if I had
> acquired anything new. In the afternoon I was taken from the cell and inter-
> viewed by several detectives. I used to dread these interviews because they
> didn't just stick to business but talked to me and among themselves about
> things that weren't so nice. Such as the toilet in the prison cell and they
> would laugh at me knowing what a dirty hole it was right in the prison cell
> and how difficult it was to use. They were sure I was married. They also made
> fun of the sign of the cross.[44]

The Maryknollers kept in touch with each other via their Korean friends
and servants who braved carrying messages between the convents. These
same friends tended to their daily needs. Sister Agneta Chang traded her
Maryknoll habit for a Korean nun's dress to make it easier to travel on regular trains. On December 23 the sisters at P'yŏngyang and Chinnamp'o were
moved north to the Ŭiju convent. This made seven altogether, and they
took turns cooking and cleaning indoors. When detectives visited and
started questions, Sister Eugenia had a hard time taking them seriously,
much to the irritation of Sister Gabriella, who worried about giving offense
and inviting even more hostile attentions. Sister Eugenia also annoyed Sister Gabriella by refusing to cut her food intake, a problem that brought a
scolding for Sister Gabriella from the police, who were trying to enforce rationing. These stresses were like family problems, natural enough in such
close confinement.

Sister Agneta, though suffering from a progressive spinal deterioration
that was already causing her much pain, brightened the American Sisters'
confinement with her visits and news of life on the outside. One day a Japanese detective let it slip that there were talks under way about a prisoner
exchange. Immediately the Sisters started planning for Sister Agneta to
take charge of the Maryknoll work and property if they should suddenly be
ordered to travel. Agneta did her part by lining up nuns to teach in the
school, work in the hospital, and train the new recruits.[45]

Escape to the West: The *Asama/Gripsholm* Repatriation

In Seoul on April 10 there was a commotion in the concentration camp on
the seminary compound. The American detainees were suddenly sent

44. Memorandum by Sr. Elenita Barry, M.M., H3.7a, Box 1, file F-2, "Personal
Narratives of WWII: Chinnampo, Korea," in the Maryknoll Mission Archives.
45. Sister Mary Eugenia (Mary Agnes Gorman), M.M., Memorandum on Six
Months' Internment, no date, and Mulherin to Rogers, Personal Narratives of
WWII, Maryknoll Mission Archives.

Korea missionary internees returning to America on the *Gripsholm*, 1942. (Dick, Horace, Joan, and Grace Underwood in the front row) From Harry A. Rhodes and Archibald Campbell, *History of the Korea Mission, Presbyterian Church in the U.S.A., II (1935-1959)* (New York: Commission on Ecumenical Mission and Relations of the United Presbyterian Church in the U.S.A., 1964), p. 25.

home to prepare for repatriation— and then just as suddenly re-arrested. This was unsettling but it also seemed to indicate movement somewhere in the negotiations to get them home. On May 31, again without any warning, they were told that they had one day to pack and be ready for transportation to Japan. On June 1, a special evacuation train made its way down the peninsula collecting American and British citizens including the Southern Presbyterians in Kwangju, conveying all 101 civilians to Pusan for the ferry ride to Kobe. The Underwoods took with them Eddie and Alice Crowe, Seoul Foreign School classmates of Dick and Grace Underwood, put in Ethel's care by their American father and Korean mother who chose to stay behind. Henry Davidson, recovering slowly from his pneumonia, spent most of the time lying down. One Catholic priest actually died on the trip.

In Kobe, the evacuees were put in a dormitory and held without any explanation for two long weeks. Unbeknownst to them, the plans that had been so carefully negotiated by the International Red Cross for their repatriation had suddenly been put on hold by the Battle of Midway, June 3-6, 1942. There, in the mid-Pacific, the Imperial Japanese Navy had lost the decisive naval engagement of the war and it was no longer clear how safe the waters around Japan would be or whether the Japanese could guarantee the safety of the evacuees at sea.

The Americans from Korea knew nothing of these developments. However, one day they were abruptly mustered out, searched, and marched through the streets to the station for an overnight train trip to Yokohama. There they boarded the *Asama Maru*, a special repatriation ship with huge white crosses painted on the sides. They joined a large group of American residents in Japan who were already on board, including Ambassador and Mrs. Joseph Grew.[46] The *Asama* was a combination freighter/passenger vessel designed for many fewer than the 945 people who eventually boarded it.[47] Women and children were assigned to the cabins while the men were sent to an improvised dormitory in one of the cargo holds. The evacuees learned that their ship would be picking up additional "enemy nationals" at ports along the China coast, after which they it would head for a neutral port where the passengers would be traded for Japanese evacuees from the West.

But apparently there were still problems with the arrangements and the *Asama* just sat in Tokyo Bay. On June 17 it changed position, first exiting the breakwater and then returning to the Tokyo waterfront to drop anchor within sight of the internment camp where many on board had spent the preceding six months. Fear swept the ship that they were being taken back after all. One woman threatened suicide if she was returned to the camp. Meanwhile, the Japanese officials on board said nothing. Conditions worsened in the June heat and the *Asama* started looking like a slave ship. Then, in the wee hours of the morning on June 25, a navy escort appeared, the engines came to life, floodlights shone on the painted crosses, and the ship headed out to sea.

At sea the passengers revived and got busy devising coping routines. The missionaries organized worship services. The crew stopped trying to segregate the passengers. The Japanese chefs worked at meals resembling Western food, while the passengers learned to choke down rehydrated fish

46. The crosses were to protect the ship from submarine attack. After the war, an American naval officer told Ambassador Grew that his submarine had taken aim one foggy dawn at what looked like a Japanese transport but was actually the *Asama*. He was seconds away from launching his torpedoes when the periscope handler sighted the white crosses through the haze. John Coventry Smith, *From Colonialism to World Community* (Philadelphia: The Geneva Press, 1982), p. 105.

47. The *Asama Maru* was familiar to some of the evacuees who had traveled aboard it in peacetime. It was built by the Mitsubishi dockyard in Nagasaki in 1929. At 17,000 tons with twin screws, it was the largest ship built in the Far East at that time and the fastest on the Pacific. Its passenger capacity was 222 in first class, 96 in second class, and 504 in steerage. After the evacuation it was used as a troop ship. It was sunk in the China Sea by an American submarine on November 1, 1944. William H. Miller Jr., *Pictorial Encyclopedia of Ocean Liners, 1860-1994* (New York: Dover Publications, 1995), p. 9.

and rice. People timed their washing for the half hour each day when there was fresh running water.

Though things got tighter by stages as the *Asama* took on more passengers—370 in Hong Kong and 125 more in Saigon for a total that was 123 more than capacity—there was rising excitement as the ship made progress. Off Singapore the *Asama* was joined by the Italian ship *Conte Verde* carrying 600 Western evacuees from China, and together the two vessels steamed through the Strait of Sunda and across the Indian Ocean to Lourenço Marques in Portuguese East Africa—now known as Maputo, in Mozambique—the place chosen for an exchange of civilian detainees between the East and West.

On July 22, as the *Asama* and *Conte Verde* glided through the green waters of Delagoa Bay to the dock at Lourenço Marques, the other ships in the harbor sounded their foghorns in welcome: three short and one long—the Morse Code "V" for "victory"—something the returning Americans did not realize had become a wartime theme in the West. Already waiting at the dock was the Swedish M/V *Gripsholm* bearing fifteen hundred Japanese refugees from the United States, and as the *Asama* and *Conte Verde* tied up ahead and astern of the *Gripsholm*, Western civilization came sailing over the railing in the form of oranges and cigarettes thrown by the Scandinavian crewmen of the *Gripsholm*. In the morning, the ships traded passengers, and then it was time for lunch. To the delight of the famished *Asama*ns the *Gripsholm* laid on four full-scale smorgasbords. And in the afternoon they disembarked—no longer under guard—to explore the town while the Lourenço Marques American community took the children on sightseeing tours.

Two days later the *Gripsholm* sailed for New York. Soon enough, when freed from the pressures of captivity, the different Western personalities aboard the *Gripsholm* began to assert themselves. With fifteen hundred Americans from all over the East ranging from nuns to soldiers of fortune, there was considerable sharing and not a little friction. First came a mix-up about cabin assignments. When that was settled there were recriminations about things that had happened in captivity. Then came the inevitable feud between the missionary and non-missionary contingents over liquor and entertainment, with objections to card games from one side and disparaging remarks about Sunday hymn-singing from the other. One missionary, after objecting to the consumption of liquor in an adjacent cabin, entered the cabin and threw the occupants' bottles out the porthole. But by the first port call at Rio de Janeiro, the passengers had sorted themselves out. The voyage from Rio to New York was spent with U.S. Navy intelligence officers aboard debriefing the evacuees on conditions in East Asia. With time on their hands, several wrote memoirs of their internment and the last months in East Asia. The Americans from Korea composed meticulous inventories of personal possessions that had been left, in preparation for claims against the Japanese when the war ended. Finally, on the morning of Monday, August 25, the *Gripsholm* entered New York harbor and delivered its passengers safely home at last.[48]

The Dark Valley in Korea

Between 1942 and 1945, the common people of the Japanese empire experienced great privation. The last year of the war brought a rain of bombs upon the cities of Japan proper, culminating in the firebombing of Tokyo in March 1945 and the nuclear attacks on Hirōshima and Nagasaki in August. There were shortages of everything. There were endless antiwaste and recycling campaigns. People had to give up their metal objects— not only their jewelry but also their pots and pans. There was an ever-expanding labor draft. Wages plummeted. Protein consumption dropped when the fishing fleet ran out of fuel. Medical services deteriorated. The educational system collapsed. City people fled to the countryside and had to bargain away their heirlooms just to get food from farmers. It was, as the Japanese call it, their "Dark Valley."[49]

Japan's colonies also suffered during the war, and though Korea never was a target for American bombs, the Korean people suffered in other ways. The Government-General of Chōsen, hard-pressed to support the war machine with food, minerals, energy, and people for military and labor drafts, squeezed the last ounce of effort from them. Japan took the Koreans' rice and left them to eat barley and millet. The Koreans had to do without fuel and had to gather every stick of wood off their hillsides, completely denuding their land. They were taken to Japan by boatloads to work in mines and factories. Respected Korean leaders, including former leaders of the Independence Movement, were forced to exhort their people to work harder for Japanese victory in the war.[50] Able-bodied Korean men were drafted into the army. In time the sacrifices fell even more heavily on the young. The schools closed, the boys were drafted as laborers and soldiers, and many of the girls were drafted as laborers also and as "comfort women" to serve the troops in military brothels.

During the war, the Koreans heard only what the Japanese let them to hear. The government-controlled press published only rosy ac-

48. Smith, *From Colonialism to World Community*, p. 108.

49. See Thomas R. Havens, *Valley of Darkness: The Japanese People and World War Two* (Lanham, Md.: University Press of America, 1986). For wartime Korea, see Kajiyama Toshiyuki, *The Clan Records: Five Stories of Korea* (Honolulu: University of Hawaii Press, 1995).

50. Among these were the writer Yi Kwangsu; Ch'oe Namsŏn, the primary writer of the 1919 declaration of independence, Methodist Bishop Chŏng Ch'unsu, and educators Helen Kim, Yun Ch'iho, and L. George Paik. These well-known figures were denounced later on for "collaboration," though they had had little choice but to speak "patriotically" or go to prison.

counts of victories against the Allies. Ordinary Koreans got their war news from rumors. They wondered how their overseas independence leaders were doing: Kim Ku and the Korean Provisional Government in Chungking; Syngman Rhee and the Korean National Association in America; and the Restoration Army (*Kwangbok-kun*) and Independence Army (*Tongnip-kun*) said to be fighting on the battlefields of China and Manchuria.

A few Western sojourners remained to share life in Korea's own Dark Valley. In Seoul, the Soviet consulate carried on with nine officers, while businessman Emile Martel continued to represent France. Though the American Maryknollers had gone home on the *Gripsholm*, the other Catholic orders stayed put: Bishop Bonifacius Sauer continued to head the German Benedictine contingent at Tōgwŏn, near Wŏnsan, that included seventeen priests, twenty brothers, and fourteen nuns including Sister Immaculata Martel, Emile Martel's daughter. French and Irish missionaries at various locations, including Seoul (twenty-seven), Mokp'o (eleven), and Taegu (nine), were put under house arrest and their missions turned over to Korean or Japanese priests who could be held accountable for their actions and whereabouts.

And the war years were the last years for Novina. The Swiss Family Robinson-like existence of the Yankovskys and their entourage of White Russians started changing in 1936, when clan matriarch Daisy Yankovsky died of cancer at the age of fifty-two. George Yankovsky remarried in 1939, at which point daughter Victoria, disliking her stepmother, married one of her father's retainers and moved away to Hsinking (Changchun), in Japanese-controlled Manchuria. For Victoria it was a radical change to live in the city with her husband working for a Ford dealer. There was also the joy and tragedy of motherhood. Her first child died as a toddler. Her second child Orr was born in 1944.

At Novina, meanwhile, conditions deteriorated and the settlement became a virtual concentration camp. By 1944, when it seemed that the Japanese were likely to lose the war, George Yankovsky arranged a kind of family escape. He purchased a homestead a hundred kilometers north of the Korean-Manchurian border at what he called "the crossroads of the world for boar and tiger," and made plans to move there after the war. Meanwhile he sent Valery to occupy it and persuaded Victoria to follow.

In P'yŏngyang the only Westerners—eleven Russians and one Irish priest—were kept at home. In Seoul, some of the White Russian families in the market started claiming safer nationalities—like the Salahudtinoffs, Tatars who changed their name to "Salahudtin," thereby increasing the number of Turks in the city by five.[51] The Tchirkines stayed put on the

51. Kim and Chung, *Catholic Korea—Yesterday and Today*, pp. 323-324, and Yŏngsin Ak'ademi, *Chosŏn chaeryu kumi'in chosarok, 1907-1942 nyŏn* (Directory

church compound and tried to watch out for their foreign friends' interests. Natalya, for example, saved some of Mary Taylor's things from Dilkusha when it was taken over by the Japanese as enemy property. Twins Vladimir and Cyril were sent to Shanghai to live with Natalya's Efremoff family relatives and attend engineering school and then, after Sergei died in 1943, Natalya was all alone. Canadian miner Alexander McFarlane, who had been interned in the Methodist seminary in 1942, was allowed to go home to the Seoul suburb of Sosa where he lived under house arrest until his death in 1945. American Charles Crowe and his Korean wife spent the war years in confinement until Charles, too, died just as the war was ending.[52]

Many Koreans who had been close to Westerners were labeled enemy sympathizers during the war and paid a heavy price. Pastor Chu Kich'ŏl of the Sanjŏng-hyŏn Church in P'yŏngyang, for example, died in prison in April 1944. Other Christians abandoned their foreign religion. Those who remained active were at pains to prove that they too were loyal to the emperor. Methodist Bishop Chŏng Ch'unsu, for example, permitted *kamidana* shrines to be put in the chancels of his denomination's churches, had Shintō *misogi* purification rituals performed alongside Christian baptisms during services, rented the Methodist seminary buildings in Seoul to the police for use as an academy, and even raised funds for the Japanese war effort by taking up collections for warplanes and donating the proceeds from sales of church-owned land.[53]

Elsewhere, at Chōsen Christian College the wartime administration of Yun Ch'iho, Matsumoto Teru, and Yu Ŏkkyŏm gamely carried on until the military authorities declared the campus enemy property in 1943 and ousted them, turning the college into a labor camp and then, in 1944, into the Japanese-run Keijō Industrial Arts School. George Paik, who lived on campus in one of the faculty houses, was kept under house arrest and allowed out only for such patriotic purposes as neighborhood meetings to hear official versions of war news and exhortations about using less fuel—and a speech he reportedly gave in 1943 over JODK radio supporting the war.[54] Other C.C.C. professors spent time in prison for activities that

of Europeans and Americans in Korea, 1907-1942) (Seoul: Yŏngsin Akademi, Han'gukhak yŏn'guso, 1981), passim.

52. Mabel McFarlane, letter to the author, February 6, 1989. Earlier the Crowes had asked Horace and Ethel Underwood to take their children, Eddie and Alice, to the United States with them on the *Gripsholm*. Edwin Crowe, letter to the author, May 3, 1990.

53. For a detailed description, see the accounts by Methodist Bishop Yang Chusam [J. S. Ryang], entitled "The Japanese Persecution of the Korean Christians," and "Chronological Records of What Was [sic] Happened," Methodist Mission Archives, Drew University.

54. L. George Paik, interview, Seoul, March 16, 1984; Yonsei taehakkyo ch'angnip p'alsimnyŏn kinyŏm saŏp wiwŏnhoe, *Yonsei taehakkyo-sa* (History of Yonsei University) (Seoul: Yonsei University Press, 1969), pp. 449-453; Cumings, *The*

were construed as unpatriotic—helping compile a dictionary of the Korean language, in one case.[55] C.C.C. vice president Matsumoto Teru and his family went back home to Hiroshima when the college closed in 1943, in time to be present when the Americans dropped the atomic bomb on August 6, 1945. When the bomb went off, Matsumoto was leading morning prayers at his school and he was injured. Elsewhere in the city his wife and daughter were killed.[56]

Lilian Ross was one of the fifteen Northern Presbyterians from Korea who volunteered for reassignment in the Philippines in 1941 rather than go all the way home to the United States. After a lonely summer in Kanggye, she left Korea in September and, after waiting weeks for transportation from Shanghai to Manila, arrived in the Philippines in November. Japan attacked the Philippines the following month, and on January 5, 1942, Lilian Ross was among the American missionaries in Manila taken for internment at the Santo Tomás concentration camp.[57]

For much of the war, life at Santo Tomás followed a routine, with the internees doing assigned tasks and helping each other. Lilian Ross took her turn on kitchen and cleaning duty and often at the end of the day gathered groups of children together for stories that were often Bible lessons. On July 8, 1944, however, the Japanese moved the Santo Tomás internees to a different concentration camp at Los Baños. Here they were put in Filipino thatch-roofed huts and set to work on camp maintenance jobs, all on two meals a day. The food was mostly gruel, and the prisoners spent much of their time looking for edible plants growing by the fence to supplement their diet. Under this starvation regimen many of the prisoners lost so much weight that they started looking like skin and bones and fell seriously ill. Lilian Ross was one of those who got by with no apparent ill effects. "A tough customer like your daughter, who makes 100% use of anything eaten and can like just about anything eatable still goes strong where many are hard hit," she wrote her mother Susan. "Tooting my own horn? Fact remains I have not lost 30-40-50 pounds. Masticating for most of an hour what could be swallowed in ten minutes helps one to feel satisfied."[58]

Origins of the Korean War, Vol. I, p. 149.

55. Lee Hi-seung (Yi Hŭisung), "Recollections of the Korean Language Society Incident," in Marshall R. Pihl, ed., *Listening to Korea* (New York: Praeger, 1973), pp. 19-42.

56. H.H. Underwood to Hooper, October 23, 1945, in the Presbyterian Historical Society, Philadelphia.

57. Lilian Ross, Interview, Duarte, California, May 28, 1987. Also see Harry A. Rhodes and Archibald Campbell, eds., *History of the Korea Mission of the Presbyterian Church in the U.S.A.*, Vol. 2, 1935-1959 (New York: United Presbyterian Church in the U.S.A., 1964), pp. 21-22.

58. Lilian Ross, "Dear Mother of Mine" letter, October 21, 1944, in the Lilian Ross papers.

On January 7, 1945, the guards suddenly disappeared from the Los Baños camp. The prisoners quickly set up a committee and discovered that the camp storehouses had considerable grain that the committee immediately distributed, five kilos per adult. Six days later the guards returned and reasserted control over the camp. They slashed the rations, telling the prisoners that "everybody is starving everywhere—even your soldiers are starving. Be glad you are given even this!" Lilian summed up the atmosphere at Los Baños in a letter to her mother:

> We spent an afternoon lined up in the hot sun for roll call—which was really barracks inspection. This last month there has been no electricity even for a bathroom light—eliminating undetected radios we suppose—no noon meal (most of the time) no personal trading (but lately the guards are rich with spoils of diamonds, watches, etc. for things can be brought in when the right person wants them in) no good supply of camp vegetables, fruit not at all, few coconuts (which rot outside) and little meat. No transportation is the reason given. Our custodians would be court marshaled [sic] if they used or allowed us to use anything but Jap. currency that is not acceptable to Phil. traders. A carrabo (water buffalo) costs Jap. P. 30-40,000 and gives the camp little more than a flavor to the stew....So it boils down to doing without. Thick mush gruel of rice and corn for breakfast, thinner mush of rice for supper with veg. soup and usually greens. Now we are allowed 200 grams per person a day of grain and that will be gone by the 19th. Many are suffering keenly who ate freely of the 5 kilo per person given out by our committee in the absence of the guards a month ago. Some bartered away their rice for smokes and deserve to be hungry.[59]

By February 1945, the internees at Los Baños could hear the war approaching. Their first clue was the sound of explosions as the Japanese started destroying their supplies to deny them to the invading Americans. American planes buzzed the camp on February 7 as food stocks were running low and it appeared that rescue might not come in time to alleviate the starvation of some prisoners such as Korea missionary Herbert Blair. In fact Blair did die of beriberi on February 20, just three days before U.S. paratroopers dropped into the camp and Marines came crashing through the fence in amphibious "Ducks." The camp guards fought a brief battle before being taken prisoner themselves. By the end of the day all 2,169 internees had been taken to a makeshift military hospital and the camp buildings had been burned to the ground. Lilian Ross saw that the Japanese had been lying about the American soldiers. "Since [being freed] we see folks not emaciated—so bronzed and sturdy and well rounded. To see them makes me laugh inside—and I laugh at the good things given us. Have just eaten [80 pesos' worth of] eggs and probably Peso 80 worth of cream and

59. Lilian Ross, "Dear Family" letter, February 25, 1945, and "Dear Mother" letter, February 7, 1945, in the Lilian Ross papers.

sugar for breakfast by [camp prices] when eggs could be seen last! Such good food should stick in a Scotsman's throat!"[60]

Back in Korea, the news blackout continued for many months longer, until the day of the Japanese surrender on August 15, 1945. However, there was no dearth of rumors, their number increasing toward the end of the war as people could see American B-29s passing overhead in broad daylight, bound for Japanese targets in Manchuria. People speculated about the time and place of a rumored Allied landing in Korea—and worried that the Japanese would react to the landing by rounding up and possibly executing Koreans who might want to help the invaders. There was even a rumored death list with the names of everyone known to have had ties to Westerners before the war, notably Christian leaders who were not already in prison.[61]

Everything changed with the war's sudden end. In Manchuria, the Japanese Army melted before a violent Soviet onslaught and within days of their entry into the war on August 8, Red Army troops were landing on the northeast coast of Korea. With the Japanese surrender a week later came the news that the United States and the Soviet Union had decided upon a joint occupation of the peninsula by zones, with the Soviets taking charge north of the thirty-eighth parallel and American forces taking charge in the south. The victorious Allies were to establish a trusteeship until the Koreans could govern themselves. In the meantime the people were to be calm and await their liberation. Some wondered: under newly arrived foreign armies, what kind of "liberation" would it be?

---

60. Lilian Ross, "Dear Family" letter, February 25, 1945.

61. "[On the eve of Liberation] the Japanese military feared that the Christians would help the American army when it landed in Korea, so they planned to massacre about 3,000 Christian leaders on the 17th of August—just two days [after the actual surrender]. For [deliverance from] this we are most grateful." Kim Kwansik, "The Present Situation of the Christian Church in Korea" (1946), in UCCA, 83. 006C, Box 5, File, 141. It was commonly believed that there was a death list of Christians, and that the war's abrupt end saved many Koreans from execution. L. George Paik, interview, Seoul, March 16, 1984.

PART II

IN POST COLONIAL KOREA
1945 — 1950

-- 14 --

Liberation and Reoccupation

Korea remained a Japanese colony through the end of World War II. The Allies recognized it as part of Japan, but they also knew that the Koreans were a separate people who ought to be liberated. The Allies made the liberation of Korea a wartime goal at the Cairo conference in December 1943, when Franklin D. Roosevelt, Winston Churchill, and Chiang Kai-shek declared that "in due course," Korea would be "free and independent."

As victory approached in the Pacific, Allied planners knew that they would have to oversee a transition from colonial rule to independence in Korea. They assumed that there was no Korean group or structure that could handle the transition. The former monarchy was discredited and no one seriously proposed restoring it. In Chungking there was a Korean Provisional Government that claimed to be ready to take the reins in Korea, but the U.S. State Department had little confidence in it. It also had grown weary of the Washington-based campaign of the aging Korean nationalist Syngman Rhee to present himself as a government-in-waiting. Rather, the planners' working assumption was that Korea was not ready for self-government, would need a period of international "trusteeship" while Korean leaders sorted themselves out,[1] and that the trusteeship would have to be-

1. For example, in a July 2, 1943, meeting of the Political Subcommittee of the State Department during a discussion of postwar foreign policy at which top officials such as Secretary of State Cordell Hull and Undersecretary Sumner Welles were present, "It was said that Korea, because of its rather unsuccessful experiment in self-government and its long oppression by Japan, would require a period of tutelage and assistance." From "Records of Harley A. Nutter, 1934-1945," in Harley A. Nutter, *Postwar Foreign Policy Preparation, 1939-1945* (Washington, D.C.: U.S. Government Printing Office, 1947), reprinted in Chŏng Yŏng'uk and Yi Kilsang, eds., *Haebang-chŏnhu miguk-ŭi chŏngch'aeksa charyojip*, Vol. I, ed. (Seoul: Tarakbang, 1994), p. 249.

gin with an outright military occupation to oversee the disarmament and repatriation of Japanese soldiers and civilians from the peninsula. No one knew how long the trusteeship would last or exactly how it would be created. Trusteeships in the past had lasted for decades, and until the victorious Allies actually assessed the situation in Korea they were in no position to announce a timetable for independence. The very idea of trusteeship, however, was at odds with public opinion among Koreans who saw no reason why the phrase "in due course" should not mean "immediately."

Little progress had been made toward defining the trusteeship idea when Japan flashed its decision to surrender to the Allies on the night of August 11, 1945, Japan time. However, by then, the short-term military situation in Korea had overtaken long-term thinking about the country's future. The Soviet Union had entered the war against Japan on August 8 as requested at Yalta by the United States and Great Britain. The Allies expected the Soviet Red Army to encounter stiff resistance as it invaded Manchuria, but instead the Japanese Manchurian Army collapsed and the Soviets rushed forward toward Korea, landing on the northeast coast within hours and massing units to enter the peninsula across the Yalu River within days. In the last hours before Japan's surrender, it dawned on Allied planners that the Soviet Union was quickly gaining the capability to reach the Japanese home islands ahead of American occupation forces. The Americans were on Okinawa preparing to implement years of careful occupation plans for Japan, but their transportation was not yet in place. Suddenly the American high command realized that if the Soviets reached Japan ahead of the U.S. Army, the occupation there would have to be shared. Given the fact that the United States was counting on a unilateral occupation, and taking into account the experience of trying to occupy Germany jointly with the Soviets, the United States was determined to keep this from happening.[2]

In Washington, D.C., the State-War-Navy Coordinating Committee (SWNCC) met in the Executive Office Building on the night of August 14 to find a way to halt the Soviet rush toward Japan. Alarmed that they might end up having to share the occupation of Japan with the Soviets, they decided instead to shift the idea of joint occupation to Korea. The trusteeship that was planned for Korea could be a Soviet-American operation while the occupation of Japan would remain unilaterally American. Assuming that any trusteeship would start with a military occupation, the question then became how to allocate occupation duty between the two powers.

2. Commenting on the choice of the XXIVth Corps for Korean occupation duty because it was the nearest available force, former foreign service officer Gregory Henderson put it very well: "General Hodge was very possibly the first man in history to wield executive powers over a nation of nearly twenty million on the basis of shipping time." *Korea: The Politics of the Vortex* (Cambridge, Mass.: Harvard University Press, 1968), p. 123.

As SWNCC pondered the division of Korea into occupation zones, the officials sent two staff colonels into an adjacent room with a small *National Geographic* map of Korea and ordered them to return with a boundary suggestion for forwarding to the Russians. The two officers looked at the map, noted that the 38th parallel nearly bisected the peninsula while putting the capital city of Seoul in the American zone, and returned to their superiors with the 38th parallel as their suggestion. The U.S. Government then flashed the 38th parallel proposal to the Soviets. The Soviets accepted it and halted their advance toward Japan as the Americans wished.[3]

Korea in the Time of Liberation

More than three weeks elapsed between the Japanese surrender on August 15, 1945, and the arrival of U.S. occupation troops in the southern zone of Korea on September 8. During that interval, officials of the Government-General of Chōsen struggled to keep order while they waited for the Americans to come from Okinawa. Keeping order was no small task. Fearing for their lives, the colonial police force, which included many Korean collaborators, went into hiding. In its place, groups of young people organized themselves into para-police units that were called *chi'andae*.[4] Governor-General Abe Nobuyuki remained in charge at the top, but he had a big problem: he needed to arrange the handover of the colonial government to the incoming Americans while keeping the Korean people under

3. For many years, the story of how Korea was divided remained a secret. Until the 1970s, the U.S. government allowed exculpatory versions of the story to go unchallenged by the facts, allowing blame to be directed against the Soviets. Koreans naturally were keen to read the American documents that became declassified in the 1980s and they were shocked to discover the offhand way their country had been divided. Later, one of the colonels, Dean Rusk (later secretary of state), published his memoirs containing the following account, in which his fellow officer, "Tic," is Charles H. Bonesteel III, the future UN commander-in-chief in Seoul (late 1960s).

"Working in great haste and under great pressure we had a formidable task: to pick a zone for the American occupation. Neither Tic nor I was a Korea expert, but it seemed that Seoul the capital, should be in the American sector. We also knew that the U.S. Army opposed an extensive area of occupation. Using a *National Geographic* map, we looked just north of Seoul for a convenient dividing line but could not find a natural geographical line. We saw instead the thirty-eighth parallel and decided to recommend that...." Dean Rusk, *As I Saw It* (New York: Penguin Books, 1990), pp. 124 and 167.

4. The first *chi'andae*, "Peace Preservation Corps," members were students who volunteered to direct traffic and perform other routine functions in place of the disappearing police. See Cumings, *The Origins of the Korean War*, Vol. I, pp. 74-76. Later they became more political, carrying out reprisals against individual Japanese and their Korean collaborators. The corresponding units in North Korea were called *po'andae*, "Peace and Security Bands."

U.S. 24th Corps marching into Seoul, 1945. U.S. National Archives, reproduced from Jon Halliday and Bruce Cumings, *Korea: The Forgotten War* (New York: Pantheon, 1988), p. 19.

control. Especially urgent was the need to protect colonial officials and Japanese residents from Korean reprisals while they were waiting for the Americans to take over the job of keeping order. Abe needed to find Korean leaders who would be willing to restrain their people, and eventually he settled on Yŏ Unhyŏng (Lyuh Woon Hyung), the sometime Shanghai Korean independence leader who had been arrested and returned to Korea and had spent the latter years of the Japanese occupation as editor of the *Chung'ang Ilbo* newspaper. Yŏ set up an organization called the Committee for the Preparation of Korean Independence (CPKI; *Chosŏn kŏn'guk chunbi wiwŏnhoe*). Leftists did not dominate the CPKI early on; however, it veered left as newly released political prisoners joined and South Korean communists succeeded in getting themselves into leadership positions. The CPKI briefly supervised the *chi'andae* but in fact lost control of both the para-police and the local organizing units of the CPKI. Instead, communities across South Korea created their own "people's committees" (*inmin wiwŏnhoe*). While in Seoul, Yŏ Unhyŏng posed as the head of a national federation of the people's committees that was called the "Korean People's Republic."[5]

The Yanks Land in Korea

During the last week of the Pacific war, an order percolated down the chain of command to Lt. Gen. John R. Hodge, leader of the U.S. XXIV Corps on the island of Okinawa, to prepare for occupation duty in the southern zone of the Korean peninsula up to the 38th parallel.[6] At the time, the men of the XXIVth Corps had been training for occupation duty in Japan and were

5. Yi Chŏngsik (Chong-Sik Lee), "Inmin Konghwaguk gwa haebang chŏnngguk," in *Han'guksa simin kangchwa*, 12 (1993), pp. 15-45.

6. Hodge's fitness for this position and his performance are subjects of continuing critical commentary. See James I. Matray, "Hodge Podge: American Occupation Policy in Korea, 1945-1948," *Korean Studies*, XIX (1995), pp. 17-38.

caught unprepared for their new assignment. In the American mind, Korea was a place that existed only in theory like a subatomic particle that no one had ever actually seen. Nor was there much that could be learned about the place. The only intelligence available on Okinawa was an introductory study along lines of an encyclopedia article.[7] Maps were scanty and inaccurate, with place names printed in romanized Japanese. The Army had taken a set of aerial photographs in 1944 but the negatives were in Washington and only a few of the prints could be found on Okinawa.[8]

The men of the XXIVth Corps got their first look at Korea during reconnaissance flights in the third week of August 1945. They observed little activity on the ground. The roads were deserted and the factories appeared idle. The political atmosphere, however, was charged with trouble. When the Americans finally made radio contact with Seoul, Japanese officials reported that chaos was imminent and pleaded with the Americans to help them keep order. The U.S. Army responded by dropping leaflets over Korea's cities telling the people to continue obeying the Japanese. "Do not let hate, excitement, or selfishness lead you into foolish actions," said the handbills that were dropped on September 1. "Maintain peaceful and orderly conduct at all times. It is only by doing these things that you may speed the lifting of restrictions on your country and your daily life."[9]

To provide for Allied prisoners of war being held in camps in Seoul, Inch'ŏn, and Hŭngnam, the Americans sent B-29's from Okinawa to drop packages of food and medical supplies. These airdrops were made from low altitudes, and when some of the parachutes failed to open there was damage. One package killed a woman in Seoul. Another pierced the roof of a barracks in Inch'ŏn, killing a Korean, injuring eight Japanese, and breaking an American prisoner's leg. At Hŭngnam in the north, newly under Soviet occupation, a relief package crashed through the roof of a building and just missed a Red Army colonel who then ordered his own planes to intercept all American planes and make them land before delivering their cargos.[10]

On September 4, 1945, a team of Army planners landed at Seoul's Kimp'o air base to arrange the arrival of the XXIVth Corps that was scheduled for September 8. A detail of Japanese officials met the Americans and

7. This item was the *Joint Army-Navy Intelligence Study of Korea*, called "JANIS 75," published in April 1945.
8. HUSAFIK, I, pp. 20-22.
9. Ibid., p. 69.
10. On August 29, four Yaks scrambled to intercept a B-29 and force it to land at Hamhŭng airfield. The B-29 found the runway too short and decided to return to base. It turned out to sea, at which point the Yaks fired on it, destroying an engine. Six of the crew bailed out and were recovered by Korean fishermen. The other seven men stayed on the plane and crash-landed the stricken bomber at Hamhŭng airfield. The Russian commanders were chagrined, apologized to the American side, and allowed the men to be flown out by C-46 on September 14. Two more airdrops followed at Hŭngnam without incident. HUSAFIK, I, p. 52.

Japanese Governor-General Abe Nobuyuki signing the surrender transferring Korea to U.S. command and occupation, September 9, 1945, in Seoul. Yi Kyu-hŏn, comp., *Sanjinŭro ponŭn tongnip undong: Imjŏnggwa kwangbok* (Seoul: Sŏmundang, 1987), p. 184.

escorted them to the Chōsen Hotel. There they sequestered themselves for four days, giving no sign of their intentions. Their visitors were almost all non-Koreans, including top-ranking Japanese officials, liberated Allied POW's, and Soviet Consul-General Alexander Poliansky, the city's only remaining Western diplomat. When a delegation of English-speaking Koreans tried to gain admittance to offer greetings and advice they were turned away. A welcome-to-Korea demonstration with a brass band went unacknowledged. Outside the hotel gate, a small group of Koreans carried on a vigil in hopes of learning news of their country's fate. One of them affirmed his patriotic wish for freedom with a minor act of vandalism. Seeing the hotel's name romanized in Japanese style on the gatepost, he changed it from the Japanese "Chosen" to the Korean "Chosun."

When the Koreans saw that the Americans were doing business with the Japanese, there was much confusion. The confusion turned to anger on

September 7 when two Koreans in a crowd of demonstrators at Inch'ŏn were shot by Japanese troops acting under American orders to keep the peace. General Hodge was quoted as having said that he saw Koreans and Japanese as "the same breed of cat."[11] "Liberation" suddenly looked like it meant being handed over from one foreign occupier to another.

On September 8, the XXIVth Corps arrived aboard a convoy of twenty-one ships at Inch'ŏn harbor. The landing took a day and a half, with the first units continuing to Seoul by train on the morning of September 9. On this final day of Japanese control in Korea no cheering throngs greeted the liberators. The first Americans to arrive at the railroad station marched into the city in silence, passing small knots of onlookers as they divided, one column to establish a command post at the Hanto (Bando) Hotel, next to the Chosun and the other to Ryūzan (Yongsan) to take over the headquarters compound of the Japanese Chōsen Army. While they marched, planes roared overhead "providing striking demonstrations of power that could hardly have failed to impress both Japanese and Koreans."[12]

The cheering came later in the day, as a motorcade of military and press vehicles led by General Hodge and Admiral Thomas Kincaid drove up Kōka-mon-dōri (today's Sejong-no) into the grounds of the Government-General Building to receive the Japanese surrender. While Japanese mounted police restrained the crowd, the Americans went into the building and upstairs to the governor-general's conference room on the second floor. The Japanese were waiting for them when they entered at a few minutes past 4:00 P.M.: Governor-General Abe Nobuyuki, Chōsen Army Commander Lt. Gen. Kozuki Yoshio, Navy Commander Vice Admiral Yamaguchi Gisaburō, and others, all in uniform but without swords or decorations, with Abe in the center seat along the far side of the table. The Japanese rose from their chairs when the Americans entered, listened glumly to a short speech by General Hodge, and watched Abe mop his brow and sign the surrender documents as ordered. After a ceremony that took less than half an hour, the Americans moved to the front steps of the building to watch as an honor guard pulled down the *hinomaru,* Rising Sun, and raised the Stars and Stripes. The Americans, who still had said nothing to the waiting Koreans, then piled into vehicles to leave the grounds at which point, according to Army historians, "the crowd of Koreans, many of whom had been looking over the wall while the flag was being raised, were almost beside themselves with enthusiasm."[13]

11. The U.S. Army later explained that Hodge had been referring only to Korean *collaborators* as "the same breed of cat" as Japanese, and not all Koreans. HUSA-FIK, I, pp. 43-44.

12. Ibid., p. 7.

13. Ibid., p. 12.

288 Living Dangerously in Korea

American Soldiers and Korean Civilians

The American military occupation created a new kind of Western presence in South Korea. Koreans were shocked to find the American occupiers simply replacing the Japanese, but some—especially those who knew some English—found that the bureaucracy of the U.S. Army Military Government in Korea ("USAMGIK," or "MG" for short) presented significant opportunities. Graduates of mission schools, notably Chōsen Christian College, avidly pursued jobs as translators and staffers, and USAMGIK quickly acquired a reputation as an "interpreters' government," with Korean personnel feeding information to the Americans and Americans' ideas being filtered through the Korean personnel.[14] To convey Korean sentiments to the American authorities, an English-language newspaper, the *Korea Times*, was begun by C.C.C. Professor M. M. Lee (Yi Myŏngmok) and Methodist church leader Hyunki Lew (Yu Hyŏnggi). The Koreans who found niches in the American occupation were generally conservative, and they did little to discourage the rightward drift of policy under the U.S. military. Like the leftists who attached themselves to the Red Army occupation in the north, pro-American Koreans in the south[15] were sometimes seen as opportunists who were betting on a lame horse. A saying went around reflecting the Koreans' lack of confidence in the occupation's staying power: "Don't trust America and don't be deceived by Russia. Japan will rise again." (*Migugŭl mitchimara; Soryŏn-e sokchimalla; Ilboni irŏnanda.*)

Closer to the ground and on a daily basis, the occupation created friction. In North Korea, Koreans learned to dread the Russian command "*Davai!*" (Give it!) as Red Army soldiers confiscated their wristwatches. In the south, the Americans started out with a certain amount of public relations capital held over from positive experiences before 1941 and the image of the United States as the winner of the war. However, many Koreans recoiled from the American soldiers with their physical size, tanned faces and big noses. GIs made Koreans nervous. They had weapons and vehicles and acted like conquerors, apparently looking down on Koreans. They conducted themselves with frightening carelessness. Koreans developed a stereotype of American soldiers speeding through villages aboard huge

14. H.H. Underwood was heard to say that "the government, as far as Koreans are concerned, is being run by C.C.C. professors and graduates." Edward Adams, "Report on Korea, 1946," (mimeographed), Presbyterian Historical Society, RG 140, Box 16, File 29. One Korean likened the U.S. Military Government to the court of Kubilai Khan, in which various competing factions from various ethnic regions of thirteenth century China doctored information flowing to and from the Great Khan, even affecting the lives of competitors whose heads rolled on many occasions. Young S. Kim, writing his reminiscences on the Internet at <http://www.kimsoft.com/Korea/US-stole.htm>.

15. *Ch'inmip'a*, adapting the term *ch'inilp'a*, the Korean term for Japanese collaborator.

trucks, oblivious to the local population even when they occasionally ran over pedestrians.[16]

The Americans commonly referred to Koreans as "gooks."[17] The term "gook" was well established in the GI vocabulary before 1945 and in Korea it was a standard slang term that Americans used even in their daily discourse with Koreans. It was part of GI pidgin, an earthy though generally harmless language that included expressions such as "numbah-one" (meaning "good"), "numbah-ten" ("bad"), "same-same" and "hubba-hubba" ("hurry up"). Much GI pidgin across the Far East originated in the American occupation of Japan, so that a Korean cook or laundress was a "mama-san," a male laborer was a "papa-san," the houseboy was called "boy-san," barmaids were "Jo-san" (for "girl," as in the Japanese o-jōsan), and mistresses were "moose."[18] Though the troops saw nothing wrong with these Japan-isms and most Koreans shrugged them off, the word "gook" was unmistakably an insult. From his headquarters in Tokyo, General Douglas MacArthur decreed an end to the use of "gook" to describe Koreans, calling it a blight on the teaching of democracy in the East; but the troops, finding it too perfect as a pejorative, never gave it up.

16. Sometimes it was more than a stereotype. Seoul National University sociologist Kim Kyŏngdong remembers "Truckloads of tanned GIs jammed the main street of our city. Even now, almost 50 years later, my mind retains the ghastly picture of a friend of mine lying dead in the street, still bleeding horribly after having been run over by one of the enormous GMC trucks. It was an accident, of course, but the gruesome image of that moment, together with the strange smell of gasoline engines, keeps coming back to nauseate me." "Korean Perceptions of America," in Clark, *Korea Briefing 1993*, pp. 163-164. Also see Mark Gayn, *Japan Diary* (Tokyo: Charles E. Tuttle, 1981), p. 410, and Agnes Davis Kim, *I Married a Korean* (New York: John Day, 1953), pp. 211-212.

17. The Army explained the term "gook" as a term applying to "all Polynesian or Oriental natives" and attributed it to the troops' need for a term to refer to all non-caucasians. HUSAFIK, ch. 5, p. 64. The term seems to have originated in the South Pacific during World War II and became a racist epithet for Asians in general and Koreans—and later Vietnamese—in particular during the Korean and Vietnamese wars. See David Roediger, "Gook: The Short History of an Americanism," *Monthly Review*, XLIII:10 (March 1992), pp. 50-54, and Harold Wentworth and Stuart Berg Flexner, *Dictionary of American Slang* (New York: Crowell, 1975), p. 223. The origins of the term remain obscure and subject to misinformation. Consider Linda Reinberg's inventive explanation that "gook" is the Korean word for "person," in *In the Field: The Language of the Vietnam War* (New York: Facts on File, 1991), p. 95.

18. "Moose" is a corruption of the Japanese "*musume*," lit., "daughter," which refers to an American soldier's mistress normally maintained off base in a "hooch" (rented room) in the "vil" (camptown; *kijich'on*) during his tour in Korea. The indispensability of this term in the military vocabulary was impressed upon the author during a U.S. Army officer candidate qualifying oral at Ft. Lewis, Washington in 1967, when the examining board of majors and colonels gave me an impromptu Korean vocabulary quiz starting with the word "moose."

"American soldiers take away our fountain pens and watches and are act-ing lewdly with our women," complained one Korean in 1946. "I saw some of them satisfying their desires in a vehicle near the front of the station."[19] To counteract this, the military started a Sisyphian campaign to get the troops to straighten up. The Army newspaper *Stars and Stripes* again ad-monished them not to use the term "gook." Nonetheless a poll taken by USAMGIK's Office of Public Opinion in March 1946 showed a disappoint-ing drop in the number of Koreans expressing positive feelings about Americans from 62 percent to 51 percent in a few months, with one of the main reasons being the way "American soldiers frequently 'beguile and frighten women on the streets.'" General Hodge reacted by ordering his commanders to lecture the troops on how to act—with results such as the following:

> Today we had another "orientation" class. The officer who conducted it warned us that the following things would not—repeat *not*—be tolerated in this command: armed robbery of civilians, rape, and appearing in public in the OD uniform without a necktie.

The U.S. Army in Korea was not the first occupation force in history to confront issues of fraternization. The troops' pursuit of female compan-ionship clashed with Korean customs that reserved respectable girls for carefully arranged marriages and absolutely forbade casual dating, espe-cially with foreigners. This social ethic actually interfered with the Army's ability to recruit qualified secretarial assistance. This was not a problem for the maids, laundresses, and cooks who tended to be married and mid-dle-aged. However, the young, educated women who worked in USAMGIK offices were often approached for dates. The women, their families, and Korean society in general misunderstood these overtures, and they put the women in a difficult position. For example, one morning an American offi-cer found that his Korean receptionist was very upset by a leaflet that a man had handed to her on the way to work. He ordered up a rough translation and found that it said:

> WE COULD NOT OVERLOOK YOU, WOMANHOOD, when you fool around with Westerners in just showing your vanity and worldly devices, which is nothing but scandalous, while you should put all your strength on establishing the state of new Korea. From now on any one of you who shows the following scandalous actions beware that you will be insulted right in front of public:
>
> 1. Those women who are quite animated in riding automobile with West-erners.
> 2. Those women who wink at the Westerners in saying "Hello gum" and "My home" and such short words.

19. This account follows HUSAFIK I, pp. 65-70.

3. Those women who chew gum and stroll all over town.
4. Those women who are whispering to the Westerners in the night.
5. Those women who go to the dance hall just because they are crazy about coffee and chocolate.

Americans afforded constant irritations, such as the failure to remove shoes upon entering a restaurant or private home, criticizing Korean food and customs, making disparaging comments about the admittedly unsanitary environment, and constantly demanding that Koreans do things the American way. The cultures clashed, for example, in contrasting attitudes toward trading gifts, the Koreans' customary way of smoothing social interaction. In an effort to avoid corruption and the incurring of awkward obligations, General Hodge, never one to do things halfway, issued an order in February 1946 forbidding "the acceptance by United States officers from Koreans of gifts, favors, or entertainment." The effect was to discourage all social contact between Americans and Koreans, because "respectable" Koreans were loath to be seen frequenting foreign military facilities and disliked accepting hospitality with no way to reciprocate. Thus the Koreans who populated the GIs' Korea turned out to be mainly base employees and the denizens of the camp towns around the bases: bar girls, hustlers, pimps, prostitutes, and the "slicky boys" who regularly stole from them all.[20]

Homecoming for the Missionaries

Korea as it appeared to the U.S. Army was quite different from the picture in the minds of the one group of Americans who wanted desperately to get to Korea in 1945: the prewar missionaries whose careers had been interrupted by the *Mariposa* evacuation and the attack on Pearl Harbor. However, any resumption of missionary work required approval by the U.S. Military Government authorities who controlled everything and everyone that went in and out of South Korea. At first the Army declared Korea a military zone and excluded American civilians altogether. Navy Commander George Z. Williams, a Methodist MK (missioner's kid) from Kongju, was

20. The significance of this base environment as a social problem attending the presence of U.S. forces in South Korea went largely unremarked for a very long time, being accepted as one price for American protection during the cold war. In the 1980s and '90s, however, it became a burning issue in U.S.-Korean relations, with reporters and scholars "exposing" life in the "vil." For example, see Pak Taesun, "U'ulhan kijich'on maŭl Sŏnyu-ri" (Sŏnyu Village: A Dreary Camp Town), *Mal* (March 1990), pp. 128-133. A leading writer of fiction on this theme is Kang Sokkyŏng. See her short story "Days and Dreams" in *Words of Farewell: Stories by Korean Women Writers*, trans. Bruce and Ju-Chan Fulton (Seattle: The Seal Press, 1989), pp. 1-27. For a summary discussion of the Korean literature, see Ji-moon Suh, "America and Americans as Depicted in Korean Fiction," *Migukhak nonmunjip*, XXVIII:2 (1996), especially pp. 376-383.

one of the few uniformed members of the former missionary community to see Korea in the fall of 1945. When he was overheard speaking Korean he quickly found himself attached to headquarters as a "political advisor."[21] Certain others also penetrated the Army blockade. The ever-resourceful Underwoods were back in force by mid-1946, Horace Senior as an advisor to General Archibald Arnold in charge of the civilian administration of Korea, Young Horace, still in the Navy, as an educational liaison, and son Dick in the ranks as an Army sergeant. Ethel Underwood was there too, having talked her way onto an Army troop ship in March.

Months before the Japanese surrender, the Board of Foreign Missions of the Presbyterian Church in the U.S.A. had convened a meeting of senior Korea missionaries to decide what to do should mission work become possible once again. Though the loss of all the mission's northern stations could not have been foreseen at that time, the conferees discussed priorities for the field, fund raising, and the most delicate question of whom to send. It had been four years since the sailing of the *Mariposa*. Many of the missionaries had been biding their time in temporary assignments, eager for news and excited that the war seemed to be grinding to a conclusion. There was heavy competition to get on the "A" list of people who would be sent first. The criteria for the top two "A" and "B" lists included language and administrative skills, type of expertise, age, health, and family situation. Priority went to males who could muster the remnants of the Presbyterian Church in Korea and help reestablish it. Medical missionaries and educators were put on a lower list.

Since his deportation from Korea in the summer of 1941, Charlie Clark had thought about little else but getting back. In 1945 he was 67 years old, had a heart condition, and was gradually losing his eyesight, but he still believed himself fit for missionary work.[22] He kept busy while waiting for the call to return by volunteering for work with Presbyterian National Missions and giving missionary sermons in churches far and wide. He and Mabel rented an apartment in Chicago where Mabel spent her days in quiet solitude. Her condition, which the Board's medical staff diagnosed as chronic vascular degeneration, also had deteriorated and she was growing senile, now incapable of handling even the smallest responsibilities. Her eccentricities had come to include making the rounds of the apartment house each morning, opening every available window. Charlie watched and fol-

21. Richard D. Robinson, "Korea: Betrayal of a Nation," typescript, 1960, p. 8.
22. He was unaware of the report that had been filed on him by Mission Chairman William N. Blair at the time of his deportation in 1941: "He came very near to having a nervous breakdown. He ought to be encouraged, I'll put it stronger, forced if necessary, to take a complete rest, something he has never done before in his life, before he is given any commission in the Philippines or elsewhere." Blair to J.L. Hooper, October 8, 1941, in C.A. Clark's correspondence file, Presbyterian Historical Society.

lowed her, closing the windows behind her as she went. She did not object to this. Opening the windows once seemed sufficient.[23]

Loyal friends from Mabel's childhood church helped Charlie take care of his wife. They made it possible for him to leave her so he could travel and give talks about Korea. Her brother DeGray Craft and his wife lived nearby and would visit her several times each day. With supervision Mabel could still cook simple meals, and Charlie enjoyed having lunch with her when he was home. The mail came around noon, and he often read her letters from friends and family, including daughter Katherine, attending seminary in New York, and son Allen, who had transferred to be a missionary in Colombia.

When word came that the Presbyterian Board was reconstituting the Korea Mission, Charlie was ecstatic. As the last prewar president of the Mission's seminary in P'yŏngyang he felt certain that he would be invited to the conference in New York. He was crestfallen, therefore, to get no further communications from the Board, even after the group had started meeting. In frustration he cabled Board Secretary Leon Hooper asking not to be forgotten. In a long letter he argued his usefulness to the "A" list, going back to his basic skills as a carpenter and potential restorer of buildings. He cited his scholarship, his mastery of the language, his knowledge of the people, his continuing series of Bible commentaries in Korean, his network of former students, and his legendary appetite for hard work.

Back from the Board came a tactful reply concurring in everything he had said. However, Dr. Hooper pointed out that the Board was concerned for Mabel's failing health and felt it best, all things considered, if younger and less-encumbered, if slightly less experienced, colleagues be chosen for the "A" list. Charlie did not read this letter to Mabel. He did sink into a short depression while he struggled to accept being turned out to pasture. As he brooded, he felt surer than ever that he was needed in Korea. If the issue was health, he had bluffed the mission doctors before and he could do it again. But there was no getting around Mabel's condition. In daily prayers he asked for the grace to accept not returning to Korea. And in any case, returning remained impossible for anyone for more than a year longer.

Charlie Clark's reaction to not making the "A" list was in character: he lost himself in work. He volunteered to take a pastorate in McAlester, Oklahoma, together with daughter Katherine, who went with him as Christian Education director. The assignment had certain attractions: a ministry in Indian country was something like going to the foreign mission field. Katherine helped take care of Mabel, making time for Charlie to keep working on the Bible commentaries that he wanted to take back to Korea with him when the time was right.

23. Marabelle Taylor, conversation, Arcadia, California, September 20, 1986.

On many days during that summer of 1946, the mercury in McAlester soared beyond 100 degrees Farenheit. Some days it was closer to 110 and occasionally even more. For most people, and especially for the elderly like Mabel Clark, the only thing to do was to sit and try not to move. Mabel withdrew ever farther into herself, often not responding even to Katherine. One steaming afternoon as Katherine was coming home she encountered her mother on the sidewalk heading for the railroad station, dressed in her winter gear with coat, hat, and gloves. Katherine hurried to her side and asked her where she was going. "Home to Chicago, to my family," said Mabel. Suddenly sick with worry, Katherine took her by the elbow and directed her back to the house.

Eventually the heat broke and it got cooler, but Mabel remained locked inside of herself. It was on a November morning while the soup was on the stove and Mabel was sitting in her customary kitchen chair, that she slumped to her left, fell from the chair, and died.

When the doctor had come and gone and the arrangements had been made to take her body to Chicago for burial in the Craft family plot, Charlie sat down and wrote a heartfelt letter to Board Secretary A.K. Reischauer. He reported Mabel's death and emphasized, as he often had before, that in her quietude she had been strong in a way that had kept keep him going through the years. It was a touching letter with much sentimental praise for Mabel and a request that the Board recognize her contribution "before her name is filed away as an insignificant bit of history." He followed this with a request for reconsideration of his status for the "A" list in his new capacity as a single man.[24] In a few days he received Reischauer's reply tactfully denying the request. Charlie knew his foreign missionary career was over.

The Army decided to permit a few missionaries to return because General MacArthur thought there was a link between Christianity and democracy. Though the presence of civilians was certain to create unwelcome logistical problems, General Hodge implemented MacArthur's policy in Korea by asking the American mission boards to assign twenty veteran male missionaries—ten Protestants and ten Catholics—to serve in USAMGIK's Department of Public Health and Welfare. There was no denying the need for their services. More than a million Koreans had been repatriated from Japan and an estimated 650,000 had come as refugees from North Korea, all without jobs and most without prospects.[25] Material conditions were such that the Military Government needed all the help it could get, and the missions were ready with men to do the work.

24. Charles Allen Clark to A.K. Reischauer, November 18, 1946, in Record Group 140, Box 18, File 10, in the Presbyterian Historical Society, Philadelphia.

25. Horace H. Underwood et al., circular to mission boards with property in Korea, April 2, 1946, and Bliss Billings, General Letter dated June 20, 1946 (UCCA, 83.006C, Box 5, File 140).

As they passed through Japan, the relief workers were amazed by the destruction caused by the American air raids on the familiar cities of Tokyo and Yokohama. Japanese friends told them how the bombers had circled the city, dropped bombs in lines across the circles, and finally saturated sections of the circles with napalm until they were infernos.[26] Ordinary Japanese people had suffered greatly, but even Bill Kerr, whose prewar work in Korea had been among Japanese Christians there and was not given to Japan-bashing, thought that justice had been served. His sentiments pointed to the near-complete agreement between American missionary opinion and the political/military objectives of the United States in East Asia:

> Personally, I don't want to see help poured in here with the idea of apology for what our armed forces have done. Particularly do I not want to see Hiroshima and Nagasaki picked out as though we were trying to make amends. That was part of what Japan brought upon itself, and we don't have to apologize. But now that it is all over we are glad to join in the work of restoration where it is welcomed with genuine appreciation.[27]

The group arrived back in Seoul on January 16, 1946. Bill Kerr made a beeline for his former home, last seen when he was arrested on the day of the Pearl Harbor attack. As he was being taken away, he had turned the house over to a Japanese friend for safekeeping. Upon his return in 1946 he found the Japanese family still there paying rent into a special account. The Korean neighbors had done them no harm. The servants were still keeping house, the furnace was working, the furniture was intact, and not a single book was missing from the Kerr family library.[28]

In June 1946, a second group of ten senior missionaries from the Presbyterian, Methodist, Canadian, Catholic, and Anglican missions crossed the Pacific to join the advance party. Greeting them on the main port building at Inch'ŏn was a huge sign that said, "WELCOME TO INCHON, BEST DAMN

26. P'yŏngyang Korea Kid Charles Phillips took part in the destruction of Tokyo as he flew B-29's during incendiary bombing raids in the spring of 1945. See Charles Phillips, *B-29's over Japan* (Moreno Park, Calif.: B-Nijuku Publishers, 1995).

27. Quoted in William Scott to A.E. Armstrong, October 21, 1946 (UCCA 83. 006C, Box 5, File 143).

28. The Kerr house was a few minutes' walk from the Capitol, and between the house furnishings, the servants, and rations from the officer's mess it was possible to live very well there. Among Kerr's carefully chosen house mates were Dexter Lutz, a Northern Presbyterian missionary agricultural expert, formerly stationed in P'yŏngyang, working in the Military Government's economic section; Maj. Clarence Weems, son of Methodist missionaries in Kaesŏng, on General Almond's staff as a political advisor; J. Earnest Fisher, a former Chōsen Christian College professor who served the Military Government in various capacities; and Southern Presbyterian "Korea Kid" Jim Levie, who was an officer in the administrative branch of the government.

Inch'ŏn welcome for returning missionaries, 1947. Florence Murray Collection, United Church of Canada Archives.

PORT IN THE PACIFIC." American uniforms were everywhere. American enlisted men took them to Seoul in Army jeeps, driving on the right, American-style, instead of the left as before. Enroute they passed American military installations: the supply depot in Pup'yŏng and the American headquarters in the old Japanese army base at Yongsan in southern Seoul. Japanese signs had largely disappeared, and along the street were new signs in rough English. One at Samgakchi said "Hawaii Laundry—Glorious Pajamas." Another across from the Chosun Hotel said "Hubba Hubba Photo Studio."[29]

Looking up at South Mountain as the jeeps entered downtown Seoul new arrivals saw the granite stairway leading up to the site of the old

29. Florence Murray, Photo Albums, Korea Mission Photo Collection, United Church of Canada Archives, Victoria University, Toronto. The Hubba Hubba Photo Studio survives (as of 1997) as the Bando-Chosun Arcade's "Hebba Hebba" Photo Studio.

Chōsen Shrine. The shrine itself was gone, having been burned in 1945, but the white stone pillars of the elegant *torii* gate remained, a sign of the American occupation troops' infatuation with Japanese aesthetics.[30] A short way down Namdaemun-no (formerly "Nandaimon-dōri") the old Mitsukoshi Department Store had become the army's Main PX.[31] The top brass of the Military Government lived in the most prized locations. Some were in the Chosun Hotel. Others lived at the Naija or Bizenya Hotels, or in the wooded Japanese bank officers' compound in An'guk-dong, or in the houses of the "Gold Coast," the Japanese housing district in Sinsŏl-dong. The former Government-General building dominated the cityscape as always, but now there were American officers toiling in its chambers, the Stars and Stripes was flying over the lawn, and Chevrolet staff cars were parked out front.

The returned missionaries' symbiosis with the military meant doing things the Army way: living where the Army put them, eating what the Army fed them, and buying what the Army sold them. There was no choice. The Korean economy, like that of Japan, was a shambles. The legal exchange rate had been three yen to the dollar in 1941. During the war the yen had inflated some; but in the last two weeks of August 1945, the Japanese had flooded Korea with currency, issuing hundreds of millions, perhaps billions, of yen until they ran out of paper.[32] Koreans had no choice but to endure the inflation. A pair of shoes was 800 yen ($53 at the legal rate). At the legal rate, a pound of meat was 75 yen ($5.00), up from ¥1 (30 cents) before the war. Soap was $1.50, up from 2.5 cents, and a bag of rice which had been $6.50 (¥20) before the war was now an astonishing $246.00 (3,700 yen).[33] Bill Kerr's servants had to be paid between 600 and 1200 yen a

30. The series of *torii* gates were finally destroyed in 1947. (A photo dated 1947 in the Florence Murray collection shows the stone pillars being taken down.) A most meaningful event for Korea's Christians was the Easter Sunrise service held directly on the site of the Chōsen Shrine in April 1947. *Korea Klipper*, IV:12 (May 1947), p. 1.

31. This was Seoul's answer to the Main PX in Tokyo, which was located on the Ginza in the old Matsuya Department Store.

32. HUSAFIK, chapter 3, p. 22. When the Americans arrived, local money (with "yen" Koreanized as "*wŏn*") was supposed to be worth ¥15=$1, but by 1946 the black market rate was ¥100 to $1 and rising. The civilians had three options: (1) live within the Army system, where the Army used its own "military yen" currency and traded it at the legal rate of ¥15=$1 so that meals in the Capitol cost them ¥12 (80 cents) a day, (2) go broke trying to live on the economy at the legal rate of ¥15=$1, or (3) live on the economy trading dollars illegally at ¥100=$1 and risk arrest and deportation.

33. Edward Fraser to Mrs. Bert Fraser, July 4, 1946. UCCA 83.006C, Box 5, File 136. The rice price owed to the disruptions of the previous autumn and the fact that South Korea was suddenly cut off from its reserve supply of alternative grains from Manchuria when Korea was divided. Hoarding and the time of year (July) also contributed to the extraordinary price, which Fraser went on to say was more like

month, an amount that posed no problem for the five men in Kerr's household earning American salaries but was a prohibitive expense for any foreign family returning to keep house on the previous standard. Not that
housing was available. All Western-style habitations had been requisitioned
as military billets at the rental rate of one "military yen" per year. The only
returnees billeted in their own houses were Bill Kerr and the Underwood
family.

Much had changed. "One is keenly aware of the absence of Japanese and
of the ubiquity, animation and cordiality of the Koreans," wrote the Canadian William Scott.

> Before the war the Japanese were everywhere, dominating the Korean scene.
> Wherever you went you heard Japanese. Whatever of import was being done,
> Japanese were doing it. Japanese officials sat in the seats of authority. Japa-
> nese police patrolled the streets. Japanese businessmen and industrialists
> controlled and exploited the country's resources. Meanwhile, the Koreans
> went about with a sullen, dispirited and resentful mien. Today, that is en-
> tirely changed....The Korean language has come into its own, and to speak it
> is an open sesame to every Korean heart."[34]

As to what had happened during the war, "Every Korean with whom we
talk tells us much, but no two have the same story," wrote Presbyterian Roscoe Coen.

> People look fairly well fed and clothed, in spite of terrible inflation and high
> prices with severe scarcity of some goods, especially rice. The worst thing for
> the Koreans is the division of their country with the Americans in the south
> with one set of ideals and methods and the Russians in the north with an op-
> posing set of ideals and methods and little hope of union.[35]

When the returning missionaries sought out their old Korean friends,
they learned much about the ordeal of the war years. There had been much
attrition in the membership and leadership of the church. Church property
had been lost, but the moral damage was worse. Christians were accusing
each other of betrayal. The Japanese had succeeded in compromising
many who now stood accused of being collaborators.[36] Those accused de-

¥5,000 ($333 at the legal rate) per bag during floods.
    34. William Scott to A.E. Armstrong, November 19, 1946. UCCA, 83.006C, Box 5,
File 143.
    35. Roscoe Coen, General Letter, July 5, 1946. Copy in UCCA 83.006C, Box 5,
File 140.
    36. Presbyterian educator George Paik and Methodist Bishop Yang Chusam were
said to have actually traveled to Japan in 1941 to bow to the spirit of the Sun Goddess at the Grand Shrine of Ise. They allegedly reported to Amaterasu, the Sun Goddess, on their appointments to the board of directors of the Christian Literature Society of Korea. Harold H. Henderson, "Post-war Problems in Korea," seminar paper, San Francisco Theological Seminary, San Anselmo, November 12, 1945 (copy
in RG 140, Box 16, File 29, Presbyterian Historical Society, Philadelphia).

fended themselves by pointing to the futility of a public "witness" against the Japanese during the war. Yun Ch'iho was singled out for vilification for a laundry list of collaborationist offenses during the war including having accepted an imperial appointment to represent Korea in the Japanese House of Peers in 1945.[37] "Indeed, it is absurd to stigmatize anybody for having been pro-Japanese," answered Yun. "[A]s subjects of Japan, what alternative could we, *who had to live* in Korea, have but to obey the orders and demands, however arbitrary, of the Japanese regime? If we had to send our sons to battlefields and our daughters to factories, could we refuse to do anything that the militarists commanded?"[38]

Meanwhile, the returning foreign missionaries faced a delicate situation of their own. The Presbyterians had separated from the Korean church over the Shintō issue in 1938 and had given up titles to schools and other former mission property. The Methodists had turned their mission property over Bishop Yang Chusam and thus had to apply to the bishop to recover their own mission residences.[39] The Canadian Mission, having served

The bitterest recriminations fell on Methodist Bishop Chŏng Ch'unsu, who had used his position to channel funds from church offerings and property sales to the Japanese government to buy warplanes. Chŏng eventually was defrocked and expelled from the Methodist church. He subsequently became a Catholic and "defected" to North Korea in 1949.

The returning missionaries appealed for a moratorium on the collaboration issue as soon as they arrived in 1946, and the Presbyterians organized a retreat for their own clergy to try to clear the air. At the September retreat, fifty survivors of the Shintō shrine struggle were persuaded to confess their sins to each other, repudiate the General Assembly's 1938 decision to go along with Shintō worship, forgive one another, and then go out to hold retreats of their own with the general membership.

37. Toyama Shigeki and Adachi Yoshiko, *Kindai Nihon seijishi hikkei* (Tokyo, 1961), p. 121; *Nippon Times* (Tokyo), April 4, 1945, p. 1; Younghi Yun Whisnant, telephone interview, November 28, 1972. Yun's brief tenure in the House of Peers came in the spring of 1945 when Japan decided to let the colonies of Taiwan and Chosen have representation in the mainly ceremonial upper chamber of the legislative Diet. Among other things contributing to Yun's reputation as a collaborator were the presidency of an "Anti-English League" to purify the national language (Japanese) of English loan words; encouraging young Koreans to enlist in the Japanese armed forces; giving speeches over the radio denouncing the Allies and "declaring war" on them. The Japanese forced many respected Korean leaders to make such public declarations.

38. Yun Ch'iho, "An Old Man's Ruminations" (October 20, 1945), in the papers of the late J. Earnest Fisher, of Bristol, Virginia.

39. Property questions were of keen interest to the missionaries and other civilians who had been forced to leave their possessions behind when they were evacuated or repatriated in 1940-42. Some prepared elaborate inventories to support claims that were later lodged with the State Department to be paid from captured Japanese assets. These settlements, when they were finally worked out, provided only fractions of the value of what was lost.

almost entirely north of the 38th parallel before the war, had to find a new role in South Korea. In effect, though the war had forced the weakened Korean church to live on its own resources independent of foreign financing and influence, the American occupation created conditions under which it was useful for the missionaries to reassert their presence and prolong their leadership. Under other circumstances this reassertion no doubt would have been less welcome than it was. However, the missionaries returned and the Korean church spent most of another generation under missionary leadership.

The interdenominational Chōsen Christian College was a case-in-point. The Japanese had declared it enemy property and ended its existence as a college in 1943. The former faculty and alumni reopened it after Liberation, using the old name but without the involvement of the supporting missions or the United Board for Christian Higher Education in Chōsen, the New York foundation that controlled the school's dollar endowment. The United Board was reluctant to release funds from the endowment to the reorganized college without a careful redefinition of the relationship. The question was whether to allow foreign control again, and how much to allow, in order to get access to the funds. Even after the college's former president Horace H. Underwood returned to Korea and was in a position to vouch for the new leadership, it took a long time to work out the new relationship with the foundation in New York. George Paik and his faculty, meanwhile, were hard-pressed to meet their expenses. It was not until April 1947 that the papers were signed and

The prewar business people lost the most. When the war began, A.W. Taylor had owned his house at Dilkusha, part of the W.W. Taylor Company and Taylor Building in Sogong-dong, and a partnership in a gold mine, which he was in the process of selling. The gold mine proceeds went into a bank account, and since all American assets were frozen in the Japanese empire there was little to do with the money but pay off debts. In 1941 the Japanese requisitioned a parcel of land at Dilkusha for a military road, paying the Taylors and then taking the money back for "back taxes." When Taylor was interned and fell behind in these tax payments in 1942, gendarmes appeared at Dilkusha to put attachment tags on every piece of furniture and item of clothing, frightening Mary into paying the entire tax bill.

Later in the spring of 1942, as he was about to be repatriated, A.W. Taylor turned his assets over to a Japanese business associate named Kondo, who left them in the hands of a former Taylor employee named K.D. Lee at the end of the war. In March 1946 when it was finally counted, the family's money came to ¥196,027, worth a fraction of the $65,000 it had been before the war. Dilkusha and the Taylor Building, having been seized by the Japanese as enemy property, were returned after the war; but Dilkusha had been devastated by looters and squatters, the grounds had been stripped of trees except for the ancient gingko, and a spontaneous village had grown up around the house. There was little choice but to sell it off.

American money began flowing again, to the newly renamed Chosun Christian University (CCU).[40]

The Fate of Christians in North Korea

The division of Korea at the 38th parallel devastated the Christian community because of the large number of Christians in the north. These Christians began migrating southward when the regime of Kim Il-sung started attacking the church. Kim's first move was to try to co-opt Cho Mansik, perhaps the most famous North Korean Christian leader.[41] Cho had spent the early liberation period as part of the Committee for the Preparation of Korean Independence (CPKI) and founder of the Korea Democratic Party (Chosŏn Minjudang). When he refused to cooperate with the leftist regime being set up by the Red Army and Kim Il-sung, he was removed from public life and put under house arrest.

Violence flared between leftists and Christians through the winter of 1945-46. Christians opposed the Soviet regime on the question of trusteeship, which the Soviets supported. Christians tried to organize an alternative celebration for March 1, 1946, the first-ever public commemoration of the 1919 Independence Movement, which the regime was planning to observe in a government rally. Many Christians were divested of their property and businesses in the land reform of March. Moreover, all property that had belonged to the Korean church, including church buildings, schools, hospitals, and income-producing lands owned by school foundations (*chaedan*), was reclassified as state property whether they had been owned by Korean Christian groups or foreign missionary societies. The methods of the land reform involved reclassification of citizens as loyal or disloyal, with special trouble in store for those who were identified as collaborators with the former Japanese colonial regime. Many intellectuals, businessmen, and others who were seen as rich or as members of pre-Lib-

40. L. George Paik, interviews, Seoul, March 1984, and minutes, Cooperating Board for Christian Education in Chōsen, Inc., April 14, 1947, in the archives of the United Board for Christian Higher Education in Asia, Day Missions Library, Yale Divinity School. Also see biographies of Yu Ŏkkyŏm, Horace H. Underwood, and Paek Nakchun (L. George Paik) in *Chilli wa chayu ŭi kisudul,* pp. 241-81.

41. Cho Mansik, known for his leadership of the self-reconstruction movement of Koreans under Japanese colonial rule, was an important Presbyterian layman and educator. He demonstrated the self-reconstruction principle through his Korean Products Promotion Society (Chosŏn Mulsan Changnyohoe), founded in 1922, through which he set a Gandhi-like example of frugality and self-support through the making of simple necessities for living. See Kenneth M. Wells, "The Rationale of Korean Nationalism under Japanese Colonial Rule, 1922-1932: The Case of Cho Mansik's Korean Products Promotion Society," *Modern Asian Studies,* XIX:4 (1985), pp. 823-859.

eration elites were open to being marked for discrimination and, in some cases, expropriation and punishment.

In November 1946, the northern regime organized an election for members of the region's people's committees, the first step in the creation of a national assembly. Candidates in the election were supposed to represent a broad spectrum of national opinion and included some Christians, but the region's Christians opposed the process as a whole because it was clearly meant to legitimize Communist political control. When Christian leaders announced a boycott on grounds that the election was scheduled for a Sunday and thus violated their strict tenet of Sunday observance, the regime took it as a kind of last straw. The government denounced the boycott as an attack on order and an effort to destabilize the system in order to promote the fortunes of the American-backed rightists and collaborators in South Korea. Christians who took this stance were to be regarded as opponents of the "revolutionary state" and its policies, and therefore as enemies of the people.

Having marginalized the existing churches in this manner, the regime created a state-recognized church resembling the nondenominational "kyodan" model employed by the Japanese when they created their state-controlled church during the war. This was the "Christian League" (the *Kidok-kyodo yŏnmaeng*), officially empowered to hold the property and supervise and limit the work of the North Korean Christian church. Kang Yang'uk, an ordained Presbyterian minister with family ties to Kim Il-sung, headed the League.[42] Thereafter, although many Christians remained in North Korea, they were subjected to official discrimination in such matters as access to schooling and the better types of jobs. The disenfranchised Christian community tried to carry on a while longer and even held a rally in April 1947 that is said to have drawn twenty thousand.[43] Churches con-

42. Kim Yangson, *History of the Korean Church in the Ten Years since Liberation,* trans. Allen D. Clark (Seoul: mimeographed, n.d.), pp. 11-14, and George M. McCune and Arthur L. Grey Jr., *Korea Today* (Cambridge, Mass.: Harvard University Press, 1950), pp. 174-175.

Kang Yang'uk was a cousin of Kang Pansŏk, Kim Il-sung's mother. The Kang family were Christians, as is well known; Kang Pansŏk herself was a Presbyterian deaconess and her cousin Kang Yang'uk was a graduate of the Presbyterian Theological Seminary in P'yŏngyang and an ordained Presbyterian pastor. He remained head of the Christian League in North Korea until his death in 1983, rising in the meantime to the rank of vice-premier of the Democratic People's Republic of Korea. Kang's son, Kang Yŏngsŏp, succeeded him as head of the League.

43. Veteran missionary William N. Blair was allowed a five-day visit to P'yŏngyang in April 1947 and was present at the rally. He found the former Presbyterian Theological Seminary in operation, though its president, Kim Injun, was in prison. Harry A. Rhodes and Archibald Campbell, eds., *History of the Korea Mission of the Presbyterian Church in the U.S.A.,* Vol. II (New York: United Presbyterian Church in the U.S.A., 1964), p. 94. (Note: Kim Injun was the father of Kim Sungha, long-time Korea librarian at the Harvard-Yenching Library in Cambridge.)

tinued to hold services and pastors continued to preach and teach. Christian families clung to their beliefs as part of their family life. But the energy and vitality that had been so impressive before the war never returned and the growth of the movement all but ceased.

In this way, Christians became enemies of the "revolutionary state" in North Korea. Thousands of them were forced to join the southward stream of landlords, merchants, and other "class enemies" who left their homes, property, jobs, and often family members to cross the 38th parallel into the relative safety of South Korea. The influx of Christian refugees put great stress on the churches of the south, many of whose members held traditional regional prejudices against northerners, lacked the means to offer them much help, and actually came to resent their aura of martyrdom. Refugee churches sprang up. One, the Yŏngnak Church, based on the congregation from Sinŭiju that followed their pastor south in a Biblical-style exodus, became one of the largest churches in the world.

Christians who remained in North Korea faced stern tests. In P'yŏngyang, Sister Agneta Chang felt torn between her desire to be reunited with her Maryknoll Sisters and her opportunity, which she saw as her duty, to serve as the last "foreign" missionary in the city. She was lonely, and her chronic back injury plagued her. It especially hurt to kneel. For a time she kept up a correspondence with Mother Mary Joseph Rogers, her superior in New York, with letters being smuggled across the 38th parallel by Catholic couriers at great risk. Mother Mary Joseph wanted to bring her back to New York for rest and medical treatment, and she pled with Father George Carroll, the Maryknoll chief in Seoul, to get her out. However, the Korean bishop in Seoul insisted that Sister Agneta stay in P'yŏngyang. By the time Bishop Patrick Byrne, as apostolic delegate to Korea, won an order to bring her south across the parallel, the border had become too dangerous to cross.[44]

Stranded in North Korea, Sister Agneta watched as the Kim Il-sung regime fired Catholic teachers and replaced them with government-approved instructors in the parochial schools. As she thought about going south she knew that her defection would simply bring more hardship to the Sisters in the P'yŏngyang convent. So she did her work, organizing the nuns into a self-governing body with their own elected leaders. The Communists did not intrude or interfere in the convent itself, even as late as 1949.

However, across the country at Tŏgwŏn, near Wŏnsan, it was a different story with the German Benedictines, who, after having been released from house arrest at the end of the war, were put back under guard in 1946. Germans, not being enemy nationals, had not had to leave Korea during the

44. This account follows correspondence appended to Sr. Gabriella Mulherin, M.M., "Flower of the Martyrs," unpublished typescript (Maryknoll, N.Y., Maryknoll Mission Archives, 1979), pp. 18-30.

war. However, as the Japanese retreated from Manchuria and northeastern Korea in the days after the surrender they burned the Catholic and Protestant missions in Lungchingtsun and the Catholic church and convent at Hoeryŏng, leaving only structural elements and heating equipment for the incoming Russians to loot.

The Soviet troops singled out German missionaries for special persecution. In the months following the surrender, they killed two Benedictines in Yenchi, two others in Hoeryŏng, and rounded up the remainder for house arrest in the Benedictine Abbey at Tŏgwŏn. While in the Abbey, the Germans lived on food grown on the Abbey's own farmlands and the persecution was not severe for many months. After the North Korean regime was established in 1948, however, the persecution resumed. In May 1949, North Korean soldiers raided the Abbey, arrested the Benedictine Mission leader Bishop Bonifatius Sauer and the entire Benedictine contingent plus four Korean priests, and shipped them all to a prison in P'yŏngyang. All students were evicted from the Catholic seminary at Tŏgwŏn and the school was turned into an agricultural college and renamed for Kim Il-sung. The Wŏnsan convent was turned into a hospital, and the Catholic middle school was turned into a school for Russian military dependents. When the purge was done, there were only two Korean priests left for the entire Korean northeast.[45]

White Russians: Homeless Again

South of Hoeryŏng, the Reds reached Novina and came upon the Yankovsky family and their colony of White Russians. The Reds had grievances against George Yankovsky, ranging from his anticommunism to his collaboration with the Japanese. Yankovsky and his son Arsenii were arrested and interrogated by SMERSH,[46] and then temporarily released. Sons Valery and Yuri soon were put to work as "volunteer" interpreters for the Red Army, while Arsenii worked part time for SMERSH and part time as a procurement officer for the Rear Services Sector of regional headquarters (YUZHMOR[47]) at Ch'ŏngjin. The Yankovsky brothers had little choice but to work for the Reds. As a SMERSH agent put it to Arsenii, the whole

---

45. Joseph Chang-mun Kim and John Jae-sun Chung, *Catholic Korea—Yesterday and Today* (Seoul: Catholic Korea Publishing Company, 1964), pp. 341-342.

46. "SMERSH" was created in 1943 as the Army counterintelligence branch (aka the *Kontrrazvedka*) of the Stalinist NKVD security organization. The nickname "SMERSH" is short for "*smyert shpionam*," meaning "Death to spies." Its Korean regional headquarters immediately after the war was in Ch'ŏngjin. SMERSH was absorbed into the Soviet NKVD security organization in 1946.

47. YUZHMOR was the Southern Naval Defense Area (*Yuzhnii Morskoi Oboronitel'nii Rayon*). One of its functions was to operate a military tribunal that tried suspected criminals, resisters, and deviants, both Russians and Koreans.

Yankovsky family was already in plenty of trouble.[48]

Before long, after things had settled down in North Korea, the Yankovskys once again were arrested for collaboration. In the summer of 1946, George and his cousin Tatiana, who had worked for the Imperial Japanese Navy in Ch'ŏngjin, were sent to prison in Tumen, on the Soviet-Manchurian border. Valery was arrested next and sent to Siberia, first to labor as a marksman shooting wolves from airplanes and then, after he tried to escape, to work in a lead mine in Magadan. When it was Yuri's turn to be arrested he was sent to a labor camp in Kazakhstan.[49]

Arsenii Yankovsky was the last of the family to leave North Korea. His job with YUZHMOR lasted into 1946, but when the Soviet supply headquarters withdrew to Vladivostok, SMERSH moved in and the interrogations began. He decided to run. Claiming to have business in P'yŏngyang, he took his wife across the country to P'yŏngyang and then caught a bus south to Sariwŏn, where the two of them hitchhiked to the border village of Hakhyŏn-ni. There they crossed the 38th parallel with a group of smugglers on the night of January 11, 1947, surrendering to South Korean police and U.S. Military Intelligence.

Meanwhile in Seoul, the last days of World War II were terrifying for Natalya Thcherkine. She and several Russian friends were arrested by Japanese gendarmes and roughly interrogated about contacts and communications among Russians in Korea. Widowed, and with her sons away at engineering school in Shanghai, Natalya Tchirkine had lived on a shoestring in seclusion on the Russian Orthodox Church compound. Her only human contact had been with next-door neighbors, the Belogolovys and their daughters Nina and Toma, and the cosmetics chemist Ivan Tikhonov. She had nothing of military significance to tell the Japanese, but for many hours she had to endure the terror of arrest in a building where she often heard the screams of other prisoners undergoing interrogation and torture.

With the coming of the U.S. occupation, Natalya acquired a job as a translator for the U.S. Army. She brought her sons back from Shanghai and the Tchirkines and Belogolovys went to work getting American visas, hoping to go to school in the United States. Vladimir and Cyril Tchirkine were first admitted to the University of California, and then the Belogolovy girls were admitted to the University of Hawaii. The children's admissions to college in America helped their parents get immigration visas, and Natalya

48. Headquarters, U.S. Army Forces in Korea, Office of the Assistant Chief of Staff, G-2, *Intelligence Summary Northern Korea*, No. 29 (1 February 1947), pp. 466-477. This account of Arsenii Yankovsky follows this document and interviews with Victoria Yankovsky, June 24, 1991, and Orr Chistiakoff, March 11, 1992.

49. According to his nephew, life at the camp was so harsh that Yuri had to dig holes at night to hide in during the day, to escape the burning sun. His captors once threw chlorine in his eyes, partially blinding him. Conversations with Orr Chistiakoff, March/April 1992.

herself moved into an apartment in Albany, California, near Berkeley, just days before the outbreak of the Korean War.

In the Russian Consulate-General, over the wall from the Orthodox Church compound, the Japanese did not arrest Alexander Poliansky or any of his retinue of thirty-six men, women, and children when the Soviet Union declared war on Japan on August 8, 1945. In fact Poliansky was among the first to visit the incoming American advance party at the Chosun Hotel later in the month. The Americans were skeptical about Poliansky from the beginning. He seemed too sure of himself, too quick to offer opinions at a time when everyone else was confused. Poliansky got all the courtesies that the Americans offered other Allied delegations: the Post Exchange, the APO mail facility, and even a plane to take him to Japan to get more money from the Soviet Embassy in Tokyo when his funds ran low. But counter-intelligence reported that Poliansky and the Russian consulate staff were keeping surreptitious contact with leftist groups in South Korea. Since the Army was dealing with Soviet Army authorities in North Korea and had no use for the diplomatic channel available through Poliansky and his staff, there was really no reason for him to remain in Seoul. The fact that the Americans were not allowed any corresponding consular facility in P'yŏng-yang made his presence in South Korea all the more irritating.

One of Poliansky's jobs was to disseminate favorable information about the USSR. This included showing movies to Korean audiences, something that the Military Government allowed until it was discovered that the movies were being used as recruiting tools for the left. Films that exaggerated the Russians' role in winning the war against Japan also galled the Americans. Friction increased until the Americans caught Poliansky's staff showing films commercially. It was diplomatic practice that films imported by embassies and consulates via the pouch not be used commercially, and the distribution of Poliansky's films to theaters was ruled a violation. Poliansky apologized, then repeated the offense, at which point the American authorities called him on the carpet and presented him with an ultimatum: either allow the Americans to open a consulate in P'yŏngyang or leave South Korea. In Moscow, Foreign Minister Vyacheslav Molotov lodged a protest, which was rejected by the Americans. On July 2, 1946, Poliansky closed the consulate, loaded his staff and dependents into vehicles, drove up to the 38th parallel and disappeared into Soviet-occupied North Korea.[50]

50. HUSAFIK, draft chapter IV, pp. 294-310. At the time of Poliansky's departure, three staffers were left behind to maintain the consulate buildings. Later, during the Korean War, the buildings were heavily damaged, and the South Korean government allowed the grounds to be turned into a refugee camp, with war victims living in shanties on the premises as late as 1958. In the 1960s the land was parceled up and sold for commercial use, some of it being purchased by the *Kyŏng-hyang Sinmun* newspaper. In 1990, when the Soviet Union and South Korea opened diplomatic relations, the Soviets tried and failed to recover the old

Poliansky's departure across the 38th parallel further hardened the division between North and South Korea. By late 1946, U.S. occupation authorities in the south were becoming resigned to failure in the effort to reunite Korea, and powerful forces were forming to create a separate Korean government in the southern zone. The American-educated Syngman Rhee was at the head of one such body of political opinion, using tokens of American support, many of them inadvertent from the U.S. point of view, to full advantage in his effort to rally the Korean people behind his leadership. Poliansky's departure thus punctuated an end to the trusteeship idea and signaled the opening of a new chapter in Korea's emergence as a symbol in the international cold war.

property and were forced to locate their new embassy in Kangnam, south of the Han River. The South Korean government refused to dislodge the companies that had built upon it and there remained only the tower of the former legation building as a historical site. In 1997 the Russian Federation and the South Korean government reached an agreement to bring the Russian Embassy back to Chŏng-dong on property formerly belonging to the Methodist-run Paejae Boys' High School.

-- 15 --

Making Korea Safe for Democracy

The American soldiers of General John Hodge's XXIVth Corps did their best to sow the seeds of democracy in South Korea. However, the Koreans themselves had competing political agendas that kept the country in a state of low-level civil war through much of the U.S. occupation. Before they could foster democracy the Americans had to establish peace, and this required repression of the uncooperative. USAMGIK authorities reorganized the police force into an instrument that looked a lot like the former Japanese colonial police in the eyes of many Koreans. The Americans supplemented this in 1946 with a "constabulary," a military force dedicated to internal stability. With these Korean instruments and with U.S. forces in the background, the U.S. Military Government set about keeping order throughout most of South Korea.

American Internationalism in South Korea

These things happened in Korea during the heyday of American Internationalism, an ideology famously defined during World War II by publisher Henry Luce in a *Life* magazine editorial entitled "The American Century." Luce, himself the son of American China missionaries, believed in the religious and political ideals that had inspired young people of his parents' generation to spread Christianity and democratic politics around the world. He believed that America was uniquely positioned to create a world where there would be peace, justice, and abundance for all. In his editorial, Luce used language similar to Josiah Strong's a generation earlier:

> [Americans] are the inheritors of all the great principles of Western Civilization—above all Justice, the love of Truth, the ideal of Charity....For the mo-

ment it may be enough to be the sanctuary of these ideals. But not for long. It now becomes our time to be the powerhouse from which the ideals spread throughout the world and do their mysterious work of lifting the life of mankind from the level of the beasts to what the Psalmist called a little lower than the angels.

America as the dynamic center of ever-widening spheres of enterprise, America as the training center of the skillful servants of mankind, America as the Good Samaritan, really believing again that it is more blessed to give than to receive, and America as the powerhouse of the ideals of Freedom and Justice—out of these elements surely can be fashioned a vision of the 20th Century to which we can and will devote ourselves in joy and gladness and vigor and enthusiasm....It is in this spirit that all of us are called, each to his own measure of capacity, and each in the widest horizon of his vision, to create the first great American Century.[1]

Korea was one place where the United States tried briefly to exercise Henry Luce's grand American vision. Liberating the Koreans from Japanese rule was the first step. However, the Military Government in South Korea fell far short of fostering democracy or prosperity. It soon became preoccupied with the basic job of keeping order and thus postponed fulfilling the promise of liberation, which was a system of self-government based on democratic ideals. Koreans resented this and expressed themselves through street demonstrators, strikes, union actions, and political agitation. Many "agitators," as Americans saw them, were leftists who wanted basic changes in the way power and wealth were distributed in Korea. Arrayed against them were propertied people who feared losing their privileged positions through mob rule. Americans increasingly were drawn to the view that moderate reforms should not give way to revolution, and they saw the "agitators" as threats to public order at best, as communist agents at worst. Accordingly, American occupation policy took the side of reaction and employed armed force to defend the status quo.

Having to suppress free expression in South Korea was highly upsetting to some of the American soldiers who had to wield military weapons to silence disaffected citizens. Many of them were war veterans who were used to justifying violence by the rightness of the American cause. But in Korea, it seemed that the U.S. Army had gotten into the business of stifling freedom. In the opinion of Harry Savage, an Army sergeant from the Midwest, the U.S. Army had been co-opted by a murderous faction of Koreans who were bent on punishing ordinary citizens for their legitimate grievances. After helping suppress the strikes in southeastern Korea in the fall of 1946 he wrote a letter of protest to President Harry Truman.

1. Henry R. Luce, "The American Century," *Life*, February 17, 1941. For a critical discussion of the political milieu and some of the principal characters in shaping "Americanism" and marrying it to the ideology of anti-communism in Asia, see Cumings, *The Origins of the Korean War*, Vol. II, pp. 82-134.

This strike proved to be the forerunner of all the riots and uprisings that were to follow. The first call that our Battalion received came from Tongyong. We arrived there at night and by that time the Communists had completely taken over the city and were actually running the City Hall. We restored law and order allright but scores of people were killed in those riots and not a word reached the American public....Three days later most of us went back to Masan and the next day a riot there broke out. Our entire battalion patrolled that town all day with dead bodies lying all over the streets, and we kept our machine guns blazing. It was then that I saw atrocities that I had never seen before, but [now] I know how it must have been to live under the Nazis. In Tongyong, I saw an athlete, a boxer, on the suspicion of being a Communist, first beaten by the Korean police until he could no longer stand up and then he was made to [do] push-ups. When he collapsed they turned him over and he was dead.

In Masan, the Korean police gathered some three hundred persons mostly at random and made them kneel in front of the police station for around four hours with an occasional pat on the back of a policeman's club. Every now and then they would take a few of them inside and then the torture would begin. Many times people would come running out to us and beg us to kill them, shoot them, anything to end this torture. Many of the GI's got very angry at this and started beating the policemen, which only added to the confusion. Most of the officers, however, stood calmly by and let the beatings go on without letup. In fact our Division Artillery sent a letter to our Battalion to the effect not to criticize what the police were doing....Most of us thought surely these things would reach American newspapers. About two weeks later the [army newspaper] *Stars and Stripes* had an article about it. They said that there had been a riot in Masan, but American troops "restored law and order without firing a shot." I ask you, what kind of propaganda is that? I did not go to Korea, with democracy in mind, and with the thought that I was going there to help the Korean people, to sit idly by and watch these things without wanting to do something about it.[2]

Sorting Out the Koreans

Few American occupation soldiers had the slightest interest in Korean politics. Koreans operated beyond the earshot of the American Military Government, focusing their efforts on creating alliances aimed at winning ultimate political power.[3] Americans were mystified by the Koreans' struggles but tended to side with Koreans who seemed to have the most familiar qualities. They befriended Koreans who spoke English, embraced Christianity, and believed in law and order and the sacredness of private prop-

2. Letter to President Harry Truman from Sgt. Harry H. Savage of Yankton, South Dakota, recently discharged from the U.S. Army, April [no date] 1947 (National Archives and Records Service, Department of State file number 895.00/4-247).
3. See Gregory Henderson, *Korea: The Politics of the Vortex* (Cambridge, Mass.: Harvard University Press, 1968), especially chapter 5, "The Gates of Chaos," pp. 113-147.

erty. Conversely, they opposed the disorder that they saw in street demonstrations and the threat of "communism" in all its forms. Right-wing Koreans soon learned how to manipulate the Americans and deflect their power toward defeating the left—those Koreans who wanted to punish collaborators, redistribute wealth and land, and establish a "people's government."

By the time the U.S. XXIVth Corps landed in September 1945, Koreans on the left and right were already locked in their high-stakes struggle. Indeed, as Bruce Cumings has shown, the Japanese had shown the Koreans how to organize in mass support of specific political goals. In terms of organization and methods, it was a short step from supporting the Japanese emperor's grand design to supporting the wealthy and powerful on the right, or those demanding revolutionary action to redistribute land and wealth on the left. The Japanese had required every Korean to be part of the war effort, to sacrifice for the common goal, and to denounce slackers and enemies of the people. Koreans had learned to see the link between their own actions and big political ideas. Liberation therefore found them primed to participate in the scramble to join the political organizations and factions that blossomed in August 1945 and to identify with their leaders, goals, and programs.

Mass action was especially effective on the left, where people had already organized small unions, or *chohaps,* of workers and farmers as early as the 1930s. The goal of the *chohaps* had been to break down the system of wealth and privilege that benefited landlords and big merchants, and they had been anathema both to the Japanese authorities and to the property-owning class of Koreans. The colonial regime had handled the *chohap*s roughly, using Korean informants to identify the *chohap* organizers so they could be singled out for punishment. The informants were among the most hated Korean collaborators. The fact that they survived after Liberation in a position to influence the American occupiers rankled the unionists and generated resentment against the American Military Government as well.

"Ideological leftists"—that is, people with enough Marxist political consciousness to make them want to overturn the social structure that privileged the rich and powerful—spawned new mass organizations along lines of the earlier *chohap* unions. They were small local organizations that enjoyed considerable local support. Their leaders were well connected in their locales, where relatives and family friends acted as support groups and hid them when the police came around. Their methods were often violent, involving attacks on police stations and government installations where agents sent by the central government in Seoul represented an ongoing effort by outsiders to rule the villages and maintain oppressive systems. In short, they were the kind of independent, politically uncontrollable local movements that the Korean government had always regarded as a threat. Half a century after the Tonghak peasant rebellion, powerful Koreans in the capital were still aware of the damage that could be caused by the blending of many local bands of malcontents.

Between the Japanese collapse and the American arrival on September 8, 1945, politically minded Koreans took the opportunity to choose up sides on the left and right. On the left, the *chohap* associations got time to organize and think about taking action against their enemies; and on the right, people with property, money, and stakes in the economic status quo got time to think about ways to protect their interests. The most important result of this period was the formation of People's Committees (*inmin wiwŏnhoe*) across South (as well as North) Korea. The People's Committees, as mentioned in the preceding chapter, were "democratic" institutions of the traditional sort: that is, they were units of self-government made up of village and district leaders whom people trusted to act in their best interests. Related to these circles of local authority were the local *chi'andae* para-police and, in Seoul, the emerging coalition of Marxist intellectuals who formed the core of the South Korean Workers Party.[4]

In the first flush of liberation, representatives of the right and left actually got together to form a pan-national moderate congress called Committee for the Preparation of Korean Independence (CPKI). The CPKI met in Seoul on September 6 to create a governmental entity that could deal with the U.S. Army that was due to arrive on September 8th. The CPKI met at Kyŏnggi Girls High School, a ten-minute walk from the Chosun Hotel where the XXIVth Corps' advance party was sequestered. The CPKI voted to create the Korean People's Republic (KPR; *Chosŏn inmin konghwaguk*), headed by a 55-person national People's Committee. A majority of the committee members had spent time in prison under the Japanese and few had any taint of collaboration about them. It was a roster of names from many shades of the political spectrum. It paid homage to the overseas independence movement by listing Syngman Rhee in the United States and Kim Ku in China. But the active members were those who had lived through the entire Japanese occupation and had experienced the war in Korea itself and were unknown in the United States, China, or the Soviet Union. Within this group there were shades of ideology from left to right. There was also a generational rift between older, more mellow conservatives in their sixties who had been part of the 1919 Independence Movement, and younger more aggressive conservatives who had come of age during the worst of

---

4. The Korean Communist Party (KCP) ordered all leftist political parties in the south to unite in August 1946 under the name of the South Korean Workers' Party. For the evolution of organized leftist ideas in South Korea as seen through editorials and articles in the KCP's official organ, the *Haebang Ilbo* (Liberation Daily), see Chong-Sik Lee, trans. and ed., *Materials on Korean Communism, 1945-1947* (Honolulu: Center for Korean Studies, University of Hawaii, 1977).

the wartime occupation and were determined not to share power with their critics, especially those on the left.[5]

Even today, Koreans and knowledgeable foreign observers disagree about the legitimacy and popular appeal of the South Korean left in the 1940s. Nevertheless, it is possible to make some observations about the environment out of which the left recruited its mass support. This environment included the following conditions:

The scene

In South Korea there was a sharp divide between the metropolis (Seoul), and the provinces. This had always been the case, and Koreans were accustomed to the difference between the politically sophisticated capital city and the ideologically primitive provinces. In the countryside, where the standard of living was extremely low, politics derived from village hierarchies, clan connections, and local history. Abstract political philosophy was only dimly understood in an environment where land tenure, weather, and crops were the main concern and all considerations were local. The converse was also true. Many of the people in Seoul were there precisely to escape the backwardness of the countryside. They relished the intrigue of capital politics and the conflicts of national factions and ideologies. Their concerns were government, finance, big business, and international affairs. They actively avoided identifying with the concerns of the rural population. The Korean left, however, though it included a good number of educated urban intellectuals, operated primarily in the countryside and made a point of identifying with rural preoccupations.

The quality of life

Given the speed of change in modern Korea, it takes some mental effort to recall the conditions of diet, health, housing, education, and living standards that prevailed in Korea at the time of liberation. In the 1930s, for example, life expectancy was thirty-six years for men and thirty-eight years for women.[6] Women were treated like chattel by their own relatives. They had little autonomy or even identity of their own. They were known as so-and-so's mother or daughter or wife and their given names were so seldom used that their family members, and sometimes the women themselves, could not remember what they were. Children suffered from malnutrition,

5. Bruce Cumings, *The Origins of the Korean War,* Vol. I, p. 85.

6. Yu Yŏng'ik (Young-Ick Lew), "Haebang-ŭi yŏksajŏk ŭiŭi," in *Han'guksa simin kangchwa,* XII (1993), p. 10. In the mid-1990s, life expectancy for men was 66 years and for women, 73 years. Donald Stone Macdonald and Donald N. Clark, *The Koreans: Contemporary Politics and Society,* 3d. ed. (Boulder, Colo.: Westview Press, 1996), p. 10.

their bellies distended, their playful energies sapped by parasites. Working-men were insulted and bullied by their "betters" and spent their days in manual labor. People stripped the hills of anything that could be used for fuel, using brushwood to cook meals made from whatever grains were left after rents and taxes.

The misery and privation of country life were products of Japanese poli-cies that took away all but the barest essentials by the end of the war. Nor was there much hope of escaping up the ladder of education, for the Japa-nese built elementary schools in the bigger villages only, and middle schools only in provincial towns. The needs of the family, especially the need for household and farm labor, together with the expense of educa-tion, often doomed the farm child's chances to go to school. Such were the endemic circumstances in rural Korea, creating an environment that was ripe for conversion to political fury in 1945.

The ideas

Land ownership, access to money and credit, and tax rates all were areas of gross inequality under the Japanese. Studies of Korea's rural economy in the early 1940s point to a volatile combination of hatreds toward land-lords, bankers, usurers, and tax collectors and their enforcers in the army and police. In the 1930s, before the Koreans experienced the worst of Japa-nese oppression, Western missionaries won many converts to Christianity. The gospel brought with it rare opportunities for dignified association and expression as well as the hope of education and advancement. Many saw Christianity as a way out of the mire; yet in the war years even Christianity was taken away, its leaders imprisoned, its adherents scattered by the po-lice, its meetings canceled, its schools closed, its churches padlocked and sometimes even appropriated for conversion to Shintō shrines.

To escape conditions in their home environments or to answer the sum-mons of labor and military drafts, many Koreans had left their country for other parts of Korea, Japan, or Manchuria. Certain areas were especially af-fected by this migration, among them the provinces of North and South Chŏlla in southwestern Korea, and the large island of Cheju off the south-west coast. The uprooting of these people, and then their return to find conditions unchanged or worsened, opened their eyes to the situation of their families and home villages and put things in political terms. The land distribution picture, job prospects, and hopes for a better life in general all added up to an even greater gap between rich and poor, with little sign that things would improve under the Americans. Disillusioned returnees with experience in other places brought the People's Committees many angry recruits with nothing to lose and much to gain by overturning the status quo. These people demanded changes in two trends that had developed under Japanese rule: the concentration of farmland in the hands of big owners, and the high rate of tenancy that had left farmers as serfs working fields that their ancestors had owned.

Western assessments of Korean political currents in the late 1940s typically used the term "communist" as a blanket label for every shade of leftist.[7] Thus "communist cells" existed in schools; "communist guerrillas" infested the hills; "communist agents" caused "communist rebellions" and in short were thought to be responsible for most of the political turmoil in liberated Korea. The long cold war encouraged this gross conflation of the most innocuous reformism with "communism." However, a more accurate assessment of what happened in Korea in the late 1940s requires an understanding of the South Korean left on its own terms, as a movement powered by the opportunities that came with liberation from Japan. The U.S. Military Government offered hope for *eventual* redress through democratic institutions. Leftist leaders—that is, urban intellectuals, north Korean agents trekking in the Taebaek Mountains back and forth across the 38th parallel, angry returnees from Japan, and local *chohap* and People's Committee leaders—all promised quicker results. They advocated sharing the wealth and meting out revolutionary justice to big landlords and collaborators. They also looked like they might win in the left-right struggle, meaning that Korea's farmers were being offered a chance to join the winning side. For many who did not grasp any other aspect of Korean "communism," getting on the leftist bandwagon seemed to be the wisest course of action.

In the eyes of the Military Government, this tentative left leaning constituted "communism." However, this is an oversimplification. It was more a matter of faction-forming and certainly not "International Communism" as the term was understood by Americans in the cold war. Taking it out of the context of the low-level conflict then occurring in the Korean countryside and interpreting it as part of the worldwide superpower confrontation was a tragic misconstruction.

If the informal alliance of the People's Republic, the People's Committees, and out-and-out Marxists created opportunities for the Korean left, the American occupation created opportunities for the Korean right. The American Military Government's stated goal of a stable and forward-looking political and economic structure won considerable popular support.

---

7. This tendency started at the top, with General Hodge. Members of his own staff noted that his basic prejudice was that "*all* liberals are communists. Hodge has a G-2 and C.I.C. [intelligence and counterintelligence] group that puts out a bunch of 'subjective bias' as 'intelligence.' They play up to his bitter antagonism to communism." [Under the circumstances, it is likely that he will be] "sold a bill of goods on immediate 'democratic' elections and South Korea will be in Syngman Rhee's pocket" (Arthur C. Bunce to Edwin Martin, 24 Feb. 1947 [895.00/2-2447]. Bunce was with the Office of the Advisor, U.S. Army Forces in Korea, and Martin was Chief of the State Department's Division of Japanese and Korean Economic Affairs.)

For some, as we have seen, there were jobs to be had. For others, the opportunities were ideological, as in the case of Christians who supported the Military Government and worked to establish a democratic government friendly to ideas of capitalism and private property. Some were waiting to buy up former Japanese property that the Americans had taken over as "vested" property during the occupation. These Koreans were not eager to see the reorganization of property or any general land reform.

South Koreans of the left and right viewed events during the first months of the liberation era quite differently. They watched the Soviet-backed communist program being put into place in North Korea while leftist organizers adapted their tactics to foster revolution in the south. It is not known how much direct assistance these organizers got from North Korea, though they got some. Nor can it be assumed that the South Korean left operated as an advance guard of the North Korean regime. Communications were too primitive and there was too much friction between leftist factions in the metropole and the provinces.[8] What is known is that by the autumn of 1946, communist-led cells of leftists existed everywhere in South Korea, comprised of students, returned Koreans from Japan, unemployed workers, and landless tenant farmers. Their frustration fed the movement; the Marxist prescription for class struggle suited them; and the opportunities for revenge (or justice) provided them with immediate targets.

If late August 1945 belonged to the CPKI and the centrist coalition, by early September the South Korean power structure had collected itself and formed an effective counter organization, the Korean Democratic Party. This group, comprised of "notables" from educated and property-owning circles, attached itself to General John R. Hodge and the top military leadership virtually from the moment of their arrival. They discredited the transitional "Korean People's Republic" leader Yŏ Unhyŏng, painting him as a collaborator because the Japanese had put him in place. They denounced the People's Committees (*inmin wiwŏnhoe*) in the countryside, painting them as communist and therefore enemies of the American plan for South Korea. In brief, the conservative Koreans who comprised the Korean right easily co-opted the American Military Government because of its predilection to abhor anything "communist." This safeguarded the future of capitalism and private property and ensured that there would be only limited reform. It did little for democratic government in the provinces, or for the early redress of grievances in Korea's towns and villages. Those currents were identified as "communist"; and being communist they could not be allowed by the U.S. occupation authorities to be part of legitimate politics or be represented in the political structure. As "communists" their leaders

---

8. Sŏ Changsŏk, "Haebanggwa nambukhan kongsanjuŭi," in *Han'guksa simin kangchwa*, XII (1993), pp. 103-107.

were enemies of the state—criminals, in effect; and as criminals they deserved repression.

Coming Home to Kwangju

In 1946, when the first returning Southern Presbyterian missionaries reached their prewar outposts in Honam, they were filled with hope that the U.S. Army occupation would be a chance "for the American forces to show by example and by precept what constitutes that righteousness which alone will exalt a nation!"[9] A substantial Army contingent had been established at Fort Sykes, a former Japanese airfield five miles outside Kwangju. Missionaries preached to the troops on Sundays and often stayed in the officers' billets, ate in the mess hall, and used the APO mail service. The U.S. military presence in Kwangju enriched the missionaries' social life and even created a new kind of mission work consisting of ministering to the military men and their wives. One missionary wrote of the fertile field provided by the International Women's Club of Kwangju, lately joined by more than sixty army wives:

> They…seated me at the table with the president and the Korean wives of high government officials to help with the interpreting. It was an astonishing experience to see so many American women in Kwangju, but I enjoyed getting acquainted with them. Several of the Army officers' families have had us over for meals and we have had them to meals in our home. Once we went on a picnic with the Chaplain and his family to a beautiful dammed-up lake in the picturesque, green mountains five or six miles from here. A group of young people also went in a truck. We have been so glad to meet and have over for meals a number of the GI's. Pray that this may lead to real conversions. We have been able to talk to Jews, Protestants, Catholics, and one Christian Scientist. I think it is evident that there is a job for us here more important than the rehabilitation of Mission property—the rehabilitation of the souls of men.[10]

As they picked up the pieces of their lives before the war, the Kwangju missionaries encountered new problems. Their buildings were much the worse for wear after years of looting, war, and occupation. Wartime squatters had stripped the houses not only of their furniture and contents but also of the fixtures, windows, flooring, plumbing, and even the wiring. The Knox family's house, less damaged than some, had been reconditioned for use by the U.S. Army as an officers' club in 1945 and then occupied by an Army colonel and his family until mid-1947. When they got it back the Knoxes found that Army trucks had ruined their lawn and garden, that the

9. Joseph Hopper, "Dear Friends" letter from Kwangju, September 5, 1946, Presbyterian Church (U.S.A.), Department of History, Montreat, North Carolina.
10. Maie B. Knox, "Dear Friends in America" letter, August 27, 1947, Presbyterian Church (U.S.A.), Department of History, Montreat, North Carolina.

building repairs had been poorly done with inferior materials and had to be done over, and that there was still no plumbing. Before they moved in, their "crowning achievement" was a drain that made it possible to empty water into the sink instead of carrying it into the backyard to be dumped.[11]

The Southern Presbyterians, once witnesses to their Korean Christians' seething anger against the Japanese, returned to Honam to new kinds of political unrest and rumor mongering. The anger now was against accused collaborators and between communists (or leftists) and anticommunists (or rightists). "The country is in constant political turmoil," wrote Maie Knox. "We hear rumors that there is a great persecution of Christians going on in the Russian zone. Also that the Korean Communist leader in [North Korea] has been killed by non-Communists. Even in the American zone Communists go to churches, demand contributions to the Communist cause, beat up the Christians who refuse to contribute, and skip out to the next place before the police can catch them."

Army contacts and local Christians painted a picture of the political scene. North Korean refugees were of two types: those escaping the cruelties of life under the communists, and agents of the communists themselves who were well trained and well paid to agitate the Honam population. According to senior missionary William A. Linton, they were also well supplied with money.

It is provided by the great communist machine that keeps agents everywhere. These refugees have money to entertain friends, buy clothes and food, and live a carefree life. They talk of contentment north of the line under a well-organized free government run by the Koreans. They claim that all have plenty of land, good houses, ample food and clothes. They tell of how imperialistic Americans have been found moving Korean rice and rice liquors, for which they have acquired such a taste, back to the United States. This, they claim, is the reason for the rice shortage in southern Korea. Americans are just stripping Korea to enrich the United States. The grain, flour, machinery, fertilizer, cloth, and other commodities that come in from America are only what the Americans can't use, just waste, that is being sold to Korea at an exorbitant price.

However, their story continues, the Koreans need not worry for the great Red Army, the most powerful in the world, is poised and waiting just north of the line ready to bring the "second liberation" to Korea. To be sure, the Americans took advantage of the good intentions of the Russians when the Red Army whipped the Japanese Army and forced it to surrender at the time of the "first liberation" in August 1945, but the Russians will not allow that to happen again. All are urged to prepare for the entry of their allies, the Red Army, when the American forces will be pushed into the ocean in twenty-four hours. On that day, the claims continue, the "faithful" will be fully rewarded and all enemies of "democracy" will be summarily dealt with. Full lists of the

11. A special indignity was the way the Army turned the chapel at Florence Root's Speer School for Girls into a GI bar. Ibid.

enemies of the "father country" (Russia) have been carefully prepared and all on the list will be liquidated and their property confiscated and divided among the "faithful."[12]

So it was not hard to understand why "Koreans feel that it is only being realistic to take into consideration the question of how one might live under the communists."[13] The missionaries praised leaders such as Syngman Rhee and Kim Ku for taking public stances against the left; and although they were aware of Syngman Rhee's opportunism and Kim Ku's record as a terrorist, the news from the Christian community in North Korea fixed their attitudes implacably against all real and imagined communists.[14]

In November 1947, Florence Root returned to Kwangju and resumed her position as principal of the Speer School for Girls. She found a city under siege, with police boxes surrounded by walls of sandbags to protect them in the night. There were frequent pitched battles in the suburbs between police patrols and leftist "guerrillas." "Communistic propaganda and activity and a mistaken idea of their recently acquired independence on the part of many Koreans are big causes of much of the disturbed conditions here," wrote Miss Florence. "Korea's troubles have only just begun, I fear. But with it all the opportunities to preach and teach are unlimited, and we feel the urgency of working 'while it is yet day, because the night cometh when no man can work.'"[15]

The missionaries circulated stories about the struggles raging between local Korean Christians and their communist enemies. Emily Winn reported that in one place, "a highly honored Elder, who was much better off than most of the Koreans, was terribly beaten up by some young communists on two charges: one that he was a rich man, and the other that he was a Christian." Miss Winn made no bones about the Christians' fighting back:[16]

An encouraging thing happened in a village six miles out...where the communists had grown strong and no church services had been held for some

12. William A. Linton, "Dear Friends" letter October 4, 1947, Presbyterian Church (U.S.A.), Department of History, Montreat, North Carolina.

13. Ibid.

14. Though the missionaries sided strongly against the leftists, they were aware of the haphazard quality of law enforcement under the Americans and the Korean constabulary and police, and they intervened upon occasion. "The other day Rob [Knox] was able to get a Christian released from jail who had been arrested as a Communist. Rob told the American police adviser that this man was not a Communist, was a good Christian and that he had known him all his life. The adviser immediately ordered his release. This was Cho Il Whan, the son of an elder, known and beloved by all the missionaries." Maie Knox, letter, August 27, 1947.

15. Florence Root, "Dear Friends" letter, September 1, 1948, Presbyterian Church (U.S.A.), Department of History, Montreat, North Carolina.

16. Ibid.

time. When the communists there attacked and injured the police, the whole village rose up and drove them completely out of that neighborhood. The women of the village, we were told, were so aroused they, themselves, chopped away at the supporting pillars of the communists' homes and made the houses collapse, while the men of the place ran them out of town. The church is opened again and Christians are worshipping unmolested.[17]

The 1948 Election

In 1947 the arrangements for joint administration of the Korean peninsula by the United States and the Soviet Union finally broke down. After having been divided into occupation zones for two years, North and South Korea began moving toward the establishment of two permanent regimes north and south of the 38th parallel. The Soviet Union, backing the leftist Korean faction headed by Kim Il-sung in P'yŏngyang, professed opposition to the idea of separate regimes. The United States, backing rightist factions in the south and facing rising political pressure within the United States for a firm stand against communist expansion, proposed a Korea-wide plebiscite to be managed by the United Nations, to establish the machinery for a constitutional assembly and the construction of a democratic government. The Soviet Union and the North Koreans, believing the United Nations to be under American domination and suspecting a plot to use the population advantage in the south to win the election for the right-wing, balked and refused to cooperate. When the United Nations election commission arrived to begin organizing the plebiscite, the P'yŏngyang regime barred its members from crossing northward across the 38th parallel. UN-sponsored elections, therefore, went forward only in southern Korea. Despite the lack of North Korean participation, the United Nations, clearly under American direction, went on to recognize the legitimacy of the political process in the southern zone that created the Republic of Korea with its president Syngman Rhee and its capital in Seoul.

Primarily because of their own refusal to be part of this process, the leftists under the P'yŏngyang regime were left out of the process and actively opposed it. Looking south, they were alarmed at the way the American occupation had tolerated Japanese collaborators and allowed the Syngman Rhee group to take a commanding position in southern politics. They were disgusted that Syngman Rhee unceasingly claimed credentials as a nationalist even though his group contained many landlords, businessmen, and officials who had prospered under the Japanese regime. Charging that Rhee was conniving with the Americans to split Korea permanently in order to keep these people in power, the North Koreans set out to disrupt the South Korean elections of 1948.

17. Emily Winn, "Dear Friends Back Home" letter, August 12, 1948, Presbyterian Church (U.S.A.), Department of History, Montreat, North Carolina.

In the two Chŏlla Provinces, the Southern Presbyterians carried on their mission work amid the worst of the violence. Every week brought rumors of police officers being killed by communists in this or that village, and police actions aimed at arresting and sometimes killing communists.

The election process was designed to proceed by stages through the spring and summer of 1948, with May 10 as the date for the election of representatives to a legislative assembly, local leaders who would meet in Seoul to write a constitution and elect a president.[18] As the process developed, voters across the southern zone, men and women, chose their representatives as planned, the representatives met in Seoul, and after a certain amount of wrangling and a tense choice between Syngman Rhee and Kim Ku for president, Syngman Rhee was inaugurated on the steps of the former Government-General Building on August 15, the third anniversary of liberation from Japan. General Hodge relinquished his authority to President Syngman Rhee, the Republic of Korea was recognized by the Western

18. The U.S. Military Government in Korea originally set the date for Sunday, May 9, whereupon the Christian community, like the Christian community in North Korea in the elections of 1946, protested having to vote on Sunday. American missionaries were particularly voluble in expressing to the U.S. military the inappropriateness of scheduling an election on Sunday.

In a dispatch to Washington, State Department advisor (and former U.S. consul-general in Seoul) William Langdon reported that Roscoe C. Coen, claiming to represent the Northern and Southern Presbyterians, the United Church of Canada, the Salvation Army, and the Methodists, had visited him to demand that the date be changed. Langdon's reaction was not unlike that of O. Gaylord Marsh, U.S. consul-general in the late 1930s, when the American missionaries in Korea were asserting religious principles against decisions by the then-government. He wrote,

"General Hodge is ignoring these petitions since proclaimed date cannot be changed in any event as [the] election date was determined after consideration by experts of all factors that might contribute to [the] widest possible participation in [the] election, and in agreement with UNTCOK [the UN election commission] as well as in consultation with Korean political leaders. The possibility of criticisms from [a] religious viewpoint of [the] selection of [the] Sabbath for [the] election was not overlooked. However, Christian communities in Korea [are] relatively tiny although extremely influential and esteemed, and it was not allowable that the possible hurt to religious scruples of [a] small part of this community should override all other considerations mentioned.

"General Hodge feels that the association of certain American Protestant groups with native groups opposing [the] election proclamation is not helpful to [the] present critical and difficult task of United States in Korea and suggests that [the] Department in its discretion may wish to discuss with [the] home [mission] boards this activity of their local representatives. Reverend Coen [has] also associated himself with [a] petition of [the] Korean National Christian Council to the United Nations Temporary [Election] Commission."

(Acting U.S. Political Advisor to SecState March 10, 1948 [National Archives and Records Service, Department of State file number 895.00/3-948]).

democracies, and the new American Ambassador, John J. Muccio, became the senior American official in Korea.

Throughout the election campaign, leftists kept up their violent efforts to block the creation of a separate state in South Korea. In Kwangju, Florence Root was glad for the patrols of American soldiers and Korean constabulary but noted that out beyond the suburbs, railroad bridges and telephone lines had been "injured by communists" and that mail service was more irregular than ever.[19] In Taegu, U.S. Army authorities told the Northern Presbyterian missionaries to stay indoors through Election Day to avoid entanglement in the "labor troubles" that were plaguing the city at the time. Apparently they did so: missionary sources say little about the way the power lines were cut along with rail and telegraph lines on May 8, the same day a leftist newspaper was blown up; or how fighting broke out on May 9, with more deaths and arrests; or how on election day itself the electric power was sabotaged and youthful demonstrators on both sides were shot, both by police and by each other.

Given the atmosphere of American politics at the dawn of the cold war, it is not hard to see why Christians would have chosen sides against communism. In Korea, however, a certain irony attaches to the fact that many of the Westerners who knew the country best and once had run considerable risks to resist Japanese curbs on freedom of religion and had loathed the colonial regime for the violence it committed against the Koreans, did not question the use of violence by American forces and the police and constabulary under the U.S. Military Government as the appropriate means to deal with peasant dissension. Communism seemed to be a worldwide infection that had spread to Korea, and its agents were not to be considered players in Korean politics or to have a voice in their country's future. Communist terror tactics in Korea presented a problem that was to become familiar by the end of the twentieth century. The response then was the same as the response later on. There would be no negotiating with terrorists. Unfortunately this also meant resistance to discussing the grievances that lay behind the choice of terror tactics.

19. Florence Root, "Dear Friends" letter, May 10, 1948, Presbyterian Church (U.S.A.), Department of History, Montreat, North Carolina.

-- 16 --

Soldiers of Freedom

In 1994, the South Korean government opened a grand-scale War Memorial museum on the site of the former Japanese army regimental headquarters in Seoul, to honor the Republic's military and identify the South Korean cause in the Korean War with the heroic military traditions of the ancient Korean kingdoms of Koguryŏ, Silla, Koryŏ, and Chosŏn.[1]

The museum is a tour de force of signs and symbols. Its heroic exterior is reminiscent of the architecture of Mussolini's Italy, masculine and intended to inspire a feeling of pride and triumph. Inside the building, the exhibits are arranged to establish a sense of the Korean military as the defenders of Korean national identity, and they are stunningly effective. Ultimately, however, the subject of the museum is the South Korean military as national savior in the late twentieth century, and here the exhibits are remarkable for what they omit. For example, there is virtually no mention of the Allied effort in defeating Japan and liberating Korea during World War II (though due credit is given to the United Nations and United States for participation in the Korean War itself).

In the museum version of history, the South Korean Army is descended from the China-based Kwangbok and Tongnip armies, its officers and men veterans of campaigns fought shoulder-to-shoulder with the Nationalist Chinese against Japan during World War II. Though photographs in the exhibits show the Korean soldiers in Japanese-style uniforms, there is little else to indicate that many of them actually served in the Japanese imperial forces and not in Korean or Chinese units. Nor does the museum account for the fact that it was American advisors who chose South Korea's first army officers in 1945-46. Or that it was a pragmatic American decision to

1. For the War Memorial museum, see Sheila Miyoshi Jager, "Manhood, the State and the Yongsan War Memorial, South Korea," *Museum Anthropology: Journal for the Council of Museum Anthropology*, XXI:3 (1997), pp. 33-39.

find the best officer material available without regard to the fact that many of the most promising candidates had recently served in the Japanese armed forces.

The Korean Constabulary

The objective of the U.S. Military Government in Korea was to contain communist expansion at all costs and win the hearts and minds of the Korean people if possible. However, the Americans often had to resort to force simply to keep the peace. In order to do this, they created a national police force and a military constabulary, predecessors of South Korea's National Police (KNP) and the Republic of Korea Army (ROKA). The Americans sought experienced policemen for the KNP—veterans of the Japanese colonial police who had been trained by the Japanese to use Japanese methods such as torture and thought control. The Americans created the constabulary to assist and protect the KNP, having discovered that the police were widely hated as Japanese collaborators. For the constabulary, they recruited officers from private armies that had been organized by certain wealthy Koreans essentially as bodyguards, from among former members of the China-based Kwangbok Army, and from the ranks of Korean officers who had served in Japanese military. Because they had better experience, the Japanese-trained officers soon emerged as the constabulary elite.[2] In order to train them in American weapons and tactics the Americans taught them military expressions in English at a language school set up in December 1945, one of the schools that was eventually combined into the Korean Military Academy (KMA).[3]

2. The reasons for the Manchurian-trained officers' emerging as the best officers in the constabulary are clear enough. The private armies had little formal training and the troops from the Independence armies in China likewise were ragged in their experience. But the Japanese-trained soldiers had experience, even if very little of it was combat experience, with the Manchurian Army.

3. The school was set up in the buildings of the Methodist Theological Seminary in Naengch'ŏn-dong, where the Japanese had interned Western civilians in Seoul following the attack on Pearl Harbor.

One American officer's account serves to illustrate the training atmosphere at the Academy, as follows:

"My company ('C') was given the mission of teaching a company-sized group of Korean constabulary the nomenclature, assembly, and disassembly of the M-1 rifle. The ROKs were to be taught the English nomenclature to avoid language problems in the supply channels in future times. There were about 200 in the class. I had made several charts with the picture of the part labeled in English and Korean [*Han'gŭl* alphabet]. There were at least ten assistant instructors to help. The Hangul was great since it could convey most American sounds. Within *two days* all the Korean soldiers could disassemble and assemble the M-1 rifle calling each part by [its] proper U.S. name! There were some problems with the sounds of F and P. 'Follower' came out 'Pollower,' etc. Needless to say, I was quite impressed."

The constabulary, which was launched in mid-1946 as the Chosŏn kyŏng-bidae, was not originally meant to be a national army since South Korea was not yet a nation. Its function was strictly to keep domestic order, and the soldiers in the constabulary were trained in riot control and counterinsurgency.[4] Nor were the Americans much concerned that they were using former Japanese collaborators who had been schooled in Japanese rightwing ideology. The Americans did not blacklist everyone who had served the Japanese during the colonial period. On the contrary, since military experience was a main qualification for appointment to the constabulary and could only have been acquired under the Japanese at that time, collaboration in effect was a qualification. The Americans applied the pragmatic criterion of military ability without taking politics into account, and the Korean candidates were happy to be given a second chance at a military career. In time, mentor-protégé bonds developed between American trainers and the Korean candidates—ties that fitted both the Americans' military needs and Korean patterns of hierarchy and authority.

The Korean Constabulary existed from 1946 to 1948, when it became the Republic of Korea Army. Of the American advisors who shaped the constabulary and laid the foundation for the ROK Army, none played a more important role than James Harry Hausman, a veteran of the Battle of the Bulge who arrived in Korea in July 1946 at the age of twenty-eight.[5] When he landed in Seoul, fresh from a month of military government training at Carlisle Barracks, Captain Hausman was assigned to duty with the new constabulary's 8th Regiment in Ch'unchŏn.[6] A month later he was trans-

Lt. Col. Charles Wesolowsky USA (Ret.) to Allan R. Millett, September 16, 1995. I am indebted to Professor Millett for sharing this letter with me.

Among the school's first graduates were some of South Korea's most illustrious figures including Generals Paek Sŏnyŏp and Chŏng Ilgwŏn, future president Park Chung-hee (Pak Chŏnghŭi), and the man destined to be Park's assassin, Kim Chaegyu. Park and Kim were members of the school's second class that graduated after eighty days' training in December 1946.

4. For the early history of the Korean constabulary, see Robert K. Sawyer, *Military Advisors in Korea: KMAG in Peace and War* (Washington, D.C.: US Government Printing Office, 1969).

5. Allan R. Millett, "Captain James H. Hausman and the Formation of the Korean Army, 1945-1950," *Armed Forces and Society*, XXIII:4 (summer 1997), pp. 507-508. I am grateful to Professor Millett for his help in uncovering documents concerning James Hausman and the origins of the Korean Army, as well as to Colonel Hausman himself for lending me his papers and materials during our series of interviews in 1995 and for giving me permission to use them for this book.

6. Hausman was given a Japanese-American Nisei interpreter to help him communicate with the Koreans. In Ch'unch'ŏn his work was mainly logistical, arranging for equipment and such for the regiment. However, he also made contact with the Irish Catholic mission in Ch'unch'ŏn and formed a friendship with Father Thomas Quinlan. Quinlan, with fifteen years' experience in Korea, persuaded him to get rid of his Nisei interpreter, arguing that it would be better to speak in broken

James H. Hausman (second from right) listening to Chief of Staff Chae Pyŏngdŏk, 1950. U.S. National Archives, reproduced from Halliday and Cumings, *Korea*, p.45.

ferred to Seoul as "executive officer" to Col. Russell D. Barros, the Chief of the Korean Constabulary. He then moved up to become advisor to Brig. Gen. William L. Roberts, the constabulary commander; and finally, when the Koreans acquired their own general staff, he was assigned to be advisor to the Korean chief of the constabulary. In 1948 when South Korea became a republic and the constabulary became the ROK Army, the Americans were downgraded from occupiers to advisors. Hausman became part of the Provisional Military Advisory Group (PMAG, pronounced "P-mag"), forerunner of the better-known Korea Military Advisory Group (KMAG, pronounced "Kaymag"), with a position as advisor to the ROK Army Chief of Staff. By this time Hausman had earned a solid reputation not only as an outstanding army organizer but also as someone who got along well with Koreans and understood them well enough to get things done, a rare and vital quality in the U.S. Military Government.[7]

Korean, English, or even GI pidgin than to speak Japanese to the Koreans. Hausman repaid Fr. Quinlan's good advice by getting him access to the Army PX system. (James H. Hausman, transcript of a 1988 interview with author John Toland in the Hausman papers, now at the Korea Institute, Harvard University.)

7. Brigadier General William L. Roberts to the commanding general, U.S. Army Forces in Korea, "Award of the Legion of Merit, Recommendation for Hausman, Capt. James Harry, 10 January 1949," in the Hausman papers.

Hausman thus became the link between the U.S. Army and the South Korean military. He was completely attuned to American objectives in Korea and considered himself a thoroughly patriotic soldier. He stopped counting the days until the end of his Korean tour and settled down to make Korea his home. Working with the Korean constabulary gave him an important job to do in the peacetime army. American officers never went beyond speaking pidgin Korean and indeed, Hausman never became fluent in the language, but he learned enough to recognize what was being said around him and he could communicate using a Korean-English officers' patois that was sufficient for daily work and friendships. More important, he learned how to convey his own sincerity. Other Americans shunned Korean food, but Hausman liked it. He crisscrossed the country, traversing muddy tracks in his Jeep, fording rivers, balancing on paddy dikes, and clinging to cliff-sides to reach remote locations and meet the soldiers in the field. He learned to sleep on hot Korean *ŏndol* floors, to sit through endless ceremonial meals (and drinking sessions), and to take his turn singing for group entertainment. He marched and ran with the troops, engaged in wrestling and strength tests, told jokes, and established a reputation as a sincere and understanding American officer.

Hausman nurtured the Korean constabulary from a desk in the office of General Song Hosŏng, the constabulary's first chief.[8] On his first field tour as advisor to General Song, Hausman drove his own jeep to visit every one of the *kyŏngbidae*'s fifteen regiments.[9] One of his top concerns was the way the rivalry between the police and the military was becoming a nationwide turf battle. Another was the discovery that entire counties of certain provinces were not under central control but were ruled by local leaders and in some cases by people he took to be communists. The worst areas

8. Song Hosŏng was a veteran of the Kwangbok Army in China, a former constabulary section chief appointed by the Americans to be the chief of staff. Song's reputation in Korea is tarnished by the fact that after his capture during the North Korean invasion in 1950 he was heard on the radio making speeches supporting the Kim Il-sung regime. Hausman believes that he was forced to make the broadcasts, but Koreans consider him a communist for having done it. Jim Hausman and Chŏng Ilhwa, *Han'guk Taet'ongnyŏng'ŭl umjigin migun taewi Hausman* (Seoul: Han'guk Munwŏn, 1995), pp. 140-148, and Hausman interview, Austin, Texas, August 5, 1995.

9. Hausman was accompanied by Yi Hyŏnggun, a graduate of the Japanese Imperial Military Academy, who spoke English and was a favorite of the U.S. advisors. He rose by 1947 to the rank of brigadier general at the age of 28. (His father-in-law was Yi Ungjun, the former Japanese army colonel who advised Col. John Marshall, the first chief of the Korean constabulary, on selection of the first 110 Korean Military Academy students and later served briefly as the ROK Army chief of staff.) Millett, "Captain James H. Hausman and the Formation of the Korean Army, 1945-1950," pp. 511-512.

were in the southwest near the Chiri Mountains. The Chiri Mountains, which divide southwest Korea from the southeast, are connected to the main mountain ranges that form the spiny backbone of the Korean peninsula. High along this north-south mountain system ran trails that formed a transportation and communication system between the Soviet-occupied north and the American-occupied south. Along the trail traveled agents, organizers, supplies, and weapons, reinforcing the local resistance to government control deep in South Korean territory. Hausman's trip taught him something of the difficulty of controlling the Korean countryside and impressed upon him the importance of discipline and loyalty among the units assigned to the southern provinces. It also gave him a chance to meet the man who would be his best Korean friend for more than thirty years, Chŏng Ilgwŏn, commanding officer of the constabulary's 4th Regiment at Kwangju.[10]

Hausman also discovered the presence within the constabulary of a large number of leftist soldiers and officers who had not been screened for political reliability. General Hodge and the top command at Military Government headquarters had decreed a rapid expansion of the constabulary with little attention to the political associations of the men. This was understandably the result of the Americans' frustration with the mélange of political groups that had blossomed after Liberation, but it set the constabulary up to be divided between left and right. Hausman's American bosses did not have much patience for his warnings about leftists in the constabulary because they sounded like the all-too-familiar complaints that flowed from the right-wing National Police. However, Hausman realized that the constabulary members themselves constantly were having to test each other's loyalties, creating tensions that complicated the constabulary's inner workings from the start. The officer training school's second class in particular was afflicted by this left-right schism, with graduates who were actually part of the South Korean Labor Party.[11]

But under orders from the top the constabulary kept expanding, from 5,000 men to 25,000 and then 50,000. U.S. advisors organized recruiting teams to attract men to the ranks, and the teams competed with each other for numbers, with the Americans continuing to ignore the recruits' politics.

10. Chŏng Ilgwŏn was a northerner who attended the Canadian Mission's Myongdong Academy in Lungchingtsun and who later served in the Japanese Manchurian Army. Hausman was so impressed with him that he had him transferred up to Seoul when he got back and installed him as the constabulary's vice-chief. Hausman had been looking for someone compatible with himself for the number two staff position, since it was clear that the chief's job was going to be a political football and no one was going to occupy it long enough to become really effective. The continuity and stability would have to be at the vice-chief level, and Hausman and Chŏng occupied offices across the hall from each other. James Hausman, interview, Austin, Texas, Sept. 5, 1995.

11. Millett, "Captain James H. Hausman," pp. 513-514.

As Hausman explained it, "The Korean idea of checking every recruit, police records, local files from the
man's village, talk to the village elders, who could
vouch for a given family many generations back—this
was much too slow. We actually created a safe haven for
communists [and] we suffered the ill effects of this
many times in the months and years ahead."[12]

James H. Hausman
(1960s). Internet
photograph.

Nor were a few weeks of American training enough
to change the Korean military culture that had been
created largely by the Japanese. Infiltrating the mascu-
line military culture of the Korean Constabulary was Hausman's special tal-
ent, but there were times when he recoiled at the Koreans' own harsh
methods. He disliked the beatings that were Standard Operating Procedure when officers wanted to punish enlisted men. Caught between American and Japanese/Korean military cultures, he suggested a choice: instead
of being whacked across the stomach with a baseball bat, let the culprit
choose a loss of pay, jail time, and/or a black mark on his military record.
Hausman was surprised to observe that the men always chose the whack.[13]

Writing discipline manuals was one of Hausman's jobs as he sat at his
desk in the constabulary Chief's office. One of these was the protocol for
firing squads. Once he had the Signal Corps film an execution to have a record of the proper procedure. In this silent 16-millimeter movie, a truck
bearing five prisoners, constabulary soldiers who have been found to be
communists, enters the execution ground at Susaek, west of Seoul. The
prisoners look like university students, clean-cut and intelligent, some
wearing glasses. They are wearing white prisoners' garb, and their hands
are tied. As they are led to the edge of the field to be tied to a row of posts in
the ground, one asks for a moment to speak to Hausman. He is Lt. Col. Kim
Chŏngsuk, an intelligence officer who had worked with Hausman from the
earliest days of the Korean Constabulary and who had been regarded by
the Americans as prime officer material until he was exposed as a left-wing
plotter.[14] A military policeman leads Kim to Hausman and Kim apologizes,
saying, "I'm sorry for all the trouble I have caused you." Then he and the
others are tied to the posts and small targets are pinned over their hearts.

12. James Hausman, Toland interview transcript, p. 37, in the Hausman papers.
Colonel Terrill ("Terrible") Price, in charge of the recruitment effort, gave prizes to
the recruiting teams that brought in the most men, but he made little effort to check
the backgrounds of the new recruits. James Hausman, interview, August 5, 1995.

13. James Hausman, interview, Austin, Texas, August 19, 1995, and note cards
for a speech on the early days of the constabulary (no date), in the Hausman
papers.

14. Hausman, interview, August 19, 1999; also "My Early Days in Korea," type-
script in the Hausman papers at the Korea Institute, Harvard University, p. 6. Kim
Chongsuk was assigned to be the Korean Constabulary's first chief of intelligence
(G-2) when Hausman started building the KC Headquarters staff in 1946.

In Hausman's narration of the film they sing "the North Korean national anthem" following which five-man squads face each prisoner, take aim, and fire. As they slump to the ground a constabulary officer strides smartly toward them and administers the *coup de grace* to each.[15]

Hausman's staff work taught him much about the Korean personnel, values and traits, and the degree to which American ways could be adapted to Korean organizations. Knowing the officers who commanded the constabulary's fifteen regiments meant repeated trips out into the provinces on the country's dirt-and-gravel roads. As the local units built airstrips, Hausman started flying in PMAG's tiny spotter planes, two-seater L-5's that flew at less than a hundred miles per hour and could be maneuvered at tree-top level down narrow valleys to put down on abbreviated landing strips and even, when necessary, on roads. Since they belonged to PMAG, the L-5's bore American markings, something that seemed to discourage guerrillas in the countryside from taking potshots at them as they flew overhead. On one occasion, however, PMAG headquarters ordered a change in the markings, even on planes manned by Americans, to the Korean *taegŭk* symbol. The planes with Korean markings drew much more fire from the ground. Hausman's plane was hit one day, and after landing he found a bullet hole in the belly of the plane—but no corresponding bullet hole out the top. The bullet was found lodged in the folded parachute under Hausman's seat.[16] U.S. Army insignia were quickly repainted on his plane.

As the time approached for the 1948 election in South Korea, no area was more beset by violence than South Chŏlla Province and the island of Cheju, sixty miles off the Chŏlla coast. At the time, Cheju was undergoing a demographic ordeal. Under Japanese rule, many islanders had been recruited for hard labor in Japan, so that by 1938 as many as 50,000 islanders were living in the Osaka area alone. Push factors accounted for this out flux, since the Japanese neglected the island's primitive economy and a late 1930s development plan was never put into effect.[17]

After Liberation, many natives of Cheju Island returned home to unemployment and hopeless futures, ripe for recruitment into an antigovernment resistance. The island's population suddenly swelled to almost 300,000, completely disrupting the economy. Meanwhile, though the island's resident Japanese were taken home by ship, the U.S. Military Gov-

15. Hausman, interviews, August 5 and 19, 1995; Toland interview, p. 70; and VHS videotape made from 16mm Army Signal Corps film showing scenes of Hausman's early years in Korea, in Hausman's memorabilia in Austin, Texas. The film presents a scene reminiscent of photos taken of Japanese gendarmes executing white-clad Korean "righteous troops" in the protectorate years of 1904-05.

16. James Hausman, interview, Austin, Texas, August 5, 1995.

17. Hermann Lautensach, *Korea*, trans. Katherine and Eckert Dege (Helmstedt, Germany: Springer-Verlag, 1988), pp. 378-379.

ernment was slow to establish a presence on Cheju, leaving ample time for the villagers to be organized by leftist elements into autonomous people's committees (*inmin wiwŏnhoe*). Disbanding these and reestablishing central government authority on Cheju proved to be a daunting task that was not fully accomplished for many years.

For the first five months of 1948, all politics in South Korea became focused on the national elections that were destined to create the Republic of Korea. Pak Hŏnyŏng, the leader of the South Korean Workers' Party, had been in North Korea since the autumn uprising of 1946, sending orders from his base in Haeju. In February he called a general strike in the South, which produced four days of work stoppages, rallies, and sabotage, challenging the U.S. Military Government's ability to keep order. On Cheju Island, strikers attacked police stations after police had seized Workers' Party membership lists, setting off a much longer period of turmoil. Units of an ad-hoc "People's Liberation Army" that earlier had been active in uprisings in South Kyŏngsang Province, rose up on Cheju armed with old Japanese rifles, grenades, swords, and even farm tools, and began attacking government installations and right-wing youth elements who were ferried to the island to stop them.[18]

The youth elements included groups from the notorious Northwest Youth Corps (*Sŏbuk ch'ŏngnyŏnhoe*), which included refugees from North Korea, some of them Christians, who were motivated by a blood debt against the communists and were fully committed to wiping them out wherever they could be found. Organized partly as a response to the late 1946 uprisings in the Taegu area, the youth corps were funded by the U.S. military as well as by right-wing political groups and wealthy individuals who feared communism most and were determined to maintain the South as a sanctuary from communist rule. American authorities knew that the South Korean propertied class was behind the right-wing youth who operated like Chiang Kai-shek's Blue Shirts in China or Hitler's Brown Shirts, intimidating people who otherwise did not fear the police.

On Cheju Island the Northwest Youth earned a fearsome reputation. In 1947, the Korean police dispatched an 800-man youth contingent to Cheju to help deal with violence related to a March First independence holiday celebration. The Northwest Youth took out their anger on anyone suspected of being a communist sympathizer. Beginning as government-spon-

---

18. Jim Hausman explained that the sudden appearance of so many weapons on Cheju Island came from the fact that after the American occupation authorities had found stockpiled Japanese weapons and ammunition in the island's mountain caves and had dumped the materiel into the sea, island residents surreptitiously recovered them. "Cheju-do is famous for its women divers, and the communists made good use of them. They had them dive and recover considerable weapons and ammunition. This was used against the ROK troops (the 9th Regiment)." Hausman, Toland interview transcript, p. 15, in the Hausman papers.

sored thugs, they quickly evolved into organized criminals who engaged in protection rackets and terrorized the populace. It is no surprise that leftist organizers had little trouble finding volunteers to fight as antigovernment guerrillas on the slopes of Mt. Halla, the island's great volcano.

The main guerrilla attack began on April 3, 1948, when the SKWP's forces came down the slopes of Mt. Halla to attack the police.[19] Enjoying the support of an estimated 80 percent of the island's people and with help from the self-defense units of the island's people's committees and defectors from the Korean Constabulary, their attack posed a formidable challenge to the central government. However, the guerrillas retreated to the slopes after the initial attack, allowing time for the government, still under American occupation control, to respond. The Americans ordered three thousand police and constabulary troops to the island, many of whom were captured in the fighting, subjected to people's trials, and executed, sometimes reportedly by women "who had suffered most from them."[20] There were reprisals as government troops swept the larger towns looking for communist sympathizers and engaging in counterterror. At night within their sandbag forts on the mountainside, however, they shivered in fear of guerrilla attacks.

In Seoul, American authorities were alarmed that the situation on Cheju was so far out of control. Maj. Gen. William F. Dean, the military governor, flew to the island on an inspection trip and then dispatched more constabulary troops. American advisors accompanied them as they slowly fought to gain the upper hand. Jim Hausman recalled the view from headquarters in Seoul:

> General Roberts flew to Cheju-do to pin the Third Mugunghwa (colonel's rank) on the Ninth [constabulary] Regiment's commander. That night an NCO [non-commissioned officer in the constabulary] (a communist) killed the colonel as he slept. Needless to say, General Roberts refrained from taking part in all future ROKA promotions.

> Then there was the occasion when ROKA personnel on Cheju-do speared to death about twenty civilians (allegedly communists) without benefit of trial. Unfortunately, a picture was taken and later was given to Ambassador Muccio. I might add, a KMAG sergeant had witnessed this act and he was plainly recognizable in that picture. I was ordered to report to the Ambassador. When confronted with the facts about this incident I told the Ambassador that this was a good sign because in the past, similar groups of two

19. Standard accounts of the Cheju Island rebellion are John Merrill, "The Cheju-do Rebellion," *The Journal of Korean Studies,* II (1980), pp. 139-197, and Cumings, *The Origins of the Korean War,* Vol. II, pp. 250-267. For the standard American military account (and the role of James Hausman), see Sawyer, *Military Advisors in Korea,* pp. 39-40.

20. This account follows John Merrill, *Korea: The Peninsular Origins of the War* (Newark, Del.: University of Delaware Press, 1989), pp. 65-68 and passim.

hundred or more had been summarily executed—and now the number was down to twenty. This was progress. I won't repeat the Ambassador's reply to me—I wouldn't want to give you the impression that he was short-tempered and uncouth.

Ironically, the greatest guerrilla leader [in all Korea] was a native of Cheju-do —Kim Chi Hae. ROK troops chased him and his band of guerrillas throughout the Chiri-san area for many months. When his capture appeared imminent, we issued strict instructions to bring his body to Seoul. (It was customary to mutilate bodies and display them for people to see. In addition, we ceased insisting on capture as this caused too many friendly casualties.) One morning I found a square five-gallon gas can in my office. On inspection, I found it contained one highly bloated human head—Kim Chi Hae's.[21]

Trouble raged on Cheju Island for the rest of 1948 and early 1949, and when it was over it had taken the lives of an estimated thirty thousand islanders, mostly men, about 10 percent of the total population. Through the summer and fall of 1948, responsibility for the suppression of the insurrection on Cheju passed from the U.S. Army to the Republic of Korea Government under President Syngman Rhee. In the fall, Rhee ordered additional units of the Korean Constabulary to Cheju Island to join in the fight. These included a part of the 14th Infantry Regiment in the south coast port of Yŏsu, immediately across from Cheju. The 14th Infantry was one of the units that had worried Jim Hausman because of the way it had been put together, helter-skelter, with no review for the new recruits' political reliability.

There were a number of trouble signs surrounding the 14th Regiment in October 1948. The men had just been issued a supply of American-made rifles (M-1s) and ammunition to add to their existing Japanese arsenal. Though it was known that the ranks contained a potentially troublesome number of leftists and even Communists, the high command issued the new weapons in the belief that the officers could keep the men in line, and because the unit was about to be dispatched to Cheju for suppression duty.

21. Hausman, "My Earliest Memories of Korea," typescript, pp. 47-48, in the Hausman papers. "Kim Chi Hae" in Hausman's account is almost certainly Kim Chihoe, a leading figure in the guerrilla warfare that followed the Yŏsu-Sunch'ŏn rebellion in the Chiri Mountains. He was killed in a government raid on April 9, 1949. Merrill, *Korea: The Peninsular Origins of the War*, pp. 120 and 122. Memories differ on the identity of the guerrilla whose head was presented to Hausman. Some recall that it was that of Kim Talsam, organizer of the Cheju branch of the Korean "People's Liberation Army" in 1947 and the architect of the support system by which the Communist guerrillas were sustained by villagers throughout the island. Kim Talsam eluded capture on Cheju and went on to fight for months during 1949-50 in the mountains of Kangwŏn Province. He was killed by government troops while trying to cross into North Korea on March 21, 1950 (Cumings, *The Origins of the Korean War*, Vol. II, p. 403). Thanks to Professor Allan Millett for drawing my attention to this alternative version of the story.

334 Living Dangerously in Korea

The regimental commander, Major Oh Tonggil, was a notorious rightist and supporter of Syngman Rhee's archrival Kim Ku. Major Oh was suddenly removed from his command on October 5, 1948, and charged with plotting a coup. This gave the left-wing soldiers in the ranks a golden opportunity to organize their comrades, drawing, ironically, on the support of right-wing soldiers who were loyal to Kim Ku and Major Oh. In mid-October the order came down for two battalions of the 14th Regiment to embark for Cheju Island. Shortly thereafter, the regiment rose up in rebellion.

No more than forty men began the mutiny that started on the night of October 19, 1948, but within hours they had murdered a number of their officers and gathered several thousand supporters, both soldiers and civilians. Encouraged by local people who turned out to cheer and wave them on with red flags, they attacked the police headquarters, helped themselves to the weapons, and then sent a trainload of rebels inland to the city of Sunch'ŏn. There they attacked the police headquarters and government tax and post offices, as well as the government school, robbed the bank, and then set up their headquarters with the North Korean flag flying. As the rebellion spread across the area, people's committees were formed, people's courts were convened, and posses went to impose revolutionary justice on landlords, rich merchants, government officials, and former Japanese collaborators.

In Seoul, General Roberts ordered Jim Hausman into the air at the head of an American team headed for Kwangju and Yŏsu. Hausman's mission was to take operational control of the suppression of the rebellion if he thought the Korean command was taking insufficient action, to establish and run a task force headquarters, to report to Seoul, and to create and execute a plan to overcome the rebellion.[22] Hausman's counterpart, Korean Constabulary Chief Song Hosŏng, was instructed by General Roberts to recapture Sunch'ŏn and Yŏsu without delay. "The liberation of these cities from the rebel forces will be moral and political victories of great propa-

---

22. "The choice of Jim Hausman as senior advisor was based on two points: (1) he was the Advisor to the Commanding General, Korean Constabulary, (2) his long association with the Korean Constabulary, his knowledge of their strength and weaknesses to include most of the Korean officers." Roberts to CG USAFIK, "Award of the Legion of Merit, Recommendation for Hausman, James Harry," 10 January 1949, in the Hausman papers.

Hausman earlier had asked General William F. Dean, the military governor, whether he should hesitate to give orders to officers of the newly established Republic of Korea's constabulary instead of merely "advising" them. The situation apparently called for abandoning pretenses, for General Dean replied, "You will advise the Koreans in such a manner as to assure that they carry out your orders." (James Hausman, note cards for a speech on the early days of the constabulary, in the Hausman papers.)

ganda value. You should therefore put a first priority on an operation to liberate both these cities."[23]

The Americans landed at Kwangju to news from the local commander that the units that had already been sent to Yŏsu had been "lost," much to Hausman's disgust. It was said that the entire 14th was in revolt, and that the 4th Regiment in Kwangju was not going to be reliable because its men were disloyal. "In essence," wrote Hausman, "all hell had broken loose and we had nothing at hand to stop the onslaught."[24]

With Chŏng Ilgwŏn and Paek Sŏnyŏp, his two most trusted Korean officers, Hausman conferred with the American advisors stationed in Kwangju. They ordered the rails ripped up north of Sunch'ŏn to keep the rebels from using trains to get any farther than they had on the first night of the rebellion. Before long the "lost" units were found in the hills west of Sunch'ŏn, where they had gone instead of attacking the city. They had not obeyed orders, but they also had not defected to the side of the mutineers, much to Hausman's relief. On October 21 the Task Force commanders decided to send General Song at the head of a hastily constructed patchwork of Korean Constabulary units to Sunch'ŏn, and to move units into the area from the north and east. On the 23rd the Army closed in on Sunch'ŏn, taking the city in the mid-afternoon and discovering that the mutineers had killed as many as five hundred police and civilians, including women and children. Government troops pursued the rebels toward Yŏsu, taking the high ground to the north of the city by the afternoon of the 25th and continuing the attack on the 26th and 27th, when they reported the city retaken in the afternoon. There were many casualties, and upwards of two thousand prisoners were taken. As many as a thousand rebels escaped into the hills, being seen heading toward Paegun-san, northeast of Sunch'ŏn, and the Chiri mountains, where they stayed, just as Hausman had feared,

---

23. The legal basis for Americans commanding Korean forces in the early days of the Republic was an agreement between General John R. Hodge and President Syngman Rhee, signed on August 24, 1948, "whereby the ROK Government would gradually assume command of the nation's security forces. Until the task was completed and the American troops withdrew from Korea, the United States would retain operational control of the Korean forces." Sawyer, *Military Advisors in Korea*, p. 34. This should be remembered as a precedent for the "Taejŏn Agreement" of July 1950 whereby the American commanding general of the UN Command took operational control of South Korean armed forces during wartime.

The Korean Constabulary officially became the Republic of Korea Army on 15 December 1948 following enactment of the ROK Armed Forces Organization Act the previous month, legislation that created the ROK Ministry of National Defense and the ROK Army and Navy.

24. "History of the Rebellion, 14th Constabulary Regiment," written but not signed by James Hausman, in the Hausman papers.

for the better part of a decade.[25]

Blood and Water in Sunch'ŏn

Sunch'ŏn was a Southern Presbyterian Mission station, and six missionaries lived through the Yŏsu/Sunch'ŏn uprising. The morning of October 20 brought the sound of small arms and mortar fire as the train full of rebels from Yŏsu pulled into the station. Many teenaged students from Sunch'ŏn joined the rebels as they attacked the police. Elmer Boyer, who was in charge of the mission's leprosarium near Yŏsu but lived in Sunch'ŏn, accidentally drove into the fighting on his way to work that morning and quickly turned around. Over the next several days mortar shells fell on the mission compound. Bullets scarred the houses and drilled holes in Boyer's Ford, but none of the Americans was hurt.

When the ROK soldiers came into Sunch'ŏn to enforce order, the missionaries opened their homes to their American advisors. Elmer Boyer cooked for them in the kitchen of the compound's "saxie house." "I am running a 'Mess Hall' and Billet for the American men, advisors to the Korean Army," he wrote. "We have had as many as fourteen, and will have a few for some time." The Americans took to the roof of John and Florence Crane's house waving a bedsheet at low-flying government spotter planes, wanting to show that the mission compound was friendly territory and inhabited by American citizens who needed quick relief. A flag would have been better, but there was none until Louise Miller, Janet Crane, and Meta Biggar fashioned the Stars and Stripes from red cloth and some blue-and-white feed sacks. They named the flag "Betsy" and photographs of it became staples of the news coverage that followed when Sunch'ŏn became accessible to American reporters.[26]

Boyer wrote,

> Had the National Army been a day later coming in, we would likely not have survived....Most of the police were killed and hundreds of civilians. In one

25. Headquarters, U.S. Army Forces Korea, "G-2 Periodic Report, March 18, 1948 to December 12, 1948," facsimile in *Chuhanmigun chŏngbo ilchi* (Ch'unch'ŏn: Institute of Asian Culture Studies, Hallym University, 1990), pp. 531-559.

In Hausman's opinion, the Yŏsu mutiny had been in the planning stages when headquarters ordered the battalions to Cheju Island. The plotters had been forced to begin their uprising prematurely, greatly reducing their chances for success against superior Army forces. However, their purpose had not been to take over the army in South Chŏlla or to start a general uprising. Hausman believed that their intention had been to put well-armed guerrillas in unit strength into the Chiri Mountains, positioned to help North Korean forces if there ever was an invasion of the South. In this respect, therefore, Hausman saw the mutiny as a partial success. James Hausman, Toland interview transcript, p. 13, in the Hausman papers.

26. Meta Biggar, "Dear Friends" letter, November 3, 1948, in the Presbyterian Church (U.S.A.), Department of History, Montreat, North Carolina.

pile of bodies, where they had been shot, bound and tied in bunches of about ten, I counted ninety-eight five days after they had been shot. In the Police yard, there were about eighty bodies. I have several pictures of this group, mainly policemen. Just below our house, twenty-four were shot. I buried these and another Christian young man together in a long grave near here. There were many small groups of dead scattered all over Soonchun. Well, that is over, and all this part of Korea seems to be under control.[27]

Florence Root passed along what was to become the most famous missionary story of the rebellion.

Horrible atrocities have been committed causing sorrow and suffering in many families. In one community alone, twenty-five or more Christian homes were burned. But the testimony of our Leper Colony's pastor and his two sons is one to thrill and inspire the hearts of all of us. Many of their schoolmates were incited by communistic teachers to kill the Christian boys. When one boy started to kill the oldest son, he called him by name saying he was not afraid to die because he knew Christ as his Savior and urging him too, to turn to Christ for salvation. The second son ran to protect his brother, saying he had done nothing wrong, and asking them to kill him instead. Both died as real witnesses for Jesus. [After the rebellion] Their father went to the home of his son's murderer, who was imprisoned awaiting the death penalty, to try to comfort those parents and lead them to Christ. He even urged the police to pardon the boy and put him in his care that he might train him in the true faith, a faith that brings life and not death to all it touches. The police did not consent to this plan, but were deeply impressed with the witness of this bereaved father. Out of this new testing may the Korean Church emerge cleansed and strengthened to bring glory to their great Head.[28]

According to the missionaries, the weeks following the rebellion saw a resurgence in the Christian churches of South Chŏlla province. In Sunch'ŏn itself, where many had been attacked, robbed, or taxed by the incoming armies on both sides, sacrificial offerings were taken in the churches to send relief to the burned-out citizens of Yŏsu. Many new members joined the churches. "Another noticeable result of this terrible tidal wave of hatred and murder, is the extremely cordial attitude of the people, non-Christians, whom one meets on the street and in places of business since that time. At least locally the evil-doers have had to 'flee to the mountains,' as a regiment of loyal troops keep martial law and train vigilance Committees...."[29]

27. Elmer T. Boyer, Sunch'ŏn, to "Dear Friends in the Homeland," October 28, 1948.
28. Florence Root, "Dear Friends" letter, October 4-November 26, 1948, in the Presbyterian Church (U.S.A.), Department of History, Montreat, North Carolina.
29. J. Curtis Crane, "Dear Folks at Home" letter, November 29, 1948, in the Presbyterian Church (U.S.A.), Department of History, Montreat, North Carolina.

Vouching for a Future President

The Yŏsu rebellion created many heroes and villains and has gone down as a major episode in modern Korean history. It was the last serious communist uprising in South Korea before the outbreak of the Korean War in June 1950. Jim Hausman was decorated for his role in it, and the investigation that followed led to the purge in the Korean Army that Hausman had wanted for many months. Paek Sŏnyŏp supervised the housecleaning, which led to the dismissal of more than 10 percent of the eighty thousand men in the ROK military, including sixty members of the third graduating class of the Korean Military Academy.

Among the officers arrested and charged as communists in the aftermath of the Yŏsu rebellion was Park Chung-hee, the future coup leader and president of South Korea. Park came from humble beginnings in a village near Taegu, in North Kyŏngsang Province. He had first worked as a primary school teacher and then had joined the Japanese military as a cadet in the Manchurian Army's officer training school, going by the Japanese name Masaō Takaki and holding the rank of first lieutenant when the war ended in August 1945. After being disarmed by Chinese forces, Park and his fellow Korean officers briefly served with a Korean "liberation army" in the Peking-Tientsin area before making their way home. In the fall of 1946, Park was recruited as a cadet in the second class of the Korean Constabulary's officer training school, the future Korean Military Academy.[30]

Soon after Park entered training, the October 1946 uprisings broke out in Taegu and vicinity. Rioters routed the Korean police, seized weapons, and liberated prisoners. They used their weapons on landlords, suspected collaborators, and police whenever they found them, and in the process many innocent people lost their lives. The uprisings and the repression that they brought have already been described. Before they were over, the killing had spread throughout North Kyŏngsang Province. In the town of Kumi, Park Chung-hee's brother Park Sang-hee, then the secretary-general of the Sŏnsan County People's Front, led an attack on the police station. Park Sang-hee himself had once been a prisoner of the Japanese, had led attacks on Japanese properties in the days after liberation, had organized protesters in antitrusteeship demonstrations against the Americans, and had organized citizens' arrests of rightists. To the police and their American advisors, he was a communist troublemaker. When police reinforcements arrived along with U.S. Army units to restore order, Park Sang-hee was killed while trying to escape.

30. Details of Park Chung-hee's life in this account are taken from Cho Kapchae, *Spit on My Grave*, an English translation of *Nae mudŏm-e ch'imŭl paetchyŏra*, installment 123, in the English edition of the *Chosŏn Ilbo* (March 3, 1998), on the World Wide Web at <http:www.chosunilbo.com/w21data/html/news/199803/1998 03060364.html>.

The news of his brother's death reached Park Chung-hee in Seoul where he was attending classes at the constabulary's academy. In retrospect, it seems that Sang-hee's death soured Park on Americans for life, but at the time, he remained in place, pursuing his army career. He graduated in December 1946 and he was assigned to the 8th constabulary regiment in Ch'unch'ŏn where he served for more than a year. In the meantime, however, he kept up friendly contacts with many former members of the Manchurian Army and the liberation army in China. These were fraternal ties, and at the time the political situation was sufficiently confused to permit many kinds of political views in the constabulary. Some of his associates were members of the South Korean Workers' Party, and Park Chung-hee allowed himself to be recruited as a Party member. Notwithstanding this, Park was assigned early in 1948 to be company commander at the constabulary academy and promoted to the temporary rank of major, a position he lost when two men in his company died of heat exhaustion during an ill-advised run in the mountains during the hottest part of August. His next assignment came during the Yŏsu rebellion in October, when he was assigned to be an operations officer on the staff of the 5th Brigade.

When Jim Hausman arrived to fight the Yŏsu rebels, he was aware that Park Chung-hee, the operations officer, disliked Americans and had friends and family members who were known communists. There has been much conjecture about whether Park himself believed in the communist cause or whether he was simply reacting to his brother's death at the hands of the rightist police and their American advisors. In any event, though there is no sign that Park protected or sheltered any of the Yŏsu rebels, communist officers who were rounded up after the incident named him as a fellow traveler, and he was arrested on November 11. During his interrogation Park claimed that he had been recently disillusioned by reports of life under communism in North Korea and had long since abandoned thoughts of being a communist. In a statement given during military police interrogation, he insisted that he had joined the South Korean Workers' Party in anger over his brother's death and not for ideological reasons. Park's biographer asserts that his Japanese-trained interrogator tortured him with electric shocks to force him to give up more names of communists in the Army. Park "cooperated" and named many, including some who were never shown to be communists at all. His cooperation under torture was later cited as a reason to give him lenient treatment, and although he later destroyed the records of his trial, those familiar with the case recall that he was convicted of treason and sentenced to death. The sentence was reduced to ten years in prison when he turned over the names of others in the army who were members of the South Korean Workers' Party.

By 1949, Jim Hausman had become a trusted confidant of President Syngman Rhee, close enough to be moved into a house on the presidential compound. Rhee used Hausman as a lever on his own military officers in

340 Living Dangerously in Korea

the newly reorganized Republic of Korea Army, knowing that he was respected and popular, and mindful of his familiarity with the officers as individuals. The president was worried about the presence of communists in the army and afraid that personal ties would corrupt the prosecution of those responsible for the trouble in the southwest. Rhee ordered Hausman to attend the more important trials, including that of Park Chung-hee, and to report directly back. Thus Hausman was able to endorse leniency for Park, arguing that he was the victim of army factionalism and did not deserve death. President Rhee agreed to commute Park Chung-hee's sentence on condition that Paek Sŏnyŏp, then head of Army Intelligence (G-2), would take personal responsibility for him. Park was discharged from the army and stayed out until the Korean War, when he was recommissioned as an Army counterintelligence agent under Kim Jong-pil (Kim Chŏngp'il), a nephew-by-marriage who had graduated from the fifth class of the Korean Military Academy. Park eventually rose to major general and together with Kim Jong-pil masterminded the May 16, 1961, military coup. Park emerged as head of the ruling junta and then, after formally retiring from the army, served as president of the Republic from 1963 until his assassination in October 1979.

-- 17 --

Living in the ROK

The U.S. Army finished pulling out of Korea in the middle of 1949, leaving behind only the Korea Military Advisory Group (KMAG) to support the Republic of Korea Army. Many signs of abandonment accompanied the exodus. Earlier on, the Pentagon had asked what the Koreans would need in order to turn their constabulary into a decent national army. The military advisors in Seoul had recommended creating a force of 100,000 men with sufficient equipment, organized into divisions of suitable types. Their request had called for substantial expenditures on new equipment, expenses that the U.S. government, in the midst of a worldwide foreign policy reorganization, could not afford. General Douglas MacArthur had intervened with a counterproposal, suggesting that the Koreans get all the arms and equipment that had been used by the U.S. Army's XXIVth Corps during the occupation since it was uneconomical to ship it home. He wanted to follow this with an announcement that the United States had left South Korea with a well-trained, mobile force capable of defending the country.

Ultimately the United States followed MacArthur's suggestion, essentially dumping the equipment already on hand in Korea regardless of its condition. The American military advisors who were being left behind with the ROK Army worried about intelligence estimates that the North Koreans were likely to use their superior forces to invade the south as soon as the U.S. Army pulled out. Jim Hausman, who was staying in Korea with KMAG, complained to a departing general that the Americans were "leaving my wife and children here without anything to protect them." Another officer leaned over, gave him a pat and said, "Hausman, that is what your shoulder patch is all about: 'KMAG,' for <u>K</u>iss <u>M</u>y <u>A</u>ss <u>G</u>oodbye."[1]

The military pullout left the American diplomatic and economic aid missions as the most visible Western elements in Korea, with religious missionaries in distant third place. The British Consulate-General in Chŏng-dong became a full-fledged legation once again, though no longer the most prestigious foreign establishment in the country. The United States was now the dominant foreign player and American Ambassador John J. Muccio was

1. James Hausman, notes for a speech on the early days of the constabulary, and Toland interview transcript, p. 37, in the Hausman papers. For a different view of what the Americans left the ROK Army, see Cumings, *The Origins of the Korean War*. Vol. II, pp. 472-478.

An Army document dated 26 June 1950, the day after the North Korean invasion, gives the total American aid to Korea between 1945 and June 1950 as $495 million, $141 million of it in surplus military equipment. The remainder is relief and economic assistance through GARIOA and ECA. Thanks to Professor Allan Millett for sharing this document with me.

When the U.S. Army withdrew from South Korea in 1949 it transferred to the Republic of Korea under the Surplus Property Act, military equipment that had cost the U.S. approximately $56 million and had a 1949 replacement value of $110 million. The ground equipment was enough for a force of 50,000 men. It included 100,000 small arms, 50,000,000 rounds of small arms ammunition, more than 2,000 rocket launchers, more than 40,000 vehicles of all types, and a number of light artillery pieces and mortars with over 700,000 rounds of ammunition for them. Other equipment sufficient for an additional 15,000 men subsequently arrived in Korea from American stocks in Japan. (U.S., Senate, Committee on Armed Services and Senate Committee on Foreign Relations, 82nd Congress, 1st Session, *Hearings on the Military Situation in the Far East and the Relief of General MacArthur, 1951*, pp. 1992-93, quoted on the Internet at <http://www.army.mil/cmh-pg/books/pd-c-02.htm>.)

The Central Intelligence Agency gave the following estimate of South Korea's chances after a US Army withdrawal in early 1949:

"Withdrawal of US forces from Korea in the spring of 1949 would probably in time be followed by an invasion timed to coincide with Communist-led South Korean revolts, by the North Korean People's Army possibly assisted by small battle-trained units from Communist Manchuria. Although it can be presumed that South Korean security forces will eventually develop sufficient strength to resist such an invasion, they will not have achieved that capability by the spring of 1949. It is unlikely that such strength will be achieved before January 1950. Assuming that Korean communists would make aggressive use of the opportunity presented them, US troop withdrawal would probably result in a collapse of the US-supported Republic of Korea, an event which would seriously diminish US prestige and adversely affect US security interests in the Far East.

"In contrast, continued presence in Korea of a moderate US force, would not only discourage the invasion but would assist in sustaining the will and ability of the Koreans themselves to resist any future invasion once they had the military force to do so and, by sustaining the new Republic, maintain US prestige in the Far East."

the ranking foreigner.[2] Ambassador Muccio appropriated all of the former U.S. Consulate compound in Chŏng-dong—the compound bought in 1882 by Lucius Foote—for his own residence and garden and bought adjacent properties to house his deputies.[3] He installed the embassy offices just off City Hall Plaza in Noguchi Jun's former hotel, the Bando, and across the street in the former Mitsui Building. These buildings housed the various sections of the embassy as well as offices of the Economic Cooperation Administration (ECA), the U.S. aid mission. The United Nations had observer teams and aid officials as well, and there were frequent visits by fact-finding teams and congressional delegations that came to meet with President Syngman Rhee and Prime Minister Yi Pŏmsŏk. Cultural delegations stopped by Seoul and touring orchestras gave concerts. Though the rest of the world learned little about Korea from these encounters, the Koreans became highly conscious of the West, and particularly the United States, whose official presence in downtown Seoul and military presence on the former Chōsen Army compound in Yongsan emphasized America's role as South Korea's main international patron.

So omnipresent were Americans that by 1948 all Caucasians were being referred to simply as *Miguk saram*, "Americans."[4] They took up residence in all parts of the city. The missionaries reoccupied their compounds. The American Embassy annexed a former Japanese bank executives' compound near the Capitol Building to house staffers, while other officials used their housing allowances to rent the homes of Korea's former colonial elite wherever they could be found. KMAG housed its military advisors at "Camp Sŏbinggo," forerunner of today's South Post in Yongsan.[5] Seoul's

2. The United States formally recognized the Republic of Korea on January 1, 1949, and Muccio, who had been in Korea as President Harry Truman's "special representative" since the founding of the Republic of Korea on August 15, 1948, formally assumed the position of U.S. ambassador on March 21, 1949.

3. The American Embassy residence area in Chŏng-dong (commonly called Compound I) was enlarged on September 20, 1948, through the purchase from the new Korean government of three plots of land that lay adjacent to the existing U.S. consulate compound (originally purchased by Lucius Foote). These consisted of .66 acre that had once belonged to the Seoul Union Club, 1.13 acres formerly owned by the Northern Presbyterian Mission, and a 2.73 acre addition that had housed Japanese officials during the colonial period and before then had been an area of the Tōksu Palace that housed palace women in the years between 1897 and 1919. The State Department paid US$149,345.88 for the package.

4. Or, alternatively, *Miguk-nom*, "American SOBs."

5. Yongsan (lit. "Dragon Hill") was a suburb of Seoul as recently as the 1940s and comfortably accommodated the sprawling military reservation that was constructed there by the Japanese as the headquarters of the Chōsen Army until 1945.

The United States Army's 7th Infantry Division occupied Yongsan upon arrival in Korea in September 1945. The area was then known as Camp Sobinggo (lit. "West Ice House"), and on September 11, 1948, after the U.S. military occupation ended and Korea became a sovereign nation, the United States formally acquired

prime real estate market inflated steadily as officials found ways to bring their families and put them in unofficial housing to live "on the economy."[6]

U.S. government organizations discouraged bringing families to Korea and, except for the most senior officials, did not pay for dependents' transportation, housing, schooling, or medical care. Korea thus was far down the list of desirable assignments. This had always been the case in East Asia, where ports like Hong Kong, Shanghai, and Tientsin had been famous for their masculine culture. These were places where men often saved money and even amassed fortunes to be spent back home, but their time in-country was lonely and boring. The men were temporary residents with little interest in learning about the host culture or its language or people. Instead, after a long day's work, they sought each other's company in bars and expatriate clubs. They played cards and went to sporting events. They formed liaisons with local women, which sometimes led to permanent attachments and even marriage. And not a few spent too many nights alone with the bottle. Korea was just the latest example of this familiar way of life.

Storytelling was one good way to pass the time, and since life in Asia was what they had in common, the men of the foreign community traded stories about Asians. Considerable information, misinformation, and disinformation was transmitted in this manner by old-timers to newcomers—"old-timers" being those who had been in country longer than a year, or

the compound as a result of ROK-U.S. agreements. The Americans pulled out in 1949 and left only KMAG to share the fifty-six buildings of the Yongsan military reservation with the ROK Army.

The Yongsan military reservation suffered extensive damage during the Korean War and when the U.S. military headquarters returned to Seoul, the U.S. Eighth Army established itself on the then-campus of Seoul National University near East Gate, using the nearby Presbyterian Mission compound as quarters for top officers. The Eighth Army moved back to Yongsan on September 15, 1953 and has been there ever since.

The Yongsan military reservation eventually came to encompass four distinct areas: Main Post, which contains the headquarters buildings; South Post, which contains support facilities, housing, and elements such as the 121st Evacuation Hospital (formerly at ASCOM City in Pup'yŏng), Seoul American High School, the officer's club and a hotel called Dragon Hill Lodge; an annex to South Post that contains the commissary and housing for officers and U.S. Embassy families; and Camp Coiner, north of Main Post, which houses the 304th Signal Corps Battalion. The most significant change to overtake Yongsan was the cession of the South Post golf course to the City of Seoul as a public park in 1991. Otherwise it remains intact, now very much in the middle of the city of Seoul. Though the rest of the city has changed dramatically, many of the structures that are still in use at Yongsan date from the Japanese period—making it in effect a museum of colonial-era architecture.

6. For an amusing account of life on the economy in Korea in the late 1940s see Irma Materi, *Irma and the Hermit* (New York: W.W. Norton, 1949).

sometimes just longer than the listener.[7] They gathered on Saturday night in the bars of the Chosun and Naija hotels to drink commissary liquor and trade their lore and in-joke humor. Someone suggested that Korea should be known not only as the "Land of the Morning Calm" but also as the "Land of the Afternoon Student Demonstration and Night Soil."[8] They also did much complaining. *Chicago Daily News* reporter Keyes Beech captured the mood in his account of a conversation with a British trader in the Chosun Hotel bar. The trader, according to Beech, was a bitter man:

> "Do you realize," he said, "that in this whole bloody country, either north or south of the 38th parallel, there is not a single golf course?"
>
> I admitted [wrote Keyes Beech] that this intelligence was new to me. The trader contemplated his gin and tonic morosely and added,
>
> "What are you going to do with a country that hasn't one golf course and a prime minister named Lee Bum Suk?"
>
> I confessed I didn't know.[9]

For the rare American woman who managed to get to Korea, the country sometimes was a delightful surprise. Getting away from the American ghetto took a certain courage, but it was worth it. One KMAG colonel's wife wrote a book about her adventures riding public buses and hitching rides on army jeeps to get around the city, exploring markets and historic sites and drinking in the local scene. She was enchanted by the Koreans' love of music:

> Until you've heard a Korean folksong you've never heard real Oriental singing. It is a wavering on a note, held and wiggled in the throat between the head voice and the throat voice. It is very plaintive, tuneless, and interesting. Some of the songs are melodic and the Americans learn them immediately. The boys sing around the house all the time. The melodies are plaintive. These warm nights we have music provided until quite late by the Korean apartment house adjacent to us. There is a loud speaker which broadcasts the music all over the area. The little Korean children are allowed to stay up no telling how late, and we can hear them running, playing, yelling, and laughing. Some of the tunes I've heard I surely would like to buy and bring home.[10]

7. For accounts of this lifestyle on in the treaty ports of the China coast, see John K. Fairbank, *Trade and Diplomacy on the China Coast: The Opening of the Treaty Ports, 1842-1854* (Stanford, Calif.: Stanford University Press, 1953), passim.

8. John Curtis Perry, Peter W. Stanley, and James C. Thomson Jr., *Sentimental Imperialists: The American Experience in East Asia* (New York: Harper and Row, 1982), p. 237.

9. Keyes Beech, *Tokyo and Points East* (Garden City, N.Y.: Doubleday, 1954), p. 135. "Lee Bum Suk" was the romanization chosen for his own name by Prime Minister Yi Pŏmsŏk.

10. Dorothy House Vieman, *Korean Adventure: The Inside Story of an Army Wife* (San Antonio: The Naylor Company, 1951), p. 22.

Taech'ŏn Beach. From Rhodes and Campbell, *History of the Korea Mission,* p. 32.

Such agreeable feelings about Korea, however, were rare. Most Americans avoided going out "on the economy" and never wandered the alleys of a "kimch'i market," or rode a "kimch'i bus" and few indeed ever sampled kimch'i itself. Forays from the base were in vehicles driven by Korean drivers who could navigate the streets and take responsibility for parking and guarding the vehicle when it was out and about. As a result they suffocated in boredom and counted the days until they could leave Korea. The ennui was alleviated only slightly by small-time social events such as the "dog banquet" given by KMAG Commanding General William L. Roberts and his wife for the pets of the KMAG officers' wives. The invitations announced that there would be prizes for the cutest puppy costumes.[11]

Being a male-only hardship post contributed to Korea's attracting more than its share of bureaucratic deadwood, and the more gung-ho embassy and ECA staffers grew bitter about having to suffer colleagues who were merely marking time until retirement.[12] But in their midst were some who turned their Korean duty to career advantage. These included President Syngman Rhee's American advisors Preston Goodfellow, Harold Lady, and

11. Vieman, ibid., pp. 71-72. It should be mentioned that the transportation situation in Korea was primitive by any standard at the time. Even as late as 1958, no less intrepid and curious a group than the Royal Asiatic Society regarded the chartering of a bus for an overnight trip to a temple as a major adventure full of uncertainties. Today the Society periodically offers day trips to the same temple via air-conditioned motor coach on an divided highway, and the main obstacle is the traffic jam at the toll gate getting back into the city in the evening. In other words, it is incomparably easier for an expatriate in Korea today to learn a little about the local culture without risking life and limb.
12. This is the opinion of John C. Caldwell, a China MK assigned to ECA duty in Seoul, in *The Korea Story* (Chicago: Henry Regnery, 1952).

Robert Oliver.[13]   Rhee's American advisors earned notoriety as promoters of their own fortunes no less than Rhee's. Harold Lady, for example, who joined Rhee's staff on the recommendation of his brother-in-law John Staggers, Rhee's Washington lawyer, spent his time in Korea trying to set up a tungsten mining concession.[14] Lady often sat in on meetings between Rhee and American officials and helped him drive hard bargains with the United States. He was instrumental in numerous negotiations—for trade deals with Japan, for example, and weapons for the South Korean military—through which he was thought to have made a considerable amount of money for himself.[15]

Many Americans who turned out to play important roles in U.S.-Korean relations started gathering their experience during these early postwar years. In addition to Jim Hausman of KMAG and Harold Lady, who returned after the Korean War to serve as President Rhee's chief economic advisor, diplomats Gregory Henderson and Donald S. Macdonald, sometime aid official and army liaison officer Robert Kinney, and businessman Carl Ferris Miller were a few who joined longtime missionaries such as Horace G. Underwood as the leading American residents in Korea. As a newly discovered American interest in the East, Korea also attracted its first generation of American academic specialists during this period, among them Edward W. Wagner of Harvard, Samuel Martin of Yale, and Fred Lukoff of the University of Washington.

Paradise Regained

In the summer of 1948, a young Methodist missionary named James Moore accompanied some students on a camp retreat at a beach near the west coast town of Taech'ŏn. The setting was idyllic and Moore was enchanted. His wife Margaret, daughter of Canadian missionary Stanley Martin, had spent her childhood summers at Wŏnsan Beach, and Moore had heard innumerable stories about Sorai, Wŏnsan, and Hwajinp'o, all of which were now in the northern zone and inaccessible to the missionary community. Sorai, in fact, lay just across the thirty-eighth parallel, tantalizingly within sight of the offshore island called "White Wings" (Paengnyŏng-do) which

13. Robert T. Oliver, longtime communications professor at Pennsylvania State University befriended Rhee during his exile in Washington, D.C., and eventually wrote several Korea-related books including an authorized biography entitled *Syngman Rhee: The Man behind the Myth* (New York: Dodd Mead, 1954).

14. For Goodfellow et al., see Bruce Cumings, *The Origins of the Korean War*, vols. I and II, passim. For Oliver's slant on Syngman Rhee see Robert T. Oliver, *Syngman Rhee and American Involvement in Korea, 1942-1960* (Seoul: Panmun Books, 1978).

15. Harold Lady left Korea on the day the Korean War broke out and was blocked by U.S. officials from returning until after the armistice. Cumings, *The Origins of the Korean War*, Vol. II, pp. 62-64 and passim.

lay just across the line in the south. Taech'ŏn Beach looked like a dream come true: two miles of clean sand—unusual on a coastline that was mainly mud flats—along a two-mile peninsula that was uninhabited except for a fishing hamlet at the near end.

Back in Seoul, Jim Moore learned that the peninsula at Taech'ŏn was actually for sale. After having been owned by the Japanese, it had been appropriated as "vested property" by the U.S. Military Government after Liberation, and in 1948 it had just been turned back to the new government of the Republic of Korea. The Protestant missions—the Presbyterians, Methodists, Canadians, Oriental Missionary Society, and Seventh Day Adventists—quickly organized a consortium to buy part of the property to replace what had been lost in the north. The parcel consisted of the farthest kilometer of beach front along with a wooded headland overlooking the bay with its reef and offshore islands. By the summer of 1949 six families had already built beach houses, and construction was under way for tennis courts, a lodge with rooms for rent, and other facilities. A year later, when the Korean War began, there were nearly twenty cabins ready for occupancy.[16]

Later on, Taech'ŏn Beach was to become a sacred retreat for the foreign community. The resort lasted well into the 1990s. Korea Kids of the second, third, fourth, and even fifth generations collected memories of Taech'ŏn Beach as the best part of growing up in Korea, just as earlier generations remembered, and pined for, Sorai and Wŏnsan.[17] In the annals of ci-

16. Horace G. Underwood, interview, Seoul, July 19, 1997.

17. Taech'ŏn was the foreign (mainly missionary) community's summertime retreat through the 1990s. However, in 1990 the local government more-or-less forcibly took the section along the beach front for resale to Korean developers, and the shrinking Taech'ŏn Beach Association constituency retreated to the headland. Meanwhile, the opposite end of the beach developed slowly as a raffish weekend hangout between 1955 and 1980, referred to by the denizens of the foreign beach as the "Korean Beach," or "KB." Between the KB and the foreign beach was a buffer area that continued to serve as a campground for Methodist schools such as Paejae.

In its heyday, between 1955 and 1990, the foreign beach had more than a hundred family-owned cabins built in rows along the beach and on the slopes of "the Point," or headland. Those without cabins could rent, or they could take no-frills rooms and meals in the lodge, which also served as the beach community's central facility. Since many foreign residents spent the entire summer at Taech'ŏn Beach, there was time for many forms of recreation. The lodge auditorium was the site of Saturday night skits and concerts, Sunday church services, a midsummer Bible conference, and an annual play with beach goers as the cast, performing everything from Gilbert and Sullivan to Rodgers and Hammerstein. Outdoors were tennis courts, with an annual championship, and swimming lessons and lifeguard-supervised swimming hours. The atmosphere faithfully replicated the mood of an American church camp.

For many older beach goers, Taech'ŏn was a reconstruction of the delights of Sorai and Wŏnsan. Vesper services on Thursday and Sunday evenings in the

vilian life in Korea, therefore, the name of James Moore, finder of Taech'ŏn, has a place of special honor.

Patrick Byrne, Vatican Diplomat

In 1948, the pioneer Maryknoll missionary Patrick Byrne, one of the original group of American priests who had started Catholic work in P'yŏngyang in the 1920s, was elevated to an auspicious new job. He was made a monsignor and appointed by the Vatican as its apostolic delegate to the newborn Republic of Korea. President Syngman Rhee, though famous as a Methodist, had learned the political uses of Catholic connections during his lean years currying American support in Washington, D.C. At a time when the State Department wanted nothing to do with him, Francis Cardinal Spellman of New York had honored the Korean leader with a dinner at the Waldorf-Astoria, in effect anointing him as the church's choice for leadership in Korea against the forces of godless communism. As vicar apostolic, Byrne had been the only religious figure invited to speak at Rhee's inauguration and had used the opportunity to chide Rhee's critics on the platform.

The Vatican's ambassador in Seoul had few responsibilities and many privileges. The cardinals in Rome bought Byrne an elegant house at No. 2 Kungjŏng-dong, a quiet spot backing up on the wall of the Ch'il-gung royal shrine. Byrne's property included a large Japanese garden with trees, paths, decorative rocks, and ponds stocked with carp, all visible from a parlor that had floor-to-ceiling glass on three sides, which Byrne said made the house feel like an aquarium. A long corridor interrupted by right-angle turns connected the parlor with the front door of the house, with rooms opening off the corridor. Byrne's kitchen was staffed by the ancient "Cookie," who long before had learned Western cooking from Dr. Lillias Underwood, and Cookie's septuagenarian sister, who had fled her own house when her husband tried to kill her for refusing to sell cigarettes on the street. The cleaning woman was "Agnes" and the outside man was

amphitheater atop the point were moments of surpassing beauty, as the audience watched the sun set beyond the islands in the Yellow Sea, much as Sorai-goers once had watched it set past "White Wings." Parents who once had learned to swim so a Sorai "S" could be sewn on their bathing suits had their children go through swimming lessons for the Taech'ŏn "T," followed by the intermediate Circle, then Wings for swimming the thousand yards to the reef, and for a hardy few, a Chevron for swimming to "The Monster," three miles off shore. Many families had boats, and sailing, water skiing, and exploring the outer islands were an important part of life at Taech'ŏn. In 1957, the Underwood family donated a trophy, the Underwood Cup, to the resort's best swimmer. Soon thereafter, the DeCamp family donated a trophy for the best all-around girl athlete. In 1959, U.S. Ambassador Walter C. Dowling donated the Embassy Cup, an annual citizenship award for beach teenagers.

"Ardok," named for King Nebuchadnezzar's captain of the guard,[18] which naturally turned into "Our Duck" in daily usage. "Our Duck" was a genial Korean who would have worked for nothing in exchange for English lessons if Byrne had permitted it. ("I would rather pay anybody double than get 'em at reduced rates plus English," wrote Byrne to his family.) Byrne communicated with his household staff in Japanese, since he had forgotten his Korean during the war.[19]

Among Byrne's perks as a member of the diplomatic corps was access to the U.S. Army Post Exchange (PX), commissary, and APO mail service. This marked him as a source for precious imported goods through Army channels. For decades, the possession of PX privileges was an informal mark of rank among foreign civilians in Korea, and any unofficial American who had them and was foolish enough to let it be known could expect to be importuned constantly by friends and even strangers who did not.[20] Byrne was continually being surprised by the audacity of visitors who came on pretexts of doing business and ended by asking him to get them things at the PX.

Cookie, however, never bothered to ask. On Saturday afternoons Byrne customarily shopped at the Army commissary, a task he did himself be-

18. The reference is to Arioch (sometimes spelled Ariock, sounding like "Ardok" in Korean) is in the Book of Daniel, chapter 2, verse 14. Thanks to former Korea missionaries Court and Sally Robinson and Julie Sansom for identifying this reference.

19. Patrick Byrne, "Dear Mother" letter, undated [early summer. 1949], in the Maryknoll Mission Archives, Maryknoll, New York. This section follows this remarkable 23-page, single-spaced description of Byrne's life in Seoul, written in highly colloquial, and humorous, language. Variations in spelling are Byrne's and in most cases intentional.

20. At the beginning of the American occupation of South Korea in 1945, the Army sponsored all American citizens in Korea and gave them access to Army post exchange (PX), commissary, and Army Post Office (APO) facilities. As the number of civilians in Korea swelled, they put a burden on the Army's ability to supply the goods. After the handover of sovereignty from the U.S. Army to the Republic of Korea in August 1948, access to the PX , commissary, and APO was restricted in principle to U.S. military personnel and government employees and their dependents. A major exception was the entire diplomatic corps, which enjoyed access to the PX as a courtesy of the U.S. government. Monsignor Byrne fell in this category.

Extension of privileges to civilians who would not normally be entitled to them has always been at the discretion of the U.S. commanding general in Korea, and different commanders have been more or less generous with exceptions. Meanwhile, the foreign community has been resourceful in appealing for exceptions. In the 1950s, for example, when the press enjoyed PX and APO privileges so American reporters could buy film and file stories, certain missionaries won PX privileges by claiming to be contributors to religious publications in the United States. Chaplains historically have been useful to missionaries in winning access to military facilities for those who give guest sermons or volunteer to help counsel the troops.

cause no one else in the household was allowed into Camp Sŏbinggo. On Saturday mornings, the wizened Cookie would glance anxiously at the clock and remind him to go if it got to be past lunchtime. She had children and grandchildren, and on Sundays she would take them "souvenirs" consisting of soap and ends of ham, etc. Byrne was not unwilling to be used, at least to a point. He wrote, "But still, Cookie was the finest outside of the Waldorf, so I was not crabbing about the graft....So I would hie me to the commissary and get the soap, and put it in the pantry; and after she had left on Sunday I would count the bars wot were left, and compare the depredation with the previous Sunday's, and everything was lovely." Byrne told the story in a highly colloquial family letter:

> But Cookie made a sad mistake. Our Duck got a tummy ache and was laid up for about a week; and all the trouble he caused Cookie was to have her make thin rice gruel for him; but she got tired of it; and said to him says she: "Why the dickens don't you go on home and let them take care of you there and not be bothering us here?" (Which was cruel on Cookie's part, because his home ... has a wife and four kids in ONE ROOM. No place to be sick!) So Our Duck got sore, he swore a mighty oath of revenge, and bided his time.

> When Our Duck got on his pins again, he laid a trap and waited for the next Sunday excursion of Cookie; grabbed her with the boodle in her arms; and hauled her to judgment. Poor Cookie...she resigned. And as she was leaving says I to her says I: "Cookie, you-all haint been puttin' nuthin over on we-uns; I know you've been taking those things; your previous boss, a Colonel & Mrs., told me you used to swipe things. But I haint fired you, and iffen you-all wish to remain, you may."

> Then Cookie gave her ultimatum, just like Grant at Valley Forge, I mean Yorktown, and I'm not too sure about Grant, maybe it was Foch, but anyhow it was a grandult...says Cookie, "I'll not work in the same house with that lousy skunk Our Duck"...and Our Duck, who was present, just grinned from year to year.

> [So Cookie's sister took over.] During these years as "slave" (I am NOT being sarcastic...in the oriental way, the younger member of the family is under the older...all his life or hers), Sister had picked up quite a bit....So, says I, I'll do my best with young Seventy [year-old], while looking for another Cookie...so I did, and I couldn't find another Cookie, they are scarce as scarce can be, and passed on like treasures from departing family to staying family....So one day when I was feelin' adventuresome I invited a couple of bozos, and Sis did the thing up in grand style; so I invited six; and that didn't faze her either; and last week she covered herself with glory by taking care of eleven guests plus mesel." And is Young Sis having the time of her life! The saddest blow that could happen to her would be to have Cookie, the ole Slave Driver, return. She makes [Our Duck] nifty tidbits all the time to show her appreciation—[and I am] saving the six thousand yen paid monthly to Cookie.

Thus did Monsignor Byrne solve several problems at once. However, many other challenges remained, such as the thievery that was endemic in late 1940s Korea. Burglars, pickpockets, and petty thieves were everywhere. Not even the American ambassador was safe: his shoes were taken from the threshold of a *kisaeng* restaurant one night and he had to walk to his car in stocking feet. The rampant stealing amazed Byrne:

> It didn't used to be like this in the old days; why we never lost a cent. I remember when we lived up north, where the Soviets are now, I went a whole summer without even locking my door, and never lost a thing. We would ride our nifty bikes up to the store or the saloon and stay inside two, yes three hours, and come out...if we could...and find the bike, without any lock at all, just where we had left it in relation to terra firma. Of course in relation to the stellar spaces, its position had inevitably changed somewhat owing to the procession of the celestial spheres...but to get back to earth, this was a honest land.

Byrne's house was hit numerous times. In a single raid a thief made off with his typewriter, socks, fountain pen, some underwear, and his cassock ("The doggone thief must intend to enter the seminary this next term; but I don't think he expects to become a Maryknoller, because he didn't take my cincture.") The obvious remedy was a guard dog. Byrne got two, both of which turned out to be "the kind of watch-dog who watches for burglars so he can play with them." One night he heard the "plop" of someone dropping in over the wall, followed by the clink of a falling tile.

> Says I to [myself], "Robbers have jumped down (this was at 2 A.M.) from the temple wall into my garden and dislodged a tile from the top of the wall. They are now prowling around in my garden: where the heck are Butch and Tabi?" So I stole softly through my miles of corridor to the front door where the kennel is and called "Butch." Well sir, after three calls, Butch comes out yawning, stretching, and yawning some more. "Come on, Butch," says I, and started for the garden. "Aw, what's your hurry," said Butch, or sniffs to that effect, and do you know, that fierce mastiff MADE ME LEAD HIM through the garden; he came four or five feet behind me, and very reluctantly at that....So I ruffled his fur and sicced 'm on to the robbers as fiercely and encouragingly as I could. What happened? Not a doggone thing. Butch wouldn't even bark; he just wasn't interested; he went back into his kennel...and was I off Butch for life. Why, I wouldn't give that hound a hamberg if it was the last one I had on earth.

Byrne's car was a 1946 Pontiac that he drove himself.[21] Twice he lost his headlights. Once his hubcaps were stolen while the car was parked in front

---

21. "I am my own chauffeur, which to the Koreans is a scandal and a disgrace....The British Minister is a pal of mine in this scheme; he too drives his own car. The American would, but he doan know how. The Chinese [Shao Chang-hsu] would but he ain't gotta car, not now. In fact he has just lost his job, in consequence of the communist victories in China. It is too bad, for he used to give such amazing dinners; with soup made of walnuts."

of a building filled with American soldiers and officers. One morning he
went to his garage and found that "during the night some bozos had broken in and taken not only the four tires, but the wheels as well." He wrote,

> Poor ole Ponty Ack, … he was lying there on the ground all spread out like a
> hen on thirteen eggs, the fenders touching the ground and with a look of
> such profound dejection and helplessness that you'll never forget till your
> dying day, no sir.

> Well, I went to the Chief of Police and he jumped up and said, "Gosh Mon
> Seenyer, not YOUR car; surely they never DARED touch YOUR car!" …
> "Whew," said he, "… my reputation is at stake; if I can't get back your wheels
> I'll resign from the police force!" … and we both wept on one another's
> shoulders till lunch time … but do you know, the Chief called all of his men
> offen everything else (and what a crime wave there was just THEN) … and
> put 45 detectives on the track of my four wheels, and … one day after the
> thieves had put the wheels on the black market they were recovered and
> brought to me in triumph. I didn't even have to put another pound of air in
> 'em; just slip 'em on and tighten the lugs and off I could sail, as bravely as of
> yore.

Byrne's sense of humor got him through most of life's minor crises, but
when it came to politics he was a very serious man. He blamed Franklin
Roosevelt for giving North Korea to the Russians and thought the Americans were being beaten in a world struggle between democracy and athe-
ism whose battle line ran along the 38th parallel. He was happy that the
armed forces were pacifying Cheju Island, that the "commies" there were
"surrendering actually in crowds, sometimes as many as a thousand in one
day, and the whole commy campaign has come to a nignominious end."
But he was also worried about the threat of invasion from the north, as he
wrote to his family back in Washington, imagining an escape and homecoming that was fated never to happen:

> The battle surges back and forth….Now, if the commies who are scaring Mrs.
> President [Mme. Rhee] into cat-fits by their charges on the 38th parallel cities
> actually come the 20 miles they need to get to Seoul, I suppose we'll have to
> put off [my consecration ceremony] till kingdom come. It's a political affair,
> you see….So don't be surprised if I run in on you some dark night saying,
> "Hot dog, they run me away, Folks, can I please come in outa the rain?" And
> [my sister] will shout, "Doggone it, now I know why I was makin' that Chili
> Sauce all day yesterday; Something just TOLD ME!" And we shall live happily
> ever after.

Death in the Afternoon

For the Underwood family, South Korea's passage from occupation zone to
independent republic was the fulfillment of a cherished wish. The turmoil

in the southern provinces and talk of war from North Korea were merely the adversities of the moment. Horace and Ethel Underwood had never known Korea when it did not face some kind of adversity, and the secret was to endure, adjust, and make life bearable.

By 1949, the Underwood clan had found their way back and were planning to stay. Young Horace and his wife Joan were in language school preparing for the Presbyterian Mission's Korean competency test. John, one of the twins, had already passed and was serving as a missionary in Ch'ŏngju. Richard, now a sergeant, was still in Seoul with the Army. Together they cooked up family projects. One year it was restoring the old Chrysler convertible which they found abandoned

Ethel Underwood (1888-1949). From Rhodes and Campbell, *History of the Korea Mission*, p. 297.

alongside a country road, its top shredded, its upholstery stripped, and its engine block cracked. Another year it was designing and building a new *Black Duck* for use at Taech'ŏn Beach. For the senior Underwoods it was like getting a new lease on life to be able to resume their careers in their fifties, teaching at their beloved college, surrounded by family and friends.

The politics, however, were worrisome. As an advisor to General Arnold, the Military Governor of South Korea, Dr. Underwood had shared the American command's concerns about communist infiltration and he had agonized over having to use so much force against the "communists" in the south. In his opinion, the terrorist episodes in Taegu and the Chŏlla Provinces were not likely to merge into anything that would lead to a national revolution but they had to be stopped because they encouraged disorder and terrorism elsewhere. But some of the terrorism hit close to home. The child of a C.C.U. professor was killed in what appeared to be a random attack on his house in Seoul.[22] Elsie Caldwell, a Presbyterian MK whose husband was serving with ECA, was hit by a stray bullet one day on the missionary compound near East Gate.[23] There was no way to prevent such inci-

22. Horace G. Underwood, interview, November 11, 1983.
23. Caldwell, *The Korea Story*, p. 160.

dents. They would simply have to take precautions and live reasonably and normally, letting it be known that basically things were going to turn out all right in Korea.

On March 17, 1949, Ethel Underwood gave a tea in the library of the family home for a group of university women. The featured speaker was Mo Yunsuk, a poet who had just returned from a trip with the South Korean observer mission to the UN General Assembly. Mo was a charter member of the Syngman Rhee regime, an anticommunist former North Korean married to An Hosang, the German-educated head of Rhee's anticommunist youth network.

Earlier that month, in a move to end the violent skirmishing between left- and right-wing youth organizations in South Korea, An Hosang had outlawed all student groups that were not under his own control. This was an intentionally one-sided step, for it was only the leftist groups that were outlawed. That may have been an additional reason for making An Hosang's wife, the poet Mo Yunsuk, a target for the assassins who forced their way into the Underwood House on the afternoon of March 17.

As Mo Yunsuk was speaking in the library, four young men from the left-wing Democratic Patriotic Students League came to the house, donned masks, and entered, intending to kill her with their sawed-off U.S. 30 caliber carbine. The youth who entered first via the front door upset the Underwoods' dog, whose barking brought the houseboy. His scuffle with the assailant then brought Mrs. Underwood out of the library to see what was the matter. In the hallway she confronted the intruder and tried to shove him out the front door, while from the kitchen there emerged a second intruder with the gun, wrestling with the Underwoods' cook. When Mrs. Underwood turned to see what was happening behind her the gunman fired two shots and she fell, mortally wounded.

The attackers then dashed into the library where the guests lay prostrate on the floor. By this time Mo Yunsuk was hiding in another part of the house, and when they failed to find her the assailants fled down the hill and disappeared into the village below. Ethel Underwood, meanwhile, lay bleeding to death on the hallway floor, her head cradled in the lap of George Paik's wife Ch'oe Ikwŏn. By the time a college car could be summoned to take her to Severance Hospital she was dead.

The Korean National Police and American M.P.'s were at the Underwood House within the hour to begin the investigation, which turned out to be inconclusive. An M.P. spied a Korean police officer pocketing one of the spent carbine shells as a souvenir and took it from him as an aid in finding the murder weapon, but the gun was already being passed hand to hand through the cells of the underground and never was recovered.[24]

24. Everett Drumright to SecState, April 29, 1949 (395.1113), with copies of Korean National Police investigative reports and newspaper articles.

An estimated three thousand people attended Ethel Underwood's funeral on March 22 at Seoul's West Gate Church. Thousands more lined the route to the foreigners' cemetery at Yanghwajin for the burial in a touching demonstration of respect for the Underwood family.[25] There is no evidence that her murder was anything but a botched attack on Mo Yunsuk, part of the endemic political violence of the time. But the idea that Ethel Underwood had died a random death in the crossfire was too painful for her husband to bear. Grasping for meaning he wrote to family and friends in America that he thought it "entirely possible" that someone in P'yŏngyang, or perhaps even in Moscow, had ordered his wife's murder in order to frighten other Americans into leaving Korea.[26] If that was the assailants' purpose, the ensuing police investigation did not reveal it. However, Ethel Underwood's murder dispelled all illusions that life in Korea could ever return to normal. The prewar style was gone for good, and though the birth of the South Korean republic had felt like a new beginning that might usher in a time of peace and stability, Ethel's death was a sign that the future would be a time of permanent crisis.

In August 1949, Homer Hulbert returned on a sentimental journey to see Korea for the first time since 1907—only to fall ill and die within days of his arrival—another omen of an era's ending. A.W. Taylor also died while trying to resume his trading business in Seoul. The Frenchman Emile Martel, sometime mine concessionaire, trader, and consul, passed away in September. The Benedictine Bishop Bonifacius Sauer died in a P'yŏngyang jail in January 1950, and in February, Alice Appenzeller suffered a fatal stroke while giving a chapel talk at Ewha.

In March, Monsignor George Carroll found a courier who was willing to smuggle Sister Agneta Chang out of North Korea for 70,000 wŏn, "C.O.D., F.O.B., Seoul." "As soon as she arrives," wrote Patrick Byrne to Mother Mary Columba in New York, "we are going to make her look like an olive, i.e., stuffed with red (not pimento, but real steaks). She probably hasn't had a decent meal in years." Byrne tried twice to send the instructions, written on silk and stitched into the courier's coat lining, but there was no answer from Sister Agneta.[27]

Thinking the Unthinkable

The short-wave radio, the air link with Tokyo, and the comings and goings of official journalists brought worrisome news from abroad. The fall of

25. Horace G. Underwood, letters to Mrs. Edwards Cleaveland (undated) and John Coventry Smith, March 21, 1949, PHS RG 140, Box 18, file 15.
26. Horace H. Underwood, "Death of a Missionary," undated memorandum (probably late March, 1949), PHS RG 140, Box 18, file 15.
27. Byrne to Mother Mary Columba, M.M. (New York), March 3, 1950, in Gabriella Mulherin, "Flower of the Martyrs," correspondence, p. 22.

China to communism in 1949, the Soviets' acquisition of the atomic bomb, and worries about communist gains in Europe all made it seem that the world including Korea was engulfed in a struggle that no one could control. The Korean communists with their Soviet backers had thwarted unification and now there was an aggressive regime in P'yŏngyang bent on wiping out the westward-leaning republic in South Korea. Along the 38th parallel there were constant skirmishes and firefights between opposing forces. Could the Syngman Rhee government survive?

In the American Embassy in Seoul, officials monitored the progress of the Korean aid legislation that had to be approved by Congress before South Korea could be organized and built into a self-supporting nation. Congress rejected one version of the Korean aid bill in January but passed a different one the following month.[28] On January 12, Secretary of State Dean Acheson addressed the National Press Club in Washington and drew a line describing a "perimeter" that excluded South Korea and Taiwan from the list of countries United States would defend from communist attack. Korea and Taiwan were United Nations problems, Acheson said, and the United Nations should assume primary responsibility for their defense. John Foster Dulles, the future Secretary of State, visited Korea as a special representative of President Harry Truman less than a week before the North Korean invasion and continued giving the ambiguous message. He said that the American people would support South Korea "consistent with your own self-respect and primary dependence on your own efforts," and ended by declaring, "You are not alone; you will never be alone, as long as you continue to play worthily your part in the great design of human freedom."[29]

General MacArthur said that if North Korea attacked the south, American strategic considerations would "force abandonment of any pretense of active [U.S.] military support."[30] Utterances like these were disturbing to the expatriates in Korea, and they fretted about what to do in case of war. The American Embassy and KMAG together worked out an evacuation plan code-named "CRULLER" for American citizens that would be activated upon orders from the ambassador. An alert would be signaled by the repetition of the word "FIRESIDE" over Armed Forces Radio Station WVTP, while the word "HIGHBALL" would mean that "CRULLER" was in effect and people should move as quickly as possible to pickup points for evacuation from the country. Fifteen different assembly points were established across the city for those needing evacuation, including the Naija Hotel, Embassy

28. Dean Acheson, *Present at the Creation* (New York: W.W. Norton, 1969), p. 358.

29. John Foster Dulles, Speech to the Republic of Korea National Assembly, June 19, 1950, quoted in ibid.

30. CINCFE (commander-in-chief, Far East; i.e., MacArthur) to Department of the Army, January 19, 1949, quoted on the Internet at <http://www.army.mil/cmh-pg /books/pd-c-02.htm>.

Compounds I and II, and various billets in the Camp Sŏbinggo area. From
the assembly points, depending on the time and means of transportation
available, they would be transported to the port of Inch'ŏn, Kimp'o Airport, or possibly the railroad station and eventually be taken to Japan.[31]
Optimists thought it might work. Everyone prayed that they would never
need to find out.

31. Sawyer, *Military Advisors in Korea,* pp. 110-112. In the State Department archives there is a version of this plan called "LIONIZE JUNIOR," dated 1 June 1949.
(395.1115/7-5549).

-- 18 --

A Country Ripped by War

The first shots of the Korean War were exchanged across the 38th parallel in the predawn darkness of Sunday, June 25, 1950, on the Ongjin Peninsula not far from Sorai Beach. The North Korean invasion of South Korea itself began not long thereafter with two thrusts through the north-south corridors on either side of the Pukhan Mountains north of Seoul.

Just south of the parallel in the western corridor lay the ancient capital of Kaesŏng and its Methodist Mission compound. When the invasion began, there were six American civilians asleep on the compound including Kris Jensen, a visitor from Seoul. The first gunshots in the distance sounded so much like routine skirmishing that neither Jensen nor his host, Larry Zellers, paid much attention. They waited until daylight to get up for breakfast and then they were startled to see heavily armed soldiers passing outside their window. Kris Jensen opined that this was a South Korean drill, though it seemed very well staged. The soldiers were wearing North Korean uniforms and kept firing their rifles into the air. Other realistic effects had also been achieved, such as a cutoff of electric power. The two Americans went outdoors and saw that the power lines had been pulled down and were lying on the ground. And suddenly it struck them: probably—no, *certainly*—the moving soldiers were North Koreans, and they were already caught behind North Korean lines.[1]

In Seoul, the first Americans to hear of the invasion war were KMAG radio operators who relayed reports from the 38th parallel to their officers at Camp Sŏbinggo. At first it seemed to be nothing more than a coincidence of skirmishes, but by breakfast the reports clearly added up to more. South Korean defenses in the corridors north of the city were organized to form a

1. Larry Zellers, *In Enemy Hands: A Prisoner in North Korea* (Lexington, Ky.: The University Press of Kentucky, 1991), pp. 1-3.

tripwire on the parallel itself, positioned in a way to buy time for main units to the rear to collect themselves for a proper stand. On June 25, the tripwire was triggered before dawn, and by mid-morning an all-out effort was being mounted to bolster ROK Army units at the front. There was no assurance that they could hold the line. KMAG telephoned the news to the American Embassy at 7:00 A.M., and by nine o'clock, American officials were convinced that this was in fact the dreaded general assault.[2]

On base at Camp Sŏbinggo, KMAG advisor Jim Hausman and his wife Bertha were looking forward to a quiet Sunday. However, Hausman was awakened by his telephone: a call from ROK Army headquarters with news that there was fighting all along the front. He jumped up, threw on some clothes, and jogged the three minutes over Dragon Hill to headquarters. There he found the phones crackling with news from the front. One call was from the American advisors attached to the ROK 17th Regiment on the Ongjin Peninsula, urgently requesting air evacuation.[3] The Ongjin Peninsula was a part of Hwanghae Province on the west coast that sagged below the 38th parallel and thus was part of South Korea but had no land contact with the southern zone. It was the North Koreans' first conquest on June 25 and many southern defenders were lost waiting for evacuation that day.

Hausman quickly concluded that the general assault was on. He saw North Korean YAK fighters buzzing Seoul and coming uncomfortably close to Army headquarters. While he was watching, a small group of U.S. Air Force planes also appeared but dropped their wing tanks and fled when they saw the YAKs, apparently because they had not been told to fight back. As Ambassador John J. Muccio made his way to Yongsan to be with the generals, a YAK buzzed the street near his car. One of his escorts got lucky and hit the plane with rifle fire, to no apparent effect.

All through the day on Sunday, June 25, the residents of Seoul city struggled with fright and denial. By nightfall, however, the word was out that North Korea was likely to capture Seoul before any meaningful resistance could be organized. Around midnight, the American Embassy's section chiefs were ordered to their offices to start pulling files for burning. Nearby at the British Legation, Minister Vyvyan Holt and his deputy George Blake did the same, spending most of Sunday night and Monday preparing for the fall of Seoul. The Americans and British disagreed, however, about the degree of the danger. While the Americans were getting ready to evacuate, British Ambassador Vyvyan Holt (aka "Captain Holt") argued that anyone

2. Harold Joyce Noble, *Embassy at War* (Seattle: University of Washington Press, 1975), pp. 10-15.

3. Two American officers, Maj. Lloyd Swink and Lt. Frank Brown, volunteered to bring them out. American LSTs that had been in the water between Inch'ŏn and the Ongjin Peninsula brought out two surviving battalions of the 17th regiment. James Hausman, "Dear Jung" letter to Chŏng Ilhwa, May 17, 1991, in the Hausman papers, covering faxed notes for the Chŏng Ilhwa book on Hausman.

with diplomatic status would be quite safe and said that he did not intend to leave the city. He acknowledged that North Koreans might search the British Embassy but that things would have to get a lot worse than that before he decided to leave. Captain Holt seemed to believe that if he chose to leave later, he would be free to do so.

Operation Highball

The American Ambassador was not so sanguine. At 2:00 A.M. on Monday, June 26, he ordered the code word "highball" broadcast over army radio station WVTP, beginning the general evacuation.[4] American citizens were given one hour to report to their pickup points for transportation via army bus to the mustering point at ASCOM City, the military logistics depot on the road to Inch'ŏn, and then to the port itself to board ships for the journey to Japan. They were to come to the American ambassador's compound immediately, bringing only what they could carry. Margaret Moore had her hands full with a three-week-old baby, two rambunctious sons, and her prized violin. Her husband, Jim, the discoverer of Taech'ŏn Beach, remained behind.[5]

Outside Seoul, foreigners got the invasion news by telephone or telegraph. At Taech'ŏn Beach, where the Northern Presbyterian Mission was having its annual meeting, the eighty Americans were slow to get the word. The beach had no electricity or telephone service, and the nearest telegraph was in Taech'ŏn town, eight miles inland. Most had just fallen asleep when they were awakened by the sound of a jeep approaching at high speed. It was embassy staffer Bob Kinney bringing news of the invasion. Kinney, whose wife Gail and her parents were at the beach that weekend, believed that a general evacuation order was coming and had known that there was no way to get the word to them other than to drive the 135 miles from Seoul through rainy-season mud and washouts. A discussion buzzed in the dark around Kinney's jeep. Had the "highball" evacuation actually been ordered? No one was sure. For the time being they decided not to wake their families. Some of the men took baseball bats and commenced a patrol of the resort perimeter in search of alarming signs. Others fiddled with teenager Eddie Adams's AM radio trying to pick up station WVTP through the static. The question was settled at 8:00 A.M. when another Embassy staffer, Frank Barnhart, drove in with the news that the "highball" evacuation had indeed been ordered and that the Americans must be on the move immediately.[6]

4. Noble, *Embassy at War*, pp. 250-252 and 254-256.
5. David J. Moore, family memoir/memorandum enclosed with correspondence to the author, April 11, 1997.
6. Robert and Gail Kinney, interview, Kailua, Hawaii, July 27, 1994. This account of the Taech'ŏn Beach evacuation follows Edward B. Adams, "June 25, 1950...Forty Years after," *Korea Times*, June 23, 1990, p. 5, and "Nation Survives

In Seoul, the recipients of the "highball" evacuation order did their best
to get to the collection points within one hour as ordered, but it took much
longer to find the necessary vehicles and to prepare the 682 evacuees for
the 22-mile trip to ASCOM City and Inch'ŏn. It was 9:00 A.M. under gray
and rainy skies when the convoy of army buses filled with American civilians pulled out of the Chŏng-dong street in front of Ambassador Muccio's
compound and made its way across the Han River toward ASCOM City. The
evacuees were already suffering from lack of sleep and food. Older children sensed the drama and were fascinated; younger children squirmed
and whimpered until they fell asleep; but the grownups had to stay awake
thinking about what was being left behind. Veterans of the 1940 *Mariposa*
evacuation muttered glumly that this time it was more disorganized and
worse in every way. They repeated these sentiments when they saw the
evacuation ship: a freshly unloaded Norwegian fertilizer ship named the SS
Reinholt. It took all day to get the people out to where the *Reinholt* lay at
anchor and a while longer to board an additional 181 latecomers. At 6:00
P.M. the captain ordered his ship into motion and by late evening the
Reinholt was in the Yellow Sea en route to Fukuoka, Japan. The stench of
nitrate fertilizer was everywhere in the ship making it seem that the soggy
deck would be better sleeping space than the dry but chemical-smelling interior. Bert Hausman and her three children picked a spot beneath an overhanging structure and snacked on what was left of their supply of bread
and cheese before curling up together to go to sleep. During the night the
overhanging structure turned out to be a water tank that overflowed and
drenched them and their suitcases. Disgusted, Mrs. Hausman heaved the
ruined baggage, contents and all, over the railing into the blackness.[7]

Escape from Taech'ŏn Beach

The Taech'ŏn Beach contingent got under way at 11:00 A.M. on Monday
the 26th, in a convoy of nine jeeps, trailers, and rented trucks. Their first
leg was the 85-mile stretch over the mountains to Taejŏn, a bruising journey of eight hours. In Taejŏn they put down for the night at the KMAG compound and assorted missionary houses, planning to take a morning train
to Pusan. During the evening, however, the news grew dramatically worse.
Just after midnight there was a report that North Koreans had landed on
the east coast and might be about to disrupt road and rail traffic all along
the main line to Pusan. So at one o'clock in the morning the Presbyterians

War with Fortitude," *Korea Times,* June 24, 1990, p. 5, as well as Rhodes and Campbell, *History of the Korea Mission,* pp. 30-35, Smith, *From Colonialism to World
Community,* pp. 146-150, and Arthur Emmons, "War Comes to Korea," *Foreign Service Journal* (August 1950), pp. 11-14.
    7. Bertha Hausman, attachment to John Toland's interview with James Haus-
man, in the Hausman papers.

set out once more, taking the road over the mountains to Taegu. Every aspect of the situation was depressing. Most of the baggage had been abandoned for lack of space. Tires kept blowing every few miles and had to be fixed. It had started raining during the night, and talk of a landslide up ahead forced a 60-mile detour. At 8:00 A.M. someone measured on a map and found that they had made only fifty miles in seven hours.

Tuesday morning, June 27, brought a letup in the rain, but then came dust. Horace G. Underwood described it this way:

> We had our jeep full plus were pulling the trailer with seven people in it. It must have been sheer hell to have bumped along in the trailer, and I shall never forget poor Nat and Mary Bercovitz. They were both small people, had just arrived on the field, and riding in the trailer they were covered with dust except for two huge round eyes each, staring out at us. I felt very sorry for them, and in fact they never came back to Korea.[8]

And there was a new kind of delay. Planes were flying overhead, but there was no way to tell whether they were friendly or hostile. It was necessary to stop and hit the ditch at every sound of approaching aircraft. It was an adventure for the children but not for the adults, many of whom had been through the *Mariposa* and *Gripsholm* evacuations. At mid-afternoon, having abandoned yet another jeep and trailer by the side of the road, what was left of the caravan pulled into the Taegu Presbyterian compound. One of the jeeps was down to three tires and a rim.

In Taegu there was only time for sandwiches before news came that Seoul had fallen to the North Koreans. There were more hasty arrangements, a quick ride to the train station, a 5:30 p.m. departure from Taegu and a 10:30 P.M. arrival at Pusan. A hot rain was falling as the Americans reached the pier and stumbled onto the waiting Liberty Ship SS *Lone Star State*. As they boarded, they stuffed their leftover Korean money, over a million wŏn in all, into a pillowcase for the six men who had decided to stay behind to help with refugees. As the *Lone Star State* put out into the dark waters of the Korea Strait, the rain turned into a midnight storm. It took most of the next day to reach the safety of Japan and the ministrations of the American Red Cross.[9]

8. Horace G. Underwood, "Reminiscences," unpublished typewritten autobiographical notes, p. 73.

9. The Northern Presbyterians were not the only group to have this experience. The Southern Presbyterians were also having their annual meeting that weekend, in Chŏnju, North Chŏlla Province, when the American Embassy telephoned with the evacuation order. The Southern Presbyterians, with one suitcase per person, rode across the Chiri mountains to Pusan in Jeeps, and then embarked for Japan. Elmer T. Boyer, *To Build Him a House* (Norfolk, Va., family memoir, 1976), pp. 92-94, and George Thompson Brown, *Mission to Korea* (Atlanta: Board of World Missions, Presbyterian Church in the U.S., 1962), pp. 187-189.

Last Flight From Kimp'o

Back in Seoul, the first phase of the evacuation on Monday, June 26, was
the only one that went remotely according to plan. As the North Korean
Army approached from the northeast, things simply fell apart. Early on
Tuesday the 27th, Ambassador John Muccio and the last of the American
Embassy staff abandoned the capital and headed for Suwŏn, twenty-five
miles south of the Han River, which was the Syngman Rhee government's
chosen fallback position. On the embassy compounds the Americans left
an estimated $4.5 million in personal effects, not counting vehicles,
$100,000 worth of food, and $40,000 worth of duty-free liquor in the commissary—and a considerable number of documents including personnel
records.[10] Looters struck in full force, as Kris Jensen's wife Maud later
learned when she returned to Seoul in the autumn of 1950 to survey the
wartime damage.

> As soon as the Americans left...the first mobs entered. Nothing is left in our
> whole house—nothing but some of the coal in the cellar and the stove in the
> kitchen. Mission furniture, the refrigerator, relief materials in the attic, stored
> foods sufficient for a year or more ahead—everything is gone. Besides such
> items, of course, there are all the things it takes to run a home—good pic-
> tures, photographs, bedding, linens, silver, dishes, kitchen equipment, ta-
> bles, curios—and worst of all, our books, for a valuable, specialized library is
> hard to replace. Everything is gone: from our wedding silver to the newly ac-
> quired bowl of beautiful hand-hammered brass, a rare Korean curio; from
> our winter clothing to files of papers and records accumulated through the
> years. Our prized Bo-bo, faithful army-trained watchdog to the last, was
> killed by the first mob.[11]

The few American civilians remaining in Seoul on Tuesday, June 27,
crowded into line at Kimp'o Airport for space on the relay of U.S. Air Force
C-54's making runs to Japan. Enemy YAKs kept buzzing the field and straf-
ing the runway, making the evacuation extremely dangerous. Two C-54's
that had been hit earlier lay broken on the ground with thick smoke pouring from their hulks. The planes that came in from Japan and continued to
land between YAK raids kept their engines running on the tarmac and lingered only long enough to load. Their prop wash scattered contents from
the sorry heap of suitcases that built up in front of the terminal as people
were ordered to leave their baggage behind. One C-54, thought to be the
last one out, was so heavily loaded that it barely cleared the fence at the
end of the runway—and still left more than fifty Americans stranded, to be
evacuated, fortunately, on one last plane. Cars were simply abandoned in

10. Caldwell, *The Korea Story,* pp. 166-176.
11. Maud K. Jensen, "Korea Evacuation 1950," undated pamphlet printed for
family and friends.

the airport parking lot, some with keys conveniently left in the ignition.[12]

The next-to-last C-54 brought in four reporters—Keyes Beech of the *Chicago Daily News,* Frank Gibney of *TIME,* Marguerite Higgins of the New York *Herald-Tribune,* and Burton Crane of the *New York Times.* The plane's crew chief was aghast when the foursome told him they were staying to cover the fall of Seoul. "So this is what it's like when we run," thought Beech to himself as they came in through the deserted airport:

> Everywhere were signs of the white man's flight. Punctured beer cans, universal symbol of American culture, lay where they had been tossed on the concrete runway. Abandoned suitcases had burst open, spilling their contents on the ground. Three army trucks, loaded with more trunks and bags that the evacuation planes had refused to take for fear of overloading, were packed with their backs to the field.[13]

In the terminal parking lot the journalists chose their vehicles: a Studebaker for Higgins, a Dodge for Keyes Beech, and a jeep for Gibney and Crane. Picking their way through the crowds in Yŏngdŭngp'o they made their way across the Han River bridge to Camp Sŏbinggo. A skeleton crew of twenty-two KMAG officers was still present, obeying orders from Tokyo to stay with the ROK Army north of the Han River. One of them took Gibney, Crane, and Beech to his house for what turned out to be a very short night.

Blowing Up the Han River Bridge

At ROK Army headquarters, Jim Hausman, Chief of Staff Ch'ae Pyŏngdŏk, and Defense Minister Shin Sŏngmo watched the map throughout the day on the 26th, glumly noting the progress of the North Koreans toward Seoul. It worried them that there was only one bridge suitable for heavy vehicles across the Han River, and that the bridge was choked with traffic. Late in the day they decided that it would be best to move the general staff headquarters south across the river to Sihŭng. Feeling uneasy about leaving Seoul so precipitously, Minister Shin Sŏngmo made a heartfelt speech ending with "We will fight until the end—let's pledge that!" Hausman sent his driver home to get a bottle of whiskey, and the men raised their glasses in a solemn promise.

Ch'ae, however, thought that he should not leave the city just yet and decided to stay behind. When Hausman left him in the conference room, the Korean chief was seated at the head of the table with the bottle of whiskey and his .45 caliber pistol at his elbow. During the evening, as the staff

12. J. Elmer Kilbourne, Conversation, Taech'ŏn Beach, Korea, July 28, 1990. O.H.P. King, *Tail of the Paper Tiger* (Caldwell, Idaho: The Caxton Printers, 1961), pp. 100-112.

13. Beech, *Tokyo and Points East,* p. 108.

convoy traveled south of the Han, the radio on one of the KMAG jeeps crackled to life with a message from Tokyo:

REPAIR TO YOUR FORMER LOCATION. YOU HAVE LIMITED USE OF US AIR AND NAVAL FORCES IN YOUR AREA. MOMENTOUS DECISIONS ARE IN THE OFFING. BE OF GOOD CHEER.

MACARTHUR.[14]

Heeding MacArthur, early the next morning Minister Shin, Hausman, and the ROK Army general staff made their way back to Seoul. As they returned over the Han River bridge, Hausman was surprised to see that ROK Army engineers were stacking cases of dynamite on the approach to the bridge and were getting ready to rig the structure for demolition. MacArthur's message had filled Hausman with hope that the Americans were returning in force, and he hoped against hope that there would be time to save Seoul from North Korean occupation. He picked up a case of dynamite and carried it away from the bridge, emphasizing to the officer in charge that the bridge was not to be blown. The Koreans politely waited until he had gotten back in his Jeep and resumed driving before retrieving the box and resuming their work.

When he got back to headquarters, Hausman found Ch'ae seated where he had left him many hours earlier, at the table with the whiskey bottle, now completely empty, and his .45 caliber pistol. When Hausman gave him MacArthur's message the Korean chief rose heavily to his feet. "Just at that time, as if to underscore what I had just said, a U.S. Air Force bomber flew high over our headquarters, headed for the north. Ch'ae was like a new man. He smiled and then he gave me a bear hug."[15] Then they discussed the bridge. Hausman told Ch'ae that he expected the two of them to be out visiting forward units, and that Vice Chief of Staff Kim Paegil should be ordered to stay at headquarters and exercise sole authority to destroy the bridge if that should prove necessary.

By Tuesday the 27th, however, it was clear that nothing could save the city from North Korean occupation. In the afternoon, Hausman drove a jeep downtown and actually saw a North Korean tank cruising the street near the old royal palace. By midnight the ROK general staff was packing up again, the officers using their aides to move their families out of the city across the bridge that was by then fully prepared for demolition. With

14. Receipt of this message was burned into Hausman's memory as one of the most important moments of his life. Years later he and General Paek Sŏnyŏp visited MacArthur in the general's suite at the Waldorf-Astoria in New York. "I told General MacArthur about receiving his message while displacing to our new command post in Sihŭng. Then I quoted the message....The General was quite impressed. He stood up and gave me the famous MacArthur handshake, one hand shaking the other on my elbow." James Hausman, Toland interview transcript, pp. 32-33, in the Hausman papers.
15. Ibid., p. 41.

other members of the Korean military brass Hausman set out in his jeep during the night, threading his way through crowds of Seoulites thronging the bridge until he reached the southern side. Back in the crush of humanity at the northern end of the bridge, another jeep carried reporters Gibney, Beech, and Crane, who had been rousted by news that North Korean troops were in the city. They were part way across the bridge when everything came to a halt. "We sat in the Jeep, waiting....Then it seemed the whole world exploded in front of us," wrote Keyes Beech. "I remember a burst of orange flame; silhouetted against the flame was a truckload of Korean soldiers. The truck lifted into the air. I felt our own jeep in motion—backwards." It never entered Beech's mind that the South Koreans had blown their own bridge. He assumed it was a lucky hit from North Korean guns. "I was thinking: 'What a beautiful shot it was. Those tanks must have had the bridge zeroed in.'"[16]

Hausman's group was luckier. They were safely across the river when the bridge blew. "It was a tremendous explosion," he later recounted. "Our Jeep actually left the road, vertically. With such a short wheelbase, it's a wonder it didn't overturn."[17] He always insisted that no one in his party had given the order to detonate the explosives and that he was as horrified

16. Beech, *Tokyo and Points East,* pp. 113-114. Eventually the trio made their way upstream along the riverbank and safely across by ferryboat.

The destruction of the Han River highway bridge was a moral and political disaster for the ROK Army and its American advisors, and the controversy about it has never fully been settled. There is no question that the entire Rhee government was in a panic about the advancing North Koreans and desperate for any measure that would stop or slow them. The problem, of course, was that there were people on the bridge when it exploded, and they were simply sacrificed. Many believe that it was ROK Army Chief Ch'ae Pyŏngdŏk who gave the order to blow the bridge with the full knowledge of what would happen. Some believe that he did this despite Hausman's advice and others believe that Hausman lied later when he claimed to have tried to stop the explosion. Ch'ae himself did not live long enough to testify in his own defense. He was shot and killed in an ambush during the summer. Instead, in September the Rhee regime found a scapegoat, Colonel Ch'oe Changsik, the chief army engineer on the bridge that night. Col. Ch'oe was executed by an army firing squad on September 21, 1950. A reinvestigation of the incident after the May 16, 1961, coup d'etat revealed that Col. Ch'oe had orders from the chief of staff to blow the bridge but had done his best to clear the roadway of people before doing so; that subsequent orders not to blow the bridge had been issued but had failed to reach Col. Ch'oe in time, partly because of poor telephone communications and partly because Army MPs blocked the messengers' access to the engineers on the bridge.

To this debacle must also be added the fact that the explosion on the highway bridge, while it no doubt inconvenienced the invading Korean People's Army, did not stop North Korean tanks from crossing the Han River. They were able to do so on the adjacent railroad bridge that remained intact.

17. James Hausman, Toland interview transcript, p. 35, in the Hausman papers.

as anyone to realize that hundreds, perhaps thousands, of innocent people had died in the explosion.

Retreat and Recriminations

The retreat from Seoul was traumatic for all involved. On the morning of the invasion, President Syngman Rhee had ordered his cabinet into session. George Paik had gotten the word by phone at home in Ahyŏn-dong, but having no car had been obliged to walk downtown to the meeting. The news was bad and it had quickly gotten worse. By Monday it had become clear that the families of the cabinet ministers should leave the city as soon as possible. Preoccupied with the survival of their own loved ones, the leading echelon of the Seoul government were less than effective in devising plans to cope with the emergency. As the government broke down, President Rhee gathered up his wife and bodyguards and headed south himself.

On his way to what had been decided would be a temporary government headquarters, he passed Sihŭng where Hausman was camped with the ROK Army brass. Inside a small building he and Hausman sat down at a rickety table. From his pocket the president drew the rumpled clipping about Secretary of State Acheson's "perimeter" speech and let loose his anger about the American's slowness to send aid. "'I will never forgive the Americans,' and his finger almost touched my nose. He asked me, 'Where are my arms, my ten million dollars?' I told him that Congress had just recently approved the money. They must approve the expenditure. And then comes the procurement. That usually takes months. I assured [him that things would move more quickly now]. Several times Rhee would say, 'You Americans,' so I asked if I had done something wrong. He replied in the negative saying, 'You are not an American. You are a worm like us. But someday the worm will turn!' At that point the president opened the palm of his hand and with one finger he moved as though a worm was turning." [18]

General MacArthur arrived at the Suwŏn airstrip a little before noon on Thursday, June 29, and proceeded immediately to the temporary headquarters at Suwŏn Agricultural College. President Rhee, Ambassador Muccio, and Chief of Staff Ch'ae were waiting for him. After a short briefing, he departed for the front, which was still the south bank of the Han River at Yŏngdŭngp'o. The trip was dangerous and subject to YAK attacks. "One YAK, of the two which flew over, dropped a small bomb on the far end of the runway where MacArthur's plane was parked. Some shells came in while [we] were traveling to the front. Most of us hit the ground, but MacArthur didn't even flinch." [19]

18. Ibid., p. 30.
19. James Hausman, notes faxed to Chŏng Ilhwa, attached to cover letter dated 17 May 1991, in the Hausman papers.

By the end of the day, after MacArthur had taken off for Tokyo, it was understood that the U.S. military were about to intervene in force. The question was whether the Americans would be able to establish a strong enough presence in Korea quickly enough to stop the North Korean advance. On the other side of the world, the United Nations was voting to create the international peacekeeping force that would fight the war for more than three years and restore the border between North and South, essentially, to what it had been before the invasion. However, until the UN Command could be established and the beachhead secured in what came to be called the Pusan Perimeter, the North Koreans rolled southward across the Han and down the main transportation arteries, preceded by large numbers of refugees and retreating ROK troops. The defeats demoralized the soldiers and the people. A force of American defenders was hurriedly brought in and sent to the front, then near Osan, to engage the North Koreans. Task Force Smith, as it was called, had the distinction of being the first American unit to tangle with the enemy and prove that it was a mistake to underestimate the Korean People's Army. On July 5 it engaged the invaders and lost a total of 150 dead, wounded, and missing in action before being sent reeling southward toward Ch'ŏnan. The U.S. 24th Infantry Division joined the war soon after and made a stand at Taejŏn, only to be overcome by the North Koreans. Its commander, Major General William F. Dean, the former military governor in occupied South Korea, was taken as a prisoner of war.

The invasion route followed the main north-south highway, the same path taken by thousands of refugees who streamed southward ahead of the fighting. As they trudged toward Pusan, the refugees had to cross the central mountain massif of the peninsula, the range of wooded hills that had been in constant use by North Korean infiltrators and were thought still to be infested with communist guerrillas. Fearing that these enemy agents would recruit a rear-guard force from among the moving refugees, commanders alerted American troops south of Taejŏn to be on the lookout for suspicious people trying to join refugee groups. These orders planted the idea that virtually anyone in Korean "white pajamas" was a potential enemy, and they frightened the American soldiers as they beat their own retreat through the mountains. These conditions led to the killings of Korean civilians by American soldiers between July 25 and 29, 1950, the most notorious incident of which was the massacre in the concrete tunnel of a railroad overpass in Nogŭn-ni, a village in the Yŏngdong district of North Ch'ungch'ŏng Province.[20] In this bitterly remembered incident, American troops of the 7th Cavalry Regiment of the 1st Cavalry Division rounded up and shot as many as three hundred Korean civilian noncombatants, alleg-

20. For Yŏngdong as a "thoroughly Red" area, see Cumings, *The Origins of the Korean War*, Vol. II, p. 279.

edly because they were harboring North Korean agents, possibly KPA sol-diers in disguise.[21] Though the story was reported in the West at the time, little was made of it, and it certainly was not the only such atrocity, since mass killings were committed by all sides in the Korean War.

The Disappearance of Miss Florence

For Florence Root, the significance of Korean politics in the late 1940s was that they created the conditions in which she had to carry out her work of village visitations and women's evangelism in the environs of Kwangju. As guerrilla activity slacked off, she happily reported a surge of activity in rural conversions and church buildings. Her visits drew crowds of Sunday School children and their mothers and her women's Bible classes often drew many more than could fit in the cramped church sanctuaries. The ac-cordion she carried with her was a great drawing card. "I feel like the Pied Piper of Hamlin when I see the children come racing to the place from which the music issues!" she wrote. "Everywhere doors are open to the Gospel. Truly we must work while it is day."[22]

When the North Korean invasion came, it seemed far away from the rou-tine in Honam. The American Embassy sent word to evacuate, however, and the Southern Presbyterians decided once again that it would be best to pull out for the duration. Unlike the *Mariposa* evacuation of 1940, how-ever, there was some question about how long the emergency would last, whether it would affect the Chŏlla provinces, and how soon it would be possible to return. Mothers and children were told to leave, but a skeleton crew of men and single women missionaries remained.

By mid-July, the Presbyterians were feeling the effects of the invasion in the form of refugees. "Economic conditions were making it impossible to

21. The Nogŭn-ni (also written Nogŭn-ri) massacre was reported at the time by John Osborne and other Western journalists (see *Life* magazine, 21 August 1950, pp. 77-85). The story was revived by an Associated Press account that was published on the front page of the *New York Times* on September 30, 1999, which forced a bi-national investigation, the final report from which attributed the incident to poor training and discipline in the American ranks and the general fright associated with the retreat.

During the years that intervened between the incident itself and the story that broke in the *Times* in 1999, Koreans who knew of the massacre kept the story alive in Korea and from time to time raised the issue of compensation and a possi-ble apology from the American side. The South Korean government did not press the American side for any kind of an investigation and appeared to collude in a gen-eral "war is hell" explanation of what had happened, while Korean dissidents de-manded to know about the orders under which the American soldiers had been op-erating in July of 1950 and whether they included instructions to kill Korean civilians.

22. Florence Root, "Dear Friends" letter, May 5, 1950, in the Presbyterian Church (U.S.A.), Department of History, Montreat, North Carolina.

continue the reconstruction program and the growing tenseness of the situation [made] it difficult to carry on most of our work," wrote Chŏnju hospital worker Gene Lindler.

> The end came for us about July 15, when the Communists broke through the Kŭm River line near Taejŏn. Just in case we had to leave suddenly, we had already packed as many of our personal things, hospital equipment and expensive drugs that we could conveniently carry in three jeeps and a quarter ton truck. So in less than three hours after we received the word that we must leave, we were on our way to Pusan by way of Kwangju and Soonchun.

Florence Root, however, refused to obey the evacuation order. She had seen it before and remembered that the Irish Columbans in her district had stayed in Korea through all of World War II. She did not think that a person such as herself, involved in charitable work and educating Korean women and children, would give political offense to the North Koreans even if they caught her. The last departing missionary left Kwangju on July 17, and several Koreans who left on July 20 reported having heard that Miss Florence had gone into hiding in the mountains. That was the last word anyone had of her. Her fellow missionaries hoped that since the communists had taken Honam area with ease and there was comparatively little fighting, she might actually have managed to hide successfully. But no one knew.[23]

In Enemy Hands

Foreigners who elected to stay in Seoul after the invasion faced the oncoming North Koreans with a mixture of dread and resignation. Monsignor Patrick Byrne was one of the highest ranking members of this group. Byrne had spent the entire Second World War in Japan and he did not think that the communist occupation of Seoul could be worse than what he had already been through. More important was the principle: his commitment was to the Korean church, and that obligation transcended his American nationality. He was within easy hearing distance when the ROK Army blew the Han River bridge early Wednesday morning, and he was at home waiting when the North Koreans arrived later in the day to take stock of the Catholic Mission compound.

Journalist Maurice Chanteloup also chose to stay in Seoul to cover the invasion for Agence France Presse. He was in the French Legation with Charles Martel, the acting French Minister, when the North Koreans came. Chanteloup, Martel, Holt, and Byrne all were among the Westerners who were permitted to stay at home for the first few days of North Korean occupation before being loaded onto a train to be taken to P'yŏngyang for "pro-

---

23. Charlotte B. Linton, "Dear Friends" letter, September 10, 1950. In the Presbyterian Church (U.S.A.), Department of History, Montreat, North Carolina.

tective custody" from American bombers.[24]

For Kris Jensen and his hosts on the Methodist Mission compound in Kaesŏng who were stranded on the morning of the invasion, captivity came within hours of the North Korean assault. There were several days of house arrest after which the six Americans were transported to P'yŏngyang and held for interrogation, men and women, three to a cell. They knew nothing of significance to tell their captors but the questioning sessions continued without resolution. Meanwhile they could hear shots coming from the sandbag-lined execution box in one corner of the prison compound as Korean prisoners were put to death.

On July 13, Captain Vyvyan Holt and the contingent of Western diplomats and civilians from Seoul arrived to join the Jensen party in captivity, forcing a move to larger quarters. The North Koreans found a school in the outskirts of P'yŏngyang that they transformed into a concentration camp for Westerners. Larger numbers seemed to afford safety from immediate execution, and although the prisoners were forbidden to communicate between rooms, they got to know their roommates and passed the time trading life stories. In the communal toilet facilities the guards paid no attention to the occasional conversations by means of which the various rooms' inmates shared information. U.S. Air Force planes ruled the sky, and a constant topic of conversation was the meaning of the B-29 raids on the city. The daylight B-29 raids on the P'yŏngyang rail yards were especially spectacular.

On September 5, as P'yŏngyang was being pounded by the bombers, the North Koreans announced that they were moving the group again for protection against the "bloodthirsty Americans." At P'yŏngyang Station they boarded a special train full of captured American soldiers and rode northward through the mountains, moving only at night. Each dawn for five days the train stopped and its occupants were ordered to spend the daylight hours among the trees along the track. One day a pair of P-51 Mustangs strafed the parked train, but no one was hurt.

> On September 11 the train passed Kanggye and pulled into the Yalu River border town of Manp'ojin. Here, too, there was little inkling of the ordeal ahead; in fact, the prisoners had considerable freedom to roam and even bathe in the river. One day a North Korean officer called them together and announced a "be happy" campaign. He told them to sing the song that every North Korean schoolchild knew praising the Great Leader Kim Il-sung. Salvation Army Commissioner Herbert Lord, who was translating, was obliged to tell him, "I regret to tell you that we do not know that song."
>
> "What? How can anyone not know that song? ... Well, what about the song praising the glorious success of our railroad system?" he asked.

24. Letter, Maurice Chanteloupe to Frank Baldwin quoted in Harold Noble, *Embassy at War*, p. 261.

"I regret to say that we do not know that song either," Lord announced, pretending to be sad. The officer looked dumbfounded for a moment but quickly recovered.

"I will permit you to sing any song you wish from your own culture. I will permit this, even though some of your songs may be decadent."[25]

Holding the Pusan Perimeter

During the summer of 1950 and after many defeats and debacles in the southward retreat to the Naktong River, General Douglas MacArthur at the head of the United Nations response to what the Security Council had branded as international aggression gathered his forces in Japan and began landing troops in South Korea. The port of entry was Pusan, and by the middle of August the UN Command, consisting primarily of the U.S. Eighth Army and a patchwork of ROK Army units, had gathered enough strength to stop the North Korean onslaught short of its goal of total conquest.

MacArthur's man in Korea was Lt. Gen. Walton H. Walker, commander of the Eighth Army. Walker arrived on July 13, just after the Task Force Smith disaster, and caught up with General William F. Dean south of Ch'ŏnan. Walker was shocked to see the disarray in the ROK forces and wanted to stiffen their resistance. Days passed with no effective stand against the invaders and debacle upon debacle during the retreat past Taejŏn and southeast through the mountains. On July 17 General MacArthur radioed from Tokyo that Syngman Rhee had put the ROK Army back under direct American command for the duration of the war.[26] After days of trying to communicate with the ROK military, Walker discovered that his subordinates thought of Capt. Jim Hausman as holding the key link. He made for Taegu where Hausman was in charge of G-3 (Operations) and strode into his office. In tones of irony mixed with resignation he demanded,

"Are you the captain I have to see in order to move a ROK unit?!"

"I *hope* not, sir!" answered Hausman, saluting.

With his face in a scowl General Walker sat down and allowed Hausman to teach him some things about the workings of the Korean Army. In sum,

25. Zellers, *In Enemy Hands,* pp. 70-71.
26. This was the "Taejŏn Agreement," by which South Korean armed forces (with certain exceptions) are part of a combined command (originally the UN Command, now the US-ROK Combined Forces Command) led by an American commander-in-chief, historically the individual who commands U.S. Forces in Korea (USFK), the remnants of the UN Command (UNC), and the Eighth United States Army (EUSA), all headquartered since the Korean War in the American military compound in the Yongsan district of Seoul. Under the Taejŏn Agreement and its successors, the American CFC commander has "Operational Control" (OPCON) over ROK forces in wartime and nominal OPCON over main defensive units in peacetime. For a discussion see Donald N. Clark, ed., *The Kwangju Uprising: Shadows over the Regime in South Korea* (Boulder, Colo.: Westview Press, 1988), pp. 68-76.

Hausman advised the general to communicate with the Koreans through him. He remembered it this way:

> I explained fully how we operated as advisors to the ROK Army....I suggested that the ROK G-3 could work with his G-3 [Hausman]. I told him to tell me what he wanted and I would be certain that it is carried out because I would have the order issued by the ROK Army Chief of Staff. If he orders a unit to move and it doesn't, the unit commander will be shot on the spot. [And] that is how I first met General Walker.[27]

Though the ROK Army is given scant credit for its discipline in the early weeks of the war and many units were in fact assigned to labor duty to support the better-mechanized Americans as they arrived from Japan, the Korean Army did accomplish something formidable in holding communist forces at bay in North Kyŏngsang Province. With the help of naval gunfire from the USS *Juneau* the ROK Second Division was able to regain some territory north of Pohang. Walker, meanwhile, moved his headquarters south from Taegu to Pusan and mounted a concentrated defense against a major thrust by the Korean People's Army at Masan, on the southern coast. The North Koreans threw everything they had into this battle to take the remaining corner of the peninsula, including a new tool—psychological warfare broadcasts by "Seoul City Sue" aimed at convincing the troops that their cause was hopeless.[28] General Walker was forced to deliver several

27. James Hausman, John Toland interview transcript, p. 42, in the Hausman papers.
28. The propaganda broadcasts by "Seoul City Sue" began several weeks into the war and continued for at least a year. The voice was that of an unidentified American woman who reminded the Americans of "Tokyo Rose," the Japanese-American nisei named Iva Toguri who broadcast propaganda throughout the South Pacific during World War Two. In Korea, the GIs were both fascinated and repelled that an American woman could support the North Korean side.
Seoul City Sue's scripts were almost certainly authored by the speaker herself, a person with a standard American accent and enough familiarity with American culture and society to be able to invent stingingly effective taunts. She is remembered, for example, by black soldiers in segregated units of the U.S. 24th Division for one particular broadcast in which she claimed that if she, a white traitor, were to return home to the United States, she would get better treatment from ordinary Americans than they would, as black veterans. "And we had to swallow that," they later said. "We knew she was right." (Interviews with former soldiers of the 24th Infantry Division broadcast by ABC News on May 26, 1996.)
Attempts to identify "Seoul City Sue" have suggested that she was Anna Wallis Suhr, an American who originally went to Korea as a Methodist missionary in 1937 to do social work. One version of the story is that Anna Wallis had just ended an unhappy love affair when she decided to leave America and work overseas. Whatever the case, after she arrived in Seoul she took up with a politically active young Korean named "Suhr" (the surname Sŏ) and married him, an act that in those days cost her both her job with the Methodist Mission and her American citizenship.

versions of his famous "Stand or Die" speech making clear that the Eighth Army would *not* allow its lines to be breached by the North Koreans. Reinforcements pouring in from Japan helped stiffen the resistance, and by the middle of August the line was holding.

Korea Kids in the Inch'ŏn Landing

But instead of confronting the North Koreans directly and pushing them back from the Pusan Perimeter, MacArthur's command devised a dramatic strategy that took a large amphibious force around the peninsula to the port of Inch'ŏn, landing it there on September 15. The Inch'ŏn Landing began with artillery barrages against the harbor's outer defenses, and proceeded according to plan, overcoming the defending North Koreans and putting elements of the U.S. and South Korean Marines and the U.S. 7th Infantry Division into the city during the day. This began a thrust toward Seoul that trapped a large part of the Korean People's Army in South Korea. The Inch'ŏn landing therefore stopped the North Korean invasion in its tracks. By October 1950 the UN forces under MacArthur were poised for a counterinvasion of the North.[29]

Anna Wallis Suhr and her husband spent the World War II years in China, where they experienced many hardships. They returned to Seoul after Liberation in 1945 and rejoined his family, which had not fared well in the interim. With the return of the first Methodist missionaries in 1946 Anna found occasional work as a typist at the Methodist Social Service Center (the Taehwa-gwan) in Insa-dong. With help from her mission friends and sympathetic American officials she tried to recover her American citizenship in a campaign that was complicated by her husband's reputation as a leftist. Even J. Harold Berrean, an American advisor to the Korean National Police, was unable to overcome the handicap of Suhr's reputation as a communist, and the matter was still unresolved when the Korean War broke out in June 1950.

Being ineligible for American emergency transportation out of Korea, Anna Wallis and her husband were caught in Seoul when the Korean People's Army entered the city on June 28. Their fate after that is unclear, but acquaintances later reported that they were arrested and taken to North Korea, ostensibly against their will. If Anna Wallis Suhr was in fact "Seoul City Sue," her former missionary friends do not attribute her making the broadcasts to any motive other than fear from her life and that of her husband. (Nell Dyer, letter to author, June 14, 1996; conversations and correspondence with Insong Lee, January 25, 1999, Regina Weaver, January 25, 1999, J. Dennis Berrean, July 2, 1996, and Margaret Martin Moore, January 19, 1998.)

29. For the Inch'ŏn Landing see Robert Debs Heinl Jr., *Victory at High Tide* (Philadelphia: J. B. Lippincott, 1968), and Walt Sheldon, *Hell or High Water* (New York: MacMillan, 1968), as well as the standard military history: Roy E. Appleman, *South to the Naktong, North to the Yalu*, Department of the Army, Office of the Chief of Military History (Washington, D.C.: U. S. Government Printing Office, 1961).

Three Korea Kids, all of with the U.S. Navy, served on General MacArthur's staff in Tokyo helping plan the Inch'ŏn Landing: Presbyterians Horace G. Underwood and Jim Lampe, and Methodist William Shaw. Underwood had gotten himself reactivated in Japan after his escape from Taech'ŏn Beach in June. Jim Lampe and Bill Shaw had both rejoined the Navy in the United States in order to get to the action in Korea, Shaw having interrupted his graduate studies at Harvard in order to do so. All three were familiar with the treacherous tides of the Yellow Sea, having spent their boyhood summers boating to and from Sorai Beach. The tidal fluctuation at Inch'ŏn made any planned landing especially problematic because the water rose or fell an average of twenty-eight feet every six hours. At low tide, many rocks and reefs were exposed or just under the surface, greatly limiting the movement of ships. Any attempt to put landing craft on the beach at Inch'ŏn would require going in at the moment of high tide and leaving the landing craft grounded until they could be unloaded and removed on the next tide. Plans for the landing therefore called for dodging obstructions in the approach along Flying Fish Channel and then pounding Inch'ŏn's artillery defenses into silence in time for the landing craft to go in on the high tide to the beach and seawall. The Marines on the boats would then have to scramble ashore and strike at all the enemy's positions at once in order to keep the landing craft from being destroyed as they lay stuck on the beach. Timing was crucial and there was no room for error.

Horace Underwood and Bill Shaw were assigned to the first wave of the First Marines' assault on Inch'ŏn, because they knew the territory and could speak the language. They remained in the forefront as the Marines approached Seoul on the night of September 19, Horace Underwood being part of a 14-man advance party that set out to cross the Han River between Kimp'o Airport and the town of Haengju. As Underwood recalled the events of that night:

I was assigned to go with the team—very tough Marine Ranger scouts—and we all swam across the river with our equipment in a rubber raft. On the Haengju side the fellows spread out looking for any North Korean troops, but did not find any, so the signal was given for the assault troops to start across. They had come only a little way when heavy fire broke out from the hill behind the village and the banks just above us. The assault craft turned back and we were stuck on the wrong side of the river, so quietly (VERY quietly) we slipped into the water and swam back across, naturally without our equipment or even our clothes. All I had on was underwear and socks....

The next day air strikes were put on the defenses and the assault went across with little difficulty....I followed along with the Regimental HQ as they advanced—with very little opposition—along the north bank of the Han. About the second night across we had camped in a little village just west of Susaek. That afternoon Frank Gibney, a Japanese language colleague from Pearl Harbor days and now a reporter, Keyes Beech, and Marguerite Higgins (reporters) joined us so I went to spend the night with them. That night a shell fell on the house where the HQ was located, killing one man and wounding several, so I guess I missed my chance for a Purple Heart....[30]

On the morning of the 22nd, Underwood's unit continued eastward toward the Seoul suburb of Moraenae. In the meantime, Bill Shaw, who had crossed the river with another unit of the First Marine Division, turned north toward the suburb of Hongje-dong beyond the mountain called An-san. That afternoon his unit was ambushed in the village of Nokpŏn-ni, and Shaw was killed by a sniper.[31]

Horace Underwood did not hear of Bill Shaw's death until late in the day, when he returned to division headquarters. In the meantime, however, he had nearly reached "Hill 104," the spur of An-san beside the Yŏnhi-dong valley that was the site of his parents' home. The North Koreans had decided to make Hill 104 their defense line for Western Seoul and from the ridge above the Underwood House had pinned down a considerable number of South Korean Marines. As the Americans joined the battle, Horace Underwood was obliged to use his knowledge of the terrain to help direct artillery fire along the ridge, hitting his house in the process and burning it so completely that only the rock walls were left. It took four all-out assaults to take Hill 104, and in the fighting a large number of men on both sides were killed.[32]

Street fighting consumed the rest of the week until the 29th, when General MacArthur "delivered" the recaptured city of Seoul to President Syngman Rhee in the great hall of the former Japanese Government-General Building.[33]

The Death March in North Korea

The Inch'ŏn Landing stopped North Korea's invasion in its tracks, interrupted lines between the North and its army in the South, and raised the possibility that the North might be vulnerable to a counterinvasion. Westerners looking for reasons to invade the North began arguing that this was the opportunity to carry out the original United Nations mandate of 1948

30. Horace G. Underwood, "Reminiscences," pp. 78-79.
31. Allan R. Millett, "The Martyr," memorandum dated 1994-98; letter from Ambassador William Sherman to Allan R. Millett, February 10, 1997. I am grateful to Professor Millett for sharing these materials with me.
32. Horace G. Underwood estimates that no fewer than 150 North Korean soldiers were buried on the hillside more or less where they fell. Interview, November 11, 1983; Horace G. Underwood, "Reminiscences," pp. 78-79; and Sheldon, *Hell or High Water*, pp. 252-262, 298.
33. General MacArthur's ceremonial return of the South Korean capital to President Syngman Rhee is one of the unforgettable scenes of the Korean War. See Appleman, *South to the Naktong, North to the Yalu*, p. 537.

to create a united Korea. The attempt to do so then had been frustrated by Soviet and North Korean communist intransigence. Now the war had opened the door to reunification under an internationally recognized government.

This rationale proved irresistible to President Harry Truman who was hungry for an opportunity to "roll back" communism. On October 7 the United Nations approved a British resolution to send General MacArthur's UN army across the 38th parallel to reunite the peninsula, and within hours, with the ROK Army in the foreground, UN forces were in North Korea headed for P'yŏngyang.[34]

Meanwhile, the Western civilian prisoners in North Korea had been encamped at Kosan near the Yalu River. On October 21, the day the UN army reached P'yŏngyang, they were ordered to march twelve miles farther up the Yalu to Chŭi'am-ni. Here the guards seemed to turn friendlier, asking what kind of treatment they would get if the tables turned and UN forces captured *them*. A squad of prisoners—mostly from the diplomatic contingent—even managed to persuade two guards to go with them a distance downstream along the Yalu River in search of advance units of the UN army. Instead, however, they ran into soldiers of the Chinese People's Liberation Army (PLA) infiltrating southward through the mountains. The Korean guards were just as surprised as the prisoners, and they quickly returned to camp.

A week later the prisoners were ordered back to Kosan. As they marched they ran into more PLA soldiers in khaki uniforms carrying burp guns, grenades, and ammunition belts. The North Koreans seemed intimidated. They had no information about the incoming Chinese and did not even know whether to regard them as friendly. For a day or two it seemed that some of the guards were deserting and the Western prisoners were virtually free—though with nowhere to go and no means to get there.

The order then came to march the prisoners back downstream to Manp'ojin, and as they were starting out they got a new commandant. He started out by searching the prisoners and confiscating anything that could be used as a weapon, including the 82-year-old Fr. Paul Villemot's cane, leaving the aged priest to stumble along on the arm of another captive. Then he gave a speech. "We are going on a long march," he said. "I am in command, and I have the authority to make you obey. From now on you will be under military orders....Everyone must march." When Father Thomas Quinlan pleaded that the Father Villemot would die if he tried to

---

34. Jim Hausman believed that Syngman Rhee would have ordered his own troops to invade the north with or without the United Nations. James H. Hausman, interview, August 5, 1995, Austin, Texas.

march without his cane the commandant answered, "Then let him march till he dies. That is a military order."[35]

And so at dusk on October 31 they set out, the civilians and nearly 850 G.I.'s. Chilled to the bone and marching in darkness to escape detection by UN planes, many prisoners straggled and failed to keep up the pace. In the morning the new commandant, whom the prisoners had nicknamed "The Tiger," formed them into groups and made them responsible for each other. Later in the day several American soldiers dropped back. The Tiger immediately stopped the march and sent for their group leader, an Army lieutenant named Cordus Thornton. In a scene burned into the memory of everyone on the Death March, The Tiger convened an impromptu court martial. He hailed some passing KPA soldiers and asked them what to do to a soldier who disobeys an order. "Shoot him!" they shouted. And with that The Tiger blindfolded and bound Lt. Thornton and stepped around behind him. Larry Zellers and Nell Dyer watched transfixed from the side of the road. Beside them Sagida Salahudtin felt tears streaming down her face.

"You see," said The Tiger, "I have the authority to do this." With his pistol muzzle he pushed up the back of Thornton's hat and pulled the trigger at point-blank range.[36]

The cold-blooded murder of Lieutenant Thornton broke whatever spirit was left in the hearts of the captives. Soon their physical stamina also left them. As they marched, passing Manp'ojin and continuing to Chunggang-jin at the northernmost tip of Korea, nearly one hundred POW's died of dysentery, cold, and abuse despite heroic efforts to survive and help each other. Father Hunt of the Anglican Mission, who was overweight and had problems with his feet, was supported as he walked by Father Quinlan. The men took turns carrying the Irish Sister Mary Clare, who had shriveled to eighty pounds. Mother Beatrix, 75, kept falling behind and finally was ordered left by the side of the road. People died of exhaustion during the day and froze to death at night. Someone suggested that the missionary doctor from Kaesŏng be asked to certify each death before the body could be left behind. Instead, The Tiger ordered that his guards "certify" deaths by shooting motionless bodies through the heart.

Amid the life-threatening conditions of the Death March the White Russians displayed special resilience. They seemed somehow tougher and more adaptable than the other Westerners. When it got unbearably cold,

35. Zellers, *In Enemy Hands,* p. 85. In Zellers's account, the quote is "Let them march till they die," a version of the conversation appropriated by Fr. Philip Crosbie for the title of his book, *March Till They Die* (Westminster, Md.: The Newman Press, 1956).

36. All Death March memoirs describe this scene. This account follows Zellers, *In Enemy Hands,* pp. 88-91.

they taught the others how to insulate their summer clothes with straw and tie off pants around the ankles to keep their legs warm. Ivan Tikhonoff made himself useful by fashioning stoves out of mud and rock and then cooking quite palatable food, mainly soups. His sense of chemistry, the sense that had created the jasmine-and-herbs perfume that he had always peddled door-to-door to the wealthy ladies of Seoul, was put to medical use: he gathered oak leaves and distilled from them a bitter remedy for dysentery.[37] And these were not Tikhonoff's only survival skills: he would carry on perfectly good conversations with the guards until they turned to politics. Then he would cup his ear and shout, "Eh? Speak louder, you know I'm deaf."[38]

Many more died. Natalya Funderat, a stout Polish woman who was having great difficulty keeping up, was helped for a time by Commissioner Lord who tied a rope around her waist and pulled her along like a farmer with an ox; but when she finally could not stand, she had to be abandoned. Others fell deathly ill. Patrick Byrne like many others was stricken by dysentery on top of an already serious cold. He was never warm enough, having only his summer-weight clothes and a blanket but no coat, with hands so numb that others had to tie his shoes for him.

On November 8, nine days after starting the Death March, the surviving prisoners limped into the border town of Chunggangjin. Sister Mary Clare lived for only minutes after their arrival. Father Villemot died three days later, and the Gombert brothers, both priests, two days after that. The Tiger, however, insisted that the prisoners go outdoors to exercise, and Monsignor Byrne was among those forced to take off his blanket and exercise in the freezing weather in his summer shirtsleeves. Byrne's cold quickly developed into pneumonia and in the cramped house where he and twenty other men were kept, the rasping of his breathing gave little hope that he would survive for very long. The Tiger ordered one short march to the next town, Hajang-ni, at the end of which those who were deathly ill were put into a "people's hospital," an abandoned farmhouse with a mud floor covered with straw. When there was a fire in the kitchen, smoke rose through the cracks in the floor and made breathing even more painful.

Father Quinlan appealed to The Tiger for help for Monsignor Byrne and the other dying prisoners. He argued that Byrne was the papal representative in Korea and had done much good for the Korean people during his quarter-century of service. Quinlan begged for a hen to make chicken soup, and perhaps some milk. For once The Tiger seemed human, promising to see what he could do; but he also noted that there was little for anyone to eat there in the freezing mountains and milk, certainly, was out of

37. Jim Atkinson, "Story of Ivan Nikolaevitch Tikhonoff," typescript furnished by Margaret Storey, pp. 1-2.
38. Crosbie, *March Till They Die,* p. 118.

the question. Byrne, however, failed quickly. When he died on November 25, Father Quinlan dressed him in his own summer cassock and along with Byrne's secretary, Father William Booth, took Byrne's body to a nearby field, dug a grave with a North Korean guard looking on, and laid Byrne to rest. Quinlan kept his rosary and later presented it to Francis Cardinal Spellman in New York.[39]

Foreign Civilians Held Captive by the North Koreans, 1950-53[40]
(*) = died in captivity; (?) = disappeared in captivity

Diplomats
Captain Vyvyan Holt, minister, British Legation
George Blake, vice consul
Norman Owen, secretary
Georges Perruche, consul general, French Legation
Jean Meadmore, French vice consul
Charles Martel, French Chancellor
Catholic missionaries
Bishop Patrick Byrne, apostolic delegate (USA, Maryknoll)(*)
Fr. William Booth, Byrne's secretary (USA, Maryknoll)
Monsignor Thomas Quinlan (Irish Columban)
Fr. Philip Crosbie (Irish Columban)
Fr. Francis Canavan (Irish Columban)(*)
Fr. Antoine Gombert, 76 (French, Paris SME)(*)
Fr. Julien Gombert, 74 (French, Paris SME; Brother)(*)
Fr. Celestine Coyos, 42 (French, Paris SME; Basque)
Fr. Joseph Bulteau, 50 (French, Paris SME)(*)
Fr. Joseph Cadars, 70 (French, Paris SME)(*)
Mother Therese Bastin (French, prioress, Carmelite)(*)
Mother Henriette de Lobit (French, sub-prioress, Carmelite)
Mother Mechtilde Devriese (French, Carmelite)(*)
Sister Marie-Madeleine, 59 (blind; French, Carmelite)
Sr. Bernadette Descayaux (French, Carmelite)
Frau Charlotte Gliese (German laywoman)

39. This account of Patrick Byrne's death follows Thomas Quinlan's "Message Recorded in Berlin by Monsignor Quinlan, S.S.C., after his Release from Communist Captivity, April 1953," transcript of a statement made in Berlin, in the Maryknoll Mission Archives, New York.
After the winter at Hajang-ni, the civilian prisoners were transferred back to Manp'ojin, where they spent the remainder of the war. The Tiger was replaced in January 1951 as camp commandant and reportedly court-martialed and sentenced to two years in prison himself for embezzling the funds given him to care for the prisoners during the Death March.
40. Crosbie, *March Till They Die,* passim.

Maisara Daulatsch (Korean-born Turkish laywoman)
Helena (Polish-Korean laywoman) (?)
Fr. Paul Villemot, 82 (French; chaplain, St. Paul of Chartres Sisters'
Orphanage beside Seoul Cathedral)(*)
Mother Beatrix Edouard, 76 (French; St. Paul Orphanage, superior)(*)
Mother Eugenie Demeusy (French; St. Paul Orphanage)

Protestant missionaries
Herbert A. Lord, O.B.E., British, lieutenant-commissioner in the
Salvation Army
Bishop Cecil Cooper, 70 (Anglican Mission)
Rev. Charles Hunt, Anglican Mission (*)
Sr. Mary Clare, Irish, Anglican Mission, Seoul (*)
Bertha Smith, USA, Methodist Mission, Kaesŏng
Helen Rosser, USA, Methodist Mission, Kaesŏng
Nell Dyer, USA, Methodist Mission, Kaesŏng
A. Kristian Jensen, USA, Methodist Mission, Seoul
Ernst Kisch, Austrian, Methodist Hospital, Kaesŏng (*)
Lawrence Zellers, USA, Methodist Mission, Kaesŏng

Business and miscellaneous occupations
Alfred Matti, general manager, Chosun Hotel (Swiss) (*)
Maurice Chanteloup, French, Agence France Presse reporter
Mme. Amelia Martel, French, longtime Seoul resident
Mlle. Marguerite Martel, French; daughter of Amelia Martel
Walter Eltringham, USA, ECA official, Seoul (*)
Louis Dans, 37, USA, Traders Exchange, Seoul
William Evans, 50, USA, mining engineer, Seoul (*)
George Hale, USA, engineer (*)
Philip Deane, British, *London Observer* correspondent
Andrea(s) (White Russian), ECA engineer, Seoul (?)
Evgenii Smirnov, 60 (White Russian) (*)
Ilian Kichakov, 58 (White Russian) (*)
Mikhail Leonov, 70 (White Russian)(*)
Mme Natalya Funderat, 60 (White Russian)(*)
Ivan Tikhinov, 68 (White Russian)
Dimitri Vorosiv, 59 (White Russian)

Families
Salahudtin Family (Turks/White Russians; formerly "Salahudtinoff")
Salim Salahudtin, father, mid-fifties
Faiza, wife, Turkish, much younger
Sagid, son, 18
Sagida, daughter, 17
Farid, son, 13
Shaucat, son, 9

Murat, son, 6
Hamid, son, 1
Ahmet Sultan, 30, Turkish, Mrs. Salahudtin's brother
Sophia Sultan, Turkish, Mrs. Salahudtin's sister
Ivan Kilin, 36 (White Russian)
Marusya Kilin, wife, 29 (White Russian)
Olga, daughter, 8
Nikolai, son, 6
Georgi, son, 2

Finding Miss Florence

It was on July 23, as Florence Root was taking a bath in the "saxie house" on the Kwangju Presbyterian Mission compound, that Ansikie, her servant, burst in to announce that the Korean People's Army was on the city's outskirts. "I received it as information," she later wrote, "as that seemed about all there was left for me to do."

> A few minutes later Cho Yong Tack [Cho Yŏngtaek] came in to say that "X" and he had prepared a cave, out at his orphanage just out of town, for me, and would I trust myself to them. I agreed, and in the stream of refugeeing people followed him out the hospital gate....[T]hey put me on an improvised stretcher and carried me out over past ["Y village"] but found that so many people were milling around there that they could not possibly hide me at the place prepared. So I hid in a locust thicket all day—and at dusk they put me in a [chige A frame] and carried me, with several hours' stop in the middle of the night under Moodung San [Kwangju's mountain], and a few minutes' rest twice during the next day, down into Neungju [Nŭngju] County...where I was given supper and a few hours rest—and then before daybreak the next morning, we climbed a steep rough mountain to a lonely house about ten *li* [2.5 miles] from ["Z village"] where that group farms and cares for several children and young people. Yes, this was the much talked-about ["A"] group, who, out of love for their Master, willingly offered to keep me safe from the enemy. Just a little ways from our destination, we were met by *three* Communist soldiers or police—but the Lord sent the right ones to us, who examined us and let us go, and then closed their own mouths and never reported where we were. They knew Chung In Sul, who was our leader there, and knew the self-sacrificing lives those people live for others and so that was the first miracle of many![41]

For eleven weeks Florence Root hid in the mountains, moving when necessary but only at night. Ultimately she was taken to the mountain village of Tonggwang, where a Christian family hid her in a closet. It was a special concern of the villagers that children, who might not be able to

---

41. Florence Root, "Dear Maie and Rob, Mary, Anna, Ginny and Mike" letter, October 22, 1950, in the Presbyterian Church (U.S.A.), Department of History, Montreat, North Carolina.

keep the secret, not see her. She emerged from the closet around dawn each day to stretch her legs and eat breakfast while the children were still asleep. The closet was a most uncomfortable place with little air or light, made especially unpleasant by the odor of unwashed bedding and dirty household items. At times she could not bear it and had to step out into the room. Even these sorties were fraught with risks.

Naturally there was no way to learn any news of the war or how long Florence Root might have to hide in the closet. Neither she nor the Tonggwang villagers had heard anything about the Inch'ŏn Landing, and though the villagers knew something had changed because there were South Korean troops to be seen during the day, they considered their area to be occupied by the Korean People's Army and behaved accordingly. Miss Root certainly had no inkling of what it meant when her host burst into the house one October morning, threw open the closet door, and acting as if he had never seen her before, took hold of her and pushed her out into the courtyard into the presence of a group of South Korean national police. The host and the police together took rope and bound her hands behind her back, insulting her all the while, and shoved her into a waiting police truck to be driven away. Uncomprehending and frightened beyond words, Miss Florence rode with her eyes tightly shut, praying for mercy. Yet when the truck had driven well out of the village, it stopped. The policemen came back, untied her hands, and then, in a completely different tone of voice, explained that the "arrest" had been faked to protect the Tonggwang villagers, in case communist troops should occupy the area again and accuse them of harboring an American spy. Their "surprise" at finding her and their enthusiasm to get rid of her were meant to protect them, and they were supposed to say that they thought she had been taken away to be executed. Within days Miss Root was back in her house on the Kwangju compound. In December she presided at the reopening of the Speer School for Girls. Looking back she realized how fortunate she had been. Some of the people who had helped her, including evangelist Cho Yŏng-taek who took her from her house and put her in touch with the people who eventually saved her life, had not survived the communist occupation.[42]

The Liberation of P'yŏngyang

The UN force that invaded North Korea was made up primarily of South Korean and U.S. Army and Marine units augmented by brigade-level forces from the British Commonwealth. It struck north along two routes: straight up along the railroad to the Manchurian border at Sinŭiju, and northeast

---

42. Young Roh Ahn, *Rain for a Parched Land* (Seoul: Qumran Publishing, 1997), pp. 189-199; Ronald Detrick, notes and correspondence, 1998.

Former Presbyterian Boys School Building with communist murals, P'yŏngyang, 1950. From Rhodes and Campbell, *History of the Korea Mission*, p. 99.

toward Wŏnsan, Hamhŭng, and the inland central part of North Korea. Hundreds of thousands of men were involved in these two main thrusts, and it is of little military significance that Korea Kids were involved in both of them. Yet the Korea MKs' accounts are especially poignant as they bear witness to a military campaign gone seriously wrong, with devastating results for the Korean people.

The U.S. Eighth Army encountered little difficulty going north from Seoul via Sariwŏn to P'yŏngyang on the main road. Advance units of the U.S. First Cavalry Division entered from the south on October 19 as the ROK First Division approached from the east, and by ten o'clock in the morning on October 20 P'yŏngyang was firmly in the hands of the UN Command.

In the advance units entering P'yŏngyang was Lieutenant Howard F. Moffett (PYFS class of '35), son of pioneer missionary Samuel A. Moffett, a U.S. Navy doctor temporarily assigned to the staff of Air Force Major General Earle Partridge. On the afternoon of October 21 General Partridge sent Lieutenant Moffett to P'yŏngyang to find a suitable headquarters for the U.S. 5th Air Force in northern Korea. Moffett relished the assignment and he was determined to be the first to reclaim the former Presbyterian Mission compound in the northwestern corner of the city for his boss—and for himself.

As his plane approached the airstrip south of the Taedong River, Moffett could see that a span of the main highway bridge on the north side was missing, blown up two days earlier by the retreating North Koreans. Vehicles were crossing on a temporary pontoon bridge across the sandbar a little upstream from Moranbong, where the Moffett family had moored their houseboat when Howard was a boy. "It doesn't matter," Moffett thought to himself. "I know the way anyway."

It was late in the day, and to make it to the compound before dark he hitched a ride over the bridge on a passing tank. On the northern side he swung off the tank and began loping through the city streets in the direction of his boyhood home. Moffett was fast on his feet, a challenge to some of the children he passed who ran alongside to see if they could keep up. "Hello!" they called up to him, using every Korean child's first English word. "Hello," Moffett called back to them; and then, in his remembered boyhood Korean, "Does anyone remember Reverend Moffett?" "I am his son!" Someone said yes, and he stopped.

"Are you a Christian?" he asked the bystander.

"Oh, yes," was the reply. "I was baptized by Reverend Moffett."

Moffett resumed running, cutting into the city and then north along the main street to the old Presbyterian Mission compound. Suddenly there it was: the big church, a strange new communist headquarters building where the Bernheisels' house had been, and behind that, the Hill, Roberts, Blair, Swallen, and Hamilton houses all still standing. Across the road was his own family's house, Pyeng Yang Foreign School, and the Union Christian College. "I'm home," he said to himself.

Exploring the headquarters building by twilight, Moffett felt sure that he had found Kim Il-sung's personal lair. Hanging on the outside were huge portraits of Stalin and Kim Il-sung. Inside was a spacious lobby and an inner office suite. Groping in the dark because there was no electricity, he found a long leather sofa and stretched out. Excited and tired at the same time, he fell asleep.

In the morning he awoke and looked around. Surely this must be Kim Il-sung's own office, judging from the size of the desk, the quality of the furniture, and the portrait of Stalin hanging over his sofa. In the outer office, Moffett found he had company: an American colonel sent by the Eighth Army to find a suitable headquarters for General Walton Walker. Moffett, a mere lieutenant, was obliged to negotiate a deal: General Walker and the Eighth Army would get everything east of the road, including the North Korean headquarters; General Partridge and the Fifth Air Force would take everything on the west side including Pyeng Yang Foreign School and the old Moffett home. The Air Force side thus acquired Kim Il-sung's personal quarters in the former home of missionary Margaret Best. Moffett found food still on the table and some unexpected capital improvements. One was a nine-bank Czechoslovakian-made organ. Another was a shaft leading to a subterranean chamber that contained a wood-paneled suite with a living room, bedroom, barber shop, and another tunnel leading over to what Moffett remembered as the Presbyterian Women's Bible Institute.

Other longtime Korea missionaries meanwhile got themselves to P'yŏng-yang by any and all means. Edward Adams, Harry Hill, Archibald Campbell, and Francis Kinsler arrived by truck and jeep on October 25 with a group of North Korean refugee pastors—Yun Hayŏng, Han Kyŏngjik, Yi Insik, Kim Yangsŏn, and Yu Hojun. Howard Moffett got them one of the compound houses and they set to work planning the "Christian reoccupation" of P'yŏngyang. They celebrated their return with standing-room-only services in P'yŏngyang's biggest churches. One service, at the Sanjong-hyŏn Presbyterian Church on October 29, drew three thousand worshippers to hear a sermon by Han Kyŏngjik on Isaiah 60:1, "Arise, shine, for thy light is come." One of the hymns was "A Mighty Fortress Is Our God," the same hymn that had been sung so defiantly in the same church on Easter Sunday 1940, during the showdown with the Japanese over Shintō worship.

The returning American missionaries savored the idea of resuming their work in North Korea. They had a joking argument over how to use the new communist headquarters building. Being a doctor, Howard Moffett thought it should be a hospital. Francis Kinsler, a minister, thought it should be made part of the Presbyterian Theological Seminary. Ned Adams, an educator, thought it should be a college.[43]

But the reoccupation of North Korea was no joking matter. Howard Moffett found that many Koreans were shying away from the Americans, fearing to be seen with them, and he had to turn to loyal Christians in the city to recruit houseboys and helpers to staff the newly reoccupied mission houses. In fact there was reason to be fearful. Between the Inch'ŏn Landing on September 15 and the fall of P'yŏngyang on October 19, many surviving noncommunists had perished. A reign of terror had swept the city as the retreating communists meted out wartime justice to persons likely to welcome the liberation by the United Nations. Thus, when the advance units of the UN army entered the city they came upon hundreds of fresh corpses in open fields, basements, and shallow mass graves. Christians—already marked as anti-communists—had died by the hundreds. They were taken by troops, by uniformed police, and by plainclothesmen like the ones who took Sister Agneta Chang from the Catholic convent on October 4. Finding her in bed and too sick to walk, they took her away on an oxcart. The last friends to see her alive reported that she had been taken north along a bumpy dirt road, groaning prayers as she went.[44]

43. The preceding account is based on an interview with Howard Moffett in Seoul, July 21, 1990 and personal correspondence and reports of Moffett and other missionaries who saw P'yŏngyang in 1950 on file at the Presbyterian Historical Society, Philadelphia.

44. Sr. Agneta was in double jeopardy, not only because she was the senior Catholic nun and American-trained, but because her brother, John M. Chang (Chang Myŏn), South Korean ambassador to Washington at the time, had been making

P'yŏngyang City celebration to welcome UN forces, October 1950. From J. H. Song, comp., *Sajinŭro ponŭn Taehan Min'guk simnyŏnsa* (Seoul: Taehan Min'guk podo yŏnmaeng, 1958), p. 47.

In return for the slaughter of anticommunist elements in North Korea by the retreating Kim Il-sung forces, UN forces discovered, and in some cases participated in, bloody reprisals against communist collaborators. South Korean police and reinvigorated rightist youth organizations, some of them North Koreans returned from the South, meted out their own war-time justice in the occupied areas. The United States and United Nations had no means of controlling the violence that followed.[45]

President Syngman Rhee was one of the first South Korean visitors to P'yŏngyang after it fell to the United Nations. Accompanying him was KMAG advisor Jim Hausman. U.S. Army authorities organized a rally for Rhee, who addressed the crowd of liberated North Koreans from the balcony of Kim Il-sung's headquarters on October 29. Rhee was supposed to appear alone, front and center, as the legitimate leader of the unified Korean people. Not fully appreciating the theatrical purpose of the moment, Hausman stepped out onto the balcony with him.

radio speeches to the people of Korea celebrating the defeat of the North Korean Army in Seoul, and promising liberation to the people above the 38th parallel.

45. The story of the violence against Christians and the moral toll it took on what was left of the Korean church in North Korea was written in the form of a novel by North Korean-born writer Richard E. Kim. See *The Martyred* (New York: G. Braziller, 1964; republished by the University of California Press, 1997).

I remember while I was on the balcony…, a Second Division officer tapped me on the shoulder and told me that General MacArthur had ordered that no American was to be seen with President Rhee as this trip was of his own volition, and was not supported by the U.S. I left the balcony to talk to the officer. Actually I laughed at him. I told him that the whole affair was farcical, inasmuch as the plane that had brought us to P'yŏngyang was ours, and the pilot was an American.…I also told him that at least several thousand pictures had already been taken, showing me with the president on the balcony. I suggested that he could try confiscating those pictures![46]

For a number of the top officers of the South Korean Army, the liberation of P'yŏngyang was a homecoming, and Hausman delighted in their happiness at finding friends and relatives. He spent several evenings with General Paek Sŏnyŏp visiting citizens of P'yŏngyang who told of the desperate retreat of Kim Il-sung's forces and their murderous vendettas against suspected sympathizers. From these same people Hausman repeatedly heard about the communists' promise that they would be returning with the Chinese army behind them to punish anyone who collaborated with the UN forces. He realized that their hosting him, in itself, would mark them for death if the threat held true, so it was with deep dread that he heard the first rumors from these same relatives of his South Korean officers, that Chinese uniforms were being sighted in the northern mountains. As the rumors turned into reliable reports, the UN Command learned that regular Chinese units had already infiltrated through the mountains as far south as Unsan County, the location of the old American gold mines.[47] While the generals pondered these signs, they allowed their advance units to continue toward the Yalu River in the northwest and the central mountains toward the Chosin Reservoir.[48] General MacArthur continued to think that the Chinese would never dare to confront his army. In October at their meeting on Wake Island, he had assured President Truman that the war was almost over. "Organized resistance will be terminated by Thanksgiving," he had declared. The North Koreans "are thoroughly whipped. As for the Chi-

46. James H. Hausman, Toland interview transcript, p. 51; "My Earliest Memories of Korea" typescript, p. 80.
47. Navy Lt. Jim Lampe was sent to P'yŏngyang especially to interview one of these difficult prisoners, whom the U.S. Army insisted were Korean even though they claimed to be Chinese and spoke no Korean. Horace G. Underwood, "Reminiscences," p. 81-A.
48. This famous battle site is often referred to wartime lore as the "Chosin Reservoir." However, "Chosin" is the Japanese reading of the characters for "Changjin," the name of the Korean town at the southern end of the reservoir. The Japanese name "Chosin" is close enough to the Japanese name for Korea ("Chōsen") to have created the confusion that led to a Western habit of calling the reservoir "Frozen Chosen," a term that is sometimes used in military history to refer to all of Korea. I use the word "Chosin" for its name recognition, but the correct name is Changjin.

nese, MacArthur told the President that if they intervened they knew "there would be the greatest slaughter." MacArthur's post-Inch'ŏn hubris was just too great to allow him to consider the alternative interpretation: that the Chinese were preparing a force big enough to rout the UN army and rescue Kim Il-sung's communist republic.[49]

Chinese Surprise in North Korea

As late as the last week of October 1950, U.S. intelligence was continuing to report that the communist side was no longer capable of organized defense. In mid-November, South Korean units were photographed on the heights overlooking the Yalu River, evidence of the UN side's triumph. However, a week later, the remnants of the North Korean army together with their Chinese reinforcements emerged westward out of the mountains to attack the UN forces all along their northward route of advance. MacArthur's forces suddenly had to retreat. In the eastern mountains, where the communist side actually cut off the route of escape, they had to fight their way southward through communist troops just to get to their evacuation point of Hŭngnam.[50]

In the western corridor of the peninsula along the main transportation arteries between P'yŏngyang and the Yalu, Chinese forces attacked from the inland mountains and threatened to segment the UN armies as they pulled back to P'yŏngyang. It was not long before it was obvious that P'yŏngyang, so recently liberated, would have to be abandoned. From Taegu, where he had requisitioned a house on the Presbyterian compound, Ambassador John Muccio sent a transport plane to the P'yŏngyang airstrip to evacuate the American civilians in the city.

Lieutenant Howard Moffett, meanwhile, was gripped with fear for his family's Christian friends, the ones who had recognized him and exposed themselves for retribution as collaborators with the American invaders. He did not leave on Muccio's airplane. Instead he used a car that he had requisitioned—the 1939 Plymouth that once had belonged to his neighbors, the Phillips family—and began ferrying carloads of Koreans on the pontoon bridge across the Taedong River. His final carload was the family of a long-time Presbyterian Mission employee jammed into the Plymouth for the seventeen-hour drive to Seoul.

49. MacArthur's miscalculations are the subject of Stanley Weintraub's *MacArthur's War: Korea and the Undoing of an American Hero* (New York: The Free Press, 2000), especially chapters 11 and 12.

50. For first-person accounts of this phase of the war, see Donald Knox, *The Korean War: Pusan to Chosin—an Oral History* (New York: Harcourt Brace Jovanovich, 1985), pp. 617-680.

To Choose between Life and Death

Back in P'yŏngyang, the Americans employed a scorched earth policy to deny the communist invaders what they had left behind. Cpl. Leonard Korgie of the U.S. 21st Infantry Division, one of the last Americans out of the city, recalled the scene:

> We went through P'yŏngyang at night and the whole city looked like it was burning. In one place the engineers burned a rations dump about the size of a football field. God, it was a shame to see in a land of hunger all the food going up in smoke. There was US military equipment everywhere. I don't know how much was destroyed....I believe we set on fire most of the villages we passed through. We weren't going to give the Chinese too many places to shelter in during the rest of the winter.[51]

All along the western corridor of North Korea the UN forces were in full retreat. A UN stand at the Ch'ŏngch'ŏn River failed to halt the communist advance.[52] A bombing campaign to destroy everything military between the Ch'ŏngch'ŏn and Yalu Rivers also failed to save the UN's fortunes. As the Americans set fire to P'yŏngyang, they created a general panic. Anyone who had been seen at Syngman Rhee's rally or had welcomed or worked with the Americans and South Koreans grabbed whatever could be carried and headed south on foot.[53]

Living in a house over the ridge from the old Presbyterian Mission compound in P'yŏngyang was a 19-year-old student named Hong Kyŏngsŏn and his grandmother. Theirs was a Christian household that belonged to the West Gate Presbyterian Church and Hong identified himself as a Christian, a fact that did not bar him from attending school though it did subject him to official discrimination. Like many Christians in the city of P'yŏngyang, Hong Kyŏngsŏn was part of the welcoming crowd that greeted the UN liberation of the city. And when Howard Moffett turned to the city's churches for people to work for the U.S. military on the mission compound, it was natural for Hong to volunteer for a job as a houseboy.

Believing that the Americans were omnipotent, Hong Kyŏngsŏn had not worried much about the dire predictions of reprisals after a communist re-

51. Ibid., p. 659.
52. The account of this campaign follows S.L.A. Marshall, *The River and the Gauntlet* (New York: William Morrow, 1953).
53. This account is based on an interview with Timothy Kyung-Sun Hong, Duarte, Calif., January 9, 1999. For other accounts of what happened to Christians and others who fell victim to the North Korean regime during the war, see See Chulho Awe, *Decision at Dawn: The Underground Witness in Korea* (New York: Harper and Row, 1965), pp. 145-168. The novelist Richard Kim also gave a gripping account of the situation faced by Christians in P'yŏngyang in his novel *The Martyred*.

turn. The news that the Americans were pulling out thus came as a shock to him, and he was caught without having made any preparations to flee in such an eventuality. He hardly knew what to do when a group of fellow Christian workers swung by in a jeep on the afternoon of December 1 and offered him a ride out of the city. Kyŏngsŏn begged them to wait just a few minutes while he went over the hill to say goodbye to his grandmother, but by the time he got back the jeep was gone. Instead, though the last American had been gone for only a few minutes, looters had started raiding the compound houses. In a daze, Kyŏngsŏn entered the house where he had been working and emerged with his own share of the take: two commissary cans of peaches in syrup.

By the following day, it was clear that the Hong household had no time to lose if they were going to escape the communist reoccupation of P'yŏngyang. The thunder of artillery was audible to the north and most members of the West Gate Church had already left. Hong Kyŏngsŏn's grandmother pondered how best to travel. Money was worthless, so she took two bolts of silk—a recognized medium of exchange in the traditional Korean economy—and wound them tightly around her grandson's middle. The silk was very thin and the bolts were only about two feet wide. Wrapped around the skinny boy they would be useful as warm underclothing even if they never had to be used to buy food. Over the cloth, Kyŏngsŏn donned a shirt and jacket. He also put on two pairs of pants. With only one pair of socks in rubber shoes, walking would be his biggest problem, but it was still better than wearing sandals.

On the night of December 2, Hong Kyŏngsŏn and his grandmother made their way in the dark to the bank of the Taedong River. Upstream was the bombed-out railroad bridge. The bridge itself was under water but the steel framework stuck up and had been serving as an icy crossing for the bravest of the refugees for several days. Even in daylight, hundreds, or maybe thousands, of people had slipped off the girders and fallen, most of them to their deaths. Farther downstream was the pontoon bridge constructed by the U.S. Army Engineers in October, now recently destroyed during the retreat. Not realizing that the departing UN forces had removed the southern half of the pontoon bridge, the fleeing refugees pressed out onto the structure in the midnight darkness. They reached the middle of the river only to discover that the bridge ended there, and they screamed in panic at the people behind them to stop shoving. But the shoving came all the way from the bridgehead and could not be resisted, so in twos and threes they fell off the broken end of the bridge into the freezing black water and were swept away.

On the northern bank, Hong Kyŏngsŏn and his grandmother found themselves part of a group of refugees trying to figure out how to cross the Taedong. In their party was a hardware merchant, and together with young

Hong he hit upon a plan to fashion a raft. Using cast-off wood, some abandoned gasoline drums, and spools of baling tape from the merchant's shop, Hong and the hardware man lashed together a thing that would float. On the first crossing they paddled across unrolling a spool of the baling tape to serve as a ferry rope. Then, leaving the merchant on the southern bank, Hong pulled himself back along the tape to the city side to get his grandmother. This proved impossible: a crush of refugees piled on immediately almost sinking the raft, and it was not until the fourth crossing that Hong was able to insist that the crowd put his grandmother aboard. On that crossing, the Hongs abandoned the raft and set off on the southward road, hoping that someone else would pull it back to the northern side for more passengers.

Turning Out the Lights in North Korea

Downstream at Chinnamp'o at the mouth of the Taedong River, Navy Lt. Jim Lampe worked frantically to evacuate as many Korean civilians as possible before the Americans abandoned the port. For Lampe, as for Howard Moffett, the return to P'yŏngyang had been filled with personal significance. He had been born in Sŏnch'ŏn, had attended Pyeng Yang Foreign School from sixth grade on, and would have graduated in 1942 if the Pacific War had not intervened. The return to North Korea had been a personal odyssey; but now, in the December chill, he was participating in yet another American abandonment of Korea and he was bitter about it. The Navy had already loaded the most valuable supplies on landing craft and the skippers wanted to be under way. Lampe, however, struggled to postpone the pullout while he commandeered sampans and junks to fill with refugees and power craft to pull them south to Inch'ŏn. Keeping control was difficult.

> I had the police form a line of all those who had worked for us, who hadn't gotten out on the junks, to form a line, four abreast, with their families, along the pier area, to be taken out to an LST by our small boats. It was morning now and that line was the most pathetic thing I had seen.

> We got into trouble when a group of several thousand who hadn't worked for us, but wanted to get out, crashed through the guards and into the line... Each of these people had a pitiable small bundle with them—[and] each thought that their life depended on their getting on one of those boats.

> Noon passed....One LST still had room for more. All but 12 of our guards were pulled out and we backed down to the loading ramp. The crowd had absolutely no semblance of order now; it was just a solid mass of people, several thousand, all pushing. The demolition people had not had time to de-

stroy much of the stores left behind and it was decided that the destroyers would shell the areas where they were piled. Word was sent in to stop and get off the beach before the destroyers opened fire....Word came that the destroyers wanted to fire while there was still light and that the LST could take only one more load ....[We] shoved off all but six of us on that boat as there was one more—the last one—on its way in for the last load. We had to be on that boat.

For some time, women were begging on their knees, crying, praying for their lives to be put on that boat. ROK sailors and Marines...would have to turn away [and] brace themselves, [then] turn again and start beating the crowd back with their rifle butts. Some laid down their rifles and joined the crowd. I pulled these out, told them they had to fight for their country and put them on the next boat out.

Women, the old ones, young girls and half naked babies in the cold, all crying, pleading....The last boat out. I felt like a monstrous murderer. A devil with a gun and pistol condemning these people to death....I was ashamed and embarrassed to be leaving and these helpless ones had to stay. Had to actually kick my foot free from a woman's hand as I stepped in the boat. I felt like killing these people for making me feel like a murderer, and I wanted to blow my brains out for being the murderer. Big, warm, well armed American!

...[Out] on the ship I couldn't talk to anyone. I went aft on top of the after gun mount and watched the bombardment—I didn't want to see it but I had to. I *knew* some of those several thousand left behind and pushing each other in the water as though by will power they could make another boat come in for them.

Some must have been hurt in the bombardment. It couldn't be avoided. It was quite spectacular as large gas and oil storages went up, throwing flames 250-300 feet in the air. Hell could hold no greater terrors. I vowed never to go near Chinnamp'o again. How could I look these people in the eyes?[54]

Meanwhile, Korean refugees trekking southward through the battle lines reported that their worst fears were coming true in P'yŏngyang as the communists meted out people's justice to those who had opposed them. But it was not enough to escape the communists. There were scenes of inhuman brutality on the refugee road itself. Refugees fought and stole from each other. When refugees asked for food and water along the way, villagers attacked them and drove them away. Planes—some of them with South Korean markings and some from the U.S. Air Force—cruised along the roads and attacked the refugees at will.

Hong Kyŏngsŏn and his grandmother were on the road headed south when a P-51 Mustang with South Korean markings swooped low over his

54. James Sharrocks Lampe, Letter to "Peg" (his wife Margaret Bowman Lampe), March 8, 1951. I am indebted to Fran Lampe Peterson for permission to use the letter.

group of travelers. He could clearly see the pilot's face as he buzzed the refugees, waggling the wings and eliciting waves of greeting from below. The plane passed behind them and disappeared briefly behind a hill, then turned and reemerged along the road with guns blazing, spraying the civilians with machine gun bullets. Terrified, Hong could feel the heat from the bullets and their impact as they hit the dirt around him. He grabbed his grandmother and dove for the ditch as others fell, some of them dead before they hit the ground. Hong later said he thought the airman's target had been the oxcart that was traveling with them and carrying some of the oldest people, since all vehicles were suspected of transporting enemy weapons and ammunition. The airman succeeded in killing several of the riders, the driver, and the ox.[55]

In the remaining thirty-two months of the Korean War, the U.S. Air Force made a point of punishing every part of North Korea by bombing. On December 14-15, 1950, the Air Force hit the city of P'yŏngyang with seven hundred 500-pound bombs, 175 tons of delayed-fuse demolition bombs, and thousands of gallons of napalm. Two more rounds of bombing on January 3 and 5, 1951, were aimed, in the words of General Matthew Ridgway, at "burning the city to the ground."[56] By spring, refugees had described the results to Americans in the south. As Archibald Campbell wrote in a letter in April, "Pyeng Yang was in such fine shape when we were there last fall, but since then most of the compound has been destroyed—the college, the academy buildings, the Women's Higher Bible Institute, the Foreign School, the Reiners' and Miss Best's houses at least."[57] As more information came in, the destruction turned out to be total: everything was gone except one seminary building that the Reds were using as a courthouse. American bombing was so thorough that the planes ran out of targets and started aiming as if by caprice, for example, using a B-29 to bring down a North Korean soldier on a motorcycle.[58] In the words of the North Koreans themselves, "... everything was destroyed: factories, businesses, schools, health facilities, government offices, and people's homes—everything. The American imperialists removed P'yŏngyang from the map, and it seemed that it

55. Timothy Kyung-Sun Hong, interview, Duarte, Calif., January 9, 1999. Hong believes that some of the air attacks along North Korean roads during this period were not aimed at destroying communist supplies but actually intended to discourage the refugees themselves from streaming south to overwhelm the already scarce resources of South Korea.

56. Cumings, *The Origins of the Korean War.* Vol. II, p. 753.

57. Quoted in Rhodes and Campbell, *History of the Korea Mission,* vol. II, pp. 102-103.

58. It was a B-29 of the U.S. Air Force's 92nd Bombardment Group that actually "chased an enemy soldier on a motorcycle dropping bombs until one hit the hapless fellow." Robert Frank Futrell, *The United States Air Force in Korea, 1950-53* (New York: Duell, Sloan, and Pierce, 1961), p. 195.

would take more than a century to rebuild."[59] Beyond P'yŏngyang, up north in Unsan, even the work of the old Oriental Consolidated Mining Company was ruined as the bombers hit the town of Pukchin and the mineshafts filled with water over time, so that former OCMC engineers were certain that they could never be pumped out well enough to be used again.[60]

59. Kang Kunjo, *P'yŏngyang-ŭi ŏje wa onŭl* (P'yŏngyang: Sahoe kwahak ch'ulp'ansa, 1986), p. 105.

60. Spencer J. Palmer, "American Gold Mining in Korea's Unsan District," *Pacific Historical Review*, XXXI:4 (November 1962), p. 390. Since the early 1990s, the DPRK government has been working on draining the mineshafts and creating possibilities for a new gold mining industry, without significant results. C. Kenneth Quinones, conversation, Seoul, Korea, July 21, 2002.

--19--

Epilogue

In 1951 at the height of the Korean War when U.S. Air Force bombers were pounding the DPRK into rubble, a North Korean writer named Han Sŏrya penned an anti-American story entitled *Sungnyangi* ("The Jackals").

"The Jackals" is about a Korean boy named Sugil and his widowed mother who live on a missionary compound where the mother is the cleaning lady for an American family. The foreigners in the story are grotesque. They keep weapons in the house and have a terrifying bulldog as a pet. They are physically ugly. The American wife has a long canine snout and slitty eyes, and the missionaries' son moves like an insect on "long grasshopper legs."

One day the boy Sugil finds a discarded rubber ball and starts playing with it, only to get into a scuffle with the American boy in which Sugil is injured. He requires hospitalization and while in the mission hospital, dies. To cover up what's happened, the missionary doctors cremate Sugil's body and announce that he's died of a contagious disease. This is too much for Sugil's mother, who storms into her employers' house. As translated by Brian Myers:

> Like a tornado she flung open the heavy door of the missionary's brick house to find her three enemies around their dinner table. As if fixing on a target she looked around at their faces, which grew and shrank before her eyes as if shown on a movie screen. The old jackal's spade-shaped eagle's nose hung villainously over his upper lip, while the vixen's teats jutted out like the stomach of a snake that has just swallowed a demon, and the slippery wolf cub gleamed with poison like the head of a venomous snake that has just shed its skin. Their six sunken eyes seemed to Sugil's mother like open graves constantly waiting for corpses. Like demons before the king of the underworld

this pack of wolves quaked at the sight of Sugil's mother, with her tangled hair, bloodshot eyes, bloodsoaked feet, and torn skirt.[1]

The missionaries lamely try to convince Sugil's mother that her son has gone to live with Jesus in heaven. When this fails they accuse her of being possessed by the devil. But Sugil's mother will not be distracted. Brian Myers continues his translation:

> "Give me back my boy!" Sugil's mother put her head down and lunged forward in an effort to get past, but the vixen, taking a few steps backward, blocked her way.
>
> "God will forgive you for this," she said.
>
> Just then the old jackal stood straight up. "Out devil," he shouted at the top of his voice.
>
> "Devil?" [screamed Sugil's mother]. "You son of a bitch, you kill someone for taking a ball you've thrown away. *You* bastards get out! Who gave you the right to come to another country and kill innocent people? This is *our* Korean land, *Korean land* ... [and there are still plenty of Koreans left]."

During the fracas the missionaries produce their rifle. Sugil's mother manages to wrest it away from them and break it over the stove. But just as she is getting the best of them, the Japanese colonial police arrive at the house to subdue her, thwarting her revenge. "It was bitterly mortifying to be taken away before exacting vengeance on her enemies," concludes the writer.

> "Just you wait," she said. ["There are plenty of Koreans left!"] As she walked, it seemed the darkening street would never end. The birds were flying back and forth across the low sky in search of their nests.

It is not hard to see why Han Sŏrya would have written such a bitter story in 1951. North Korea's wartime experience with Americans is certainly one reason for the xenophobia of the P'yŏngyang regime under Kim Il-sung and his son Kim Jong-il. The prewar experience also includes many things that are painful for the West to remember. After all, the story of Dr. Haysmeir and the apple thief, variations of which arise whenever Koreans speak critically of the missionary era, is true. So are the stories about the gold mines at Unsan. However, "Jackals" is nonetheless a mere caricature of Westerners in Korea and, like the actions of Dr. Haysmeir, an injustice to the majority who did so much that was good. If the organized forgetting is such that the only memories of the West that remain in North Korea in the

---

1. Brian Myers, *Han Sorya and North Korean Literature: The Failure of Socialist Realism in the DPRK* (Ithaca, N.Y.: Cornell University East Asia Program, 1994), pp. 157-188.

twenty-first century are those of Dr. Haysmeir, *nodaji*, and death from the skies, the purpose of history as a testimony of truth has not been served.

The Human Legacy

The Westerners in this book crossed the ocean keen to make a difference to the people of Korea. Little did they realize how much Korea was bound to change them in return. For those who came to regard Korea as their true home, their tenuous belonging was an illusion as we have seen. When Charlie Clark was deported from Korea in 1941, for example, he suffered an emotional loss that diminished him forever. For the rest of his life he pined to go back to a homeland that was not, and never had been, his own. There were many, many others like him.

Korea's relations with the West also wrought profound changes in the lives of innumerable Koreans. The missionary connections that enabled Yun Ch'iho and George Paik to get their modern educations are just examples. The professional and social advancement provided by mission schools and seminaries to a whole echelon of Korean leaders must always be included in any assessment of the Western impact on Korea. The transformation of Korean collaborators who had served in the Japanese armed forces into South Korean army officers is another case of life-altering interventions by Westerners in the lives of individual Koreans. Adoptees and Korean-American immigrants can offer many more recent examples of ways in which external forces have changed Korean lives, often as if by accident, in more recent times.

Changes such as these awaited Hong Kyŏngsŏn as he lifted his grandmother out of the ditch beside the road from P'yŏngyang and surveyed the carnage created by the Mustang that had strafed their refugee caravan that day in December 1950. He knew they had to keep moving, and his grandmother suggested a change in course, southwest toward Haeju. After several days of walking and begging food along the way, they arrived in the city and purely by accident ran into members of their own family. The family decided that Kyŏngsŏn should continue southward on his own, to avoid being drafted into the Korean People's Army, or worse, if he was recognized as a collaborator with the Americans. Hong made for the coastline, reaching the sea at a point north of Kanghwa Island on the Han-Imjin estuary. From there he hitched a series of rides on fishing boats for more than a hundred miles before going ashore. Not far from Taech'ŏn Beach he headed inland, seeking out Christian homes to take him in, until he finally reached the city of Taegu. There he stopped and moved into a tiny room in a Christian orphanage to work for room and board as an attendant. He was too malnourished to pass the Army physical and did not wear any uniform for the balance of the war.

As a church volunteer and later as a student in the Taegu Bible Institute, Hong Kyŏngsŏn had a chance to work in the school's drama program. There he encountered an American missionary, Katherine Clark, the daughter of Charlie and Mabel, now returned to Korea as a teacher. Learning English and taking the name of Timothy, Hong became Kay Clark's assistant and eventually the couple were married. In 1968 they left Korea, changed careers, and went into the restaurant business in Chicago. In 1987 they retired to Southern California. In all that time Timothy Hong has heard nothing at all about his family in North Korea. Living in Los Angeles in his seventies, he still yearns for news and dreams about his father and mother in Kanggye.

For Kris Jensen and the other civilian prisoners of the North Koreans the death march under the tyranny of The Tiger was the worst, but they had to endure more than two years in POW camps until being released just prior to the July 1953 armistice. The American and European missionaries in the group were taken by rail through China and Siberia and ultimately released to the West via Berlin. After his release, Kris Jensen returned with his wife Maud to the Methodist Mission in Seoul, and there he died in 1956.

The Salahudtin family and certain other civilians were released into the South through P'anmunjŏm, as were all UN military POWs. All the Salahudtins' children were taken under the wing of the Turkish forces in the UN Command and educated in Seoul's foreign schools before finding their way to the United States as immigrants. Sagid Salahudtin, who studied geometry and physics with Larry Zellers in the prison camp, later earned a Ph.D. in nuclear physics and worked for the U.S. Atomic Energy Commission.

Horace H. Underwood was not in Korea when the war broke out in June 1950. He had a heart condition that was aggravated by the pain of Ethel's murder, and his doctors had advised him to retire and return to the United States for better medical care. He was in New York when the North Koreans invaded, and he insisted on returning. When the Army spurned his offers of advice he turned his attention to repairing the damage at Chosun Christian University. But then came the Chinese Communists, the second fall of Seoul, and a retreat to refugee life in Pusan. It was in February 1951, in the bleakest hours of the Korean War, that his heart finally failed him. He died in the company of his sons Richard and John, at the age of sixty. When the United Nations recaptured Seoul a few weeks later, the brothers buried their father in the grave next to Ethel's in the Foreigners' Cemetery at Yanghwajin.

Horace and Ethel's eldest son Horace G. Underwood, third in the succession of Horace Underwoods in Korea, spent the war years in uniform serving together with his brother Richard as a staff interpreter for the United Nations at the truce negotiations in P'anmunjŏm. In 1955 he returned to Korea with his wife Joan. Horace G. taught on the English faculty of Chosun Christian University and served as acting president of the newly renamed Yonsei University in 1960-61, replacing L. George Paik who was elected to the National Assembly. Joan Davidson Underwood taught English at Yonsei and Latin at Seoul Foreign School until her death in 1976. Later Horace married Australian missionary Dorothy Watson and after retirement remained on the Yonsei campus, serving on the Board of Trustees and living in a house across the street from where the news first came of the attack on Pearl Harbor in December 1941.

Richard Underwood represented the American-Korean Foundation in Seoul during the 1950s and in 1962 began a 30-year career as headmaster of Seoul Foreign School, where his mother had come to be the first teacher in 1912. A third Underwood brother, John, served with the Presbyterian Mission for forty-six years in Andong, Ch'ŏngju, and Kwangju.

Of the fourth generation of Korea Underwoods, Horace and Joan's son H.H. Underwood II joined the English faculty of Yonsei University in 1976 and taught there for more than twenty years before becoming executive director of the Fulbright Commission in Seoul. His younger brother Peter returned in the 1980s as a businessman. All their children attended Seoul Foreign School but none of them yet has attempted to continue the Underwood dynasty of missionary educators into the twenty-first century.

Among the others whose stories are told in this book, Charlie Clark never returned to Korea. He did remarry, and he spent the last fifteen years of his life in a second career as an itinerant pastor on Indian reservations in Oklahoma, being driven to services after his eyesight failed. He died in 1961 at the age of 83.

Lilian Ross was reassigned to Taegu after World War II and worked with church women in the Taegu environs until her retirement in the 1970s, after which she retired in place and lived with her Korean protégés until osteoperosis forced her to retire again to a nursing facility in California. She lived to the age of 93. Florence Root likewise stayed "home" in Korea after her mandatory mission retirement age until her infirmities required relocation to a retirement home in Harrisonburg, Virgina. She was 102 years old when she died there in 1995.

A few survivors of the *Mariposa* and *Gripsholm* evacuations still live in the United States and Canada. Mary Linley Taylor and her sister Una Mouat-Biggs lived for many years in northern California. Natalya Tchirkine lived in the San Francisco Bay Area with her sons Cyril and Vladimir until her death in 1989 at the age of 96. The Tchirkines' former neighbor Nina Belogolovy lived in Fremont, in the East Bay, and her sister Toma lived in Orange County. None of them ever returned to Korea.

No doubt the longest odyssey was Victoria Yankovsky's circuit back to the family homestead at Sidemi in the Primorsk region south of Vladivostok. Victoria spent ten years in Chile with her husband and son waiting for a visa to the United States. In 1953 they took jobs in New York State at Leo Tolstoy Farm, a home for displaced White Russians. In 1968 they moved to California and bought a small hotel in Healdsburg on the Russian

River. In 1991, after her husband died and she had sold the hotel, Victoria and her son and granddaughter Orr and Alora Chistiakoff were invited back to Sidemi for the unveiling of a set of statues commemorating the original pioneers of the Primorsk region, Mikhail Yankovsky foremost among them.[2]

James Hausman left Korea in March 1951 to serve in the Pentagon as chief of Korea-related military intelligence during the war.[3] He returned to Seoul in March 1956 as special advisor to the commander-in-chief of the UN Command (CINC/UNC), who was always an American general. After retiring from the Army as a lieutenant colonel, he remained as a civilian in the position of special advisor to CINC/UNC, serving Generals Lyman Lemnitzer, George Decker, Carter Magruder, Guy Meloy Jr., Hamilton Howze, Dwight Beach, Charles H. Bonesteel III, John Michaelis, Donald Bennett, Richard Stilwell, John Vessey, and John A. Wickham Jr. Though the U.S. official "country team" in Korea is nominally headed by the American ambassador, it was these commanding generals who represented America's primary interest in Korea. They rotated on the average of every two years. Hausman briefed them when they arrived and after they left he continued to feed them trustworthy information back at the Pentagon, where several of them became chiefs of staff. It is no exaggeration to say that for more than twenty years Hausman functioned as the institutional memory of the U.S. government on Korean military affairs.

Walking in the Cemetery at Yanghwajin

Today, Westerners in Korea live in wholly different ways. Gone are the missionary compounds and landmarks of yesteryear along with the attributes of life in Korea before the Pacific War: the servants, the resorts, and the social distance between Koreans and Westerners. With land prices soaring, Korea's foreign sojourners live in apartments and do their own housework. With the advent of subways and fleets of taxis, they take public transportation. In the summer they leave the country on vacation—something that would have been a dream for the early missionaries who did not see their families for many years at a time. The earlier eras have ended—the missionary era, the era of the foreign aid official, and that of the military advisor. Seoul's two best international schools, both founded by members of leading missionary families, are now attended mostly by well-traveled Korean children. The foreign children who attend are from the business and

2. Victoria's brother Valery is a poet near Moscow. Brother Arsenii ("Andy Brown") found a position with TRW after he was fired by the U.S. Army and rose to the position of vice president. Brother Yuri died after being released from the Gulag. Sister Muza worked for many years as a secretary with the U.S. Civil Service and retired in San Francisco.

3. He was the executive officer of the Japan/Korea Section, Eastern Branch, Strategic Intelligence, G-2, and chief of the Korea Section.

diplomatic communities. Missionary children are rare, and no one ever uses the term "Korea Kid."

None of the descendants of North Korea's prewar foreign community live there now, though a handful of former Pyeng Yang Foreign School students have found their way back to visit the site of the P'yŏngyang Presbyterian Mission. In 1997, two delegations of Pyeng Yang Foreign School alumni visited North Korea on emergency famine assitance missions. Like other visitors to North Korea they reported that the city is preternaturally clean and orderly. The geographical landmarks such as the Taedong River and Peony Point are there to help them get their bearings but the only trace of the forrmer mission compound is the intersection of the streets that were cut through it in the late 1930s.[4] The site of PYFS itself is inaccessible, since it is now the location of the DPRK Foreign Ministry.

When the Reverend Billy Graham visited North Korea at President Kim Il-sung's invitation in 1992, he made a sentimental pilgrimage to the site of Pyeng Yang Foreign School. His wife, Ruth, daughter of China missionary L. Nelson Bell, had attended PYFS as a boarding student in the thirties. So had Dwight Linton, a member of Graham's entourage in 1992. They were disappointed to find no relics of the former Western establishment in the PYFS environs. Linton, however, did manage to find some Koreans who could remember what had been there before the war.

Not far away, in Shanghai, Tianjin, and other China Coast cities, the visitor can still find many structures that recall the prewar era when Western expatriates flourished as transplanted aristocrats. Not so in Seoul. With the destruction and reconstruction of the Korean War era and generations of urban reconstruction, the traces are much harder to find. Korea has changed in ways that would have been inconceivable to the prewar foreign residents. Under Korean direction the missionaries' churches, schools, and hospitals have proliferated and evolved in astonishing ways, sometimes bearing scant resemblance to the original foreign vision. Though the thousands of Christian churches might trace their beginnings to the early missionaries, the red neon crosses that illuminate the city's hillsides at night are a Korean adaptation, Koreans regard Christianity as a Korean religion now. The role of foreigners in the promotion of Christianity has been reduced largely to stereotype in the national memory.

But there is still one place where the air is still heavy with the earlier intentions: Yanghwajin, the spot by the Han River where the original Horace Underwood and James Scarth Gale once built a summertime shack in which they drafted the first *Han'gŭl* dictionary, and the gravesite of the Protestant community's first casualty, John Heron. Today Yanghwajin re-

4. *North Korean Journey: Billy Graham in the Democratic People's Republic of Korea* (Minneapolis: World Wide Publications, 1993). Ruth Bell Graham herself visited P'yŏngyang at the invitation of the Kim Jong-il government in September 1997.

The Rev. Billy Graham with President Kim Il-sung (to Graham's left) in North Korea, 1992, together with representatives of the North Korean Christian community. Courtesy of a member of the Graham party.

mains the site of the Seoul Foreigners' Cemetery, a wooded spot enclosed by a wall, hemmed in by the bridge of the Green Line, the Riverside expressway, and the avenue leading to the Yanghwa Grand Bridge. Around the cemetery the modern city rumbles: huge trucks shake the ground; cement mixers growl and spit concrete for the buildings that keep going up; and every few minutes a subway train clatters up from underground to cross the Green Line bridge. Inside the cemetery in winter, when the trees are bare and the wind whips uphill from the Han River, one can imagine the desolation that must have attended the dreary gatherings of Seoul's foreign residents as they came together over the years to bury friends and loved ones.

In the spring, the groundskeeper tends beds of blooming flowers. When the weather is warm, students like to sit on the benches to do their homework. Neighborhood housewives hold picnics under the shade trees, and at sundown the custodian has to chase couples out of the park so he can close the gate. In autumn, the leaves crumple under foot as visitors pass tombstones of different heights and styles with the names of Korea's earliest foreign residents: royal advisors Charles LeGendre and Clarence Greathouse; educators Mary Scranton and Alice Appenzeller; diplomats Henry B. Joly and Georges Ulrich. They went for their own reasons; they established themselves and created a unique way of life; many of them regarded Korea as home; and they died—though many of them live on in their work as evidenced by Underwood Hall at Yonsei University and Appenzeller Hall at Ewha.

For a while, even these graves were endangered. In the early 1980s, Seoul city planners decided that the land should be used for something more productive. Only the timely intervention of a committee of Korean clergymen saved the cemetery with a compromise: the city would declare it a "cemetery park" and give the public access to it, in return for which historians and descendants of the early Western residents would be able to keep their monuments and memories. To mark the centennial of Protestant Christianity in Korea, the committee built a memorial chapel on the site, which is now the home of Seoul Union Church, the oldest foreign congregation in the city. Nowadays the congregation is comprised mainly of short-term foreign residents who only plan to live in Seoul for a year or two.

One Sunday every spring there is a congregational picnic. Except for the rare occasions when there is an actual funeral, this is the day when the cemetery gets the most attention. The church members eat and spend some time wandering among the tombstones before going home. They recognize a few names like the Underwoods, who have a cluster of matching monuments beside the lower path, because their descendants still belong to the church. Someone sees the Orthodox crosses and exclaims, "Imagine all those Russians in Korea!" They look at the rows of tiny tombstones in the infants' and children's section, and say, "How sad! Good thing our doctors are better now." And someone notes Homer Hulbert's tombstone with his deathbed quote, "I would rather be buried in Korea than in Westminster Abbey."

"Not me!" jokes a companion. "I'll take Westminster Abbey any day!"

Bibliography

ARCHIVES AND MUSEUM COLLECTIONS

Catholic Foreign Mission Society of America (Maryknoll), Maryknoll Mission Archives, Maryknoll (Ossining), New York.

Day Missions Library, Yale Divinity School, New Haven, Connecticut.

Eli Barr Landis Collection, Yonsei University Library, Seoul.

Korean Christian Museum, Soongsil University, Seoul.

Eighth U.S. Army Command Reference Library, Yongsan [Seoul]. Koreana Collection.

United Methodist Church Archives, Drew University, microfilm records of the Korea Mission of the Methodist Episcopal Church in the possession of Professor Yi Manyŏl, Sookmyung University, Seoul.

National Museum of Korea, Seoul. Research Room records on the history of the Government-General Building.

Presbyterian Church in the U.S.A., Department of History, Montreat, North Carolina.

Presbyterian Historical Society, Philadelphia, Pennsylvania.

Republic of Korea War Memorial Museum, Yongsan [Seoul].

Roanoke College Archives, Salem, Virginia.

United Church of Canada Archives, Victoria University of the University of Toronto, Canada.

United Kingdom, Public Record Office, Kew, Surrey.

United States National Archives and Records Service, Washington, D.C., College Park, and Suitland, Maryland.

YMCA Archives, University of Minnesota, Minneapolis, Minnesota.

REFERENCE WORKS

Calkin, Homer L., comp. *Catalog of Methodist Archival and Manuscript Collections*. (Part II: Asia) N.p.: World Methodist Historical Society, 1982.

Ch'ŏnjukyo P'yŏngyang Kyogusa P'yŏnch'an Wiwŏnhoe, *Ch'ŏnjukyo P'yŏng-yang Kyogusa* (History of the Catholic Diocese of P'yŏngyang) Seoul: Pundo Ch'ulp'ansa, 1981.

Clark, Allen D., comp. *Protestant Missionaries in Korea, 1893-1983*. Seoul: Christian Literature Society of Korea, 1987.

Clark, Donald N. *The Seoul Foreigners' Cemetery at Yanghwajin: An Informal History*. Seoul: Seoul Union Church, 1998.

Gore, Michael, and Won Pyong-oh. *The Birds of Korea*. Seoul: Royal Asiatic Society, 1969.

Han'guk kyohoe inmulsa (Biographical History of the Korean Church), I: *Sŏn'gyosa p'yŏn* (Volume on missionaries). Seoul, 1975.

Hoare, James E., and Susan Pares. *Conflict in Korea: An Encyclopedia*. Santa Barbara: ABC-Clio, 1999.

Howard, Richard, and Alick Moore. *A Complete Checklist of the Birds of the World*. Oxford: Oxford University Press, 1980.

Kidokkyo Tae-Paekkwa-sajŏn P'yŏnch'an Wiwŏnhoe, *Kidokkyo Tae-Paekkwa-sajŏn* (Encyclopedia of Korean Christianity). 16 vols. Seoul: Kidokkyomunsa, 1980-85.

Kim Sung-t'ae and Pak Hye-jin, comps. *Naehan sŏn'gyosa ch'ongnan, 1884-1984* (Sketches of Missionaries in Korea, 1884-1984). Seoul: Han'guk Kidokkyo Yŏksa Yŏn'guso, 1994.

The Korea Mission Year Book, 1928. Seoul: Christian Literature Society, 1928.

Lee, Helen F. MacRae Parker. *The Helen F. MacRae Collection: A Bibliography of Korean Relations with Canadians and Other Western Peoples, Which Includes a Checklist of Documents and Reports, 1898-1975*. Occasional Paper No. 12, School of Library Service, Dalhousie University, Halifax, N.S., 1976.

Lipp, Charles H., and Peter W. Williams, eds. *Encyclopedia of American Religious Expression*. 3 vols. New York: Charles Scribner's Sons, 1988.

Miller, William H., Jr. *Pictorial Encyclopedia of Ocean Liners, 1860-1994*. New York: Dover Publications, 1995.

Murphy, Sunny, and Yi Myung-hui. *Koreana Collection*. Yongsan [Seoul]: Eighth U.S. Army Command Reference Library, 1982.

Pak Taehŏn. *Sŏyangini pon Chosŏn—Chosŏn kwan'gye sŏyang sŏji* (Korea as Seen by Westerners: Western Books on Korea, 1655-1949) 2 vols. Seoul: Sosanbang Rare Books, 1996.

Sajinŭro Pon Tongnip Undong (The Independence Movement in Photographs), I: *Woech'im gwa t'ujaeng* (Crying-out and Struggle) and II: *Imjŏng gwa kwangbok* (Provisional Government and Liberation). Seoul: Sŏmundang, 1987-1988.

Seoul Mining Company, *Director's Report and Statement of Accounts for the Year Ended December 31st, 1922*.

Sungjŏn [Soongjun] University. *Sungjŏn Taehakkyo 80-nyŏnsa* (Eighty-year History of Sungjŏn [now Sungsil] University). Seoul: Sungjŏn Taehakkyo, 1982.

Wentworth, Harold, and Stuart Berg Flexner, *Dictionary of American Slang*. New York: Crowell, 1975.

Yŏngsin Ak'ademi. *Chosŏn chaeryu kumi'in chosarok, 1907-1942 nyŏn* (Directory of Europeans and Americans in Korea, 1907-1942). Seoul: Yŏngsin Akademi, Han'gukhak yŏn'guso, 1981.

Yonsei taehakkyo ch'angnip p'alsimnyŏn kinyŏm saŏp wiwŏnhoe, *Yonsei taehakkyo-sa* (History of Yonsei University). Seoul: Yonsei University Press, 1969.

Yi Hŭisŭng, comp. *Han'guk Inmyŏng Taesajŏn* (Biographical Dictionary of Korea). Seoul: Shin'gu Munhwasa, 1972.

Yu Yŏngyŏl, comp. *Kuksa Taesajŏn* (Historical Dictionary of Korea). Seoul: Tong'a Munhwasa, 1970.

PRIVATELY PRINTED, UNPUBLISHED, AND NON-PRINT MATERIALS, AND PRIVATE COLLECTIONS

"Ataman (Hetman) of the Don," English translation by Cyril Tchirkine of an article in *Russian Life*. Typescript, n.d.

Atkinson, Jim. "Story of Ivan Nikolaevitch Tikhonoff," unpublished manuscript, n.d.

Baird, Richard H., comp. *William M. Baird of Korea: A Profile*. Private print, 1968.

Blair, William N. *Precious Memories of Dr. Samuel A. Moffett*. Private print, n.d.

Boyer, Elmer T. *To Build Him a House*. Private print, 1976.

Bruen, Clara Hedberg. *40 Years in Korea*. Private print, 1987.

Chesshir, Rand. *Sacred Halls*. VHS Video. Los Angeles: SCL Productions, 1995.

Clark, Allen D. Papers and albums in the possession of the author.

Clark, Charles Allen. Papers and albums in the possession of the author.

Clark, Kathleen M., comp. *All Our Family in the House*. Private print, 1975.

Collier, Jeanne Avison. "My Childhood Memories of Korea, 1927-1938," unpublished family memoir, 1991.

Crane Family papers and albums, Presbyterian Church (U.S.A.), Department of History, Montreat, North Carolina.

Crane, Paul Shields. "Memoirs," unpublished family memoir, 2 vols. 1989.

DeCeuster, Koen. "From Modernization to Collaboration, the Dilemma of Korean Cultural Nationalism: The Case of Yun Ch'i-ho (1865-1945)." Unpublished Ph.D. diss. (Katholieke Universiteit Leuven, 1994).

Grierson, Robert. "Episodes on a Long, Long Trail," unpublished family memoir, n.d.

Hausman, James H. Personal papers, photos, and memorabilia connected with life and work in Korea, 1945-1950, in Hausman's possession until 1996, now in the possession of the Korea Institute, Harvard University.

Intemann, Marian A. Sharrocks. *In Syen Chun, Korea, during the Russo-Japanese War of 1904, Letters of Dr. A.M. Sharrocks and Diaries of Mrs. Mary Ames Sharrocks*. Santa Rosa, California, private print, 1984.

Jensen, A. Kristian. *Internment, North Korea.* Private print, n.d.

Jensen, Maud Keister. *Korea Evacuation, 1950.* Private print, n.d.

Kim, David Chu Hang, and Agnes Davis Kim. Personal papers in the possession of the author.

Kim Yang-son, *History of the Korean Church in the Ten Years since Liberation (1945-1955),* trans. Allen D. Clark. Seoul, mimeograph, n.d.

Lee, Jong Hyeong. "Samuel Austin Moffett: His Life and Work in the Development of the Presbyterian Church of Korea, 1890-1936." Ph.D. diss. (Union Theological Seminary, Richmond, Virginia, 1983).

Lyon, William B. 16mm home movie films of life in Korea in the 1930s.

Martin, Stanley Haviland. Papers in the possession of Margaret Martin Moore, Wilmore, Kentucky.

McCune, Evelyn Becker. *Michigan and Korea, 1899-1914,* compiled and edited from the journals of Arthur Becker. San Francisco: McAllister Street Press, 1977.

Moffett, Samuel Austin. Letters in the possession of Samuel Hugh Moffett, Princeton, New Jersey.

Moffett, Samuel Hugh. Papers, Seoul, 1976, and Princeton, New Jersey, 1988.

Moskowitz, Karl. "Current Assets: The Employees of Japanese Banks in Korea." Ph.D. diss.(Harvard University, 1979).

Paik, Lak-Geoon George (Paek Nak-chun). Personal papers and papers in the Paik collection at Yonsei University, Seoul.

Pollard, Harriet. "The History of the Missionary Enterprise of the Presbyterian Church, U.S.A., in Korea, with Special Emphasis on the Personnel." M.A. thesis, Northwestern University, 1927.

Rand, Laurance B., III. "American Venture Capitalism in the Former Korean Empire: Leigh S.J. Hunt and the Unsan Gold Mines." Paper presented at the Columbia University Seminar on Korea, May 1984.

Rankin, Jessie, and Marianne Hirst. Papers in the possession of the author.

Roberts, A. Josephine. Papers in the possession of the author.

Roberts, Stacy Lippincott, and Evelyn Millen Roberts. Papers and albums in the possession of the author.

Roberts, Stacy Lippincott, Jr. Papers and albums and papers in the possession of the author.

Roberts, W. Dayton, comp. "Stacy and Evelyn Roberts as Remembered by their Children," unpublished family memoir, 1991.

Robinson, Richard D. "Korea: Betrayal of a Nation." Typescript, 1960.

Ross, Lilian. Papers in the possession of Katherine Clark Hong, Duarte, California.

Scott, William. "Canadians in Korea: A Brief Historical Sketch." Manuscript dated 1975, United Church of Canada Archives, Victoria University of the University of Toronto.

Southall, Lillian Crane. "The Journey Is Our Home," unpublished family memoir, n.d.

Stokes, Marion B., "Autobiography of Marion Boyd Stokes, D.D.," unpublished family memoir, 1998.

Suh, David Kwang-sun [Sŏ Kwangsŏn]. "American Missionaries and a Hundred Years of Korean Protestantism." Unpublished paper, Seoul, 1984.

Underwood, Horace G. Personal papers, photographs, and 16mm films. Yonsei University, Seoul.

Underwood, Horace H. Papers in the possession of Horace G. Underwood, Yonsei University, Seoul.

Underwood, John T. Papers in the possession of the author.

Wilson, John, comp. *Pyeng Yang Foreign School*. Commemorative booklet on the history of Pyeng Yang Foreign School, presented by the PYFS alumni delegation to officials of the Democratic People's Republic of Korea on the occasion of their visit to P'yŏngyang, February 1997.

Yi Paeyŏng. "Ku Hanmal Migugi-ŭi Unsan kŭmgwang ch'aegŭlgwŏn hoedŭge taehayŏ" (Concerning the American Gold Mining Concession at Unsan at the End of the Chosŏn Kingdom). History thesis. Seoul: Ewha Womans University, 1971.

Yun Ch'iho, *Yun Ch'iho Ilgi* (Yun Ch'iho's Diary), comp. National History Compilation Committee. 10 vols. Seoul: Kuksa p'yŏnch'an wiwŏnhoe, 1983-1990.

INTERVIEWS AND CORRESPONDENCE

Avison, Ella Sharrocks. Interview, 9 June 1976, Seoul, Korea.

Baird, Richard H. Interview, 27 May 1987, Duarte, California.

Chistiakoff, Orr. Telephone interviews, March/April 1992; interview, 19 December 1992, Santa Rosa, California.

Ch'oe Ikwŏn [Mrs. L. George Paik]. Interview, 4 May 1990, Seoul, Korea.

Choung, Dominicus (Cheju National University). Conversations, April 1990, Cheju Island.

Crane, Paul Shields, and Sophie Montgomery Crane, Interview/conversation, 13 August 1995, Black Mountain, North Carolina.

Crowe, Edwin. Correspondence, 1990.

Deal, Paul. Telephone interview, 26 July 1989, Columbia City, Indiana.

DeCamp, E. Otto. Interview, 22 July 1983, Duarte, California.

Dyer, Nell. Correspondence, June 1996.

Fleck, Cleon. Recorded interview with Paul Fleck, 24 December 1991, Columbia City, Indiana.

Fisher, J. Earnest. Correspondence, 1972-73; Interviews, May 1985, Seoul, Korea.

Harkness, Grace Underwood. Interview, 12 June 1999, Minneapolis, Minnesota.

Hausman, James H. Interviews, August-October, 1995, Austin, Texas, and telephone conversations, 1995-96.

Hong, Katherine Clark. Interviews, 1994-2000, Duarte, California.

Hong, Timothy Kyung-Sun. Interview, 9 January 1999, Duarte, California.

Jacobson, Nina Belogolovy. Correspondence, July-August 1989.

Kessie, Barbara Amendt. Correspondence, 2 August 1993.

Kilbourne, J. Elmer. Interview, 28 July 1990, Taech'ŏn Beach, Korea.

Kim, Dong-gil [Kim Tonggil]. Interview, 2 August 1984, Seoul, Korea.

Kinney, Robert A., and Abigail Genso Kinney. Interview, 27 July 1994, Kailua, Hawaii.

Kinsler, Francis. Interview, 28 May 1987, Duarte, California.

Lee, Insong. Department of Defense POW and Missing Persons Office, The Pentagon, Arlington, Virginia. Telephone conversations, January 1999.

Lyon, William. Interview, 28 May 1987, Duarte, California.

Macdonald, Donald Stone. Interviews, correspondence, and conversations, 1985-1993, Seoul, Washington, D.C., San Francisco, and Berkeley.

Mackenzie, Catherine and Helen. Conversation, July 1996, Melbourne, Australia.

McFarlane, Mabel. Correspondence, 1988.

McLaren, Rachel (Rachel McLaren Human). Conversation, July 1996, Melbourne, Australia.

Min Kyŏngbae. Interviews, November 1982, November 1983, and April 1984, Seoul, Korea.

Moffett, Howard F. Interview, 21 July 1990, Seoul, Korea.

Moffett, Samuel H. and Eileen F. Correspondence, 2001.

Moon, Fr. Boris. Interviews, May-June 1984, Seoul, Korea.

Moore, David James. Correspondence, 1997.

Moore, John V. and Katherine Boyer. Interviews in Seoul, Korea, 1990-91, and Black Mountain, North Carolina, 1995.

Moore, Margaret Martin. Interviews, 1984, Seoul, Korea, and 1998, San Antonio, Texas, and correspondence, 1991-92.

Neumann, Lola Tyulkin. Telephone interview, 19 June 1991, San Francisco, California.

Paek Nakchun [Lak-Geoon George Paik]. Interviews, 1976, 1982, and 1983-84, Seoul, Korea.

Peterson, Fran Lampe. Interview, 8 May 1990, Seoul, Korea.

Potapoff, Muza Yankovsky [Eva Potapoff]. Interview, 16 August 1989, Healdsburg, California.

Quinones, C. Kenneth. Interview, 21 July 2002, Seoul, Korea.

Roberts, Stacy Lippincott, Jr. Interview, 9 January 1999, Duarte, California.

Ross, Lillian. Interviews, 27-28 May 1987, Duarte, California.

Somerville, John, and Virginia Bell Somerville. Interviews/conversations, 1969-1990, Taejŏn, Seoul, and Taech'ŏn Beach, Korea, and 1995, Montreat, North Carolina, and correspondence, 2002.

Taylor, Bruce and Joyce Phipps Taylor. Interview, 10 August 1989, Santa Rosa, California.

Tchirkine, Cyril. Telephone interview, 28 September 1989 and interview, 24 June 1991, Hayward, California.

Underwood, Horace G. Interviews and conversations, Seoul and Taech'ŏn Beach, Korea, and New York, and correspondence, 1982-2002.

Underwood, John T. Interviews, 1983-84, Seoul, Kwangju, and Taech'ŏn Beach, Korea.

Underwood, Richard F. Interviews, Seoul and Taech'ŏn Beach, Korea, and correspondence, 1983-1990.

Whisnant, Younghi Yun. Interview, 26 December 1972, Riverdale, New York.
Williams, George Z. Correspondence, 1990.
Yankovsky, Victoria [Victoria Chistiakoff]. Interviews, 16 August 1989, 24 June 1991, 9 December 1993, and 2 August 1994 in Healdsburg, California, and 19 December 1992, Santa Rosa, California; telephone interviews, 1989-1992; and correspondence, 1989-1994.

PUBLIC DOCUMENTS AND DOCUMENTARY COLLECTIONS

Government-General of Tyosen [Chōsen]. *Annual Report on Administration of Tyosen, 1937-38*. Keizyo [Seoul], 1938.
United Kingdom, Public Record Office, Kew, Surrey. Foreign Office Record Group No. 262.
United States. Department of the Army. Office of the Chief of Military History. *South to the Naktong, North to the Yalu*. Washington, D.C.: U.S. Government Printing Office, 1961.
United States. Department of the Army, Special Staff, U.S. Army Historical Division (Historical Manuscript File) *History of United States Armed Forces in Korea*, Part I, Chapters I-VIII. Draft Typescript, microfilm, n.d.
United States. Department of State. *Records Relating to the Internal Affairs of Korea*, a part of Record Group 59, Department of State Archives, National Archives and Records Service, Washington, D.C.
United States Embassy, Seoul, Korea. *American Legation Building in Seoul, Korea, Historic Structures Report*. Seoul: Samsung Architects Co., Ltd., 2000.
United States. Headquarters, United States Army Forces in Korea, Office of the Assistant Chief of Staff, G-2, *G-2 Periodic Reports*. Reprinted under the title *Chuhan Migun Chŏngbo Ilchi*, 15 vols. Ch'unch'ŏn, Korea: Hallym Institute of Asian Cultural Studies, Hallym University, 1989.
United States. Headquarters, United States Army Forces in Korea, Office of the Assistant Chief of Staff, G-2, *Intelligence Summary Northern Korea*, No. 29 (1 February 1947).
United States. Headquarters, United States Army Forces in Korea, Counter Intelligence Corps, *Civil Disturbances, September 1945-June 1948*, reprinted together with selected facsimile materials from Army G-2, USAMGIK Bureau of Public Information, U.S. Air Force reports, USAFIK Office of Civil Information, and U.S. Department of State reports as "Migunjŏng kijŏngbo charyochip: Shimin soyo, yŏron chosa pogosŏ" (Materials on the U.S. Military Government: Civil Disturbances, Public Opinion Reports), vols. 1 and 2, being item 6 in the series Hallim Taehakkyo Asia munje yŏn'guso charyo ch'ongsa. Ch'unch'ŏn, Korea: Institute of Asian Culture, Hallym University, 1995.
United States. Headquarters, United States Forces, Korea. *The U.S. Military Experience in Korea, 1871-1982: In the Vanguard of ROK-US Relations*. Yongsan [Seoul]: USFK/ EUSA Command Historian's Office, 1983.

BOOKS AND MONOGRAPHS

Abelmann, Nancy. *Echoes of the Past, Epics of Dissent: A South Korean Social Movement*. Berkeley and Los Angeles: University of California Press, 1996.

Academy of Korean Studies (Han'guk chŏngshin munhwa yŏn'guwŏn). *Han-Misugyo han segi-ŭi Hoego wa Chŏnmang/Reflections on a Century of Korean-United States Relations*. Seoul: Academy of Korean Studies/The Wilson Center, 1983.

Ahn, Young Roh. *Rain for a Parched Land : Biography of Florence R. Root, Missionary to Korea*. Seoul: Qumran Publishing House, 1997.

Allen, Horace N. *Korea: Fact and Fancy*. Seoul: Methodist Publishing House, 1904.

————. *Things Korean*. New York: Fleming H. Revell, 1908.

Awe, Chulho. *Decision at Dawn: The Underground Witness in Korea*. New York: Harper and Row, 1965.

Barr, Pat. *The Deer Cry Pavilion: Westerners in Japan, 1868-1905*. New York: Macmillan, 1968.

Beale, Howard K. *Theodore Roosevelt and the Rise of America to World Power*. Baltimore: The Johns Hopkins University Press, 1956.

Beech, Keyes. *Tokyo and Points East*. Garden City, N.Y.: Doubleday, 1954.

Bergman, Sten. *In Korean Wilds and Villages*, trans. Frederic Whyte. London: John Gifford, 1938.

Blair, William N. *Gold in Korea*. New York: Presbyterian Church in the U.S.A., 1946.

Bolshakoff, Serge. *The Foreign Missions of the Russian Orthodox Church*. London: Society for Promoting Christian Knowledge, 1943.

Brouwer, Ruth Compton. *New Women for God: Canadian Presbyterian Women and India Missions, 1876-1914*. Toronto: University of Toronto Press, 1990.

Brown, Arthur Judson. *The Mastery of the Far East*. London: G. Bell and Sons, 1919.

Brown, George Thompson. *Mission to Korea*. Atlanta: Board of World Missions, Presbyterian Church in the U.S.A., 1962.

Brynner, Rock. *Yul: The Man Who Would Be King*. New York: Simon and Schuster, 1989.

Caldwell, John C. *The Korea Story*. Chicago: Henry Regnery, 1952.

Chandra, Vipan. *Imperialism, Resistance, and Reform in Late Nineteenth-Century Korea*. Berkeley: University of California Press, 1988.

Chilliwa chayu ŭi kisudŭl (Standardbearers of Truth and Freedom). Seoul: Yonsei University Press, 1982.

Choe, Ching Young. *The Rule of the Taewŏn'gun, 1864-1873*. Harvard East Asian Monographs No. 45. Cambridge: Harvard University Press, 1972.

Ch'oe Yŏnghŭi. *Kyoktong-ŭi haebang samnyŏn* (Three Violent Years of Liberation). Ch'unch'ŏn: Hallim taehakkyo asea munje yŏn'guso, 1996.

Ch'oe Yŏnghŭi, Kim Sŏngjik, Kim Yunhwan, and Chŏng Yosŏp. *Ilcheha-ŭi minjok undongsa* (History of the People's Movement under Japanese Colonial Rule). Seoul: Hyŏnumsa, 1982.

Chŏng Unhyŏn. *Sŏul-sinae Ilche yusan tapsagi* (Former Japanese Properties in the City of Seoul). Seoul: Hanŭl, 1995.

Chōsen Christian College [Yŏnhi College]. Catalogues in English and Korean, 1914-1932.

Clark, Allen D. *Avison of Korea*. Seoul: Yonsei University Press, 1979.

――――. *A History of the Church in Korea*. Seoul: Christian Literature Society, 1972.

――――, comp. *Protestant Missionaries in Korea, 1884-1983*, ed. Donald N. Clark, Kim Kwang-tak, and Horace G. Underwood. Seoul: Christian Literature Society of Korea, 1985.

Clark, Charles Allen. *First Fruits in Korea*. New York: Fleming H. Revell, 1921.

――――. *The Korean Church and the Nevius Method*. New York: Fleming H. Revell, 1930.

――――. *Religions of Old Korea*. New York: Fleming H. Revell, 1932.

Clark, Donald N. *Christianity in Modern Korea*. America's Asian Agenda Series No. 5. Lanham, Md.: University Press of America/The Asia Society, 1986.

――――, ed. *The Kwangju Uprising: Shadows over the Regime in South Korea*. Boulder, Colo.: Westview Press, 1987.

―――― and James Huntley Grayson. *Discovering Seoul*. Seoul: Royal Asiatic Society, Korea Branch, 1986.

Clifford, Nicholas R. *Spoilt Children of Empire: Westerners in Shanghai and the Chinese Revolution of the 1920s*. Hanover, N.H.: University Press of New England, 1991.

Conroy, Hilary. *The Japanese Seizure of Korea: 1868-1910. A Study of Realism and Idealism in International Relations*. Philadelphia: University of Pennsylvania Press, 1960.

Cook, Harold F. *Pioneer American Businessman in Korea: The Life and Times of Walter Davis Townsend*. Seoul: Royal Asiatic Society, 1981.

Crane, Florence Hedleston. *Flowers and Folklore from Far Korea*. Tokyo: Shiseido, 1936.

Croly, Herbert. *Willard Straight*. New York, Macmillan, 1925.

Crosbie, Philip. *March Till They Die*. Westminster, Maryland: The Newman Press, 1956.

Cumings, Bruce, ed. *Child of Conflict: The Korean-American Relationship, 1943-1953*. Seattle: University of Washington Press, 1983.

――――. *Korea's Place in the Sun*. New York: W.W. Norton, 1997.

――――. *The Origins of the Korean War*. Vol. I: *Liberation and the Emergence of Separate Regimes, 1945-1947*. Princeton: Princeton University Press, 1981.

――――. *The Origins of the Korean War*. Vol. II: *The Roaring of the Cataract, 1947-1950*. Princeton: Princeton University Press, 1990.

―――― and Jon Halliday. *Korea: The Unknown War*. New York: Pantheon Books, 1988.

Dallet, Charles. *Histoire de l'église de Corée*. 2 vols. Paris: Libraire Victor Palme, 1874.

Davies, Daniel M. *The Life and Thought of Henry Gerhard Appenzeller (1858-1902)*. Lewiston, New York: The Edwin Mellen Press, 1988.

De Medina, Juan Ruiz, S.J. *The Catholic Church in Korea: Its Origins, 1566-1784*. Trans. John Bridges, S.J. Seoul: Royal Asiatic Society, Korea Branch, 1994.

Deane, Philip. *I Was a Captive in Korea*. Tokyo: Charles E. Tuttle, 1954.

Detrick, Ronald B. *Great Is Thy Faithfulness: The Life and Times of Florence Elizabeth Root*. Wilmington, N.C.: Alpha-Omega Mission Press, 2000.

Deuchler, Martina. *Confucian Gentlemen and Barbarian Envoys: The Opening of Korea, 1875-1885*. Seattle: University of Washington Press, 1977.

Duus, Peter. *The Abacus and the Sword*. Stanford: Stanford University Press, 1995.

———, Myers, Ramon H., and Peattie, Mark R., eds. *The Japanese Informal Empire in China, 1895-1937*. Princeton: Princeton University Press, 1989.

Dzirkals, Lilita I. *"Lightning War" in Manchuria: Soviet Military Analysis of the 1945 Far East Campaign*. Rand Paper Series No. P-5589. Santa Monica: The Rand Corporation, 1976.

Eckert, Carter J. *Offspring of Empire: The Koch'ang Kims and the Colonial Origins of Korean Capitalism, 1876-1945*. Seattle: University of Washington Press, 1991.

Etherton, Percy Thomas, and Tiltman, H. Hessell. *Manchuria: The Cockpit of Asia*. London: Jarrolds Publishers, 1932.

Fairbank, John King. *Chinabound: A Fifty-Year Memoir*. New York: Harper and Row, 1982.

———. *Chinese-American Interactions: A Historical Summary*. New Brunswick, N.J.: Rutgers University Press, 1975.

———, ed. *The Missionary Enterprise in China and America*. Cambridge, Mass.: Harvard University Press, 1974.

Feuerwerker, Albert. *The Foreign Establishment in China in the Early Twentieth Century*. Ann Arbor: Center for Chinese Studies, University of Michigan, 1976.

Finley, James P. *The US Military Experience in Korea, 1871-1982: In the Vanguard of ROK-US Relations*. Seoul: Eighth U.S. Army Command Historian's Office, 1983.

Fisher, J. Earnest. *Pioneers of Modern Korea*. Seoul: Christian Literature Society of Korea, 1977.

Gale, James Scarth. *Korea in Transition*. New York: Young People's Missionary Movement of the United States and Canada, n.d.

———. *The Vanguard: A Tale of Korea*. New York: Fleming H. Revell, 1904.

Gayn, Mark. *Japan Diary*. Tokyo: Charles E. Tuttle, 1981.

Hall, Basil. *Voyage of Discovery to the West Coast of Korea and the Great Loo-Choo Island*. London, 1818; reprinted by the Royal Asiatic Society, Korea Branch, 1976.

Hall, Sherwood. *With Stethoscope in Asia: Korea*. McLean, Virginia: MCL Associates, 1978.

Hamel, Hendrik. *Hamel's Journal and a Description of the Kingdom of Korea, 1653-1666*. trans. Jean-Paul Buys of Taizé. Seoul: Royal Asiatic Society, Korea Branch, 1994.

Hamgyŏngpuktoji p'yŏnch'an wiwŏnhoe, *Hamgyŏngpuktoji* (Gazetteer of North Hamgyŏng Province). Seoul: Kwangmyŏng, 1970.

Han Kyung-chik [Han Kyŏngjik]. *Special Address upon Receipt of the Templeton Prize*. Berlin, 1992.

Hart-Landsberg, Martin. *Korea: Division, Reunification, and U.S. Foreign Policy*. New York: Monthly Review Press, 1998.

Hausman, Jim, and Chŏng Ilhwa, *Han'guk Taet'tongnyŏng'ŭl umjigin Migun taewi* (The American Army Captain Who Guided Korea's Presidents). Seoul: Han'guk Munwŏn, 1995.

Hardacre, Helen. *Shintō and the State, 1868-1988*. Princeton: Princeton University Press, 1989.

Harrington, Fred Harvey. *God, Mammon, and the Japanese*. Madison: University of Wisconsin Press, 1944.

Havens, Thomas R. *Valley of Darkness: The Japanese People and World War Two*. Lanham, Md.: University Press of America, 1986.

Heinl, Robert Debs, Jr. *Victory at High Tide*. Philadelphia: J. B. Lippincott, 1968.

Henderson, Gregory. *Korea: The Politics of the Vortex*. Cambridge, Mass.: Harvard University Press, 1968.

Higgins, Marguerite. *War in Korea: The Report of a Woman Combat Correspondent*. Garden City, N.Y.: Doubleday, 1951.

Hoare, James E. *The British Embassy Compound, Seoul*. Seoul: Korean-British Society, 1984.

—— and Susan Pares. *Conflict in Korea: an Encyclopedia*. Santa Barbara: ABC-Clio, 1999.

Hong, Harold S., et al. *Korea Struggles for Christ: Memorial Symposium for the Eightieth Anniversary of Protestantism in Korea*. Seoul: Christian Literature Society, 1966.

Hulbert, Homer. *The Passing of Korea*. Garden City, N.Y.: Doubleday, 1906.

Hunt, Everett N. *Protestant Pioneers in Korea*. Maryknoll, N.Y.: Orbis Books, 1980.

Hunter, Jane. *The Gospel of Gentility*. New Haven: Yale University Press, 1984.

Huntley, Martha. *To Start a Work: The Foundations of Protestant Mission in Korea (1884-1919)*. Seoul: Presbyterian Church of Korea, 1987.

Ienaga, Saburō. *The Pacific War: World War II and the Japanese, 1931-1945*, trans. Frank Baldwin. New York: Pantheon Books, 1978.

Ion, A. Hamish. *The Cross and the Rising Sun: The Canadian Protestant Missionary Movement in the Japanese Empire, 1872-1931*. Waterloo, Ontario: Wilfrid Laurer University Press, 1990.

———. *The Cross and the Rising Sun*, Vol II: *The British Protestant Missionary Movement in Japan, Korea, and Taiwan, 1865-1945*. Waterloo, Ontario: Wilfrid Laurer University Press, 1993.

Japan Christian Yearbook, 1940, ed. Charles W. Iglehart. Tokyo: Christian Literature Society, 1940.

Johnston, Geoffrey, and A. Hamish Ion. *Canadian Missionaries and Korea: Two Case Studies in Public Opinion*. Working Paper Series No. 52, University of Toronto-York University Joint Centre for Asia Pacific Studies, 1988.

Johnston, Tess, and Deke Erh. *A Last Look: Western Architecture in Old Shanghai*. Hong Kong: Old China Hands Press, 1998.

———. *Far from Home: Western Architecture in China's Northern Treaty Ports*. Hong Kong: Old China Hands Press, 1996.

———, eds. *Hallowed Halls: Protestant Colleges in Old China*. Hong Kong: Old China Hands Press, 1998.

———. *Near to Heaven: Western Architecture in China's Old Summer Resorts*. Hong Kong: Old China Hand Press, 1994.

Kajiyama, Toshiyuki. *The Clan Records: Five Stories of Korea*. Honolulu: University of Hawaii Press, 1995.

Kang, Kun-jo. *P'yŏngyang ŭi ŏje wa onŭl* (P'yŏngyang Yesterday and Today). P'yŏngyang: Sahoe kwahak ch'ulp'ansa, 1986.

Kang Tong-jin. *Ilche ŭi Han'guk ch'imnyak chŏngch'aek sa* (A History of Japanese Occupation Policy in Korea). Seoul: Han'gilsa, 1984.

Kang, Younghill. *The Grass Roof*. New York: Charles Scribner's Sons, 1931.

Katz, Herman. *Brigadier General William McEntire Dye: A Pioneer of U.S. Military Contributions to Korea*. Yongsan [Seoul]: Office of the Military Historian, Eighth United States Army, 1982.

Kerr, Edith A., and George Anderson. *The Australian Presbyterian Mission in Korea, 1889-1941*. Sydney: Australian Presbyterian Board of Missions, 1970.

Kessler, Lawrence D. *The Jiangyin Mission Station: An American Missionary Community in China, 1895-1951* (Chapel Hill: University of North Carolina Press, 1996).

Kho, Songmoo (Ko Sŏngmu). *Koreans in Soviet Central Asia*. Studia Orientalia No. 61. Helsinki: Finnish Oriental Society, 1987.

Kim, Agnes Davis. *I Married a Korean*. New York: John Day, 1953.

Kim, C.I. Eugene, and Doretha E. Mortimore. *Korea's Response to Japan: The Colonial Period, 1910-1945*. Kalamazoo: Center for Korean Studies, Western Michigan University, 1977.

Kim, Choong Soon. *A Korean Nationalist Entrepreneur: A Life History of Kim Sŏngsu, 1891-1955*. Albany: State University of New York Press, 1998.

Kim, Helen (Kim Hwallan). *Grace Sufficient*. Nashville: The Upper Room, 1964.

Kim Ilsŏng [Kim Il-sung], *Segiwa tŏburŏ* (With the Century—Memoirs), vol. II. P'yŏngyang: Chosŏn nodongdang ch'ulp'anbu, 1992.

Kim, Joseph Chang-mun, and John Jae-sun Chung, *Catholic Korea—Yesterday and Today*. Seoul: Catholic Korea Publishing Company, 1964.

Kim, Richard E. *Lost Names: Scenes from a Korean Boyhood*. New York: Praeger, 1970.

———. *The Martyred: A Novel*. New York: G. Braziller, 1964.

Kim Samŭng. *Ch'inilp'a paegin-paengmun* (A Hundred Collaborators with Japan: Biographies and Documents). Seoul: Tolpegae, 1995.

———. *Haebanghu yangmin haksalsa* (Massacres of Civilians Since Liberation). Seoul: Karam Kihwek, 1995.

———. *Han'guk hyŏndaesa twi-yaegi* (Underground History of Modern Korea). Seoul: Karam Kihwek, 1995.

Kim Sŏkjun, *Migunjŏng sidaeŭi kukkawa haengjŏng* (State and Administration under the American Military Government). Seoul: Ewha yŏja taehakkyo ch'ulp'anbu, 1996.

Kim Sujin. *Honam Sŏn'gyo paengnyŏn gwa kŭ sayŏkjadŭl* (Missionaries in Honam: A Hundred Years of Life and Work). Seoul: Koryŏ Kŭlpang, 1992.

Kim Yurak, *Insul-ŭi Sado* (Apostles of Mercy). Seoul: Kidokkyo sŏhoe, 1973.

King, O.H.P. *Tail of the Paper Tiger*. Caldwell, Idaho: Caxton Printers, 1961.

Knox, Donald. *The Korean War: Pusan to Chosin—An Oral History*. New York: Harcourt Brace Jovanovich, 1985.

The Korea Missions Yearbook, 1928. Seoul: Christian Literature Society, 1928.

The Korean Conspiracy Trial: Full Report of the Proceedings in Appeal, by the Special Correspondent of the "Japan Chronicle." Kobe: The Japan Chronicle, 1913.

Koo, Youngnok, and Suh, Dae-Sook, eds. *Korea and the United States: A Century of Cooperation*. Honolulu: University of Hawaii Press, 1984.

Krasno, Rena. *That Last Glorious Summer, 1939—Shanghai-Japan*. Hong Kong: Old China Hand Press, 2001.

Ku, Dae-Yeol. *Korea under Colonialism: The March First Movement and Anglo-Japanese Relations*. Seoul: Royal Asiatic Society, Korea Branch, 1985.

Ladd, George Trumbull. *In Korea with Marquis Ito*. London: Longmans Green, 1908.

Latourette, Kenneth Scott. *A History of Christian Missions in China*. London: Society for Promoting Christian Knowledge, 1929.

Lattimore, Owen. *Manchuria: Cradle of Conflict*. New York: Macmillan, 1932.

Lautensach, Hermann. *Korea*. Trans. Katherine and Eckert Dege. Helmstedt, Germany: Springer-Verlag, 1988.

Ledyard, Gari K. *The Dutch Come to Korea*. Seoul: Royal Asiatic Society, Korea Branch, 1969.

Lee Chae-jin. *China's Korean Minority: The Politics of Ethnic Education*. Boulder, Colo.: Westview Press, 1986.

Lee, Chong-Sik. *Japan and Korea: The Political Dimension*. Stanford: Hoover Institution Press, 1985.

———. *The Korean Workers' Party: A Short History*. Stanford: Hoover Institution Press, 1978.

————, trans. and ed. *Materials on Korean Communism, 1945-1947*. Honolulu: Center for Korean Studies, University of Hawaii, 1977.

————. *The Politics of Korean Nationalism*. Berkeley and Los Angeles: University of California Press, 1963.

————. *Revolutionary Struggle in Manchuria*. Berkeley and Los Angeles: University of California Press, 1983.

Lee, Jung Soon, and Tae Ho Lee, *Father John E. Morris, M.M.* (Seoul: Sisters of Our Lady of Perpetual Help, 1994), an English translation of Yi Kat'arina (Chŏngsun), *Mok Yo'an Shinbu* (Seoul: Yŏngwŏnhan to'ŭm'ŭi sŏngmo sunyŏhoe, n.d.).

Lensen, George Alexander. *Japanese Recognition of the U.S.S.R.: Soviet-Japanese Relations, 1921-1930*. Tokyo: Sophia University Press, 1970.

————. *The Russian Push toward Japan: Russo-Japanese Relations, 1697-1875*. New York: Octagon Books, 1971.

————. *The Strange Neutrality: Soviet-Japanese Relations during the Second World War, 1941-1945*. Tallahassee: The Diplomatic Press, 1972.

Lone, Stewart, and Gavan McCormack. *Korea since 1850*. New York: St. Martin's Press, 1993.

McCormack, Gavan. *Chang Tso-lin in Northeast China, 1911-1928*. Stanford: Stanford University Press, 1977.

McCune, George M., and Arthur L. Grey Jr. *Korea Today*. Cambridge: Harvard University Press, 1950.

————, and Harrison, John A., eds. *Korean-American Relations: Documents Pertaining to the Far Eastern Diplomacy of the United States*, Vol. I: The Initial Period, 1883-1886. Berkeley and Los Angeles: University of California Press, 1951.

McKenzie, F.A. *Korea's Fight for Freedom*. New York: Fleming H. Revell, 1920.

————. *The Tragedy of Korea*. New York: E.P. Dutton, 1908.

McNamara, Dennis L. *The Colonial Origins of Korean Enterprise, 1919-1945*, Cambridge: Cambridge University Press, 1990.

McWilliams, Wayne C. *Homeward Bound: Repatriation of Japanese from Korea after World War II*. Hong Kong: Asian Research Service, 1988.

Malozemoff, Andrew. *Russian Far Eastern Policy, 1881-1904*. New York: Octagon Books, 1977.

Marshall, S.L.A. *The River and the Gauntlet*. New York: William Morrow, 1953.

Materi, Irma. *Irma and the Hermit*. New York: W.W. Norton, 1949.

Memmi, Albert. *The Colonizer and the Colonized*. Boston: Beacon Press, 1965.

Merrill, John. *Korea: The Peninsular Origins of the War*. Newark: University of Delaware Press, 1989.

Min Kyŏngbae. *Han'guk Kidokkyohoe-sa* (History of the Korean Christian Church). Seoul: Taehan Kidokkyo ch'ulp'ansa, 1982, and rev. ed., Seoul: Yonsei University Press, 1993.

Moffett, Samuel A. *First Letters from Korea, 1890-1891*. Seoul: Presbyterian Theological Seminary Institute of Missions, 1975.

Moon, Katherine. *Sex among Allies: Military Prostitution in U.S.-Korean Relations*. New York: Columbia University Press, 1997.

Murray, Florence. *At the Foot of Dragon Hill*. New York: E. P. Dutton, 1975.

Myers, Brian. *Han Sŏrya and North Korean Literature: The Failure of Socialist Realism in the DPRK*. Ithaca: East Asia Program, Cornell University, 1994.

Myers, Ramon H., and Peattie, Mark R., eds. *The Japanese Colonial Empire, 1895-1945*. Princeton: Princeton University Press, 1984.

Nahm, Andrew, ed. *Korea under Japanese Colonial Rule*. Kalamazoo, Michigan: Center for Korean Studies, Western Michigan University, 1973.

————. ed. *The United States and Korea: American-Korean Relations, 1866-1976*. Kalamazoo: Center for Korean Studies, Western Michigan University, 1979.

Nemeth, David J. *The Architecture of Ideology: Neo-Confucian Imprinting on Cheju Island, Korea*. Berkeley and Los Angeles: University of California Press, 1987.

Nish, Ian. *The Origins of the Russo-Japanese War*. London: Longman, 1985.

Noble, Harold Joyce. *Embassy at War*. Seattle: University of Washington Press, 1975.

North Korean Journey: Billy Graham in the Democratic People's Republic of Korea. Minneapolis: World Wide Publications, 1993.

Oliver, Robert T. *Syngman Rhee and American Involvement in Korea, 1942-1960*. Seoul: Panmun Books, 1978.

————. *Syngman Rhee: The Man behind the Myth* (New York: Dodd Mead, 1954).

Oppert, Ernest. *A Forbidden Land: Voyages to the Corea*. New York: G. P. Putnam's Sons, 1880.

Paek Nakchun [L. George Paik]. *Na-ŭi hoegorok* (Reminiscences). Seoul: Chongum Munhwasa, 1972.

Pahk, Induk. *September Monkey*. New York: Harper & Brothers, 1954.

Paik, Lak-Geoon George [Paek Nakchun]. *The History of Protestant Missions in Korea, 1832-1910*. P'yŏngyang: Union Christian College Press, 1929, repr. Seoul: Yonsei University Press, 1971.

Paik, Sun-yup [Paek Sŏnyop]. *Pusan to Panmunjom*. Washington, D.C.: Brassey's, 1993.

Pak Sŏngt'ae, Chŏng Sŏngju, and Mun Chuyong. *Sŏul yukpaengnyŏn ŏje, onŭl, naeil* (Six Hundred Years of Seoul, Yesterday, Today, and Tomorrow. Seoul: Han'guk Ilbo, 1993.

Pak Yŏngsŏk. *Chaeman Han'in tongnip undongsa yŏn'gu* (Studies on the Korean Independence Movement in Manchuria). Seoul: Ilchogak, 1993.

Palais, James B. *Politics and Policy in Traditional Korea*. Cambridge, Mass.: Harvard University Press, 1975.

Palmer, Spencer J. *Korea and Christianity*. Seoul: Royal Asiatic Society, Korea Branch, 1967.

————, ed. *Korean-American Relations: Documents Pertaining to the Far Eastern Diplomacy of the United States*, Vol. II, *The Period of Growing*

Influence, 1887-1895. Berkeley and Los Angeles: University of California Press, 1963.

Perevalov, Theodosi. *The Orthodox Church in Korea, 1900-1925.* Harbin: n.p., 1926.

Petrov, Victor. *Shanhai na Vampu* (Shanghai on the Huangpu). Washington, D.C.: Russkovo Amerikanskovo Istorichenskovo Obshchestva, 1985.

Phillips, Clifton Jackson. *Protestant America and the Pagan World.* Harvard East Asian Monographs No. 32. Cambridge, Mass.: Harvard University Press, 1968.

Pihl, Marshall, ed. and trans. *Listening to Korea.* New York: Praeger, 1972.

Price, Eva. *China Journal, 1889-1900: An American Missionary Family during the Boxer Rebellion.* New York: Scribners, 1988.

Rabe, Valentin. *The Home Base of American China Missions, 1880-1920.* Cambridge, Mass.: Harvard University Press, 1978.

Rand, Laurance B. *High Stakes: The Life and Times of Leigh S.J. Hunt.* New York: Peter Lang , 1989.

Reinberg, Linda. *In the Field: The Language of the Vietnam War.* New York: Facts on File, 1991.

Reischauer, Edwin O. *My Life between Japan and America.* New York: Harper and Row, 1986.

Rhodes, Harry A., and Archibald Campbell, eds. *History of the Korea Mission of the Presbyterian Church in the U.S.A.,* 2 vols. New York: United Presbyterian Church in the U.S.A., 1964.

Robinson, Michael Edson. *Cultural Nationalism in Colonial Korea, 1920-1925.* Seattle: University of Washington Press, 1988.

Rusk, Dean. *As I Saw It.* New York: Penguin Books, 1990.

The Russo-Japanese War: A Photographic and Descriptive Review of the Great Conflict in the Far East. New York: P.F. Collier and Son, 1905.

Rutt, Richard. *James Scarth Gale and His History of the Korean People.* Seoul: Royal Asiatic Society, Korea Branch, 1972.

Said, Edward W. *Orientalism.* New York: Pantheon, 1978.

Sands, William Franklin. *Undiplomatic Memories.* London: John Hamilton, n.d.

Sauer, Charles A. *Methodists in Korea.* Seoul: Christian Literature Society, 1935.

———. *Seoul Union Church, 1886-1961.* Seoul, n.p., 1961.

Sawyer, Robert K. *Military Advisors in Korea: KMAG in Peace and War.* Washington, D.C: U.S. Government Printing Office, 1962.

Scott, William. *Canadians in Korea.* Mimeograph, 1975.

Sergeant, Harriet. *Shanghai: Collision Point of Cultures, 1918-1939.* New York: Crown Publishers, 1990.

Shabshina, Panya Isaakovna. *V Kolonial'noi Koree (1940-1945)* (In Colonial Korea, 1940-1945). Moscow: Glavnaya redaktsia vostochnoi literaturi, 1992, trans. into Korean as *Sikminji Chosŏnesŏ.* trans. Kim Myŏngho. Seoul: Han'ŭl, 1996.

Shearer, Roy E. *Wildfire: Church Growth in Korea*. Grand Rapids, Mich.: William B. Eerdmans, 1966.

Sheldon, Walt. *Hell or High Water: MacArthur's Landing at Inch'on*. New York: Macmillan, 1968.

Sherman, A.J. *Mandate Days: British Lives in Palestine, 1918-1948*. New York: Thames and Hudson, 1997.

Shin, Gi-Wook. *Peasant Protest and Social Change in Colonial Korea*. Seattle: University of Washington Press, 1996.

Sidemi (Russian-language brochure commemorating the unveiling of a statue of Mikhail Yankovsky at Bezverhovo, Russia), September 1991.

Smith, Canfield. *Vladivostok under Red and White Rule*. Seattle: University of Washington Press, 1975.

Smith, John Coventry. *From Colonialism to World Community*. Philadelphia: The Geneva Press, 1982.

Stephan, John J. *The Russian Far East: A History*. Stanford, California: Stanford University Press, 1994.

Strong, Josiah. *Our Country: Its Possible Future and Its Present Crisis*. 2d ed. New York: Baker and Taylor, 1891.

Suh, Sang-Chul. *Growth and Structural Changes in the Korean Economy, 1910-1940*. Cambridge, Mass.: Council on East Asian Studies, Harvard University, 1978.

Suh, Dae-Sook. *Kim Il Sung: The North Korean Leader*. New York: Columbia University Press, 1988.

———. *The Korean Communist Movement, 1918-1948*. Princeton: Princeton University Press, 1967.

———, ed. *Koreans in the Soviet Union*. Honolulu: Center for Korean Studies, University of Hawaii, 1987.

———, and Edward J. Shultz, eds. *Koreans in China*. Honolulu: Center for Korean Studies, University of Hawaii, 1990.

Sutlive, Vinson H., Nathan Altshuler, Mario D. Zamora, Virginia Kerns, eds. *Missionaries, Anthropologists, and Cultural Change*, vols. I and II. Studies in Third World Societies, Nos. 25 and 26. Williamsburg, Virginia: Department of Anthropology, College of William and Mary, 1985.

Swartout, Robert R. *Mandarins, Gunboats, and Power Politics: Owen Nickerson Denny and the International Rivalries in Korea*. Honolulu: University of Hawaii Press, 1980.

Taehan Yesukyo Changnohoe Shinhak-taehak. *Ch'odaehakjang Map'o Samyŏl paksa naehan paekchunyŏn kinyŏm kangyŏnhoe* (Papers from the Centennial Symposium Commemorating Samuel A. Moffett's Arrival in Korea). Seoul: Presbyterian Theological Seminary, 1990.

Taylor, Mary Linley. *Chain of Amber*. Lewes, Sussex: The Book Guild, 1992.

———. *The Tiger's Claw: The Life-story of East Asia's Mighty Hunter*. London: Burke Publishing Company, 1956.

Toland, John. *In Mortal Combat: Korea 1950-1953*. New York: William Morrow, 1991.

Toyama Shigeki, and Adachi Yoshiko. *Kindai Nihon seijishi hikkei* (Handbook of Modern Japanese Politics). Tokyo, 1961.

Underwood, Horace G. *The Call of Korea*. New York: Fleming H. Revell, 1908.

Underwood II, Horace G. *Korea in War, Revolution, and Peace: The Recollections of Horace G. Underwood*, ed. and annotated Michael J. Devine. Seoul: Yonsei University Press, 2001.

Underwood, Horace H. *Modern Education in Korea*. New York: International Press, 1926.

———. *Korean Boats and Ships*. Reprint. Seoul: Yonsei University Press, 1979.

———. *The Seoul Union: Fifty Years a Community Center, 1889-1939*. Seoul: n.p., 1939.

Underwood II, Horace H. *Seoul Foreign School, 1912-1978*. Seoul: Seoul Foreign School, 1978.

Underwood, Lillias Horton. *Fifteen Years among the Topknots*. Boston: American Tract Society, 1904.

———. *Underwood of Korea*. New York: Fleming H. Revell, 1918.

Underwood, Peter A., et al. *First Encounters*. Seoul: Dragon's Eye Graphics, 1982.

Varg, Paul A. *Missionaries, Chinese and Diplomats*. New York: Octagon Books, 1977.

Vieman, Dorothy House. *Korean Adventure: The Inside Story of an Army Wife*. San Antonio, Texas: The Naylor Co., 1951.

Weems, Clarence Norwood, ed. *Hulbert's History of Korea*. 2 vols. New York: Hilary House, 1962.

Wells, Kenneth M. *New God, New Nation: Protestants and Self-Reconstruction in Korea, 1896-1937*. Honolulu: University of Hawaii Press, 1990.

White, William Lindsay. *The Captives of Korea*. New York: Charles Scribner's Sons, 1959.

Yankovsky, Valery. *From the Crusades to Gulag and Beyond*. Michael Hintze, trans. 2d ed. Sydney: n.p., 2001.

———. *Potomki nenun* (Four Eyes' Descendants). Moscow: Sovremennik, 1986.

Yankovsky, Victoria. *Po stranam rasseyaniya* (Through Lands of Exiles). New York: Am-izdat, 1977.

Yankovsky, Yura Mikhailovich. *Polyeka okhoti n tigrov* (Half a Century of Hunting Tigers). Reprint. Series Arsenevskaya Biblioteka. Vladivostok: Ussuri, 1990.

Yi Kwangnin [Lee Kwang-rin]. *Ch'odae Ŏndŏ'udu sŏn'gyosa-ŭi saengae* (The Life of Horace G. Underwood). Seoul: Yonsei Taehakkyo Ch'ulp'anbu, 1991.

———. *Han'guk kaehwasasang yŏn'gu* (Studies on Korean Enlightenment Thought). Seoul: Ilchogak, 1979.

———. *Ŏllibŏ R Ebisŭn-ŭi Saengae* (The Life of Oliver R. Avison). Seoul: Yonsei University Press, 1992.

Yi, Kyu-tae. *Modern Transformation of Korea*. Seoul: Sejong Publishing Company, 1970.

Yi Manyŏl. *Chonggyo kyoyuk t'ujaeng* (The Struggle for Religious Education [Under Japan]). Seoul: Minjok Munhwa Hyŏphoe, 1981.

Yi Paeyŏng. *Han'guk kŭndae kwang'ŏp ch'imt'alsa yŏn'gu* (Studies on the History of Mine-plundering in Modern Korea). Seoul: Ilchogak, 1989.

Yŏksa hakhoe. *Ilbon-ŭi ch'imnyak chŏngch'aeksa yŏn'gu* (Studies on Japanese Imperialist Aggression in Korea). Seoul: Ilchogak, 1984.

————. *No-Il chŏnjaeng chŏn-hu Ilbon-ŭi Han'guk Chimnyak* (Japanese Aggression in Korea during the Russo-Japanese War). Seoul: Ilchogak, 1986.

Young, Arthur N. *China and the Helping Hand*. Cambridge: Harvard University Press, 1963.

Yu Yŏng'ik (Lew Young-ick). *Yi Sŭngman-ŭi salm gwa kkum* (The Life and Dreams of Syngman Rhee). Seoul: Chung'ang Ilbosa, 1996.

————, Song Pyŏnggi, Yang Homin, and Im Hŭisŏp. *Han'gugin-ŭi taemi insik* (Korean Attitudes toward America). Seoul: Minumsa, 1994.

Yun Il-chu. *Han'guk Yangsik kŏnch'uk p'alsimnyŏn-sa: haebang-jŏn p'yŏn* (History of Eighty Years of Western-style Architecture in Korea: Before Liberation). Seoul: Yajŏng munwhasa, 1965.

Yun Kyŏngno. *Paek-o-in sakŏn gwa Shinminhoe yŏn'gu* (Studies on the "105 Incident" and the New People's Association). Seoul: Ilchisa, 1990.

Zellers, Larry. *In Enemy Hands: A Prisoner in North Korea*. Lexington, Ky.: The University Press of Kentucky, 1991.

ARTICLES

Baldwin, Frank. "Missionaries and the March First Movement: Can Moral Men Be Neutral?" in *Korea under Japanese Colonial Rule*, ed. Andrew Nahm. Kalamazoo: Center for Korean Studies, Western Michigan University, 1973, pp. 193-219.

Bishop, Donald M. "Shared Failure: American Military Advisors in Korea, 1888-1896," *Transactions of the Korea Branch of the Royal Asiatic Society*, LVIII (1983), pp. 53-76.

Buruma, Ian. "Will the Wall Come Tumbling Down? *The New York Review of Books*, XLI:18 (3 November 1994), pp. 24-31.

Cabot, John Moors. "The Last Days of Shanghai: 1949," *Foreign Service Journal*, May 1967, pp. 28-29.

Ch'oe, Yong-ho. "Christian Background in the Early Life of Kim Il-song," *Asian Survey*, XXVI:10 (October 1986), pp. 1082-1091.

Choi, Chungmoo. "Korean Women in a Culture of Inequality," in *Korea Briefing 1992*, ed. Donald N. Clark. Boulder, Colo.: Westview Press, 1992, pp. 97-116.

Choi, Hyaeweol. "Women's Work for 'Heathen Sisters': American Women Missionaries and their Educational Work in Korea," *Acta Koreana*, 2 (July 1999), pp. 1-22.

————. "Missionary Zeal in a Transformed Melodrama: Gendered Evangelicalism in Korea," *Asian Journal of Women's Studies*, VII:1 (2001), pp. 7-39.

Choi, Jin Young. "Dr. Frank William Schofield and His Place in Korean History," *Transactions of the Korea Branch of the Royal Asiatic Society*, LXV (1990), pp. 23-34.

Chong, Chin-sok. "E.T. Bethell and the Taehan Maeil Shinbo," *Korea Journal*, XXIV:4 (April 1984), pp. 39-44.

Clark, Donald N. "Surely God Will Work Out Their Salvation: Protestant Missionaries in the March First Movement," *Korean Studies* (University of Hawaii), XIII (1989), pp. 42-75.

———. "Yun Ch'i-ho (1864-1945): Portrait of a Korean Intellectual in an Era of Transition," *Occasional Papers on Korea* (University of Washington), IV (September 1975), pp. 36-76.

Cory, Ralph M. "Some Notes on Fr. Gregorio de Cespedes, Korea's First European Visitor," *Transactions of the Korea Branch of the Royal Asiatic Society*, XXXIII (1957), pp. 41-54.

Cumings, Bruce. "The Legacy of Japanese Colonialism in Korea," in *The Japanese Colonial Empire, 1895-1945*, ed. Ramon H. Myers and Mark R. Peattie. Princeton: Princeton University Press, 1984.

Eckert, Carter J. "Total War, Industrialization and Social Change in Late Colonial Korea," in *The Japanese Wartime Empire, 1931-1945*, ed. Peter Duus, Ramon H. Myers, and Mark Peattie. Princeton: Princeton University Press, 1996. Pp. 3-39.

Emmons, Arthur B., III. "War Comes to Korea." *The American Foreign Service Journal*, XXVII:8 (August 1950), pp. 11-14.

Gompertz, G. St. G.M. "Archbishop Mutel: A Biographical Sketch." *Transactions of the Korea Branch of the Royal Asiatic Society*, XXVII (1937), pp. 55-132.

Hahm Pyong-choon [Ham Pyŏngch'un]. "The Korean Perception of the United States," in *Korea and the United States: A Century of Cooperation*, ed. Youngnok Koo and Dae-sook Suh. Honolulu: University of Hawaii Press, 1984.

Henderson, Gregory. "A History of the Chong Dong Area and the American Embassy Residence." *Transactions of the Korea Branch of the Royal Asiatic Society*, XXXV (1959), pp. 1-31.

Ion, Andrew Hamish. "British and Canadian Missionaries and the March 1st 1919 Movement," *Hokkaido Law Review* (December 1977), pp. 586-68.

Jager, Sheila Miyoshi. "Manhood, the State and the Yongsan War Memorial, South Korea," *Museum Anthropology: Journal for the Council of Museum Anthropology*. XXI:3 (1997), pp. 33-39.

Kim, Kyong-dong. "Korean Perceptions of America," in *Korea Briefing 1993*, ed. Donald N. Clark. Boulder, Colo.: Westview Press, 1993, pp. 163-184.

Lee, Hi-seung (Yi Hŭisŭng). "Recollections of the Korean Language Society Incident," in *Listening to Korea*, ed. Marshall R. Pihl. New York: Praeger, 1973, pp. 19-42.

Lee, See-jae. "A Study on Korean Rumors during Wartime Japanese Colonial Occupation." *Korea Journal*, VII:8 (August 1987), pp. 4-19.

Liefer, Walter. "Paul-Georg von Moellendorff—Scholar and Statesman." *Transactions of the Korea Branch of the Royal Asiatic Society*, LVII (1982), pp. 41-52.

MacDonald, Callum. "'So Terrible a Liberation'—The U.N. Occupation of North Korea," *Bulletin of Concerned Asian Scholars*, XXIII:2 (April-June 1991), pp. 3-19.

McCune, George M., and Edwin O. Reischauer. "The Romanization of the Korean Language Based on its Phonetic Structure." *Transactions of the Korea Branch of the Royal Asiatic Society*, XXIX (1939), pp. 57-82.

McNamara, Dennis. "The Keisho and the Korean Business Elite," *Journal of Asian Studies*, XLVIII (May 1989), pp. 310-23.

Merrill, John. "The Cheju-do Rebellion." *Journal of Korean Studies*, II (1980), pp. 139-97.

Millett, Allan R. "Captain James H. Hausman and the Formation of the Korean Army, 1945-1950," *Armed Forces and Society* XXIII (summer 1997), pp. 503-539.

Mills, Edwin. "Gold Mining in Korea," *Transactions of the Korea Branch of the Royal Asiatic Society*, VII:1 (1916), pp. 5-39.

Moffett, Samuel H. "The Independence Movement and the Missionaries," *Transactions of the Korea Branch of the Royal Asiatic Society*, LIV (1979), pp. 13-32.

Molony, Barbara. "Japan's Strategic Investment in High Technology in Colonial Korea, 1925-1945: The Role of Noguchi Jun." *The Journal of Modern Korean Studies*, IV (May 1990), pp. 78-93.

Mortimore, Doretha E. "Dr. Frank W. Schofield and the Korean National Consciousness," in *Korea's Response to Japan: The Colonial Period, 1910-1945*, ed. C.I. Eugene Kim and Doretha E. Mortimore. Kalamazoo: Center for Korean Studies, Western Michigan University, 1977, pp. 245-61.

Myŏng Ch'ŏl. "Ma'ŭl saramdŭl" (Village People) published in installments in *Lenin kich'i* (Flag of Lenin), the Korean newspaper of Alma Ata (Alamaty), Kazakhstan, 30 September- 3 October 1980.

No Myŏngsik. "Kim Chaejun ŭi Kidokkyojŏk kŏn'guk inyŏm," in *Han'guksa Simin Kangchwa*, (Kim Chaejun's Ideology of Christian Nation-building), XVII (1995), pp. 115-29.

Paek Nakchun (L. George Paik). "Na-ŭi salmŭl toetorapomyŏ" (Looking Back over My Life), in *Chilli wa chayu-ŭi kisudŭl* (Standardbearers of Truth and Freedom), Seoul: Yonsei University Press, 1982, pp. 241-81.

Paik, L. George (Paek Nakchun). "Seventy Years of the Royal Asiatic Society in Korea," *Transactions of the Korea Branch of the Royal Asiatic Society*, XLVII (1972), pp. 25-39.

Palmer, Spencer J. "American Gold Mining in Korea's Unsan District," *Pacific Historical Review*, XXXI:4 (November 1962), pp. 379-91.

Phillips, Clifton Jackson. "The Student Volunteer Movement and Its Role in China Missions, 1886-1920," in *The Missionary Enterprise in China and*

America, ed. John King Fairbank. Cambridge, Mass.: Harvard University Press, 1974.

Price, Willard. "Jap Rule in the Hermit Kingdom," *National Geographic*, LXXXVIII:4 (October 1945), pp. 429-451.

Roediger, David. "Gook: The Short History of an Americanism." *Monthly Review*, XLIII:10 (March 1992), pp. 50-54.

Schofield, Frank. "What Happened on Sam Il Day, March 1, 1919," in *The Feel of Korea*, ed. Inha Jung. Seoul: Hollym, 1967, pp. 271-80.

Sŏ Chungsŏk. "Haebang gwa nambukhan kongsanjuŭi" (Liberation and Communism in South and North Korea). *Han'guksa simin kangchwa*, XII (1993), pp. 87-108.

Song, Seok Choong. "Grammarians or Patriots: Han'gul Scholars' Struggles for the Preservation of Their Linguistic Heritage." Unpublished paper, Department of Linguistics and Oriental and African Languages, Michigan State University, n.d.

Underwood, Horace H. "A Korean Black Duck," parts I and II. *Yachting*, L:5 (November 1931), pp. 47-49, and L:6 (December 1931), pp. 55-58, 98, 100.

Wright, Mary Clabaugh. "The Adaptability of Ch'ing Diplomacy: The Case of Korea," *Journal of Asian Studies*, XVII:3 (May 1958), pp. 363-81.

Yi Chŏngsik [Chong-Sik Lee]. "Inmin konghwaguk gwa haebang chŏngguk" (The People's Republic in the Political Context of Liberation). *Han'guksa simin kangchwa*, XII (1993), pp. 15-45.

Yu Yŏng'ik (Young-Ick Lew). "Haebang-ŭi yŏksajŏk ŭiŭi" (The Historical Significance of Liberation). *Han'guksa simin kangchwa*, XII (1993), pp. 1-14.

———. "Yi Sŭngman-ŭi kŏn'guk isang" (Syngman Rhee's Ideal of National Construction), *Han'guksa simin kangchwa*, XVII (1995), pp. 1-24.

NEWSPAPERS AND PERIODICALS

Bulletin of the Whitley County Historical Society (Columbia City, Indiana)
Japan Chronicle (Kobe, Japan)
Korea Herald (and its predecessor, the *Korean Republic*) (Seoul)
Korea Journal (UNESCO, Seoul)
Korea Klipper (Newsletter for former missionaries in Korea, 1942-present)
Korea Mission Field (Seoul, 1905-1941)
Korea Review (Seoul, 1902-1906)
Korea Times (Seoul)
Korean Repository (Seoul, 1895-1898)
National Geographic
New York Times
Nippon Times (predecessor of the *Japan Times*)
Pacific Century (San Diego)
Presbyterian Tribune

Russian Life (San Francisco)
Seoul Press (Seoul, 1911-1937)
Taehan Mae'il Shinbo (Seoul)
The Times (London)
Tong'a Ilbo (Seoul)
Tongnip Sinmun (*The Independent*, Seoul)
Toronto Globe and Mail
Transactions of the Korea Branch of the Royal Asiatic Society (Seoul, 1901-
   present)

Index

A

Acheson, Dean, 356, 368
Albion College, 68
Allen, Horace
  first mission doctor, 14, 169-70
  mining industry, 223-24, 225, 238-39
  Russo-Japanese War (1904-1905), 29, 30, 32
Allen, Young J., 110, 112
American Embassy. *See* United States
American Internationalism, 308-10
American Legation (Chŏng-dong). *See* United States
American Methodist Episcopal Church, 181
American Trading Company (Yokohama), 223-24
An Ch'angho, 203
Anglican Church, 207
Anglican Mission, 249
  allied occupation (1945-1950), 294-97
  Korean War (1950-1953), 379
Anglo-Chinese College (China), 107, 110
Anglo-Japanese Alliance (1902), 27-28, 34, 100-101, 143
Anglo-Korean School (Kaesŏng), 112, 113
An Hosang, 355
Anna Davis Industrial Shops (P'yŏngyang), 72, 123

Appenzeller, Alice
  death of (1950), 356, 405
  missionary assignment
    Ewha Womans University, 183-84, 243-44
    foreigner evacuation (1940-1941), 256
    school management, 184, 243-44
  missionary background, 183-84
Appenzeller, Ella, 14, 19
Appenzeller, Henry, 14, 183-84, 256
Arick, Melvin, 237
Armstrong, A. E., 58-59
Arnold, Archibald, 292
Asama Maru, 270-71
Aston, W. B., 71
Australian Presbyterian Mission, 90, 252
Automobile hazards, 86-88
Avison, Oliver R., 109

B

Baird, William, 209
Barker, A. H., 55
Barnhart, Frank, 361
Barros, Russell D., 325-26
Barry, Sister Elenita, 267-68
Battle of Midway (1942), 269-70
Beach, Dwight, 402
Beech, Keyes, 365, 367
Bell, Eugene, 87-88

Pearl Harbor prelude
  Canadian Presbyterian Mission, 261
  International Women's Day of
    Prayer, 259-60
  kamidana shrines, 258, 260-61
  media response, 259-60
  police arrests, 258, 259, 261
  Presbyterian Mission, 258-62
  Protestants, 259-60
  police arrests, 258, 259, 261
  police surveillance, 255
  Pyeng Yang Foreign School
    (P'yŏngyang), 251-52
  Western observations, 252-53, 255-56,
    257
  See also World War II
Foreigners' Cemetery (Yanghwajin), 20,
  21, 26, 356
  contemporary Korea, 403-5
  cemetery park declaration, 405
  memorial chapel, 405
Foreign trade
  Japanese imports, 38
  open door policy, 38
  United States, 32
France
  Catholics, 14-15
  Korean-French treaty (1886), 14-15
  Korean protection, 28
  media, 371-72
  mining industry, 229-30, 236, 239n.39
  residential compound (Chŏng-dong),
    13, 65
  Société des Missions Étrangères-de
    Paris (SME), 15, 19n.16, 136-37
Fukuzawa Yukichi, 16, 110
Funderat, Natalya, 380

G

Gale, James Scarth
  Christian Literature Society, 19
  Independence Movement (1919), 53
  Korean Tract Society, 19
  language dictionary, 18-19, 20
  P'yŏngyang, 122
Gek, Fridolf, 148
General Sherman, 122, 141
Genso, John, 108
Genso, Mabel, 108

Germany, 28
Gibney, Frank, 365, 367
Gold industry. *See* Oriental Consoli-
  dated Mining Company, Inc. (West
  Virginia)
Goodfellow, Preston, 346-47
Good Life Society, 103
Graham, Billy, 403
Graham, Ruth Bell, 403
Great Britain
  foreigner evacuation (1940-1941),
    252, 254
  Japanese domination
  Anglo-Japanese Alliance (1902),
    27-28, 34, 100-101, 143
  resistance to, 34
  Sŏngjin evacuation, 29-30
  Korean War (1950-1953)
  British Embassy evacuation, 360-61
  P'yŏngyang liberation, 384
  mining industry, 229, 230, 231
  repatriation (World War II), 269
  Republic of Korea (ROK), 342
  residential compounds (Chŏng-
    dong), 13
  Saitō regime
  British consulate, 71, 100-102
  Empire Day, 71
  International Settlement, 101
  Korean relations, 100-102
  Shanghai incident (1929), 101-2
Greater East Asia Co-Prosperity Sphere
  (Japan)
  China Incident (1937), 195
  foreigner evacuation (1940-1941),
    254
  Methodist Church reorganization, 243
  mining industry, 237
Greathouse, Clarence, 405
Great Revival (1907), 38-41, 122
Greirson, Robert, 55
Grew, Joseph, 236, 247, 250, 270
Guatemala, 207

H

Haggin, James B., 227
Hague Conference, 202
Hall, Ada B., 241
Hall, Sherwood, 241-42

Northern occupation zone, 283
North Korean missionaries, 301-4
Speer School for Girls (Kwangju)
democratization, 319
Kwangju Rising (1929), 92
Shintō shrine worship, 219-20
Western women, 179
Spellman, Francis Cardinal, 349, 381
Squeeze payments, 159-60
SS *Lone Star State*, 363
SS *Mariposa*, 250, 253, 254-55, 256-57,
291, 292, 362, 363, 370
SS *Monterey*, 250
SS *Reinholt*, 362
SS *Washington*, 250
St. Andrew's Hospital, 55, 57, 59, 261
Standard-Vacuum Oil Co., 201
Stars and Stripes, 290, 310
State-War-Navy Coordinating Committee (SWNCC), 282-83
Stilwell, Richard, 402
Student Volunteer Movement (SVM),
6-7
Sugiyama Seishakushō Company, 72
Suh, David, 97-98
Suyang Tong'uhoe, 108, 203, 204
Swallen, William, 209
Syngman Rhee
administration duration, 340
army discharge, 340
assassination (1979), 340
Cheju Island, 333
democratization
inauguration, 321-22
Korean Peoples's Republic (KPR),
312
left-wing politics, 312, 319, 320-22
South Korea elections (1948),
320-22
Industry Promotion Club, 203, 204
Korean War (1950-1953)
P'yŏngyang liberation, 388-89
Seoul evacuation, 368
Seoul liberation, 377
Suwŏn Agricultural College, 368
Korea trusteeship, 281, 307
media censorship, 273
military coup (1961), 340
Republic of Korea Army (ROKA), 324,
325, 339-40
Republic of Korea (ROK)

Korea Military Advisory Group
(KMAG), 346-47
Vatican connections, 349
Tongjihoe, 203

T

Taehan Mae'il Sinbo, 34
Taft, William Howard, 31
Talmage, Eliza, 263
Talmage, John V., 263
Taxation, mining industry
exports, 224, 235-37
imports, 237
income tax, 236
tax-free status, 226, 229, 236-37
transportation, 236
Taylor, A. W.
Che'am-ni massacre (1919), 51-52
children (Bruce), 70
death of (1949), 356
Dilkusha residency, 70-71
Pearl Harbor Day, 264, 265, 267
Taylor, Mary Linley
California residency, 401
children (Bruce), 70, 266-67
Dilkusha residency, 70-71, 75
Pearl Harbor Day, 264, 265, 266-67
theater productions, 70-71, 75, 153
Taylor, W. W., 70, 103
Tchirkine, Cyril, 144, 263, 274, 305-6,
401
Tchirkine, Natalya Efremoff, 143-44,
153, 274, 305-6
children, 144, 263, 274, 305-6, 401
death of (1989), 401
Tchirkine, Sergei, 143-44, 274
children, 144, 263, 274, 305-6, 401
Tchirkine, Vladimir, 144, 263, 274,
305-6, 401
Terauchi Masatake
church-state separation, 41
Conspiracy Case (1911), 44, 45, 50
Governor-General appointment
(1910), 31, 41, 42
Theological Review, 120
Thievery, 352-53, 364
Thornton, Cordus, 379
Tikhonoff, Ivan, 380
TIME, 365

Tŏksu-hoe, 91-92
Tokyo firebombing (1945), 272
Tong'a Ilbo, 189, 192
Tongjihoe, 203
Tragedy of Korea, The (McKenzie), 35
Transactions (Royal Asiatic Society), 103
Transportation
  foreigner evacuation (1940-1941)
    financial costs, 253
    Inch'ŏn harbor, 254-55, 256-57
    living conditions, 255
    pick-up points, 250
  mining industry taxation, 236
  missionary travel conditions, 5, 10-12,
    15, 22-23, 24-25
  repatriation (World War II), 270-72
  See also specific passenger ships;
    railways
Trans-Siberian Railroad, 29, 143
Travel. *See* Transportation
Troitzki, Aleksandr, 146
Trollope, Mark, 103
True Doctrine of the Lord of Heaven
  (Ricci), 133, 135
Truman, Harry, 309, 357, 378, 389
Trusteeship. *See* Allied occupation
  (1945-1950)

U

Ubico, Jorge, 207
Uchimura Kanzō, 98
Ugaki Kazushige
  administration tenure, 156
  mining industry, 236
  Shintō shrine worship, 212-13, 214
Ŭibyŏng, 35-36
Ulrich, Georges, 405
Underwood, Ethel Van Wagoner
  death of (1949), 355-56
  marriage (1916), 68
  missionary assignment
    allied occupation (1945-1950), 292
    Chōsen Christian College (Seoul),
    69
    comfort women, 200
    foreigner evacuation (1940-1941),
    253
    Pearl Harbor Day, 264, 265-66, 267

Pearl Harbor prelude, 259, 261, 262
  repatriation, 269
  Republic of Korea (ROK), 353-54,
    355-56
  Seoul Foreign School, 68
  World Day of Prayer case, 259, 261
  Yŏnhi Village, 67-70
  missionary background, 68, 69
  missionary residency
    Imun-dong, 68
    Yŏnhi-dong, 69-70
Underwood, Grace, 261, 265, 267, 269
Underwood, Horace Grant, I
  Korean communication
    catechism, 19
    Chemulp'o, 13, 14
    Christian Literature Society, 19
    education policy, 131-32
    Han'gŭl alphabet, 19-20
    Korean Tract Society, 19
    language dictionary, 18-19, 20
    location decision, 14
    school foundings, 14
    Seoul (Korean communication),
    18-20
  missionary background
    Dutch Reformed Seminary (New Jer-
    sey), 14
    missionary calling, 14
    missionary recruitment, 7-8, 13-14
    New York University, 14
    Presbyterian Board of Foreign Mis-
    sions, 8, 14
Underwood, Horace Grant, II
  Korean War (1950-1953)
    Inch'ŏn Landing, 376-77
    Taech'ŏn evacuation, 363
  marriage
    first (1941), 261-62
    second, 401
  missionary assignment
    allied occupation (1945-1950),
    292
    Chosun Christian University, 400
    Pearl Harbor Day, 264
    Republic of Korea (ROK), 354
    Yonsei University, 400, 401
Underwood, Horace Horton
  death of (1951), 400
  marriage (1916), 68

LIVING DANGEROUSLY IN KOREA
The Western Experience, 1900–1950

Donald N. Clark is Professor of History and Director of International Studies at Trinity University in San Antonio, Texas. The son and grandson of Presbyterian missionaries in Seoul, he began learning about Korea in the 1950s and went on to earn his Ph.D. in East Asian history at Harvard University. His experience in Korea includes periods as a Peace Corps Volunteer, Social Science Research dissertation fellow, and Fulbright scholar, most recently at Yonsei University in 1990. His publications include *Christianity in Modern Korea* (1986), *The Kwangju Uprising* (1988), the Asia Society's *Korea Briefings* series which he edited in the early 1990s, and a contribution to the *Cambridge History of China*.

EastBridge

The Missionary Experience in Asia
Kathleen L. Lodwick, Imprint Editor

Protestant and Catholic missionaries in Asia left an enduring legacy in the countries where they worked. **The Missionary Enterprise In Asia** focuses on describing and exploring their experiences, legacy, and impact. The imprint encompasses the fields of history, sociology, religion, anthropology; memoirs of those who served as missionaries in Christian missions in Asia; and writings of indigenous scholars and converts whose lives were impacted by missionary activities.

Kathleen L. Lodwick, is Professor of History at Pennsylvania State University and holds a Ph.D. in Chinese History from the University of Arizona. Professor Lodwick is currently writing a history of the Nanjing Theological Seminary.